RADIO NAVIGATIONAL AIDS

PUB. 117
2005

**IMPORTANT
THIS PUBLICATION SHOULD
BE CORRECTED EACH WEEK
FROM THE
NOTICE TO MARINERS**

Published by the
NATIONAL GEOSPATIAL-INTELLIGENCE
AGENCY Bethesda, Maryland

Prepared by
Paradise Cay Publications
Arcata, California

© COPYRIGHT 2005 BY THE UNITED STATES GOVERNMENT
NO COPYRIGHT CLAIMED UNDER TITLE 17 U.S.C.

THE PRUDENT MARINER

a. Warning On Use Of Floating Aids To Navigation and on Aids to Navigation in General, to Fix a Navigational Position.

The aids to navigation depicted on charts comprise a system consisting of fi ed and floatin aids with varying degrees of reliability. Therefore, prudent mariners will not rely solely on any single aid to navigation, particularly a floatin aid. An aid to navigation also refers to any device or structure external to a craft, designed to assist in determination of position. This includes celestial, terrestrial, and electronic means, such as Global Positioning System (GPS) and Differential GPS (DGPS). Here, too, the prudent mariner will not rely soley on any single aid to navigation.

The buoy symbol is used to indicate the approximate position of the buoy body and the sinker which secures the buoy to the seabed. The approximate position is used because of practical limitations in positioning and maintaining buoys and their sinkers in precise geographical locations. These limitations include, but are not limited to, inherent imprecisions in position fixin methods, prevailing atmospheric and sea conditions, the slope of and the material making up the seabed, the fact that buoys are moored to sinkers by varying lengths of chain, and the fact that buoy and/or sinker positions are not under continuous surveillance but are normally checked only during periodic maintenance visits which often occur more than a year apart. The position of the buoy body can be expected to shift inside and outside the charting symbol due to the forces of nature. The mariner is also cautioned that buoys are liable to be carried away, shifted, capsized, sunk, etc. Lighted buoys may be extinguished or sound signals may not function as the result of ice or other natural causes, collisions, or other accidents. Many of these factors also apply to articulated lights.

For the foregoing reasons, a prudent mariner must not rely completely upon the position or operation of floatin aids to navigation, but will also utilize bearings from fixed objects and aids to navigation on shore. Further, a vessel attempting to pass close aboard always risks collision with a yawing buoy or with the obstruction the buoy marks.

b. Use of Foreign Charts.

1. In the interest of safe navigation, caution should be exercised in the use of foreign charts not maintained through U.S. Notice to Mariners.

2. Foreign produced charts are occasionally mentioned in NGA Sailing Directions when such charts may be of a better scale than U.S. produced charts. Mariners are advised that if or when such foreign charts are used for navigation it is their responsibility to maintain those charts from the Notice to Mariners of the foreign country producing the charts.

3. The mariner is warned that the buoyage systems, shapes, colors, and light rhythms used by other countries often have a different significance than the U.S. system

4. Mariners are further warned about plotting positions, especially satellite-derived positions such as from GPS, onto foreign charts where the datum is unknown or the conversion from WGS-84 is unknown.

c. Chart Notes Regarding Different Datums.

Particular caution should be exercised during a passage when transferring the navigational plot to an adjacent chart upon a different geodetic datum or when transferring positions from one chart to another chart of the same area which is based upon a different datum. The transfer of positions should be done by bearings and distances from common features.

Notes on charts should be read with care, as they give important information not graphically presented. Notes in connection with the chart title include the horizontal geodetic datum which serves as a reference for the values of the latitude and longitude of any point or object on the chart. The latitudes and longitudes of the same points or objects on a second chart of the same area which is based upon a different datum will differ from those of the firs chart. The difference may be navigationally significant Additionally, datum changes between chart editions could significantl affect the positions of navigational aids found in the List of Lights and other NGA publications.

Positions obtained from satellite navigation systems, such as from GPS, are normally referred to the World Geodetic System 1984 (WGS-84) Datum. The differences between GPS satellite-derived positions and positions on some foreign charts cannot be determined: mariners are warned that these differences MAY BE SIGNIFICANT TO NAVIGATION and are therefore advised to use alternative sources of positional information, particularly when closing the shore or navigating in the vicinity of dangers.

(NGA/MISC)

PREFACE

The 2005 edition of Pub. 117, Radio Navigational Aids, is a list of selected worldwide stations which provide electronic services to the mariner. This edition cancels all previous editions of Pub. 117. The listing is divided into chapters according to the nature of the service performed by the stations. The firs numeral (hundreds digit) of section numbers of text and the firs numeral (thousands digit) of station numbers correspond to the chapter number.

Radiobeacons, the only category of radio navigational aids not listed in this book, are grouped geographically and carried in the NGA Lists of Lights, Pub. 110 - 116, and USCG Light Lists.

References to publications produced or sold by NGA will be followed by the stock number in parentheses.

Times quoted herein are, unless otherwise stated, in Coordinated Universal Time (UTC) and hours are reckoned from 0000 to 2359.

All bearings are true and are measured in degrees clockwise from 000° (true north) to 359°. The sectors of radio direction finder stations are given as looking from the station to seaward in accordance with international practice; it should be noted that this is the reverse of the method used in the light lists for expressing the sectors of lights.

Distances are reckoned in nautical miles unless otherwise stated.

When the term "plain language" is used in the description of the services rendered by a station, it signifie that the service is in the language of the country controlling the station, unless stated to be otherwise.

The hertz is the unit for the operating frequencies of communications-electronics equipment. Frequencies will normally be expressed as follows:

(1) In kilohertz (kHz) up to and including 300 kHz.
(2) In megahertz (MHz) up to and including 300 MHz.
(3) In gigahertz (GHz) up to and including 300 GHz.
Note: In practice, kilohertz may be used up to 30,000 kHz.

Nothing in the manner of presentation or arrangement of information in this publication implies endorsement or acceptance by NGA in matters affecting the status and boundaries of states and territories.

This edition contains information available to the National Geospatial-Intelligence Agency up to 27 November 2004, including Notice to Mariners No. 48 of 2004. Corrections which have accumulated since that date will be in Section II of the Notice to Mariners which announces the issuance of this publication. Subsequent corrections are included weekly in Section II. All of these corrections should be applied in the appropriate places and their insertion noted in the "Record of Corrections" on the next page.

Mariners and other users are requested to forward new or corrective information useful in the correction of this publication to:

MARITIME DIVISION
ST D 44
NATIONAL GEOSPATIAL-INTELLIGENCE AGENCY
4600 SANGAMORE ROAD
BETHESDA MD 20816-5003

CAUTION

Plans for air defense of the United States may require temporary suspension of the operations of certain electronic aids to navigation with little or no advance notice.

CONTENTS

Preface I
Table of Symbols VI

CHAPTER 1

Radio Direction Finder and Radar Stations 1-3

CHAPTER 2

Radio Time Signals 2-3

CHAPTER 3

Radio Navigational Warnings 3-3

CHAPTER 4

Distress, Emergency, and Safety Traffic 4-3

CHAPTER 5

Stations Transmitting Medical Advice 5-3

CHAPTER 6

Long Range Navigational Aids 6-3

CHAPTER 7

Amver 7-3

CHAPTER 8

Communication Instructions For U.S. Merchant Ships 8-3

Index I—Radio Aids to Navigation by Country I-1
Index II—Radio Aids to Navigation by Station I-5
Index III—Cross Reference—International vs. U.S. Radio Aids I-13

QUICK REFERENCE

Amver 7-3

DISTRESS, SEARCH, AND RESCUE
    Assistance by SAR Aircraft and Helicopters.. 4-14
    Distress and Safety Communications Procedures 4-7
    Emergency Position Indicating Radiobeacons (EPIRBs).. 4-18
    Frequencies for Distress and Safety 4-3
    Global Maritime Distress and Safety System (GMDSS) 4-28
    Urgency and Safety Communications Procedures.. 4-11

ELECTRONIC NAVIGATION
    LORAN-C 6-3
    Satellite Navigation.. 6-10

EMERGENCY
    U.S. Naval Cooperation and Guidance for Shipping (NCAGS).. 8-3
    Contamination Prediction System for Merchant Ships at Sea and the MERWARN System 8-9
    Reports of Hostile Activities... 4-15
    Requests for U.S. Navy Assistance in Emergency Situations 4-94

NAVIGATIONAL WARNINGS
    Coastal and Local, Long Range, and Worldwide Warnings 3-3
    Ice Information 3-16
    NAVTEX... 3-6
    Reporting Navigational Safety Information to Shore Establishments... 4-14
    SPECIAL WARNINGS and Broadcast Stations 3-6

The National Geospatial-Intelligence Agency's Maritime Safety Information Website...................................... V

THE NATIONAL GEOSPATIAL-INTELLIGENCE AGENCY
MARITIME DIVISION WEBSITE

The National Geospatial-Intelligence Agency (NGA) Maritime Division Website provides worldwide remote query access to extensive menus of maritime safety information 24 hours a day.

Databases made available for access, query and download include Chart Corrections, Publication Corrections, NGA Hydrographic Catalog Corrections, Chart and Publication Reference Data (current edition number, dates, title, scale), NGA List of Lights, USCG Light Lists, WorldWide Navigational Warning Service (WWNWS) Broadcast Warnings, Maritime Administration (MARAD) Advisories, Department of State Special Warnings, Mobile Offshore Drilling Units (MODUs), Anti-Shipping Activity Messages (ASAMs), World Port Index, and Radio Navigational Aids. Publications that are also made available as PDF file include the U.S. Notice to Mariners, U.S. Chart No. 1, The American Practical Navigator (Bowditch), International Code of Signals, Radio Navigational Aids, World Port Index, Distances Between Ports, Sight Reduction Tables for Marine and Air Navigation, and the Radar Navigation and Maneuvering Board Manual.

The Maritime Division Website can be accessed via the NGA Homepage (http://www.nga.mil) or directly at http://pollux.nss.nga.mil/. Any questions concerning the Maritime Division Website should be directed to:

>MARITIME DIVISION
>ATTN: NSS STAFF
>ST D-44
>NATIONAL GEOSPATIAL-INTELLIGENCE AGENCY
>4600 SANGAMORE ROAD
>BETHESDA MD   20816-5003
>
>Telephone: (1) 301-227-3296 or DSN 287-3296
>Fax: (1) 301-227-4211
>E-mail: webmaster_nss@nga.mil

TABLE OF SYMBOLS

LEGEND

Example: A   1   A
               (1) (2) (3)

(1) Type of modulation of the main carrier:
A   Double sideband
F   Frequency modulation
G   Phase modulation
H   Single sideband (full carrier)
J   Single sideband (suppressed carrier)
N   Emission of unmodulated carrier
R   Single sideband (reduced or variable level carrier)

(2) Nature of signal(s) modulating the main carrier:
0   No modulating signal
1   Single channel containing quantized/digital information without modulating subcarrier, excluding time division multiplex
2   Single channel containing quantized/digital information with modulating subcarrier, excluding time division multiplex
3   Single channel containing analog information
9   Multiple channels, separately containing quantized/digital information and analog information

(3) Type of information to be transmitted. "Information" does not include information of a constant, unvarying nature, such as provided by standard frequency emissions, continuous wave and pulse radars, etc.:
A   Telegraphy (aural reception)
B   Telegraphy (automatic reception)
C   Facsimile
D   Data transmission, telemetry, telecommand
        Note: With 6 kHz, EDW operation in the bands below 30 MHz allocated exclusively for maritime mobile service (FC, MO)
E   Telephony (including sound broadcasting)
N   No information transmitted
W   Telegraphy and telephony

AMPLITUDE MODULATION

A1A   Continuous wave telegraphy, Morse code
A2A   Telegraphy by on/off keying of tone-modulated carrier, Morse code: double sideband
A3E   Radiotelephony using amplitude modulation: double sideband
A3C   Facsimile
A9W   Composite emission of telegraphy and telephony: double sideband
G1D   Data transmission
G3E   Radiotelephony
H2A   Telegraphy by on/off keying of tone-modulated carrier
H2B   Selective calling using sequential single frequency code
H3E   Radiotelephony: single sideband, full carrier
J3C   Facsimile: single sideband, suppressed carrier
J3E   Radiotelephony using amplitude modulation: single sideband, suppressed carrier
N0N   Unmodulated continuous wave emission
R3E   Radiotelephony

FREQUENCY (or PHASE) MODULATION:

F1B	Narrow band direct printing (NBDP); Radioteletype
F2A	Telegraphy by on/off keying of tone-modulated carrier
F3C	Facsimile
F3E	Radiotelephony using frequency modulation

Pulse Modulation:
kHz = kilohertz
MHz = megahertz
GHz = gigahertz

TERMS AND ABBREVIATIONS

AOR-E	Atlantic Ocean Region-East
AOR-W	Atlantic Ocean Region-West
CES	Coast Earth Station
DSC	Digital Selective Calling
EPIRB	Emergency position-indicating radio beacon
GEOLUT	Local user terminal in a GEOSAR system
GEOSAR	Geostationary satellite system for SAR
HF	High Frequency
IOR	Indian Ocean Region
LEOLUT	Local user terminal in a LEOSAR system
LEOSAR	Low Earth Orbit satellite system for SAR
LUT	COSPAS-SARSAT Local User Terminal
MCC	COSPAS-SARSAT Mission Control Center
MF	Medium Frequency
MRCC	Maritime Rescue Co-ordination Center
MRSC	Maritime Rescue Sub-Center
NBDP	Narrow band direct printing
NCS	Network Coordinating Station
N.I.	No Information
NM	Nautical Miles
POR	Pacific Ocean R gion
RCC	Rescue Coordination Center
R_x	Receiver
SAR	Search and rescue
T_x	Transmitter
UTC	Coordinated Universal Time

CHAPTER 1

RADIO DIRECTION FINDER AND RADAR STATIONS

PART I RADIO DIRECTION FINDER STATIONS

100A.	General.	1-3
100B.	Accuracy of Bearings Furnished by Direction Finding Stations.	1-3
100C.	Obligations of Administrations Operating Direction Finding Stations.	1-3
100D.	Procedure to Obtain Radio Direction Finder Bearings and Positions.	1-4
100E.	Plotting Radio Bearings.	1-5
100F.	Radio Bearing Conversion.	1-5
100G.	Direction Finding Station List.	1-6
	Station List.	1-8

PART II RADAR STATIONS

110A.	Coast and Port Radar Station List.	1-16
	Station List.	1-17

CHAPTER 1

RADIO DIRECTION FINDER AND RADAR STATIONS

PART I RADIO DIRECTION FINDER STATIONS

100A. General

Radio bearings may be employed for fixin a ship's position in the same manner as other lines of position if due regard is given to the facts that they, like other lines of position, may not be absolutely accurate, and that the bearings are portions of great circles, not rhumb lines.

Radio bearings are obtained using radio direction finde sets installed on either shore stations or ships, and also by certain special radiobeacons.

Radio direction finde (RDF)stations are equipped with apparatus for determining the direction of radio signals transmitted by ships and other stations.

SECTOR OF CALIBRATION: The sector of calibration of a direction finde station is the sector around the receiving coil in which the deviation of radio bearings is known. In this book, the sectors are measured clockwise from 000° (true north) to 359° and are given from the station to seaward. Bearings which do not fall within the sector of calibration of the station should be considered unreliable.

100B. Accuracy of Bearings Furnished by Direction Finding Stations

The bearings obtained by RDF stations and reported to ships are corrected for all determinable errors except the difference between a great circle and a rhumb line (See sec. 100F.) and are normally accurate within 2° for distances under 150 miles. However, this error may be increased by various circumstances, some of which are:

STRENGTH OF SIGNALS: The most accurate bearings result from ships whose signals are steady, clear, and strong. If the signals are too weak, accurate bearings cannot be obtained.

TRANSMITTER ADJUSTMENT: The transmitter of the ship requesting bearings should be tuned carefully to the frequency of the station. If the tuning is off, it will be difficul for the station to obtain bearings sufficientl accurate for navigational purposes.

COASTAL REFRACTION (LAND EFFECT): Bearings which cut an intervening coastline at an oblique angle, or cross high intervening land, may produce errors of 4° to 5°. RDF stations normally know the sectors in which such refraction may be expected. Such sectors may not be included in the published sectors of calibration or may be marked "sectors of uncertain calibration."

SUNRISE, SUNSET, OR NIGHT EFFECTS: Bearings obtained from about half an hour before sunset to about half an hour after sunrise are occasionally unreliable because of the polarization error introduced. Changes in the intensity of the signals received occur at sunset and sunrise.

CAUTION: When RDF stations use such words as doubtful, approximate, second-class, or the equivalents in foreign languages, the bearings reported must be treated with suspicion as considerable error may exist.

DANGER FROM RECIPROCAL BEARINGS: When a single station furnishes a bearing, there is a possibility of an error of approximately 180°, as the operator at the station cannot always determine on which side of the station the ship lies. Certain direction finde stations, particularly those on islands or extended capes, are equipped to furnish two corrected true bearings for any observation. Such bearings may differ by approximately 180° and whichever bearing is suitable should be used.

CAUTION: Mariners receiving bearings which are evidently the approximate reciprocal of the correct bearings should never attempt to correct these bearings by applying a correction of 180°, as such a correction would not include the proper correction for deviation at the direction finde station. An error as large as 30° may be introduced by an arbitrary correction of 180°. Ships receiving bearings requiring an approximate 180° correction should request both bearings from the direction finder station

100C. Obligations of Administrations Operating Direction Finding Stations

The obligations of RDF station operators are given in Article 35 of the manual for use by the Maritime Mobile Satellite Services of the International Telecommunications Union (1992). They include the following:

– Effective and regular service should be maintained, but no responsibility is accepted for these services.
– Serviced stations shall be advised of doubtful or unreliable observations.
– RDF station operators shall make daily notificatio of any temporary modification or irregularities in service. Permanent modification shall be published as soon as possible in the relevant notices to mariners.
– All RDF stations shall be able to take bearings on 410 kHz and 500 kHz.
– When RDF service is provided in authorized bands between 1605 kHz and 2850 kHz, RDF stations

providing that service should be able to take bearings on 2182 kHz.
- When RDF service is provided in the bands between 156 MHz and 174 MHz, the RDF station should be able to take bearings on VHF 156.8 MHz and VHF digital selective calling frequency 156.525 MHz.

100D. Procedure to Obtain Radio Direction Finder Bearings and Positions

TO OBTAIN A BEARING: The vessel should call the RDF station or the RDF control station on the designated watch frequency. Depending on the type of information wanted, the vessel should transmit the appropriate service abbreviation(s):

- QTE: What is the true bearing from you (or designated vessel)?
- QTH: Follows the above abbreviation when the request is made to a mobile RDF station.

The vessel should also indicate the frequency it will use to enable its bearing to be taken.

The RDF station called should request the vessel to transmit for the bearing by means of the service abbreviation QTG (Will you send two dashes of ten seconds each (or carrier) followed by your call sign (repeated __ times) on ___ kHz (or MHz)?).

After shifting, if necessary, to the new transmitting frequency, the vessel should transmit as instructed by the RDF station.

The RDF station should determine the direction, sense (if possible), and classificatio of the bearing and transmit to the vessel in the following order:

- QTE.
- Three digits indicating true bearing in degrees from the RDF station.
- Class of bearing.
- Time of observation.

- If the RDF station is mobile, its own position preceded by QTH.

When the vessel has received this information, it should repeat it back, if considered necessary for confirmation The RDF station should confir or correct the information. When the RDF station is sure the information has been correctly received, it will transmit AR (end of transmission). The vessel will respond with AR.

Unless otherwise indicated, the vessel may assume that the sense of the bearing was indicated. If not, the RDF station should indicate this or report the bearing and its reciprocal.

CLASSSIFICATION OF BEARINGS: To estimate the accuracy and determine the corresponding class of a bearing:

- An operator should generally, and particularly in the maritime mobile RDF service on frequencies below 3000 kHz, give the observational characteristics of bearings shown in the table below.
- The RDF station, when facilities and time permit, may take into account the probability of error in the bearing. A bearing is considered as belonging to a particular class if there is a probability of less than 1 in 20 that the bearing error would exceed the numerical values specifie for that class in the table below. This probability should be determined from an analysis of the f ve components that make up the total variance of the bearing (instrumental, site, propagation, random sampling and observational components).

TO OBTAIN A POSITION (DETERMINED BY TWO OR MORE RDF STATIONS ORGANIZED AS A GROUP): The vessel should call the RDF control station and transmit QTF (Will you give me my position according to the bearings taken by the RDF stations you control?).

The control station shall reply and, when the RDF stations are ready, request that the vessel transmit using the service abbreviation QTG.

Classification of Bearing

Class	Bearing Error (Degrees)	Observational Characteristics					
		Signal Strength	Bearing Indication	Fading	Interference	Bearing Swing (Degrees)	Duration of Observation
A	±2°	very good or good	definit (sharp null)	negligible	negligible	less than 3°	adequate
B	±5°	fairly good	blurred	slight	slight	more than 3° less than 5°	short
C	±10°	weak	severely blurred	severe	strong	more than 5° less than 10°	very short
D	more than ±10°	scarcely perceptible	ill-define	very severe	very strong	more than 10°	inadequate

RADIO DIRECTION FINDER AND RADAR STATIONS

When the position has been determined, the control station should transmit to the vessel:
– QTF.
– The position in latitude and longitude, or in relation to a known geographic point.
– Class of position.
– Time of observation.

According to its estimate of the accuracy of the observations, the control station shall classify the position in one of the four following classes:
– Class A - positions which the operator may reasonably expect to be accurate to within 5 nautical miles.
– Class B - positions which the operator may reasonably expect to be accurate to within 20 nautical miles.
– Class C - positions which the operator may reasonably expect to be accurate to within 50 nautical miles.
– Class D - positions which the operator may not expect to be accurate to within 50 nautical miles.

For frequencies above 3000 kHz, where the distance limits specifie in the preceding subparagraph may not be appropriate, the control station may classify the position in accordance with current International Telecommunications Union-Radiocommunications Sector (ITU-R) recommendations.

TO OBTAIN SIMULTANEOUS BEARINGS FROM TWO OR MORE RDF STATIONS ORGANIZED AS A GROUP: On a request for bearings, the control station of a group of RDF stations shall proceed as indicated above. It then should transmit the bearings observed by each station of the group, each bearing being preceded by the call sign of the station which observed it.

100E.   Plotting Radio Bearings

A fix by radio bearings is defined as fol ws:
– Three or more bearings taken simultaneously.
– Two bearings and a sounding.
– Two bearings and an LOP from a celestial body.
– Two bearings and a synchronized air or submarine signal.
– Two bearings on the same station and the measure of distance run (solve as if doubling the angle on the bow) between bearings.

Radio bearings are great circle azimuths (the bearing is the angle between the meridian of the ship or station taking the bearing and the great circle, not the rhumb line). They can be plotted directly upon gnomonic charts, but they cannot be plotted on a Mercator chart without firs being corrected as described in sec. 100F.

WEIGHT TO BE GIVEN TO RADIO BEARINGS: Before using a radio bearing for navigational purposes, the mariner should consider the conditions under which it was taken and should compare the conditions with those given in sec. 100B on accuracy.

Land-based marine radiobeacon signals received by ships may only provide a bearing accuracy relative to vessel heading of ±3° - 10°. This is not satisfactory for navigation in restricted channels or harbors.

TRANSMITTERS AND RECEIVERS: Bearings reported by a direction findin station ashore must be plotted from the geographical position of the receiving antenna of the station. Bearings taken by a ship on a shore station must be plotted from the geographical position of the station's transmitting antenna.

CAUTION: These two positions are not the same for all stations.

SHIP'S PROBABLE POSITION: As radio bearings are not absolutely accurate, lines should be drawn on both sides of each radio bearing at an angular distance from the bearing equal to the estimated probable error. In the case of intersecting radio bearings, the ship's most probable position is the area enclosed by these outer lines.

In figur 1 the broken lines are radio bearings obtained on a ship by three radio stations. The solid lines are drawn at angles of 2° from the bearings (it is assumed that all the bearings are probably accurate within 2°). The black triangle in the illustration lies within the 2° error of all three bearings and is the most probable position of the ship. However, with the possibility that one of the bearings may be off by more than 2°, the areas shaded with parallel lines give other possible positions. If one of the bearings is suspected to be less accurate, the outer lines should be offset from this bearing the same number of degrees as the estimated error, and the area or areas partially enclosed by these lines should be given less weight than the other areas.

In figur 2, a ship on course 000° obtains bearings of 031° and 065° on a radio station. The lines drawn as long dashes show the bearings and the continuous lines are their limits of accuracy. It is assumed that the bearings are both accurate within 2°. The lines AB drawn with dashes and dots are equal to the distance run between bearings. The distance run is fitte to the lines showing the limits of accuracy of the bearings. This can be done easily by means of parallel rulers and dividers. The shaded quadrilateral shows the ship's probable position at the time of the second bearings, if both bearings are accurate within 2°.

Information on various kinds of land-based radiobeacons, their accuracy, and use may be found in the NGA Lists of Lights (LLPUB110 - 116), Coast Guard Light Lists (COMDTM165021 - 165027), and "The American Practical Navigator" (Bowditch) (NVPUB9).

100F.   Radio Bearing Conversion

The table on pg. 1-7 may be used to convert radio or great circle bearings into Mercator bearings for plotting on a Mercator chart. The table should be used when the distance between the ship and station is over 50 miles. The arguments used to fin the correction are the middle latitude (Lm) and the difference of longitude (DLo) between the position of the radio station and the dead reckoning (DR) position of the vessel.

EXAMPLE: A vessel in DR position 56°04'N, 142°43'W takes a bearing on the radiobeacon at Cape Spencer Light Station at 58°12.0'N, 136°38.3'W. The bearing observed is 057.5°. Find the Mercator bearing.

   Lm (to nearest whole degree) = 57°
   DLo (to nearest half degree) = 6°

With Lm 57° and the DLo 6° enter the conversion table and extract the correction 2.5°. The receiver (ship) is in N

RADIO DIRECTION FINDER AND RADAR STATIONS

latitude; the transmitter (radiobeacon) is eastward. Following the rule given at the bottom of the table, the correction is to be added:

Great circle bearing . . . . 057.5°
Correction . . . . +2.5°
Mercator bearing . . . . 060.0°

To plot the bearing, add 180° to Mercator bearing, giving 240°, the rhumb line bearing of the ship from the radiobeacon.

EXAMPLE: A vessel in DR position 42°20'N, 66°14'W requests a bearing from a direction finde station at 42°08'N, 70°42'W. The bearing given is 081°. Find the Mercator bearing.

Lm (to nearest whole degree) = 42°
DLo (to nearest half degree) = 4.5°

With Lm 42° and DLo 4.5°, enter the conversion table and extract the correction 1.5°. The receiver (RDF station) is in N latitude; the transmitter (ship) is eastward. Following the rule given at the bottom of the table, the correction is to be added:

Great circle bearing . . . . 081.0°
Correction. . . . . +1.5°
Mercator bearing . . . . 082.5°

100G. Direction Finding Station List

The station list starting on pg. 1-8 shows the names, positions, and characteristics of radio direction findin stations.The frequencies used are broken down as follows:

A–Frequency on which station (or control station) keeps watch.
B–Frequency for transmission of signals on which bearings are observed.
C– Frequency on which results are transmitted.

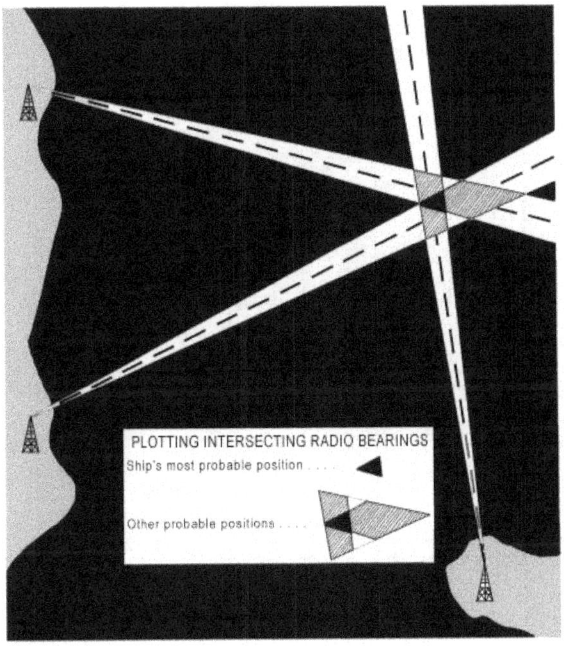

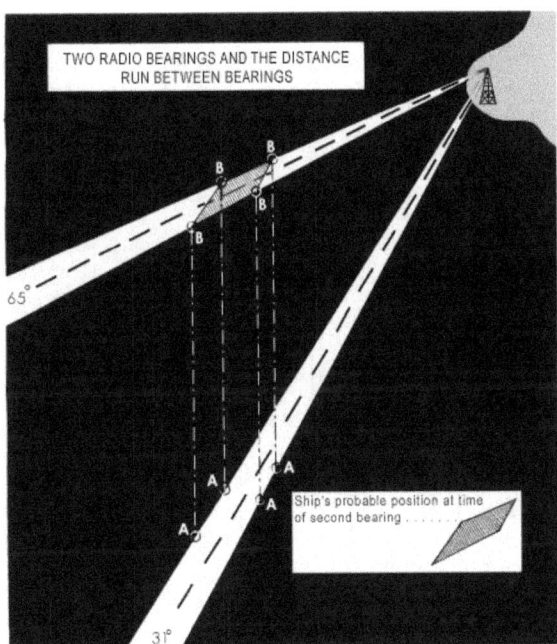

Figure 1.

Figure 2.

RADIO DIRECTION FINDER AND RADAR STATIONS

Radio Bearing Conversion Table

Correction to be applied to radio bearing to convert to Mercator bearing

Difference of Longitude

Mid Lat.	0.5°	1°	1.5°	2°	2.5°	3°	3.5°	4°	4.5°	5°	5.5°	6°	6.5°	7°	7.5°	Mid Lat.
4						0.1	0.1	0.1	0.1	0.2	0.2	0.2	0.2	0.2	0.3	4
5		0.1	0.1	0.1	.1	.1	.2	.2	.2	.2	.2	.3	.3	.3	.3	5
6		.1	.1	.1	.1	.2	.2	.2	.2	.3	.3	.3	.3	.4	.4	6
7		.1	.1	.1	.2	.2	.2	.3	.3	.3	.3	.4	.4	.4	.5	7
8		.1	.1	.1	.2	.2	.2	.3	.3	.4	.4	.4	.5	.5	.5	8
9		.1	.1	.1	.2	.2	.2	.3	.3	.4	.4	.5	.5	.6	.6	9
10		.1	.1	.1	.2	.2	.3	.4	.4	.4	.5	.5	.6	.6	.6	10
11		.1	.1	.2	.2	.3	.3	.4	.4	.5	.5	.6	.6	.7	.7	11
12	0.1	.1	.1	.2	.3	.3	.4	.4	.5	.5	.6	.6	.7	.7	.8	12
13	.1	.1	.2	.2	.3	.3	.4	.4	.5	.6	.6	.7	.7	.8	.8	13
14	.1	.1	.2	.2	.3	.4	.4	.5	.6	.6	.7	.7	.8	.8	.9	14
15	.1	.1	.2	.3	.3	.4	.4	.5	.6	.6	.7	.8	.8	.9	1.0	15
16	.1	.1	.2	.3	.4	.4	.5	.6	.6	.7	.8	.8	.9	1.0	1.0	16
17	.1	.2	.2	.3	.4	.4	.5	.6	.6	.7	.8	.9	1.0	1.0	1.1	17
18	.1	.2	.2	.3	.4	.5	.5	.6	.7	.8	.8	.9	1.0	1.1	1.2	18
19	.1	.2	.2	.3	.4	.5	.6	.6	.7	.8	.9	1.0	1.1	1.1	1.2	19
20	.1	.2	.2	.3	.4	.5	.6	.7	.8	.8	.9	1.0	1.1	1.2	1.3	20
21	.1	.2	.3	.4	.5	.5	.6	.7	.8	.9	1.0	1.1	1.2	1.2	1.4	21
22	.1	.2	.3	.4	.5	.6	.6	.8	.8	.9	1.0	1.1	1.2	1.3	1.4	22
23	.1	.2	.3	.4	.5	.6	.7	.8	.9	1.0	1.1	1.2	1.3	1.4	1.5	23
24	.1	.2	.3	.4	.5	.6	.7	.8	.9	1.0	1.1	1.2	1.3	1.4	1.5	24
25	.1	.2	.3	.4	.5	.6	.7	.8	1.0	1.1	1.2	1.3	1.4	1.5	1.6	25
26	.1	.2	.3	.4	.6	.6	.8	.9	1.0	1.1	1.2	1.3	1.4	1.5	1.6	26
27	.1	.2	.3	.4	.6	.7	.8	.9	1.0	1.1	1.2	1.4	1.5	1.6	1.7	27
28	.1	.2	.4	.5	.6	.7	.8	.9	1.1	1.2	1.3	1.4	1.5	1.6	1.8	28
29	.1	.2	.4	.5	.6	.7	.8	1.0	1.1	1.2	1.3	1.4	1.6	1.7	1.8	29
30	.1	.2	.4	.5	.6	.8	.9	1.0	1.1	1.2	1.4	1.5	1.6	1.8	1.9	30
31	.1	.2	.4	.5	.6	.8	.9	1.0	1.2	1.3	1.4	1.6	1.7	1.8	1.9	31
32	.1	.3	.4	.5	.7	.8	.9	1.1	1.2	1.3	1.4	1.6	1.7	1.8	2.0	32
33	.1	.3	.4	.6	.7	.8	1.0	1.1	1.2	1.4	1.5	1.6	1.8	1.9	2.0	33
34	.1	.3	.4	.6	.7	.8	1.0	1.1	1.2	1.4	1.5	1.7	1.8	2.0	2.1	34
35	.1	.3	.4	.6	.7	.9	1.0	1.2	1.3	1.4	1.6	1.7	1.9	2.0	2.2	35
36	.1	.3	.4	.6	.7	.9	1.0	1.2	1.3	1.5	1.6	1.8	1.9	2.1	2.2	36
37	.2	.3	.4	.6	.8	.9	1.1	1.2	1.4	1.5	1.6	1.8	2.0	2.1	2.2	37
38	.2	.3	.5	.6	.8	.9	1.1	1.2	1.4	1.5	1.7	1.8	2.0	2.2	2.3	38
39	.2	.3	.5	.6	.8	1.0	1.1	1.2	1.4	1.6	1.7	1.9	2.1	2.2	2.4	39
40	.2	.3	.5	.6	.8	1.0	1.1	1.3	1.4	1.6	1.8	1.9	2.1	2.2	2.4	40
41	.2	.3	.5	.6	.8	1.0	1.2	1.3	1.5	1.6	1.8	2.0	2.1	2.3	2.5	41
42	.2	.3	.5	.7	.8	1.0	1.2	1.3	1.5	1.7	1.8	2.0	2.2	2.3	2.5	42
43	.2	.3	.5	.7	.8	1.0	1.2	1.4	1.5	1.7	1.9	2.1	2.2	2.4	2.6	43
44	.2	.4	.5	.7	.9	1.1	1.2	1.4	1.6	1.7	1.9	2.1	2.2	2.4	2.6	44
45	.2	.4	.5	.7	.9	1.1	1.2	1.4	1.6	1.8	2.0	2.1	2.3	2.5	2.6	45
46	.2	.4	.5	.7	.9	1.1	1.3	1.4	1.6	1.8	2.0	2.2	2.3	2.5	2.7	46
47	.2	.4	.6	.7	.9	1.1	1.3	1.5	1.7	1.8	2.0	2.2	2.4	2.6	2.8	47
48	.2	.4	.6	.8	.9	1.1	1.3	1.5	1.7	1.8	2.1	2.2	2.4	2.6	2.8	48
49	.2	.4	.6	.8	1.0	1.1	1.3	1.5	1.7	1.9	2.1	2.3	2.5	2.6	2.8	49
50	.2	.4	.6	.8	1.0	1.1	1.3	1.5	1.7	1.9	2.1	2.3	2.5	2.7	2.9	50
51	.2	.4	.6	.8	1.0	1.2	1.4	1.6	1.8	2.0	2.1	2.3	2.5	2.7	2.9	51
52	.2	.4	.6	.8	1.0	1.2	1.4	1.6	1.8	2.0	2.2	2.4	2.6	2.8	3.0	52
53	.2	.4	.6	.8	1.0	1.2	1.4	1.6	1.8	2.0	2.2	2.4	2.6	2.8	3.0	53
54	.2	.4	.6	.8	1.0	1.2	1.4	1.6	1.8	2.0	2.2	2.4	2.6	2.8	3.0	54
55	.2	.4	.6	.8	1.0	1.2	1.4	1.6	1.8	2.1	2.2	2.4	2.7	2.9	3.1	55
56	.2	.4	.6	.8	1.0	1.2	1.4	1.7	1.9	2.1	2.3	2.5	2.7	2.9	3.1	56
57	.2	.4	.6	.8	1.1	1.2	1.5	1.7	1.9	2.1	2.3	2.5	2.7	2.9	3.2	57
58	.2	.4	.6	.8	1.1	1.3	1.5	1.7	1.9	2.1	2.3	2.6	2.8	3.0	3.2	58
59	.2	.4	.6	.8	1.1	1.3	1.5	1.7	1.9	2.2	2.4	2.6	2.8	3.0	3.2	59
60	.2	.4	.6	.9	1.1	1.3	1.5	1.7	2.0	2.2	2.4	2.6	2.8	3.0	3.2	60
	0.5°	1°	1.5°	2°	2.5°	3°	3.5°	4°	4.5°	5°	5.5°	6°	6.5°	7°	7.5°	

Receiver (latitude)	Transmitter (direction from receiver)	Correction Sign	Receiver (latitude)	Transmitter (direction from receiver)	Correction Sign
North	Eastward	+	South	Eastward	−
North	Westward	−	South	Westward	+

RADIO DIRECTION FINDER AND RADAR STATIONS

1-8

(1) No.	(2) Name	(3) Type	(4) Position Rx / Tx	(5) Frequency	(6) Range	(7) Procedure	(8) Remarks
				CANADA			

The VHF direction finding stations of Canada are for emergency use only. All stations are remotely controlled by a Marine Communications and Traffic Services Center (MCTS). The following details of operation are common to all of these stations:

A. Ch.16.
B. Ch.16 (distress only).
C. Ch.16 (distress only).

(1) No.	(2) Name	(3) Type	(4) Position Rx / Tx	(8) Remarks
1001	Cap-aux-Meules.	RDF	47 23 14 N / 61 51 40 W	MCTS Riviere-au-Renard (VCG).
1001.3 2-4326	Fortune Head.	RDF	47 03 54 N / 55 51 04 W	MCTS Placentia (VCP).
1001.35 2-4326	Grosses-Roches.	RDF	48 54 51 N / 67 06 38 W	MCTS Les Escoumins (VCF).
1001.45 2-4326	Havre St.-Pierre.	RDF	50 16 15 N / 63 40 44 W	MCTS Riviere-au-Renard (VCG).
1001.6 2-4326	Lac D'aigle (Sept Iles).	RDF	50 17 21 N / 66 18 43 W	MCTS Les Escoumins (VCF).
1001.85 2-4326	Mont-Louis.	RDF	49 12 48 N / 65 46 27 W	MCTS Les Escoumins (VCF).
1001.9 2-4326	Montmagny.	RDF	46 55 42 N / 70 30 45 W	MCTS Quebec (VCC).
1001.95 2-4326	Natashquan.	RDF	50 08 40 N / 61 48 00 W	MCTS Riviere-au-Renard (VCG).
1002 2-4326	Newport.	RDF	48 13 37 N / 64 47 33 W	MCTS Riviere-au-Renard (VCG).
1002.1 2-4326	Pointe Heath.	RDF	49 05 05 N / 61 42 09 W	MCTS Riviere-au-Renard (VCG).
1002.15 2-4326	Riviere-au-Renard.	RDF	49 00 29 N / 64 24 00 W	MCTS Riviere-au-Renard (VCG).
1002.2 2-4326	Riviere du Loup.	RDF	47 45 26 N / 69 36 14 W	MCTS Quebec (VCC).
1002.35 2-4326	Twillingate.	RDF	49 41 16 N / 54 48 03 W	MCTS St. Anthony (VCM).
1002.36	Banks.	RDF	44 28 30 N / 80 20 56 W	MCTS Thunder Bay (VBA).

Seasonal operation: April 1-December 31.

1002.37	Brougham.	RDF	43 55 13 N / 79 06 51 W	MCTS Prescott (VBR).

Seasonal operation: April 1-December 31.

1002.38	Cape Croker.	RDF	44 57 30 N / 80 57 53 W	MCTS Thunder Bay (VBA).

Seasonal operation: April 1-December 31.

1002.4	Cobourg.	RDF	44 04 02 N / 78 12 38 W	MCTS Prescott (VBR).

Seasonal operation: April 1-December 31.

1002.45	Pointe au Baril.	RDF	45 33 50 N / 80 19 18 W	MCTS Thunder Bay (VBA).

Seasonal operation: April 1-December 31.

1002.5	Tobermory.	RDF	45 09 42 N / 81 29 55 W	MCTS Thunder Bay (VBA).

Seasonal operation: April 1-December 31.

RADIO DIRECTION FINDER AND RADAR STATIONS

(1) No.	(2) Name	(3) Type	(4) Position Rx / Tx	(5) Frequency	(6) Range	(7) Procedure	(8) Remarks
1002.55	Trafalgar.	RDF	43 29 41 N 79 43 47 W				MCTS Prescott (VBR).
	Seasonal operation: April 1-December 31.						
1002.6 2-3510	Barry Inlet.	RDF	52 34 30 N 131 45 13 W				MCTS Prince Rupert (VAJ).
1002.65 2-3510	Calvert Island.	RDF	51 35 21 N 128 00 43 W				MCTS Prince Rupert (VAJ).
1002.7 2-3510	Cumshewa.	RDF	53 09 33 N 131 59 47 W				MCTS Prince Rupert (VAJ).
1002.75 2-3510	Dundas Island.	RDF	54 31 16 N 130 54 55 W				MCTS Prince Rupert (VAJ).
1002.8 2-3510	Klemtu.	RDF	52 34 45 N 128 33 45 W				MCTS Prince Rupert (VAJ).
1002.85 2-3510	Mount Gil.	RDF	53 15 46 N 129 11 42 W				MCTS Prince Rupert (VAJ).
1002.9 2-3510	Mount Hays.	RDF	54 17 12 N 130 18 49 W				MCTS Prince Rupert (VAJ).
1002.95 2-3510	Naden Harbor.	RDF	53 57 18 N 132 56 30 W				MCTS Prince Rupert (VAJ).
1003 2-3510	Van Inlet.	RDF	53 15 08 N 132 32 31 W				MCTS Prince Rupert (VAJ).

UNITED KINGDOM

The VHF direction finding stations of the United Kingdom are for emergency use only. Except for Guernsey and Jersey, all are remotely controlled by a HM Coast Guard Maritime Rescue Coordination Center or Sub-Center (MRCC/MRSC). The following details of operation are common to all of these stations:

A. Ch.16.
B. Ch.16 (distress only).
Ch.67. Ch.82 (Jersey only).
C. Ch.16 (distress only).
Ch.67. Ch.82 (Jersey only).

(1) No.	(2) Name	(3) Type	(4) Position Rx / Tx	(5) Frequency	(6) Range	(7) Procedure	(8) Remarks
1055 2-0001	Barra.	RDF	57 00 49 N 7 30 25 W				MRSC Stornoway.
1060 2-0001	Bawdsey.	RDF	51 59 36 N 1 25 00 E				MRSC Thames.
1065 2-0001	Berry Head.	RDF	50 23 58 N 3 29 03 W				MRSC Brixham.
1066 2-0001	Boniface.	RDF	50 36 13 N 1 12 02 W				MRSC Solent.
1070 2-0001	Compass Head.	RDF	59 52 03 N 1 16 18 W				MRSC Shetland.
1072 2-0001	Crosslaw.	RDF	55 54 29 N 2 12 19 W				MRSC Forth.
1073 2-0001	Cullercoats.	RDF	55 04 00 N 1 28 00 W				MRSC Humber.
1075 2-0001	Dunnet Head.	RDF	58 40 19 N 3 22 31 W				MRCC Aberdeen.
1080 2-0001	Easington.	RDF	53 39 08 N 0 05 54 E				MRSC Humber.

RADIO DIRECTION FINDER AND RADAR STATIONS

(1) No.	(2) Name	(3) Type	(4) Position Rx Tx	(5) Frequency	(6) Range	(7) Procedure	(8) Remarks
1082 2-0001	East Prawle.	RDF	50 13 06 N 3 42 30 W				MRSC Brixham.
1086 2-0001	Fairlight.	RDF	50 52 11 N 0 38 44 E				MRCC Dover.
1087 2-0001	Fife Ness.	RDF	56 16 42 N 2 35 18 W				MRSC Forth.
1088 2-0001	Flamborough.	RDF	54 07 05 N 0 05 13 W				MRSC Humber.
1089 2-0001	Great Ormes Head.	RDF	53 19 58 N 3 51 15 W				MRSC Holyhead.
1090 2-0001	Grove Point.	RDF	50 32 56 N 2 25 12 W				MRSC Portland.
1090.5 2-0155	Guernsey.	RDF	49 26 16 N 2 35 46 W				
1091 2-0001	Hartland.	RDF	51 01 13 N 4 31 24 W				MRCC Swansea.
1091.2 2-0001	Hartlepool.	RDF	54 41 47 N 1 10 34 W				MRSC Humber.
1092 2-0001	Hengistbury Head.	RDF	50 42 57 N 1 45 38 W				MRSC Portland.
1093 2-0001	Inverbervie.	RDF	56 51 06 N 2 15 39 W				MRSC Forth.
1093.5 2-0155	Jersey.	RDF	49 10 51 N 2 14 18 W				
1094 2-0001	Kilchiaran.	RDF	55 45 54 N 6 27 11 W				MRCC Clyde.
1094.1 2-0001	Lands End.	RDF	50 08 08 N 5 38 11 W				MRCC Falmouth.
1094.2 2-0001	Langdon Battery.	RDF	51 07 58 N 1 20 35 E				MRCC Dover.
1094.5 2-0001	Law Hill.	RDF	55 41 46 N 4 50 28 W				MRCC Clyde.
1095 2-0001	Lizard.	RDF	49 57 36 N 5 12 04 W				MRCC Falmouth.
1095.5 2-0001	Lowestoft.	RDF	52 28 36 N 1 42 12 E				MRCC Yarmouth.
1096 2-0001	Newhaven.	RDF	50 46 56 N 0 03 01 E				MRSC Solent.
1097 2-0001	Newton.	RDF	55 31 01 N 1 37 06 W				MRSC Humber.
1098 2-0001	North Foreland.	RDF	51 22 32 N 1 26 43 E				MRCC Dover.
1098.2 2-0001	Noss Head.	RDF	58 28 48 N 3 03 00 W				MRCC Aberdeen.
1098.3 2-0001	Portnaguran.	RDF	58 14 49 N 6 09 44 W				MRSC Stornoway.

RADIO DIRECTION FINDER AND RADAR STATIONS

(1) No.	(2) Name	(3) Type	(4) Position Rx Tx	(5) Frequency	(6) Range	(7) Procedure	(8) Remarks
1098.5 *2-0175*	Orlock Head.	RDF	54 40 25 N 5 34 58 W				MRSC Belfast.
1105 *2-0001*	Rame Head.	RDF	50 19 02 N 4 13 12 W				MRSC Brixham.
1105.2 *2-0001*	Rhiw.	RDF	52 50 00 N 4 37 49 W				MRSC Holyhead.
1106 *2-0001*	Rodel.	RDF	57 44 54 N 6 57 25 W				MRSC Stornoway.
1108 *2-0001*	St. Ann's Head.	RDF	51 40 58 N 5 10 31 W				MRSC Milford Haven.
1109 *2-0001*	St. Mary's, Isles of Scilly.	RDF	49 55 44 N 6 18 15 W				MRCC Falmouth.
1115 *2-0001*	Selsey.	RDF	50 43 48 N 0 48 13 W				MRSC Solent.
1116 *2-0001*	Shoeburyness.	RDF	51 31 23 N 0 46 30 E				MRSC Thames.
1117 *2-0001*	Skegness.	RDF	53 09 00 N 0 21 00 E				MRCC Yarmouth.
1120 *2-0001*	Snaefell.	RDF	54 15 50 N 4 27 40 W				MRSC Liverpool.
1150 *2-0001*	Tiree.	RDF	56 30 37 N 6 57 41 W				MRCC Clyde.
1155 *2-0001*	Trevose Head.	RDF	50 32 55 N 5 01 59 W				MRCC Falmouth.
1160 *2-0001*	Trimingham.	RDF	52 54 34 N 1 20 36 E				MRCC Yarmouth.
1165 *2-0001*	Tynemouth.	RDF	50 01 04 N 1 24 59 W				MRSC Humber.
1170 *2-0001*	Walney Island.	RDF	54 06 37 N 3 16 00 W				MRSC Liverpool.
1171 *2-0175*	West Torr.	RDF	55 11 42 N 6 05 12 W				MRSC Belfast.
1172 *2-0001*	Whitby.	RDF	54 29 24 N 0 36 18 W				MRSC Humber.
1175 *2-0001*	Wideford Hill.	RDF	58 59 17 N 3 01 24 W				MRSC Shetland.
1180 *2-0001*	Windyhead.	RDF	57 38 54 N 2 14 30 W				MRCC Aberdeen.

RADIO DIRECTION FINDER AND RADAR STATIONS

(1) No.	(2) Name	(3) Type	(4) Position Rx / Tx	(5) Frequency	(6) Range	(7) Procedure	(8) Remarks
				FRANCE			
	The VHF direction finding stations of France are for emergency use only. The following details of operation are common to all of these stations:			CROSS Stations: A. Ch.11, 16 (67 when 11 is in use for distress traffic) B. Ch.11, 16 (67). C. Ch.11, 16 (67). Signal and lookout stations: A. Ch.16 and 7 additional frequencies (swept by scanner) from Ch.1-29, 36, 39, 48, 50, 52, 55, 56, 60-88. B. Ch.11, 16. C. Ch.11, 16.			
1182 2-0815	Gris-Nez.	RDF	50 52 12 N 1 35 00 E				Controlled by CROSS.
1182.1 2-0815	Jobourg.	RDF	49 41 06 N 1 54 36 W				Controlled by CROSS.
1182.2 2-0815	Roches-Douvres.	RDF	49 06 30 N 2 48 48 W				Controlled by CROSS-Jobourg.
1182.3 2-0815	Dunkerque.	RDF	51 03 24 N 2 20 24 E				Controlled by signal station.
1182.4 2-0815	Boulogne.	RDF	50 44 00 N 1 36 00 E				Controlled by signal station. Day service only.
1182.5 2-0815	Ault.	RDF	50 06 30 N 1 27 30 E				Controlled by signal station. Day service only.
1182.6 2-0815	Dieppe.	RDF	49 56 00 N 1 05 12 E				Controlled by signal station. Day service only.
1182.7 2-0815	Fecamp.	RDF	49 46 06 N 0 22 12 E				Controlled by signal station.
1182.8 2-0815	La Heve.	RDF	49 30 36 N 0 04 12 E				Controlled by signal station.
1182.9 2-0815	Villerville.	RDF	49 23 12 N 0 06 30 E				Controlled by signal station. Day service only.
1183 2-0815	Port-en-Bessin.	RDF	49 21 06 N 0 46 18 W				Controlled by signal station.
1183.05 2-0815	Saint-Vaast.	RDF	49 34 30 N 1 16 30 W				Controlled by signal station. Day service only from Jun. 1 to Sep. 30.
1183.1 2-0815	Barfleur.	RDF	49 41 54 N 1 15 54 W				Controlled by signal station.
1183.2 2-0815	Homet.	RDF	49 39 30 N 1 37 54 W				Controlled by lookout station.

RADIO DIRECTION FINDER AND RADAR STATIONS

(1) No.	(2) Name	(3) Type	(4) Position Rx Tx	(5) Frequency	(6) Range	(7) Procedure	(8) Remarks
1183.25 *2-0815*	La Hague.	RDF	49 43 36 N 1 56 18 W				Controlled by signal station. Day service only.
1183.3 *2-0815*	Carteret.	RDF	49 22 24 N 1 48 18 W				Controlled by signal station.
1183.35 *2-0815*	Le Roc.	RDF	48 50 06 N 1 36 54 W				Controlled by signal station. Day service.
1183.45 *2-0815*	Le Grouin (Cancale).	RDF	48 42 36 N 1 50 36 W				Controlled by signal station. Day service only from Jun. 1 to Sep. 15.
1183.5 *2-0815*	Saint-Cast.	RDF	48 38 36 N 2 14 42 W				Controlled by signal station. Day service only.
1183.55 *2-0815*	S. Quay Portrieux.	RDF	48 39 18 N 2 49 30 W				Controlled by signal station.
1183.6 *2-0815*	Brehat.	RDF	48 51 18 N 3 00 06 W				Controlled by signal station. Day service only.
1183.65 *2-0815*	Ploumanach.	RDF	48 49 30 N 3 28 12 W				Controlled by signal station.
1183.7 *2-0815*	Batz.	RDF	48 44 48 N 4 00 36 W				Controlled by signal station. Day service only.
1183.75 *2-0815*	Brignogan.	RDF	48 40 36 N 4 19 42 W				Controlled by signal station.
1183.8 *2-0815*	Le Stiff (Ile d'Ouessant).	RDF	48 28 36 N 5 03 06 W				Controlled by CROSS-Corsen.
1183.85 *2-0815*	Saint-Mathieu.	RDF	48 19 48 N 4 46 12 W				Controlled by lookout station.
1183.9 *2-0815*	Toulinguet (Camaret).	RDF	48 16 48 N 4 37 30 W				Controlled by signal station. Day service only.
1183.95 *2-0815*	Cap de la Chevre.	RDF	48 10 12 N 4 33 00 W				Controlled by signal station. Day service only.
1184 *2-0815*	Pointe du Raz.	RDF	48 02 18 N 4 43 48 W				Controlled by signal station.
1184.05 *2-0815*	Penmarc'h.	RDF	47 47 54 N 4 22 24 W				Controlled by signal station.
1184.1 *2-0815*	Beg-Meil.	RDF	47 51 18 N 3 58 24 W				Controlled by signal station. Day service only.
1184.15 *2-0815*	Etel.	RDF	47 39 48 N 3 12 00 W				Controlled by CROSS.
1184.2 *2-0815*	Beg Melen.	RDF	47 39 12 N 3 30 06 W				Controlled by signal station. Day service only.

RADIO DIRECTION FINDER AND RADAR STATIONS

(1) No.	(2) Name	(3) Type	(4) Position Rx Tx	(5) Frequency	(6) Range	(7) Procedure	(8) Remarks
1184.3 2-0815	Saint-Julien.	RDF	47 29 42 N 3 07 30 W				Controlled by signal station. Day service only.
1184.4 2-0815	Le Talut.	RDF	47 17 42 N 3 13 00 W				Controlled by signal station.
1184.45 2-0815	Piriac.	RDF	47 22 30 N 2 33 24 W				Controlled by signal station. Day service only.
1184.5 2-0815	Chemoulin.	RDF	47 14 06 N 2 17 48 W				Controlled by signal station.
1184.55 2-0815	Saint-Sauveur.	RDF	46 41 42 N 2 18 48 W				Controlled by signal station.
1184.6 2-0815	Les Baleines.	RDF	46 14 36 N 1 33 42 W				Controlled by signal station. Day service only.
1184.65 2-0815	Chassiron.	RDF	46 02 48 N 1 24 30 W				Controlled by signal station.
1184.75 2-0815	Pointe de Grave.	RDF	45 34 18 N 1 03 54 W				Controlled by signal station.
1184.8 2-0815	Cap Ferret.	RDF	44 37 30 N 1 15 00 W				Controlled by signal station.
1184.82 2-0815	Messanges.	RDF	43 48 48 N 1 24 00 W				Controlled by signal station. Day service only.
1184.85 2-0815	Socoa.	RDF	43 23 42 N 1 41 06 W				Controlled by signal station.
1185.5 2-1040	La Garde.	RDF	43 06 18 N 5 59 30 E				Controlled by CROSS.
1185.6 2-1040	Cap Bear.	RDF	42 30 48 N 3 08 00 E				Controlled by signal station.
1185.7 2-1040	Cap Leucate.	RDF	42 55 06 N 3 03 42 E				Controlled by signal station.
1185.8 2-1040	Sete.	RDF	43 29 54 N 3 41 30 E				Controlled by signal station.
1185.9 2-1040	L'Espiguette.	RDF	43 23 54 N 3 41 36 E				Controlled by signal station.
1186 2-1040	Cap Couronne.	RDF	43 20 06 N 5 03 18 E				Controlled by signal station.
1186.2 2-1040	Bec de L'Aigle.	RDF	43 10 30 N 5 34 36 E				Controlled by signal station. Day service only.
1186.3 2-1040	Cap Cepet.	RDF	43 04 48 N 5 56 30 E				Controlled by lookout station.
1186.4 2-1040	Porquerolles.	RDF	43 00 00 N 6 13 42 E				Controlled by signal station.

RADIO DIRECTION FINDER AND RADAR STATIONS

(1) No.	(2) Name	(3) Type	(4) Position Rx / Tx	(5) Frequency	(6) Range	(7) Procedure	(8) Remarks
1186.5 2-1040	Cap Camarat.	RDF	43 12 06 N 6 40 30 E				Controlled by signal station.
1186.6 2-1040	Cap du Dramont.	RDF	43 24 48 N 6 51 12 E				Controlled by signal station. Day service only.
1186.7 2-1040	La Garoupe.	RDF	43 34 00 N 7 08 12 E				Controlled by signal station.
1186.8 2-1040	Cap Ferrat.	RDF	43 41 12 N 7 19 30 E				Controlled by signal station.
1186.9 2-1040	Cap Corse.	RDF	43 00 18 N 9 21 36 E				Controlled by signal station. Day service only.
1187 2-1040	Ile Rousse.	RDF	42 37 54 N 8 55 24 E				Controlled by signal station. Day service only.
1187.1 2-1040	La Parata.	RDF	41 54 06 N 8 36 48 E				Controlled by signal station. Day service only.
1187.2 2-1040	Pertusato.	RDF	41 22 24 N 9 10 42 E				Controlled by signal station.
1187.3 2-1040	La Chiappa.	RDF	41 35 36 N 9 21 54 E				Controlled by signal station.
1187.4 2-1040	Alistro.	RDF	42 15 36 N 9 32 30 E				Controlled by signal station.
1187.5 2-1040	Sagro.	RDF	42 47 48 N 9 29 24 E				Controlled by signal station.
			BULGARIA				
1187.61 2-1282	Nos Galata Lt.	RDF	43 10 17 N 27 56 49 E	297.5 kHz, A2A.	5	On request to Hydrographic Service, Varna.	Transmits **DG**.
			PAKISTAN				
1188 2-2147	Karachi (ASK).	RDF	24 52 44 N 24 51 05 N 67 09 50 E 67 02 32 E	A. 410, 500 kHz, A1A. B. 410, 500 kHz, A1A. C. 410, 500 kHz, A1A, A2A, 1.5 kW.			CALIBRATED SECTOR: 360°.

RADIO DIRECTION FINDER AND RADAR STATIONS

PART II RADAR STATIONS

110A. Coast and Port Radar Station List

Details concerning shore-based radar stations rendering navigational assistance to ships on request are given in the listings which follow. These stations are indicated on charts by the abridged description: Ra.

These stations provide information of interest to the mariner. They have a limited range of transmission and usually broadcast traffic navigational, weather and other information concerning only their port limits and approaches. The provision of such information does not relieve the Master of his responsibility for the safe navigation of his ship.

Mariners are warned that port radar stations may suspend operation without notice for varying periods because of minor defects, maintenance work, etc.

Many of these stations provide radar information in conjunction with Vessel Traffi Service (VTS) operations. In many ports participation in VTS may be compulsory for certain classes of vessels. For further information on VTS in specifi ports, refer to National Ocean Service Coast Pilots (NOSPBCP1 - 9), NGA Sailing Directions (SDPUB or CDPUBSD 120 - 200), and other applicable guides.

RADIO DIRECTION FINDER AND RADAR STATIONS

(1) No.	(2) Name	(3) Type	(4) Position Rx Tx	(5) Frequency	(6) Range	(7) Procedure	(8) Remarks
				RUSSIA			
1190	Sankt-Peterburg.	RA		Ch.12.		Call Sankt-Peterburg Radio-12.	Vessels can obtain assistance between sea buoy and heads of Severnaya and Yuzhnaya Dambas.
1192	Novorossiysk.	RA		Ch.09,95.		Call Novorossiysk 17.	Continuous radar guidance is compulsory for vessels over 200 GRT. Covers area N of 44-37.7N, between 37-48.0E 37-52.9E.
1194	Nakhodka.	RA		Ch.12,16.		Call Traffic Control Center (Kamenskiy 17).	Mandatory radar control of vessels N of line joining 42-44.0N 132-51.6E and 42-42.9N 132-59.9E.
1196	Murmansk.	RA		Ch.12,18,67.		Call Coast Radar Station (Murmansk Radio 9).	When visibility is less than 0.5M, navigation will only be conducted under radar control. Covers area S of 60-02.7N and should be requested 2 hrs. in advance.
				LATVIA			
1198	Ventspils.	RA		Ch.14,16.		Call Radio 9.	Compulsory when visibility is less than 2M or vessel is over 150m in length or 12000 DWT.
				LITHUANIA			
1199	Klaipeda.	RA		Ch.09.		Call Radio 17.	Compulsory when visibility is less than 0.5M or for ferries, tankers, vessels with dangerous cargos and vessels constrained by their draft.
				POLAND			
1200	Leba.	RA		Ch.12,16.		Call Leba Port Radar.	Covers area of port and roads.
1201	Darlowo.	RA		Ch.12,16, or Witowo Radio (SPS) 2182kHz.		Call Darlowo Port Radar Station.	
1202	Kolobrzeg.	RA		Ch.12,16.		Call Kolobrzeg Port Radar Station.	Covers area of port and roads.
				SWEDEN			
1203	Goteborg.	RA		Ch.09,13,16.		Call Goteborg Trafik.	Available on request for large tankers and other vessels with defective radar in poor visibility. Covers the area seaward of Alvsborgsbron (57-41.5N 11-54.2E).
				NORWAY			
1204	Fedje.	RA		Ch.16,80.			Compulsory for all vessels over 200 GRT or 24m. in length (including tows) or carrying dangerous cargos. Permission to navigate within the VTS area should be obtained at least 1 hr. before entering the area. Covers the approaches of the Sture and Mongstad oil terminals.

RADIO DIRECTION FINDER AND RADAR STATIONS

(1) No.	(2) Name	(3) Type	(4) Position Rx Tx	(5) Frequency	(6) Range	(7) Procedure	(8) Remarks
				GERMANY			
1205	Die Elbe.	RA		Cuxhaven Control: Elbe Approach West Ch.65. Elbe Approach East Ch.19. Scharhorn Ch.18. Neuwerk Ch.05. Cuxhaven Ch.21. Belum Ch.03. Brunsbuttel Control: Brunsbuttel I Ch.04. II Ch.67. S. Margarethen Ch.18. Freiburg Ch.22 Rhinplatte Ch.05 Pagensand Ch.66 Hetlingen Ch.21 Wedel Ch.60.		Call Cuxhaven Elbe Traffic on Ch.71,16; Brunsbuttel Elbe Traffic on Ch.68,16; or the appropriate Control Area.	Radar information provided on request. Vessels exempt from compulsory pilotage should use this service when visibility is less than 2000m (on the Lower Elbe, W of Seemannshoft, less than 3000m).
1210	Hamburg.	RA		Light buoy No.123 to 129 Ch.19. Light buoy No.129 to Seemannshoft Ch.03. Seemannshoft to Vorhafen Ch.63. Parkhafen to Kuhwerder Vorhafen Ch.07. Kuhwerder Vorhafen to Norderelbbrucke Ch.05. Kohlbrand to Harburger harbors Ch.80.		Call Cuxhaven Elbe Traffic on Ch.71; Brunsbuttel Elbe Traffic on Ch.68; or Hamburg Radar.	Radar service provided on request. Vessels exempt from compulsory pilotage should use this service when visibility is less than 2000m (W of Seemannshoft, less than 3000m).
1215	Die Weser.	RA		Alte Weser Ch.22. Hohe Weg I,II Ch.02. Robbenplate I,II Ch.04. Blexen Ch.07. Luneplate I Ch.05. II Ch.82. Dedesdorf Ch.82. Sandstedt Ch.21. Harriersand I Ch.21. II Ch.19. Elsflethe Ch.19. Ronnebeck, Ritzenbutteler, Schonebecker Ch.78. Ochtumer, Seehausen, Lankenau Ch.81. All stations Ch.16.		Call Bremerhaven Weser Radar or Bremen Weser Radar on Ch.16.	Radar information is provided on request or if instructed by the VTS Center (in German and English). Radar service is provided when visibility is less than 3000m (Bremerhaven Weser) or 2000m (Bremen Weser); when pilot vessel is in a sheltered position; when light buoys are withdrawn due to ice; when required by traffi situation or when requested by a vessel. VTS compulsory for all vessels over 50m in length and all vessels carrying dangerous cargo.
1216	Die Jade.	RA		Jade I,II: Light buoy 1b/Jade 1 to 33 Ch.63. Light buoy 33 to 60 Ch.20.		Call Jade Radar Ch.16.	Radar information provided when visibility is less than 3000m; when pilot vessel is in a sheltered position; when light buoys are withdrawn due to ice; when required by traffi situation or when requested by a vessel. VTS compulsory for vessels (including tows) over 50m in length and all vessels carrying dangerous cargo.
1217	Die Ems.	RA		Borkum: Light buoy No.1 to 35 Ch.18. Knock: Light buoy No.35 to 57 Ch.20. Wybelsum: Light buoy No.57 to Emden harbor entrance Ch.21.		Call Ems Traffic.	Radar information is provided on request or if instructed by the VTS Center (in German and English). Radar service is provided when visibility is less than 2000m; when pilot vessel is in a sheltered position; when light buoys are withdrawn due to ice; when required by traffi situation or when requested by a vessel. VTS compulsory for all vessels over 40m in length and all vessels carrying dangerous cargo.

RADIO DIRECTION FINDER AND RADAR STATIONS

(1) No.	(2) Name	(3) Type	(4) Position Rx / Tx	(5) Frequency	(6) Range	(7) Procedure	(8) Remarks
				NETHERLANDS			
1218	Eemshaven.	RA		Ch.19.		Available on request of the pilot 1 hr. in advance to Verkeersdienst Eemsmonding on Ch.14 or Delfzijl Pilot Vessel on Ch.06,16. Call Eemshaven Radar.	Covers Lt buoy 31 or 35 to Eemshaven.
1218.5	Delfzijl.	RA		Ch.66.		Requests should be made by the master of any sea going or inland vessel through the VHF Channel appropriate for the port. Call Delfzijl Radar.	When visibility falls below 2000m within the jurisdiction of the Delfzijl VTS area. Under special circumstances assistance can be given when visibility is good, for example if navigational aids are not working correctly.
1219	Den Helder.	RA		Ch.12.		Call Yerkeerscentrale, Den Helder.	Vessels equipped with VHF are requested to participate. Vessels should make notificatio when navigating in area or passing Moormanbrug.
1220	Ijmuiden.	RA		West of Ijmuiden light buoy Ch.12. Ijmuiden light buoy to North Sea Locks Ch.09.		Call Traffic Center Ijmuiden west of Ijmuiden light buoy; call Ijmuiden Port Control from Ijmuiden light buoy to North Sea Locks.	Radar information provided to vessels within 13M of Ijmuiden light buoy (52-28.7N 04-23.9E) which do not have a pilot aboard.
1225	Scheveningen.	RA		Ch.21.	9.5	Call Radar Scheveningen.	In reduced visibility vessels may request information on their position and traffic
1226	Dordrecht.	RA		Ch.19.		Call Post Dordrecht.	

Nieuwe (Rotterdamsche) Waterweg is covered by the following five Radar Stations. The Traffic Management and Information Service is compulsory for all vessels navigating in the area. Inbound vessels with draft 20.7m and over should make notification to HCC Rotterdam through Scheveningen (PCH) 24 hrs. in advance. Vessels with draft 17.4m and over navigat- ing Nieuwe Waterweg should make notification to Traffic Center Hook through Scheveningen 6 hrs. in advance; vessels 250m and over 4 hrs. in advance. Inbound vessels with dangerous cargo should report to Central Traffic Control (HCC) 24 hrs. in advance (1 hr. in advance of unberthing). All other vessels should make notification to Hoek van Holland 3 hrs. in advance of arrival and notify their area Radar Station 1 hr. in advance of unberthing.

(1) No.	(2) Name	(3) Type	(4) Position	(5) Frequency	(6) Range	(7) Procedure	(8) Remarks
1230	Hoek van Holland (VCH).	RA		Ch.01,02,03,13,65, 66; 2182kHz.		Call Traffic Center Hoek van Holland.	Covers Maas Traffi Separation Schemes, Europoort and Nieuwe Waterweg to Kilometer Post 1023.
1231	Botlek (VCB).	RA		Ch.13,61,80.		Call Traffic Center Botlek.	Covers Nieuwe Waterweg to Kilometer Post 1011 Nieuwe Maas, 1005 Oude Maas.
1232	Hartel (VPH).	RA		Ch.62.		Call Traffic Center Hartel.	Covers Oude Maas to Buoy O12 and Hartelkanal.
1233	Stad (VCS).	RA		Ch.13,60,63.		Call Traffic Center Stad.	Covers Nieuwe Maas to Kilometer Post 998.
1234	Maasboulevard (VPM).	RA		Ch.21,81.		Call Traffic Center Maasboulevard.	Covers Nieuwe Maas to Kilometer Post 993.

RADIO DIRECTION FINDER AND RADAR STATIONS

(1) No.	(2) Name	(3) Type	(4) Position Rx Tx	(5) Frequency	(6) Range	(7) Procedure	(8) Remarks
				UNITED KINGDOM			
1237	Lerwick.	RA		Ch.12.		Call Lerwick Harbour Radio.	Vessels should report at N and S Entrances. Covers N Entrance, S Entrance and Inner Harbour.
1240	Sullom Voe Harbour.	RA		Ch.14,16.		Call Sullom Voe Harbour Radio.	Vessels arriving should make notificatio 24 hrs. in advance. Covers Yell Sound and Sullom Voe. VHF reception is poor W and N of Yell Sound.
1245	Tees.	RA		Ch.14,22.	10	Call Tees Harbour Radio.	All vessels navigating when "Channel Closed" signals are displayed or when visibility is less than 1000m must obtain prior permission from Harbour Master; all vessels with dangerous cargo must make 24 hr. advance notification all vessels over 20m must make 6 hrs. advance notification Covers Tees Bay, Tees River to tidal limits and Hartlepool.
1250	Medway.	RA		Ch.22.		Call Medway Radio.	All inbound vessels should contact Medway Navigation Service 24 hrs. in advance; outbound vessels should make 1 hr. advance notification
1254	Gravesend Radio.	RA		Thames seaward approaches to Sea Reach No.4 light buoy Ch.13. Sea Reach No.4 light buoy to Crayford Ness Ch.12. Secondary Ch.09,16, 18,20.		Call Port Control London or Gravesend Radio.	Inbound and outbound vessels should make notificatio 24 hrs. in advance. Covers Thames R. from Erith to seaward limits of the Port of London.
1255	Woolwich Radio.	RA		Ch.14,16,22.			Inbound and outbound vessels should make notificatio 24 hrs. in advance. Covers Thames R. from Crayford Ness to Greenwich.
1262	Harwich.	RA		Ch.14,20.			Inbound and outbound vessels should make notificatio 24 hrs. in advance.
1265	Southampton Vessel Traffic Services Centre.	RA		Ch.16(calling). Ch.18,20,22 (working).		Call Southampton VTS.	Compulsory for vessels 20m or over. Inbound vessels should contact VTS on Ch.12 when approaching the Nab or the Needles. Covers the Solent and Southampton waters.
1270	Liverpool.	RA		Ch.18,22. Ch.19(tankers to or from Tranmere).		Call Mersey Radio.	Vessels over 50 GRT carrying dangerous cargo should make notificatio 48 hrs. in advance of arrival/departure. All other vessels over 50 GRT should make notificatio 24 hrs. in advance of arrival and 4 hrs. in advance of departure. Covers River Mersey including Liverpool, Birkenhead, Eastham and Garston.

RADIO DIRECTION FINDER AND RADAR STATIONS

(1) No.	(2) Name	(3) Type	(4) Position Rx Tx	(5) Frequency	(6) Range	(7) Procedure	(8) Remarks
				FRANCE			
1273	Dunkerque.	RA		Dunkerque Pilots: Ch.16 (calling). Ch.72 (working). Dunkerque Port: Ch.73.		Call Dunkerque Pilots or Dunkerque Port.	Radar coverage of the pilot embarkation zone at the entrance to the Passe de l'Ouest is provided by the Pilot Station (50-59.2N 01-58.0E). Radar coverage of the access channels is provided by the port.
1274	Gris-Nez (CROSS).	RA		Ch.13,79.		Call Gris-Nez Traffic.	Radar assistance provided on request. Two radar stations at Gris-Nez (50-52.2N 01-35.1E) and Saint-Frieux (50-36.6N 01-36.6E) provide coverage extending approximately SW up to 00-30E and NE up to 30 miles from Gris-Nez.
1275	Le Havre.	RA		Ch.12.		Call Havre Port.	Radar assistance provided on request in poor visibility for Le Havre or Antifer. The area of radar coverage is a circular zone 12.5 miles radius centered on 49-39.0N 00-08.0W (approx.). Inbound vessels should make notificatio 48 hrs. in advance. Outbound vessels should make notificatio 24 hrs. in advance.
1280	La Seine.	RA		Ch.13,73.		Call Honfleur Radar.	Radar assistance provided in poor visibility and on request. The area of radar coverage extends to 20 miles W of Radar Honfleu (49-25.7N 00-14.1E) up to 00-36.2E.
1285	Rouen.	RA		Ch.13,73.		Call Radar Honfleur.	Radar assistance provided in poor visibility and on request. Coverage area extends to 20 miles W of Radar Honfleu (49-25.7N 00-14.1E) up to 00-36.2E.
1287	Corsen (CROSS).	RA		Ch.13,79.		Call Ouessant Traffic.	Coverage area is a circular zone up to 35 miles from Le Stiff Radar Tower (48-28.6N 05-03.1W).
1288	La Loire.	RA		Ch.12.		Call Saint-Nazaire Port.	Radar assistance provided on request. Coverage area from the pilot boarding point (47-07.5N 02-21.5W) to Saint-Nazaire Roads.
1290	La Gironde.	RA		Ch.16 (calling). Ch.12,14 (working).		Call Radar Verdon 3 hrs. in advance of ETA on Ch. 12.	Covers La Gironde and approaches (a circular zone 34 miles radius centered on (45-39.8N 01-07.2W). Radar information is supplied on Ch. 12 or 14 for the area between BXA lightbuoy and Le Verdon's roads. Notificatio of arrival should be made 48 hrs. in advance to Bordeaux Traffi through agent, 24 hrs. and 12 hrs. in advance direct to Bordeaux Traffic
				PORTUGAL			
1295	Aveiro.	RA		Ch.14,16.		Call Pilotosaveiro.	In bad weather pilot vessel assists vessel's approach to harbor entrance. Arrival notificatio should be made 6 hrs. in advance.

1 - 21

RADIO DIRECTION FINDER AND RADAR STATIONS

(1) No.	(2) Name	(3) Type	(4) Position Rx Tx	(5) Frequency	(6) Range	(7) Procedure	(8) Remarks
				SPAIN			
1300	Strait of Gibraltar.	RA		Ch.10,16.	19	Call Tarifa Traffic.	Tarifa Vessel Traffi Service is compulsory for VHF-equipped vessels which are Spanish flag intend to enter Spanish territorial seas, have dangerous cargo or limitations to maneuverability or navigation. Vessels should call when within 21M of Tarifa (36-01.1N 05-34.8W) or on leaving a port within that area.
				UKRAINE			
1305	Odessa.	RA		Ch.14,16.		Call Odessa Port Control.	
1310	Yuzhnyy.	RA		Ch.16,74.		Call Yuzhnyy Radio 5.	
1315	Mariupol (Zhdanov).	RA		Ch.14,16.		Call Zhdanov Radio 1.	Provides radar assistance in restricted visibility and in the absence of navigational aids. Covers from approach channel buoys 15 and 16 to berths in Port Zhdanov.
				MOROCCO			
1320	Casablanca.	RA		Ch.12.		Call CNP2.	Vessels should send notificatio of arrival to the Port Captain through Casablanca (CNP) 24 hrs. in advance.
				THAILAND			
1480	Laem Chabang.	RA		500kHz,A1A,A2A;2182 kHz,A3E,H3E;Ch.13, 14,16.			Pilotage is compulsory. ETA should be sent 24 hrs. in advance. Radar-equipped VTS station is located at Laem Krabang Hill.
				REPUBLIC OF KOREA			
1520	Busan.	RA		Ch.12,14,16,20,22.		Call Busan Port Control.	Radar assistance is available during limited visibility.
				JAPAN			
1530	Osaka.	RA		2182,2130,2150, 2394.5kHz,H3E,J3E; Ch.14,16,22.	8	Call Osaka Harbor Radar.	Information on position, traffi and weather provided for area within 4M of Osaka Central Pier (within 8M for vessels over 1000 GRT).
1540	Kanmon Kaikyo.	RA		1651kHz,H3E;Ch.13, 14,16,22.		Call Kanmon MARTIS.	All vessels should report on entering the Radar Service Area. Covers Kanmon Kaikyo, including W and E approaches and area N and E of Mutsure Shima.
1550	Bisan Seto.	RA		1651kHz,H3E;Ch.13, 14,16,22.		Call Bisan MARTIS.	All vessels should report on entering the Radar Service Area. Covers all traffi routes between 133-37.5E and 133-55E except Bisan Seto N traffi route W of Takami Shima.
1555	Nagoya.	RA		1665kHz,H3E;Ch.14, 16,22.	11	Call Nagoya Harbor Radar.	All vessels should report on entering the Radar Service Area. Covers Nagoya port, including its approaches.

RADIO DIRECTION FINDER AND RADAR STATIONS

(1) No.	(2) Name	(3) Type	(4) Position Rx / Tx	(5) Frequency	(6) Range	(7) Procedure	(8) Remarks
1560	Tokyo Wan.	RA		1665kHz,H3E;Ch.13, 14,16,22.		Call Tokyo MARTIS.	All vessels over 100 GRT or carrying more than 30 people should report when entering the Radar Service Area. Covers Tokyo Wan N of 35-10N.
1570	Kushiro.	RA		2182,2150,2245, 2394.5,2785.9kHz, H3E,J3E;Ch.14,16, 22.	10	Call Kushiro Harbor-Radar.	Radar assistance provided within 2M of 42-58.0N 144-22.6E (within 10M for vessels over 1000 GRT).
				NEW ZEALAND			
1625	Auckland.	RA		2182,2012kHz,H3E, J3E; Ch.12,16.	45		Provides vessel's range and bearing from Signal Station (36-51S 174-49E) in restricted visibility. Vessels over 100 NRT should make notificatio 24 hrs. in advance of arrival.
1630	Otago Harbour.	RA		2182,2012,2045,2129, 2162,4125,4417, 6215,6224kHz,H3E, J3E;Ch.12,14,16.	20	Call ZMH32 (Taiaroa Head).	Provides range and bearing from Taiaroa Head Signal Station (0.1M S of lighthouse) in restricted visibility. Vessels over 100 NRT should make notificatio 72 hrs. in advance of arrival, through Wellington (ZLW) or Awarua (ZLB).
1635	Wanganui.	RA		2012,2045,2162,2182, 4125,4417,6215, 6224kHz,H3E,J3E; Ch.09,12,14,16,67, 69.	20	Call Wanganui Harbour Radio (ZMH211).	Provides range and bearing from Pilot Station (39-56.9S 174-59.5E).
1640	Westport.	RA		2012,2045,2162,2182, 4125,4417kHz,H3E, J3E;Ch.12,16.	15		Provides range and bearing from Signal Station (41-44.9S 171-35.7E) in restricted visibility. Vessels should make notificatio 12 hrs. in advance of arrival.
				AUSTRALIA			
1665	Port Hedland.	RA		Ch.06,08,09,12,13, 16,67.	64		Provides range and bearing from Control Tower (20-19.0S 118-34.5E). All foreign vessels and Australian vessels over 6500 GRT should make notificatio 48 hrs. in advance of arrival.
1675	Port Dampier.	RA		Ch.11,13,16,68,78, 79. Ch.67(emergency).		Call Dampier Port Control.	Provides range and bearing from Port Control (20-37.2S 116-45.0E). All vessels over 150 GRT should make notificatio of arrival 72 hrs. in advance (7 days for vessels arriving from overseas.

RADIO DIRECTION FINDER AND RADAR STATIONS

(1) No.	(2) Name	(3) Type	(4) Position Rx Tx	(5) Frequency	(6) Range	(7) Procedure	(8) Remarks
				UNITED STATES			
	United States VTS Vessel Movement Reporting System (VMRS) rules, VTS frequency monitoring requirements and General VTS operating rules are mandatory for power-driven vessels 40 meters or more in length, vessels certificated to carry 50 or more passengers for hire, and towing vessels 8 meters or more in length engaged in towing. VTS frequency monitoring requirements and General VTS operating rules are mandatory for vessels covered by the Vessel Bridge-to-Bridge Radiotele- phone Act.						
1720	New York, NY.	RA		Ch.11,12,13,14,16.		Call New York Traffic.	Vessels should make notificatio 15 mins. before navigating within the VTS area and upon entering or getting underway within the VTS area. Covers the Upper New York Bay E to the Brooklyn Bridge in the East River and N to 40-43.7N and 74-01.6W in the Hudson River, and includes the Kill Van Kull S to the AK Railroad Bridge, Newark Bay N to the Lehigh Valley Draw Bridge, and portions of the Lower New York Bay S to the entrance buoys at Ambrose, Sandy Hook, and Swash Channels.
1730	Berwick Bay, LA.	RA		Ch.11,13,16.			Vessels should make notificatio 15 mins. before navigating within the VTS area and upon entering or getting underway within the VTS area. Covers various Intracoastal Waterway Routes converging at Berwick and Morgan City.
1735	LOOP Deepwater Port (Louisiana Offshore Oil Port).	RA		Ch.10,16,74.		Call LOOP Radar.	Compulsory for all vessels; tankers must report to COTP and Vessel Traffi Supervisor 24 hrs. before arrival. Covers vicinity of port (28-53.2N 90-01.5W), anchorage and safety fairway to SE and S.
	NOTE: LOOP Deepwater Port is not a VTS.						
1740	Houston-Galveston, TX.	RA		Ch.11,12,13,16.		Call Houston Traffic.	Vessels should make notificatio 15 mins. before navigating within the VTS area and upon entering or getting underway within the VTS area. Covers the Galveston Bay Channels and Houston Ship Channel to the Houston Turning Basin.
1750	San Francisco, CA.	RA		Ch.12,13,14,16.		Call San Francisco Traffic.	Vessels should make notificatio 15 mins. before navigating within the VTS area and upon entering or getting underway within the VTS area. Covers the waters of San Francisco Bay and its approaches S of 38N, E of 123-07W and N of 37-27N, and its tributaries as far as Stockton and Sacramento.
1760	Puget Sound, WA.	RA		Ch.05A,13,14,16.		Call Seattle Traffic.	Vessels should make notificatio 15 mins. before navigating within the VTS area and upon entering or getting underway within the VTS area. Covers the Strait of Juan de Fuca E of 124-40W, Rosario Strait, the San Juan Islands, Admiralty Inlet, and Puget Sound.

NOTE: Puget Sound Vessel Traffic Service is one sector of a Cooperative Vessel Traffic Management System (CVTMS), which is a joint U.S. and Canadian vessel traffic management effort. Canada administers the two remaining sectors of CVTMS.

RADIO DIRECTION FINDER AND RADAR STATIONS

(1) No.	(2) Name	(3) Type	(4) Position Rx Tx	(5) Frequency	(6) Range	(7) Procedure	(8) Remarks
1770	Prince William Sound, AK.	RA		Ch.13,16.		Call Valdez Traffic.	Vessels should make notificatio 15 mins. before navigating within the VTS area and upon entering or getting underway within the VTS area. Covers Prince William Sound North of Cape Hinchinbrook, including Valdez Arm, Valdez Narrows and Port Valdez.
				COLOMBIA			
1850	Puerto Covenas, Floating Storage Unit.	RA		Ch.10,13,16.		Call FSU Covenas.	Compulsory for all vessels. Vessels should contact FSU 30M from terminal.
				CHILE			
1895	Valparaiso.	RA		2182,2738kHz,H3E, J3E; 4143.6kHz,J3E; Ch.09,14,16.		Call CBV 20 (Port Captain).	Radar assistance provided on request in fog.
1900	Primera Angostura.	RA		Ch.11,13,16,68.		Eastbound vessels requiring radar assistance should call Magallanes Zonal Radio (CBM), Ch.16, when abeam Punta Arenas, or call CBM5 (Punta Delgada), Ch.68,11,13, when 20M from Punta Baxa. Westbound vessels should call Magallanes 24 hrs. before arrival at 52-35.0S 68-10.5W, or call CBM71 (Punta Dungeness), Ch.16, or CBM72 (Cabo Espiritu Santo), Ch.16, when 20M from that point.	Covers area between Banco Triton and E approaches to the Strait of Magellan.

CHAPTER 2

RADIO TIME SIGNALS

200A.	General.	2-3
200B.	The United States System	2-3
200C.	The Old International (ONOGO) System	2-3
200D.	The New International (Modified ONOGO) System	2-3
200E.	The English System	2-3
200F.	The BBC System	2-3
200G.	Codes for the Transmission of UTC Adjustments.	2-5
200H.	Shortwave Services Provided by the National Institute of Standards and Technology WWV-WWVH Broadcasts	2-6
	Station List.	2-11

CHAPTER 2

RADIO TIME SIGNALS

200A. General

The system of Coordinated Universal Time (UTC), described fully in "The American Practical Navigator" (Bowditch) (NVPUB9), came into use on 1 January 1972. Most countries have agreed to use the revised transmission procedures recommended by the the International Telecommunications Union-Radiocommunications Sector (ITU-R). Users are advised that some stations not specificall operating in the Standard Frequency and Time Signal Services may not be able to conform exactly to the current recommendations.

Stations use various systems to broadcast time signals. The more commonly used systems are described below and referred to in the station listings at the end of this chapter. Special systems are described under their respective stations.

ACCURACY OF SIGNALS: The majority of radio time signals are transmitted automatically and are referenced to standards at the various national standards labs such as the National Institute of Standards and Technology (NIST) in the U.S. Absolute reliance may be had in these signals; they should be correct to 0.05 second. Some stations transmit by a combination of manual and automatic signals. Care should be exercised to differentiate between the two at the time of actual comparison to a chronometer.

Other radio stations, however, have no automatic transmission system installed. In this instance, the operator is guided by the standard clock at the station. The clock is checked by either astronomical observations or by reliable time signals. The hand transmission should be correct to 0.25 second.

STATIONS MUST AVOID INTERFERENCE: During the transmission of time signals, stations are prohibited from making any transmissions which might interfere with the reception of these signals.

HIGH PRECISION: For ordinary navigational purposes no special precautions need be observed in receiving the signals other than to avoid those signals which are marked in the station schedule as unsatisfactory for navigational purposes.

200B. The United States System

The transmission of signals begins at 55 minutes, 0 seconds of a given hour and continues for 5 minutes. Signals are transmitted on every second during that time, except that there is no signal on the 29th second of any minute, nor on certain seconds at the ends of the minutes, as shown in the diagram.

The dashes in the diagram indicate seconds on which signals are transmitted. The seconds marked "60" are the zero seconds of the following minutes. The dash on the beginning of the hour (shown as 59 minutes, 60 seconds) is much longer than the others.

In all cases, the beginning of the dash indicates the beginning of the second; the end of the dash is without significanc .

Note that the number of dashes sounded in the group at the end of any minute indicates the number of minutes of the signal yet to be sent.

200C. The Old International (ONOGO) System

The time signal is usually preceded by a preparatory signal, described where necessary in the station listings.

The signal itself is described in the following table. In the transmission of the ONOGO signals, each dash (–) =1 second and each dot (•) = 0.25 second.

200D. The New International (Modified ONOGO) System

This is identical to the old system except that six dots are sent at the 55th through 60th seconds of each minute (instead of the old system of three 1 second dashes that commenced at the 55th, 57th, and 59th seconds), which constitute the time signals.

200E. The English System

The time signal on the hour is preceded by 5 minutes of a preparatory signal consisting of a 0.1 second dot at each second, 1 through 59, and a 0.4 second dash at each exact minute. The beginning of each dot or dash is the time reference point.

200F. The BBC System

The time signal on the hour is preceded by f ve 0.1 second dots sent at seconds 55 through 59. The hour marker is a 0.5 second dash. The beginning of each dot or dash is the time reference point.

RADIO TIME SIGNALS

The United States System

Minute	Second										
	50	51	52	53	54	55	56	57	58	59	60
55	—		—	—	—	—					—
56	—	—		—	—	—					—
57	—	—	—		—	—					—
58	—	—	—	—		—					—
59	—										—

Old International (ONOGO) System

Signal	Times				Morse Symbols
	m.	s.	m.	s.	
Letter X sent once every 10 seconds	57	00	to 57	49	— • • — — • • — — • • — — • • — — • • —
Letter O	57	55	to 58	00	— — —
Letter N sent once every 10 seconds	58	08	to 58	10	— • — • — • — • — •
Letter O	58	55	to 59	00	— — —
Letter G sent once every 10 seconds	59	06	to 59	10	— — • — — • — — • — — • — — •
Letter O	59	55	to 60	00	— — —

New International (Modified ONOGO) Syste

Signal	Times				Morse Symbols
	m.	s.	m.	s.	
Letter X sent once every 10 seconds	57	00	to 57	49	— • • — — • • — — • • — — • • — — • • —
Six dots	57	55	to 58	00	• • • • • •
Letter N sent once every 10 seconds	58	08	to 58	10	— • — • — • — • — •
Six dots	58	55	to 59	00	• • • • •
Letter G sent once every 10 seconds	59	06	to 59	10	— — • — — • — — • — — • — — •
Six dots	59	55	to 60	00	• • • • •

The English System

M.	Seconds: 1-59	60
55	• •	—
56	• •	—
57	• •	—
58	• •	—
59	• •	—

The BBC System

minute	seconds 1-54	55	56	57	58	59	60
59	(silence)	•	•	•	•	•	—

RADIO TIME SIGNALS

200G. Codes for the Transmission of UTC Adjustments

Currently the rate of departure between UTC and Greenwich mean time (UT1), used in celestial navigation, is 2.5 milliseconds a day. However, it is planned that UTC will not normally deviate from UT1 by more than 0.9 seconds. Provision has been made to maintain this relativity by means of step adjustments to the time signals of exactly 1 second. These adjustments, known as leap seconds, will normally be effected at 2400 on 30 June or 31 December. (A positive leap second begins at 23 hours, 59 minutes, 60 seconds, ending at 0 hours, 0 minutes, 0 seconds of the firs day of the following month. For a negative leap second, 23 hours, 59 minutes, 58 seconds will be followed one second later by 0 hours, 0 minutes, 0 seconds of the first day of the foll wing month.)

However, it is also quite possible that these dates may be varied depending upon any unpredicted variations in the earth's rate of rotation.

The difference between UTC and UT1 is known as D (for delta) UT1, the relationship being DUT1 = UT1 - UTC. By means of a coding system incorporated in the actual emissions, primary time signal sources will promulgate DUT1 in integral multiples of 0.1 second.

In most cases the coding will be in the form of a ITU-R code with emphasized second markers in the firs 16 seconds following the minute marker. The emphasis of the second markers can take the form of lengthening, doubling, splitting or tone modulating of the normal second markers. Each emphasized second represents a DUT1 value of 0.1 second, the total value of DUT1 being indicated by the number of emphasized seconds. The sign of DUT1 is determined by the position of the coded signals within the 16 second period, positive values being indicated by emphasis of the firs 8 seconds and negative values being indicated by emphasis of seconds 9 to 16.

A zero value of DUT1 will be indicated by the absence of emphasized second markers.

Time signal emissions of Russia follow this system; additionally, they carry a similar coding of seconds 21 to 24 or 31 to 34. The extra coding indicates a further figur (known as dUT1) to be added to the DUT1 value; the total value of the UT1 - UTC corrections being DUT1 + dUT1. Each emphasized second represents a dUT1 value of 0.02 second.

Positive values of dUT1 are indicated by emphasizing a number of consecutive second markers from seconds 21 through 24.

Negative values of dUT1 are indicated by emphasizing a number of consecutive second markers from seconds 31 through 34.

A zero value of dUT1 is indicated by the absence of emphasized second markers.

Time signals originating from Russia will also include a Morse code transmission of DUT1 + dUT1. The information is broadcast by means of a three digit group. The firs number indicates the sign of the difference (1 means a positive value and 0 means a negative value). The two numbers following give the absolute value (e.g., 072 = -0.72 second; 128 = +0.28 second). The numbers are transmitted with an interval corresponding to the length of three dashes (approximately 0.9 second).

The information is repeated 10 to 15 times during 1 minute, each group of three digits being separated from each other by a separation marker (• – •).

DUT1 may also be given by voice announcement or in Morse code. For example, U.S. Naval Radio Stations use standard Morse code from seconds 56 through 59 each minute (not used for time signals) to indicate the sign and value in tenths of a second of DUT1.

Positive values will be indicated by the letter "A" and the appropriate digit (e.g., • – • • • – – "A3": add 0.3 second).

Negative values will be indicated by the letter "S" and the appropriate digit (e.g., • • • – – – – • "S9": subtract 0.9 second).

EXAMPLES:

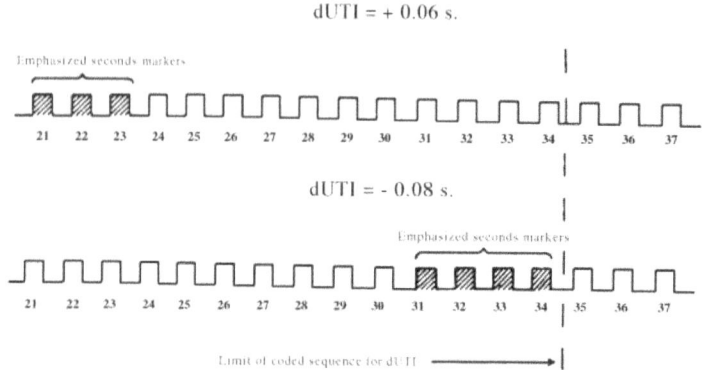

The appropriate seconds markers may be emphasized, for example by lengthening, doubling, splitting or tone modulation of normal seconds markers.

EXAMPLES:

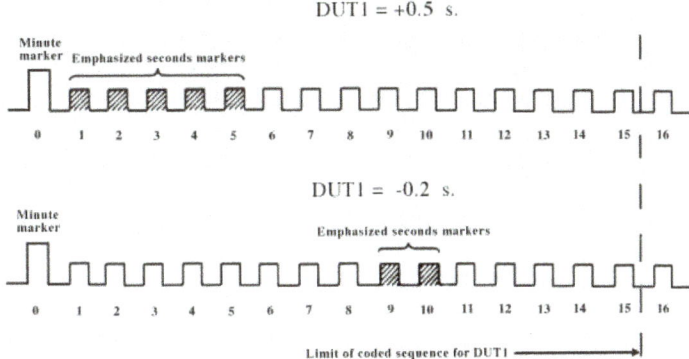

200H. Shortwave Services Provided by the National Institute of Standards and Technology WWV-WWVH Broadcasts

SHORTWAVE SERVICES: NIST broadcasts time signals continuously from the two high-frequency (shortwave) radio stations WWV, near Fort Collins, Colorado, and WWVH, Kekaha, Kauai, Hawaii on frequencies of 2.5, 5, 10, and 15 MHz (also 20 MHz from Fort Collins only). All frequencies provide the same information. Services include time announcements, standard time intervals, standard frequencies, UT1 time corrections, BCD time code, geophysical alerts, marine storm warnings, and GPS navigation system status information. The accompanying diagrams give the hourly broadcast schedules of WWV and WWVH. Station locations, radiated power, and details of antennas and modulation are given in the station listings which follow. The NIST also broadcasts time and frequency signals from its low frequency station, WWVB, also located at Fort Collins, Colorado, and from two geostationary GOES satellites.

The NIST Time and Frequency Division is internet accessible through the World Wide Web at:
http://www.boulder.nist.gov/timefreq/index.html

ACCURACY AND STABILITY: The time and frequency broadcasts are controlled by the NIST Frequency Standard, which realizes the internationally define cesium resonance frequency with an accuracy of 1 part in 10^{14}. The frequencies as transmitted by WWV and WWVH are accurate to about 1 part in 100 billion (1 x 10^{-11}) for frequency and about 0.01 millisecond (ms) for timing. The day-to-day deviations are normally less than 1 part in 1,000 billion (1 x 10^{-12}). However, the received accuracy is far less due to various propagation effects (Doppler effect, diurnal shifts, etc.) that cause fluctuation in the carrier frequencies. The usable received accuracy is about 1 part in 10 million (1 x 10^{-7}) for frequency and about 1 ms for timing.

TIME ANNOUNCEMENTS: Once per minute, voice announcements are made from WWV and WWVH. The two stations are distinguished by a female voice from WWVH and a male voice from WWV. The WWVH announcement occurs first at 15 seconds before the minute, while the WWV announcement occurs at 7.5 seconds before the minute. Coordinated Universal Time is used in these announcements.

STANDARD TIME INTERVALS: The most frequent sounds heard on WWV and WWVH are the pulses that mark the seconds of each minute, except for the 29th and 59th second pulses which are omitted completely. The firs pulse of every hour is an 800-ms pulse of 1500 Hz. The firs pulse of every minute is an 800-ms pulse of 1000 Hz at WWV and 1200 Hz at WWVH. The remaining second pulses are brief audio bursts (5-ms pulses of 1000 Hz at WWV and 1200 Hz at WWVH) that resemble the ticking of a clock. Each pulse commences at the beginning of each second. They are given by means of double-sideband amplitude modulation.

Each second's pulse is preceded by 10 ms of silence and followed by 25 ms of silence to avoid interference which might make it difficul or impossible to pick out the pulses.

STANDARD AUDIO FREQUENCIES: In alternate minutes during most of each hour, 500 or 600 Hz audio tones are broadcast. A 440 Hz tone, the musical note A above middle C, is broadcast once each hour. In addition to being a musical standard, the 440 Hz tone can be used to provide an hourly marker for chart recorders or other automated devices.

"SILENT" PERIODS: These are periods with no tone modulation. However, the carrier frequency, second pulses, time announcements, and 100 Hz BCD time code continue. The main silent periods extend from 43 to 46 and from 47 to 52 minutes after the hour on WWV and from 8 to 11 and from 14 to 20 minutes after the hour on WWVH. Minutes 29 and 59 on WWV and minutes 00 and 30 on WWVH are also silent.

BCD TIME CODE: A modifie IRIG-H time code occurs continuously on a 100 Hz subcarrier. The format is 1 pulse per second with a 1 minute time frame. It gives year (2 digits), day of the year, hours, and minutes in binary coded decimal form. Indicators for daylight saving time and leap seconds are also included in the code.

RADIO TIME SIGNALS

UT1 TIME CORRECTIONS: The UTC time scale operates on atomic frequency, but by means of resets is made to approximate the astronomical UT1 scale. It may disagree with UT1 by as much as 0.9 second before resets in steps of exactly 1 second are made. For those who need astronomical time more accurate than 0.9 second, a UTC correction is applied through the ITU-R code described earlier, using double ticks as emphasized markers.

GEOPHYSICAL ALERTS: Current geophysical alerts (Geoalerts) are broadcast in voice at 18 minutes after the hour (for WWV) and at 45 minutes after the hour (for WWVH). The messages are less than 45 seconds in length and are updated every three hours, i.e., 0000, 0300, 0600 UTC, etc. Part A of the message gives the solar-terrestrial indices for the day: specificall the 2000 UTC solar flu from Penticton, B.C., Canada at 2800 MHz, the estimated A-index for Boulder, CO and the current Boulder K-index. Part B gives the solar-terrestrial conditions for the previous 24 hours. Part C gives optional information on current conditions that may exist (that is, major flares proton or polar cap absorption [PCA] events, or stratwarm conditions). Part D gives the expected conditions for the next 24 hours. For example:

A) Solar-terrestrial indices for 26 October follow:
   Solar flu 173 and estimated Boulder A-index 20, repeat: Solar flu one-seven-three and estimated Boulder A-index two-zero.
   The Boulder K-index at 1800 UTC on 26 October was four, repeat: four.
B) Solar-terrestrial conditions for the last 24 hours follow:
   Solar activity was high.
   Geomagnetic field as unsettled to active.
C) A major flar occurred at 1648 UTC on 26 October. A satellite proton event and PCA are in progress.
D) The forecast for the next 24 hours follows:
   Solar activity will be moderate to high. The geomagnetic field will be act ve.

Solar activity is define as transient perturbations of the solar atmosphere as measured by enhanced x-ray emission, typically associated with flares Five standard terms are used to describe solar activity:

- Very low: x-ray events less than C-class.
- Low: C-class x-ray events.
- Moderate: isolated (one to four) M-class x-ray events.
- High: several (f ve or more) M-class x-ray events, or isolated (one to four) M5 or greater x-ray events.
- Very High: several M5 or greater x-ray events.

The geomagnetic fiel experiences natural variations classifie quantitatively into six standard categories depending upon the amplitude of the disturbance. The Boulder K and estimated A indices determine the category according to the following table:

Condition	Range of A-index	Typical K-indices
Quiet	$0 \leq A < 08$	usually no K indices > 2
Unsettled	$08 \leq A < 16$	usually no K indices > 3
Active	$16 \leq A < 30$	a few K indices of 4
Minor storm	$30 \leq A < 50$	K indices mostly 4 and 5
Major storm	$50 \leq A < 100$	some K indices 6 or greater
Severe storm	$100 \leq A$	some K indices 7 or greater

Solar Flares are classified by their x-ray emission as

Peak Flux Range (0.1 - 0.8 nm)

Class	mks system (Wm^{-2})	cgs system ($erg\ cm^{-2}s^{-1}$)
A	$f < 10^{-7}$	$f < 10^{-4}$
B	$10^{-7} \leq f < 10^{-6}$	$10^{-4} \leq f < 10^{-3}$
C	$10^{-6} \leq f < 10^{-5}$	$10^{-3} \leq f < 10^{-2}$
M	$10^{-5} \leq f < 10^{-4}$	$10^{-2} \leq f < 10^{-1}$
X	$10^{-4} \leq f$	$10^{-1} \leq f$

The letter designates the order of magnitude of the peak value. Following the letter the measured peak value is given. For descriptive purposes, a number from 1.0 to 9.9 is appended to the letter designation. The number acts as a multiplier. For example, a C3.2 event indicates an x-ray burst with peak flux of $3.2 \times 1^{-6}\ Wm^{-2}$.

Forecasts are usually issued only in terms of the broad C, M, and X categories. Since x-ray bursts are observed as a full-sun value, bursts below the x-ray background level are not discernible. The background drops to class A level during solar minimum; only bursts that exceed B1.0 are classifie as x-ray events. During solar maximum the background is often at the class M level, and therefore class A, B, or C x-ray bursts cannot be seen. Data are from the NOAA GOES satellites, monitored in real time by the Space Weather Operations (SWO) branch at the Space Environment Center (SEC). Bursts greater than $1.2 \times 10^{-3} Wm^{-2}$ may saturate the GOES detectors. If saturation occurs, estimated peak flux alues are reported.

The remainder of the report is as follows:
- MAJOR SOLAR FLARE: a flar which produces some geophysical effect; usually flare that have x-rays $\geq$ M5 class.
- PROTON FLARE: protons detected by satellite detectors (or polar cap absorption by riometer) have been observed in time association with H-alpha flar
- SATELLITE LEVEL PROTON EVENT: proton enhancement detected by Earth orbiting satellites with measured particle flu of at least 10 protons $cm^{-2}s^{-1}ster^{-1}$ at $\geq$ 10 MeV.

RADIO TIME SIGNALS

- SATELLITE LEVEL PROTON EVENT: proton enhancement detected by Earth orbiting satellites with measured particle flu of at least 10 protons cm^{-2}s^{-1}ster^{-1} at $\geq$ 10 MeV.
- POLAR CAP ABSORPTION: proton-induced absorption $\geq$2 dB during the daytime, 0.5 dB at night, as measured by a 30 MHz riometer located within the polar ice cap.
- STRATWARM: reports of stratospheric warming in the high latitude regions of the winter hemisphere of the earth associated with gross distortions of the normal circulation associated with the winter season.

The Geophysical Alert messages are also available by dialing: (1) 303-497-3235.

Inquiries regarding these messages should be addressed to:

SPACE WEATHER OPERATIONS
NOAA
325 BROADWAY R/E/SE
BOULDER CO   80303-3328

Telephone: (1) 303-497-5127.
Fax: (1) 303-497-3137.

The Space Environment Center (SEC) provides real-time monitoring and forecasting of solar and geophysical events, conducts research in solar-terrestrial physics, and develops techniques for forecasting solar and geophysical disturbances. Information on SEC products and data is internet accessible through the World Wide Web at:
   http://www.sec.noaa.gov

PROPAGATION FORECASTS: Users interested in further reading material on the effect of solar and geophysical activity on radio propagation should consult the latest edition of the Amateur Radio Handbook, published by the American Radio Relay League.

MARINE STORM WARNINGS: Weather information about major storms in the Atlantic and eastern North Pacifi are broadcast in voice from WWV at 8 through 10 minutes after each hour. Similar storm warnings covering the eastern and central North Pacifi are given from WWVH at 48 through 51 minutes after each hour. An additional segment (at 11 minutes after the hour on WWV and at 52 minutes on WWVH) may be used when there are unusually widespread storm conditions. The brief messages are designed to tell mariners of storm threats in their areas. If there are no warnings in the designated areas, the broadcasts will so indicate. The ocean areas involved are those for which the U.S. has warning responsibility under international agreement. The regular times of issue by the National Weather Service are 0500, 1100, 1700, and 2300 UTC for WWV and 0000, 0600, 1200, and 1800 UTC for WWVH. These broadcasts are updated effective with the next scheduled announcement following the time of issue.

Mariners might expect to receive a broadcast similar to the following:

"North Atlantic weather west of 35 West at 1700 UTC: Hurricane Donna, intensifying, 24 North, 60 West, moving northwest, 20 knots, winds 75 knots; storm, 65 North, 35 West, moving east, 10 knots; winds 50 knots, seas 15 feet."

Information regarding these announcements may be obtained from:

METEOROLOGICAL OPERATIONS DIVISION
MARINE FORECAST BRANCH
NATIONAL METEOROLOGICAL CENTER
5200 AUTH ROAD
CAMP SPRINGS MD   20746

or:

MARINE AND APPLIED SCIENCES BRANCH
NATIONAL WEATHER SERVICE
1325 EAST WEST HIGHWAY
SILVER SPRING MD   20910

GLOBAL POSITIONING SYSTEM (GPS) STATUS ANNOUNCEMENTS: Since March 1990 the U.S. Coast Guard has sponsored two voice announcements each hour on both WWV and WWVH. These give current information about GPS Satellites and related operations. The announcements are at 14 through 15 minutes after the hour on WWV and at 43 through 44 minutes after the hour on WWVH. For further information contact:

COMMANDING OFFICER
U.S. COAST GUARD NAVIGATION CENTER
7323 TELEGRAPH ROAD
ALEXANDRIA VA   22315-3998

Telephone: (1) 703-313-5900.
Fax: (1) 703-313-5920.

The Navigation Information Service (NIS) is internet accessible through the U.S. Coast Guard Navigation Center Website at:
   http://www.navcen.uscg.gov/
   http://www.navcenter.org (Mirror site)

WWVB: This station (located at 40°40'28.3"N, 105°02'39.5"W; radiated power 13 kW) broadcasts on 60 kHz. Its time scale is the same as for WWV and WWVH, and its frequency accuracy and stability as transmitted are the same. Its entire format consists of a 1 pulse per second special binary time code giving minutes, hours, days, the current year (two digits), and the correction between its UTC time scale and UT1 astronomical time. Indicators for daylight saving time, leap seconds, and leap year are also included. Identificatio of WWVB is made by its unique time code and a 45° carrier phase shift which occurs for the period between 10 minutes and 15 minutes after each hour. The useful coverage area of WWVB is within the continental United States. Propagation fluctuation are much less with WWVB than with high frequency reception, permitting frequency comparisons to be made to a few parts in 10^{11} per day.

RADIO TIME SIGNALS

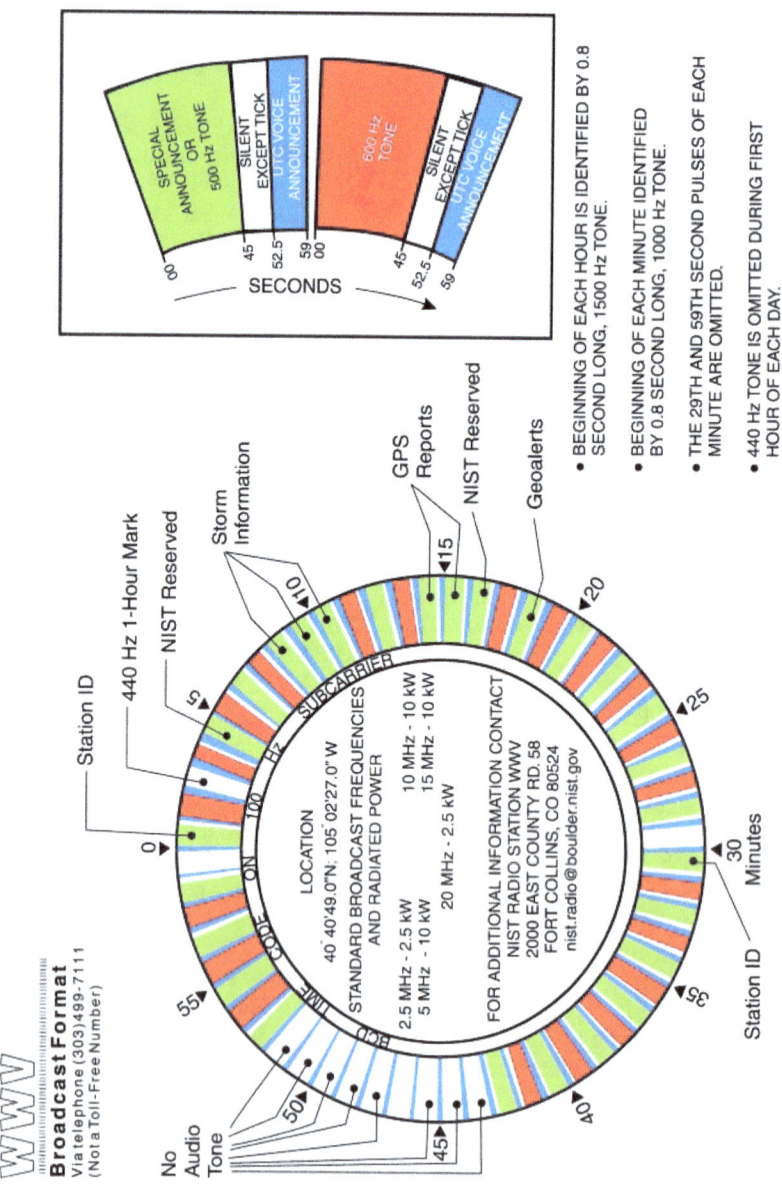

The hourly broadcast schedules of WWV.

2 - 9

RADIO TIME SIGNALS

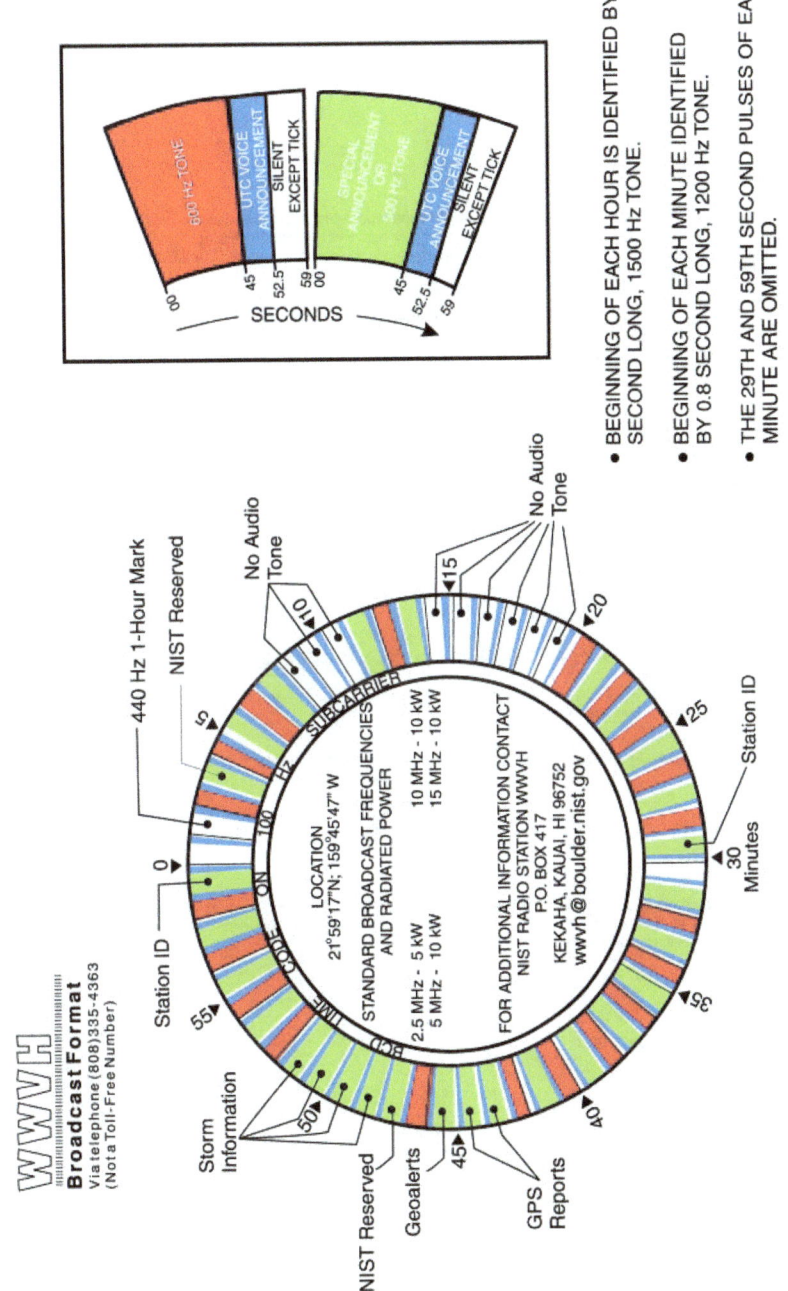

The hourly broadcast schedules of WWVH.

RADIO TIME SIGNALS

(1) No.	(2) Name	(3) Hours of Transmission	(4) System	(5) Frequency

UNITED STATES

The United States Frequency and Time Standard is maintained by the Time and Frequency Division, National Institute of Standards and Technology, Boulder, CO. Services include time announcements, standard time intervals, standard frequencies, geophysical alerts, marine storm warnings, Global Positioning System (GPS) information, UT1 time corrections and BCD Time Codes.

2000 Fort Collins, CO (WWV). Continuous. U.S. 2.5 MHz, A9W, 2.5 kW; 5.0 MHz, A9W, 10.0 kW; 10.0 MHz, A9W, 10.0 kW; 15.0 MHz, A9W, 10.0 kW; 20.0 MHz, A9W, 2.5 kW.

2001 Kekaha, Kauai, HI (WWVH). Continuous. U.S. 2.5 MHz, A9W, 5.0 kW; 5.0 MHz, A9W, 10.0 kW; 10.0 MHz, A9W, 10.0 kW; 15.0 MHz, A9W, 10.0 kW.

ANTENNAS MODULATION: At both WWV and WWVH, double sideband amplitude modulation is employed with 50 percent modulation on steady tones, 25 percent for the BCD Time Code, 100 percent for second pulses and 75 percent for voice. The broadcasts on 5, 10 and 15 MHz from WWVH are phased from vertical half-wave dipole arrays. They are designed and oriented to radiate a cardioid pattern directing maximum gain in a westerly direction. The 2.5 MHz antenna at WWVH and all antennas at WWV are half-wave dipoles that radiate omnidirectional patterns.

CANADA

2020 Ottawa, Ont. (CHU). Continuous. (See below) 3330 kHz, A2A, H3E, 3 kW; 7335 kHz, A2A, H3E, 10 kW; 14670 kHz, A2A, H3E, 3 kW.

DUT1: Marked seconds indicated by split pulses.
SYSTEM: 00s.: 500ms second marker. From 01s. to 28s.: Second markers of 300ms each. 29s.: Silence. From 30s. to 50s.: Second markers of 300ms each. From 51s. to 59s.: Station identification and time (+5R). At the beginning of the hour the first second marker lasts for 1s. and 500ms markers for seconds 01 to 09 are omitted. A binary time code is included in second markers 31-39.
ANTENNAS: CHU broadcasts from 45-17-47N 75-45-22W using vertical antennas designed to give the best possible coverage for Canadian users.

MEXICO

2040 Chapultepec (XDD)(XDP). Weekdays: 0155-0200, 1555-1600, 1755-1800; Sun. and holidays: 1755-1800. U.S. XDP: 4800 kHz, A1A; XDD: 13043 kHz, A1A.

SYSTEM: From 54m. to 55m.: "VVV DE" station call sign ("XPD" or "XDD"). From 55m. to 60m.: U.S. system, except that the second marker at 28s. is omitted each minute.

2041 Tacubaya (XBA). Weekdays: 0155-0200, 1555-1600, 1755-1800; Sun. and holidays: 1755-1800. U.S. 6976.74 kHz, A1A; 13953.6 kHz, A1A.

SYSTEM: From 54m. to 55m.: "VVV DE XBA". From 55m. to 60m.: U.S. system, except that the second marker at 28s. is omitted each minute.

VENEZUELA

2043 Observatorio Naval Caracas (YVTO). Continuous. U.S. 5000 kHz, A9W, 10 kW.

SYSTEM: From 01s. to 29s.: second markers of 100ms each. 30s.: silence. From 31s. to 40s.: second markers of 100ms each. From 40s. to 50s.: station identification, in Spanish. 51s. and 52s.: second markers of 100ms each. From 52s. to 57s.: time announcement, in Spanish. 57s. and 59s.: second markers of 100ms each. 00s.: minute marker of 500ms (800 Hz). Second markers are 1000 Hz tone.

BRAZIL

2050.5 Rio de Janeiro (PPEI). 0025-0030, 1125-1130, 1325-1330, 1925-1930, 2325-2330. English 8721 kHz, A1A, 2 kW.

DUT1: Marked seconds indicated by double pulse.

ECUADOR

2051 Guayaquil (HD210A). 0000-1200. (See below) 3810 kHz, A1A, A3E, 1 kW.

1200-1300. 5000 kHz, A1A, A3E, 1 kW.

1300-2400. 7600 kHz, A1A, A3E, 1 kW.

SYSTEM: 00s.: minute marker of 300ms. From 01s. to 28s.: second markers of 100ms each. 29s.: silence. From 30s. to 50s.: second markers of 100ms each. From 50s. to 52s.: silence. From 52s. to 58s.: time announcement. 59s.: silence. Call sign transmitted on 3810 kHz, 7600 kHz from 59m.-15s. to 59m.-50s. of each hour. In addition to time signals on 5000 kHz, a 600 Hz tone is transmitted 1200-1215 and a 400 Hz tone is transmitted 1215-1230.

RADIO TIME SIGNALS

(1) No.	(2) Name	(3) Hours of Transmission	(4) System	(5) Frequency
		ARGENTINA		
2080	Buenos Aires (LOL).	0055-0100, 1255-1300, 2055-2100.	(See below)	4856 kHz, A1A; 8030 kHz, A1A; 17180 kHz, A1A.
		1100-1200, 1400-1500, 1700-1800, 2000-2100, 2300-2400.		5000 kHz, A1A, A2A, A3E, 2 kW; 10000 kHz, A1A, A2A, A3E, 2 kW; 15000 kHz, A1A, A2A, A3E, 2 kW.

A1A-ONLY FREQUENCIES:
DUT1: Marked seconds indicated by double pulse.
SYSTEM: English. The marker at 29s. is omitted each minute.
OTHER FREQUENCIES:
DUT1: Marked seconds indicated by lengthened signal.
SYSTEM: From 01s. to 58s.: second markers of 5ms each. 59s.: silence. 00s.: minute marker of 5ms.
CARRIER MODULATION: From 00m. to 03m., 10m. to 13m., 20m. to 23m., 30m. to 33m., 40m. to 43m., 50m. to 53m.: 1000 Hz tone. From 03m. to 05m., 08m. to 10m., 13m. to 15m., 18m. to 20m., 23m. to 25m., 28m. to 30m., 33m. to 35m., 38m. to 40m., 43m. to 45m., 48m. to 50m., 53m. to 55m., 58m. to 60m.: "LOL" in morse code, station identification and time (+3P) in voice. From 05m. to 08m., 15m. to 18m., 25m. to 28m., 35m. to 38m., 45m. to 48m.: 440 Hz tone.

| 2081 | Buenos Aires (LQB)(LQC). | 2200-2205, 2345-2350. | (See below) | LQB9: 8167.5 kHz, A2A, A3E, 10 kW. |
| | | 1000-1005, 1145-1150. | | LQC20: 17550 kHz, A2A, A3E, 10 kW. |

DUT1: Marked seconds indicated by double pulse.
SYSTEM: From 55m. to 00m./40m. to 45m.: "CQCQCQ DE" followed by call sign ("LQB" or "LQC") repeated three times. From 00m. to 05m./45m. to 50m.: second markers of 300ms each (except omitted on 59s. of each minute); minute markers of 500ms each. After 05m./50m., "OKOKOK" is broadcast if time signals were valid, "NVNVNV" if invalid.

| | | **CZECH REPUBLIC** | | |
| 2091 | Liblice (OMA). | Continuous. | (See below) | 50 kHz, A1A, 7 kW. |

50 kHz FREQUENCY:
SYSTEM: Carrier interruptions of 100ms each second, 500ms each minute.
TRANSMITTER: Backup transmitter, 0.05kW, used 0600-1200 first Wed. each month.

| | | **BELARUS** | | |
| 2150 | Molodechno (RJH69). | Daylight savings time in effect:
0836-0855, 2136-2155;
Daylight savings time not in effect:
0736-0755, 1936-1955.

Not transmitted on 2nd, 12th, 22nd of each month. | (See below) | 25 kHz, A1A, 300 kW. |

SYSTEM: From 36m. to 37m.: call sign. From 37m. to 40m.: carrier. From 40m. to 43m.: sub-second markers of 12.5ms every 25ms. From 43m. to 52m.: sub-second markers of 25ms every 100ms; second markers of 100ms each; 10-second markers of 1s. each; minute markers of 10s. each. From 52m. to 55m.: sub-second markers of 12.5ms every 25ms.

| | | **RUSSIA** | | |
| 2202 | Moskva (RWM). | Continuous. | (See below) | 4996 kHz, A1A, 5 kW;
9996 kHz, A1A, 5 kW;
14996 kHz, A1A, 8 kW. |

DUT1 AND dUT1: Marked seconds indicated by double pulse with 100ms separation, between 10m.-20m. and 40m.-50m.
SYSTEM: From 00m. to 08m.: carrier. From 08m. to 09m.: silence. From 09m. to 10m.: call sign. From 10m. to 20m.: second markers of 100ms each, minute markers of 500ms each. From 20m. to 30m.: sub-second markers of 20ms every 100ms, second markers of 40ms each, minute markers of 500ms each. From 30m. to 38m.: carrier. From 38m. to 39m.: silence. From 39m. to 40m.: call sign. From 40m. to 50m.: second markers of 100ms each, minute markers of 500ms each. From 50m. to 00m.: sub-second markers of 20ms every 100ms, second markers of 40ms each, minute markers of 500ms each. Markers omitted between 56s. and 59s. at 14m., 19m., 24m., 29m., 44m., 49m., 54m., 59m.
TRANSMITTERS: 4996 kHz off-air 0500-1300 first Wed. each quarter. 9996 kHz off-air 0500-1300 second Wed. each quarter. 14996 kHz off-air 0500-1300 third Wed. every odd month.

| 2202.5 | Moskva (RBU). | January-June: 0252-0313, 0852-0913, 1452-1513, 2052-2113;
July-December: 0852-0913, 2052-2113. | (See below) | 66.67 kHz, A1A, 10 kW. |

DUT1 AND dUT1: Marked seconds indicated by double pulse with 100ms separation, between 00m.-05m.
SYSTEM: From 52m. to 59m.: carrier. From 59m. to 00m.: sub-second markers of 20ms every 100ms, second markers of 40ms, minute markers of 500ms each. From 00m. to 05m.: second markers of 100ms each, minute markers of 500ms each. From 05m. to 06m.: call sign. From 06m. to 13m.: carrier.
TRANSMITTER: Off-air 0500-1300 third Tues. each month.

RADIO TIME SIGNALS

(1) No.	(2) Name	(3) Hours of Transmission	(4) System	(5) Frequency
2203	Gorky (RJH99).	Daylight savings time in effect: 0736-0755, 1436-1455, 1936-1955; Daylight savings time not in effect: 0536-0555, 1336-1355, 1836-1855.	(See below)	25 kHz, A1A, 300 kW.
		Not transmitted on 8th, 18th, 28th of each month.		

SYSTEM: From 36m. to 37m.: call sign. From 37m. to 40m.: carrier. From 40m. to 43m.: sub-second markers of 12.5ms every 25ms. From 43m. to 52m.: sub-second markers of 25ms every 100ms, second markers of 100ms each, 10-second markers of 1s. each, minute markers of 10s. each. From 52m. to 55m.: sub-second markers of 12.5ms every 25ms.

2204	Novosibirsk (RTA).	0000-0530, 1400-2400.	(See below)	10000 kHz, A1A, 5 kW.
		0630-1330.		15000 kHz, A1A, 5 kW.
		Transmission times 1 hr. later on both frequencies when daylight savings time in effect.		

DUT1 AND dUT1: Marked seconds indicated by double pulse with 100ms separation, between 00m.-10m. and 30m.-40m.
SYSTEM: From 00m. to 10m.: second markers of 100ms each, minute markers of 500ms each. From 10m. to 20m.: sub-second markers of 20ms every 100ms, second markers of 40ms each, minute markers of 500ms each. From 20m. to 28m.: carrier. From 28m. to 29m.: silence. From 29m. to 30m.: call sign. From 30m. to 40m.: second markers of 100ms each, minute markers of 500ms each. From 40m. to 50m.: sub-second markers of 20ms every 100ms, second markers of 40ms each, minute markers of 500ms each. From 50m. to 58m.: carrier. From 58m. to 59m.: silence. From 59m. to 00m.: call sign. Markers omitted between 56s. and 59s. at 04m., 09m., 14m., 19m., 34m., 39m., 44m., 49m.
TRANSMITTERS: Both frequencies off-air 0000-1000 first and third Thurs. each month.

2205	Irkutsk (RID).	Continuous.	(See below)	5004 kHz, A1A, 1 kW; 10004 kHz, A1A, 1 kW; 15004 kHz, A1A, 1 kW.

DUT1 AND dUT1: Marked seconds indicated by double pulse with 100ms separation, between 20m.-30m. and 50m.-00m.
SYSTEM: From 00m. to 10m.: sub-second markers of 20ms every 100ms, second markers of 40ms each, minute markers of 500ms each. From 10m. to 18m.: carrier. From 18m. to 19m.: silence. From 19m. to 20m.: call sign. From 20m. to 30m.: second markers of 100ms each, minute markers of 500ms each. From 30m. to 40m.: sub-second markers of 20ms every 100ms, second markers of 40ms each, minute markers of 500ms each. From 40m. to 48m.: carrier. From 48m. to 49m.: silence. From 49m. to 50m.: call sign. From 50m. to 00m.: second markers of 100ms each, minute markers of 500ms each. Markers omitted between 56s. and 59s. at 04m., 09m., 24m., 29m., 34m., 39m., 54m., 59m.
TRANSMITTERS: 5004, 15004 kHz off-air 0000-0800 second Tues. and third Sun. each month. 10004 kHz off-air 0000-0800 third Tues. and third Sun. each month.

2205.5	Irkutsk (RTZ).	0000-2100, 2200-2400.	(See below)	50 kHz, A1A, 10 kW.

DUT1 AND dUT1: Marked seconds indicated by double pulse with 100ms separation, between 00m.-05m.
SYSTEM: From 00m. to 05m.: second markers of 100ms each, minute markers of 500ms each. From 05m. to 06m.: call sign. From 06m. to 59m.: carrier. From 59m. to 00m.: sub-second markers of 20ms every 100ms, second markers of 40ms each, minute markers of 500ms each.
TRANSMITTER: Transmitter off-air 0000-0800 first, third, fourth Mon. each month.

2206	Khabarovsk (UQC3).	Daylight savings time in effect: 0236-0255, 0636-0655, 1836-1855; Daylight savings time not in effect: 0036-0055, 0636-0655, 1736-1755.	(See below)	25 kHz, A1A, 300 kW.
		Not transmitted on 10th, 20th, 30th of each month.		

SYSTEM: From 36m. to 37m.: call sign. From 37m. to 40m.: carrier. From 40m. to 43m.: sub-second markers of 12.5ms every 25ms. From 43m. to 52m.: sub-second markers of 25ms every 100ms, second markers of 100ms each, 10-second markers of 1s. each, minute markers of 10s. each. From 52m. to 55m.: sub-second markers of 12.5ms every 25ms.

2209	Arkhangel'sk (RJH77).	0836-0855, 1136-1155; 1 hr. later when daylight savings time in effect.	(See below)	25 kHz, A1A, 300 kW.
		Not transmitted on 4th, 14th, 24th of each month.		

SYSTEM: From 36m. to 37m.: call sign. From 37m. to 40m.: carrier. From 40m. to 43m.: sub-second markers of 12.5ms every 25ms. From 43m. to 52m.: sub-second markers of 25ms every 100ms, second markers of 100ms each, 10-second markers of 1s. each, minute markers of 10s. each. From 52m. to 55m.: sub-second markers of 12.5ms every 25ms.

KYRGYZSTAN

2211	Frunze (RJH66).	Daylight savings time in effect: 0536-0555, 1136-1155, 2336-2355; Daylight savings time not in effect: 0436-0455, 0936-0955, 2136-2155.	(See below)	25 kHz, A1A, 300 kW.
		Not transmitted on 6th, 16th, 26th of each month.		

SYSTEM: From 36m. to 37m.: call sign. From 37m. to 40m.: carrier. From 40m. to 43m.: sub-second markers of 12.5ms every 25ms. From 43m. to 52m.: sub-second markers of 25ms every 100ms, second markers of 100ms each, 10-second markers of 1s. each, minute markers of 10s. each. From 52m. to 55m.: sub-second markers of 12.5ms every 25ms.

RADIO TIME SIGNALS

(1) No.	(2) Name	(3) Hours of Transmission	(4) System	(5) Frequency
		UZBEKISTAN		
2212	**Tashkent (ULW4).**	0000-0400, 0500-2400.	(See below)	2500 kHz, A1A, 1 kW.
		0000-0400, 1400-2400.		5000 kHz, A1A, 1 kW.
		0500-1330.		10000 kHz, A1A, 1 kW.
		1 hr. later when daylight savings time in effect.		

DUT1 AND dUT1: Marked seconds indicated by double pulses with 100ms separation, between 00m.-10m. and 30m.-40m.
SYSTEM: From 00m. to 10m.: second markers of 100ms each, minute markers of 500ms each. From 10m. to 20m.: sub-second markers of 20ms every 100ms, second markers of 40ms each, minute markers of 500ms each. From 20m. to 28m.: carrier. From 28m. to 29m.: silence. From 29m. to 30m.: call sign. From 30m. to 40m.: second markers of 100ms each, minute markers of 500ms each. From 40m. to 50m.: sub-second markers of 20ms every 100ms, second markers of 40ms each, minute markers of 500ms each. From 50m. to 58m.: carrier. From 58m. to 59m.: silence. From 59m. to 00m.: call sign. Markers between 56s. and 59s. omitted at 04m., 09m., 14m., 19m., 34m., 39m., 44m., 49m.
TRANSMITTERS: All off-air 0100-1100 third Mon. each month.

		GERMANY		
2320	**Mainflingen (DCF77).**	Continuous.	(See below)	77.5 kHz, A1A, A3E, 38 kW.

SYSTEM: Carrier interruptions act as second markers. From 00s. to 19s.: second markers of 100ms each. 20s.: second marker of 200ms. From 21s. to 27s.: second markers of 100ms or 200ms each; these markers are used to send binary time code information. 100ms marker—binary 0, 200ms marker—binary 1. 28s.: second marker of 100ms. From 29s. to 34s.: binary second markers of 100ms or 200ms each. 35s.: second marker of 100ms. From 36s. to 57s.: binary second markers of 100ms or 200ms each. 58s.: second marker of 100ms. 59s.: uninterrupted carrier. Station call sign transmitted twice using audio modulation of the carrier at 19m., 39m., 59m.; second markers are not interrupted.
ANTENNAS: When backup antenna is used, marker at 15s. is lengthened.

		UNITED KINGDOM		
2351	**Rugby (MSF).**	Continuous.	(See below)	60 kHz, A1A, 27 kW.

SYSTEM: National Physical Laboratory (NPL) Computer Time Service via Modem (NPL Truetime). NPL offers a service which allows a computer to set its clock to within 1/50th of a second by direct telephone connection to the National Time Scale at the NPL in Teddington, Middlesex. A call to the service, at any time of the day or night, allows a computer equipped with a suitable modem and software to correct its clock. The service uses a premium-rate telephone number. For further information contact the Time and Frequency Services, NPL at:
Inquiries telephone.....(011) 44-01819436880
NPL Truetime Telephone.....0891 516333 (UK only)
Fax.....(011) 44-01819436458
E-mail.....time@npl.co.uk
Internet.....http://www.npl.co.uk/npl/ctm/index.html
TRANSMITTER: Transmitter off-air 1000-1400 (1 hr. earlier when daylight savings time is in effect) first Tues. each month.

2360	**BBC-Radio 1.**	Mon.-Fri.: 0700, 0800; Sat.: 1300; Sun.: Nil.	(See below)	1053 kHz, A3E, 1-150 kW; 1089 kHz, A3E, 1-150 kW; 97.6-99.8 MHz, F3E (97.1 MHz for Channel Islands).
		1 hr. earlier when daylight savings time in effect.		

SYSTEM: From 59m.-55s. to 59m.-59s.: second markers of 100ms each. 00m.-00s.: minute marker of 500ms.

2361	**BBC-Radio 2.**	Mon.-Fri.: 0000, 0700, 0800, 1300, 1700; Sat.: 0000, 0700, 0800; Sun.: 0000, 0800, 0900, 1900.	(See below)	88-90.2 MHz, F3E (89.6 MHz for Channel Islands).
		1 hr. earlier when daylight savings time in effect.		

SYSTEM: From 59m.-55s. to 59m.-59s.: second markers of 100ms each. 00m.-00s.: minute marker of 500ms.

2362	**BBC-Radio 3.**	Mon.-Fri.: 0700, 0800; Sat.: 0600, 0700.	(See below)	90.2-92.4 MHz, F3E (91.1 MHz for Channel Islands).
		1 hr. earlier when daylight savings time in effect.		

SYSTEM: From 59m.-55s. to 59m.-59s.: second markers of 100ms each. 00m.-00s.: minute marker of 500ms.

RADIO TIME SIGNALS

(1) No.	(2) Name	(3) Hours of Transmission	(4) System	(5) Frequency
2363	BBC-Radio 4.	Mon.-Fri.: 0600, 0700, 0800, 0900, 1000, 1100, 1200, 1300, 1400, 1500, 1600, 1700, 1900, 2200; Sat.: 0700, 0800, 0900, 1000, 1100, 1300, 1400, 1600; Sun.: 0600, 0700, 0800, 0900, 1300, 1700, 2100.	(See Below)	198 kHz, A3E, 50-400 kW; Tyneside: 603 kHz, A3E, 2 kW; London: 720 kHz, A3E, 0.5 kW; N. Ireland: 720 kHz, A3E, 0.25-10 kW; Redruth: 756 kHz, A3E, 2 kW; Plymouth: 774 kHz, A3E, 1 kW; Aberdeen: 1449 kHz, A3E, 2 kW; Carlisle: 1485 kHz, A3E, 1 kW; 92.4-94.6 MHz, F3E (94.8 MHz for Channel Islands).

1 hr. earlier when daylight savings time in effect.

SYSTEM: From 59m.-55s. to 59m.-59s.: second markers of 100ms each. 00m.-00s.: minute marker of 500ms.

(1) No.	(2) Name	(3) Hours of Transmission	(4) System	(5) Frequency
2370	BBC-World Service.	0000, 0200, 0300, 0400, 0500.	(See below)	198 kHz.
		0000, 0200, 0300, 0600, 0700, 0800, 0900, 1100, 1200, 1300, 1500, 1600, 1700, 1900, 2000, 2200, 2300.		648 kHz.
		0200, 0300, 0600, 2200, 2300.		1296 kHz.
		0400, 0500, 0600.		3955 kHz.
		0200, 0300, 0400, 0500, 0600, 0700, 1500, 1600, 1700, 1800, 1900, 2000, 2200.		6195 kHz.
		0600, 0700, 0800.		7150 kHz.
		0300, 0400.		7230 kHz.
		0000, 0200, 0300, 0700, 0800, 0900, 2000, 2200, 2300.		7325 kHz.
		0200, 0300, 0400, 0500, 0600, 0700, 0800, 0900, 1100, 1200, 1300, 1500, 1600, 1700, 1800, 1900, 2000, 2200, 2300.		9410 kHz.
		0900, 1100, 1200, 1300, 1500.		9750 kHz.
		0700, 0800, 0900, 1100, 1200, 1300, 1500, 1600.		9760 kHz.
		0000, 0200, 0300, 2200, 2300.		9915 kHz.
		0000, 0200, 0300, 0400, 0500, 0600, 0700, 0800, 0900, 1100, 1200, 1300, 1500, 1600, 1700, 1800, 1900, 2000, 2200, 2300.		12095 kHz.
		0000, 0500, 0600, 0700, 0800, 0900, 1100, 1200, 1300, 1500, 1600, 1700, 1800, 1900, 2000, 2200, 2300.		15070 kHz.
		2200, 2300.		15340 kHz.
		0700, 0800, 0900, 1100, 1200, 1300, 1500.		17640 kHz.
		0800, 0900, 1100, 1200, 1300, 1500, 1600.		17705 kHz.

SYSTEM: From 59m.-55s. to 59m.-59s.: second markers of 100ms each. 00m.-00s.: minute marker of 500ms.
NOTE: Not intended for precise use. Direct transmissions from United Kingdom will normally be received within 0.1s. of UTC, but signals from overseas relay stations may have additional errors of up to 0.25s.

FRANCE

(1) No.	(2) Name	(3) Hours of Transmission	(4) System	(5) Frequency
2380	France Inter (Allouis) (TDF).	Continuous, except 0100-0500 each Tues.	(See below)	162 kHz, A3E.

SYSTEM: From 00s. to 20s.: second markers of 100ms each. From 21s. to 58s.: time and date announcement. 59s.: emphasized second marker of 100ms. Other second markers are emphasized to indicate the following: 13s. - the day preceding a holiday; 14s. - holiday; 17s. - local time is -2B; 18s. - local time is -1A.

SWITZERLAND

(1) No.	(2) Name	(3) Hours of Transmission	(4) System	(5) Frequency
2400	Prangins (HBG).	Continuous in the absence of telegraph traffic	(See below)	75 kHz, A1A, 20 kW.

SYSTEM: Carrier interruptions act as markers. From 01s. to 59s.: second markers of 100ms each. 00s.: minute marker of double pulse, 100ms each. 00m.-00s.: hour marker of triple pulse, 100ms each. 12h./24h.-00m.-00s.: 12-hour marker of quadruple pulse, 100ms each.

RADIO TIME SIGNALS

(1) No.	(2) Name	(3) Hours of Transmission	(4) System	(5) Frequency
		ITALY		
2410	Roma (IAM).	Mon.-Sat.: 0730-0830, 1030-1130.	(See below)	5000 kHz, A2A, A3E, 1 kW.
		1 hr. earlier when daylight savings time in effect.		

DUT1: Marked seconds indicated by double pulse.
SYSTEM: From 01s. to 59s.: second markers of 5ms each. 00s.: minute marker of 20ms. At 00m., 15m., 30m., 45m.: station identification in morse code and Italian. At 05m., 20m., 35m., 50m.: "IAM IAM IAM", time in morse code.

2411	Torino (IBF).	0545-0600, 0645-0700, 0845-0900, 0945-1000, 1045-1100, 1145-1200, 1245-1300, 1345-1400, 1445-1500, 1545-1600, 1645-1700.	(See below)	5000 kHz, A2A, A3E, 5 kW.
		1 hr. earlier when daylight savings time in effect.		

DUT1: Marked second indicated by double pulse.
SYSTEM: 45m.: station identification. From 45m. to 00m.: second markers of 5ms each, minute markers of septuple pulses of 5ms each. 50m.: "IBF IBF IBF", time (-1A) in morse code. 00m.: "IBF IBF IBF", time (-1A) in morse code, station identification.

		CHILE		
2445	Valparaiso Playa Ancha Radiomaritima (CBV).	0055-0100, 1155-1200, 1555-1600, 1955-2000.	U.S.	4228 kHz, A2A; 8677 kHz, A2A.
		PERU		
2461	Peru National Radio.	0300, 1300, 1700, 2300.	U.S.	609.5 kHz, A3E; 850 kHz, A3E; 103.9 MHz, F3E.

SYSTEM: The hour marker of 1s. commences at 59m.-59s.

2462	Radio Victoria.	0300, 1300, 1700, 2300.	U.S.	780 kHz, J3E.

SYSTEM: The hour marker of 1s. commences at 59m.-59s.

		INDIA		
2476	New Delhi (ATA).	1230-0330.	(See below)	5000 kHz, A1A, 8 kW.
		Continuous.		10000 kHz, A1A, A3E, 8 kW.
		0330-1230.		15000 kHz, A1A, 8 kW.

SYSTEM: 00m.: call sign and time in morse code. From 00m. to 04m.: second markers of 5ms 1000 Hz modulation each, minute markers of 100ms 1000 Hz modulation each. From 04m. to 15m.: second markers of 5ms each, minute markers of 100ms each. 15m.: call sign and time in morse code. From 15m. to 19m.: second markers of 5ms 1000 Hz each, minute markers of 100ms 1000 Hz each. From 19m. to 30m.: second markers of 5ms each, minute markers of 100ms each. 30m.: call sign and time in morse code. From 30m. to 34m.: second markers of 5ms 1000 Hz each, minute markers of 100ms 1000 Hz each. From 34m. to 45m.: second markers of 5ms each, minute markers of 100ms each. 45m.: call sign and time in morse code. From 45m. to 49m.: second pulses of 5ms 1000 Hz each, minute markers of 100ms 1000 Hz each. From 49m. to 00m.: second markers of 5ms each, minute markers of 100ms each. All time signals are sent 50ms in advance of UTC.

		SRI LANKA		
2480	Colombo (4PB).	0555-0600, 1325-1330.	English	482 kHz, A2A, 1 kW; 8473 kHz, A1A, 2.5 kW.

SYSTEM: From 53m./23m. to 55m./25m.: "CQ DE 4PB TIME SIGNALS AS". From 55m./25m. to 00m./30m.: second markers of 100ms each, minute markers of 400ms each.

		CHINA		
2485.1	Shanghai (XSG).	0256-0856.	(See below)	458 kHz, A1A, A2A; 4290 kHz, A1A; 6414.5 kHz, A1A; 6454 kHz, A1A; 8487 kHz, A1A; 8502 kHz, A1A; 12871.5 kHz, A1A; 12954 kHz, A1A; 17002.4 kHz, A1A.

SYSTEM: From 59m.-55s. to 59m.-59s.: second markers of 100ms each. 00m.-00s.: minute marker of 100ms.

RADIO TIME SIGNALS

(1) No.	(2) Name	(3) Hours of Transmission	(4) System	(5) Frequency
2490	Xian (BPM).	0730-0100.	(See below)	2500 kHz, A1A, A3E.
		Continuous.		5000 kHz, A1A, A3E.
		Continuous.		10000 kHz, A1A, A3E.
		0100-0900.		15000 kHz, A1A, A3E.

SYSTEM: From 00m. to 10m.: UTC second markers of 10ms each, UTC minute markers of 300ms each. From 10m. to 15m.: carrier. From 15m. to 25m.: UTC second markers of 10ms each, UTC minute markers of 300ms each. From 25m. to 29m.: UT1 second markers of 100ms each, UT1 minute markers of 300ms each. From 29m.-00s. to 29m.-40s.: "BPM" in morse code. From 29m.-40s. to 30m.-00s.: "BPM" and other station identification in Chinese. From 30m. to 40m.: UTC second markers of 10ms each, UTC minute markers of 300ms each. From 40m. to 45m.: carrier. From 45m. to 55m.: UTC second markers of 10ms each, UTC minute markers of 300ms each. From 55m. to 59m.: UT1 second markers of 100ms each, UT1 minute markers of 300ms each. From 59m.-00s. to 59m.-40s.: "BPM" in morse code. From 59m.-40s. to 00m.-00s.: "BPM" and other station identification in Chinese. All UTC signals are broadcast 20ms in advance of UTC.

JAPAN

2500	Sanwa (JG2AS).	Continuous in the absence of telegraph traffic	(See below)	40 kHz, A1A, 10 kW.

SYSTEM: From 00m.-01s. to 00m.-58s.: second markers of 500ms each. 00m.-59s.: second marker of 200ms. 01m.-00s.: minute marker of 500ms. At 15m. and 45m.: "JG2AS JG2AS JG2AS" in morse code.

2501	Sanwa (JJY).	Continuous.	(See below)	2500 kHz, A9W, 2 kW; 5000 kHz, A9W, 2 kW; 8000 kHz, A9W, 2 kW; 10000 kHz, A9W, 2 kW; 15000 kHz, A9W, 2 kW.

DUT1: Marked seconds indicated by 45ms pulses.
SYSTEM: Second markers of 5ms 1600 Hz tone each are used. The second marker indicating the minute is preceded by an annunciatory marker: from 59.000s. to 59.005s. a second marker of 5ms 1600 Hz tone; from 59.005s. to 59.045s. silence; from 59.045s. to 59.700s. annunciatory marker of 655ms 600 Hz; from 59.700s. to 00.000s. silence; from 00.000s. to 00.005s. a second marker of 5ms 1600 Hz. The carrier is modulated by a 1000 Hz tone as well as the second markers during alternating 5m. periods. From 00m. to 05m.: second markers and 1000 Hz tone. From 05m. to 09m.: second markers only. From 09m. to 10m.: second markers; "JJY JJY" and time (-9I) in morse code and then in voice; radio propagation warnings in morse code: "N" - normal, "U" - unstable, "W" - disturbed. This 10m. cycle is repeated throughout each hour except for 35m. to 39m., which is a silent period.

REPUBLIC OF KOREA

2505	Taedok (HLA).	Mon.-Fri.: 0100-0800.	(See below)	5000 kHz.

DUT1: Marked seconds indicated by double pulse.
SYSTEM: 00s.: minute marker of 500ms 1800 Hz tone. From 01s. to 28s.: second markers of 5ms 1800 Hz tone each. 29s.: silence. From 30s. to 52s.: second markers of 5ms 1800 Hz tone each. From 53s. to 58s.: time announcement by voice. 59s.: silence. 00m.: hour marker of 500ms 1500 Hz tone. A binary time code is transmitted continuously on a 100 kHz subcarrier.

PHILIPPINES

2530	Manila (DUW21).	Every even hour +55m. to +60m.	U.S.	3650 kHz, A1A, 0.5 kW.

RADIO TIME SIGNALS

(1) No.	(2) Name	(3) Hours of Transmission	(4) System	(5) Frequency
		AUSTRALIA		
2600	Radio Australia.	0700, 0800, 0900, 1000, 1100, 1200.	(See below)	6020 kHz.
		1500, 1700, 1800, 1900, 2000.		6060 kHz.
		0700, 0800, 0900, 1000, 1100, 1200, 1500, 1700, 1800, 1900, 2000.		6080 kHz.
		0900, 1000, 1100, 1200, 1300, 1400, 1500, 1600, 1700, 1800, 1900, 2000.		7240 kHz.
		1500, 1600, 1700, 1800, 1900, 2000.		7260 kHz.
		0900, 1000, 1100.		9510 kHz.
		0900, 1000, 1100, 1200, 1300, 1400, 1500, 1600, 1700, 1800, 1900, 2000.		9580 kHz.
		2100, 2200.		9645 kHz.
		0700, 0800, 0900, 1000, 1100, 1200.		9710 kHz.
		1500, 1600.		9770 kHz.
		1500, 1600, 1700, 1800, 1900, 2000.		11660 kHz.
		1500, 1600, 1700, 1800, 1900, 2000.		11695 kHz.
		0000, 0100, 0200, 0300, 0700, 0800, 0900, 1000, 1100, 1900, 2000, 2100, 2200, 2300.		11720 kHz.
		1300, 1400, 1500.		11800 kHz.
		2100, 2200.		11855 kHz.
		0000, 0100, 0200, 0300, 0700, 0800, 1700, 1800, 1900, 2000, 2200, 2300.		11880 kHz.
		0700, 0800.		11910 kHz.
		0000, 0900, 1000, 1100.		13605 kHz.
		1300, 1400.		13755 kHz.
		0900, 1000, 1100.		15170 kHz.
		0000, 0100, 0200, 0300, 2300.		15240 kHz.
		0000, 0100, 0200, 0300, 2100, 2200, 2300.		15320 kHz.
		0000, 0700, 0800, 2100, 2200, 2300.		15365 kHz.
		0100, 0200, 0300.		15510 kHz.
		1200.		15530 kHz.
		1200.		15565 kHz.
		0700, 0800.		17695 kHz.
		0100, 0200, 0300.		17715 kHz.
		0000, 0100, 0200, 0300, 0700, 0800.		17750 kHz.
		0000, 2200, 2300.		17795 kHz.
		0000, 0100, 0200, 0300.		17880 kHz.
		0700, 0800.		21525 kHz.
		0100, 0200, 0300, 0700, 0800.		21595 kHz.
		0900, 1000, 1100.		21725 kHz.
		0000, 0400, 0500, 0600, 2200, 2300.		21740 kHz.

SYSTEM: From 59m.-55s. to 59m.-59s.: second markers of 100ms each. 00m.-00s.: minute marker of 500ms. In addition a warning signal consisting of a single dot is transmitted 5s. before the first series of six dots (at ten seconds before the hour).

RADIO TIME SIGNALS

(1) No.	(2) Name	(3) Hours of Transmission	(4) System	(5) Frequency
2601	Llandilo, Penrith (VNG).	Continuous.	(See below)	2500 kHz, H9W, 1 kW; 5000 kHz, B9W, 10 kW; 8638 kHz, A1A, 10 kW; 12984 kHz, A1A, 10 kW.
		2200-1000.		16000 kHz, B9W, 5 kW.

DUT1: Marked seconds indicated by a double pulse.
SYSTEM: 00s.: minute marker of 500ms. From 01s. to 16s.: second markers of 50ms each, lengthened (as necessary) by 50ms of 900 Hz tone to indicate the current value of DUT1. From 17s. to 19s.: second markers of 50ms each. 20s.: second marker of 200ms. From 21s. to 46s.: second markers of 100ms or 200ms each, indicating the time of day and the day of the year in machine readable CCIR code. From 47s. to 49s.: second markers of 50ms each. From 50s. to 54s.: second markers of 5ms each. From 55s. to 58s.: second markers of 50ms each. 59s.: silent. Every 5th minute from 50s. to 58s.: second markers of 5ms each. Second markers of 1000 Hz tone are used. On frequencies 2500, 5000 and 16000 kHz from 01s. to 03s. of each minute a female voice announces the time of day of the preceding minute marker. On frequencies 2500, 5000 and 16000 kHz from 21s. to 49s. on every 15th minute a male voice announces the details of the service. On frequencies 8638 and 12984 kHz for one minute following 14m.-00s., 29m.-00s., 44m.-00s. and 59m.-00s. the call sign VNG (which may be distorted) is transmitted in slow morse at an audio tone of about 400 Hz.

INDONESIA

(1) No.	(2) Name	(3) Hours of Transmission	(4) System	(5) Frequency
2633	Jakarta (PKI)(PLC).	0055-0100.	Modified ONOGO	PKI: 8542 kHz, A1A, 1-3 kW; PLC: 11440 kHz, A1A.

TAIWAN

(1) No.	(2) Name	(3) Hours of Transmission	(4) System	(5) Frequency
2635	Chung-Li (BSF).	Continuous.	(See below)	5000 kHz, A1A, A2A; 15000 kHz, A1A, A2A.

DUT1: Marked seconds indicated by lengthened pulse.
SYSTEM: Second markers of 5ms each and minute markers of 300ms each are used. A 1000 Hz tone is transmitted constantly except from 40ms before to 40ms after each marker during alternating 5m. periods. From 00m. to 05m.: markers with 1000 Hz tone. From 05m. to 10m.: markers without the 1000 Hz tone. This 10m. cycle is repeated throughout the hour except for 35m. to 40m., which is a silent period.

CHAPTER 3

RADIO NAVIGATIONAL WARNINGS

300A.	General.	3-3
300B.	Coastal and Local Warnings	3-3
300C.	Long Range Warnings	3-3
300D.	Worldwide Warnings.	3-3
300E.	Worldwide Warnings Message Content	3-3
300F.	Warning Message Format	3-6
300G.	SPECIAL WARNINGS and Broadcast Stations.	3-6
300H.	NAVTEX.	3-6
300I.	U.S. NAVTEX Transmitting Stations	3-7
300J.	Worldwide NAVTEX Transmitting Stations	3-11
300K.	Ice Information	3-16
300L.	Navigational Warning Station List	3-27
300M.	WorldWide Navigational Warning Service NAVAREA Coordinators	3-78

CHAPTER 3

RADIO NAVIGATIONAL WARNINGS

300A. General

Radio navigational warning broadcasts are designed to provide the mariner with up-to-date marine information vital to safe navigation. These warnings are described as follows:
– Worldwide - Important worldwide marine information.
– Long Range - Important worldwide information issued by geographic area.
– Coastal and Local - Short-range marine information, including items of interest to small craft.

300B. Coastal and Local Warnings

These broadcasts are generally restricted to ports, harbors, and coastal waters, and involve items of local interest. Usually, local or short-range warnings are broadcast from a single coastal station, frequently by voice as well as radiotelegraph, to assist small craft operators in the area. The information is often quite detailed. Foreign area broadcasts are frequently in English as well as the native language. In the United States, short-range radio navigational warnings are broadcast by the U.S. Coast Guard Districts via NAVTEX and subordinate coastal radio stations.

300C. Long Range Warnings

These warnings are intended primarily to assist mariners on the high seas by promulgating navigational safety information concerning port and harbor approaches, coastlines, and major ocean areas. Long-range radio navigational warnings are usually broadcast by means of radiotelegraphy, and in many instances by radio-teletypewriter.

The NAVAREA system of 16 navigational warning areas has been developed by a joint committee of the International Hydrographic Organization and the International Maritime Organization. The NAVAREA system provides worldwide coverage in English using standard format and procedures.

Each NAVAREA is under the jurisdiction of an Area Coordinator. The Area Coordinator assimilates information from the coastal countries within the NAVAREA. Accountability is maintained through annual serialization and notificatio of cancellation. National Coordinators are charged with collecting warning information from sources within their national boundaries. National Coordinators often broadcast local or coastal warnings.

The United States participates as Area Coordinator for both NAVAREA IV and NAVAREA XII. NAVAREA IV includes the Western North Atlantic. NAVAREA XII includes the Eastern North Pacific

The National Geospatial-Intelligence Agency (NGA) acts as the NAVAREA IV and XII Coordinator and the United States Coast Guard (USCG) acts as the U.S. National Coordinator.

300D. Worldwide Warnings

The United States also maintains worldwide coverage using the HYDROLANT/HYDROPAC Navigational Warning System outside of NAVAREAs IV and XII. HYDROLANTs cover the eastern North Atlantic, South Atlantic, North Sea, Baltic Sea, English Channel, Mediterranean Sea, and contiguous areas. HYDROPACs include the western North Pacific South Pacific South China Sea, Indian Ocean, Red Sea, Persian Gulf, and contiguous areas. The combination of HYDROLANTs, HYDROPACs, NAVAREA IVs and NAVAREA XIIs provides worldwide notificatio of the more important marine incidents and navigational changes.

300E. Worldwide Warnings Message Content

NAVAREA IV, NAVAREA XII, HYDROLANT, and HYDROPAC Warnings normally include:

– Casualties to major and outermost aids to navigation such as primary lights, lightships, large navigational buoys (LNBs), approach or sea buoys, etc. Mariners should monitor local broadcasts for information concerning inshore, harbor and inland waterways, and aids which otherwise may not affect offshore navigation.
– Establishment of new aids that could affect the safety of offshore navigation. Alterations of an established aid where the change might be confusing are also broadcast.
– Floating dangers, such as those drifting in or near sea-lanes and large derelicts adrift on the high seas. Following the end of the ice season, all reports of ice below 52°N which endanger the North Atlantic shipping lanes are also broadcast. Trees, timbers, and drifting buoys do not normally constitute a danger for oceangoing ships and are not broadcast on the long-range systems. They may be promulgated in local broadcasts.
– New or amended shoal depths, or other changes in hydrography.
– Dangerous wrecks, obstructions, etc.
– Selected exercises and hazardous operations conducted by units of the armed forces are normally broadcast. Specificall , these include the use of flares searchlights or pyrotechnics that may be mistaken for distress signals, night firin exercises, darken-ship exercises, submarine exercises, missile launches, space missions, and nuclear tests. Such warnings are purely cautionary and are not intended to obstruct the right of innocent passage upon the high seas.

RADIO NAVIGATIONAL WARNINGS

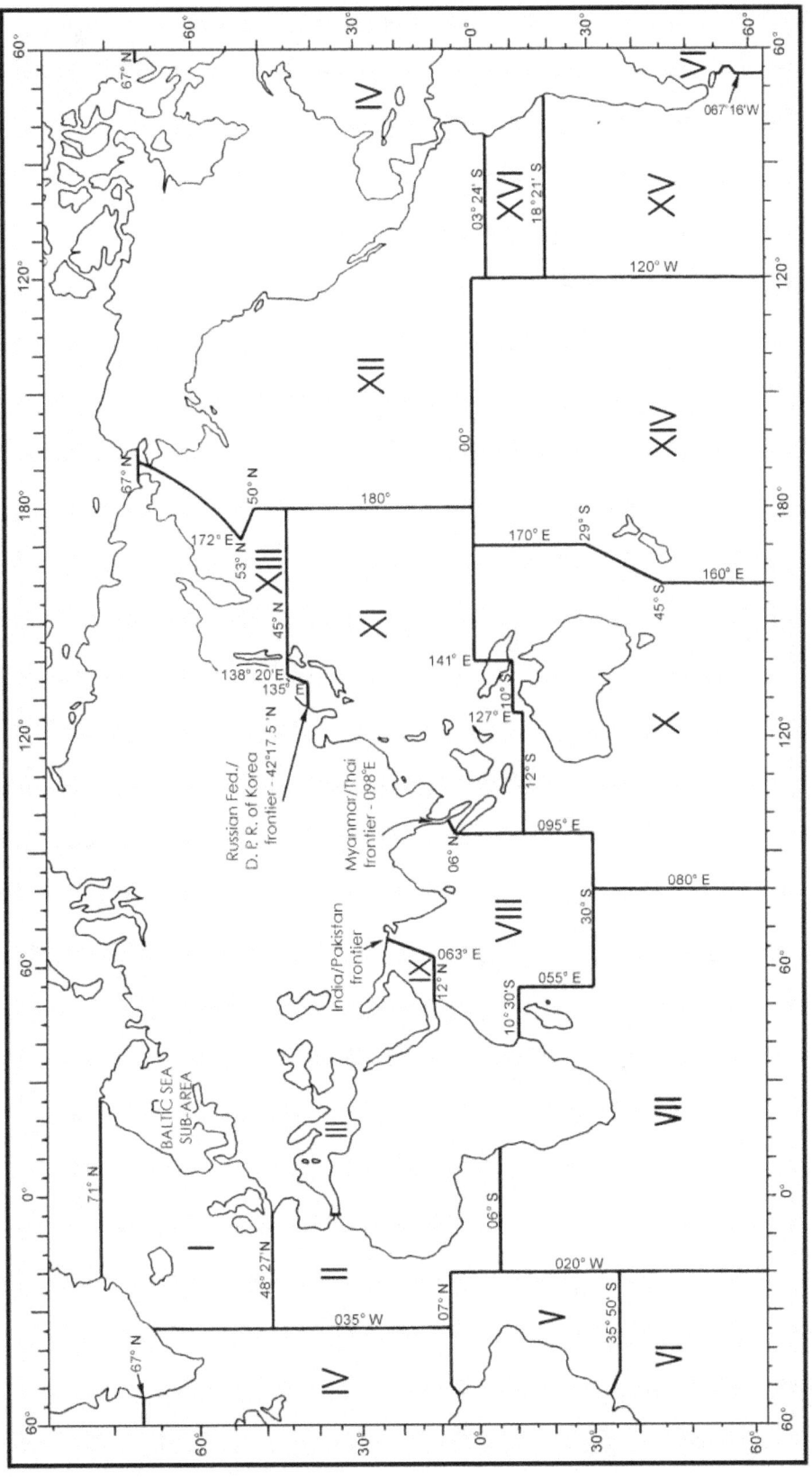

RADIO NAVIGATIONAL WARNINGS

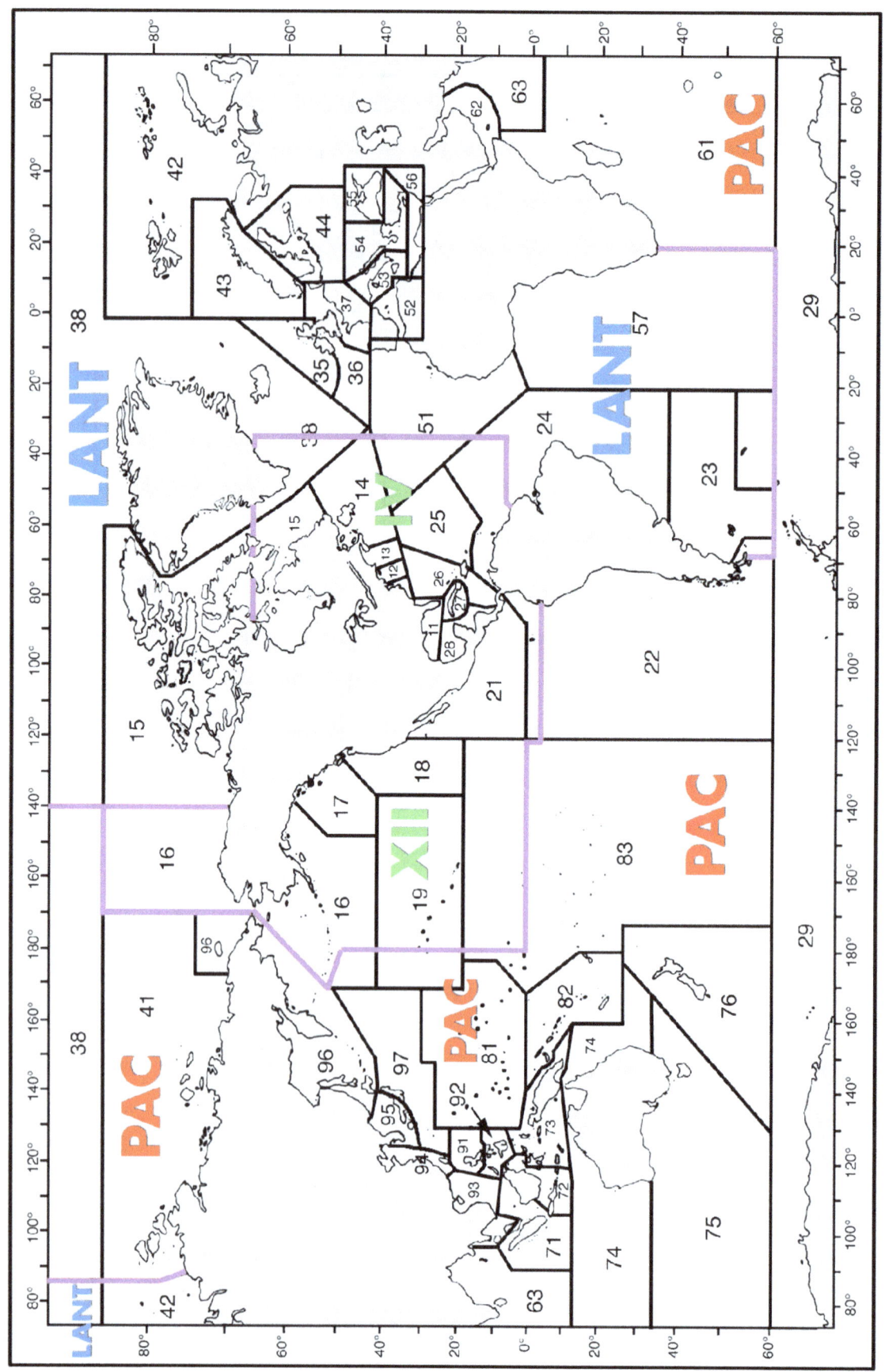

U.S. RADIO NAVIGATIONAL WARNING SYSTEMS

RADIO NAVIGATIONAL WARNINGS

– Information regarding drifting mines and unexploded ordnance at depths of less than 100 fathoms is broadcast when there is a clear danger to shipping.
– Vessels engaged in seismic operations, which often detonate explosives and tow extremely long cables.
– Malfunctions, scheduled off-air time for maintenance, and other information concerning electronic aids to navigation, including marine radiobeacon, LORAN-C, GPS, DGPS service, and satellite navigation systems.
– Establishment of offshore structures in or near shipping lanes.
– The presence of large unwieldy tows in congested waters.
– Notificatio of special changes or events such as alteration or suspension of mandatory traffi separation schemes or activation of a new buoyage system.

In accordance with IMO guidelines (COMSAR/Circ.3, dated 19 April 1996), NGA no longer promulgates messages for distress, search and rescue, man overboard, overdue vessels, EPIRBs, etc., in NAVAREA IV and XII. Rescue Coordination Centers (RCCs) are responsible for promulgating messages concerning distress and search and rescue as SafteyNET broadcasts via Inmarsat-C. Distress messages outside the limits of NAVAREA IV and XII will continue to be promulgated as HYDROLANT and HYDROPAC Warnings.

300F. Warning Message Format

Each of the four different types of Radio Navigational Warnings issued by NGA uses the same format. The firs word of the heading identifie what series is involved: NAVAREA IV, NAVAREA XII, HYDROLANT, or HYDROPAC. Following the series title is the annual serial number, used for identificatio and record keeping purposes. Following the serial number and year, and enclosed by parentheses, are two more digits: the geographic subregion locator. This is the same as the subregion system used for numbering charts. The limits of the subregions appear on the inside back cover of each Notice to Mariners. Last, a brief geographic description is included.

The second line contains a chart number if the message concerns an aid to navigation. This chart is selected to identify the aid. It is not necessarily the largest-scale chart of the area, but is usually the best for determining how the warning will affect the mariner. It is usually the chart the mariner would select for navigation when approaching the aid.

Times are always expressed in Universal Time Coordinated (UTC).

Navigation safety messages are canceled when no longer applicable. Messages are always canceled by specifi notification A message pertaining to an exercise or event of known duration includes its own cancellation, usually one hour after conclusion of the event. Warnings which are sufficientl permanent in nature to warrant promulgation in the Notice to Mariners are canceled no sooner than six weeks after publication of that printed Notice.

Section III of the Notice to Mariners includes a listing of the serial numbers for all Radio Navigational Warnings in force. Each week, NGA promulgates a general Radio Navigation Warning message for each series which lists the serial number of each message issued during the last six weeks and in force at the time the message is compiled.

300G. SPECIAL WARNINGS and Broadcast Stations

SPECIAL WARNINGS are limited series broadcasts by U.S. Navy and Coast Guard radio stations primarily for the dissemination of officia government proclamations affecting shipping.

The texts of all SPECIAL WARNINGS in force are published in Notice to Mariners No. 1 each year. SPECIAL WARNINGS may be broadcast throughout the year. NGA promulgates SPECIAL WARNINGS 24 hours, 48 hours and for the next f ve Fridays after their initial release. Their text appears in the next published Notice to Mariners following their broadcast. Each Notice to Mariners lists all in-force SPECIAL WARNINGS.

Masters are urged to provide themselves with an accurate list of all radio navigational warning messages and SPECIAL WARNINGS prior to sailing.

Radio Navigational Warnings issued by NGA are broadcast by the following stations:

– HYDROLANT Warnings are transmitted from Boston, MA (NMF).
– NAVAREA IV Warnings are transmitted from Boston, MA (NMF).
– HYDROPAC and NAVAREA XII warnings are transmitted from Port Reyes, CA (NMC), Honolulu, HI (NMO); Guam (NRV).

300H. NAVTEX

NAVTEX is an international automated direct printing service for the promulgation of navigational and meteorological warnings and urgent information to ships. It provides a low cost, simple means for the automatic reception of Marine Safety Information (MSI) by narrow band direct-printing telegraphy. NAVTEX is a component of the WorldWide Navigational Warning Service (WWNWS) and is an essential element of the Global Maritime Distress and Safety System (GMDSS). Vessels regulated by the Safety of Life at Sea (SOLAS) Convention, as amended in 1988 (cargo vessels over 300 tons and passenger vessels, on international voyages), and operating in areas where NAVTEX service is available, have been required to carry NAVTEX receivers since 1 August 1993. The USCG discontinued broadcasts of safety information over MF Morse frequencies on that date. The USCG voice broadcasts (Ch. 22A), often of more inshore and harbor information, will remain unaffected by NAVTEX.

A NAVTEX user's placard, which is intended to be laminated and either hung or posted near the NAVTEX reciver, can be found on pgs. 3-9 and 3-10.

RADIO NAVIGATIONAL WARNINGS

NAVTEX FEATURES: NAVTEX messages are broadcast on a single frequency, 518 kHz, using the English language. Nominated stations within each NAVAREA transmit on a time-sharing basis to eliminate mutual interference. All necessary information is contained in each transmission. The power of each transmitter is regulated in order to avoid the possibility of interference between transmitters.

A dedicated NAVTEX receiver has the ability to select messages to be printed according to:
– a technical code ($B_1B_2B_3B_4$) which appears in the preamble of each message; and
– whether or not the particular message has already been printed.

By International agreement, certain essential classes of safety information such as navigational and meteorological warnings and search and rescue information are non-rejectable to ensure that ships using NAVTEX always receive the most vital information.

NAVTEX coordinators exercise control of messages transmitted by each station according to the information contained in each message and the geographical coverage required. Therefore, the mariner may choose to accept messages, as appropriate, either from the single transmitter which serves the sea area around his position or from a number of transmitters.

MESSAGE PRIORITIES: Three message priorities are used to dictate the timing of the firs broadcast of a new warning in the NAVTEX service. In descending order of urgency they are:
–VITAL–for immediate broadcast, subject to avoiding interference of ongoing transmissions;
–IMPORTANT– for broadcast at the next available period when the frequency is unused;
–ROUTINE–for broadcast at the next scheduled transmission period.

Both VITAL and IMPORTANT warnings will normally need to be repeated, if still valid, at the next scheduled transmission period.

TRANSMITTER IDENTIFICATION CHARACTER (B_1): The transmitter identificatio character B_1 is a single unique letter which is allocated to each transmitter. It is used to identify the broadcasts which are to be accepted or rejected by the receiver. Two stations having the same B_1 character must have a sufficien geographical separation so as to minimize interference with one another. NAVTEX transmissions have a designed range of about 400 nautical miles.

SUBJECT INDICATOR CHARACTERS (B_2): Information in the NAVTEX broadcast is grouped by subject. The subject indicator character B_2 is used by the receiver to identify the different classes of messages listed below. The indicator is also used to reject messages concerning certain optional subjects which are not required by the ship (e.g., LORAN-C messages might be rejected by a ship which is not fitte with a LORAN-C receiver). Receivers also use the B_2 character to identify messages, which because of their importance, may not be rejected.

A:	Navigational warnings[1]
B*:	Meteorological warnings[1]
C:	Ice reports
D:	Search and rescue information, and pirate attack warnings[1]
E:	Meteorological forecasts
F*:	Pilot service messages
G*:	DECCA messages
H:	LORAN messages
J:	SATNAV messages
K:	Other electronic navaid messages
L:	Navigational warnings (additional to A)[2]
V to Y:	Special services (allocation by NAVTEX Panel)
Z:	No messages on hand

[1] Cannot be rejected by the receiver
[2] Should not be rejected by the receiver
*Normally not used in the United States

NOTE: Since the National Weather Service normally includes meteorological warnings in forecast messages, meteorological warnings are broadcast using the subject indicator character E. U.S. Coast Guard District Broadcast Notices to Mariners affecting ships outside the line of demarcation, and inside the line of demarcation in areas where deep draft vessels operate, use the subject indicator character A. Two subject indicator characters for non-MSI messages in the United States were established 1 October 1995, but currently are not in use: V for Notice to Fisherman and W for Environmental messages.

MESSAGE NUMBERING (B_3B_4): Each message within a subject group is assigned a serial number, B_3B_4, between 01 and 99. This number will not necessarily relate to series numbering in other radio navigational warning systems. On reaching 99, numbering should restart at 01 but avoid the use of message numbers still in force.

300I.   U.S. NAVTEX Transmitting Stations

NAVTEX coverage is reasonably continuous off the U.S. East, Gulf, and West Coasts, as well the area around Puerto Rico, Kodiak Alaska, Hawaii and Guam. The U.S. has no coverage in the Great Lakes, though coverage of much of the Lakes is provided by the Canadian Coast Guard. U.S. Coast Guard NAVTEX broadcast stations are as follows:

– Boston (NMF) (Station F)
– Chesapeake (Portsmouth) (NMN) (Station N)
– Savannah (NMN) (Station E)
– Miami (NMA) (Station A)
– Isabella (San Juan) (NMR) (Station R)
– New Orleans (NMG) (Station G)
– Cambria (NMQ) (Station Q)
– Point Reyes (San Francisco) (NMC) (Station C)
– Astoria (NMW) (Station W)
– Kodiak (NOJ) (Station J)
– Honolulu (NMO) (Station O)
– Guam (NRV) (Station V)

RADIO NAVIGATIONAL WARNINGS

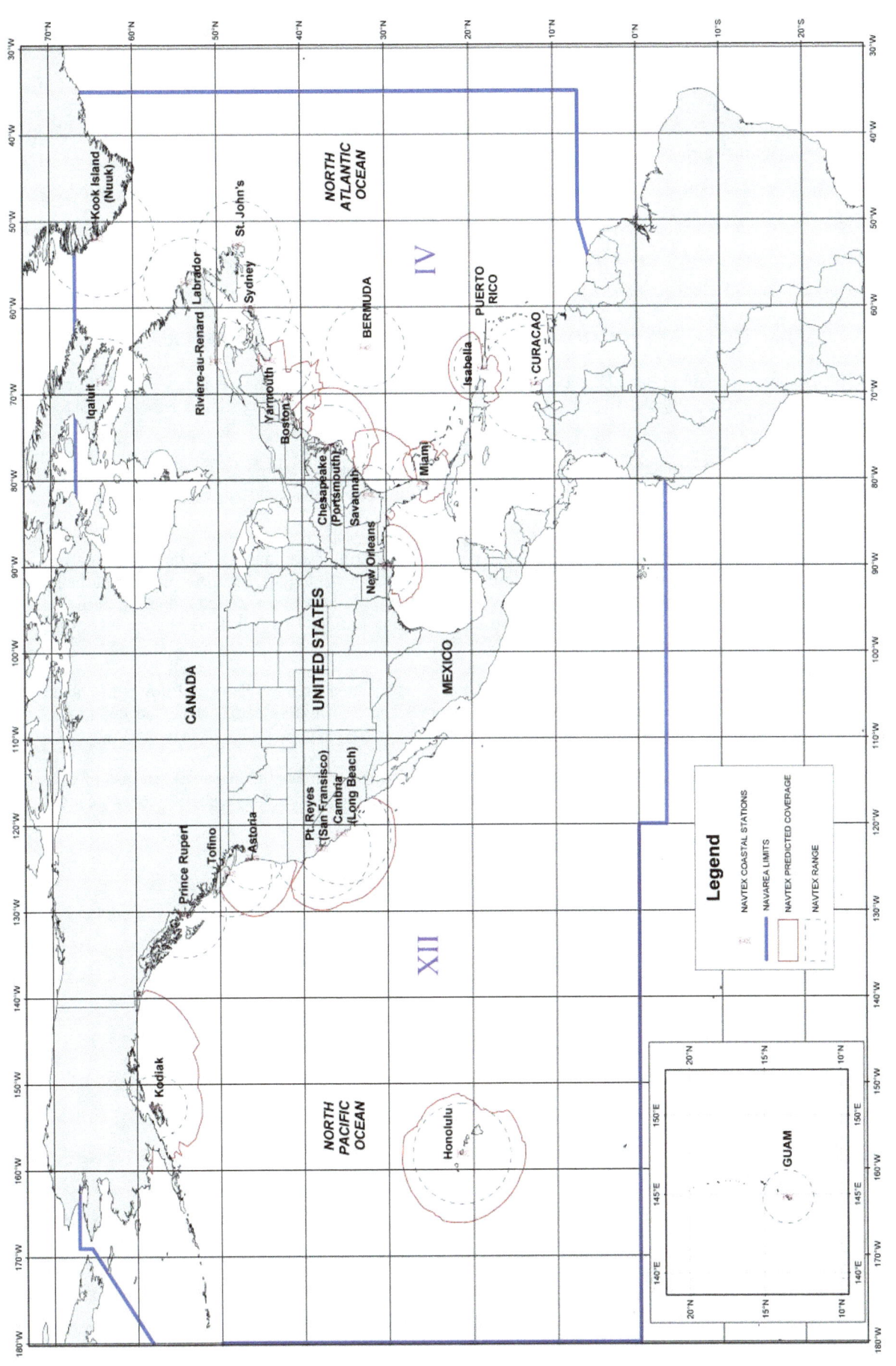

NAVTEX COVERAGE WITHIN NAVAREAS IV AND XII

RADIO NAVIGATIONAL WARNINGS

PRACTICAL INSTRUCTIONS FOR THE USE OF A NAVTEX RECEIVER

The NAVTEX receiver is a Narrow Band Direct Printing (NBDP) device operating on the frequency 518 kHz (some equipment can also operate on 490 and 4209.5 kHz), and is a vital part of the Global Maritime Distress and Safety System (GMDSS).

It automatically receives Maritime Safety Information such as Radio Navigational Warnings, Storm/Gale Warnings, Meteorological Forecasts, Piracy Warnings, Distress Alerts, etc. (full details of the system can be found in IMO Publication IMO-951E - The NAVTEX Manual).

The information received is printed on the receiver's own paper recorder roll. Each message begins with a start of message function (ZCZC) followed by a space then four B characters. The first (B_1), identifie the station being received, the second, (B_2), identifie the subject i.e. Navigational Warning, Met Forecasts, etc., and the third and fourth, ($B_3 + B_4$), form the consecutive number of the message from that station. This is followed by the text of the message and ends with an end of message function (NNNN).

The NAVTEX system broadcasts COASTAL WARNINGS that cover the area from the Fairway Buoy out to about 250 nautical miles from the transmitter; the transmissions from some transmitters can be received out to 400 nautical miles and even further in unusual propagational conditions.

The practical advice on the other side of this card will help to ensure that you make the most efficien use of your NAVTEX receiver, guaranteeing the reception of Maritime Safety Information within the respective coverage areas of the NAVTEX stations being used.

RADIO NAVIGATIONAL WARNINGS

NAVTEX RECEIVER CHECK-OFF LIST

For a NAVTEX receiver to function effectively, it is essential that the operator should have a sound knowledge of how to programme and operate his particular receiver. This is not difficul provided the following practical steps are followed:

1. Make sure that there are sufficient rolls of AVTEX paper on board.

2. Check that there is paper in the receiver.

3. Turn the NAVTEX receiver on at least four hours before sailing, or better still, leaves it turned on permanently. This avoids the chance of losing vital information that could affect the vessel during its voyage.

4. Make sure that the Equipment Operating Manual is available close to the equipment, paying particular attention to the fact that your equipment may be programmed differently from other makes and models.

5. Using the Equipment Operating Manual, make a handy guide for programming, status and autotesting procedures for your vessel's equipment, place it in a plastic cover and keep it with the equipment.

6. Have available next to the equipment a plasticised copy of the NAVAREAs/METAREAs in which the vessel is likely to sail, showing the NAVTEX stations, their coverage ranges, their respective time schedules and B_1 characters.

7. Programme your receiver to accept only those messages identifie with the B_1 character of the NAVTEX station which covers the area in which your vessel is currently sailing and the one covering the area into which you are about to sail. This will avoid the equipment printing information which has no relevance to your voyage and will avoid unnecessary waste of paper.

8. Programme your receiver to accept only those messages identifie with the B_2 characters (type of message) you wish to receive. It is recommended that most B_2 characters (A to Z) be programmed, but you may exclude those for navaid equipments (Decca or Loran for example) with which your vessel is NOT fitted Be aware that the characters A, B and D MUST be included, as they are mandatory.

9. Take extra care not to confuse the programming of B_1 characters (station designators) with those of B_2 characters (type of messages). It is very easy for an operator to believe that he/she is programming B_1 characters when in fact they are programming B_2 characters. After programming ALWAYS CHECK the programme status to ensure that it is correct.

10. If information is received incomplete/garbled, inform the relevant NAVTEX station, giving the time of reception (UTC) and your vessel's position. By so doing, not only will you obtain the information you require, but you will also help to improve the system. In the same way, any safety-critical occurrences observed during the voyage must be passed immediately to the nearest (or most convenient) Coast Radio Station and addressed to the relevant NAVAREA/METAREA or National Co-ordinator responsible for the area in which you are sailing.

RADIO NAVIGATIONAL WARNINGS

300J. Worldwide NAVTEX Transmitting Stations

The following operational coast radio stations, extracted from ANNEX 7 of the IMO GMDSS Master Plan, provide NAVTEX service. The frequency is 518 kHz unless otherwise indicated. For scheduled Maritime Safety Information (MSI) broadcast times of a particular coast radio station see sec. 300L.

NAV/MET Area	Country	NAVTEX Coast Station	Position	Range (NM)	Transmitter Identificatio (B_1) Character
I	Belgium	Oostende	51-11N 02-48E	150	M
				55	T
	Denmark (Greenland-East Coast)	Reykjavik	64-05N 21-51W	550	X
	Estonia	Tallinn	59-30N 24-30E	250	U
	France	Niton (U.K.)	50-35N 01-18W	270	K
					T (French)[1]
	Iceland	Reykjavik	64-05N 21-51W	550	R
					R (Icelandic)[1]
	Ireland	Valentia	51-27N 09-49W	400	W
		Malin Head	55-22N 07-21W	400	Q
	Netherlands	Netherlands Coast Guard (Den Helder)	52-57N 04-47E	250	P
	Norway	Bodø	67-16N 14-23E	450	B
		Rogaland	58-48N 05-34E	450	L
		Vardø	70-22N 31-06E	450	V
		Svalbard	78-04N 13-38E	450	A
		Ørlandet	63-40N 09-33E	450	N
	Russian Federation	Murmansk	68-46N 32-58E	300	C
		Arkhangel'sk	64-51N 40-17E	300	F
	Sweden	Stockholm (Bjuröklubb)	64-28N 21-36E	300	H
		Stockholm (Gislövshammer)	55-29N 14-19E	300	J
		Stockholm (Grimeton)	57-06N 12-23E	300	D
	United Kingdom	Cullercoats	55-04N 01-28W	270	G
					U[1]
		Portpatrick	54-51N 05-07W	270	O
					C[1]
		Niton	50-35N 01-18W	270	E
					I[1]
II	France	Corsen (CROSS)	48-28N 05-03E	300	A
					E (French)[1]
	Portugal	Horta (Azores)	38-32N 28-38W	640	F
					J (Portuguese)[1]
		Monsanto	38-44N 09-11W	530	R
					G (Portuguese)[1]
	Spain	Coruna	43-21N 08-27W	400	D
		Tarifa	36-01N 05-34W	400	G
		Las Palmas	28-10N 15-25W	400	I

[1] 490 kHz broadcast service.

RADIO NAVIGATIONAL WARNINGS

NAV/MET Area	Country	NAVTEX Coast Station	Position	Range (NM)	Transmitter Identificatio (B₁) Character
III	Bulgaria	Varna	43-04N 27-46E	350	J
	Croatia	Split	43-30N 16-29E	85	Q
	Cyprus	Cyprus	35-03N 33-17E	200	M
	Egypt	Alexandria	31-12N 29-52E	350	N
	France	La Garde (CROSS)	43-06N 05-59E	250	W
					S (French)[1]
	Greece	Iraklion	35-20N 25-07E	280	H
		Kerkira	39-37N 19-55E	280	K
		Limnos	39-52N 25-04E	280	L
	Israel	Haifa	32-49N 35-00E	200	P
	Italy	Roma	41-48N 12-31E	320	R
		Augusta	37-14N 15-14E	320	V
		Cagliari	39-14N 09-14E	320	T
		Trieste	45-41N 13-46E	320	U
	Malta	Malta	35-49N 14-32E	400	O
	Romania	Constanta	44-12N 28-40E	250	L (Romanian)[1]
	Russian Federation	Novorossiysk	44-36N 37-58E	300	A
		Astrakhan (Caspian Sea)	45-47N 47-33E	250	W
	Spain	Cabo de la Nao	38-43N 00-09E	300	X
	Turkey	Istanbul	41-04N 28-57E	300	D
		Samsun	41-17N 36-20E	300	E
		Antalya	36-53N 30-42E	300	F
		Izmir	38-21N 26-35E	300	I
	Ukraine	Kerch	45-23N 36-28E	120	B
		Odessa	46-29N 30-44E	280	C
IV	Bermuda	Bermuda	32-23N 64-40W	280	B
	Canada	Riviere-au-Renard	50-15N 66-10W	300	C
					D (French)
		Wiarton	44-20N 81-10W	300	H
		St. John's	47-30N 52-40W	300	O
		Thunder Bay	48-25N 89-20W	300	P
		Sydney	46-10N 60-00W	300	Q
					J (French)
		Yarmouth	43-45N 66-07W	300	U
					V (French)
		Labrador	53-42N 57-02W	300	X
		Iqaluit	63-43N 68-33W	300	T
					S (French)[1]
	Denmark (Greenland-West Coast)	Nuuk (Kook Island)	64-04N 52-01W	400	W
	Netherlands Antilles	Curaçao	12-10N 68-52W	400	H
	United States	Miami	25-37N 80-23W	240	A
		Boston	41-43N 70-30W	200	F

[1] 490 kHz broadcast service.

RADIO NAVIGATIONAL WARNINGS

NAV/MET Area	Country	NAVTEX Coast Station	Position	Range (NM)	Transmitter Identificatio (B_1) Character
IV	United States (cont.)	New Orleans	29-53N 89-57W	200	G
		Chesapeake (Portsmouth)	36-43N 76-00W	280	N
		Isabella	18-28N 67-04W	200	R
		Savannah	32-08N 81-42W	200	E
VI	Argentina	Ushuaia	54-48S 68-18W	280	M
		Rio Gallegos	51-37S 65-03W	280	N
		Comodoro Rivadavia	45-51S 67-25W	280	O
		Bahia Blanca	38-43S 62-06W	280	P
		Mar del Plata	38-03S 57-32W	280	Q
		Buenos Aires	34-36S 58-22W	560	R
	Uruguay	La Paloma	34-40S 54-09W	280	F
					A (Spanish)[1]
VII	Namibia	Walvis Bay	23-03S 14-37E	378	B
	South Africa	Cape Town	33-40S 18-43E	500	C
		Port Elizabeth	34-02S 25-33E	500	I
		Durban	30-00S 31-30E	500	O
VIII	India	Bombay	19-05N 72-50E	250	G
		Madras	13-08N 80-10E	250	P
	Mauritius	Mauritius	20-10S 57-28E	400	C
IX	Bahrain	Hamala	26-09N 50-28E	300	B
	Egypt	Ismailia (Serapeum)	30-28N 32-22E	400	X[2]
		Quseir (Kosseir)	26-06N 34-17E	350	V
	Iran	Bushehr	28-59N 50-50E	300	A
		Bandar Abbas	27-07N 56-04E	300	F
	Saudi Arabia	Dammam	26-26N 50-06E	390	G
		Jiddah	21-23N 39-10E	390	H
	Oman	Muscat	23-36N 58-30E	270	M
	Pakistan	Karachi	24-51N 67-03E	400	P
X	Australia is only providing coastal warnings through the International SafetyNET Service (AUSCOAST).				
XI	China	Sanya	18-14N 109-30E	250	M
		Guangzhou	23-08N 113-32E	250	N
		Fuzhou	26-01N 119-18E	250	O
		Shanghai	31-08N 121-33E	250	Q
		Dalian	38-52N 121-31E	250	R
	Indonesia	Jayapura	02-31S 140-43E	300	A
		Amboina (Ambon)	03-42S 128-12E	300	B
		Makassar	05-06S 119-26E	300	D
		Jakarta	06-06S 106-54E	300	E
	Japan	Otaru	43-19N 140-27E	400	J
		Kushiro	42-57N 144-36E	400	K
		Yokohama	35-14N 139-55E	400	I

[1] 490 kHz broadcast service.
[2] Includes 4209.5 kHz broadcast service.

RADIO NAVIGATIONAL WARNINGS

NAV/MET Area	Country	NAVTEX Coast Station	Position	Range (NM)	Transmitter Identificatio (B_1) Character
XI	Japan (cont.)	Moji	34-01N 130-56E	400	H
		Naha	26-05N 127-40E	400	G
	Malaysia	Pinang	05-26N 100-24E	350	U
		Miri	04-28N 114-01E	350	T
		Sandakan	05-54N 118-00E	350	S
	Korea, Republic of	Chukpyon	37-03N 129-26E	200	V
					J (Korean)[1]
		Pyonsan	35-36N 126-29E	200	W
					K (Korean)[1]
	Singapore	Singapore	01-25N 103-52E	400	C
	Taiwan	Chi-lung (Keelung)	25-08N 121-45E	540	P[2]
					V (Chinese)[2]
		Linyuan	22-29N 120-25E	540	P[2]
					X (Chinese)[2]
		Yenliaoken	23-54N 121-36E	350	P
					X (Chinese)[1]
		Lintou	23-33N 119-38E	350	P
					V (Chinese)[1]
	Thailand	Bangkok	13-43N 100-34E	200	F
	United States	Guam	13-29N 144-50E	100	V
	Vietnam	Ho Chi Minh City	10-47N 106-40E	400	X
		Da Nang	16-05N 108-13E	400	K
	Hong Kong (China)	Hong Kong	22-13N 114-15E	400	L
XII	Canada	Prince Rupert	54-17N 130-25W	300	D
		Tofin	48-55N 125-32W	300	H
	United States	Pt. Reyes (San Francisco)	37-55N 122-44W	350	C
		Kodiak	57-46N 152-34W	200	J
		Honolulu	21-22N 158-09W	350	O
		Cambria (Long Beach)	35-31N 121-03W	350	Q
		Astoria	46-10N 123-49W	216	W
XIII	Russian Federation	Vladivostok	43-23N 131-54E	230	A
		Kholmsk	47-02N 142-03E	300	B
		Petropavlovsk	53-15N 158-25E	300	C
		Magadan	59-41N 150-09E	120	D
		Okhotsk	59-22N 143-12E	300	G
XV	Chile	Antofagasta	23-40S 70-25W	300	A
					H (Spanish)
		Valparaiso	32-48S 71-29W	300	B
					I (Spanish)
		Talcahuano	36-42S 73-06W	300	C
					J (Spanish)

[1] 490 kHz broadcast service.
[2] 4209.5 kHz broadcast service.

RADIO NAVIGATIONAL WARNINGS

NAV/MET Area	Country	NAVTEX Coast Station	Position	Range (NM)	Transmitter Identificatio (B₁) Character
XV	Chile (cont.)	Puerto Montt	41-30S 72-58W	300	D
					K (Spanish)
		Punta Arenas (Magallanes)	53-09S 70-58W	300	E
					L (Spanish)
		Isla de Pascua	27-09S 109-25W	300	F
					G (Spanish)
XVI	Peru	Paita	05-05S 81-07W	400	S
		Callao	12-03S 77-09W	400	U
		Mollendo	17-01S 72-01W	400	W

RADIO NAVIGATIONAL WARNINGS

300K. Ice Information

INTERNATIONAL ICE PATROL: In February or March, the International Ice Patrol (IIP) will commence its annual service of providing maritime safety information on ice conditions in the vicinity of the Grand Banks of Newfoundland. Reports of ice in this area will originate from various sources, including passing ships and IIP reconnaissance flights Pending ice severity, the IIP will broadcast the southeastern, southern, and southwestern limits of all known ice in two message bulletins each day and a daily graphical chart containing ice information, to inform ships of the extent of the estimated limits of all known ice. The IIP continually monitors ice conditions in the vicinity of the Grand Banks and will commence iceberg warning information when appropriate; however, regardless of ice density, the IIP will begin broadcasting at least weekly (Friday) updates beginning on the Friday nearest 15 February at 1200UTC.

Broadcasts of IIP bulletins are as follows:

BROADCAST STATION	BROADCAST TIME (UTC)	FREQUENCIES
NAVTEX Broadcast		
USCG Communication Station Boston/NMF.	0045, 0445, 0845, 1245, 1645, 2045.	518 kHz, F1B.
	Special Broadcast during next available time slot.	518 kHz, F1B.
Canadian CG Marine Communications and Traffic Services St. John s/VON.	1820 (winter), 2220 (summer).	518 kHz, F1B.
SITOR Broadcast		
USCG Communication Station Boston/NMF. (NIK via NMF)	0030.	6314, 8416.5, 12579 kHz, F1B.
	1218.	8416.5, 12579, 16806.5 kHz, F1B.
RADIOFACSIMILE Broadcast		
USCG Communication Station Boston/NMF. (NIK via NMF)	1600, 1810.	6340.5, 9110, 12750 kHz, F3C.
Offenbach (Main), Germany via Pinneberg/DDK/DDH.	0930, 2100.	3855, 7880, 13882.5 kHz, F1C.
Radio Telephone		
Canadian CG Marine Communications and Traffic Services St. Antho y/VCM. (Iceberg Bulletin for NFLD Coast and Belle Isle)	0107, 0907, 1907.	2598 kHz, J3E.
	Continuous.	VHF Channel 21B, 83B.
Special Broadcasts		
Canadian CG Marine Communications and Traffic Services St. John s/VON.	0007, 0837, 1637, 2207 and as required.	2598 kHz, J3E.
	Continuous.	VHF Channel 21B, 28B, 83B.
Inmarsat SafetyNET Broadcasts		
AOR-E and AOR-W Satellites.	0000, 1200.	Inmarsat-C SafetyNET.
	Special Broadcasts of targets outside limits sent upon receipt.	
World Wide Web		
International Ice Patrol Web Page.	Updated after 0000, 1200.	http://www.uscg.mil/lantarea/iip/home.html
National Weather Service.	Updated daily after 1600.	http://weather.noaa.gov/pub/fax/PIEA88.gif
Automated Weather Network		
Automated Weather Network (AWN).	Updated daily at 0000, 1200.	Header: STNT41 KNIK.
Telefacsimile upon Demand		
Fax On Demand.	Updated daily after 1600.	Fax: (1) 860-441-2773.
E-mail On Demand.	Updated daily after 1600.	ftpmail@weather.noaa.gov

RADIO NAVIGATIONAL WARNINGS

Mariners should note that NAVTEX ice reports may be programmed for rejection at the receiver. Mariners desiring to receive IIP NAVTEX ice reports must ensure that their receivers are appropriately programmed for reception.

The Ice Chart Facsimile and the 0000Z and 1200Z Ice Bulletins are available on the World Wide Web at the International Ice Patrol's products section. IIP's homepage can be found at:

http://www.uscg.mil/lantarea/iip/home.html

The Ice Chart Facsimile is also available via Fax on Demand from the IIP's telefax machine. Dial (1) 860-441-2773 from a fax phone, and press "Copy" after successful connection.

The Ice Chart Facsimile is also available via E-mail on Demand from the National Weather Service's FTP e-mail system. Send an e-mail to ftp@weather.noaa.gov with any subject line. The body of the text should read as follows:
    open
    cd fax
    get PIEA88.gif   ---or---   get PIEA88.tif
    quit

The e-mail server will then automatically send a GIF or TIF formatted image of the facsimile back to the sender's e-mail address.

The Ice Bulletin is now posted to the Automated Weather Network, a weather service bulletin board accessible by U.S. Department of Defense and NATO units. Use header STNT41 KNIK to access IIP's products.

The 0000Z and 1200Z Ice Bulletins will be broadcast over the AOR-E and AOR-W Satellites. The 0000Z bulletin is broadcast between 2000 and 2359Z, and the 1200Z bulletin is broadcast at 1130Z. In addition, safety broadcasts regarding icebergs outside of the limits of all known ice will be transmitted over both satellites upon receipt.

COMMUNICATIONS WITH COMMANDER, INTERNATIONAL ICE PATROL: All ships are encouraged to immediately report sightings of ice to COMINTICEPAT GROTON CT, when near or within the "estimated limits of all known ice." Ships are encouraged to make reports even if no ice is sighted. The following information should be included when reporting ice:

– Ship name and call sign.
– Iceberg position [specify either the geographic coordinates (latitude, longitude) or range/bearing from ship's stated geographic position (latitude, longitude)].
– Time of sighting (in UTC).
– Method of detection (visual, radar, or both).
– Size and shape of iceberg (see tables below).
– Sea ice concentration (in tenths).
– Sea ice thickness in feet or meters (specify units).

The following tables describe size and shape criteria used by the Ice Patrol:

DESCRIPTIVE NAME	HEIGHT		LENGTH	
	(ft)	(m)	(ft)	(m)
Growler	< 17	< 5	< 50	< 15
Small Berg	17-50	5-15	50-200	15-60
Medium Berg	51-150	16-45	201-400	61-122
Large Berg	151-240	46-75	401-670	123-213
Very Large Berg	> 240	> 75	> 670	> 213

SHAPE	DESCRIPTION
Non-Tabular	This category covers all icebergs that are not tabular-shaped as described below. This includes icebergs that are dome-shaped, sloping, blocky, and pinnacle.
Tabular	Flat topped iceberg with length-height ratio greater than 5:1.

In addition to ice reports, sea surface temperature and weather reports are important to the Ice Patrol in predicting the drift and deterioration of ice and in planning aerial patrols. If you make routine weather reports to METEO WASHINGTON, please continue to do so. If your vessel does not normally make these reports, it is requested that you make special reports directly to the Ice Patrol every 6 hours when within the area between latitudes 40°N to 52°N and between longitudes 39°W to 57°W. Ships with one radio operator may prepare the reports every 6 hours and hold them for transmission when the radio operator is on watch. When reporting, please include the following:

– Ship position.
– Course.
– Speed.
– Visibility.
– Air and sea surface temperature.
– Barometric pressure.
– Wind direction and speed.

RADIO NAVIGATIONAL WARNINGS

Report ice sightings, weather, and sea surface temperature to COMINTICEPAT GROTON CT through Inmarsat, U.S. Coast Guard Communication Stations or Canadian Coast Guard Marine Communications and Traffic Services Centers. If reporting iceberg sightings to IIP through Inmarsat-A or -C, use service code 42. This will ensure the ice information immediately reaches the COMINTICEPAT GROTON CT. There is no charge to the user for iceberg reports sent using service code 42.

INMARSAT-A (General Instructions):
– Select Telenor (global identification code 01)
– Select routine priority.
– Select duplex telex channel.
– Initiate the call.
– Upon receipt of GA (Go Ahead), select the desired two-digit prefix access code foll wed by at + sign (42+).
– Send the report.
– The message will be forwarded at NO CHARGE from the mariner to International Ice Patrol by Telenor Satellite Services, Inc.

INMARSAT-C (General Instructions):
– Access the two-digit code service on SES as instructed in the manufacturer's information.
– Using the SES text editor, prepare the message.
– Enter the two-digit code of the service required (42).
– Select the CES (01, Telenor, AORW).
– Transmit the message.
– Wait for acknowledgment from the CES.
– The message will be forwarded at NO CHARGE from the mariner to International Ice Patrol by Telenor Satellite Services, Inc.

Iceberg sightings may also be reported on the guarded frequencies listed below:

Canadian Coast Guard
Marine Communications and Traffic Service

Receiving Station	Bands Guarded/ Transmit Frequency (Day/Night)
St. John's (VON), Newfoundland (St. John's Coast Guard Radio)	VHF Ch. 16 2182 kHz, H3E
St. Anthony (VCM), Newfoundland (St. Anthony Coast Guard Radio)	VHF Ch. 16 2182 kHz, H3E
Labrador (VOK) (Labrador Coast Guard Radio)	VHF Ch. 16 2182 kHz, H3E
Placentia (VCP), Newfoundland (Placentia Coast Guard Radio)	VHF Ch. 16 2182 kHz, H3E

Canadian Coast Guard
Marine Communications and Traffic Service

Receiving Station	Bands Guarded/ Transmit Frequency (Day/Night)
Port aux Basques (VOJ), Newfoundland (Port aux Basques Coast Guard Radio)	VHF Ch. 16 2182 kHz, H3E
Sydney (VCO), Nova Scotia (Sydney Coast Guard Radio)	VHF Ch. 16 2182 kHz, H3E
Dartmouth (VCS), Nova Scotia (Halifax Coast Guard Radio)	VHF Ch. 16 2182 kHz, H3E
Saint John (VAR), New Brunswick (Fundy Coast Guard Radio)	VHF Ch. 16 2182 kHz, H3E

U.S. Coast Guard
Communication Stations

DIRECT PRINTING RADIOTELETYPE
SELCALL 1097 (NMN)
(Assigned Frequency)

Ship Transmit	Shore Transmit	
4174 kHz	4212 kHz	On request
6264.5 kHz	6316 kHz	2300-1100
8388 kHz	8428 kHz	Continuous
12490 kHz	12592.5 kHz	Continuous
16696.5 kHz	16819.5 kHz	Continuous
22297.5 kHz	22389.5 kHz	1100-2300

SSB VOICE FREQUENCIES
(Carrier Frequency)

Ship Transmit	Shore Transmit	NMF	NMN
4134 kHz	4426 kHz	2230-1030	2300-1100
6200 kHz	6501 kHz	Continuous	Continuous
8240 kHz	8764 kHz	Continuous	Continuous
12242 kHz	13089 kHz	1030-2230	1100-2300
16432 kHz	17314 kHz	On request	On request

NOTE that USCG CAMSLANT Chesapeake (NMN) provides all U.S. east coast ON-CALL SITOR service.

Telephone communications are available to the Ice Patrol Offic in Groton, CT throughout the season. The numbers are: (1) 860-441-2626 (Ice Patrol Duty Office, 0700-1630 EST) or (1) 757-398-6231 (USCG Atlantic

Area Command Center, Portsmouth, VA, after working hours); IIP fax: (1) 860-441-2773.

CAUTIONS: The IIP attempts to locate and track icebergs south of 52°N, especially those south of 48°N, which may pose a hazard to shipping in the vicinity of the Grand Banks of Newfoundland. When the position, time of sighting, size, and description of icebergs are reported to IIP, the data is entered into a computer program that predicts their drift. Please note that the iceberg positions reported in all IIP products are always the predicted position for the date and time of that product. As the time after sighting increases, so does the probability of error in the icebergs' predicted positions. This probability of error is taken into account when the limits of all known ice are determined.

The purpose of the Ice Patrol's messages and charts is to advise mariners of the best estimate of the extent of icebergs in the region of the Grand Banks of Newfoundland. The iceberg positions represented within the estimated limits are intended only to give the mariner an understanding of the relative densities of icebergs. Any attempt to navigate among icebergs within the estimated limits on the basis of the facsimile charts or the message bulletins is strongly discouraged.

While the IIP attempts to be as accurate as possible in reporting the presence of icebergs to mariners, it is not possible to assure that all icebergs are reported. Mariners are strongly urged to use radar carefully, but not to rely entirely upon it to detect icebergs, since icebergs often are not detected distinctly with radar. There is no substitute for vigilance and prudent seamanship, especially when navigating near sea ice and icebergs.

The IIP earnestly solicits comments, particularly concerning the value and effectiveness of its services. Additionally, facsimile charts annotated with the ship's position, frequency used, and time of receipt can also help the IIP to better serve its customers. Comments can be provided using the phone and/or fax numbers above, or by mail to:

COMMANDER
INTERNATIONAL ICE PATROL
1082 SHENNECOSSETT ROAD
GROTON CT 06340-6095

NATIONAL ICE CENTER (NIC): The National Ice Center is a multi-agency operational center representing the Department of Defense (U.S. Navy), the Department of Commerce (NOAA), and the U.S. Coast Guard under the Department of Homeland Security. The NIC mission is to provide worldwide operational sea ice analyses and forecasts for the armed forces of the U.S. and Allied nations, the Department of Commerce, the U.S. Coast Guard under the Department of Homeland Security, and other U.S. government and international agencies, and the civil sector. The NIC produces analyses and forecasts of Arctic, Antarctic, Great Lakes and Chesapeake Bay ice conditions to support customers with global, regional and tactical scale interests. These products are available, in the following formats, on the World Wide Web at the NIC Website:

http://www.natice.noaa.gov

- Global sea ice edge products consisting of latitude/longitude pairs.
- JPG image file using the World Meteorological Organization's (WMO) Ice Egg Code.
- Geographic Information System (GIS) ARC/INFO coverages.

Some of the NIC's products are also transmitted as text messages.

The NIC is located at:

NATIONAL ICE CENTER
FEDERAL BUILDING 4
4251 SUITLAND ROAD
WASHINGTON DC 20395

Telephone: (1) 301-394-3100.

GULF OF ST. LAWRENCE, ST. LAWRENCE RIVER, SOUTH AND EAST COASTS OF NEWFOUNDLAND AND LABRADOR COAST: Commencing December 15 each year, and until ice in the Gulf of St. Lawrence is no longer likely to hinder shipping, an experienced ship Master will be attached to ECAREG CANADA as Ice Operations Officer. During this period, vessels inbound to the Gulf of St. Lawrence should report using the address ECAREG CANADA through any Marine Communications and Traffic Services (MCTS) Center 24 hours prior to their expected entry into the Cabot Strait, stating their position, destination, whether loaded or in ballast, ice class (if any), and classification society. This procedure will facilitate the passing of ice information and a suggested shipping track as necessary. Ships bound for ports on the south and east coasts of Newfoundland and along the coast of Labrador should also report to ECAREG CANADA for ice information, routing and escort as necessary. Gulf shipping interests are requested to maintain close contact with the Ice Operations Office so that all routing and escort assistance needed may be provided as circumstances permit.

All radio communications addressed to ECAREG CANADA and passed through a MCTS Center will be handled free of charge to the ship.

Ships outbound from Canadian ports east of Sept-Iles should report to the Ice Operations Office ECAREG CANADA through any MCTS Center 24 hours in advance of sailing time, if possible, for ice information, suggested routing, and escort if deemed necessary.

Ships outbound from Sept-Iles and ports west of Sept-Iles may obtain the latest bulletin pertaining to reported ice conditions, forecast, and recommended routing for the Gulf and River St. Lawrence by calling Quebec, Les Escoumins or Montreal MCTS Center on the control frequency of the sector in which the vessel is located. Vessels bound seaward when passing off Sept-Iles should also contact ECAREG CANADA through any MCTS Center for up-to-date ice information, routing, and icebreaker escort if required.

RADIO NAVIGATIONAL WARNINGS

During the winter navigation season, MTCS Centers broadcast ice advisories and forecasts on a regular schedule as indicated in the station listings. Ice forecasts will normally be for five-day periods when ice is light and of no immediate concern to shipping. Frequency of issue will be increased and forecast periods shortened when direct tactical support to shipping is required. Ice advisories will normally include a summary of existing ice conditions, a forecast of ice conditions for an appropriate period (2 to 5 days), and may include a suggested shipping track. This information is also broadcast in the form of charts by facsimile from stations so equipped.

GREAT LAKES: The Fisheries and Oceans Canada operates a service for the support of vessels navigating in Canadian waters of the Great Lakes during the season in which navigation is restricted by ice. This service includes the promulgation of up-to-date information on ice conditions, routing advice, aids to navigation, and the provision of icebreaker support when available and considered necessary, as well as the formation of convoys when conditions dictate. The following information outlines the service and facilities provided by the Canadian Coast Guard:

– Assembly and distribution of ice advisories, forecasts, and synoptic ice charts.
– Routing advice through light ice conditions, upon request.
– Coordination and direction of icebreaker support activities.

The service is known as Ice Sarnia and will commence December 1 each year, terminating when ice conditions permit unrestricted navigation. The address is:

ICE SARNIA
CANADIAN COAST GUARD
105 CHRISTINA STREET SOUTH
SARNIA ONTARIO N7T 7W1

Telephone: (1) 519-383-1855.
Fax: (1) 519-337-2498.

The Canadian Coast Guard has a limited number of icebreakers available for the support of shipping, and these are heavily committed. Therefore, it is emphasized that icebreaker support can not always be provided on short notice. In order to make the most efficien use of available resources it is most important that Ice Sarina be kept informed about the position and projected movements of vessels on the Great Lakes. Masters or agents should notify Ice Sarnia as soon as their sailing time is known, giving their ETD and destination in order to receive the most up-to-date information

ARCTIC AND HUDSON STRAIT AND BAY: The Canadian Coast Guard operates a service for the support of ships navigating in the ice-congested Canadian Arctic and other ice-free northern waters during the summer navigation season. Access to this service can be obtained by calling NORDREG CANADA. This support includes the promulgation of up-to-date information on ice conditions, advice on routes, aids to navigation, icebreaker support when available and considered necessary, and organization of convoys when conditions dictate.

Throughout the navigation season ice advisories, forecasts, and synoptic ice charts are issued by Ice Central in Ottawa and broadcast daily by radio and radio facsimile.

The Canadian Coast Guard has established a MCTS Center at Iqaluit, Nunavut. The Center opens in early June and is staffed until the end of December, or as long as ships are at sea in the area. The address is:

FISHERIES AND OCEANS
CANADIAN COAST GUARD
NORDREG CANADA
PO BOX 189
IQALUIT NUNAVUT   X0A 0H0

Telephone: (1) 867-979-5724 or 979-5269.
Fax: (1) 867-979-4236.
Telex (Telefax): 063-15529
Telegraphic Identifier: NORDREG CDA.

The Canadian Coast Guard has a limited number of icebreakers for the support of shipping. Because of heavy commitments, it is emphasized therefore that icebreaker support cannot always be provided at short notice. It is important that the Arctic Canada Traffi System (NORDREG CANADA) is as well informed as possible about the position and movements of ships in the Canadian Arctic. Ships bound for or leaving Hudson Bay or the High Arctic are required to contact NORDREG CANADA in accordance with reporting procedures specifie in the latest edition of either of the following publications:

– Pub. 140, Sailing Directions (Planning Guide) for the North Atlantic Ocean, Baltic Sea, North Sea, and the Mediterranean Sea.
– Pub. 180, Sailing Directions (Planning Guide) Arctic Ocean.
– Canadian Radio Aids to Marine Navigation (Atlantic, St. Lawrence, Great Lakes, Lake Winnipeg and Eastern Arctic).

BALTIC SEA ICE CODE: This code is used by the following countries: Denmark, Finland, Germany, Netherlands, Norway, Poland, Sweden, Russia, Estonia, Lithuania, and Latvia. The general form of the message code is:

ICE: AA 1A$_B$S$_B$T$_B$K$_B$2A$_B$S$_B$T$_B$K$_B$ ... nA$_B$S$_B$T$_B$K$_B$
      BB 1A$_B$S$_B$T$_B$K$_B$2A$_B$S$_B$T$_B$K$_B$ ... nA$_B$S$_B$T$_B$K$_B$
      CC etc.

Letter Symbols:

AA, BB, etc.	Index letters defining districts fo fairway sections or sea areas to which the following f ve-figure groups refe .
1, 2, ... n	Identifier figures of code grou referring to fairway sections or sea areas within the districts defined by AA, BB CC, etc. The number cannot exceed 9.
A$_B$	Amount and arrangement of sea ice (Table I).
S$_B$	Stage of ice development (Table II).
T$_B$	Topography or form of ice (Table III).

RADIO NAVIGATIONAL WARNINGS

K_B   Navigational conditions in ice (Table IV).

Notes:
- When a section is free of ice, the corresponding group may be omitted from the report. It should, however, always be coded as $n0//K_B$ the firs 2 days after it has become ice-free and only omitted the third day if the ice-free conditions continue.
- When all sections within a district are ice-free, the whole district shall be omitted from the report.
- The districts for which ice information is issued by countries using this code are indicated for each country in the following pages.

Table I
A_B - Amount and arrangement of sea ice

0	Ice-free
1	Open water - concentration less than 1/10
2	Very open pack ice - concentration 1/10 to less than 4/10
3	Open pack ice - concentration 4/10 to 6/10
4	Close pack ice - concentration 7/10 to 8/10
5	Very close pack ice - concentration 9/10 to 9+/10*
6	Very close pack ice, including consolidated pack ice - concentration 10/10
7	Fast ice with pack ice outside
8	Fast ice
9	Lead in very close or compact pack ice or along the ice edge
/	Unable to report
*	9+/10 means 10/10 ice concentration with small openings

Note: The higher code figure has greater priority i reporting.

Table II
S_B - Stage of ice development

0	New ice or dark nilas (less than 5 cm thick)
1	Light nilas (5 to 10 cm thick) or ice rind
2	Gray ice (10 to 15 cm thick)
3	Gray-white ice (15 to 30 cm thick)
4	Thin first-year ice, first stage (30 to 50 cm thic
5	Thin first-year ice, second stage (50 to 70 cm thick
6	Medium first-year ice (70 to 120 cm thick
7	Ice predominantly thinner than 15 cm with some thicker ice
8	Ice predominantly 15 to 30 cm with some ice thicker than 30 cm
9	Ice predominantly thicker than 30 cm with some thinner ice
/	No information or unable to report

Note: If $A_B = 0$, S_B should be reported as /.

Table III
T_B - Topography or form of ice

0	Pancake ice, ice cakes, brash ice—less than 20 m across
1	Small ice floes - 20 to 100 m acros
2	Medium ice floes - 100 to 500 m acros
3	Big ice floes - 500 to 2000 m acros
4	Vast or giant ice floe - more than 2000 m across, or level ice
5	Rafted ice
6	Compacted slush or shuga, or compacted brash ice
7	Hummocked or ridged ice
8	Thaw holes or many puddles on the ice
9	Rotten ice
/	No information or unable to report

Notes: Figures 0 to 4 only to be used if ice concentration is less than 7/10 with no compacted ice present ($T_B = 4$: vast floes). 4 to 9 to be used if ice concentration i greater 7/10 ($T_B = 4$: level ice). If $A_B = 0$, T_B should be reported as /.

Table IV
K_B - Navigation conditions in ice

0	Navigation unobstructed
1	Navigation difficult or dangerous for ooden vessels without ice sheathing
2	Navigation difficult for unstrengthened o low-powered vessels built of iron or steel; navigation for wooden vessels even with ice
3	Navigation without icebreaker assistance possible only for high-powered vessels of strong construction and suitable for navigation in ice
4	Navigation proceeds in lead or a broken ice-channel without the assistance of icebreaker
5	Icebreaker assistance can only be given to vessels suitable for navigation in ice and of special size
6	Icebreaker assistance can only be given to vessels of special ice class and of special size
7	Icebreaker assistance can only be given to vessels after special permission
8	Navigation temporarily closed
9	Navigation has ceased
/	Unknown

Baltic District Designators
Denmark
AA
(1) Sea area N of Hammaren
(2) Fairway to Ronne
(3) Sea area between Ronne and Falsterbo
(4) Sea area off Falsterbo Rev
(5) Fairway through Drogden
(6) Fairway to Kobenhavn

BB
(1) Sea area W of Ven
(2) Sea area E of Ven
(3) Sea area off Helsingor
(4) Sea area off Nakkehoved
(5) Sea area S of Hesselo
(6) Fairway to Isefjorden-Kynbyvaerkets

CC
(1) Sea area off Mon lighthouse (Route T)
(2) Sea area S of Gedser (Route T)
(3) Sea area S of Rodby Havn (Route T)

RADIO NAVIGATIONAL WARNINGS

(4) Sea area SE of Keldsnor (Route T)
(5) Sea area off Sprodsbjerg (Route T)
(6) Sea area W of Omo (Route T)

DD
(1) Agerso Sund—Stignaes
(2) Store Baelt channel, W part
(3) Store Baelt, E part (Route T)
(4) Sea area E of Romso (Route T)
(5) Fairway to Kalundborg oil harbor
(6) Sea area W of Rosnaes (Route T)

EE
(1) Sea area W of Sjaellands Rev (Route T)
(2) Sea area W of Hesselo (Route T)
(3) Sea area E of Anholt (Route T)
(4) Sea area W of Fladen Lt (Route T)
(5) Sea area NW of Kummelbanke (Route T)
(6) Sea area N of Skagen (Route T)

FF
(1) S entrance to Lille Baelt, Skjoldnaes
(2) Sea area off Helnaes
(3) Fairway to Abenra—Enstedvaerket
(4) Sea area off Assens
(5) Kolding Yderfjord to the bridges
(6) Fairway to Esbjerg

GG
(1) Fairway at Fredericia to the bridges
(2) Sea area N of Aebelo
(3) Fairway to Odense
(4) Sea area at Vesborg lighthouse
(5) Sea area S of Sletterhage
(6) Fairway to Aarhus

HH
(1) Sea area off Fornaes
(2) Fairway to Randers
(3) Entrance at Hals Barre
(4) Fairway to Aalborg
(5) Sea area NW of Laeso
(6) Sea area off Hirsholmene

Estonia

AA
(1) Narva-Yyesu—Kunda
(2) Kunda harbor and bay
(3) Kunda harbor—Tallinn
(4) Muuga harbor and bay
(5) Tallinn harbor and bay
(6) Tallinn—Osmussaar
(7) Osmussaar—Ristna
(8) Ristna—Irbenskiy Strait

BB
(1) Parnu harbor and bay
(2) Parnu—Irbenskiy Strait (eastern end)
(3) Irbenskiy Strait

CC
(1) Muhuvain

Finland

AA
(1) Roytta harbor
(2) Roytta—Etukari
(3) Etukari—Ristinmatala
(4) Ajos harbor
(5) Ajos—Ristinmatala
(6) Ristinmatala—Nukkujanmatala
(7) Nukkujanmatala—Kemi lighthouse
(8) Sea area SW of Kemi lighthouse
(9) Nukkujanmatala—Ulkokrunni

BB
(1) Virpiniemi—Ulkokrunni
(2) Oulu harbor
(3) Oulu—Kattilankalla
(4) Kattilankalla—Oulu Lt 3
(5) Oulu Lt 3—Oulu Lt 1
(6) Sea area W of Oulu Lt 1
(7) Open sea N of latitude of Marjaniemi

CC
(1) Raahe harbor and vicinity
(2) Heikinkari—Raahe lighthouse
(3) Raahe lighthouse—Nahkiainen
(4) Open sea between latitudes of Marjaniemi and Ulkokalla

DD
(1) Rahja harbor
(2) Rahja—Valimatala
(3) Sea area from Valimatala to the line Ulkokalla—Ykskivi
(4) Open sea between latitudes of Ulkokalla and Pietarsaari

EE
(1) Ykspihlaja harbor and vicinity
(2) Repskaret—Kokkola lighthouse
(3) Sea area off Kokkola lighthouse
(4) Pietarsaari harbor and vicinity
(5) Masskar—Kallan
(6) Sea area off Kallan
(7) Open sea between latitudes of Pietarsaari and Nordvalen

FF
(1) Sea area NE of Nordvalen
(2) Sea area from Nordvalen to W of Norrskar
(3) Vaskiluoto harbor
(4) Vaskiluoto—Storhasten
(5) Storhasten—Ensten
(6) Ensten—Korso
(7) Korso—Norrskar
(8) Fairway NW of Norra Gloppsten—Skvattan
(9) Sea area off Skvattan

GG
(1) Kaskinen harbor
(2) Sea area off Salgrund
(3) Sea area farther off Salgrund
(4) Open sea N of latitude of Yttergrund

HH
(1) Tahkoluoto harbor
(2) Mantyluoto harbor
(3) Kallo—Kolmikulma
(4) Sea area from Kolmikulma to the line Sappi—Kaijakari
(5) Sea area W of Sappi
(6) Sea area beyond that visible from Sappi

RADIO NAVIGATIONAL WARNINGS

(7) Open sea between the latitudes of Yttergrund and Rauma

II
(1) Rauma harbor and vicinity
(2) Valkeakari—Kylmapihlaja
(3) Kylmapihlaja—Raumanmatala
(4) Sea area W of Raumanmatala
(5) Open sea S of latitude of Rauma

JJ
(1) Uusikaupunki harbor and vicinity
(2) Kirsta—Isokari
(3) Isokari—Sandback
(4) Sea area off Sandback

KK
(1) Sea area off Salskar
(2) Sea area N of Market
(3) Sea area W of Market
(4) Sea area S of Market

LL
(1) Maarianhamina harbor and vicinity
(2) Sea area off Kobbaklintar and Nyhamn
(3) The middle Aland Sea
(4) Sea area off Lagskar

MM
(1) Naantali harbor
(2) Naantali—Rajakari
(3) Turku harbor
(4) Turku—Rajakari
(5) Rajakari—Orhisaari
(6) Orhisaari—Lovskar

NN
(1) Lovskar—Korra
(2) Korra—Iso Hauteri
(3) Iso Hauteri—Isokari
(4) Lovskar—Berghamn
(5) Berghamn—Gustav Dalen
(6) Gustav Dalen—Stora Sottunga
(7) Stora Sottunga—Brandokobben
(8) Brandokobben—Ledskar
(9) Sea area off Rodhamn

OO
(1) Lovskar—Grisselborg
(2) Grisselborg—Norparskar
(3) Sea area at Vidskar
(4) Uto
(5) Sea area S of Uto
(6) Sea area beyond that visible from Uto
(7) Sea area near Bogskar
(8) Sea area S of Bogskar
(9) Sea area beyond that visible southward from Bogskar

PP
(1) Hanko harbor
(2) Sea area E of Russaro
(3) Sea area S of Russaro
(4) Sea area beyond that visible S from Russaro
(5) Hanko—Jarngrynnorna
(6) Jarngrynnorna—Uto

QQ
(1) Koverhar harbor and vicinity
(2) Hasto Buso—Langden
(3) Langden—Ajax
(4) Sea area S of Ajax
(5) Sea area S of Jussaro

RR
(1) Inkoo harbor and vicinity
(2) Kantvik harbor and vicinity
(3) Sea area at Porkkala
(4) Porkkala Ronnskar—Sommaro
(5) Sea area off Sommaro
(6) Sea area farther off Sommaro

SS
(1) Helsinki harbor
(2) Suomenlinna—Harmaja
(3) Harmaja—Svartbaden
(4) Svartbaden—Helsinki lighthouse
(5) Helsinki lighthouse—sea area S of Porkkala
(6) Archipelago fairway Helsinki—Porkkala Ronnskar

TT
(1) Porvoo harbor and vicinity
(2) The S point of Emsalo—Porvoo lighthouse
(3) Porvoo lighthouse—Kalbadagrund
(4) Sea area Kalbadagrund—Helsinki lighthouse
(5) Valkom harbor and vicinity
(6) Archipelago fairway Boisto—Glosholm
(7) Archipelago fairway Glosholm—Helsinki

UU
(1) Kotka harbor and vicinity
(2) Viikari—Boisto
(3) Boisto—Orrengrund
(4) Orrengrund—Tiiskeri
(5) Sea area Tiiskeri—Kalbadagrund
(6) Hamina harbor and vicinity
(7) Suurmusta—Merikari
(8) Merikari—Kaunissaari

Germany

AA
(1) Stralsund to Palmer Ort
(2) Palmer Ort to Freesendorfer Haken
(3) Osttief
(4) Landtief fairway
(5) Sassnitz, port
(6) Sea area off Sassnitz
(7) Sea area off Arkona

BB
(1) Wolgast to Peenemunde
(2) Peenemunde to Ruden

CC
(1) Rostock to Warnemunde
(2) Rostock, Seehafen
(3) Warnemunde, Seekanal
(4) Sea area off Warnemunde
(5) Rostock, sea area N of navigation buoy

DD
(1) Wismar to Walfisc
(2) Walfisch to immendorf
(3) Timmendorf to Wismar navigation buoy
(4) Lubeck to Travemunde

RADIO NAVIGATIONAL WARNINGS

(5) Travemunde, harbor
(6) Sea area off Travemunde
(7) Sea area off Dahmeshovede

EE
(1) Holtenau to Laboe
(2) Sea area off Bulk
(3) Sea area NE of Kiel lighthouse
(4) Sea area off Westermarkeldorf
(5) Sea area off Marienleuchte
(6) E entrance of Fehmarnbelt

FF
(1) Flensburg to Holnis
(2) Holnis to Neukirchen
(3) Neukirchen to Kalkgrund
(4) Sea area off Falshoft

GG
(1) Holtenau, Kanalzufahrt
(2) Kanal, Holtenau to Rendsburg
(3) Kanal, Rendsburg to Brunsbuttel
(4) Brunsbuttel, Kanalzufahrt

HH
(1) Hamburg—Landungsbrucken, Elbe
(2) Stadersand (Elbe)
(3) Brunsbuttel (Elbe)
(4) Cuxhaven to Neuwerk
(5) Sea area off Elbe lightship

II
(1) Bremen (Weser)
(2) Brake (Weser)
(3) Bremerhaven (Weser)
(4) Hohe Weg lighthouse, channel
(5) Alte Weser, channel
(6) Neue Weser, channel

KK
(1) Wilhelmshaven harbor entrance
(2) Wilhelmshaven oil pier (Jade)
(3) Schillig (Jade)
(4) Wangerooge channel

LL
(1) Emden (Ems) and outer harbor
(2) Emden to Randzelgat (Ems)
(3) Borkum, Randzelgat (Ems)
(4) Borkum, Westerems

Latvia

AA
(1) Riga harbor
(2) Riga harbor—Mersrags entrance
(3) Mersrags—Irbenskiy Strait
(4) Irbenskiy Strait

BB
(1) Ventspils harbor
(2) Irbenskiy Strait—Ventspils harbor

CC
(1) Liepaja harbor
(2) Ventspils harbor—Liepaja harbor
(3) Liepaja harbor—Lithuanian waters

Lithuania

AA
(1) Klaipeda harbor
(2) Klaipeda—Latvian waters
(3) Klaipeda—Russian waters

Netherlands

AA
(1) Delfzijl
(2) Eemshaven
(3) Eems; Oterdum—Eemshaven
(4) Eems; Eemshaven—Hubertgat

BB
(1) Harlingen
(2) Along Pollendam
(3) Blauwe Slenk
(4) Vliestroom and Stortemelk

CC
(1) Den Helder
(2) Texelstroom and Marsdiep
(3) Schulpengat

DD
(1) Branch canal G and Zaandam harbors
(2) Amsterdam E harbors
(3) Amsterdam W harbors
(4) Branch canal A (Beverwijk)
(5) Nordseekanal
(6) Ijmuiden locks—fairway buoy

EE
(1) Nieuwe Maas and harbors
(2) Botlek harbors
(3) Europoort
(4) Nieuwe Waterweg
(5) Hoek van Holland—fairway buoy

FF
(1) Moerdijk
(2) Moerdijk—Dordrecht
(3) Dordrecht
(4) Oude Maas
(5) Noord

GG
(1) Antwerpen harbors
(2) Schelde: Antwerpen—Hansweert
(3) Schelde: Hansweert—Vlissingen roads
(4) Sloehaven
(5) Oostgat
(6) Wielingen
(7) Terneuzen Canal—Gent

Norway

AA
(1) Sekken (Halden)
(2) Singlefjorden (Halden)
(3) Svinesund—Halden
(4) Torbjornskjaer light
(5) Struten light
(6) Loperen (Fredrikstad)

BB
(1) Osterelv (Fredrikstad)
(2) Leira (Fredrikstad)
(3) Vesterelv (Fredrikstad)
(4) Rauoyfjord

RADIO NAVIGATIONAL WARNINGS

(5) Verlebukta—Moss
(6) Mossesundet

CC
(1) Oslo—Steilene—Spro light
(2) Spro light—Fagerstrand—Drobak
(3) Drobak—Filtvet light
(4) Filtvet light—Gullholmen light
(5) Rodtangen— Svelvik
(6) Svelvik—Steinsbraten light
(7) Steinsbraten light—Drammen
(8) Breiangen (N of Horten)

DD
(1) Langgrunn (Horten)
(2) Gullholmen light—Mefjordbaen
(3) Mefjordbaen—Fulehuk light
(4) Fulehuk light—Faerder light
(5) W of Faerder light
(6) S of Faerder

EE
(1) Torgersoygapet (Tonsberg)
(2) Husoysund—Tonsberg channel
(3) Tonsberg inner harbor
(4) Vestfjord (Tonsberg)
(5) Leistenslop
(6) Vrengen

FF
(1) Tjomekjaela
(2) Sandefjord
(3) Inside Svenner light
(4) Off Svenner light
(5) Larviksfjorden (Stavern—Larvik)
(6) Langesundsbukta

GG
(1) Brevikfjorden
(2) Frierfjorden (Porsgrunn, Skien)
(3) Jomfrulandsrenna
(4) Off Jomfruland
(5) Skatoysundet (Kragero)
(6) Langarsund (Kragero)

HH
(1) Kragerofjorden
(2) Gronholmgapet (Risor)
(3) Stangholmgapet (Risor)
(4) Lyngorfjorden
(5) Off Lyngor
(6) Tvedestrandsfjord

II
(1) Tromsoysundet (Arendal)
(2) Galtesund (Arendal)
(3) Inside Torungen light (Arendal)
(4) Off Torungen light (Arendal)
(5) Grimstad
(6) Inside Homborsund light

JJ
(1) Off Homborsund light
(2) Lillesand
(3) Kristiansandsfjorden
(4) Off Iksoy light (Kristiansand)

Poland

AA
(1) Sea area off Krynica Morska
(2) Gdansk port
(3) Gdansk, Port Polnocny
(4) Sea area off Gdansk
(5) Gdynia, port
(6) Sea area off Gdynia
(7) Sea area S of Helu
(8) Sea area E of Helu
(9) Sea area N of Helu

BB
(1) Sea area off Rozewie
(2) Ustka, port
(3) Sea area off Ustka
(4) Darlowo port
(5) Sea off Darlowo
(6) Kolobrzeg, port
(7) Sea area off Kolobrzeg

CC
(1) Zalew Szczecinski
(2) Szczecin, port
(3) Swinoujscie—Szczecin, fairway
(4) Swinoujscie, port
(5) Sea area off Swinoujscie

Russia (Baltic Coast and Gulf of Finland Coast)

AA
(1) Sankt Peterburg harbor
(2) Sankt Peterburg—Kotlin (eastern point)
(3) Kotlin (eastern point)—Tolbukhin
(4) Tolbukhin—Shepelevskiy
(5) Shepelevskiy—Seskar
(6) Seskar—Sommers
(7) Sommers—Gogland (southern point)
(8) Gogland (southern point)—Meridian of Kunda

BB
(1) Vyborg harbor and Bay
(2) Vichrevoj—Sommers
(3) B'yerkezund
(4) Bol'shoy Berezovyy (eastern point)—Shepelevskiy

CC
(1) Luzhskaya Guba
(2) Luzhskaya Guba—Line between Moshchnyy and Seskar

DD
(1) Kaliningrad harbor
(2) Kaliningrad—Lithuanian waters
(3) Kaliningrad—Polish waters

Sweden

AA
(1) Karlsborg—Maloren
(2) Sea area off Maloren
(3) Lulea—Bjornklack
(4) Bjornklack—Farstugrunden
(5) E and SE of Farstugrunden
(6) Sandgronn fairway
(7) Rodkallen—Norstromsgrund

BB

RADIO NAVIGATIONAL WARNINGS

(1) Haraholmen—Nygran
(2) Sea area off Nygran
(3) Skelleftehamn—Gasoren
(4) Sea area off Gasoren
(5) Sea area off Bjuroklubb
CC
(1) NE of Nordvalen
(2) SW of Nordvalen
(3) Vastra Kvarken (W of Holmoarne)
(4) Umea—Vaktaren
(5) SE of Vaktaren
(6) Sea area NE and SE of Sydostbrotten
DD
(1) Fairway to Husum
(2) Ornskoldsvik—Hornskaten
(3) Hornskaten—Skagsudde
(4) Sea area off Skagsudde
(5) Fairway W of Ulvoarna
(6) Sea area off Ulvoarna
EE
(1) Angermanalven above Sando bridge
(2) Angermanalven below Sando bridge
(3) Harnosand—Harnon
(4) Sea area off Harnon
(5) Sundsvall—Draghallan
(6) Draghallan—Astholmsudde
(7) Sea area off Astholmsudde
(8) Sea area off Bramon
FF
(1) Hudiksvallsfjarden
(2) Iggesund—Ago
(3) Sea area off Ago
(4) Sandarne—Hallgrund
(5) Sea area off Hallgrund
(6) Ljusnefjarden—Storjungfrun
(7) Sea area off Storjungfrun
GG
(1) Gavle—Eggegrund
(2) Sea area off Eggegrund
(3) Sea area off Orskar
(4) Oregrundsgrepen
(5) Passage at Grundkallen
HH
(1) Passage at Understen
(2) Sea area off Svartklubben
(3) Hallstavik—Svartklubben
(4) Sea area at Soderarm and Tjarven
(5) Sea area off Svenska Hogarna
II
(1) Stockholm—Tralhavet—Klovholmen
(2) Tralhavet—Furusund—Kappelskar
(3) Kappelskar—Soderarm
(4) Klovholmen—Sandhamn
(5) Sea area off Sandhamn
(6) Trollharan—Langgarn
(7) Mysingen
(8) Nynashamn—Landsort
(9) Sea area S of Landsort
KK
(1) Koping—Kvicksund
(2) Vasteras—Gronso
(3) Gronso—Sodertalje
(4) Stockholm—Sodertalje
(5) Sodertalje—Fifong
(6) Fifong—Landsort
LL
(1) Norrkoping—Hargokalv
(2) Hargokalv—Vinterklasen—Norra Krankan
(3) OxelosundHarbor
(4) Jarnverket—Lillhammaren— Norra Krankan
(5) Sea area off Gustafe Dalen
MM
(1) Sea area W of Gotska Sandon
(2) Sea area off Visby
(3) W of Stora Karlso
(4) Sea area off Hoburgen
(5) Sea area off Mago (Slite)
(6) Sea area off Faro
NN
(1) Vastervik—Marsholmen—Ido
(2) Sea area off Ido
(3) Oskarshamn—Furon
(4) Furon—Olands Norra Udde
(5) Sea area off Olands Norra Udde
OO
(1) Bla Jungfrun—Kalmar
(2) Kalmar—Utgrunden
(3) Utgrunden—Olands Sodra Udde
(4) Sea area SE of Olands Sodra Udde
PP
(1) Karlskrona—Aspo
(2) Sea area off Aspo
(3) Fairway to Karlshamn
(4) Fairway to Ahus
(5) Sea area off Sandhammaren
(6) Fairway to Trelleborg
(7) Sea area SE of Falsterbo Rev
RR
(1) Sea area N of Falsterbo Rev
(2) Drogden Passage
(3) Flintrannan
(4) Fairway to Malmo
(5) The Sound between Malmo and Ven
(6) The Sound E of Ven
(7) The Sound off Halsingborg
(8) W and S of Kullen
SS
(1) Fairway to Halmstad
(2) Fairway to Valberg
(3) Sea area W of Nidingen
(4) Knippelholmen—Botto
(5) Vinga Sand and Danafjord
(6) Buskar—Trubaduren—Vinga
(7) Off Trubaduren and Vinga
TT
(1) Uddevalla—Stenungsund
(2) Stenungsund—Hatteberget
(3) Sea area off Hatteberget
(4) Sea area off Maseskar
(5) Brofjorden—Dynabrott

RADIO NAVIGATIONAL WARNINGS

(6) Sea area off Dynabrott and Gaven
(7) Kosterfjorden
(8) Sea area off Nordkoster

UU

(1) Gota Alv
(2) Trollhatte canal—Dalbo bridge
(3) Vanersborgsviken
(4) Fairway through Luro archipelago
(5) Fairway to Gruvon
(6) Fairway to Karlstad
(7) Fairway to Kristinehamn
(8) Fairway to Otterbacken
(9) Fairway to Lidkoping

300L. Navigational Warning Station List

The stations in the following list broadcast navigational warnings, including ice information. Where these stations also provide weather and other miscellaneous information, those broadcast times and frequencies are included. Stations providing only weather information, however, are omitted. For information and schedules of marine weather broadcasts made primarily in English, refer to the Selected Worldwide Marine Weather Broadcasts (WWMARWETHRBC), a joint publication of the National Weather Service (NWS) and Naval Oceanography Command.

Broadcasts are in English unless otherwise indicated.

NOAA Weather Radio is a service providing specialized weather broadcasts for maritime users along the U.S. coastline, Great Lakes, Puerto Rico, the Virgin Islands, Guam and Saipan. It provides continuous broadcasts of the latest weather information directly from National Weather Service (NWS) offices Taped weather messages are repeated every four to six minutes and are routinely revised every one to three hours, or more frequently if needed. During severe weather, NWS forecasters can interrupt the routine weather broadcasts and substitute special warning messages.

NOAA Weather Radio broadcasts are received on one of seven VHF channels listed below. These channels are generally designated on marine VHF equipment as WX-1 through WX-7. These broadcasts usually can be received within 40 miles of the antenna site.

NOAA Weather Radio VHF Channels	
WX-1	162.550 MHz
WX-2	162.400 MHz
WX-3	162.475 MHz
WX-4	162.425 MHz
WX-5	162.450 MHz
WX-6	162.500 MHz
WX-7	162.525 MHz

A list of broadcast stations and frequencies may be obtained from the NOAA Weather Radio Website at:

http://www.nws.noaa.gov/nwr/

or from the NWS at the following address:

NATIONAL WEATHER SERVICE
ATTN: W/OM12
NOAA
1325 EAST WEST HIGHWAY
SILVER SPRING MD 20910

The NWS Marine Product Dissemination Information Homepage is internet accessible through the World Wide Web at:

http://www.nws.noaa.gov/om/marine/home.htm

Information available includes forecasts and warnings, up-to-date marine weather charts, including those broadcast by the Coast Guard over HF radiofacsimile, and the NOAA Weather Radio Guide.

RADIO NAVIGATIONAL WARNINGS

(1) No.	(2) Name	(3) Frequency	(4) Times	(5) Nature of Broadcast
		GREENLAND		
3001.5	Qaqortoq (OXF).	2129, 2225, 2265 kHz, J3E.	0035, 0335, 0635, 0935, 1235, 1535, 1835, 2135.	Local navigational warnings.
		2129, 2225, 2265 kHz, J3E, Ch. 01, 02, 03, 04, 23, 24, 25, 26, 27, 28, F3E.	0805, 1305, 1805, 2305 (1 hr. earlier when daylight savings in effect).	Weather.
		2129, 2225, 2265 kHz, J3E, Ch. 01, 02, 03, 04, 23, 24, 25, 26, 27, 28, F3E.	On request.	Weather and ice.
3002	Ammassalik (OZL).	2250, 3250 kHz, J3E.	0120, 0420, 0720, 1020, 1320, 1620, 1920, 2220.	Local navigational warnings.
		2250, 3250, 4381 kHz, J3E, Ch. 25, 26, 27, F3E.	0805, 1305, 1805, 2305 (1 hr. earlier when daylight savings in effect).	Weather.
		2250, 3250, 4381 kHz, J3E, Ch. 25, 26, 27, F3E.	On request.	Weather and ice.
3003	Greenland Radio.	570, 650, 720, 810, 900 kHz, A3E, 90.5, 92, 95, 95.2, 95.4, 95.5, 96, 96.25, 97, 98.5, 98.7 MHz, F3E.	2030 (Mon. - Fri.), 2100 (Sat., Sun.).	Local navigational warnings.
		570, 650, 720, 810, 900 kHz, A3E, 90.5, 92, 95, 95.2, 95.4, 95.5, 96, 96.25, 97, 98.5, 98.7 MHz, F3E.	0200, 1000, 1145, 1545, 2030 (Mon. - Sat.).	Weather.
		570, 650, 720, 810, 900 kHz, A3E, 90.5, 92, 95, 95.2, 95.4, 95.5, 96, 96.25, 97, 98.5, 98.7 MHz, F3E.	0200, 1100, 1500, 2100 (Sun., Hol.).	Weather.
3005	Nuuk (Kook Island).	518 kHz, F1B.	0340, 0740, 1140, 1540, 1940, 2340.	NAVTEX [W]. On trial.
3015	Aasiaat (OYR).	2116, 2304, 2400, 3125, 3276, 3280 kHz, J3E.	0235, 0535, 0835, 1135, 1435, 1735, 2035, 2335.	Local navigational warnings.
		2116, 2304, 2400, 3125, 3276, 3280, 4381, 6522 kHz, J3E, Ch. 01, 02, 03, 04, 23, 24, 25, 26, 27, 28, 60, 63, F3E..	0805, 1305, 1805, 2305 (1 hr. earlier when daylight savings in effect).	Weather.
		2116, 2304, 2400, 3125, 3276, 3280, 4381, 6522 kHz, J3E, Ch. 01, 02, 03, 04, 23, 24, 25, 26, 27, 28, 60, 63, F3E..	On request.	Weather and ice.

RADIO NAVIGATIONAL WARNINGS

(1) No.	(2) Name	(3) Frequency	(4) Times	(5) Nature of Broadcast
		CANADA - ARCTIC AND ATLANTIC		
3017	Iqaluit, N.T. (VFF).	2514, 6513 kHz, J3E.	0110, 1320, 1705.	Local navigational warnings, weather and ice (ice only at 1705).
		2514, 2582, 4363 kHz, J3E.	1340, 1705, 2235.	Local navigational warnings, weather and ice (ice only at 1705).
		3251.1, 7708.1 kHz (USB), J3C.	1000, 2100.	Weather FAX; 120/576.
		3251.1, 7708.1 kHz (USB), J3C.	0500, 2125.	Ice FAX; 120/576.
		2582, 4363 kHz, J3E.	1240, 1705, 2310.	Local navigational warnings, weather and ice (ice only at 1705) (Resolute).
		3251.1, 7708.1 kHz (USB), J3C.	1100, 2330.	Weather FAX; 120/576 (Resolute).
		3251.1, 7708.1 kHz (USB), J3C.	0010, 0700.	Ice FAX; 120/576 (Resolute).
		490 kHz, F1B.	0300, 0700, 1100, 1500, 1900, 2300.	NAVTEX [S] in French.
		518 kHz, F1B.	0310, 0710, 1110, 1510, 1910, 2310.	NAVTEX [T].
	NOTE: Station open during navigation season only, Jun. - Dec.			
3018	Inuvik, N.W.T. (VFA).	2558, 4363, 6218.6 kHz, J3E, Ch. 26, F3E.	0235, 1435.	Local navigational warnings and weather.
		4363, 5803 kHz, J3E, Ch. 26, F3E.	0115, 1315.	Local navigational warnings and weather.
		8457.8 kHz (USB), J3C.	0200, 1630.	Weather and ice FAX; 120/576.
	NOTE: During navigation season only, May - Oct.			
3019.5	Labrador, Labr. (VOK).	2598 kHz, J3E.	0137, 1007, 1437, 2037.	Weather and ice.
		2598 kHz, J3E.	1107, 2307.	Local navigational warnings.
		Ch. 21B, 83B, F3E.	Continuous.	Local navigational warnings, weather and ice.
		518 kHz, F1B.	0350, 0750, 1150, 1550, 1950, 2350; 0910, 2110 (Jul. - Oct.).	NAVTEX [X].
3020	St. Anthony, Nfld (VCM).	2598 kHz, J3E.	0107, 0907, 1337, 1937.	Weather and ice (ice at 0107, 0907).
		2598 kHz, J3E.	1237, 1907.	Local navigational warnings and ice (ice at 1907).
		Ch. 21B, 83B, F3E.	Continuous.	Local navigational warnings, weather and ice.
3021	Port aux Basques, Nfld (VOJ).	2598 kHz, J3E.	0207, 0807, 1507, 2107.	Weather and ice (ice at 0807).
		2598 kHz, J3E, Ch. 21B, 28B, 83B, F3E.	1207, 1837.	Local navigational warnings and ice (ice at 1837).
		Ch. 21B, 28B, 83B, F3E.	Continuous.	Local navigational warnings, weather and ice.
3023	St. John's, Nfld (VON).	2598 kHz, J3E.	0007, 0837, 1637, 2207.	Weather and ice.
		2598 kHz, J3E.	1307, 2007.	Local navigational warnings.
		Ch. 21B, 28B, 83B, F3E.	Continuous.	Local navigational warnings, weather and ice.
		518 kHz, F1B.	0220, 0620, 1020, 1420, 1820, 2220.	NAVTEX [O].
3027.5	Placentia, Nfld (VCP).	2598 kHz, J3E.	0048, 0737, 1607, 2137.	Weather and ice (ice at 0737, 2137).
		2598 kHz, J3E.	1137, 1807.	Local navigational warnings.
		Ch. 21B, 23B, 28B, 83B, F3E.	Continuous.	Local navigational warnings, weather and ice.

RADIO NAVIGATIONAL WARNINGS

(1) No.	(2) Name	(3) Frequency	(4) Times	(5) Nature of Broadcast
3032	Quebec, Que. (VCC).	Ch. 21B, 83B, F3E.	Continuous.	Local navigational warnings, weather and ice.
3036	Montreal, Que. (VFN).	Ch. 21B, 25B, 83B, F3E.	Continuous.	Local navigational warnings, weather and ice. (Seasonal operation May - Oct. on Ch. 83B.)
3038	Les Escoumins, Que. (VCF).	Ch. 21B, 83B, F3E.	Continuous.	Local navigational warnings, weather and ice.
3040	Riviere-au-Renard, Que. (VCG).	2598, 2749 kHz, J3E.	0937, 1737.	Local navigational warnings and ice.
		2598, 2749 kHz, J3E.	0437, 0847, 1407, 2317.	Weather.
		Ch. 21B, 25B, 83B, F3E.	Continuous.	Local navigational warnings, weather and ice.
		518 kHz, F1B.	0020, 0420, 0820, 1220, 1620, 2020.	NAVTEX [C].
		518 kHz, F1B.	0035, 0435, 0835, 1235, 1635, 2035.	NAVTEX [D] in French.
3042	Sydney, N.S. (VCO).	2749 kHz, J3E, Ch. 21B, 83B, F3E.	0040, 1440.	Local navigational warnings and weather.
		2749 kHz, J3E.	0740, 1940.	Weather.
		Ch. 21B, 83B, F3E.	1010.	Local navigational warnings.
		Ch. 21B, 83B, F3E.	Continuous.	Local navigational warnings, weather and ice.
		4416 kHz, J3C.	2200, 2331.	Ice FAX; 120/576.
		6915.1 kHz, J3C.	1121, 1142, 1741.	Ice FAX; 120/576.
		518 kHz, F1B.	0240, 0640, 1040, 1440, 1840, 2240.	NAVTEX [Q].
		518 kHz, F1B.	0255, 0655, 1055, 1455, 1855, 2255.	NAVTEX [J] in French.
3045	Halifax, N.S. (VCS) (CFH).	2749 kHz, J3E.	0240, 1540.	Local navigational warnings.
		2749 kHz, J3E.	0240, 0810, 1540, 2010.	Weather.
		Ch. 21B, 83B, F3E.	0240, 1110, 1540.	Local navigational warnings.
		Ch. 21B, 83B, F3E.	Continuous.	Weather.
		122.5 MHz, 4271, 6496.4, 10536, 13510 kHz, F1B.	0000, 0100, 0300, 0600, 0700, 0800, 0900, 1100, 1400, 1500, 1700, 1900, 2000, 2100, 2300.	Weather.
		122.5 MHz, 4271, 6496.4, 10536, 13510 kHz, J3C.	Continuous.	Weather FAX*; 120/576.
		122.5 MHz, 4271, 6496.4, 10536, 13510 kHz, J3C.	0001, 2222, 2301.	Ice FAX*; 120/576.
	*NOTE: CFH broadcast schedule at 1101.			
3047	Saint John, N.B. (VAR).	2749 kHz, J3E, Ch. 21B, 83B, F3E.	0140, 1040, 1640, 2040.	Weather.
		2749 kHz, J3E, Ch. 21B, 83B, F3E.	0140, 1640.	Local navigational warnings.
		Ch. 21B, 83B, F3E.	1240.	Local navigational warnings.
		Ch. 21B, 83B, F3E.	Continuous.	Weather
		518 kHz, F1B.	0320, 0720, 1120, 1520, 1920, 2320.	NAVTEX [U].
		518 kHz, F1B.	0335, 0735, 1135, 1535, 1935, 2335.	NAVTEX [V] in French.

ST. PIERRE AND MIQUELON

3050	St. Pierre Radio.	1375 kHz, A3E.	1050, 1130, 1515, 2150.	Weather in French.

RADIO NAVIGATIONAL WARNINGS

(1) No.	(2) Name	(3) Frequency	(4) Times	(5) Nature of Broadcast
		UNITED STATES AND CANADA - LAKES		
3068	Wiarton, Ont.	518 kHz, F1B.	0110, 0510, 0910, 1310, 1710, 2110.	NAVTEX [H].
3069	Prescott, Ont. (VBR).	Ch. 21B, 83B, F3E.	Continuous.	Local navigational warnings, weather and ice.
3070	Sarnia, Ont. (VBE).	Ch. 21B, 83B, F3E.	Continuous.	Local navigational warnings, weather and ice.
	LOCAL WARNINGS: Local Notice to Mariners: Original reports to nearest Coast Guard station for relay to District Commander (oan).			
3074	Sault St. Marie, MI (NOG) U.S. Coast Guard.	Ch. 22A, F3E.	0005, 1205.	Local Notice to Mariners and weather.
3076	Buffalo, NY (NMD-47) U.S. Coast Guard.	Ch. 22A, F3E.	0255, 1455.	Local Notice to Mariners and weather.
3077	Detroit, MI (NMD-25) U.S. Coast Guard.	Ch. 22A, F3E.	0135, 1335.	Local Notice to Mariners and weather.
3078	Grand Haven, MI (NMD-32) U.S. Coast Guard.	Ch. 22A, F3E.	0235, 1435.	Local Notice to Mariners and weather.
3079	Milwaukee, WI (NMP-9) U.S. Coast Guard.	Ch. 22A, F3E.	0255, 1455.	Local Notice to Mariners and weather.
3080	Thunder Bay, Ont. (VBA).	2582 kHz, J3E, Ch. 26, F3E.	0040, 1410.	Local navigational warnings and weather.
		2582 kHz, J3E, Ch. 26, F3E.	0040, 1520.	Ice.
		Ch. 19, 26, F3E.	0140, 0840, 1240, 1640, 2140.	Local navigational warnings and weather.
		Ch. 21B, 83B, F3E.	Continuous.	Local navigational warnings, weather and ice.
		518 kHz, F1B.	0230, 0630, 1030, 1430, 1830, 2230.	NAVTEX [P].
		UNITED STATES - ATLANTIC AND GULF		
	LONG-RANGE WARNINGS: NAVAREA IV: Original reports to NAVAREA IV Coordinator, National Geospatial-Intelligence Agency, Attn: PVM (Mail stop D-44). HYDROLANT: Original reports to National Geospatial-Intelligence Agency. LOCAL WARNINGS: Local Notice to Mariners: Original reports to nearest Coast Guard Station for relay to District Commander (oan).			
3083	Southwest Harbor, ME (NMF-44) U.S. Coast Guard.	2670 kHz, J3E, Ch. 22A, F3E.	1135, 2335.	Local Notice to Mariners and weather.
3084	Portland, ME (NMF-31) U.S. Coast Guard.	2670 kHz, J3E, Ch. 22A, F3E.	1105, 2305.	Local Notice to Mariners and weather.

RADIO NAVIGATIONAL WARNINGS

(1) No.	(2) Name	(3) Frequency	(4) Times	(5) Nature of Broadcast
3086	Boston, MA (NMF) (NIK) (NMF-7) U.S. Coast Guard.	6314, 8416.5, 12579 kHz, F1B.	0030.	Ice (seasonal).
		6314, 8416.5, 12579 kHz, F1B.	0140.	Maritime Safety Information (MSI) (HF NBDP) (NAVAREA IV, HYDROLANT and weather).
		8416.5, 12579, 16806.5 kHz, F1B.	1218.	Ice (seasonal).
		8416.5, 12579, 16806.5 kHz, F1B.	1630.	Maritime Safety Information (MSI) (HF NBDP) (NAVAREA IV, HYDROLANT and weather).
		4235 kHz, F3C.	0230, 0745.	Weather FAX*; 120/576.
		6340.5, 9110 kHz, F3C.	0230, 0745, 1400, 1720, 1900.	Weather FAX*; 120/576.
		12750 kHz, F3C.	1400, 1900.	Weather FAX*; 120/576.
		6340.5, 9110, 12750 kHz, F3C.	1600, 1810.	Ice FAX; 120/576 (Feb. - Aug.).
		2670 kHz, J3E, Ch. 22A, F3E.	1035, 2235.	Local Notice to Mariners and weather.
		518 kHz, F1B.	0045, 0445, 0845, 1245, 1645, 2045.	NAVTEX [F].
	*NOTE: Broadcast schedule at 0243, 1405.			
3087	Woods Hole, MA (NMF-2) U.S. Coast Guard.	2670 kHz, J3E.	0440, 1640.	Local Notice to Mariners and weather.
		Ch. 22A, F3E.	1005, 2205.	Local Notice to Mariners and weather.
3088.5	Long Island Sound, CT (NMY-15) U.S. Coast Guard.	Ch. 22A, F3E.	1120, 2320.	Local Notice to Mariners and weather.
3088.6	Moriches, NY (NMY-42) U.S. Coast Guard.	2670 kHz, J3E, Ch. 22A, F3E.	0010, 1210.	Local Notice to Mariners and weather.
3088.7	New York, NY (NMY-3) U.S. Coast Guard.	Ch. 22A, F3E.	1050, 2250.	Local Notice to Mariners and weather.
3090.7	Atlantic City, NJ (NMK-2) U.S. Coast Guard.	2670 kHz, J3E, Ch. 22A, F3E.	1103, 2303.	Local Notice to Mariners and weather.
3092	Baltimore, MD (NMX) U.S. Coast Guard.	Ch. 22A, F3E.	0130, 1205.	Local Notice to Mariners and weather.
3093	Chincoteague, VA (NMN-70) U.S. Coast Guard.	2670 kHz, J3E.	0233, 1403.	Local Notice to Mariners and weather.
		Ch. 22A, F3E.	0200, 1145.	Local Notice to Mariners and weather.
3096	Chesapeake, VA (NMN) (NMN-80) U.S. Coast Guard.	4426, 6501, 8764, kHz, J3E.	0330, 0500, 0930.	Maritime Safety Information (MSI).
		6501, 8764, 13089 kHz, J3E.	1130, 1600, 2200, 2330.	Maritime Safety Information (MSI).
		8764, 13089, 17314 kHz, J3E.	1730.	Maritime Safety Information (MSI).
		2670 kHz, J3E.	0203, 1333.	Local Notice to Mariners and weather.
		Ch. 22A, F3E.	0230, 1120.	Local Notice to Mariners and weather.
		518 kHz, F1B.	0130, 0530, 0930, 1330, 1730, 2130.	NAVTEX [N].
3099	Cape Hatteras, NC (NMN-13) U.S. Coast Guard.	2670 kHz, J3E.	0133, 1303.	Local Notice to Mariners and weather.
		Ch. 22A, F3E.	0100, 1055.	Local Notice to Mariners and weather.
3099.5	Fort Macon, NC (NMN-37) U.S. Coast Guard.	2670 kHz, J3E, Ch. 22A, F3E.	0103, 1233.	Local Notice to Mariners and weather.
3100	Charleston, SC (NMB) U.S. Coast Guard.	2670 kHz, J3E.	0420, 1620.	Local Notice to Mariners and weather.
		Ch. 22A, F3E.	1200, 2200.	Local Notice to Mariners and weather.
3101	Savannah, GA (NMN) U.S. Coast Guard.	518 kHz, F1B.	0040, 0440, 0840, 1240, 1640, 2040.	NAVTEX [E].

RADIO NAVIGATIONAL WARNINGS

(1) No.	(2) Name	(3) Frequency	(4) Times	(5) Nature of Broadcast
3102	Mayport, FL (NMV) U.S. Coast Guard.	2670 kHz, J3E.	0620, 1820.	Local Notice to Mariners and weather.
		Ch. 22A, F3E.	1215, 2215.	Local Notice to Mariners and weather.
3104	Miami, FL (NMA) (NCF) U.S. Coast Guard.	2670 kHz, J3E.	0350, 1550.	Local Notice to Mariners and weather.
		Ch. 22A, F3E.	1230, 2230.	Local Notice to Mariners and weather.
		518 kHz, F1B.	0000, 0400, 0800, 1200, 1600, 2000.	NAVTEX [A].
3106	Key West, FL (NOK) U.S. Coast Guard.	Ch. 22A, F3E.	1200, 2200.	Local Notice to Mariners and weather.
3107.8	St. Petersburg, FL (NME) U.S. Coast Guard.	2670 kHz, J3E.	0320, 1420.	Local Notice to Mariners and weather.
		Ch. 22A, F3E.	1300, 2300.	Local Notice to Mariners and weather.
3108	New Orleans, LA (NMG) (NMG-2) U.S. Coast Guard.	2670 kHz, J3E.	0550.	Local Notice to Mariners and weather.
		2670 kHz, J3E, Ch. 22A, F3E.	1035, 1235, 1635, 2235.	Local Notice to Mariners and weather.
		4316, 8502, 12788 kHz, J3E.	0330, 0500, 0930, 1130, 1600, 1730, 2200, 2330.	Local Notice to Mariners and weather.
		4317.9, 8503.9, 12789.9 kHz, F3C.	0000, 0600, 1200, 1800.	Weather FAX*; 120/576.
		17146.4 kHz, F3C.	1200, 1800.	Weather FAX*; 120/576.
		518 kHz, F1B.	0300, 0700, 1100, 1500, 1900, 2300.	NAVTEX [G].
	*NOTE: Broadcast schedule at 2025.			
3111	Mobile, AL (NOQ) U.S. Coast Guard.	2670 kHz, J3E, Ch. 22A, F3E.	1020, 1220, 1620, 2220.	Local Notice to Mariners and weather.
3112	Galveston, TX (NOY) U.S. Coast Guard.	2670 kHz, J3E, Ch. 22A, F3E.	1050, 1250, 1650, 2250.	Local Notice to Mariners and weather.
3116	Corpus Christi, TX (NOY-8) U.S. Coast Guard.	2670 kHz, J3E, Ch. 22A, F3E.	1040, 1240, 1640, 2240.	Local Notice to Mariners and weather.
	MEXICO			
3118	Veracruz (XFU).	451 kHz, A1A.	0300, 1600, 2100.	Local navigational warnings.
		8656 kHz, A1A.	1600, 2100.	Local navigational warnings.
		451, 8656 kHz, A1A.	0400, 1600, 2100.	Weather.
	CUBA			
3119	Santiago de Cuba (CLM).	2760 kHz, J3E.	2340.	Local navigational warnings in Spanish.
	NOTE: Frequency 2760 kHz has been reported as temporarily out of service. Navigational warnings will be transmitted on VHF Ch. 64 after prior announcement on VHF Ch. 16 until further notice.			
3121	Cienfuegos (CLC).	2760 kHz, J3E.	2305.	Local navigational warnings in Spanish.
3131	Habana (CLT).	2760 kHz, J3E.	2310	Local navigational warnings in Spanish.
		2760 kHz, J3E.	0403, 2203.	Military exercise warnings in Spanish.
		2760 kHz, J3E.	0105, 1305.	Weather in Spanish.

3 - 33

RADIO NAVIGATIONAL WARNINGS

(1) No.	(2) Name	(3) Frequency	(4) Times	(5) Nature of Broadcast
		BERMUDA		
3135	Bermuda Harbor (ZBM).	2582 kHz, J3E, Ch. 27, F3E.	0035, 0435, 0835, 1235, 1635, 2035.	Local navigational warnings and weather.
		162.4 MHz (WX2), J3E.	Continuous.	Local navigational warnings and weather.
		518 kHz, F1B.	0010, 0410, 0810, 1210, 1610, 2010.	NAVTEX [B].
		JAMAICA		
3135.5	Jamaica Coast Guard (6YX).	2738 kHz, A3E, Ch. 13, F3E.	1330, 1830.	Local navigational warnings and weather.
		Ch. 13, F3E.	0130, 1430, 1930.	Weather.
		PUERTO RICO		
3138	San Juan, PR (NMR) (NMR-1) U.S. Coast Guard.	2670 kHz, J3E.	0305, 1505.	Local Notice to Mariners and weather.
		Ch. 22A, F3E.	1210, 2210.	Local Notice to Mariners and weather.
		518 kHz, F1B.	0200, 0600, 1000, 1400, 1800, 2200.	NAVTEX [R].
		MARTINIQUE		
3140	Fort de France (CROSSAG) (MRCC).	Ch. 79, F3E; Ch. 80, F3E.	0020, 0040, 1450, 1510; 0030, 0050, 1500, 1520.	Local navigational warnings and weather in French for Martinique, St. Lucia and Dominica.
		Ch. 79, F3E; Ch. 80, F3E; Ch. 64, F3E.	1530, 2300; 1540, 1600, 2310, 2330; 1550, 2320.	Gunfir warnings and weather in French for Guadeloupe.
		Ch. 64, F3E.	0000, 1630.	Local navigational warnings and weather in French for St. Martin and Antigua.
		2545 kHz, J3E.	1215, 2133.	Weather in French.
		2545 kHz, J3E.	Every even hour.	Weather.
		Ch. 64, 79, 80, F3E.	Every hour.	Weather.
		Ch. 79, F3E; Ch. 80, F3E;	1120, 1140, 2220, 2240; 1130, 1150, 2230, 2250.	Weather in French for Martinique, St. Lucia and Dominica.
		Ch. 79, F3E; Ch. 80, F3E; Ch. 64, F3E.	0100, 1200; 0110, 0130, 1210, 1230; 0120, 1220.	Weather in French for Guadeloupe.
		Ch. 64, F3E.	0200, 1300.	Weather in French for St. Martin and Antigua.
		TRINIDAD AND TOBAGO		
3143	North Post (9YL) (Trinidad).	2735, 3165 kHz, J3E.	1250, 1850.	Local navigational warnings (weather on 3165 kHz).
		8441 kHz, A1A.	0100, 0600, 0900, 1300, 1500, 1730, 2130.	Weather.
		17184.8 kHz, A1A.	1200, 1530.	Weather.
		12885 kHz, A1A.	1330, 2050.	Weather.
		Ch. 24, 25, 26, 27, F3E.	1340, 2040.	Weather.
		6470.5 kHz, A1A.	2300.	Weather.
		NETHERLANDS ANTILLES		
3145	Curacao (PJC).	518 kHz, F1B.	0110, 0510, 0910, 1310, 1710, 2110.	NAVTEX [H].

RADIO NAVIGATIONAL WARNINGS

(1) No.	(2) Name	(3) Frequency	(4) Times	(5) Nature of Broadcast

BRAZIL

LONG-RANGE WARNINGS:
NAVAREA V:
Includes the waters west of 20°W between 7°N and 35°S, subdivided into the following areas: North Coast, East Coast and South Coast. Navigational aids are referred to by International numbers; the term "number of order" refers to Brazilian Light List numbers. Original reports are addressed "NAVEMAR" and handled by Brazilian government stations without charge.

No.	Name	Frequency	Times	Nature of Broadcast
3150	Belem (PPL).	4321 kHz, A1A.	0600.	Local navigational warnings in Portuguese, NAVAREA V.
		8462 kHz, A1A.	1800.	Local navigational warnings in Portuguese, NAVAREA V.
		8462 kHz, A1A.	1000.	Weather.
		4321 kHz, A1A.	2200.	Weather.
		4369 kHz, J3E.	0103, 0603, 1003, 1203, 1503, 2103.	Local navigational warnings and weather in Portuguese, NAVAREA V.
3151	Belem Radio Liberal (ZYI-533).	1330 kHz.	0100, 0900, 1700.	Local navigational warnings.
3152	Belem Radio Marajoara (ZYI-531).	1130 kHz.	0200, 0930, 1800.	Local navigational warnings.
3153	Ponta do Ceu.	Ch. 16, F3E.	0000, 1200, 1800.	Local navigational warnings.
3154	Radio Nacional de Macapa (ZYH-222).	630 kHz.	1100, 1600, 2130.	Local navigational warnings.
3157	Olinda (PPO).	4321 kHz, A1A.	0200.	Local navigational warnings in Portuguese, NAVAREA V.
		8462 kHz, A1A.	1400.	Local navigational warnings in Portuguese, NAVAREA V.
		8294 kHz, F3C.	0745-0830, 1745-1830.	Weather FAX; 120/576
		4321 kHz, A1A.	0430.	Weather.
		8462 kHz, A1A.	1630.	Weather.
		4369 kHz, J3E.	0103, 0603, 1003, 1203, 1503, 2103.	Local navigational warnings and weather in Portuguese, NAVAREA V.
3161	Rio de Janeiro Naval (PWZ-33).	4289, 6435, 8550, 12795, 17160, 22530 kHz, A1A.	0500, 1330, 2230.	NAVAREA V and local navigational warnings.
		4289, 6435, 8550, 12795, 17160, 22530 kHz, F1B.	0400, 1230, 2130.	NAVAREA V and local navigational warnings.
		12660, 17140 kHz, F3C.	0745-0830, 1745-1830.	Weather FAX; 120/576.
		4289, 6435, 8550, 12795, 17160, 22530 kHz, A1A.	0215, 0945, 1945.	Weather.
		4289, 6435, 8550, 12795, 17160, 22530 kHz, F1B.	0115, 0845, 1845.	Weather.
3166	Juncao (PPJ).	4321 kHz, A1A.	0800.	Local navigational warnings in Portuguese, NAVAREA V.
		8462 kHz, A1A.	2000.	Local navigational warnings in Portuguese, NAVAREA V.
		4321 kHz, A1A.	0000.	Weather.
		8462 kHz, A1A.	1200.	Weather.
		4381 kHz, J3E.	0103, 0603, 1003, 1203, 1503, 2103.	Local navigational warnings and weather in Portuguese, NAVAREA V.

RADIO NAVIGATIONAL WARNINGS

(1) No.	(2) Name	(3) Frequency	(4) Times	(5) Nature of Broadcast
		URUGUAY		
3168	La Paloma (CWC-30) (CWS-27).	2722.1, 4146 kHz, J3E, Ch. 15, F3E.	0600, 1200, 1900.	Local navigational warnings and weather in Spanish.
		490 kHz, F1B.	0000, 0400, 0800, 1200, 1600, 2000.	NAVTEX [A] in Spanish.
		518 kHz, F1B.	0050, 0450, 0850, 1250, 1650, 2050.	NAVTEX [F].
3169	Punta del Este (CWC-34).	2722.1 kHz, J3E, Ch. 15, F3E.	0133, 1503, 2133.	Local navigational warnings and weather in Spanish.
3169.5	Punta Carretas (CWF).	2768.5 kHz, H3E, J3E, R3E.	0000, 1400, 1900.	Local navigational warnings and weather in Spanish.
		4357.4, 6518.8, 8291.1, 13128.7, 17260.8, 22636.3 kHz, J3E, R3E.	0003, 1403, 1903.	Local navigational warnings and weather in Spanish.
3170	Cerrito (CWA).	421.5 kHz, A1A, A2A, 4346, 8602, 12750, 17230 kHz, A1A.	1100, 1600, 2100.	Local navigational warnings and weather in Spanish.
3176.1	Montevideo Trouville (CWC-39) (CWC).	2722.1, 4146 kHz, J3E, Ch. 15, F3E.	0103, 1133, 1903.	Local navigational warnings and weather in Spanish.
3177	Colonia (CWC-23).	2722.1 kHz, J3E, Ch. 15, F3E.	0333, 1333, 2103.	Local navigational warnings and weather in Spanish.
3178	Nueva Palmira (CWC-31).	Ch. 15, F3E.	0033, 1033, 1803	Local navigational warnings and weather in Spanish.
		ARGENTINA		
	LONG-RANGE WARNINGS: NAVAREA VI: Includes the waters between the coast of Argentina and 20°W between 35°50′S and Antarctica. Original reports to NAVAREA VI Coordinator, Hidrografi Naval, Buenos Aires.			
3182	Buenos Aires (L2B) (L2G).	4210, 8416.5, 12579, 16806.5 kHz, F1B.	0030, 1530, 2100.	Maritime Safety Information (MSI) (HF NBDP) (NAVAREA VI).
		4210, 8416.5, 12579 kHz, F1B.	1000, 1900.	Maritime Safety Information (MSI) (HF NBDP) (Local navigational warnings).
		16806.5 kHz, F1B.	1900.	Maritime Safety Information (MSI) (HF NBDP) (Local navigational warnings).
		4210, 8416.5, 12579 kHz, F1B.	0300, 1400.	Maritime Safety Information (MSI) (HF NBDP) (Weather).
		16806.5 kHz, F1B.	1400.	Maritime Safety Information (MSI) (HF NBDP) (Weather).
		Ch. 15, F3E.	0010, 0410, 0810, 1210, 1610, 2010.	Local navigational warnings and weather in Spanish.
		Ch. 21, F3E.	Every hour +00m, +15m, +30m, +45m.	Local navigational warnings and weather in Spanish.
		518 kHz, F1B.	0650, 1450, 2250.	NAVTEX [R].
		518 kHz, F1B.	0250, 1050, 1850.	NAVTEX [R] in Spanish.
3184	Mar del Plata (L2U).	Ch. 15, F3E.	0230, 0530, 1130, 1730, 2330.	Local navigational warnings and weather in Spanish.
		518 kHz, F1B.	0640, 1440, 2240.	NAVTEX [Q].
		518 kHz, F1B.	0240, 1040, 1840.	NAVTEX [Q] in Spanish.
3186	Recalada Rio de la Plata (L3Z).	Ch. 15, F3E.	0040, 0440, 0840, 1240, 1640, 2040.	Local navigational warnings and weather in Spanish.
3191	Quequen (L5B).	Ch. 15, F3E.	0010, 0410, 0810, 1210, 1610, 2010.	Local navigational warnings and weather in Spanish.

RADIO NAVIGATIONAL WARNINGS

(1) No.	(2) Name	(3) Frequency	(4) Times	(5) Nature of Broadcast
3192	Bahia Blanca (L2J) (L2N).	2065, 4149, 8294 kHz, J3E.	0010.	Local navigational warnings in Spanish.
		4149, 8294, 12353 kHz, J3E.	1210.	Local navigational warnings in Spanish.
		2065, 4149, 8294 kHz, J3E.	0440.	Weather in Spanish.
		4149, 8294, 12353 kHz, J3E.	1740.	Weather in Spanish.
		Ch. 15, F3E.	0010, 0410, 0810, 1210, 1610, 2010.	Local navigational warnings and weather in Spanish.
		518 kHz, F1B.	0630, 1430, 2230.	NAVTEX [P].
		518 kHz, F1B.	0230, 1030, 1830.	NAVTEX [P] in Spanish.
3193	Puerto Madryn (L4S).	Ch. 15, F3E.	0010, 0410, 0810, 1210, 1610, 2010.	Local navigational warnings and weather in Spanish.
3196	Comodoro Rivadavia (L2W) (L3B).	4210, 8416.5, 12579 kHz, F1B.	2300.	Maritime Safety Information (MSI) (HF NBDP) (Local navigational warnings).
		8416.5, 12579, 19680.5 kHz, F1B.	1300.	Maritime Safety Information (MSI) (HF NBDP) (Local navigational warnings).
		4210, 8416.5, 12579 kHz, F1B.	0530.	Maritime Safety Information (MSI) (HF NBDP) (Weather).
		8416.5, 12579, 19680.5 kHz, F1B.	1830.	Maritime Safety Information (MSI) (HF NBDP) (Weather).
		Ch. 15, F3E.	0350, 0750, 1050, 1650, 2250.	Local navigational warnings and weather in Spanish.
		518 kHz, F1B.	0620, 1420, 2220.	NAVTEX [O].
		518 kHz, F1B.	0220, 1020, 1820.	NAVTEX [O] in Spanish.
3204	Rio Gallegos (L3I).	2065, 4149 kHz, J3E.	0740.	Local navigational warnings in Spanish.
		4149, 8294 kHz, J3E.	2040.	Local navigational warnings in Spanish.
		2065, 4149 kHz, J3E.	0440.	Weather in Spanish.
		4149, 8294 kHz, J3E.	1740.	Weather in Spanish.
		Ch. 15, F3E.	0010, 0410, 0810, 1210, 1610, 2010.	Local navigational warnings and weather in Spanish.
		518 kHz, F1B.	0610, 1410, 2210.	NAVTEX [N].
		518 kHz, F1B.	0210, 1010, 1810.	NAVTEX [N] in Spanish.
3208	Ushuaia (L3P).	Ch. 15, F3E.	0010, 0410, 0810, 1210, 1610, 2010.	Local navigational warnings and weather in Spanish.
		518 kHz, F1B.	0600, 1400, 2200.	NAVTEX [M].
		518 kHz, F1B.	0200, 1000, 1800.	NAVTEX [M] in Spanish.
	ANTARCTICA			
3209	Casey (VLM) (Australia).	7470 kHz, F3C.	Continous.	Weather FAX*; 120/576.
	*NOTE: Broadcast schedule at 0700.			
3210	Centro Meteorologico Antartico Vcom. Marambio (LSB) (Argentina).	2401, 4807, 9951 kHz, F1B.	0025, 0325, 0625, 0925, 1225, 1525, 1825, 2125.	Weather.
		2401, 4807, 9951 kHz, F1B.	1525 (Tue., Thu.).	Ice.
3211	Palmer Station (KWB-268) (USA).	4553 kHz, F1B.	0100.	Ice.
		13553 kHz, F1B.	1500.	Ice.
		10235 kHz, F1B.	2000.	Ice.

RADIO NAVIGATIONAL WARNINGS

(1) No.	(2) Name	(3) Frequency	(4) Times	(5) Nature of Broadcast
		ICELAND		
3212	Reykjavik (TFA).	438 kHz, A1A.	0530, 1130, 1730, 2330.	Local navigational warnings, weather and ice.
		1650 kHz, A3E.	0430.	Local navigational warnings, weather and ice in Icelandic.
		1876 kHz, J3E.	0533, 1133, 1733, 2333.	Weather.
		490 kHz, F1B.	0320, 0720, 1120, 1520, 1920, 2320.	NAVTEX [R] in Icelandic.
		518 kHz, F1B.	0250, 0650, 1050, 1450, 1850, 2250.	NAVTEX [R].
		518 kHz, F1B.	0350, 0750, 1150, 1550, 1950, 2350.	NAVTEX [X]* (East Coast Greenland broadcast for Denmark).
	*NOTE: On trial.			
3212.5	Icelandic State Broadcasting Service.	209, 666, 738 kHz, A3E.	1010, 1245, 1615, 1845, 2215.	Ice in Icelandic.
		209 kHz, A3E.	0100.	Weather and ice in Icelandic.
		209, 666, 738 kHz, A3E.	0645, 0815, 1010, 1615, 1845, 2215.	Weather in Icelandic.
		JAN MAYEN		
3214	Jan Mayen (LMJ).	1743 kHz, J3E, Ch. 16, G3E.	On request.	Local navigational warnings and ice.
		1743 kHz, J3E.	1203, 2303.	Weather.
		FAROE ISLANDS		
3215	Torshavn (OXJ).	1641 kHz, A3E, Ch. 23, 24, 25, 26, F3E.	Every even hour +35m.	Local navigational warnings and weather.
		BJORNOYA		
3216	Bjornoya (LGP) (LJB).	1722 kHz, J3E, Ch. 16, G3E.	On request.	Local navigational warnings, weather and ice.
		1757 kHz, J3E, Ch. 12, G3E.	1005, 2205.	Weather.
		SVALBARD		
3218	Svalbard (LGS).	1731 kHz, J3E, Ch. 25, 26, 27, G3E.	0003, 0803, 1203.	Local navigational warnings (ice on request).
		1731, 4357 kHz, J3E.	1203, 2303.	Weather.
		518 kHz, F1B.	0000, 0400, 0800, 1200, 1600, 2000.	NAVTEX [A].
		RUSSIA - NORTHERN COASTS		
	LONG-RANGE WARNINGS: NAVIP: World-wide navigational warnings. LOCAL WARNINGS: PRIP.			
3224	Murmansk (UDK) (UDK2).	521.5, 6393.5, 13050 kHz, F1B.	0400, 1730.	PRIP warnings.
		521.5, 6393.5, 13050 kHz, F1B.	0420, 1740.	Weather in Russian.
		6446, 7907, 8444 kHz, F3C.	0700, 0800, 1400, 1430, 2000.	Weather and ice FAX*; 120/576.
		518 kHz, F1B.	0020, 0420, 0820, 1220, 1620, 2020.	NAVTEX [C].
	*NOTE: Broadcast schedule at 1850 (RPM/IOC: 90/576).			

RADIO NAVIGATIONAL WARNINGS

(1) No.	(2) Name	(3) Frequency	(4) Times	(5) Nature of Broadcast
3226	Arkhangel'sk (UGE).	446 kHz, F1B.	0510, 0530, 1710, 1730.	Local navigational warnings in Russian.
		2595 kHz, J3E.	0633, 1833.	Local navigational warnings in Russian.
		518 kHz, F1B.	0050, 0450, 0850, 1250, 1650, 2050.	NAVTEX [F].
3232	Dickson (UCI).	428.6 kHz, F1B.	0818, 2018.	Local Navigational warnings in Russian.
3235	Pevek.	148 kHz, F3C.	0530-0730, 1130-1330, 1430-1630.	Ice FAX, 90/576.

NORWAY

(1) No.	(2) Name	(3) Frequency	(4) Times	(5) Nature of Broadcast
3242	Vardo (LGV).	1635, 1695, 1713 kHz, J3E. Ch. 04, 23, 24, 25, 26, 27, G3E.	0233, 0633, 1033, 1433, 1833, 2233.	Local navigational warnings and weather (ice on request).
		1635, 1695, 1713 kHz, J3E.	1203, 2303.	Weather.
		518 kHz, F1B.	0330, 0730, 1130, 1530, 1930, 2330.	NAVTEX [V].
3244	Bodo (LGP).	1659, 1710, 1770 kHz, J3E, Ch. 01, 02, 03, 04, 05, 07, 19, 20, 21, 23, 24, 25, 26, 27, 28, 60, 62, 63, 64, 65, 81, 84, 85, G3E.	0333, 0733, 1133, 1533, 1933, 2333.	Local navigational warnings and weather (ice on request).
		1659, 1710 kHz, J3E.	1203, 2303.	Weather.
		518 kHz, F1B.	0010, 0410, 0810, 1210, 1610, 2010.	NAVTEX [B].
3248	Orlandet (LFO).	1782 kHz, J3E, Ch. 02, 03, 05, 07, 24, 25, 26, 27, 28, 61, 62, 82, G3E.	0133, 0533, 0933, 1333, 1733, 2133.	Local navigational warnings and weather (ice on request).
		1782 kHz, J3E.	1215, 2315.	Weather.
		518 kHz, F1B.	0210, 0610, 1010, 1410, 1810, 2210.	NAVTEX [N].
3251	Floro (LGL).	1680 kHz, J3E, Ch. 03, 20, 23, 27, 65, 78, G3E.	0233, 0633, 1033, 1433, 1833, 2233.	Local navigational warnings and weather (ice on request).
		1680 kHz, J3E.	1215, 2315.	Weather.
3252	Bergen (LGN).	1728 kHz, H3E, Ch. 07, 18, 21, 25, G3E.	0233, 0633, 1033, 1433, 1833, 2233.	Local navigational warnings and weather (ice on request).
		1728 kHz, H3E.	1215, 2315.	Weather.
3254	Rogaland (LGQ).	1692 kHz, J3E, Ch. 20, 24, 26, G3E.	0233, 0633, 1033, 1433, 1833, 2233.	Local navigational warnings and weather (ice on request).
		1692 kHz, J3E.	1215, 2315.	Weather.
		518 kHz, F1B.	0150, 0550, 0950, 1350, 1750, 2150.	NAVTEX [L].
3256	Farsund (LGZ).	1785 kHz, J3E, Ch. 05, 07, 27, 61, G3E.	0233, 0633, 1033, 1433, 1833, 2233.	Local navigational warnings and weather (ice on request).
		1785 kHz, J3E.	1215, 2315.	Weather.
3258	Tjome (LGT).	1665 kHz, J3E, Ch. 02, 03, 07, 24, 25, 26, 27, 62, 63, 65, 79, 81, 86, 87, G3E.	0233, 0633, 1033, 1433, 1833, 2233.	Local navigational warnings and weather (ice on request).

RADIO NAVIGATIONAL WARNINGS

(1) No.	(2) Name	(3) Frequency	(4) Times	(5) Nature of Broadcast
			SWEDEN	
	Coast radio stations (MF) operated remotely by Stockholm Radio: Tingstäde (1674 kHz) Grimeton (1710 kHz) Bjuröklubb (1779 kHz) Gislövshammar (1797 kHz) Härnösand (2733 kHz)			
3288	Stockholm (SDJ).	1674, 1710, 1779, 1797, 2733 kHz, J3E, Ch. 01, 03, 21, 22, 23, 24, 25, 26, 27, 28, 62, 64, 65, 66, 78, 81, 82, 84, F3E.	0333, 0733, 1133, 1533, 1933, 2333.	Local navigational warnings, weather and ice (ice at 1133).
		1674, 1710, 1779, 1797, 2733 kHz, J3E, Ch. 01, 03, 21, 22, 23, 24, 25, 26, 27, 28, 62, 64, 65, 66, 78, 81, 82, 84, F3E.	0633, 1433.	Weather in Swedish (May - Nov.).
		518 kHz, F1B.	0110, 0510, 0910, 1310, 1710, 2110.	NAVTEX [H] (Bjuröklubb).
		518 kHz, F1B.	0130, 0530, 0930, 1330, 1730, 2130.	NAVTEX [J] (Gislövshammar).
		518 kHz, F1B.	0030, 0430, 0830, 1230, 1630, 2030.	NAVTEX [D] (Grimeton).
			FINLAND	
	NOTE: Ships are requested to report ice and other navigational hazards by radio; ice conditions may be reported in ice code, English, Finnish, German or Swedish, and should be sent to the nearest coast radio station. Finnish icebreakers Urho (OHMS), Sisu (OHMW)*, Voima (OHLW), Apu (OHMP), Fennica (OJAD), Nordica (OJAE), Otso (OIRT), Kontio (OIRV) and Botnica (OJAK) maintain 24 hour watch on radiotelephone 2338 kHz and on VHF Ch. 16. Icebreakers will reply on the call frequency, whereafter the communication will continue on a working frequency. * Also 12 hour watch on radiotelegraphy 500 kHz.			
3314	Turku (OFK).	1638, 1677, 1719, 2810 kHz, J3E, Ch. 01, 02, 03, 04, 05, 23, 24, 25, 26, 27, 28, 68, 84, 86, F3E.	0233, 0633, 1033, 1433, 1833, 2233.	NAVAREA I, local navigational warnings and weather.
		1638, 1677, 1719, 2810 kHz, J3E, Ch. 01, 02, 03, 04, 05, 23, 24, 25, 26, 27, 28, 68, 84, 86, F3E.	0803, 1133, 1933.	Ice.
3315	Radio Finland (Yleisradio).	558, 963 kHz, A3E.	0655, 1045, 1710, 2055.	Local navigational warnings and weather in Finnish.
		93.1-100.3 MHz, F3E.	0615, 1045, 1710, 2010.	Local navigational warnings and weather in Finnish.
		558, 963 kHz, A3E, 93.1-100.3 MHz, F3E.	1045.	Ice in Finnish.
		6120 kHz, A3E.	1045 (Mon. - Sat.).	Local navigational warnings, weather and ice in Finnish.
			RUSSIA - BALTIC COAST	
	LONG-RANGE WARNINGS: NAVIP: World-wide navigational warnings. LOCAL WARNINGS: PRIP.			
3325	Kaliningrad (UIW).	4228, 8454, 12877.5, 16927, 19724.5, 22603.5 kHz, F1B.	1000, 1620.	NAVIP and NAVAREA warnings.
			LITHUANIA	
3332	Klaipeda (LYL).	3215 kHz, J3E.	0333, 0733, 1133, 1533, 1933, 2333.	Local navigational warnings.
		3215 kHz, J3E.	0758, 1555.	Weather.
		3730 kHz, A1A, F1B.	0505, 1300.	Weather.
		Ch. 04, F3E.	0503, 0703.	Weather.

RADIO NAVIGATIONAL WARNINGS

(1) No.	(2) Name	(3) Frequency	(4) Times	(5) Nature of Broadcast
		LATVIA		
3333	Riga (YLQ).	4357 kHz, J3E.	0033, 0433, 0833, 1233, 1633, 2033.	Local navigational warnings.
		Ch. 09, F3E.	0615, 1515.	Weather.
		Ch. 71, F3E.	0503, 1303.	Local navigational warnings and weather.
		ESTONIA		
3334	Tallinn (ESA).	3310 kHz, J3E.	0233, 0633, 1033, 1433, 1833, 2233.	Local navigational warnings.
		1650 kHz, J3E.	0433, 1333.	Weather.
		3310 kHz, J3E, Ch. 69, F3E.	Every hour +03m, +33m.	Weather.
		518 kHz, F1B.	0320, 0720, 1120, 1520, 1920, 2320.	NAVTEX [U] (Broadcast relayed by Stockholm (SDJ)).
		POLAND		
3336	Witowo (SPS).	2720 kHz, J3E, Ch. 24, 25, 26, F3E.	0133, 0533, 0933, 1333, 1733, 2133.	Local navigational warnings.
		2720 kHz, J3E, Ch. 24, 25, 26, F3E.	1035, 1335.	Ice.
		2720 kHz, J3E, Ch. 24, 25, 26, F3E.	0133, 0733, 1333, 1933.	Weather.
3337	Slupsk.	Ch. 12, 71, F3E.	0615, 1145, 1745.	Local navigational warnings.
		Ch. 12, 71, F3E.	0605, 1135, 1735, 2205.	Weather.
3338	Zatoka Gdansk VTS.	Ch. 71, F3E.	0605, 1205, 1805, 2305.	Local navigational warnings and weather in Polish.
		Ch. 71, F3E.	0620, 1220, 1820, 2320.	Local navigational warnings and weather in English.
		DENMARK		

NOTE: Ice information is available 24 hours on request from the Danish Ice Service at the Naval Operation Command (SOK) Århus by telephone: (45) 89 43 32 04/53, fax: (45) 89 43 32 44.

Coast radio stations (MF) operated remotely by Lyngby Radio:
  Skamlebæk (1704 kHz)
  Blåvand (1734 kHz)
  Skagen (1758 kHz)
  Rønne (2586 kHz)

(1) No.	(2) Name	(3) Frequency	(4) Times	(5) Nature of Broadcast
3359	Lyngby (OXZ).	1704, 1734, 1758, 2586 kHz, A3E, Ch. 01, 02, 03, 04, 05, 07, 23, 28, 64, 65, 66, 83, F3E.	0133, 0533, 0933, 1333, 1733, 2133.	Local navigational warnings.
		1704, 1734, 1758, 2586 kHz, A3E.	1305.	Ice.
		1704, 1734, 1758, 2586 kHz, A3E, Ch. 01, 02, 03, 04, 05, 07, 23, 28, 64, 65, 66, 83, F3E.	On request.	Weather and ice.
		Ch. 02, 04, 05, 07, 28, 64, 65, F3E.	0220, 0520, 0820, 1120, 1420, 1720, 2020, 2320.	SHIPPOS information.
3362	Danish Radio (Kalundborg).	243, 1062 kHz, A3E.	0445, 0745, 1045, 1645, 2145.	Weather in Danish.
		243 kHz, A3E.	1150.	Ice.
		243, 1062 kHz, A3E.	1530 (Mon. - Fri.).	Ice.

3 - 41

RADIO NAVIGATIONAL WARNINGS

(1) No.	(2) Name	(3) Frequency	(4) Times	(5) Nature of Broadcast

GERMANY - NORTH SEA

NOTE: Vessels encountering dangers to navigation in waters of the Federal Republic of Germany should notify Seewarndienst Emden (Sea Warning Service Emden) through the nearest Coast Radio Station. The Sea Warning service is available 24 hours and can be contacted by telephone: (49) 4927 187783, fax: (49) 4927 187788, telex: (41) 232154 SWD EM D, e-mail: seewarndienst.wsa-emd@t-online.de.

Reports of oil pollution should be sent to the Zentral Meldekopf Cuxhaven (ZMK) (Central Headquarters Cuxhaven) through the nearest Coast Radio Station. Radio telegrams must carry the legend ZMK Cuxhaven and commence with the codeword Oelunfall (Oil Accident). ZMK Cuxhaven bears the cost of the message and is available 24 hours by telephone: (49) 4721 567485, fax: (49) 4721 567404, e-mail: mlz@wsd-nord.de, frequency: through Cuxhaven Elbe Traffi Ch. 16, 71.

No.	Name	Frequency	Times	Nature of Broadcast
3370	Bremen (MRCC).	Ch. 16, F3E.	Every hour +00m, +30m.	Local navigational warnings.
3371	Offenbach/Pinneberg (DDH) (DDK).	147.3, 11039, 14467.3 kHz, F1B.	0950, 1715.	Local navigational warnings.
		4583, 7646, 10100.8 kHz, F1B.	0515, 1715.	Local navigational warnings.
		147.3, 11039, 14467.3 kHz, F1B.	0500, 0505, 0520, 0530, 0535, 0600, 0605, 0620, 0630, 0700, 0725, 0730, 0820, 0840, 0900, 0905, 0920, 0930, 1010, 1025, 1030, 1035, 1100, 1120, 1200, 1205, 1220, 1230, 1300, 1325, 1330, 1420, 1440, 1500, 1505, 1520, 1530, 1545, 1610, 1625, 1630, 1635, 1735, 1800, 1805, 1820, 1830, 1900, 1925, 1930, 2020, 2040, 2100, 2105, 2120, 2130.	Weather in German.
		4583, 7646, 10100.8 kHz, F1B.	0000, 0005, 0020, 0030, 0035, 0200, 0300, 0305, 0320, 0330, 0355, 0415, 0440, 0535, 0550, 0600, 0605, 0610, 0735, 0815, 0835, 0850, 0900, 0905, 0930, 0955, 1015, 1035, 1115, 1135, 1150, 1200, 1205, 1210, 1335, 1435, 1450, 1500, 1505, 1530, 1550, 1610, 1635, 1735, 1800, 1805, 1810, 1935, 2015, 2035, 2050, 2100, 2105, 2130, 2155, 2215, 2235, 2315.	Weather.
		3855, 7880, 13882.5 kHz, F3C.	0430-2200.	Weather FAX*; 120/576.
		3855, 7880, 13882.5 kHz, F3C.	0930, 1007, 1520, 1540, 2100, 2115.	Ice FAX*; 120/576.
	*NOTE: Broadcast schedule at 1111.			
3373	Deutschlandfunk (DLF).	1269, 6190 kHz, A3E.	0105, 0640, 1105. 2105 (Summer only).	Weather and ice in German.

NETHERLANDS

No.	Name	Frequency	Times	Nature of Broadcast
3375	Netherlands Coast Guard (PBK).	3673 kHz, J3E, Ch. 23, 83, F3E.	0333, 0733, 1133, 1533, 1933, 2333.	Local navigational warnings and weather (ice at 1133).
		3673 kHz, J3E.	0940, 2140.	Weather.
		Ch. 23, 83, F3E.	0705, 1205, 1805, 2205.	Weather.
		518 kHz, F1B.	0230, 0630, 1030, 1430, 1830, 2230.	NAVTEX [P].

BELGIUM

No.	Name	Frequency	Times	Nature of Broadcast
3378	Antwerpen (OSA).	Ch. 24, F3E.	Every hour +03m, +48m.	Local navigational warnings and weather.
3380	Oostende (OSU).	2761 kHz, J3E, Ch. 27, F3E.	0233, 0633, 1033, 1433, 1833, 2233.	Local navigational warnings.
		2761 kHz, J3E, Ch. 27, F3E.	0103, 0503, 0903, 1303, 1703, 2103.	Ice.
		2761 kHz, J3E, Ch. 27, F3E.	0820, 1720.	Weather.
		518 kHz, F1B.	0310, 0710, 1110, 1510, 1910, 2310.	NAVTEX [T].
		518 kHz, F1B.	0200, 0600, 1000, 1400, 1800, 2200.	NAVTEX [M] (Dover Strait broadcast for U.K.).

RADIO NAVIGATIONAL WARNINGS

(1) No.	(2) Name	(3) Frequency	(4) Times	(5) Nature of Broadcast
		UNITED KINGDOM		
	LONG-RANGE WARNINGS: NAVAREA I: Includes waters north to 71°N, south to 48°27′N and west to 35°W, and the Baltic Sea. Original reports to Hydrographer of the Navy, Radio Navigational Warnings, Ministry of Defence, Taunton. LOCAL WARNINGS: WZ: Original reports to Hydrographer of the Navy, Radio Navigational Warnings, Ministry of Defence.			
3390	Aberdeen (Coastguard MRCC).	2226 kHz, J3E, Ch. 23, 84, 86, F3E.	0320, 0720, 1120, 1520, 1920, 2320.	Local navigational warnings and weather.
		2226 kHz, J3E.	0820, 2020 (Oct. 1 - Mar. 31).	Weather.
3391	Forth (Coastguard MRSC).	Ch. 23, 86, F3E.	0205, 0605, 1005, 1405, 1805, 2205.	Local navigational warnings and weather.
3392	Cullercoats.	490 kHz, F1B.	0720, 1920.	NAVTEX [U] (Inshore local broadcast).
		518 kHz, F1B.	0100, 0500, 0900, 1300, 1700, 2100.	NAVTEX [G].
3394	Humber (Coastguard MRSC).	2226 kHz, J3E, Ch. 23, 84, F3E.	0340, 0740, 1140, 1540, 1940, 2340.	Local navigational warnings and weather.
		2226 kHz, J3E.	0910, 2110 (Oct. 1 - Mar. 31).	Weather.
3395	Northwood (GYA).	2618.5, 4610, 8040, 11086.5 kHz, F3C.	Continuous.	Weather FAX* (North Atlantic); 120/576.
		6834, 18261 kHz, F3C; 3289.5, 14436 kHz, F3C.	Continuous; Alternate.	Weather FAX* (Persian Gulf); 120/576.
	*NOTE: Broadcast schedule at 0100, 1300 for North Altantic and 0230, 1430 for Persian Gulf.			
3396	Yarmouth (Coastguard MRCC).	1869 kHz, J3E, Ch. 23, 84, 86, F3E.	0040, 0440, 0840, 1240, 1640, 2040.	Local navigational warnings and weather.
3397	Thames (Coastguard MRSC).	Ch. 23, 73, 84, 86, F3E.	0010, 0410, 0810, 1210, 1610, 2010.	Local navigational warnings and weather.
3397.1	Dover (Coastguard MRCC).	Ch. 23, 86, F3E.	0105, 0505, 0905, 1305, 1705, 2105.	Local navigational warnings and weather.
3397.2	Solent (Coastguard MRSC).	1641 kHz, J3E, Ch. 23, 86, F3E.	0040, 0440, 0840, 1240, 1640, 2040.	Local navigational warnings and weather.
3398	Niton.	490 kHz, F1B.	0310, 0710, 1110, 1510, 1910, 2310.	NAVTEX [T] in French.
		490 kHz, F1B.	0520, 1720.	NAVTEX [I] (Inshore local broadcast).
		518 kHz, F1B.	0040, 0440, 0840, 1240, 1640, 2040.	NAVTEX [E].
		518 kHz, F1B.	0140, 0540, 0940, 1340, 1740, 2140.	NAVTEX [K].
3400	Portland (Coastguard MRSC).	Ch. 10, F3E.	0220, 0620, 1020, 1420, 1820, 2220.	Local navigational warnings and weather.
		Ch. 73, 86, F3E.	0220, 0620, 1020, 1420, 1820, 2220.	Weather.
3400.2	Brixham (Coastguard MRSC).	Ch. 10, 23, 73, 84, 86, F3E.	0050, 0450, 0850, 1250, 1650, 2050.	Local navigational warnings and weather.
3400.3	Falmouth (Coastguard MRCC).	2226 kHz, J3E, Ch. 23, 86, F3E.	0140, 0540, 0940, 1340, 1740, 2140.	Local navigational warnings and weather.
		2226 kHz, J3E.	0950, 2150 (Oct. 1 - Mar. 31).	Weather.
3400.4	Swansea (Coastguard MRCC).	Ch. 10, 23, 73, 84, 86, F3E.	0005, 0405, 0805, 1205, 1605, 2005.	Local navigational warnings and weather.
3400.5	Milford Haven (Coastguard MRSC).	1767 kHz, J3E, Ch. 84, 86, F3E.	0335, 0735, 1135, 1535, 1935, 2335.	Local navigational warnings and weather.
3400.6	Holyhead (Coastguard MRSC).	1880 kHz, J3E, Ch. 73, 84, F3E.	0235, 0635, 1035, 1435, 1835, 2235.	Local navigational warnings and weather.
3400.7	Liverpool (Coastguard MRSC).	Ch. 10, 23, 73, 86, F3E.	0210, 0610, 1010, 1410, 1810, 2210.	Local navigational warnings and weather.

RADIO NAVIGATIONAL WARNINGS

(1) No.	(2) Name	(3) Frequency	(4) Times	(5) Nature of Broadcast
3401	Portpatrick.	490 kHz, F1B.	0820, 2020.	NAVTEX [C] (Inshore local broadcast).
		518 kHz, F1B.	0220, 0620, 1020, 1420, 1820, 2220.	NAVTEX [O].
3402	Clyde (Coastguard MRCC).	1883 kHz, J3E, Ch. 10, 23, 73, 84, 86, F3E.	0020, 0420, 0820, 1220, 1620, 2020.	Local navigational warnings and weather.
3404	Stornoway (Coastguard MRSC).	1743 kHz, J3E, Ch. 10, 67, 73, 84, F3E.	0110, 0510, 0910, 1310, 1710, 2110.	Local navigational warnings and weather.
3404.1	Shetland (Coastguard MRSC).	1770 kHz, J3E, Ch. 10, 23, 73, 84, F3E.	0105, 0505, 0905, 1305, 1705, 2105.	Local navigational warnings and weather.
		1770 kHz, J3E.	0710, 1910 (Oct. 1 - Mar. 31).	Weather.
3404.5	Belfast (Coastguard MRSC).	Ch. 73, 84, 86, F3E.	0305, 0705, 1105, 1505, 1905, 2305.	Local navigational warnings and weather.

IRELAND

(1) No.	(2) Name	(3) Frequency	(4) Times	(5) Nature of Broadcast
3405	Dublin (Coastguard MRCC).	Ch. 02, 04, 23, 83, F3E.	0033, 0433, 0833, 1233, 1633, 2033 (1 hr. earlier when daylight savings in effect).	Local navigational warnings.
		Ch. 02, 04, 23, 83, F3E.	0033, 0103, 0403, 0633, 0703, 1003, 1233, 1303, 1603, 1833, 1903, 2203 (1 hr. earlier when daylight savings in effect).	Weather.
3406	Malin Head (EJM) (Coastguard MRSC).	1677 kHz, J3E, Ch. 02, 23, 24, 26, 83, F3E.	0033, 0433, 0833, 1233, 1633, 2033 (1 hr. earlier when daylight savings in effect).	Local navigational warnings.
		Ch. 02, 23, 24, 26, 83, F3E.	0033, 0103, 0403, 0633, 0703, 1003, 1233, 1303, 1603, 1833, 1903, 2203 (1 hr. earlier when daylight savings in effect).	Weather.
		518 kHz, F1B.	0240, 0640, 1040, 1440, 1840, 2240.	NAVTEX [Q].
3408	Valentia (EJK) (Coastguard MRSC).	1752 kHz, J3E, Ch. 04, 23, 24, 26, 28, F3E.	0233, 0633, 1033, 1433, 1833, 2233 (1 hr. earlier when daylight savings in effect).	Local navigational warnings.
		1752 kHz, J3E.	0303, 0833, 0903, 1503, 2033, 2103 (1 hr. earlier when daylight savings in effect).	Weather.
		Ch. 04, 23, 24, 26, 28, F3E.	0033, 0103, 0403, 0633, 0703, 1003, 1233, 1303, 1603, 1833, 1903, 2203 (1 hr. earlier when daylight savings in effect).	Weather.
		518 kHz, F1B.	0340, 0740, 1140, 1540, 1940, 2340.	NAVTEX [W].

CHANNEL ISLANDS

(1) No.	(2) Name	(3) Frequency	(4) Times	(5) Nature of Broadcast
3410	Jersey.	Ch. 25, 82, F3E.	0433, 0833, 1633, 2033.	Local navigational warnings.
		Ch. 25, 82, F3E.	0307, 0645, 0745, 0845, 0907, 1245, 1507, 1845, 2107, 2245 (1 hr. earlier when daylight savings in effect for 0645, 0745, 0845).	Weather.

RADIO NAVIGATIONAL WARNINGS

(1) No.	(2) Name	(3) Frequency	(4) Times	(5) Nature of Broadcast

FRANCE - CHANNEL AND ATLANTIC

LONG-RANGE WARNINGS:
NAVAREA II:
Includes the waters of the eastern Atlantic between 6°S and 48°27′N, west to 20°W up to 7°N and west to 35°W to the northern boundary. Original reports to the nearest coast radio station and vessels in the vicinity. Message should be preceded by the safety signal "SECURITE" and addressed to "PREFET MARITIME". It should include the originating vessel's name and owner.
NOTE: Maritime Safety Information (MSI) broadcasts are announced by CROSS Stations on 2182 kHz or VHF Ch. 16 prior to broadcast on scheduled frequency or channel number.

No.	Name	Frequency	Times	Nature of Broadcast
3421	Gris-Nez (CROSS) (MRCC).	1650 kHz, J3E.	0733, 1933.	Local navigational warnings.
		1650, 2677 kHz, J3E.	0733, 1933.	Weather in French.
		Ch. 79, F3E.	Every hour +03m, +04m, +10m.	Weather in French.
		Ch. 79, F3E.	0603, 0610, 0620, 1433, 1445, 1503, 1803, 1810, 1820.	Weather in French.
3421.5	Jobourg (CROSS) (MRCC).	1650 kHz, J3E.	0815, 2015.	Local navigational warnings.
		Ch. 80, F3E.	Every hour +03m, +20m, +50m.	Weather.
		Ch. 80, F3E.	0603, 0615, 0633, 0645, 0703, 1433, 1445, 1503, 1515, 1533, 1803, 1815, 1833, 1845, 1903.	Weather in French.
3423	Corsen (CROSS) (MRCC).	1650, 2677 kHz, J3E.	0635, 1835.	Local navigational warnings.
		1650, 2677 kHz, J3E.	Every hour +03m., 0715, 1915.	Weather in French.
		Ch. 79, F3E.	0345, 0403, 0415, 0433, 0445, 0603, 0615, 0633, 0645, 0703, 1003*, 1015*, 1033*, 1045*, 1103*, 1433, 1445, 1503, 1515, 1533, 1803, 1815, 1833, 1845, 1903.	Weather in French.
		Ch. 79, F3E.	Every hour +03m.	Weather in French.
		490 kHz, F1B.	0040, 0440, 0840, 1240, 1640, 2040.	NAVTEX [E] in French.
		518 kHz, F1B.	0000, 0400, 0800, 1200, 1600, 2000.	NAVTEX [A].
	*NOTE: May 1 - Sep. 30.			
3423.5	Etel (CROSS) (MRCC).	2677 kHz, J3E.	Every hour +33m, 0803, 1403, 1803.	Weather in French.
		Ch. 79, F3E.	Every hour +03m, 0603, 0615, 0633, 0645, 0703, 1433, 1445, 1503, 1515, 1533, 1803, 1815, 1833, 1845, 1903.	Weather in French.
		Ch. 80, F3E.	Every hour +03m, 0603, 0615, 0633, 0645, 0703, 0715, 1433, 1445, 1503, 1515, 1533, 1545, 1803, 1815, 1833, 1845, 1903, 1915.	Weather in French.

SPAIN - NORTH COAST

No.	Name	Frequency	Times	Nature of Broadcast
3430	La Guardia.	Ch. 21, F3E.	0840, 2010.	Local navigational warnings.
		Ch. 21, F3E.	0840, 1240, 2010.	Weather in Spanish.
3430.1	Vigo.	Ch. 10, F3E.	On receipt.	Local navigational warnings.
		Ch. 10, F3E.	0015, 0415, 0815, 1215, 1815, 2015.	Weather.
		Ch. 65, F3E.	0840, 2010.	Local navigational warnings.
		Ch. 65, F3E.	0840, 1240, 2010.	Weather in Spanish.

RADIO NAVIGATIONAL WARNINGS

(1) No.	(2) Name	(3) Frequency	(4) Times	(5) Nature of Broadcast
3430.2	Bilbao.	Ch. 10, F3E.	On receipt.	Local navigational warnings.
		Ch. 10, F3E.	Every even hour +33m.	Weather.
		Ch. 26, F3E.	0840, 2010.	Local navigational warnings.
		Ch. 26, F3E.	0840, 1240, 2010.	Weather in Spanish.
3430.3	Pasajes.	Ch. 27, F3E.	0840, 2010.	Local navigational warnings.
		Ch. 27, F3E.	0840, 1240, 2010.	Weather in Spanish.
3430.4	Santander.	Ch. 24, F3E.	0840, 2010.	Local navigational warnings.
		Ch. 24, F3E.	0840, 1240, 2010.	Weather in Spanish.
		Ch. 74, F3E.	On receipt.	Local navigational warnings.
		Ch. 74, F3E.	0245, 0445, 0645, 0845, 1045, 1445, 1845, 2245.	Weather.
3430.5	Navia.	Ch. 60, F3E.	0840, 2010.	Local navigational warnings.
		Ch. 60, F3E.	0840, 1240, 2010.	Weather in Spanish.
3430.6	Cabo Ortegal.	Ch. 02, F3E.	0840, 2010.	Local navigational warnings.
		Ch. 02, F3E.	0840, 1240, 2010.	Weather in Spanish.
3430.8	Cabo Penas.	1677 kHz, J3E.	0703, 1903.	Local navigational warnings.
		1677 kHz, J3E.	0703, 1303, 1903.	Weather in Spanish.
		Ch. 23, F3E.	0840, 2010.	Local navigational warnings.
		Ch. 23, F3E.	0840, 1240, 2010.	Weather in Spanish.
3430.9	Gijon.	Ch. 10, F3E.	On receipt.	Local navigational warnings.
		Ch. 10, F3E.	Every even hour +15m.	Weather.
3433	Finisterre.	1764 kHz, J3E.	0703, 1903.	Local navigational warnings.
		1764 kHz, J3E.	0703, 1303, 1903.	Weather in Spanish.
		Ch. 11, F3E.	On receipt.	Local navigational warnings.
		Ch. 11, F3E.	0233, 0633, 1033, 1433, 1833, 2233.	Weather.
		Ch. 22, F3E.	0840, 2010.	Local navigational warnings.
		Ch. 22, F3E.	0840, 1240, 2010.	Weather in Spanish.
3434	Coruna.	1698 kHz, J3E.	0703, 1903.	Local navigational warnings.
		1698 kHz, J3E.	0703, 1303, 1903.	Weather in Spanish.
		Ch. 10, F3E.	On receipt.	Local navigational warnings.
		Ch. 12, 13, 14, F3E.	0005, 0405, 0805, 1205, 1605, 2005.	Weather.
		Ch. 26, F3E.	0840, 2010.	Local navigational warnings.
		Ch. 26, F3E.	0840, 1240, 2010.	Weather in Spanish.
		518 kHz, F1B.	0030, 0430, 0830, 1230, 1630, 2030.	NAVTEX [D].

RADIO NAVIGATIONAL WARNINGS

(1) No.	(2) Name	(3) Frequency	(4) Times	(5) Nature of Broadcast
3436	Machichaco.	1707 kHz, J3E.	0703, 1903.	Local navigational warnings.
		1707 kHz, J3E.	0703, 1303, 1903.	Weather in Spanish.

PORTUGAL

NOTE: Original reports to the nearest coast radio station. Message should be preceded by the safety signal "SECURITE" and be in English or International Code (CDPUBNV102) giving the following information: description of navigational danger, position and date/time of observation.

(1) No.	(2) Name	(3) Frequency	(4) Times	(5) Nature of Broadcast
3441	Leixoes.	Ch. 11, F3E.	0705, 1905.	Local navigational warnings and weather.
3444	Monsanto (CTV).	2657 kHz, J3E, Ch. 11, F3E.	0905, 2105.	Local navigational warnings and weather.
		490 kHz, F1B.	0100, 0500, 0900, 1300, 1700, 2100.	NAVTEX [G] in Portuguese.
		518 kHz, F1B.	0250, 0650, 1050, 1450, 1850, 2250.	NAVTEX [R].
3445	Faro.	Ch. 11, G3E.	0805, 2005.	Local navigational warnings and weather.
3456	Porto Santo, Madeira (CTQ).	2657 kHz, J3E.	0735, 1935.	Local navigational warnings.
		2657 kHz, J3E.	0935, 2135.	Weather.
		Ch. 11, F3E.	1030, 1630.	Local navigational warnings.
		Ch. 11, F3E.	0900, 2100.	Weather.

ACORES

(1) No.	(2) Name	(3) Frequency	(4) Times	(5) Nature of Broadcast
3456.2	Ponta Delgada.	Ch. 11, F3E.	0930, 2130.	Local navigational warnings and weather.
3456.3	Horta (CTH).	2657 kHz, J3E.	0935, 2135.	Local navigational warnings and weather.
		Ch. 11, F3E.	1000, 1100, 2000, 2200.	Local navigational warnings and weather.
		490 kHz, F1B.	0120, 0520, 0920, 1320, 1720, 2120.	NAVTEX [J] in Portuguese.
		518 kHz, F1B.	0050, 0450, 0850, 1250, 1650, 2050.	NAVTEX [F].

SPAIN - SOUTH AND MEDITERRANEAN

LONG-RANGE WARNINGS:
NAVAREA III:
Includes the waters of the Mediterranean and the Black Sea. Original reports to NAVAREA III Coordinator, Instituto de la Marina.

(1) No.	(2) Name	(3) Frequency	(4) Times	(5) Nature of Broadcast
3458	Cadiz.	Ch. 26, F3E.	0833, 2003.	Local navigational warnings.
		Ch. 26, F3E.	0833, 1133, 2003.	Weather in Spanish.
		Ch. 74, F3E.	On receipt.	Local navigational warnings.
		Ch. 74, F3E.	0315, 0715, 1115, 1515, 1915, 2315.	Weather.
3459	Alicante.	Ch. 85, F3E.	0910, 2110.	Local navigational warnings.
		Ch. 85, F3E.	0910, 1410, 2110.	Weather in Spanish.
3459.3	Chipiona.	1656 kHz, J3E.	0733, 1933.	Local navigational warnings.
		1656 kHz, J3E.	0733, 1233, 1933.	Weather in Spanish.

RADIO NAVIGATIONAL WARNINGS

(1) No.	(2) Name	(3) Frequency	(4) Times	(5) Nature of Broadcast
3459.35	Cabo de la Nao.	Ch. 01, F3E.	0910, 2110.	Local navigational warnings.
		Ch. 01, F3E.	0910, 1410, 2110.	Weather in Spanish.
		518 kHz, F1B.	0350, 0750, 1150, 1550, 1950, 2350.	NAVTEX [X].
3459.37	Valencia.	Ch. 10, F3E.	On receipt.	Local navigational warnings.
		Ch. 10, F3E.	Every even hour +15m.	Weather.
3459.4	Castellon.	Ch. 25, F3E.	0910, 2110.	Local navigational warnings.
		Ch. 25, F3E.	0910, 1410, 2110.	Weather in Spanish.
		Ch. 74, F3E.	On receipt.	Local navigational warnings.
		Ch. 74, F3E.	0900, 1400, 1900.	Weather.
3459.5	Tarragona.	Ch. 23, F3E.	0910, 2110.	Local navigational warnings.
		Ch. 23, F3E.	0910, 1410, 2110.	Weather in Spanish.
		Ch. 74, F3E.	On receipt.	Local navigational warnings.
		Ch. 74, F3E.	Summer: 0433, 0833, 1433, 1933; Winter: 0533, 0933, 1533, 2033.	Weather.
3459.55	Barcelona.	Ch. 10, F3E.	On receipt.	Local navigational warnings.
		Ch. 10, F3E.	Summer: 0500, 0900, 1400, 1900; Winter: 0600, 1000, 1500, 2000.	Weather.
		Ch. 60, F3E.	0910, 2110.	Local navigational warnings.
		Ch. 60, F3E.	0910, 1410, 2110.	Weather in Spanish.
3459.6	Malaga.	Ch. 26, F3E.	0833, 2003.	Local navigational warnings.
		Ch. 26, F3E.	0833, 1133, 2003.	Weather in Spanish.
3459.65	Almeria.	Ch. 74, F3E.	On receipt.	Local navigational warnings.
		Ch. 74, 76, F3E.	Every odd hour +15m.	Weather.
3459.7	Cabo de Gata.	1767 kHz, J3E.	0750, 1950.	Local navigational warnings.
		1767 kHz, J3E.	0750, 1303, 1950.	Weather in Spanish.
		Ch. 27, F3E.	0833, 2003.	Local navigational warnings.
		Ch. 27, F3E.	0833, 1133, 2003.	Weather in Spanish.
3460	Tarifa.	1704 kHz, J3E.	0733, 1933.	Local navigational warnings.
		1704 kHz, J3E.	0733, 1233, 1933.	Weather in Spanish.
		Ch. 10, F3E.	On receipt.	Local navigational warnings.
		Ch. 10, F3E.	Every even hour +15m.	Weather.
		Ch. 81, F3E.	0833, 2003.	Local navigational warnings.
		Ch. 81, F3E.	0833, 1133, 2003.	Weather in Spanish.
		518 kHz, F1B.	0100, 0500, 0900, 1300, 1700, 2100.	NAVTEX [G].

RADIO NAVIGATIONAL WARNINGS

(1) No.	(2) Name	(3) Frequency	(4) Times	(5) Nature of Broadcast
3462	Cartagena.	Ch. 04, F3E.	0910, 2110.	Local navigational warnings.
		Ch. 04, F3E.	0910, 1410, 2110.	Weather in Spanish.
		Ch. 10, F3E.	On receipt.	Local navigational warnings.
		Ch. 10, F3E.	0115, 0515, 0915, 1315, 1715, 2115.	Weather.
3462.5	Bagur.	Ch. 23, F3E.	0910, 2110.	Local navigational warnings.
		Ch. 23, F3E.	0910, 1410, 2110.	Weather in Spanish.
			ISLAS BALEARES	
3464	Palma.	1755 kHz, J3E.	0750, 1950.	Local navigational warnings.
		1755 kHz, J3E.	0750, 1303, 1950.	Weather in Spanish.
		Ch. 10, F3E.	On receipt.	Local navigational warnings.
		Ch. 10, F3E.	Summer: 0635, 0935, 1435, 1935; Winter: 0735, 1035, 1535, 2035.	Weather in Spanish.
		Ch. 20, F3E.	0910, 2110.	Local navigational warnings.
		Ch. 20, F3E.	0910, 1410, 2110.	Weather in Spanish.
3464.5	Menorca.	Ch. 85, F3E.	0910, 2110.	Local navigational warnings.
		Ch. 85, F3E.	0910, 1410, 2110.	Weather in Spanish.
3465	Ibiza.	Ch. 03, F3E.	0910, 2110.	Local navigational warnings.
		Ch. 03, F3E.	0910, 1410, 2110.	Weather in Spanish.
			FRANCE - MEDITERRANEAN	

NOTE: Maritime Safety Information (MSI) broadcasts are announced by CROSS Stations on 2182 kHz or VHF Ch. 16 prior to broadcast on scheduled frequency or channel number.

(1) No.	(2) Name	(3) Frequency	(4) Times	(5) Nature of Broadcast
3471	La Garde (CROSS) (MRCC).	1696, 2677 kHz, J3E.	0733, 1503.	Local navigational warnings.
		1696, 2677 kHz, J3E.	0550, 1333, 1750.	Weather in French.
		1696, 2677 kHz, J3E.	0003, 0403, 0803, 1203, 1603, 2003.	Weather in French.
		Ch. 79, F3E.	Every hour +03m, 0603, 0615, 1133, 1145, 1803, 1815.	Weather in French.
		Ch. 80, F3E.	Every hour +03m, 0633, 0645, 0650, 0703, 1203, 1215, 1220, 1233, 1833, 1845, 1850, 1903.	Weather in French.
		490 kHz, F1B.	0300, 0700, 1100, 1500, 1900, 2300.	NAVTEX [S] in French.
		518 kHz, F1B.	0340, 0740, 1140, 1540, 1940, 2340.	NAVTEX [W].
3473	Corse (Sous-CROSS) (MRSC).	Ch. 79, F3E.	Every hour +10m, 0633, 0645, 0703, 0715, 0733, 0745, 1133, 1145, 1203, 1215, 1233, 1245, 1833, 1845, 1903, 1915, 1933, 1945.	Weather in French.

3 - 49

RADIO NAVIGATIONAL WARNINGS

(1) No.	(2) Name	(3) Frequency	(4) Times	(5) Nature of Broadcast
		MONACO		
3474	Monaco (3AC) (3AF).	4363 kHz, J3E, Ch. 20, 22, F3E.	0703.	Local navigational warnings in French (in English on request).
		8806, 13152, 17323, 22768 kHz, J3E.	0930.	Weather.
		4363 kHz, J3E, Ch. 20, 22, F3E.	0803, 1303, 1815.	Weather.
		8728, 8806 kHz, J3E.	0715, 1830.	Weather.
		Ch. 20, 22, F3E.	Every hour +03m (during hours of service).	Weather.
		Ch. 23, 24, 25, F3E.	Continuous.	Weather.
	NOTE: Hours of service: 0600-2100 (Winter), 0500-2000 (Summer).			
		ITALY		
3475	Roma (IAR).	521.5 kHz, A1A.	0948, 1318, 1748, 2118.	Local navigational warnings and weather.
		521.5, 4292, 8530, 13011, 17160.8 kHz, A1A.	0830, 2030.	Weather.
		521.5, 4292 kHz, A1A.	0050, 0650, 1250, 1850.	Weather.
		Ch. 25, F3E.	0533, 0933, 1333, 1833, 2333.	Local navigational warnings.
		Ch. 25, F3E.	0135, 0735, 1335, 1935.	Weather.
		Ch. 68, F3E.	Continuous.	Weather.
		518 kHz, F1B.	0250, 0650, 1050, 1450, 1850, 2250.	NAVTEX [R].
3476	Cagliari (IDC).	444 kHz, A1A.	0918, 1248, 1648, 2048.	Local navigational warnings and weather.
		2680 kHz, J3E, Ch. 04, 62, 82, F3E.	0303, 0803, 1203, 1603, 2003.	Local navigational warnings.
		2680 kHz, J3E, Ch. 04, 62, 82, F3E.	0135, 0735, 1335, 1935.	Weather.
		2680 kHz, J3E.	0303, 0803, 1203, 1603, 2003.	Weather.
		Ch. 68, F3E.	Continuous.	Weather.
		518 kHz, F1B.	0310, 0710, 1110, 1510, 1910, 2310.	NAVTEX [T].
3477.2	Augusta (IQA).	2628 kHz, J3E, Ch. 85, 86, F3E.	0333, 0833, 1233, 1633, 2033.	Local navigational warnings.
		2628 kHz, J3E, Ch. 85, 86, F3E.	0135, 0735, 1335, 1935.	Weather.
		2628 kHz, J3E.	0333, 0833, 1233, 1633, 2033.	Weather.
		Ch. 68, F3E.	Continuous.	Weather.
		518 kHz, F1B.	0330, 0730, 1130, 1530, 1930, 2330.	NAVTEX [V].
3477.3	Porto Cervo.	Ch. 26, F3E.	0303, 0803, 1203, 1603, 2003.	Local navigational warnings.
		Ch. 26, F3E.	0135, 0735, 1335, 1935.	Weather.

RADIO NAVIGATIONAL WARNINGS

(1) No.	(2) Name	(3) Frequency	(4) Times	(5) Nature of Broadcast
3477.4	Porto Torres (IZN).	2719 kHz, J3E, Ch. 26, 28, 85, F3E.	0303, 0803, 1203, 1603, 2003.	Local navigational warnings.
		2719 kHz, J3E, Ch. 26, 28, 85, F3E.	0135, 0735, 1335, 1935.	Weather.
		2719 kHz, J3E.	0303, 0803, 1203, 1603, 2003.	Weather.
		Ch. 68, F3E.	Continuous.	Weather.
3477.5	Ancona (IPA).	511.5 kHz, A1A.	0948, 1248, 1718, 2118.	Local navigational warnings and weather.
		2656 kHz, J3E, Ch. 02, 25, F3E.	0433, 0933, 1333, 1733, 2133.	Local navigational warnings.
		511.5 kHz, A1A.	0148, 0748, 1348, 1948.	Weather.
		2656 kHz, J3E, Ch. 02, 25, F3E.	0135, 0735, 1335, 1935.	Weather.
		2656 kHz, J3E.	0433, 0933, 1333, 1733, 2133.	Weather.
		Ch. 68, F3E.	Continuous.	Weather.
3477.6	Ravenna.	Ch. 27, F3E.	0433, 0933, 1333, 1733, 2133.	Local navigational warnings.
		Ch. 27, F3E.	0135, 0735, 1335, 1935.	Weather.
		Ch. 68, F3E.	Continuous.	Weather.
3478	Genova (ICB).	447 kHz, A1A.	0848, 1348, 1748, 2148.	Local navigational warnings and weather.
		2722 kHz, J3E, Ch. 07, 25, 27, F3E.	0333, 0833, 1233, 1633, 2033.	Local navigational warnings.
		2722 kHz, J3E, Ch. 07, 25, 27, F3E.	0135, 0735, 1335, 1935.	Weather.
		2722 kHz, J3E.	0333, 0833, 1233, 1633, 2033.	Weather.
		Ch. 68, F3E.	Continuous.	Weather.
3480	Livorno (IPL).	2591 kHz, J3E, Ch. 26, 61, F3E.	0333, 0833, 1233, 1633, 2033.	Local navigational warnings.
		2591 kHz, J3E, Ch. 26, 61, F3E.	0135, 0735, 1335, 1935.	Weather.
		2591 kHz, J3E.	0333, 0833, 1233, 1633, 2033.	Weather.
		Ch. 68, F3E.	Continuous.	Weather.
3482	Civitavecchia (IPD).	1888 kHz, J3E, Ch. 01, 64, F3E.	0533, 0933, 1333, 1833, 2333.	Local navigational warnings.
		1888 kHz, J3E, Ch. 01, 64, F3E.	0135, 0735, 1335, 1935.	Weather.
		1888 kHz, J3E.	0533, 0933, 1333, 1833, 2333.	Weather.
		Ch. 68, F3E.	Continuous.	Weather.
3484	Napoli (IQH).	2632 kHz, J3E, Ch. 01, 25, 27, F3E.	0333, 0833, 1233, 1633, 2033.	Local navigational warnings.
		2632 kHz, J3E, Ch. 01, 25, 27, F3E.	0135, 0735, 1335, 1935.	Weather.
		2632 kHz, J3E.	0333, 0833, 1233, 1633, 2033.	Weather.
		Ch. 68, F3E.	Continuous.	Weather.

RADIO NAVIGATIONAL WARNINGS

(1) No.	(2) Name	(3) Frequency	(4) Times	(5) Nature of Broadcast
3486	Messina (IDF).	2789 kHz, J3E, Ch. 88, F3E.	0333, 0833, 1233, 1633, 2033.	Local navigational warnings.
		2789 kHz, J3E, Ch. 88, F3E.	0135, 0735, 1335, 1935.	Weather.
		2789 kHz, J3E.	0333, 0833, 1233, 1633, 2033.	Weather.
		Ch. 68, F3E.	Continuous.	Weather.
3487	Palermo (IPP).	1852 kHz, J3E, Ch. 27, 61, 81, 84, F3E.	0333, 0833, 1233, 1633, 2033.	Local navigational warnings.
		1852 kHz, J3E, Ch. 27, 61, 81, 84, F3E.	0135, 0735, 1335, 1935.	Weather.
		1852 kHz, J3E.	0333, 0833, 1233, 1633, 2033.	Weather.
		Ch. 68, F3E.	Continuous.	Weather.
3489	Mazara del Vallo (IQQ).	2600 kHz, J3E, Ch. 25, 26, 82, F3E.	0333, 0833, 1233, 1633, 2033.	Local navigational warnings.
		2600 kHz, J3E, Ch. 25, 26, 82, F3E.	0135, 0735, 1335, 1935.	Weather.
		2600 kHz, J3E.	0333, 0833, 1233, 1633, 2033.	Weather.
		Ch. 68, F3E.	Continuous.	Weather.
3490	Lampedusa (IQN).	1876 kHz, J3E, Ch. 25, 87, 88, F3E.	0333, 0833, 1233, 1633, 2033.	Local navigational warnings.
		1876 kHz, J3E, Ch. 25, 87, 88, F3E.	0135, 0735, 1335, 1935.	Weather.
		1876 kHz, J3E.	0333, 0833, 1233, 1633, 2033.	Weather.
		Ch. 68, F3E.	Continuous.	Weather.
3493	Crotone (IPC).	2663 kHz, J3E, Ch. 26, 62, 84, 88, F3E.	0333, 0833, 1233, 1633, 2033.	Local navigational warnings.
		2663 kHz, J3E, Ch. 26, 62, 84, 88, F3E.	0135, 0735, 1335, 1935.	Weather.
		2663 kHz, J3E.	0333, 0833, 1233, 1633, 2033.	Weather.
		Ch. 68, F3E.	Continuous.	Weather.
3495	Bari (IPB).	514.5 kHz, A1A.	0848, 1218, 1648, 2048.	Local navigational warnings and weather.
		2579 kHz, J3E, Ch. 01, 05, 27, F3E.	0333, 0833, 1233, 1633, 2033.	Local navigational warnings.
		514.5 kHz, A1A.	0125, 0725, 1325, 1925.	Weather.
		2579 kHz, J3E, Ch. 01, 05, 27, F3E.	0135, 0735, 1335, 1935.	Weather.
		2579 kHz, J3E.	0333, 0833, 1233, 1633, 2033.	Weather.
		Ch. 68, F3E.	Continuous.	Weather.
3496	San Benedetto del Tronto (IQP).	1855 kHz, J3E, Ch. 65, 87, F3E.	0433, 0933, 1333, 1733, 2133.	Local navigational warnings.
		1855 kHz, J3E, Ch. 65, 87, F3E.	0135, 0735, 1335, 1935.	Weather.
		1855 kHz, J3E.	0433, 0933, 1333, 1733, 2133.	Weather.
		Ch. 68, F3E.	Continuous.	Weather.

RADIO NAVIGATIONAL WARNINGS

(1) No.	(2) Name	(3) Frequency	(4) Times	(5) Nature of Broadcast
3498	Trieste (IQX).	512.5 kHz, A1A.	0848, 1218, 1648, 2048.	Local navigational warnings and weather.
		2624 kHz, J3E, Ch. 01, 26, F3E.	0433, 0933, 1333, 1733, 2133.	Local navigational warnings.
		2624 kHz, J3E, Ch. 01, 26, 83, F3E.	0135, 0735, 1335, 1935.	Weather.
		2624 kHz, J3E.	0433, 0933, 1333, 1733, 2133.	Weather.
		Ch. 83, F3E.	0333, 0833, 1233, 1633, 2033.	Local navigational warnings.
		Ch. 68, F3E.	Continuous.	Weather.
		518 kHz, F1B.	0320, 0720, 1120, 1520, 1920, 2320.	NAVTEX [U].

MALTA

(1) No.	(2) Name	(3) Frequency	(4) Times	(5) Nature of Broadcast
3498.05	Malta.	2625 kHz, J3E, R3E, Ch. 04, F3E.	1003, 1603, 2103.	NAVAREA III, local navigational warnings.
		2625 kHz, J3E, R3E, Ch. 04, F3E.	0603, 1003, 1603, 2103.	Weather.
		518 kHz, F1B.	0220, 0620, 1020, 1420, 1820, 2220.	NAVTEX [O].

ALBANIA

(1) No.	(2) Name	(3) Frequency	(4) Times	(5) Nature of Broadcast
3498.1	Durres (ZAD).	460 kHz, A1A.	0818, 1218, 1618.	Local navigational warnings.

CROATIA

(1) No.	(2) Name	(3) Frequency	(4) Times	(5) Nature of Broadcast
3499	Split (9AS).	Ch. 07, 21, 81, F3E.	0545, 1245, 1945.	Local navigational warnings and weather.
		518 kHz, F1B.	0240, 0640, 1040, 1440, 1840, 2240.	NAVTEX [Q].
3499.05	Dubrovnik (9AD).	2615 kHz, J3E, Ch. 04, 07, F3E.	0625, 1320, 2120.	Local navigational warnings and weather.
3499.1	Rijeka (9AR).	2771 kHz, J3E, Ch. 24, F3E.	0535, 1435, 1935.	Local navigational warnings and weather.

SERBIA AND MONTENEGRO

(1) No.	(2) Name	(3) Frequency	(4) Times	(5) Nature of Broadcast
3499.5	Bar (YUW).	1720.4 kHz, J3E, Ch. 20, 24, F3E.	0850, 1420, 2050.	Local navigational warnings and weather.

GREECE

(1) No.	(2) Name	(3) Frequency	(4) Times	(5) Nature of Broadcast
3500	Kerkira (SVK).	2830 kHz, J3E.	0033, 0633, 1033, 1633.	Local navigational warnings.
		2830 kHz, J3E.	0703, 0903, 1533, 2133.	Weather.
		518 kHz, F1B.	0140, 0540, 0940, 1340, 1740, 2140.	NAVTEX [K].
3502	Iraklion (SVH).	2799 kHz, J3E.	0633, 1133, 1733, 2333.	Local navigational warnings.
		2799 kHz, J3E.	0703, 0903, 1533, 2133.	Weather.
		518 kHz, F1B.	0110, 0510, 0910, 1310, 1710, 2110.	NAVTEX [H].
3503	Rodhos (SVR).	2624 kHz, J3E.	0633, 1133, 1733, 2333.	Local navigational warnings.
		2624 kHz, J3E.	0703, 0903, 1533, 2133.	Weather.

RADIO NAVIGATIONAL WARNINGS

(1) No.	(2) Name	(3) Frequency	(4) Times	(5) Nature of Broadcast
3504	Athens (SVN) (SVJ4).	2590 kHz, J3E.	0703, 0933, 1503, 2103.	Weather.
		8743 kHz, J3E.	1215, 2015.	Weather in Greek.
		8743 kHz, J3E.	0633, 1233, 1633, 2233.	Local navigational warnings.
		4481, 8105 kHz, F3C.	0845-0945.	Weather FAX; 120/576.
3506	Hellenic Radio-Television.	729 kHz, A3E.	0450.	Local navigational warnings.
		729, 927, 1008, 1044, 1404, 1485, 1494, 1512, 1602 kHz, A3E, 88.0-97.9, 101.8 MHz, F3E.	1330.	Local navigational warnings.
		729 kHz, A3E.	0430.	Weather.
		729, 927, 1008, 1044, 1404, 1485, 1494, 1512, 1602 kHz, A3E.	1330.	Weather in Greek.
3507	Hellas.	Ch. 01, 02, 04, 23, 25, 27, 60, 63, 82, 83, 85, F3E.	0500, 1100, 1730, 2330.	Local navigational warnings.
		Ch. 01, 02, 04, 23, 25, 27, 60, 63, 82, 83, 85, F3E.	0600, 1000, 1600, 2200.	Weather.
		Ch. 86, F3E.	Continuous.	Local navigational warnings and weather.
3508	Limnos (SVL).	2730 kHz, J3E.	0033, 0633, 1033, 1633.	Local navigational warnings.
		2730 kHz, J3E.	0703, 0903, 1533, 2133.	Weather.
		518 kHz, F1B.	0150, 0550, 0950, 1350, 1750, 2150.	NAVTEX [L].

CYPRUS

(1) No.	(2) Name	(3) Frequency	(4) Times	(5) Nature of Broadcast
3509	Cyprus (5BA).	2700 kHz, H3E, J3E, R3E.	0733, 1533.	Local navigational warnings.
		518 kHz, F1B.	0200, 0600, 1000, 1400, 1800, 2200.	NAVTEX [M].

BULGARIA

(1) No.	(2) Name	(3) Frequency	(4) Times	(5) Nature of Broadcast
3510	Varna (LZW).	3740 kHz, J3E.	0703, 1903.	Local navigational warnings and weather.
		4212.5 kHz, F1B.	0630, 1830.	Weather.
		12635.5 kHz, F1B.	0630, 1230, 1830.	Weather.
		Ch. 26, F3E.	0733, 1933.	Local navigational warnings and weather.
		518 kHz, F1B.	0130, 0530, 0930, 1330, 1730, 2130.	NAVTEX [J].

ROMANIA

(1) No.	(2) Name	(3) Frequency	(4) Times	(5) Nature of Broadcast
3512	Constanta (YQI).	2748 kHz, J3E.	0733, 1033, 1333, 1633, 1933.	Local navigational warnings and weather.
		Ch.12, G3E.	0703, 1003, 1303, 1603, 1903, 2203.	Local navigational warnings and weather.
		490 kHz, F1B.	0150, 0550, 0950, 1350, 1750, 2150.	NAVTEX [L] in Romanian.

NOTE: Navigational warnings are announced on MF 2182 kHz and 2187.5 kHz DSC, and on VHF Ch. 16 and Ch. 70 DSC prior to broadcast on scheduled frequency or channel number.

RADIO NAVIGATIONAL WARNINGS

(1) No.	(2) Name	(3) Frequency	(4) Times	(5) Nature of Broadcast
		UKRAINE		
3514	Odessa (UDE) (UFB).	510.5 kHz, A1A.	1718, 2318.	Local navigational warnings.
		510.5, 6341.5 kHz, A1A.	0518, 1118.	Local navigational warnings.
		3310 kHz, R3E.	0233, 0633, 1033, 1433, 1833, 2233.	Local navigational warnings.
		510.5, 6341.5 kHz, A1A.	0520, 1500, 2105.	Weather and ice (in Russian at 0520, 1500).
		6353, 8520, 12947, 17155 kHz, A1A.	0100.	Weather (Apr. 15 - Sep. 30 on 17155 kHz).
		518 kHz, F1B.	0230, 0630, 1030, 1430, 1830, 2230.	NAVTEX [C].
3516	Sevastopol (URL-8).	476 kHz, A1A.	0018, 0618, 1218, 1818.	Local navigational warnings.
		2695 kHz, H3E.	0033, 0733, 1133, 1533, 1933, 2233.	Local navigational warnings.
3517	Mariupol (USU) (UTW).	473 kHz, A1A.	0218, 0818, 1418, 2018.	Local navigational warnings.
		2805 kHz, H3E.	0233, 0633, 1033, 1433, 1833, 2233.	Local navigational warnings.
		473, 4265 kHz, A1A.	0500, 1700.	Weather and ice in Russian (ice at 1700).
		2805 kHz, H3E.	0330, 0930.	Weather and ice in Russian (ice at 0930).
		6326.5, 8422.5, 12615, 16829 kHz, F1B.	1440.	Local navigational warnings in Russian and Ukrainian (selected warnings repeated in English).
3517.5	Kerch.	518 kHz, F1B.	0100, 0500, 0900, 1300, 1700, 2100.	NAVTEX [B].
3518	Kiev.	12828.7 kHz, F3C.	1857 (on 1, 6, 11, 16, 21, 26 of each month).	Ice FAX; 120/576.
		GEORGIA		
3519	Batumi (UFA).	484 kHz, A1A.	0118, 0718, 1318, 1918.	Local navigational warnings.
		3630 kHz, H3E.	0133, 0533, 0933, 1333, 1733, 2133.	Local navigational warnings.
		484 kHz, A1A.	0507, 1307, 2030.	Weather in Russian.
		RUSSIA - BLACK SEA		
	LONG-RANGE WARNINGS: NAVIP: World-wide navigational warnings. LOCAL WARNINGS: PRIP.			
3520	Novorossiysk.	518 kHz, F1B.	0300, 0700, 1100, 1500, 1900, 2300.	NAVTEX [A].
		RUSSIA - CASPIAN SEA		
	LOCAL WARNINGS: PRIP.			
3522	Astrakhan.	518 kHz, F1B.	0340, 0740, 1140, 1540, 1940, 2340.	NAVTEX [W].

RADIO NAVIGATIONAL WARNINGS

(1) No.	(2) Name	(3) Frequency	(4) Times	(5) Nature of Broadcast
			TURKEY	
3528.1	Antalya.	Ch. 67, F3E.	0700, 1000, 1300, 1600, 1900.	Weather.
		Ch. 67, F3E.	0730, 0900, 0930, 1130, 1330, 1530, 1730, 1930.	Weather in Turkish.
		490 kHz, F1B.	0030, 0430, 0830, 1230, 1630, 2030.	NAVTEX [D] in Turkish. On trial.
		518 kHz, F1B.	0050, 0450, 0850, 1250, 1650, 2050.	NAVTEX [F].
3529	Izmir.	490 kHz, F1B.	0020, 0420, 0820, 1220, 1620, 2020.	NAVTEX [C] in Turkish. On trial.
		518 kHz, F1B.	0120, 0520, 0920, 1320, 1720, 2120.	NAVTEX [I].
3531	Samsun.	Ch. 67, F3E.	0700, 1000, 1300, 1600, 1900.	Weather.
		Ch. 67, F3E.	0730, 0900, 0930, 1130, 1330, 1530, 1730, 1930.	Weather in Turkish.
		490 kHz, F1B.	0000, 0400, 0800, 1200, 1600, 2000.	NAVTEX [A]. On trial.
		518 kHz, F1B.	0040, 0440, 0840, 1240, 1640, 2040.	NAVTEX [E].
3533	Istanbul (TAH).	4405, 8812, 13128 kHz, J3E.	1000, 1800.	Weather.
		4560, 8431, 12654 kHz, F1B.	0800, 2000.	Weather.
		Ch. 67, F3E.	0700, 1000, 1300, 1600, 1900.	Weather.
		Ch. 67, F3E.	0730, 0900, 0930, 1130, 1330, 1530, 1730, 1930.	Weather in Turkish.
		490 kHz, F1B.	0010, 0410, 0810, 1210, 1610, 2010.	NAVTEX [B] in Turkish. On trial.
		4209.5 kHz, F1B.	0200, 0600, 1000, 1400, 1800, 2200.	NAVTEX [M] in Turkish. On trial.
		518 kHz, F1B.	0030, 0430, 0830, 1230, 1630, 2030.	NAVTEX [D].
			ISRAEL	
3534	Haifa (4XO).	2649 kHz, J3E, Ch. 26, F3E.	On request.	Local navigational warnings and weather.
		518 kHz, F1B.	0020, 0420, 0820, 1220, 1620, 2020.	NAVTEX [P].
			EGYPT - MEDITERRANEAN	
3537	Alexandria.	518, kHz, F1B.	0210, 0610, 1010, 1410, 1810, 2210.	NAVTEX [N].
			LIBYA	
3538	Tripoli (5AT).	2182 kHz, H3E, J3E.	0903, 1903.	Local navigational warnings.
		2197 kHz, H3E, J3E.	0833, 1733.	Weather.
			TUNISIA	
3540	La Goulette Port (3VW).	2182 kHz, J3E.	0003, 0403, 0603, 1003, 1303, 1803, 1903, 2103.	Local navigational warnings in French.
		2182 kHz, J3E.	On receipt, every hour +03m, +33m.	Weather in French.
		1743 kHz, J3E.	0405, 1905.	Weather in French.

RADIO NAVIGATIONAL WARNINGS

(1) No.	(2) Name	(3) Frequency	(4) Times	(5) Nature of Broadcast
3542	Tunis (3VT).	1820, 2670 kHz, A3E.	0803, 1203, 2003.	Local navigational warnings in French.
		1820, 2670 kHz, A3E.	0805, 1705.	Weather in French.
		ALGERIA		
3550	Annaba (7TB).	2775 kHz, A3E.	0833, 2033.	Local navigational warnings in French.
		1745 kHz, A3E.	0920, 1033, 1720, 1833.	Weather in French.
3552	Alger (7TA).	416 kHz, A1A, A2A, 1792 kHz, A3E.	0918, 2118.	Local navigational warnings in French.
		1792 kHz, A3E.	0903, 1703.	Weather in French.
		416 kHz, A1A, A2A, 2691 kHz, A3E.	0918, 2118.	Weather in French.
3554	Oran (7TO).	1735 kHz, A3E.	0833, 2033.	Local navigational warnings and weather in French.
		1735, 2586, 2719 kHz, A3E.	0920, 1033, 1720, 1735.	Weather in French.
		MOROCCO		

NOTE: Vessels observing dangers to navigation are requested to transmit observations to the nearest coast radio station and other vessels in the vicinity. Message should be preceded by the safety signal "SECURITE" and addressed to Commander, Royal Navy, Casablanca, giving observing vessel's name and owner.

(1) No.	(2) Name	(3) Frequency	(4) Times	(5) Nature of Broadcast
3560	Tanger (CNW).	1911 kHz, H3E, J3E.	1018, 1748.	Local navigational warnings in French.
		1911 kHz, H3E, J3E.	Every hour +03m, 0915, 1635.	Weather in French.
3570	Agadir (CND).	1911 kHz, H3E, J3E.	1048, 1628.	Local navigational warnings in French.
		1911 kHz, H3E, J3E.	Every hour +33m, 0935, 1615.	Weather in French.
3572	Casablanca (CNP).	2586 kHz, H3E, J3E.	0918, 2028.	Local navigational warnings in French.
		2586 kHz, H3E, J3E.	Every hour +33m, 0945, 1645.	Weather in French.
3574	Saf (CND-3).	1743 kHz, A3E.	0928, 1648.	Local navigational warnings in French.
		1743 kHz, H3E, J3E.	Every hour +03m, 0915, 1635.	Weather in French.
		ISLAS CANARIAS		
3579	Arrecife.	1644 kHz, J3E.	0803, 1903.	Local navigational warnings.
		1644 kHz, J3E.	0803, 1233, 1903.	Weather in Spanish.
		Ch. 25, F3E.	0833, 2033.	Local navigational warnings.
		Ch. 25, F3E.	0833, 1333, 2033.	Weather in Spanish.
3579.5	Fuerteventura.	Ch. 22, F3E.	0833, 2033.	Local navigational warnings.
		Ch. 22, F3E.	0833, 1333, 2033.	Weather in Spanish.
3580	Las Palmas.	1689 kHz, J3E.	0803, 1903.	Local navigational warnings.
		1689 kHz, J3E.	0803, 1233, 1903.	Weather in Spanish
		Ch. 10, F3E.	On receipt.	Local navigational warnings.
		Ch. 26, F3E.	0833, 2033.	Local navigational warnings.
		Ch. 26, F3E.	0833, 1333, 2033.	Weather in Spanish.
		518 kHz, F1B.	0120, 0520, 0920, 1320, 1720, 2120.	NAVTEX [I].

RADIO NAVIGATIONAL WARNINGS

(1) No.	(2) Name	(3) Frequency	(4) Times	(5) Nature of Broadcast
3581	Tenerife.	Ch. 27, F3E.	0833, 2033.	Local navigational warnings.
		Ch. 27, F3E.	0833, 1333, 2033.	Weather in Spanish.
		Ch. 74, F3E.	0215, 0615, 1015, 1415, 1815, 2215.	Local navigational warnings.
		Ch. 74, F3E.	0015, 0415, 0815, 1215, 1615, 2015.	Weather.
3581.3	Gomera.	Ch. 24, F3E.	0833, 2033.	Local navigational warnings.
		Ch. 24, F3E.	0833, 1333, 2033.	Weather in Spanish.
3581.6	Hierro.	Ch. 23, F3E.	0833, 2033.	Local navigational warnings.
		Ch. 23, F3E.	0833, 1333, 2033.	Weather in Spanish.
3581.9	La Palma.	Ch. 20, F3E.	0833, 2033.	Local navigational warnings.
		Ch. 20, F3E.	0833, 1333, 2033.	Weather in Spanish.
MAURITANIA				
3583	Nouadhibou (5TA).	1881 kHz, A3E.	0833.	Weather in French.
SENEGAL				
3584	Dakar (6VA) (6VU).	1813 kHz, A3E.	0848, 1248, 1948.	Local navigational warnings in French.
		13667.5, 19750 kHz, F3C.	Continuous.	Weather FAX; 120/576.
GUINEA				
3590	Conakry (3XC).	1813 kHz, A3E.	0818, 1218, 1718.	Local navigational warnings in French.
COTE D'IVOIRE (IVORY COAST)				
3600	Abidjan (TUA).	2586 kHz, H3E.	0848, 1248, 1948.	Local navigational warnings in French.
GHANA				
3605	Tema (9GX).	1674 kHz, H3E, J3E.	0905, 2105.	Local navigational warnings and weather.
		8791 kHz, J3E.	0900, 2100.	Local navigational warnings and weather.
		Ch. 26, F3E.	0830, 2030.	Local navigational warnings and weather.
		Ch. 27, F3E.	0800, 2000.	Local navigational warnings and weather.
BENIN				
3610	Cotonou (TYA).	1813 kHz, H3E.	0818, 1218, 1718.	Local navigational warnings in French.
		1813 kHz, H3E.	1003, 1603.	Weather in French.
NIGERIA				
3615	Lagos (5OW).	2755 kHz, J3E.	0833, 1303.	Local navigational warnings.
3617	Port Harcourt (5OZ).	2630 kHz, J3E.	0820, 1220.	Local navigational warnings.
CAMEROON				
3620	Douala (TJC).	500, 519 kHz, A1A.	Every hour +48m (0500-2000).	Local navigational warnings.
		8449 kHz, A1A.	0800, 0900, 1300.	Weather.
		13069.5 kHz, A1A.	0700, 1100, 1500.	Weather.

RADIO NAVIGATIONAL WARNINGS

(1) No.	(2) Name	(3) Frequency	(4) Times	(5) Nature of Broadcast
		NAMIBIA		
3627	Luderitz (V5L).	Ch. 23, G3E.	0905, 1605.	NAVAREA VII and local navigational warnings.
		Ch. 23, G3E.	0935, 1235, 1635.	Weather.
3628	Walvis Bay (V5W).	1764, 4357 kHz, J3E, Ch. 26, 27, G3E.	0905, 1605.	NAVAREA VII and local navigational warnings.
		1764, 4357 kHz, J3E, Ch. 26, 27, G3E.	0935, 1235, 1635.	Weather.
		518 kHz, F1B.	0010, 0410, 0810, 1210, 1610, 2010.	NAVTEX [B].
		ANGOLA		
3629	Luanda (D3E).	4143.6, 8291.1 kHz, J3E, Ch. 24, F3E.	0233, 0633, 1033, 1433, 1833, 2233.	Local navigational warnings in Portuguese.
		CONGO (BRAZZAVILLE)		
3630	Pointe Noire (TNA).	2705 kHz, R3E.	0610, 0810, 1010, 1410, 1610.	Local navigational warnings in French.
		SOUTH AFRICA		

LONG-RANGE WARNINGS:
NAVAREA VII:
Includes waters of the South Atlantic and Indian Oceans, bound on the west by a line running from the African Coast at 6°S to 20°W, thence south to Antarctica, and on the east by a line running from the east African coast at 10°30′S to 55°E, thence south to 30°S, east to 80°E and south to Antarctica. Original reports to NAVAREA VII Coordinator, Hydrographer, S.A. Navy, Maritime Headquarters, Cape Town.

(1) No.	(2) Name	(3) Frequency	(4) Times	(5) Nature of Broadcast
3641	Port Elizabeth (ZSQ).	4375, 8740, 13146 kHz, J3E, Ch. 23, 24, 25, 27, 28, 83, G3E.	1015, 1333, 1815.	NAVAREA VII, local navigational warnings and weather (weather only at 1333).
		518 kHz, F1B.	0120, 0520, 0920, 1320, 1720, 2120.	NAVTEX [I].
	NOTE: HF and VHF voice broadcasts remotely controlled from Cape Town.			
3643	Durban (ZSD).	4375, 8740, 13146 kHz, J3E, Ch. 01, 03, 25, 26, 27, 28, G3E.	1015, 1333, 1815.	NAVAREA VII, local navigational warnings and weather (weather only at 1333).
		518 kHz, F1B.	0220, 0620, 1020, 1420, 1820, 2220.	NAVTEX [O].
	NOTE: HF and VHF voice broadcasts remotely controlled from Cape Town.			
3644	Cape Town (ZSC).	4375, 8740, 13146 kHz, J3E, Ch. 01, 03, 04, 23, 25, 26, 27, 84, 85, 86, G3E.	1015, 1333, 1815.	NAVAREA VII, local navigational warnings and weather (weather only at 1333).
		518 kHz, F1B.	0020, 0420, 0820, 1220, 1620, 2020.	NAVTEX [C].
3645	East London (ZSA).	Ch. 26, G3E.	1015, 1333, 1815.	NAVAREA VII, local navigational warnings and weather (weather only at 1333).
	NOTE: VHF voice broadcasts remotely controlled from Cape Town.			
3645.1	Cape Naval (NAVCOMCEN Cape) (ZSJ).	4014 kHz, F3C.	0430, 0500, 2230.	Weather FAX*; 120/576.
		7508, 13538 kHz, F3C.	0430, 0500, 0630, 0730, 1030, 1100, 1530, 2230.	Weather FAX*; 120/576.
		18238 kHz, F3C.	0630, 0730, 1030, 1100, 1530.	Weather FAX*; 120/576.
		7508, 13538, 18238 kHz, F3C.	0800.	Ice FAX; 120/576.
		4014 kHz, J2B.	1700.	Weather.
		7508, 13538 kHz, J2B.	0915, 1700.	Weather.
		18238 kHz, J2B.	0915.	Weather.

*NOTE: Broadcast schedule at 0430.

RADIO NAVIGATIONAL WARNINGS

(1) No.	(2) Name	(3) Frequency	(4) Times	(5) Nature of Broadcast
		CHILE		
	LONG-RANGE WARNINGS: NAVAREA XV: Includes the waters of the eastern South Pacifi from 18°21′S to Antarctica, bound on the west by 120°W and on the east by 67°16′W. Original reports to Director del Servicio Hidrografic y Oceanografic de la Armada de Chile, Valparaiso.			
3645.4	Puerto Montt (CBP).	2738, 4146 kHz, J3E.	1130, 2325.	Weather in Spanish.
		Ch. 10, G3E.	1150, 2345.	Weather in Spanish.
		518 kHz, F1B.	0430, 1230, 2030.	NAVTEX [D].
		518 kHz, F1B.	0030, 0830, 1630.	NAVTEX [K] in Spanish.
3645.5	Valparaiso Playa Ancha (CBV).	4214.5, 4217.5, 8420.5, 8424, 12583.5, 12587, 16811, 16814.5, 22380.5 kHz, F1B.	1430.	NAVAREA XV warnings and local navigational warnings.
		4214.5, 4217.5, 8420.5, 8424, 12583.5, 12587, 16811, 16814.5 kHz, F1B.	1210, 1610, 1845.	Weather.
		2738, 4357 kHz, J3E.	1235, 2335.	Weather in Spanish.
		Ch. 10, G3E.	1215, 2315.	Weather in Spanish.
		4228, 8677, 17146.4 kHz, F3C.	1115, 1630, 1915, 2315.	Weather FAX; 120/576.
		518 kHz, F1B.	0410, 1210, 2010.	NAVTEX [B].
		518 kHz, F1B.	0010, 0810, 1610.	NAVTEX [I] in Spanish.
3645.6	Talcahuano (CBT).	2738 kHz, J3E.	0220, 1420.	Local navigational warnings.
		2738 kHz, J3E.	0045, 1245.	Weather in Spanish.
		Ch. 10, G3E.	0055, 1255.	Weather in Spanish.
		518 kHz, F1B.	0420, 1220, 2020.	NAVTEX [C].
		518 kHz, F1B.	0020, 0820, 1620.	NAVTEX [J] in Spanish.
3645.7	Magallanes (CBM).	2738, 4146 kHz, J3E.	0035, 1235.	Weather in Spanish.
		Ch. 10, G3E.	0010, 1210.	Weather in Spanish.
		518 kHz, F1B.	0440, 1240, 2040.	NAVTEX [E].
		518 kHz, F1B.	0040, 0840, 1640.	NAVTEX [L] in Spanish.
3645.75	Antofagasta (CBA).	2738 kHz, J3E.	0045, 1250.	Weather in Spanish.
		Ch. 14, G3E.	0055, 1305.	Weather in Spanish.
		518 kHz, F1B.	0400, 1200, 2000.	NAVTEX [A].
		518 kHz, F1B.	0000, 0800, 1600.	NAVTEX [H] in Spanish.
3645.76	Isla de Pascua (Easter Island) (CBY).	2738 kHz, J3E.	0225, 1425.	Weather in Spanish.
		Ch 14, G3E.	0215, 1415.	Weather in Spanish.
		518 kHz, F1B.	0450, 1250, 2050.	NAVTEX [F].
		518 kHz, F1B.	0050, 0850, 1650.	NAVTEX [G] in Spanish.
3645.77	Centro Meteorologico Presidente Eduardo Frei, King George Island (South Shetland Islands) (CAN6D).	5302.5, 11662.5, 15470.5 kHz, F1B.	0030, 0330, 0930, 1230, 1530, 2130, 2230.	Weather.
		5302.5, 11662.5, 15470.5 kHz, F3C.	0930, 1530, 2130.	Weather FAX; 120/576.

RADIO NAVIGATIONAL WARNINGS

(1) No.	(2) Name	(3) Frequency	(4) Times	(5) Nature of Broadcast
3645.8	Base Prat, Greenwich Island (South Shetland Islands) (CBZ).	2738 kHz, J3E.	0150, 1350.	Weather.
		6439 kHz, F1B.	1400, 2200.	Weather.
		6439 kHz, F1B.	On request.	Ice.
		Ch. 14, G3E.	0155, 1355.	Weather.

ECUADOR

NOTE: Original reports to Guayaquil (HCG) Naval Radio, preceded by the word "HIDRO", or mail to Institute of the Navy, Guayaquil.

3646	Guayaquil Naval (HCG).	8474 kHz, A2A.	0000, 1200, 1700.	Local navigational warnings.

PERU

LONG-RANGE WARNINGS:
NAVAREA XVI:
Includes the waters of the eastern South Pacifi between 3°24′S and 18°21′S, west to 120°W. Original reports to Direccion de Hidrografi y Navegacion de la Marina, Callao.

3646.1	Callao (OBC).	485, 12307 kHz, A1A.	0200, 1600, 2100.	Local navigational warnings and weather in Spanish, NAVAREA XVI.
		518 kHz, F1B.	0320, 0720, 1120, 1520, 1920, 2320.	NAVTEX [U].
3646.2	Paita (OBY-2).	485, 6436 kHz, A1A.	0230, 1630, 2130.	Local navigational warnings.
		518 kHz, F1B.	0300, 0700, 1100, 1500, 1900, 2300.	NAVTEX [S].
3646.3	Mollendo (OBF-4).	156.8 MHz, F3E.	0245, 1645, 2145.	Local navigational warnings and weather.
		518 kHz, F1B.	0340, 0740, 1140, 1540, 1940, 2340.	NAVTEX [W].

UNITED STATES - PACIFIC

LONG-RANGE WARNINGS:
NAVAREA XII:
Original reports to NAVAREA XII Coordinator, National Geospatial-Intelligence Agency, Attn: PVM (Mail stop D-44).
HYDROPAC:
Original reports to National Geospatial-Intelligence Agency.
LOCAL WARNINGS:
Local Notice to Mariners:
Original reports to nearest Coast Guard Station for relay to District Commander (oan).

3646.5	Long Beach, CA (NMC) (NMQ-9) U.S. Coast Guard.	2670 kHz, J3E.	0503, 1303, 2103.	Local Notice to Mariners and weather.
		Ch. 22A, F3E.	0200, 1800.	Local Notice to Mariners and weather.
3646.6	Cambria, CA (NMQ) U.S. Coast Guard.	518 kHz, F1B.	0045, 0445, 0845, 1245, 1645, 2045.	NAVTEX [Q].

RADIO NAVIGATIONAL WARNINGS

(1) No.	(2) Name	(3) Frequency	(4) Times	(5) Nature of Broadcast
3657	Point Reyes, CA (NMC) (NMC-17) U.S. Coast Guard.	2670 kHz, J3E.	0203, 1403.	Local Notice to Mariners and weather.
		8416.5, 16806.5 kHz, F1B.	0005, 1800.	Maritime Safety Information (MSI) (HF NBDP) (NAVAREA XII, HYDROPAC and weather).
		4426, 8764, 13089 kHz, J3E.	0430, 1030.	Maritime Safety Information (MSI).
		8764, 13089, 17314 kHz, J3E.	1630, 2230.	Maritime Safety Information (MSI).
		Ch. 22A, F3E.	1630, 1900, 2330.	Local Notice to Mariners and weather.
		4346 kHz, F3C.	0245, 0800, 1100, 1430.	Weather FAX*; 120/576.
		8682, 12590.5, 17151.2 kHz, F3C.	0245, 0800, 1100, 1430, 1930, 2300.	Weather FAX*; 120/576.
		22527 kHz, F3C.	1930, 2300.	Weather FAX*; 120/576.
		518 kHz, F1B.	0000, 0400, 0800, 1200, 1600, 2000.	NAVTEX [C].
	*NOTE: Broadcast schedule at 1104, 2324.			
3661	Humboldt Bay, CA (NMC-11) U.S. Coast Guard.	2670 kHz, J3E.	0303, 1503.	Local Notice to Mariners and weather.
		Ch. 22A, F3E.	1615, 2315.	Local Notice to Mariners and weather.
3664	North Bend, OR (NOE) U.S. Coast Guard.	2670 kHz, J3E, Ch. 22A, F3E.	0603, 1803.	Local Notice to Mariners and weather.
3665	Astoria, OR (NMW) U.S. Coast Guard.	2670 kHz, J3E, Ch. 22A, F3E.	0533, 1733.	Local Notice to Mariners and weather.
		518 kHz, F1B.	0130, 0530, 0930, 1330, 1730, 2130.	NAVTEX [W].
3666	Portland, OR (NMW-44) U.S. Coast Guard.	Ch. 22A, F3E.	1745.	Local Notice to Mariners and weather.
3667	Port Angeles, WA (NOW) U.S. Coast Guard.	2670 kHz, J3E, Ch. 22A, F3E.	0615, 1815.	Local Notice to Mariners and weather.
3668	Seattle, WA (NMW-43) U.S. Coast Guard.	Ch. 22A, F3E.	0630, 1830.	Local Notice to Mariners and weather.
	CANADA - PACIFIC			
3671	Victoria, B.C. (VAK).	162.475 MHz, Ch. 21B, F3E.	Continuous (interrupted during live broadcasts at 0510, 1510, 2110).	Local navigational warnings and weather.
3672	Comox, B.C. (VAC).	162.475, 162.55 MHz, Ch. 21B, F3E.	Continuous (interrupted during live broadcasts at 0420, 1520, 2120).	Local navigational warnings and weather.
3675	Tofino B.C. (VAE).	2054 kHz, J3E, 162.4, 162.475, 162.55 MHz, Ch. 21B, F3E.	0050, 0650, 1250, 1850.	Local navigational warnings and weather.
		162.4, 162.475, 162.55 MHz, Ch. 21B, F3E.	Continuous (interrupted during live broadcasts).	Local navigational warnings and weather.
		518 kHZ, F1B.	0110, 0510, 0910, 1310, 1710, 2110.	NAVTEX [H].
3677	Prince Rupert, B.C. (VAJ).	2054 kHz, J3E.	0105, 0705, 1305, 1905.	Local navigational warnings and weather.
		162.4, 162.475, 162.55 MHz, Ch. 21B, F3E.	Continuous.	Local navigational warnings and weather.
		518 kHz, F1B.	0030, 0430, 0830, 1230, 1630, 2030.	NAVTEX [D].

RADIO NAVIGATIONAL WARNINGS

(1) No.	(2) Name	(3) Frequency	(4) Times	(5) Nature of Broadcast
		UNITED STATES - ALASKA		
	LONG-RANGE WARNINGS: NAVAREA XII: Original reports to NAVAREA XII Coordinator, National Geospatial-Intelligence Agency, Attn: PVM (Mail stop D-44). HYDROPAC: Original reports to National Geospatial-Intelligence Agency. LOCAL WARNINGS: Local Notice to Mariners: Original reports to nearest Coast Guard Station for relay to District Commander (oan).			
3692.5	Juneau, AK (NMJ) U.S. Coast Guard.	Ch. 22A, F3E.	0103, 0203, 0303, 0403, 1403, 1433, 1503, 1533.	Local Notice to Mariners and weather.
3695	Kodiak, AK (NOJ) U.S. Coast Guard.	6501 kHz, J3E.	0203, 1645.	Maritime Safety Information (MSI).
		Ch. 22A, F3E.	0133, 0233, 0533, 1433, 1603, 1803.	Local Notice to Mariners and weather.
		2054 kHz, F3C.	0950, 1600.	Weather and ice FAX*; 120/576.
		4298, 8459 kHz, F3C.	0400, 0950, 1600, 2150.	Weather and ice FAX*; 120/576.
		12412.5 kHz, F3C.	0400, 2150.	Weather and ice FAX*; 120/576.
		518 kHz, F1B.	0300, 0700, 1100, 1500, 1900, 2300.	NAVTEX [J].
		518 kHz, F1B.	0340, 0740, 1140, 1540, 1940, 2340.	NAVTEX [X]. (Weather products previously broadcast from Adak.)
	*NOTE: Broadcast schedule at 1727.			
3696.5	Valdez, AK U.S. Coast Guard.	Ch. 22A, F3E.	0115, 0133, 0715, 0733, 1315, 1333, 2115, 2133.	Local Notice to Mariners and weather.
		UNITED STATES - HAWAII		
	LONG-RANGE WARNINGS: NAVAREA XII: Original reports to NAVAREA XII Coordinator, National Geospatial-Intelligence Agency, Attn: PVM (Mail stop D-44). HYDROPAC: Original reports to National Geospatial-Intelligence Agency. LOCAL WARNINGS: Local Notice to Mariners: Original reports to nearest Coast Guard Station for relay to District Commander (oan).			
3703	Honolulu, HI (NMO) (NMO-2) U.S. Coast Guard.	8416.5, 12579, 22376 kHz, F1B.	0130, 2030.	Maritime Safety Information (MSI) (HF NBDP) (NAVAREA XII, HYDROPAC and weather).
		8416.5, 12579 kHz, F1B.	0730, 1330.	Maritime Safety Information (MSI) (HF NBDP) (NAVAREA XII, HYDROPAC and weather).
		6501, 8764 kHz, J3E.	0600, 1200.	Maritime Safety Information (MSI).
		8764, 13089 kHz, J3E.	0005, 1800.	Maritime Safety Information (MSI).
		2670 kHz, J3E.	0545, 1145, 1745, 2345.	Local Notice to Mariners.
		Ch. 22A, F3E.	0500, 0900, 1700, 2100.	Local Notice to Mariners and weather.
		518 kHz, F1B.	0040, 0440, 0840, 1240, 1640, 2040.	NAVTEX [O].
3703.5	Honolulu, HI (KVM70).	9982.5 kHz, F3C.	1132.	Weather FAX*; 120/576.
		11090 kHz, F3C.	0533, 1132, 1733.	Weather FAX*; 120/576.
		16135 kHz, F3C.	0533, 1733, 2320.	Weather FAX*; 120/576.
		23331.5 kHz, F3C.	2320.	Weather FAX*; 120/576.
	*NOTE: Broadcast schedule at 1132, 2320.			
		MAURITIUS		
3710	Mauritius (3BM).	518 kHz, F1B.	0020, 0420, 0820, 1220, 1620, 2020.	NAVTEX [C].

RADIO NAVIGATIONAL WARNINGS

(1) No.	(2) Name	(3) Frequency	(4) Times	(5) Nature of Broadcast
3710.5	Port Louis (3BB).	4402 kHz, J3E.	0115, 0730, 1315, 1930.	Weather.
		4402 kHz, J3E.	0433, 1233, 1603.	Local navigational warnings.
		Ch. 14, F3E.	0205, 1405.	Weather.
		REUNION		
3711	Reunion (COSRU) (MRCC).	2600 kHz, J3E.	0430, 1000, 1230.	Weather in French.
		2600 kHz, J3E.	0430, 1000.	Local navigational warnings in French.
		Ch. 79, F3E.	0315, 0330, 0345, 0400, 0545, 0600, 0615, 0630, 0900, 0915, 0930, 0945, 1100, 1115, 1130, 1145, 1400, 1415, 1430, 1445, 1600, 1615, 1630, 1645.	Local navigational warnings and weather in French.
		EGYPT - RED SEA		
3713.2	Quseir.	518 kHz, F1B.	0330, 0730, 1130, 1530, 1930, 2330.	NAVTEX [V].
3713.4	Ismailia (Serapeum) (SUZ).	4209.5 kHz, F1B.	0750, 1150.	NAVTEX [X].
		518 kHz, F1B.	0350, 0750, 1150, 1550, 1950, 2350.	NAVTEX [X] (Red Sea and Gulf of Suez broadcasts).
		SAUDI ARABIA - RED SEA		
3713.6	Jiddah.	1726 kHz, J3E.	0333, 0733, 1133, 1533, 1933, 2333.	Local navigational warnings.
		1726 kHz, J3E.	0503, 0533, 1133, 1703, 1733, 2333.	Weather.
		518 kHz, F1B.	0110, 0510, 0910, 1310, 1710, 2110.	NAVTEX [H].
		OMAN		
3713.8	Muscat.	518 kHz, F1B.	0200, 0600, 1000, 1400, 1800, 2200.	NAVTEX [M].
		QATAR		
3713.9	Doha.	2768 kHz, J3E, Ch. 24, F3E.	0433, 0833, 1233, 1633.	Local navigational warnings and weather.
		2768 kHz, J3E, Ch. 24, F3E.	0503, 1003, 1603.	Weather.
		SAUDI ARABIA - PERSIAN GULF		
	LOCAL WARNINGS: MENAS: Original reports to Middle Eastern Navigational Service, P.O. Box 66, Manama, Bahrain.			
3714.2	Dammam.	518 kHz, F1B.	0100, 0500, 0900, 1300, 1700, 2100.	NAVTEX [G].
		IRAN		
3715	Bandar Khomeyni (EQN).	Ch. 18, F3E.	0530, 1230.	Local navigational warnings and weather.
3715.1	Bushehr (EQM).	Ch. 18, F3E.	0530, 1230.	Local navigational warnings and weather.
		518 kHz, F1B.	0000, 0400, 0800, 1200, 1600, 2000.	NAVTEX [A].

RADIO NAVIGATIONAL WARNINGS

(1) No.	(2) Name	(3) Frequency	(4) Times	(5) Nature of Broadcast
3715.2	Bandar Abbas (EQI).	460, 8469 kHz, A1A.	0530, 1230.	Local navigational warnings and weather.
		Ch. 18, F3E.	0530, 1230.	Local navigational warnings.
		4210 kHz, F1B.	0730, 1430.	Maritime Safety Information (MSI) (HF NBDP).
		8416.5 kHz, F1B.	0330, 0530, 1230.	Maritime Safety Information (MSI) (HF NBDP).
		12579 kHz, F1B.	0830, 1030.	Maritime Safety Information (MSI) (HF NBDP).
		518 kHz, F1B.	0050, 0450, 0850, 1250, 1650, 2050.	NAVTEX [F].
3715.3	Chah Bahar (EQJ).	Ch. 18, F3E.	0530, 1230.	Local navigational warnings and weather.

BAHRAIN

3716	Bahrain.	518 kHz, F1B.	0010, 0410, 0810, 1210, 1610, 2010.	NAVTEX [B].

PAKISTAN

LONG-RANGE WARNINGS:
NAVAREA IX:
Includes the waters of the Red Sea, Persian Gulf, Suez Canal, Gulf of Oman and the Arabian Sea from Somalia to the India-Pakistan frontier. Original reports to Area Coordinator, NAVAREA IX, Hydrographer of the Pakistan Navy, Naval Headquarters, Karachi. The Middle East Navigational Aid Service is Subarea Coordinator.
LOCAL WARNINGS:
For the coast of Pakistan. Original reports to the Hydrographer of the Pakistan Navy.

3720	Karachi (ASK).	500 kHz, A2A.	0030, 0430, 1230, 2030.	Local navigational warnings and weather.
		466, 484, 13024 kHz, A1A, 500 kHz, A2A.	0830.	Local navigational warnings and weather (weather only on 484 kHz).
		466, 484, 8694 kHz, A1A, 500 kHz, A2A.	1630.	Local navigational warnings and weather (weather only on 484 kHz).
		500 kHz, A2A.	Every hour +00m.	Weather.
		518 kHz, F1B.	0230, 0630, 1030, 1430, 1830, 2230.	NAVTEX [P].
3721	Karachi Naval (AQP).	2457.5, 6390, 8490, 13011, 17093.6 kHz, A1A.	0400, 1200.	NAVAREA IX.
		2457.5, 6390, 8490, 13011, 17093.6 kHz, A1A.	0200, 0600, 1000, 1400, 1800, 2200.	Navigational warnings and weather.

INDIA

LONG-RANGE WARNINGS:
NAVAREA VIII:
Includes the waters of the Indian Ocean from 10°30'S on the African coast to 55°E, thence south to 30°S and east to 95°E. Original reports to NAVAREA VIII Coordinator, Chief Hydrographer to the Government of India, Dehra Dun.

3722	Bombay Naval (VTG).	2072, 4268, 6467, 8634, 12808.5, 16938, 22378 kHz, A1A.	0500, 0900, 1500.	NAVAREA VIII.
		2072, 4268, 6467, 8634, 12808.5, 16938, 22378 kHz, A1A.	1215 (Sun.).	NAVAREA VIII.
		4268, 8634, 12808.5, 16938, 22378 kHz, A1A.	0900.	Weather.
		2072, 4268, 6467, 8634, 12808.5 kHz, A1A.	1500.	Weather.

RADIO NAVIGATIONAL WARNINGS

(1) No.	(2) Name	(3) Frequency	(4) Times	(5) Nature of Broadcast
3722.05	Bombay (VWB).	521, 8630, 12710 kHz, A1A.	0648, 1548.	Local navigational warnings.
		521, 8630, 12710 kHz, A1A.	0420, 0820, 1220, 1620, 2020, 2320.	Weather.
		500 kHz, A2A, 8630, 12710 kHz, A1A.	0448, 0848, 1248, 1648, 2048, 2348.	Weather.
		521 kHz, A1A.	0618, 0848, 1518, 1648.	Weather.
		500 kHz, A2A, 8630, 12710 kHz, A1A.	Every hour +00m.	Weather.
		518 kHz, F1B.	0100, 0500, 0900, 1300, 1700, 2100.	NAVTEX [G].
3722.1	Vishakhapatnam (VWV).	474 kHz, A1A.	0548, 1548.	Local navigational warnings.
		474, 500 kHz, A1A.	0050, 0550, 0950, 1350, 1850, 2150.	Weather.
		474 kHz, A1A.	Every hour +00m.	Weather.
3722.2	Vishakhapatnam Naval (VTP).	2295, 4238, 6418, 8646, 12840, 16695 kHz, A1A.	0500, 0900, 1500.	NAVAREA VIII.
		2295, 4238, 6418, 8646, 12840, 16695 kHz, A1A.	1215 (Sun.).	NAVAREA VIII.
3723	Kandla (VWK).	440 kHz, A1A.	0648, 1548.	Local navigational warnings.
		440 kHz, A1A.	0420, 0820, 1220, 1620, 2020, 2320.	Weather.
		440 kHz, A1A.	Every hour +00m.	Weather.
3725	Ratnagiri (VWZ).	420.5 kHz, A1A.	0648, 1548.	Local navigational warnings.
		420.5 kHz, A1A.	0420, 0820, 1220, 1620, 2020, 2320.	Weather.
		420.5 kHz, A1A.	Every hour +00m.	Weather.
3726	Goa (VWG).	417.5 kHz, A1A.	0648, 1548.	Local navigational warnings.
		417.5 kHz, A1A.	0420, 0820, 1220, 1620, 2020, 2320.	Weather.
		417.5 kHz, A1A.	Every hour +00m.	Weather.
3727	Mangalore (VWL).	438 kHz, A1A.	0648, 1548.	Local navigational warnings.
		438 kHz, A1A.	0420, 0820, 1220, 1620, 2020, 2320.	Weather.
		438 kHz, A1A.	Every hour +00m.	Weather.
3728	Cochin (VWN).	460 kHz, A1A.	0648, 1548.	Local navigational warnings.
		460 kHz, A1A.	0420, 0820, 1220, 1620, 2020, 2320.	Weather.
		460 kHz, A1A.	Every hour +00m.	Weather.
3728.1	Tuticorin (VWT).	487 kHz, A1A.	0648, 1548.	Local navigational warnings.
		487 kHz, A1A.	0050, 0550, 0950, 1350, 1850, 2150.	Weather.
		487 kHz, A1A.	Every hour +00m.	Weather.

RADIO NAVIGATIONAL WARNINGS

(1) No.	(2) Name	(3) Frequency	(4) Times	(5) Nature of Broadcast
3728.2	Madras (VWM).	515 kHz, A1A.	0548, 1548.	Local navigational warnings.
		515 kHz, A1A.	0050, 0550, 0950, 1350, 1850, 2150.	Weather.
		500 kHz, A2A, 4301, 8674.4 kHz, A1A.	0050, 1350, 1850, 2150.	Weather.
		500 kHz, A2A, 8674.4, 12718.5 kHz, A1A.	0550, 0950.	Weather.
		500 kHz, A2A.	Every hour +00m.	Weather.
		518 kHz, F1B.	0230, 0630, 1030, 1430, 1830, 2230.	NAVTEX [P].
3728.3	Calcutta (VWC).	470, 8526 kHz, A1A.	0548.	Local navigational warnings.
		470, 4286 kHz, A1A.	1548.	Local navigational warnings.
		500 kHz, A2A, 8526 kHz, A1A.	0018, 0518, 0848, 1318, 1818, 2118.	Weather.
		470 kHz, A1A.	0050, 0550, 0950, 1350, 1850, 2150.	Weather.
		470 kHz, A1A.	0848, 0918, 1418, 1818.	Weather.
		4286 kHz, A1A.	1818.	Weather.
		500 kHz, A2A, 8526 kHz, A1A.	Every hour +00m.	Weather.
3729	Port Blair (VWP).	442 kHz, A1A.	0548, 1548.	Local navigational warnings.
		442 kHz, A1A.	0100, 0600, 1000, 1400, 1900, 2200.	Weather.
		442 kHz, A1A.	Every hour +00m.	Weather.
	SRI LANKA			
3730	Colombo (4PB).	482 kHz, A1A, A2A, 8473 kHz, A1A.	0600, 0900, 1330.	Local navigational warnings.
		482 kHz, A1A, A2A, 8473 kHz, A1A.	0530, 0600, 1300, 1330.	Weather.
	BANGLADESH			
3731	Chittagong (S3D).	466, 484, 500 kHz, A1A.	0850, 1650.	Local navigational warnings
		466, 484, 500, 8694, 13056 kHz, A1A, 2182 kHz, A3E.	0050, 0450, 0850, 1250, 1650, 2050.	Weather.
		466, 484, 500, 8694, 13056 kHz, A1A, 2182 kHz, A3E.	Every hour +00m.	Weather.
	BURMA (MYANMAR)			
3733	Rangoon (XYR).	460, 500, 8710 kHz, A1A, A2A.	0500, 0900, 1700.	Local navigational warnings (weather at 0900, 1700).
		460, 500, 8710 kHz, A1A, A2A.	0100, 0500, 1300, 2100.	Weather.
		460, 500, 8710 kHz, A1A, A2A.	Every hour +00m.	Weather.
	MALAYSIA - PENINSULAR			
3734	Pinang.	518 kHz, F1B.	0320, 0720, 1120, 1520, 1920, 2320.	NAVTEX [U].
	SINGAPORE			
3735	Singapore.	Ch. 09, F3E.	0100, 0300, 0500, 0700, 0900, 1100, 1300, 1500, 1700, 1900, 2100, 2300.	Local navigational warnings and weather.
		518 kHz, F1B.	0020, 0420, 0820, 1220, 1620, 2020.	NAVTEX [C].

RADIO NAVIGATIONAL WARNINGS

(1) No.	(2) Name	(3) Frequency	(4) Times	(5) Nature of Broadcast
		THAILAND		
3736	Bangkok.	6765.1, 8743 kHz, J3E.	0000, 0300, 0600, 0900, 1200, 1500, 1800, 2100.	Weather.
		518 kHz, F1B.	0050, 0450, 0850, 1250, 1650, 2050.	NAVTEX [F].
		VIETNAM		
3737	Hai Phong (XVG).	8470 kHz, A1A.	0618, 1018, 1418, 2018.	Local navigational warnings.
		8470 kHz, A1A.	0018, 1218.	Weather.
		8470 kHz, A1A.	Every even hour +18m.	Weather.
		8294 kHz, J3E.	0100, 1300.	Weather in Vietnamese.
		8294 kHz, J3E.	Every odd hour +00m.	Weather in Vietnamese.
3737.5	Da Nang (XVT).	8294 kHz, J3E.	0030, 1230.	Weather in Vietnamese.
		518 kHz, F1B.	0140, 0540, 0940, 1340, 1740, 2140.	NAVTEX [K].
3738	Ho Chi Minh Ville (XVS).	8590 kHz, A1A.	0018, 0418, 0818, 1218.	Local navigational warnings.
		8590 kHz, A1A.	0048, 1148.	Weather.
		8590 kHz, A1A.	Every odd hour +48m.	Weather.
		8294 kHz, J3E.	0200, 1200.	Weather in Vietnamese.
		8294 kHz, J3E.	Every even hour +00m.	Weather in Vietnamese.
		518 kHz, F1B.	0350, 0750, 1150, 1550, 1950, 2350.	NAVTEX [X].
		HONG KONG (CHINA)		
3739	Hong Kong.	518 kHz, F1B.	0150, 0550, 0950, 1350, 1750, 2150.	NAVTEX [L].
		CHINA		
3740	Guangzhou (XSQ).	445, 4288, 6382, 8458, 12973 kHz, A1A.	0248, 0548, 0848, 1148, 1748, 2048, 2348.	Local navigational warnings.
		445, 6382, 8458, 12973 kHz, A1A.	0230, 0730.	Local navigational warnings in Chinese.
		445, 4288, 8458, 12973 kHz, A1A.	1400.	Local navigational warnings in Chinese.
		6316, 8435, 16880, 22420 kHz, F1B.	0200, 0630.	Local navigational warnings in Chinese.
		4212, 8435, 12613, 16880 kHz, F1B.	1330.	Local navigational warnings in Chinese
		445, 6382, 8458, 12973 kHz, A1A.	0700.	Local navigational warnings.
		445, 6382, 8458, 12973 kHz, A1A.	0030.	Weather.
		445, 4288, 8458, 12973 kHz, A1A.	1230.	Weather.
		445, 6382, 8458, 12973 kHz, A1A.	0100.	Weather in Chinese.
		445, 4288, 8458, 12973 kHz, A1A.	1300.	Weather in Chinese.
		445, 4288, 6382, 8458, 12973 kHz, A1A.	0248, 0448, 1048, 1448, 1648, 2048, 2248.	Weather.
		518 kHz, F1B.	0210, 0610, 1010, 1410, 2210.	NAVTEX [N].

RADIO NAVIGATIONAL WARNINGS

(1) No.	(2) Name	(3) Frequency	(4) Times	(5) Nature of Broadcast
3740.1	Sanya (XSI).	518 kHz, F1B.	0200, 0600, 1000, 1400, 2200.	NAVTEX [M].
3740.2	Tianjin (XSV).	445, 8600 kHz, A1A.	Every even hour +18m.	Local navigational warnings.
		445, 8600, 12969 kHz, A1A.	0600, 2200.	Ice.
		445, 4283, 8600, 12969 kHz, A1A.	1300.	Ice.
3740.3	Dalian (XSZ).	462 kHz, A1A, A2A, 6333.5, 8694 kHz, A1A.	0050, 1050.	Weather.
		518 kHz, F1B.	0250, 0650, 1050, 1450, 2250.	NAVTEX [R].
3740.4	Fuzhou (XSL).	518 kHz, F1B.	0220, 0620, 1020, 1420, 2220.	NAVTEX [O].
3741	Shanghai (XSG).	522.5, 4290, 6454, 8487, 12954, 17002.4 kHz, A1A.	0200.	Local navigational warnings.
		522.5, 4290, 6454, 8487, 12954, 17002.4 kHz, A1A.	0300, 0900.	Weather.
		458 kHz, A1A, A2A, 522.5, 4290, 6454, 8487, 12954 kHz, A1A.	0000, 0300, 0500, 0900, 1200, 1500, 1800, 2100.	Weather.
		518 kHz, F1B.	0240, 0640, 1040, 1440, 2240.	NAVTEX [Q].
			REPUBLIC OF KOREA	
3742	Inchon (HLC).	2284 kHz, A3E.	0003.	Local navigational warnings.
3742.5	Cheju (HLE).	2299, 2583 kHz, J3E.	0902, 1702.	Local navigational warnings.
3743	Mokpo (HLM).	470 kHz, A2A.	0018, 0818.	Local navigational warnings and weather.
3744	Kunsan (HLN).	484 kHz, A2A.	0018, 0818.	Local navigational warnings and weather.
		2507 kHz, A3E.	0403.	Local navigational warnings.
3744.5	Pyonsan.	490 kHz, F1B.	0140, 0540, 0940, 1340, 1740, 2140.	NAVTEX [K] in Korean.
		518 kHz, F1B.	0340, 0740, 1140, 1540, 1940, 2340.	NAVTEX [W].
3745	Kangnung (HLK).	476 kHz, A2A.	0018, 0818.	Local navigational warnings and weather.
		2836 kHz, J3E.	0903.	Local navigational warnings.
3746	Busan (HLP).	434 kHz, A2A.	0018, 0818.	Local navigational warnings and weather.
3746.5	Chukpyon.	490 kHz, F1B.	0130, 0530, 0930, 1330, 1730, 2130.	NAVTEX [J] in Korean.
		518 kHz, F1B.	0330, 0730, 1130, 1530, 1930, 2330.	NAVTEX [V].
3747	Ullung (HLU).	458 kHz, A2A.	0018, 0818.	Local navigational warnings and weather.
3747.5	Yeosu (HLY).	447 kHz, A2A.	0018, 0818.	Local navigational warnings and weather.

RADIO NAVIGATIONAL WARNINGS

(1) No.	(2) Name	(3) Frequency	(4) Times	(5) Nature of Broadcast

RUSSIA - PACIFIC

LONG-RANGE WARNINGS:
NAVAREA XIII:
Includes the waters of the Sea of Okhotsk, North Pacifi and Bering Sea north of 45°N and east to the International Date Line. Original reports to NAVAREA XIII Coordinator, Chief, Head Department of Navigation and Oceanography, St. Petersburg.
NAVIP:
World-wide navigational warnings.
LOCAL WARNINGS:
PRIP.

No.	Name	Frequency	Times	Nature of Broadcast
3748	Vladivostok (UFL).	3165, 8595, 12729 kHz, F1B.	1100, 2300.	NAVAREA XIII, local navigational warnings, and weather.
		3165, 8595, 12729 kHz, F1B.	1130, 2330.	NAVAREA XIII, local navigational warnings, and weather in Russian.
		17175.2 kHz, F1B.	2330.	NAVAREA XIII, local navigational warnings, and weather in Russian.
		518 kHz, F1B	0000, 0400, 0800, 1200, 1600, 2000.	NAVTEX [A].
3749.5	Petropavlovsk-Kamchatskiy (UBE).	4323, 6360.5, 12603 kHz, F1B.	2200.	NAVIP and NAVAREA XIII warnings in Russian.
		518 kHz, F1B.	0020, 0420, 0820, 1220, 1620, 2020.	NAVTEX [C].
3750	Kholmsk.	518 kHz, F1B.	0010, 0410, 0810, 1210, 1610, 2010.	NAVTEX [B].
3751	Magadan.	2400 kHz, J3E.	0203, 1233.	Weather in Russian.
		2400 kHz, J3E.	1303.	Local navigational warnings in Russian.
		518 kHz, F1B.	0030, 0430, 0830, 1230, 1630, 2030.	NAVTEX [D].
3751.5	Okhotsk.	518 kHz, F1B.	0100, 0500, 0900, 1300, 1700, 2100.	NAVTEX [G].

JAPAN

LONG-RANGE WARNINGS:
NAVAREA XI:
Includes the waters of the western North Pacifi from the Equator to 45°N, east to 180°. Original reports to NAVAREA XI Coordinator, Chief Hydrographer, Japan Coast Guard, Tokyo.
Maritime Safety Information broadcasts--Storm warnings, weather messages and navigational warnings are announced by Japan Coast Guard (JCG) CRS on VHF Ch. 16, before being broadcast on the scheduled VHF channel number.

No.	Name	Frequency	Times	Nature of Broadcast
3753	Kushiro (JNX).	Ch. 12, F3E.	0103, 0125, 0703, 0725.	Local navigational warnings.
		424 kHz, F1B.	0108, 0508, 0908, 1308, 1708, 2108.	NAVTEX [K] in Japanese.
		518 kHz, F1B.	0140, 0540, 0940, 1340, 1740, 2140.	NAVTEX [K].
3754	Shiogama (JNN).	Ch. 12, F3E.	0125, 0133, 0725, 0733.	Local navigational warnings.
3756	Tokyo (JMH).	3622.5, 7305, 13597, 18220 kHz, F3C.	Continuous.	Weather FAX*; 120/576.
		3622.5, 7305, 13597, 18220 kHz, F3C.	0130 (Wed., Sat.), 1019 (Tue., Fri.).	Ice FAX; 120/576.
	*NOTE: Broadcast schedule at 0340.			
3757	Yokohama (JGC).	Ch. 12, F3E.	0120, 0720.	Local navigational warnings.
		424 kHz, F1B.	0034, 0434, 0834, 1234, 1634, 2034.	NAVTEX [I] in Japanese.
		518 kHz, F1B.	0120, 0520, 0920, 1320, 1720, 2120.	NAVTEX [I].
3760	Nagoya (JNT).	Ch. 12, F3E.	0110, 0710.	Local navigational warnings.
3764	Kobe (JGD).	Ch. 12, F3E.	0133, 0733.	Local navigational warnings.

RADIO NAVIGATIONAL WARNINGS

(1) No.	(2) Name	(3) Frequency	(4) Times	(5) Nature of Broadcast
3766	Hiroshima (JNE).	Ch. 12, F3E.	0115, 0715.	Local navigational warnings.
3767	Kagoshima (JNJ).	Ch. 12, F3E.	0120, 0720.	Local navigational warnings.
3769	Ishigaki (JNG).	Ch. 12, F3E.	0133, 0733.	Local navigational warnings.
3772	Tanabe (JNH).	Ch. 12, F3E.	0103, 0703.	Local navigational warnings.
3772.2	Kochi (JNO).	Ch. 12, F3E.	0125, 0725.	Local navigational warnings.
3772.4	Moji (JNR).	Ch. 12, F3E.	0103, 0703.	Local navigational warnings.
		424 kHz, F1B.	0017, 0417, 0817, 1217, 1617, 2017.	NAVTEX [H] in Japanese.
		518 kHz, F1B.	0110, 0510, 0910, 1310, 1710, 2110.	NAVTEX [H].
3772.5	Sasebo (JNK).	Ch. 12, F3E.	0115, 0715.	Local navigational warnings.
3772.8	Niigata (JNV).	Ch. 12, F3E.	0115, 0715.	Local navigational warnings.
3773	Maizuru (JNC).	Ch. 12, F3E.	0120, 0720.	Local navigational warnings.
3775	Otaru (JNL).	Ch. 12, F3E.	0110, 0133, 0710, 0733.	Local navigational warnings.
		424 kHz, F1B.	0051, 0451, 0851, 1251, 1651, 2051.	NAVTEX [J] in Japanese.
		518 kHz, F1B.	0130, 0530, 0930, 1330, 1730, 2130.	NAVTEX [J].
3777	Naha (JNB).	Ch. 12, F3E.	0110, 0710.	Local navigational warnings.
		424 kHz, F1B.	0000, 0400, 0800, 1200, 1600, 2000.	NAVTEX [G] in Japanese.
		518 kHz, F1B.	0100, 0500, 0900, 1300, 1700, 2100.	NAVTEX [G].
			TAIWAN	
3785	Chi-lung (XSX).	420, 8445, 8506 kHz, A1A, 8428* kHz, F1B.	0430, 1030, 1630, 2230.	Weather.
		438 kHz, A1A.	Every even hour +18m, +48m.	Local navigational warnings.
		490, 4209.5 kHz, F1B.	0330, 0730, 1130, 1530, 1930, 2330.	NAVTEX [V] in Chinese.
		490, 4209.5 kHz, F1B.	0350, 0750, 1150, 1550, 1950, 2350.	NAVTEX [X] in Chinese.
		518, 4209.5 kHz, F1B.	0230, 0630, 1030, 1430, 1830, 2230.	NAVTEX [P].
	*NOTE: Broadcast announced through DSC 8414.5 kHz.			
3787	Hua-lien (XSY).	523, 8546, 8700 kHz, A1A.	Every even hour +18m, +48m.	Local navigational warnings.
		523, 8546, 8700 kHz, A1A.	0530, 1130, 1730, 2330.	Weather.
3790	Kao-Hsiung (XSW).	448, 8582, 8632 kHz, A1A.	Every odd hour +18m, +48m.	Local navigational warnings.
		448, 8582, 8632 kHz, A1A.	0500, 1100, 1700, 2300.	Weather.
3790.5	Tai-Chung (XSW2).	476, 8511 kHz, A1A.	Every even hour +18m, +48m.	Local navigational warnings.

RADIO NAVIGATIONAL WARNINGS

(1) No.	(2) Name	(3) Frequency	(4) Times	(5) Nature of Broadcast
		PHILIPPINES		
3792	Polo (DZCA).	1170 kHz, A3E.	0030, 0930.	Local navigational warnings.
3792.5	Caloocan (DWWW).	630 kHz, A3E.	0900, 2100.	Local navigational warnings.
3793	Malolos (DZRP).	918 kHz, A3E.	0000, 1200, 1400, 2000.	Local navigational warnings.
3794	Valenzuela (DZFM).	738 kHz, A3E.	0900, 2100.	Local navigational warnings.
3795	Manila (DZS-4).	8776.8 kHz, A3E.	0030, 0330, 0630, 0930, 1230.	Local navigational warnings and weather.
		Ch. 09, 16, 20, F3E.	0030, 0330, 0630, 0930, 1230.	Weather.
3795.5	Mandaluyong (DWAD).	1098 kHz, A3E.	0900, 2100.	Local navigational warnings.
3796	Lucena (DZLT).	1188 kHz, A3E.	1030, 2230.	Local navigational warnings.
3797	Laoag (DZJC).	900 kHz, A3E.	0900, 2100.	Local navigational warnings.
3798	Puerto Princesa (DYPR).	783 kHz, A3E.	0900, 2100.	Local navigational warnings.
3799	Davao (DXMC).	819 kHz, A3E.	1030, 2230.	Local navigational warnings.
3801	Iloilo (DYRP).	1017 kHz, A3E.	1030, 2230.	Local navigational warnings.
3802	Daet (DZMD).	1161 kHz, A3E.	1030, 2230.	Local navigational warnings.
		MALAYSIA - SABAH		
3803	Sandakan.	518 kHz, F1B.	0300, 0700, 1100, 1500, 1900, 2300.	NAVTEX [S].
		MALAYSIA - SARAWAK		
3805	Miri.	518 kHz, F1B.	0310, 0710, 1110, 1510, 1910, 2310.	NAVTEX [T].
		INDONESIA - SUMATERA		
3816	Dumai (PKP).	448, 500 kHz, A1A.	Continuous.	Local navigational warnings.
		6337 kHz, A1A.	0400, 0800, 1200.	Local navigational warnings.
		8457 kHz, A1A.	0100, 0600, 1000, 1300.	Local navigational warnings.
		12682.5 kHz, A1A.	0230, 0700.	Local navigational warnings.
		17184.8 kHz, A1A.	0500, 0900.	Local navigational warnings.
		2182, 3180, 6215.5, 6515.7 kHz, R3E.	Continuous.	Local navigational warnings.
		8765.4 kHz, R3E.	0100, 0800.	Local navigational warnings.
		13125.6 kHz, R3E.	0400, 1000.	Local navigational warnings.

RADIO NAVIGATIONAL WARNINGS

(1) No.	(2) Name	(3) Frequency	(4) Times	(5) Nature of Broadcast
3817	Belawan (PKB).	474, 500 kHz, A1A.	Continuous.	Local navigational warnings.
		4295 kHz, A1A.	0100, 0400, 0700, 1500.	Local navigational warnings.
		8686 kHz, A1A.	0300, 0600, 0900, 1230.	Local navigational warnings.
		12970.5 kHz, A1A.	0000, 0600.	Local navigational warnings.
		16861.7 kHz, A1A.	0200, 1100.	Local navigational warnings.
		2182, 3180, 6215.5 kHz, R3E.	Continuous.	Local navigational warnings.
		6515.7 kHz, R3E.	0730.	Local navigational warnings.
		8746.8 kHz, R3E.	0300, 0930.	Local navigational warnings.
3819	Palembang (PKC).	448, 500 kHz, A1A.	0000.	Local navigational warnings.
		6491.5 kHz, A1A.	0000, 0500, 0800, 1230.	Local navigational warnings.
		8437 kHz, A1A.	0100, 0500, 0900, 1130.	Local navigational warnings.
		2182, 2690 kHz, R3E.	0230, 0430, 0700, 1200.	Local navigational warnings.
		6215.5 kHz, R3E.	0100, 0500, 0900, 1300.	Local navigational warnings.
		8808.8 kHz, R3E.	0200, 0600, 1000.	Local navigational warnings.
		**INDONESIA - JAVA**		
3820	Jakarta (PKX).	470, 500 kHz, A1A.	Continuous.	Local navigational warnings.
		8542, 12970.5 kHz, A1A.	0200, 1000, 1800.	Local navigational warnings.
		16861.7 kHz, A1A.	0400, 1200, 2000.	Local navigational warnings.
		22431 kHz, A1A.	0000, 0600, 1400, 2200.	Local navigational warnings.
		2182, 2690, 6215.5, 6506.4, 6218.6 kHz, R3E.	Continuous.	Local navigational warnings.
		8753, 13128.7 kHz, R3E.	0000.	Local navigational warnings.
		22698.3 kHz, R3E.	2000.	Local navigational warnings.
		8542, 12970.5 kHz, A1A, 2690 kHz, R3E.	1100.	Weather.
		518 kHz, F1B.	0040, 0440, 0840, 1240, 1640, 2040.	NAVTEX [E].
3824	Surabaya (PKD).	430, 500 kHz, A1A.	Continuous.	Local navigational warnings.
		4238 kHz, A1A.	0230.	Local navigational warnings.
		8461 kHz, A1A.	0200, 0730.	Local navigational warnings.
		12704.5 kHz, A1A.	0000, 1100.	Local navigational warnings.
		16861.7 kHz, A1A.	0100, 1000.	Local navigational warnings.
		2182 kHz, R3E.	Continuous.	Local navigational warnings.
		4379.5, 6215.5 kHz, R3E.	0000.	Local navigational warnings.
		8796.4 kHz, R3E.	0100, 0630, 0900.	Local navigational warnings.
		13134.9 kHz, R3E.	0100, 0500, 1000.	Local navigational warnings.

RADIO NAVIGATIONAL WARNINGS

(1) No.	(2) Name	(3) Frequency	(4) Times	(5) Nature of Broadcast
		INDONESIA - SULAWESI		
3830	Makasar (PKF).	465, 500 kHz, A1A.	Continuous.	Local navigational warnings.
		4295 kHz, A1A.	0200, 0900.	Local navigational warnings.
		8686 kHz, A1A.	0100, 0400, 0630, 1030, 1200.	Local navigational warnings.
		12682.5 kHz, A1A.	0430, 1000, 1230.	Local navigational warnings.
		4397.7 kHz, R3E.	0030, 0300.	Local navigational warnings.
		6215.5 kHz, R3E.	0330, 1100.	Local navigational warnings.
		8802.6 kHz, R3E.	0000, 0600.	Local navigational warnings.
		13100.8 kHz, R3E.	0730, 1330.	Local navigational warnings.
		518 kHz, F1B.	0030, 0430, 0830, 1230, 1630, 2030.	NAVTEX [D].
3832	Bitung (PKM).	438, 500 kHz, A1A.	Continuous.	Local navigational warnings.
		6428.5 kHz, A1A.	0600, 1100.	Local navigational warnings.
		8694 kHz, A1A.	0100, 0500, 0900, 1300.	Local navigational warnings.
		12704.5 kHz, A1A.	0200, 1000, 1400.	Local navigational warnings.
		2182, 2690 kHz, R3E.	0000, 0400, 0800, 1200, 1400.	Local navigational warnings.
		2182 kHz, R3E.	1000.	Local navigational warnings.
		6215.5 kHz, R3E.	0100, 0500, 0900, 2000.	Local navigational warnings.
		8808.8 kHz, R3E.	0230, 0700, 1100.	Local navigational warnings.
		INDONESIA - MOLUCCAS		
3836	Amboina (PKE).	470, 500 kHz, A1A.	Continuous.	Local navigational warnings.
		8473 kHz, A1A.	0200, 0900.	Local navigational warnings.
		12682.5 kHz, A1A.	0000, 0800.	Local navigational warnings.
		17184.8 kHz, A1A.	0600, 1200.	Local navigational warnings.
		2182, 2690 kHz, R3E.	0000.	Local navigational warnings.
		6215 kHz, R3E.	0700, 1200.	Local navigational warnings.
		8794 kHz, R3E.	0300, 2300.	Local navigational warnings.
		518 kHz, F1B.	0010, 0410, 0810, 1210, 1610, 2010.	NAVTEX [B].

RADIO NAVIGATIONAL WARNINGS

(1) No.	(2) Name	(3) Frequency	(4) Times	(5) Nature of Broadcast
		INDONESIA - IRIAN JAYA		
3840	Jayapura (PNK).	465, 500 kHz, A1A.	2200, 0000 (Mon.-Sat.), 0000, 0700 (Sun., hol.).	Local navigational warnings.
		8694 kHz, A1A.	0000, 0300 (Mon.-Sat.), 0000, 0700 (Sun., hol.).	Local navigational warnings.
		12682.5 kHz, A1A.	0100, 0530, 0900 (Mon.-Sat.), 0100, 0900 (Sun., hol.).	Local navigational warnings.
		17074.4 kHz, A1A.	0200, 0700 (Mon.-Sat.), 0200 (Sun., hol.).	Local navigational warnings.
		2182 kHz, R3E.	2200, 0000.	Local navigational warnings.
		3180 kHz, R3E.	2200, 0000 (Mon.-Sat.), 0200 (Sun., hol.).	Local navigational warnings.
		6215.5 kHz, R3E.	2200 (Mon.-Sat.), 2300, 0700 (Sun., hol.).	Local navigational warnings.
		6227 kHz, R3E.	2200, 0000, 0700 (Mon.-Sat.), 0000, 0700, 0900 (Sun., hol.).	Local navigational warnings.
		6510 kHz, R3E.	2200, 0000, 0700.	Local navigational warnings.
		8800 kHz, R3E.	0100, 0400, 0700, 1000 (Mon.-Sat.), 0200, 0800 (Sun., hol.).	Local navigational warnings.
		13110 kHz, R3E.	0000, 0300, 0600, 0900.	Local navigational warnings.
		518 kHz, F1B.	0000, 0400, 0800, 1200, 1600, 2000.	NAVTEX [A].
		PAPUA NEW GUINEA		
3866	Port Moresby (P2M).	484 kHz, A2A, 6351.5, 13042 kHz, A1A.	0100, 0900.	Local navigational warnings and weather.
		4407, 6515.7 kHz, J3E.	0603, 2203.	Local navigational warnings and weather.
		484 kHz, A2A, 6351.5, 13042 kHz, A1A.	Every odd hour +00m.	Weather.
		4407, 6515.7 kHz, J3E.	Every even hour +03m.	Weather.
		AUSTRALIA		

LONG-RANGE WARNINGS:
NAVAREA X:
Includes the waters surrounding Australia and the Solomon Islands south to Antarctica bound on the west by 80°E and on the east by 170°E south to the Tasman Sea and 160°E south to Antarctica. Original reports to RCC Australia, through any Australian Coast Radio Station (CRS).
LOCAL WARNINGS:
AUSCOAST:
Original reports to RCC Australia.

(1)	(2)	(3)	(4)	(5)
3876	Cairns.	8176 kHz, J3E.	1257, 2357.	Maritime Safety Information (MSI).
		Ch. 81, F3E.	0145, 0345, 0545, 0745, 1945, 2145, 2345.	Weather.
3876.5	Gladstone.	8176 kHz, J3E.	1157, 2257.	Maritime Safety Information (MSI).
3877	Penta Comstat, Firefly (VZX).	4483, 6522, 8713 kHz, J3E.	0625, 2125.	Weather.
		6522, 8713 kHz, J3E.	0635, 2135.	Local navigational warnings and weather.
		8713, 13176 kHz, J3E.	0700, 2200.	Weather.
		8713, 13176, 17365, 22822 kHz, J3E.	0700, 2200.	NAVAREA X warnings.
3882	Sydney.	8176 kHz, J3E.	0057, 1357.	Maritime Safety Information (MSI).
		Ch. 67, F3E.	0733, 2133.	Local navigational warnings and weather.

RADIO NAVIGATIONAL WARNINGS

(1) No.	(2) Name	(3) Frequency	(4) Times	(5) Nature of Broadcast
3883	Melbourne.	8176 kHz, J3E.	0257, 2157.	Maritime Safety Information (MSI).
		Ch. 67, F3E.	0448, 1048, 2248.	Local navigational warnings and weather.
3884	Hobart (VMT-232).	2524, 4620 kHz, J3E, Ch. 67, 68, F3E.	0345, 0903, 2145.	Weather.
		8176 kHz, J3E, Ch. 67, 68, F3E.	0557.	Maritime Safety Information (MSI).
		Ch. 82, F3E.	0803, 2233.	Weather.
3885	Adelaide.	8176 kHz, J3E.	0357, 0757.	Maritime Safety Information (MSI).
3886	Perth.	8176 kHz, J3E.	0657, 1057.	Maritime Safety Information (MSI).
		Ch. 16, 67, F3E.	1118, 2318.	Local navigational warnings and weather.
3892	Port Hedland.	8176 kHz, J3E.	0457, 0857.	Maritime Safety Information (MSI).
3900	Darwin.	8176 kHz, J3E.	0157, 0957.	Maritime Safety Information (MSI).
		Ch. 67, F3E.	0833, 2233.	Weather.
3901	Charleville (VMC).	4426, 8176, 12365, 16546 kHz, J3E.	Every hour +00m (2100-0800), 0030, 0130, 0230, 0330, 0430, 0530, 0630, 0730, 2130, 2230, 2330.	Weather.
		2201, 6507, 8176, 12365 kHz, J3E.	Every hour +00m (0800-2100), 0830, 0930, 1030, 1130, 1230, 1330, 1430, 1530, 1630, 1730, 1830, 1930, 2030.	Weather.
		2628, 5100, 11030, 13920 kHz, F3C.	0900-1900.	Weather FAX*; 120/576.
		5100, 11030, 13920, 20469 kHz, F3C.	1900-0900.	Weather FAX*; 120/576.
	*NOTE: Broadcast schedule at 0015-0045, 1215-1245.			
3902	Wiluna (VMW).	4149, 8113, 12362, 16528 kHz, J3E.	Every hour +00m (2300-1000), 0030, 0130, 0230, 0330, 0430, 0530, 0630, 0730, 0830, 0930, 2330.	Weather.
		2056, 6230, 8113, 12362 kHz, J3E.	Every hour +00m (1000-2300), 1030, 1130, 1230, 1330, 1430, 1530, 1630, 1730, 1830, 1930, 2030, 2130, 2230.	Weather.
		5755, 7535, 10555, 15615 kHz, F3C.	1100-2100.	Weather FAX*; 120/576.
		7535, 10555, 15615, 18060 kHz, F3C.	2100-1100.	Weather FAX*; 120/576.
	*NOTE: Broadcast schedule at 0015-0045, 1215-1245.			

RADIO NAVIGATIONAL WARNINGS

(1) No.	(2) Name	(3) Frequency	(4) Times	(5) Nature of Broadcast

NEW ZEALAND

LONG-RANGE WARNINGS:
NAVAREA XIV:
Includes the waters of the South Pacifi from the Equator to Antarctica bound on the west by 170°E south to the Tasman Sea and 160°E south to Antarctica and bound on the east by 120°W. Original reports to the nearest coast radio station or by mail to NAVAREA XIV Coordinator, Hydrographer, RNZN, Auckland.

No.	Name	Frequency	Times	Nature of Broadcast
3904	Taupo Maritime Radio (ZLM).	2207, 4146, 6224 kHz, J3E.	0133, 0533, 1333, 1733 (1 hr. earlier when daylight savings in effect).	Local navigational warnings and weather.
		6224, 12356 kHz, J3E.	0303, 0903, 1503, 2103 (1 hr. earlier when daylight savings in effect).	NAVAREA XIV and weather.
		8297, 16531 kHz, J3E.	0333, 0933, 1533, 2133 (1 hr. earlier when daylight savings in effect).	NAVAREA XIV and weather.
		2207, 4146, 6224 kHz, J3E.	0803, 1203, 2003 (1 hr. earlier when daylight savings in effect).	Weather.
		Ch. 67, 68, 71, F3E.	0533, 0733, 1033, 1333, 1733, 2133 (1 hr. earlier when daylight savings in effect).	Local navigational warnings and weather.

GUAM

No.	Name	Frequency	Times	Nature of Broadcast
3913	Guam (NRV) U.S. Coast Guard.	12579, 16806.5, 22376 kHz, F1B.	0230, 0500, 0900, 1500, 1900, 2315.	Maritime Safety Information (MSI) (HF NBDP) (HYDROPAC at 0230, 0900).
		2670 kHz, J3E.	0705, 2205.	Local Notice to Mariners and weather.
		13089 kHz, J3E.	0330, 2130.	Maritime Safety Information (MSI).
		6501 kHz, J3E.	0930, 1530.	Maritime Safety Information (MSI).
		Ch. 22A, F3E.	0900, 2100.	Local Notice to Mariners and weather.
		518 kHz, F1B.	0100, 0500, 0900, 1300, 1700, 2100.	NAVTEX [V].

NEW CALEDONIA

No.	Name	Frequency	Times	Nature of Broadcast
3940	Noumea (FJP).	Ch. 23, 24, 25, 26, 28, 82, 83, 87, F3E.	Every hour +03m, +33m.	Weather in French and in English on request.
		Ch. 23, 24, 25, 26, 28, 82, 83, 87, F3E.	0415, 0730, 1930, 2230.	Local navigational warnings and weather in French and in English on request.

FRENCH POLYNESIA

No.	Name	Frequency	Times	Nature of Broadcast
3943	Mahina.	2620, 8805.7 kHz, J3E.	0030, 0230, 1845, 2100.	Local navigational warnings.
		2620 kHz, J3E.	0700, 2200.	Weather in French.
		8805.7 kHz, J3E.	0640, 2100.	Weather in French.

FIJI

No.	Name	Frequency	Times	Nature of Broadcast
3945	Suva (3DP).	4372, 8746 kHz, J3E.	0003, 0403, 0803, 2003.	Local navigational warnings and weather.
		4372, 8746 kHz, J3E.	Every hour +03m.	Weather.

AMERICAN SAMOA

No.	Name	Frequency	Times	Nature of Broadcast
3948	Pago Pago (KUQ).	8585 kHz, A1A.	0000, 0400, 1600, 2000.	Local navigational warnings (weather at 0400, 2000).
		6361 kHz, A1A.	0800.	Local navigational warnings.

TONGA

No.	Name	Frequency	Times	Nature of Broadcast
3949	Nukualofa (A3A).	2080, 6230 kHz, J3E, Ch. 26, F3E.	0135, 0835, 2035.	Local navigational warnings.
		2080, 6230 kHz, J3E, Ch. 26, F3E.	0134, 0834, 2034.	Weather.

RADIO NAVIGATIONAL WARNINGS

**300M. WorldWide Navigational Warning Service
NAVAREA Coordinators**

NAVAREA I (United Kingdom)
The Hydrographer of the Navy
United Kingdom Hydrographic Offic
Admiralty Way
Taunton, Somerset TA1 2DN, United Kingdom
Phone: 44 1823 723316, Fax: 44 1823 322352
E-mail: rnwuser@ukhornw.u-net.com
Website: http://www.hydro.gov.uk

Baltic Sea Sub-Area NAVAREA I (Sweden)
Swedish Maritime Administration
BALTICO
S-601 78 Norrkoping, Sweden
Phone: 46 11 19 10 45
Fax: 46 11 238945 (07-15 UTC)
    46 8 6017969 (15-07 UTC)
Telex: 64320 BALTICO S (07-15 UTC)
    16060 STORDO S (15-07 UTC)
E-mail: ntm.baltico@sjofartsverket.se (07-15)
    baltico@stockholmradio.se (15-07)
Website: http://www.sjofartsverket.se

NAVAREA II (France)
Navarea II Co-ordinator
EPSHOM BREST
13 Rue du Chatellier
BP 30316
29603 Brest Cedex, France
Phone: 33 2 98221667, Fax: 33 2 98221432
E-mail: coord.navarea2@shom.fr
Website: http://www.shom.fr

NAVAREA III (Spain)
Mares Mediterraneo y Negro
Instituto Hidrográfico de la Marin
Plaza San Severiano, 3
11007 Cadiz, Spain
Phone: 34 956 599 409 (HJ)
    34 956 599 409 (H24)
Fax: 34 956 599 396
Telex: 76147 MEDCO E
    76102 MARIH E
E-mail: ihmesp@retemail.es (Not for Warnings)
Website: none

NAVAREA IV and XII (United States)
National Geospatial-Intelligence Agency
Attn: PVM (Mail Stop D-44)
4600 Sangamore Road
Bethesda, Maryland 20816-5003
Phone: (1) 301-227-3147, Fax: (1) 301-227-3731
Telex: 898334/EASYLINK MBS 62554950
E-mail: navsafety@nga.mil
Website: http://pollux.nss.nga.mil

NAVAREA V (Brazil)
Diretoria de Hidrografia e N vegaçao
Rua Barao de Jaceguay S/N°
Ponta da Armaçao
24048-900 Niteroi - RJ, Brazil
Phone: 55 21 2620 0073/2613 8210
Fax: 55 21 2620 7291/2613 8210
E-mail: 331@chm.mar.mil.br
Website: http://www.dhn.mar.mil.br

NAVAREA VI (Argentina)
Servicio de Hidrografia N val
Avenida Montes de Oca 2124
C 1270ABV Buenos Aires, Argentina
Phone: 54 11 4301 2249/0061/0067
Fax: 54 11 4303 2299/4301 2249
E-mail: snautica@hidro.gov.ar
Website: http://www.hidro.gov.ar

NAVAREA VII (Republic of South Africa)
Hydrographic Offic
Private Bag X1, Tokai
7966 Cape Town, South Africa
Phone: 27 21 787 2445/2444, Fax: 27 21 787 2228
E-mail: hydrosan@iafrica.com
Website: http://www.sanho.co.za

NAVAREA VIII (India)
National Hydrographic Offic
Post Box No. 75
107-A Rajpur Road
Dehradun 248001, India
Phone: 91 135 2747360/65, Fax: 91 135 2748373
E-mail: nho@sancharnet.in
Website: http://www.hydrobharat.org

NAVAREA IX (Pakistan)
Hydrographic Department
Naval Headquarters
11, Liaquat Barracks
Karachi 75530 Pakistan
Phone: 92 21 48506151/52
Fax: 92 21 9201623/9203246/9203258
Telex: 20774 HDRO PK
E-mail: hydropk@bol.edu.pk
Website: http://www.paknavy.gov.pk/hydro/

NAVAREA X (Australia)
Australian Search and Rescue (AusSAR)
Australian Maritime Safety Authority (AMSA)
GPO Box 2181
Canberra Act 2601
Australia
Phone: 61 2 6230 6811, Fax: 61 2 6230 6868
E-mail: rccaus@amsa.gov.au
Website: http://www.amsa.gov.au

RADIO NAVIGATIONAL WARNINGS

NAVAREA XI (Japan)
Notices to Mariners Division
Hydrographic and Oceanographic Department
Japan Coast Guard
3-1, Tsukiji, 5-chome
Chuo-ku, Tokyo 104-0045 Japan
Phone: 81 3 3541 3812/3817, Fax: 81 3 3542 7174
Telex: 2522222 JAHYD J
E-mail: tuho@jodc.go.jp
Website: http://www1.kaiho.mlit.go.jp/jhd-E.html

NAVAREA XIII (Russian Federation)
Department of Navigation and Oceanography
8, 11 Liniya, B-34
Saint Petersburg 199034, Russia
Phone: 7 812 277 1511, Fax: 7 812 323 7548
Telex: 121531 NAVIO RU
E-mail: gunio@homepage.ru
Website: none

NAVAREA XIV (New Zealand)
NZDF Joint Geospatial Support Facility
HMNZ Naval Base
Private Bag 32901
Devonport
Auckland 9, New Zealand
Phone: 64 9 445 5644, Fax: 64 9 445 5589
E-mail: brian.twyman@nzdf.mil.nz
Website: http://www.hydro.linz.govt.nz

NAVAREA XV (Chile)
Director del Servicio Hidrográfico y Oceanográfico de
 Armada de Chile
Casilla 324
Valparaiso, Chile
Phone: 56 32 266666, Fax: 56 32 266542
E-mail: shoa@shoa.cl
Website: http://www.shoa.cl

NAVAREA XVI (Peru)
Dirección de Hidrografia y N vegación de la Marina
Avenida Gamarra No. 500
Chucuito, Callao 1, Peru
Phone: 51 1 465 8312/429 6019/429 9063
Fax: 51 1 465 2995
E-mail: dihidronav@dhn.mil.pe
Website: http://www.dhn.mil.pe/

Chairman
IHO Commission on Promulgation of Radio
 Navigational Warnings
4 quai Antoine 1er
B.P. 445
MC 98011 MONACO CEDEX
Principality of Monaco

Telephone: 337-93-10-81-00
Fax: 337-93-10-81-40
Telex: 479164 MC INHORG
E-mail: info@ihb.mc
Website: http://www.iho.shom.fr

CHAPTER 4

DISTRESS, EMERGENCY, AND SAFETY TRAFFIC

PART I

400A.	General.	4-3
400B.	Obligations and Responsibilities of U.S. Vessels	4-12
400C.	Reporting Navigational Safety Information to Shore Establishments.	4-14
400D.	Assistance by SAR Aircraft and Helicopters.	4-14
400E.	Reports of Hostile Activities	4-15
400F.	Emergency Position Indicating Radio Beacons (EPIRBs)	4-18
400G.	Global Maritime Distress and Safety System (GMDSS)	4-28
400H.	The Inmarsat System	4-30
400I.	The SafetyNET System	4-34
400J.	Inmarsat-C SES Maintenance	4-41
400K.	Digital Selective Calling (DSC)	4-41
400L.	Use of GMDSS Equipment for Routine Telecommunications	4-47
400M.	Instructions for Canceling Inadvertent Distress Alerts	4-48
	List of Operational VHF DSC Coast Stations for Sea Areas A1.	4-55
	List of Operational MF DSC COAST Stations for Sea Areas A2.	4-82
	List of Operational HF DSC COAST Stations for Sea Areas A3 and A4.	4-91

PART II

410A.	Requests for U.S. Navy Assistance in Emergency Situations.	4-94
APPENDIX A	Ocean Areas and Command Centers/Communications Facilities	4-96
APPENDIX B	High Frequencies Guarded by Air Force, Navy, Coast Guard, and Commercial Stations	4-98
	List of Inmarsat Coast Earth Stations	4-107
	List of Rescue Coordination Centers using Ship Earth Stations	4-109

CHAPTER 4

DISTRESS, EMERGENCY, AND SAFETY TRAFFIC

PART I

400A. General

The transition period for implementation of the Global Maritime Distress and Safety System (GMDSS) began on 1 February 1992 and continued to 1 February 1999. This event marked the most important change in maritime safety since the advent of radio in 1899. The proven benefit of satellite communications (high reliability, simple operation, and multi-modal capacities) are the cornerstone of this system, which relies heavily on automation and the extensive use of Inmarsat satellites. The result will be a total transformation of the existing maritime distress communications system. For further information on GMDSS see sec. 400G.

Regulations concerning distress, emergency, and safety traffi are contained in the Radio Regulations of the International Telecommunication Union (ITU), Geneva. Pertinent information is extracted below in condensed form from the 2001 edition.

ARTICLE 30, GENERAL PROVISIONS:
Section I - Introduction: This Chapter contains the provisions for the operational use of the Global Maritime Distress and Safety System (GMDSS), which is fully define in the International Convention for the Safety of Life at Sea (SOLAS), 1974, as amended. Distress, urgency and safety transmissions may also be made, using Morse telegraphy or radiotelephony techniques, in accordance with the provisions of Radio Regulations for distress and safety communications for non-GMDSS vessels (Appendix 13), and relevant ITU-R Recommendations.

No provision of these Regulations prevents the use by a mobile station or a mobile earth station in distress of any means at its disposal to attract attention, make known its position, and obtain help.

No provision of these Regulations prevents the use by stations on board aircraft, ships engaged in search and rescue (SAR) operations, land stations, or coast earth stations, in exceptional circumstances, of any means at their disposal to assist a mobile station or a mobile earth station in distress.

Section II - Maritime provisions: The provisions specifie in this Chapter are obligatory in the maritime mobile service and the maritime mobile-satellite service for all stations using the frequencies and techniques prescribed for the functions set out herein. However, stations of the maritime mobile service, when fitte with equipment used by stations operating in conformity with Radio Regulations for distress and safety communications for non-GMDSS vessels (Appendix 13), shall comply with the appropriate provisions of those Regulations.

The International Convention for the Safety of Life at Sea (SOLAS), 1974 as amended, prescribes which ships and which of their survival craft shall be provided with radio equipment, and which ships shall carry portable radio equipment for use in survival craft. It also prescribes the requirements which shall be met by such equipment.

Ship earth stations located at RCCs may be authorized by an administration to communicate for distress and safety purposes with any other station using bands allocated to the maritime mobile-satellite service, when special circumstances make it essential, notwithstanding the methods of working provided for in these Regulations.

Mobile stations of the maritime mobile service may communicate, for safety purposes, with stations of the aeronautical mobile service. Such communications shall normally be made on the frequencies authorized, and under the conditions specified in the Radio R gulations.

ARTICLE 31, FREQUENCIES FOR THE GLOBAL MARITIME DISTRESS AND SAFETY SYSTEM (GMDSS):
Section I - General: The frequencies to be used for the transmission of distress and safety information under the GMDSS are shown in the following tables. In addition to the frequencies listed, coast stations should use other appropriate frequencies for the transmission of safety messages.

Any emission causing harmful interference to distress and safety communications on any of the discrete frequencies identifie in the following tables is prohibited.

The number and duration of test transmissions shall be kept to a minimum on the frequencies identifie below; they should be coordinated with a competent authority, as necessary, and, wherever practicable, be carried out on artificia antennas or with reduced power. However, testing on the distress and safety calling frequencies should be avoided, but where this is unavoidable, it should be indicated that these are test transmissions.

Before transmitting for other than distress purposes on any of the frequencies identifie below for distress and safety, a station shall, where practicable, listen on the frequency concerned to make sure that no distress transmission is being sent.

DISTRESS, EMERGENCY, AND SAFETY TRAFFIC

Table of Frequencies below 30 MHz

Frequency (MHz)	Description of usage	Notes
490	MSI	Used only for maritime safety information (MSI) in a national language through the international NAVTEX system.
518	MSI	Used only for MSI in the English language by the international NAVTEX system.
*2174.5	NBDP	Used only for distress and safety communications (traffic) using NBDP tel graphy.
*2182	RT	A carrier frequency used for distress and safety communications (traffic) by T. 2182 kHz uses class of emission J3E.
*2187.5	DSC	Used only for distress and safety calls using digital selective calling in accordance with the Radio Regulations.
3023	AERO-SAR	An aeronautical carrier (reference) frequency which may be used for intercommunication between mobile stations engaged in coordinated SAR operations, and for communication between these stations and participating land stations.
*4125	RT	A ship station carrier frequency for calling on RT. 4125 kHz is authorized for common use by coast and ship stations for SSB RT on a simplex basis for call and reply purposes, provided the peak power does not exceed 1 kW. The use of this frequency for working purposes is not permitted. 4125 kHz is authorized for common use by coast and ship stations for SSB RT on a simplex basis for distress and safety traffic In the United States, 4125 kHz is authorized for common use by coast and ship stations for SSB RT on a simplex basis, provided the peak power does not exceed 1 kW. Aircraft stations may use this frequency to communicate with stations of the maritime mobile service for distress and safety purposes, including SAR.
*4177.5	NBDP	Used only for distress and safety communications (traffic) using NBDP tel graphy.
*4207.5	DSC	Used only for distress and safety calls using digital selective calling in accordance with the Radio Regulations.
4209.5	MSI	Used only for NAVTEX-type transmissions.
4210	MSI-HF	Used only for the transmission of high seas MSI by coast stations to ships, by means of NBDP telegraphy, in the maritime mobile service.
5680	AERO-SAR	An aeronautical carrier (reference) frequency which may be used for intercommunication between mobile stations engaged in coordinated SAR operations, and for communication between these stations and participating land stations.
*6215	RT	A ship station carrier frequency for calling on RT. 6215 kHz is authorized for common use by coast and ship stations for SSB RT on a simplex basis for call and reply purposes, provided the peak power does not exceed 1 kW. The use of this frequency for working purposes is not permitted. 6215 kHz is authorized for common use by coast and ship stations for SSB RT on a simplex basis for distress and safety traffic Aircraft stations may use this frequency to communicate with stations of the maritime mobile service for distress and safety purposes, including SAR.
*6268	NBDP	Used only for distress and safety communications (traffic) using NBDP tel graphy.

Note: Except as provided in these Regulations, any emission capable of causing harmful interference to distress, alarm, urgency or safety communications on the frequencies denoted by an asterisk (*) is prohibited.

DISTRESS, EMERGENCY, AND SAFETY TRAFFIC

Table of Frequencies below 30 MHz

Frequency (MHz)	Description of usage	Notes
*6312	DSC	Used only for distress and safety calls using digital selective calling in accordance with the Radio Regulations.
6314	MSI-HF	Used only for the transmission of high seas MSI by coast stations to ships, by means of NBDP telegraphy, in the maritime mobile service.
*8291	RT	Used only for distress and safety communications (traffic) by T.
*8376.5	NBDP	Used only for distress and safety communications (traffic) using NBDP tel graphy.
*8414.5	DSC	Used only for distress and safety calls using digital selective calling in accordance with the Radio Regulations.
8416.5	MSI-HF	Used only for the transmission of high seas MSI by coast stations to ships, by means of NBDP telegraphy, in the maritime mobile service.
*12290	RT	Used only for distress and safety communications (traffic) by T.
*12520	NBDP	Used only for distress and safety communications (traffic) using NBDP tel graphy.
*12577	DSC	Used only for distress and safety calls using digital selective calling in accordance with the Radio Regulations.
12579	MSI-HF	Used only for the transmission of high seas MSI by coast stations to ships, by means of NBDP telegraphy, in the maritime mobile service.
*16420	RT	Used only for distress and safety communications (traffic) by T.
*16695	NBDP	Used only for distress and safety communications (traffic) using NBDP tel graphy.
*16804.5	DSC	Used only for distress and safety calls using digital selective calling in accordance with the Radio Regulations.
16806.5	MSI-HF	Used only for the transmission of high seas MSI by coast stations to ships, by means of NBDP telegraphy, in the maritime mobile service.
19680.5	MSI-HF	Used only for the transmission of high seas MSI by coast stations to ships, by means of NBDP telegraphy, in the maritime mobile service.
22376	MSI-HF	Used only for the transmission of high seas MSI by coast stations to ships, by means of NBDP telegraphy, in the maritime mobile service.
26100.5	MSI-HF	Used only for the transmission of high seas MSI by coast stations to ships, by means of NBDP telegraphy, in the maritime mobile service.

Note: Except as provided in these Regulations, any emission capable of causing harmful interference to distress, alarm, urgency or safety communications on the frequencies denoted by an asterisk (*) is prohibited.

DISTRESS, EMERGENCY, AND SAFETY TRAFFIC

Table of Frequencies above 30 MHz

Frequency (MHz)	Description of usage	Notes
*121.5	AERO-SAR	The aeronautical emergency frequency 121.5 MHz is used for the purposes of distress and urgency for RT by stations of the aeronautical mobile service using frequencies in the band between 117.975 MHz and 137 MHz. This frequency may also be used for these purposes by survival craft stations. EPIRBs use this frequency as indicated in the Radio Regulations. Mobile stations of the maritime mobile service may communicate with stations of the aeronautical mobile service on the aeronautical emergency frequency 121.5 MHz for the purposes of distress and urgency only, and on the aeronautical auxiliary frequency 123.1 MHz for coordinated SAR operations, using class A3E emissions for both frequencies. They shall then comply with any special arrangement between governments concerned by which the aeronautical mobile service is regulated.
123.1	AERO-SAR	The aeronautical auxiliary frequency 123.1 MHz, which is auxiliary to the aeronautical emergency frequency 121.5 MHz, is for use by stations of the aeronautical mobile service and by other mobile and land stations engaged in coordinated SAR operations. Mobile stations of the maritime mobile service may communicate with stations of the aeronautical mobile service on the aeronautical emergency frequency 121.5 MHz for the purposes of distress and urgency only, and on the aeronautical auxiliary frequency 123.1 MHz for coordinated SAR operations, using class A3E emissions for both frequencies. They shall then comply with any special arrangement between governments concerned by which the aeronautical mobile service is regulated.
156.3	VHF (Ch. 06)	Used for communication between ship stations and aircraft stations engaged in coordinated SAR operations. It may also be used by aircraft stations to communicate with ship stations for other safety purposes. Ship stations shall avoid harmful interference to such communications on Ch. 06 as well as to communications between aircraft stations, ice-breakers and assisted ships during ice seasons.
*156.525	VHF (Ch. 70)	Used in the maritime mobile service for distress and safety calls using digital selective calling.
156.650	VHF (Ch. 13)	Used on a worldwide basis for ship-to-ship communications relating to the safety of navigation. It may also be used for the ship movement and port operations service subject to the national regulations of the administrations concerned.
*156.8	VHF (Ch. 16)	Used for distress and safety communications by RT. It may also be used by aircraft stations for safety purposes only.
*406-406.1	406-EPIRB	This frequency band is used only by satellite EPIRBs in the Earth-to-space direction.
1530-1544	SAT-COM	In addition to its availability for routine non-safety purposes, this frequency band is used for distress and safety purposes in the space-to-Earth direction in the maritime mobile-satellite service. GMDSS distress, urgency and safety communications have priority in this band.
*1544-1545	D&S-OPS	Use of this band (space-to-Earth) is limited to distress and safety operations, including feeder links of satellites needed to relay emissions of satellite EPIRBs to earth stations and narrow-band (space-to-Earth) links from space stations to mobile stations.

Note: Except as provided in these Regulations, any emission capable of causing harmful interference to distress, alarm, urgency or safety communications on the frequencies denoted by an asterisk (*) is prohibited.

DISTRESS, EMERGENCY, AND SAFETY TRAFFIC

Table of Frequencies above 30 MHz

Frequency (MHz)	Description of usage	Notes
1626.5-1645.5	SAT-COM	In addition to its availability for routine non-safety purposes, this frequency band is used for distress and safety purposes in the Earth-to-space direction in the maritime mobile-satellite service. GMDSS distress, urgency and safety communications have priority in this band.
*1645.5-1646.5	D&S-OPS	Use of this band (Earth-to-space) is limited to distress and safety operations, including transmissions from satellite EPIRBs and relay of distress alerts received by satellites in low polar Earth orbits to geostationary satellites.
9200-9500	SARTS	Used by radar transponders to facilitate SAR.

Note: Except as provided in these Regulations, any emission capable of causing harmful interference to distress, alarm, urgency or safety communications on the frequencies denoted by an asterisk (*) is prohibited.

Section II - Survival craft stations: Equipment for radiotelephony use in survival craft stations shall, if capable of operating on any frequency in the bands between 156 MHz and 174 MHz, be able to transmit and receive on 156.8 MHz and at least one other frequency in these bands.

Equipment for transmitting locating signals from survival craft stations shall be capable of operating in the 9200-9500 MHz band.

Equipment with DSC facilities for use in survival craft shall, if capable of operating in the bands between:
– 1605 and 2850 kHz, be able to transmit on 2187.5 kHz;
– 4000 and 27500 kHz, be able to transmit on 8414.5 kHz;
– 156 and 174 MHz, be able to transmit on 156.525 MHz.

Section III - Watchkeeping:

(A) - Coast stations: Those coast stations assuming a watch-keeping responsibility in the GMDSS shall maintain an automatic DSC watch on frequencies and for periods of time as indicated in the information published in the List of Coast Stations.

(B) - Coast earth stations: Those coast earth stations assuming a watch-keeping responsibility in the GMDSS shall maintain a continuous automatic watch for appropriate distress alerts relayed by space stations.

(C) - Ship stations: Ship stations, where so equipped, shall, while at sea, maintain an automatic DSC watch on the appropriate distress and safety calling frequencies in the frequency bands in which they are operating. Ship stations, where so equipped, shall also maintain watch on the appropriate frequencies for the automatic reception of transmissions of meteorological and navigational warnings and other urgent information to ships. However, ship stations shall also continue to apply the appropriate watch-keeping provisions of the Radio Regulations for distress and safety communications for non-GMDSS vessels (Appendix 13).

NOTE: Listening watches on 2182 kHz are no longer mandatory. Until 1 February 2005, every ship while at sea shall maintain, when practicable, a continuous listening watch on VHF Ch. 16; such a watch shall be kept at the position from which the ship is normally navigated.

Ship stations complying with the provisions of the Radio Regulations should, where practicable, maintain a watch on the frequency 156.650 MHz (VHF Ch. 13) for communications related to the safety of navigation.

(D) - Ship earth stations: Ship earth stations complying with the provisions of the Radio Regulations shall, while at sea, maintain watch except when communicating on a working channel.

ARTICLE 32, OPERATIONAL PROCEDURES FOR DISTRESS AND SAFETY COMMUNICATIONS IN THE GMDSS:

Section I - General: Distress and safety communications rely on the use of terrestrial MF, HF and VHF radiocommunications and communications using satellite techniques.

The distress alert shall be sent through a satellite either with absolute priority in general communication channels or on exclusive distress and safety frequencies or, alternatively, on the distress and safety frequencies in MF, HF and VHF bands using DSC.

The distress alert shall be sent only on the authority of the person responsible for the ship, aircraft or other vehicle carrying the mobile station or the mobile earth station.

All stations which receive a distress alert transmitted by DSC shall immediately cease any transmission capable of interfering with distress traffi and shall continue watch until the call has been acknowledged.

DSC shall be in accordance with the relevant ITU-R Recommendations.

Each administration shall ensure that suitable arrangements are made for assigning and registering identities used by ships participating in the GMDSS, and shall make registration information available to RCCs on a 24-hour day, 7-day week basis. Where appropriate, administrations shall notify responsible organizations immediately of additions, deletions and other changes in these assignments. Registration information shall be in accordance with the Radio Regulations (Resolution 340).

DISTRESS, EMERGENCY, AND SAFETY TRAFFIC

Any GMDSS shipboard equipment which is capable of transmitting position coordinates as part of a distress alert message and which does not have an integral electronic position-fixin system receiver shall be interconnected to a separate navigation receiver, if one is installed, to provide that information automatically.

Transmissions by radiotelephony shall be made slowly and distinctly, each word being clearly pronounced to facilitate transcription.

The Phonetic Alphabet and Figure Code, and the abbreviations and prosigns listed below, in accordance with the Radio Regulations, should be used where applicable. The Standard Marine Communication Phrases (published by the International Maritime Organization (IMO)) and the International Code of Signals (CDPUBNV102) are also recommended for use. (NOTE: Three-letter signals (Q Code) are also listed in ACP 131, Communications Instructions, Operating Signals.)

AA - All After
AB - All Before
ADS - Address
$\overline{AR}$ - End of transmission (in telegraphy, a bar over the letters means they are sent as one signal: • – • – •)
$\overline{AS}$ - Waiting period
BK - Interruption of transmission in progress
BN - All between
BQ - Reply to RQ
$\overline{BT}$ - Separation between parts of a transmission
C - Affirmat ve
CFM - Confirm/I confi
CL - I am closing my station
COL - Collate/I collate
CORRECTION - Cancel last word or group
CP - General call to two or more specified station
CQ - General call to all stations
CS - Request for call sign
DE - From
DF - Precede time, bearing, possible error
DO - Bearing doubtful, request again at specified tim
DSC - Digital selective calling
E - East
ETA - Estimated time of arrival
INTERCO - Signals from International Code will follow
K - Invitation to transmit
$\overline{KA}$ - Starting signal
KTS - Knots
MIN - Minutes
MSG - Prefi indicating message to or from Master regarding ship's operation or navigation
MSI - Marine safety information
N - North
NBDP - Narrow band direct printing telegraphy
NIL - I have nothing to send you
NO - Negative
NW - Now
NX - Notice to Mariners
OK - It is correct
OL - Ocean letter
P - Prefix indicating pr vate radiotelegram
PBL - Preamble, used after question mark in telegraphy, RQ in telephony, or RPT, to request repetition
PSE - Please
R - Received
RCC - Rescue coordination center
REF - Reference
RPT - Repeat
RQ - Request
S - South
SAR - Search and rescue
SIG - Signature, used after question mark in radiotelegraphy, RQ in telephony, or RPT, to request repetition
SLT - Radiomaritime letter
SVC - Prefix indicating service messag
SYS - Refer to your service message
TFC - Traffi
TR - Land station request for position and next port of call; also precedes response
TU - Thank you
TXT - Text
$\overline{VA}$ - End of work
W - West
WA - Word after
WB - Word before
WD - Word(s) or group(s)
WX - Weather
XQ - Prefix indicating service not
YZ - Plain language

Section II - Distress alerting:

(A) - General: The transmission of a distress alert indicates that a mobile unit (ship, aircraft or other vehicle) or person is threatened by grave and imminent danger and requests immediate assistance. The distress alert is a digital selective call using distress call format in the bands used for terrestrial radiocommunication or a distress message format, in which case it is relayed through space stations. (The format of distress calls and distress messages shall be in accordance with the relevant ITU-R Recommendations.)

The distress alert shall provide the identificatio of the station in distress and its position. (It may also contain information regarding the nature of the distress, the type of assistance required, the course and speed of the mobile unit, the time that this information was recorded and any other information which might facilitate rescue.)

A distress alert is false if it was transmitted without any indication that a mobile unit or person was in distress and required immediate assistance. Administrations receiving a false distress alert shall report this infringement, if that alert:

– was transmitted intentionally;
– was not cancelled in accordance with the Radio Regulations (Resolution 349);
– could not be verifie as a result of either the ship's failure to keep watch on appropriate frequencies in accordance with the Radio Regulations, or its failure to respond to calls from an authorized rescue authority;
– was repeated; or
– was transmitted using a false identity.

DISTRESS, EMERGENCY, AND SAFETY TRAFFIC

Administrations receiving such a report shall take appropriate steps to ensure that the infringement does not recur. No action should normally be taken against any ship or mariner for reporting and cancelling a false distress alert.

(B) - Transmission of a distress alert:

– (B1) - Transmission of a distress alert by a ship station or a ship earth station: Ship-to-shore distress alerts are used to alert RCCs via coast stations or coast earth stations that a ship is in distress. These alerts are based on the use of transmissions via satellites (from a ship earth station or satellite EPIRB) and terrestrial services (from ship stations and EPIRBs).

Ship-to-ship distress alerts are used to alert other ships in the vicinity of the ship in distress and are based on the use of DSC in the VHF and MF bands. Additionally, the HF band may be used.

– (B2) - Transmission of a shore-to-ship distress alert relay: A station or RCC which receives a distress alert shall initiate the transmission of a shore-to-ship distress alert relay addressed, as appropriate, to all ships, to a selected group of ships or to a specifi ship by satellite and/or terrestrial means.

The distress alert relay shall contain the identificatio of the mobile unit in distress, its position and all other information which might facilitate rescue.

– (B3) - Transmission of a distress alert by a station not itself in distress: A station in the mobile or mobile-satellite service which learns that a mobile unit is in distress shall initiate and transmit a distress alert in any of the following cases:

- when the mobile unit in distress is not itself in a position to transmit the distress alert;
- when the Master or person responsible for the mobile unit not in distress considers further help is necessary.

A station transmitting a distress alert relay, in accordance with the Radio Regulations, shall indicate that it is not itself in distress.

(C) - Receipt and acknowledgment of distress alerts:

– (C1) - Procedure for acknowledgment of receipt of distress alerts: Acknowledgment by DSC of receipt of a distress alert in the terrestrial services shall be in accordance with relevant ITU-R Recommendations. (For further information on procedures for DSC distress alerts, acknowledgments and relays see sec. 400J.)

Acknowledgment through a satellite of receipt of a distress alert from a ship earth station shall be sent immediately.

Acknowledgment by radiotelephony of receipt of a distress alert from a ship station or a ship earth station shall be given in the following form:

- the distress signal MAYDAY;
- the call sign or other identificatio of the station sending the distress message, spoken three times;
- the words THIS IS (or DE spoken as DELTA ECHO in case of language difficulties)
- the call sign or other identificatio of the station acknowledging receipt, spoken three times;
- the word RECEIVED (or RRR spoken as ROMEO ROMEO ROMEO in case of language difficulties)
- the distress signal MAYDAY.

The acknowledgment by direct printing telegraphy of receipt of a distress alert from a ship station shall be given in the following form:

- the distress signal MAYDAY;
- the call sign or other identificatio of the station sending the distress alert;
- the word DE;
- the call sign or other identificatio of the station acknowledging receipt of the distress alert;
- the signal RRR;
- the distress signal MAYDAY.

The acknowledgment by direct printing telegraphy of receipt of a distress alert from a ship earth station shall be given by the coast earth station receiving the distress alert, by retransmitting the ship station identity of the ship transmitting the distress alert.

– (C2) - Receipt and acknowledgment of receipt by a coast station, a coast earth station or a RCC: Coast stations and appropriate coast earth stations in receipt of distress alerts shall ensure that they are routed as soon as possible to a RCC. Receipt of a distress alert is to be acknowledged as soon as possible by a coast station, or by a RCC via a coast station or an appropriate coast earth station.

A coast station using DSC to acknowledge a distress call shall transmit the acknowledgment on the distress calling frequency on which the call was received and should address it to all ships. The acknowledgment shall include the identificatio of the ship whose distress call is being acknowledged.

– (C3) - Receipt and acknowledgment of receipt by a ship station or ship earth station: Ship or ship earth stations in receipt of a distress alert shall, as soon as possible, inform the Master or person responsible for the ship of the contents of the distress alert.

In areas where reliable communications with one or more coast stations are practicable, ship stations in receipt of a distress alert should defer acknowledgment for a short interval so that receipt may be acknowledged by a coast station.

Ship stations operating in areas where reliable communications with a coast station are not practicable which receive a distress alert from a ship station which is, beyond doubt, in their vicinity, shall, as soon as possible and if appropriately equipped, acknowledge receipt and inform a RCC through a coast station or coast earth station.

However, a ship station receiving an HF distress alert shall not acknowledge it but shall observe the provisions of *D* below, and shall, if the alert is not acknowledged by a coast station within 3 minutes, relay the distress alert.

A ship station acknowledging receipt of a distress alert in accordance with *C3* above should:

- in the firs instance, acknowledge receipt of the alert by using radiotelephony on the distress and safety traffic frequen y in the band used for the alert;
- if acknowledgment by radiotelephony of the distress alert received on the MF or VHF distress alerting frequency is unsuccessful, acknowledge receipt of the

distress alert by responding with a digital selective call on the appropriate frequency.

A ship station in receipt of a shore-to-ship distress alert should establish communication as directed and render such assistance as required and appropriate.

(D) - Preparations for handling of distress traffic On receipt of a distress alert transmitted by use of DSC techniques, ship stations and coast stations shall set watch on the radiotelephone distress and safety traffi frequency associated with the distress and safety calling frequency on which the distress alert was received.

Coast stations and ship stations with NBDP equipment shall set watch on the NBDP frequency associated with the distress alert signal if it indicates that NBDP is to be used for subsequent distress communications. If practicable, they should additionally set watch on the radiotelephone frequency associated with the distress alert frequency.

Section III - Distress traffic

(A) - General and SAR coordinating communications: Distress traffic consists of all messages relating to the immediate assistance required by the ship in distress, including SAR communications and on scene communications. The distress traffic shall as far as possible be on the frequencies con tained in Article 31 (see above).

The distress signal consists of the word MAYDAY.

For distress traffi by radiotelephony, when establishing communications, calls shall be prefi ed by the distress signal MAYDAY.

Error correction techniques in accordance with relevant ITU-R Recommendations shall be used for distress traffi by direct printing telegraphy. All messages shall be preceded by at least one carriage return, a line feed signal, a letter shift signal and the distress signal MAYDAY.

Distress communications by direct printing telegraphy should normally be established by the ship in distress and should be in the broadcast (forward error correction) mode. The ARQ mode may subsequently be used when it is advantageous to do so.

The RCC responsible for controlling a SAR operation shall also coordinate the distress traffi relating to the incident or may appoint another station to do so.

The RCC coordinating distress traffic the unit coordinating SAR operations (the On Scene Commander (OSC) or Coordinator Surface Search (CSS)) or the coast station involved may impose silence on stations which interfere with that traffic This instruction shall be addressed to all stations or to one station only, according to circumstances. In either case, the following shall be used:
– in radiotelephony, the signal SEELONCE MAYDAY;
– in NBDP telegraphy normally using forward error correcting mode, the signal SILENCE MAYDAY. However, the ARQ mode may be used when it is advantageous to do so.

Until they receive the message indicating that normal working may be resumed, all stations which are aware of the distress traffic and which are not taking part in it, and which are not in distress, are forbidden to transmit on the frequencies in which the distress traffic is taking place

A station of the mobile service which, while following distress traffic is able to continue its normal service, may do so when the distress traffi is well established and on condition that it observes the provisions of the above paragraph and that it does not interfere with distress traffic

When distress traffi has ceased on frequencies which have been used for distress traffic the RCC controlling a SAR operation shall initiate a message for transmission on these frequencies indicating that distress traffi has finished

In radiotelephony, the message referred to in the above paragraph consists of:
– the distress signal MAYDAY;
– the call "Hello all stations" or CQ (spoken as CHARLIE QUEBEC) spoken three times;
– the words THIS IS (or DE spoken as DELTA ECHO in the case of language difficulties)
– the call sign or other identificatio of the station sending the message;
– the time of handing in of the message;
– the name and call sign of the mobile station which was in distress;
– the words SEELONCE FEENEE.

In direct printing telegraphy, the message referred to in the above paragraph consists of:
– the distress signal MAYDAY;
– the call CQ;
– the word DE;
– the call sign or other identificatio of the station sending the message;
– the time of handing in of the message;
– the name and call sign of the mobile station which was in distress; and
– the words SILENCE FINI.

(B) - On scene communications: On scene communications are those between the mobile unit in distress and assisting mobile units, and between the mobile units and the unit coordinating SAR operations (the OSC or CSS).

Control of on scene communications is the responsibility of the unit coordinating SAR operations. Simplex communications shall be used so that all on scene mobile stations may share relevant information concerning the distress incident. If direct printing telegraphy is used, it shall be in the forward error correcting mode.

The preferred frequencies in radiotelephony for on scene communications are 156.8 MHz (VHF Ch. 16) and 2182 kHz. The frequency 2174.5 kHz may also be used for ship-to-ship on scene communications using NBDP telegraphy in the forward error correcting mode.

In addition, the frequencies 3023 kHz, 4125 kHz, 5680 kHz, 123.1 MHz, and 156.3 MHz (VHF Ch. 06) may be used for ship-to-aircraft on scene communications.

The selection or designation of on scene frequencies is the responsibility of the unit coordinating SAR operations. Normally, once an on scene frequency is established, a continuous aural or teleprinter watch is maintained by all participating on scene mobile units on the selected frequency.

(C) - Locating and homing signals: Locating signals are radio transmissions intended to facilitate the findin of a mobile unit in distress or the location of survivors. These

DISTRESS, EMERGENCY, AND SAFETY TRAFFIC

signals include those transmitted by searching units, and those transmitted by the mobile unit in distress, by survival craft, by float-fre EPIRBs, by satellite EPIRBs and by SAR radar transponders to assist the searching units.

Homing signals are those locating signals which are transmitted by mobile units in distress, or by survival craft, for the purpose of providing searching units with a signal that can be used to determine the bearing to the transmitting stations.

Locating signals may be transmitted in the following frequency bands:

– 117.975-136 MHz;
– 156-174 MHz;
– 406-406.1 MHz;
– 1645.5-1646.5 MHz; and
– 9200-9500 MHz.

Locating signals shall be in accordance with the relevant ITU-R Recommendations.

ARTICLE 33, OPERATIONAL PROCEDURES FOR URGENCY AND SAFETY COMMUNICATIONS IN THE GMDSS:

Section I - General: Urgency and safety communications include:
– navigational and meteorological warnings and urgent information;
– ship-to-ship safety of navigation communications;
– ship reporting communications;
– support communications for SAR operations;
– other urgency and safety messages;
– communications relating to navigation, movements and needs of ships, and weather observation messages destined for an official meteorological service

Section II - Urgency communications: In a terrestrial system the announcement of the urgency message shall be made on one or more of the distress and safety calling frequencies as specifie using DSC and the urgency call format. A separate announcement need not be made if the urgency message is to be transmitted through the maritime mobile-satellite service.

The urgency signal and message shall be transmitted on one or more of the distress and safety traffi frequencies specified, or via the maritime mobile-satellite service or o other frequencies used for this purpose.

The urgency signal consists of the words PAN PAN.

The urgency call format and the urgency signal indicate that the calling station has a very urgent message to transmit concerning the safety of a mobile unit or a person.

In radiotelephony, the urgency message shall be preceded by the urgency signal (PAN PAN), repeated three times, and the identification of the transmitting station

In NBDP, the urgency message shall be preceded by the urgency signal (PAN PAN) and the identificatio of the transmitting station.

The urgency call format or urgency signal shall be sent only on the authority of the Master or the person responsible for the mobile unit carrying the mobile station or mobile earth station.

The urgency call format or the urgency signal may be transmitted by a land station or a coast earth station with the approval of the responsible authority.

When an urgency message which calls for action by the stations receiving the message has been transmitted, the station responsible for its transmission shall cancel it as soon as it knows that action is no longer necessary.

Error correction techniques in accordance with relevant ITU-R Recommendations shall be used for urgency messages by direct printing telegraphy. All messages shall be preceded by at least one carriage return, a line feed signal, a letter shift signal and the urgency signal PAN PAN.

Urgency communications by direct printing telegraphy should normally be established in the broadcast (forward error correction) mode. The ARQ mode may subsequently be used when it is advantageous to do so.

Section III - Medical transports: The term "medical transports," as define in the 1949 Geneva Conventions and Additional Protocols, refers to any means of transportation by land, water or air, whether military or civilian, permanent or temporary, assigned exclusively to medical transportation and under the control of a competent authority of a party to a conflic or of neutral States and of other States not parties to an armed conflict when these ships, craft, and aircraft assist the wounded, the sick and the shipwrecked.

For the purpose of announcing and identifying medical transports which are protected under the above-mentioned Conventions, the procedure of Section II of this Article (urgency communications) is used. The urgency signal (PAN PAN) shall be followed by the addition of the single word MEDICAL in NDBP and by the addition of the single word "MAY-DEE-CAL," in radiotelephony.

The use of the signals described in the above paragraph indicates that the message which follows concerns a protected medical transport. The message shall convey the following data:
– call sign or other recognized means of identificatio of the medical transport;
– position of the medical transport;
– number and type of vehicles in the medical transport;
– intended route;
– estimated time enroute and of departure and arrival, as appropriate;
– any other information, such as fligh altitude, radio frequencies guarded, languages used and secondary surveillance radar modes and codes.

The identificatio and location of medical transports at sea may be conveyed by means of appropriate standard maritime radar transponders.

The identificatio and location of aircraft medical transports may be conveyed by the use of the secondary surveillance radar (SSR) system specifie in Annex 10 to the Convention on International Civil Aviation.

The use of radiocommunications for announcing and identifying medical transports is optional; however, if they are used, the provisions of the above Regulations shall apply.

Section IV - Safety communications: In a terrestrial system the announcement of the safety message shall be made on one or more of the distress and safety calling frequencies as specifie using DSC techniques. A separate announcement need not be made if the message is to be transmitted through the maritime mobile-satellite service.

The safety signal and message shall normally be transmitted on one or more of the distress and safety traffi frequencies specified or via the maritime mobile-satellite service or on other frequencies used for this purpose.

The safety signal consists of the word SECURITE.

The safety call format or the safety signal indicates that the calling station has an important navigational or meteorological warning to transmit.

In radiotelephony, the safety message shall be preceded by the safety signal (SECURITE, spoken SECURITAY) repeated three times, and identificatio of the transmitting station.

In NBDP, the safety message shall be preceded by the safety signal (SECURITE), and the identificatio of the transmitting station.

Error correction techniques in accordance with relevant ITU-R Recommendations shall be used for safety messages by direct printing telegraphy. All messages shall be preceded by at least one carriage return, a line feed signal, a letter shift signal and the safety signal SECURITE.

Safety communications by direct printing telegraphy should normally be established in the broadcast (forward error correction) mode. The ARQ mode may subsequently be used when it is advantageous to do so.

Section V - Transmission of Maritime Safety Information (MSI): (MSI includes navigation and meteorological warnings, meteorological forecasts and other urgent messages pertaining to safety normally transmitted to or from ships, between ships and between ship and coast stations or coast earth stations.)

(A) - General: Messages from ship stations containing information concerning the presence of cyclones shall be transmitted, with the least possible delay, to other mobile stations in the vicinity and to the appropriate authorities at the firs point of the coast with which contact can be established. These transmissions shall be preceded by the safety signal.

Messages from ship stations containing information on the presence of dangerous ice, dangerous wrecks, or any other imminent danger to marine navigation, shall be transmitted as soon as possible to other ships in the vicinity, and to the appropriate authorities at the firs point of the coast with which contact can be established. These transmissions shall be preceded by the safety signal.

The operational details of the stations transmitting MSI in accordance with the provisions of B, C, D, and E below shall be indicated in the List of Radiodetermination and Special Service Stations. (In Pub. 117, see station listings in sec. 300J, 300L and 400I.)

The mode and format of the transmissions mentioned in B, C and D below shall be in accordance with the relevant ITU-R Recommendations.

(B) - International NAVTEX system: MSI shall be transmitted by means of NBDP telegraphy with forward error correction using the frequency 518 kHz in accordance with the international NAVTEX system.

(C) - 490 kHz and 4209.5 kHz: The frequency 490 kHz may be used for the transmission of MSI by means of NBDP telegraphy with forward error correction.

The frequency 4209.5 kHz is used exclusively for NAVTEX-type transmissions by means of NBDP telegraphy with forward error correction.

(D) - High seas MSI: MSI is transmitted by means of NBDP telegraphy with forward error correction using the frequencies 4210 kHz, 6314 kHz, 8416.5 kHz, 12579 kHz, 16806.5 kHz, 19680.5 kHz, 22376 kHz and 26100.5 kHz.

(E) - MSI via satellite: MSI may be transmitted via satellite in the maritime mobile-satellite service using the band 1530-1545 MHz.

Section VI - Intership navigation safety communications: Intership navigation safety communications are those VHF radiotelephone communications conducted between ships for the purpose of contributing to the safe movement of ships.

The frequency 156.650 MHz (VHF Ch. 13) is used for intership navigation safety communications.

Section VII - Use of other frequencies for distress and safety: Radiocommunications for distress and safety purposes may be conducted on any appropriate communications frequency, including those used for public correspondence. In the maritime mobile-satellite service, frequencies in the bands 1530-1544 MHz and 1626.5-1645.5 MHz are used for this function as well as for distress alerting purposes.

Section VIII - Medical advice: Mobile stations requiring medical advice may obtain it through any of the land stations shown in the List of Radiodetermination and Special Service Stations. (In Pub. 117, see sec. 500B.)

Communications concerning medical advice may be preceded by the urgency signal.

ARTICLE 34, ALERTING SIGNALS IN THE GMDSS:

Section I - EPIRB and Satellite EPIRB Signals: The EPIRB signal transmitted on 156.525 MHz and satellite EPIRB signals in the band 406-406.1 MHz or 1645.5-1646.5 MHz shall be in accordance with relevant ITU-R Recommendations.

Section II - Digital selective calling (DSC): The characteristics of the "distress call" in DSC system shall be in accordance with relevant ITU-R Recommendations.

400B. Obligations and Responsibilities of U.S. Vessels

It is the accepted normal practice of seamen (and there are obligations upon Masters), to render assistance when a person or persons are in distress at sea. These obligations are set out in Regulation 10 of Chapter V of the 1974 SOLAS Convention (1974), to which the United States is signatory:

DISTRESS, EMERGENCY, AND SAFETY TRAFFIC

Distress Messages—Obligations and Procedures

(a) The Master of a ship at sea, on receiving a signal from any source that a ship or aircraft or survival craft thereof is in distress, is bound to proceed with all speed to the assistance of the persons in distress, informing them, if possible, that he is doing so. If he is unable or, in the special circumstances of the case, considers it unreasonable or unnecessary to proceed to their assistance, he must enter in the logbook the reason for failing to proceed to the assistance of the persons in distress.

(b) The Master of a ship in distress, after consultation, so far as may be possible, with the Masters of the ships which answer his call for assistance, has the right to requisition such one or more of those ships as he considers best able to render assistance, and it shall be the duty of the Master or Masters of the ship or ships requisitioned to comply with the requisition by continuing to proceed with all speed to the assistance of persons in distress.

(c) The Master of a ship shall be released from the obligation imposed by paragraph (a) of this Regulation when he learns that one or more ships other than his own have been requisitioned and are complying with the requisition.

(d) The Master of a ship shall be released from the obligation imposed by paragraph (a) of this Regulation, and, if his ship has been requisitioned, from the obligation imposed by paragraph (b) of this Regulation, if he is informed by the persons in distress or by the Master of another ship which has reached such persons that assistance is no longer necessary.

(e) The provisions of this Regulation do not prejudice the International Convention for the unificatio of certain rules with regard to Assistance and Salvage at Sea, signed at Brussels on 23 September 1910, particularly the obligation to render assistance imposed by Article 11 of that Convention.

U.S. IMPLEMENTATION OF THE GMDSS: The Federal Communications Commission (FCC) adopted the GMDSS requirements of the SOLAS Convention on 16 January 1992. (The GMDSS revisions to the Radio Regulations were developed by the International Maritime Organization (IMO) and ITU, and adopted by the ITU in 1987. The IMO adopted GMDSS requirements to the 1974 SOLAS Convention in 1988.) GMDSS requirements apply to the following U.S. vessels on international voyages or on the open sea:

– Cargo ships of 300 gross tons and over.
– Ships carrying more than 12 passengers.

Compliance will be required according to the following schedule:

– 1 February 1992 - Voluntary compliance by any ships.
– All ships constructed after 1 February 1992 must carry a radar transponder and two-way VHF radiotelephone for survival craft.
– 1 August 1993 - Applicable ships must have satellite EPIRB and NAVTEX.
– All ships constructed before 1 February 1992 to carry a radar transponder and two-way VHF radiotelephone for survival craft by 1 February 1995.
– 1 February 1995 - Newly constructed applicable ships must be GMDSS-equipped.
– All applicable ships to carry 9GHz radar by 1 February 1995.
– 1 February 1999 - All applicable ships must be GMDSS-equipped.

The FCC has exempted GMDSS-equipped U.S. ships from the Communications Act of 1934 requirements to carry (and provide operators for) Morse telegraphy equipment. This exemption is effective once the FCC, or its designee, has determined and certifie that the vessel has GMDSS equipment installed and in good working condition. This exemption was mandated by the Telecommunications Act of 1996.

FCC rules applicable to the GMDSS include the following:

– Required equipment must be inspected once every 12 months.
– Ships must carry at least two persons with GMDSS Radio Operators licenses, designated as primary and backup(s), to act as dedicated radio operator in case of distress and carry out normal communications watch routines (including selection of HF DSC channels, reception of MSI, and entering ship's position in DSC equipment every 4 hours).
– At-sea maintenance, if employed (the alternatives being system redundancy or shore maintenance), must be provided by licensed GMDSS radio maintainers.
– Ships operating in Sea Area A3 (beyond NAVTEX coverage: see sec. 400H) must carry equipment capable of receiving MSI via Inmarsat Enhanced Group Calling (EGC) (SafetyNET).
– GMDSS equipment must be approved by the FCC and carry labels indicating compliance.
– Inmarsat antennas should be installed so as to minimize masking.
– A dedicated, non-scanning radio installation capable of maintaining a continuous DSC watch on VHF 156.525 MHz (Ch. 70) must be installed.

These changes are found in Parts 13 and 80 of Title 47 of the Code of Federal Regulations.

INFORMATION REQUIRED CONCERNING NAVIGATIONAL DANGERS AND CYCLONES: Vessels encountering imminent dangers to navigation or cyclones should notify all ships in the vicinity and the nearest coast station, using the safety signal. The following information should be provided for navigational dangers:

– The kind of ice, derelict or danger observed.
– The position of the danger when last observed.
– The time and date the observation was made.

The following information should be provided for hurricanes in the Atlantic and eastern Pacific typhoons in the western Pacific cyclones in the Indian Ocean, and storms of a similar nature in other regions:

– A statement that a cyclone has been encountered, transmitted whenever the Master has good reason to believe that a cyclone exists in his vicinity.

– Time, date, and position of ship when the observation was taken.
– As much of the following information as possible should be included in the message:
– Barometric pressure.
– Barometric tendency during the past 3 hours.
– True wind direction and force.
– Sea state (smooth, moderate, rough, high).
– Swell (slight, moderate, heavy), with direction and period.
– Course and speed of ship.

When a Master has reported a dangerous cyclone, it is desirable that subsequent observations be made and transmitted hourly, if possible, but in any case at intervals of not more than 3 hours, so long as the ship remains under the influence of the cyclone.

For winds of Force 10 or above on the Beaufort Scale for which no storm warning has been received (storms other than the cyclones referred to above) a message should be sent containing similar information to that listed above but excluding details concerning sea and swell.

For sub-freezing air temperatures associated with gale force winds, causing severe ice accretion on superstructures, send a message including:
– Time and date.
– Air temperature.
– Sea temperature.
– Wind direction and force.

400C. Reporting Navigational Safety Information to Shore Establishments

Masters should pass navigational safety information to cognizant shore establishments by radio. This information may include, but is not limited to, the following:
– Ice.
– Derelicts, mines, or other floating dangers
– Casualties to lights, buoys, and other navigational aids.
– The newly discovered presence of wrecks, rocks, shoals, reefs, etc.
– Malfunction of radio navigational aids.
– Hostile action or potential hostile action which may constitute a hazard to shipping.

MESSAGES ADDRESSED TO THE U.S. COAST GUARD: In the waters of the United States and its possessions, defects noted in aids to navigation should be addressed to COAST GUARD and transmitted direct to a U.S. government coast station for relay to the Commander of the nearest Coast Guard District.

Merchant ships should send messages about defects in aids to navigation through commercial facilities only when they are unable to contact a government coast station. Charges for these messages will be paid by the Coast Guard.

Vessels reporting distress, potential distress, groundings, hazards to navigation, medicos, failures of navigational aids, etc. to the Coast Guard, should include the following information in their initial report to expedite action and reduce the need for additional message traffic

– Particulars regarding the reporting vessel: name, position, course, speed, destination, and estimated time of arrival.
– Particulars concerning the vessel or object reported: position, name, color, size, shape, and other descriptive data.
– Particulars concerning the case: nature of the case, conditions, and action taken, if any.

MESSAGES ADDRESSED TO NGA (INFORMATION CONCERNING OTHER THAN U.S. WATERS): Messages describing dangers on the high seas or in foreign waters should be addressed to NGA NAVSAFETY BETHESDA MD, which may decide to issue a safety broadcast. Whenever possible, messages should be transmitted via the nearest government radio station. If that is impractical, a commercial radio station may be used. Navigational warning messages to the U.S. government should always be sent through U.S. radio stations, government or commercial, but never through foreign stations.

Although any coast station in the mobile service will handle without charge messages relative to dangers to navigation or defects in aids to navigation, it is requested that, where practicable, ships address their messages to NGA and send them through the nearest U.S. station. Ship to shore Coast Guard radio stations are available for long-range communications. The AMVER Bulletin should be consulted for the latest changes to the communications network.

Warning information may also be reported directly to the NGA NAVSAFETY Radio Broadcast Watch Desk by the following methods:
– Telephone: (1) 301-227-3147.
– Fax: (1) 301-227-3731.
– E-mail: navsafety@nga.mil.

400D. Assistance by SAR Aircraft and Helicopters

SAR aircraft may drop rescue equipment to ships in distress. This may include equipment containers connected in series by a buoyant line. The following may be dropped:
– Individual life rafts or pairs linked by a buoyant line.
– Buoyant radiobeacons and/or transceivers.
– Dye and smoke markers and flame float
– Parachute flares for illumination
– Salvage pumps.

A helicopter may be used to supply equipment and/or evacuate persons. In such cases the following information will be of value:
– An orange smoke signal, signal lamp, or heliograph can be used to attract the attention of the helicopter.
– A clear stretch of deck should be made available as a pickup area, if possible, marked out with a large letter H in white. During the night the ship should be illuminated as brightly as possible, particularly any obstructions (masts, funnels, etc.). Care should be taken that illumination will not blind the helicopter pilot.
– The helicopter will approach from abaft the beam and come to a hover over the cleared area.

DISTRESS, EMERGENCY, AND SAFETY TRAFFIC

- The ship should, when possible, maintain a constant speed through the water and keep the wind 30° on the port bow. If these conditions are met, the helicopter can hover and use its hoist in the cleared area. If a vessel is on fir or making smoke it is an advantage to have the wind 30° on the bow. The above procedure may be modified on instructions from the pilot
- An indication of wind direction is useful. Pennants, flags or a small amount of smoke from the galley funnel may be helpful.
- The length of the helicopter's winch cable is about 15 meters (50 feet) minimum.
- The lifting device on the end of the winch cable should never be secured to any part of the ship or become entangled in the rigging or fixtures Ships' personnel should not attempt to grasp the lifting device unless requested to do so by the helicopter. In this case, a metal part of the lifting device should firs be allowed to touch the deck in order to avoid possible shock due to static electricity.
- If the above conditions cannot be met, the helicopter may be able to lift a person from a boat or life raft secured on a long painter. Cases have occurred of life rafts being overturned by the downdraft from a helicopter. It is advisable for all persons in a raft to remain in the center of the raft until they are about to be lifted.
- In cases of injured persons a special stretcher may be lowered by the helicopter. The stretcher should be unhooked while the casualty is being strapped in.

400E. Reports of Hostile Activities

SHIP HOSTILE ACTION REPORT (SHAR): NGA has established SHAR procedures to disseminate information within the U.S. Government on hostile or potentially hostile actions against U.S. merchant ships. Shipmasters should send a SHAR message to NGA by whatever means available immediately after they have encountered hostile actions or become aware of potential hostile actions which may constitute danger to U.S. shipping.

The text of a SHAR message should include the acronym SHAR, the location or position of the incident, a brief description of the situation, the Inmarsat identity of the ship transmitting the SHAR, the Inmarsat Ocean Region guarded, and the call sign of the coast radio station being guarded, if any. An example of the procedure vessels can use to send a SHAR message to NGA via either Inmarsat-A or -B telex follows on pg. 4-16.

If circumstances are such that only minimum essential data can be transmitted, a second SHAR message should be sent as soon afterward as possible containing amplifying information, such as:
- Latitude, longitude, course, and speed.
- Bearing and distance from nearest geographic point.
- Description of event.
- Next port of call and ETA.
- Date and time last message sent regarding this incident.

SHAR messages can be transmitted to NGA via Inmarsat-A, -B, or -C telex:
NGA NAVSAFETY BETHESDA MD
TELEX 898334

SHAR delivery may also be made by the following methods:
- NBDP via telex.
- Telephone: (1) 301-227-3147.
- E-mail: navsafety@nga.mil.

Rapid dissemination of a SHAR is vital so that a radio broadcast warning, if needed, may be promulgated as soon as possible. When a SHAR is received by NGA, it is reviewed and (if appropriate) immediately sent to the Department of State and other relevant government authorities and official for action. A SHAR can result in the promulgation of NAVAREAs, HYDROLANTs, HYDROPACs, and SPECIAL WARNINGS (See chap. 3.) to help ensure the safety of any other U.S. fla vessels in the affected area.

A SHAR is not a distress message. U.S. fla and effective U.S. controlled (EUSC) vessels, under attack or threat of attack, may request direct assistance from the U.S. Navy following the procedures in Part II of this chapter.

DISTRESS, EMERGENCY, AND SAFETY TRAFFIC

Procedure to Send a SHAR via Inmarsat-A or Inmarsat-B Telex

IDB A INMARSAT 12/JLY/99 21:30:46 ← *Land Earth Station and Date-Time Group*

1514205 MMAA X ← *Answer back identifying vessel*
GA+ ← *Go ahead from Land Earth Station*
0023898334+ ←
NGA USA ← *Answer back from NGA*

> "00" Auto service code for Inmarsat
> "23" Telex country code for the United States
> "898334" NGA's telex number
> "+" Completes dialing string

```
FM M/V HYDRO
TO NGA NAVSAFETY
   BETHESDA  MD
   TELEX 898334

SHAR SHAR SHAR

AMERICAN FREIGHTER OBSERVED HIT BY SEVERAL ROCKETS FIRED
FROM UNKNOWN LAND BASED SOURCE WHILE TRANSITTING
NORTH MITSIEWA CHANNEL.

INCIDENT OCCURRED AT 132300Z NOV 99 IN POSITION 16-24N 039-13E.

GUARDING COASTAL STATION JEDDAH/HZH AND AOR-EAST SATELLITE,
INMARSAT ID 1514205.

CAPTAIN SMITH
```
} *Text*

NGA USA ← *Answer back from NGA*

1514205 MMAA X ← *Answer back from vessel*

..... ← *Sequence of five periods terminating the transmission*

IDB A ILXACD SN4252
CALL 0023898334   } *Summary of call*
2 MINS 6 SECS

DISTRESS, EMERGENCY, AND SAFETY TRAFFIC

PIRACY ATTACK ALERT: The international format for a piracy attack alert includes the following:
- The distressed vessel's name and call sign (and Inmarsat ID, if applicable, with ocean region code).
- Distress signal MAYDAY or SOS (MAYDAY need not be included in the Inmarsat system when distress priority (3) is used).
- The text heading PIRACY ALERT.
- Position and time.
- Nature of event.

This message should be sent to the nearest RCC, national or regional piracy center, or nearest coast radio station.

A follow-up message should be sent when time permits, including the following:
- Reference to the initial Piracy Alert.
- Details of the incident.
- Last observed movements of the pirate vessel.
- Assistance required.
- Preferred methods for future communication.
- Date and time of report.

A regional Piracy Reporting Center in Kuala Lumpur, Malaysia, has been established by the International Maritime Bureau (IMB) in the Southeast Asia Region. The center maintains watch 24-hours a day and, in close collaboration with law enforcement, acts on reports of suspicious shipping movements, piracy, and armed robbery at sea anywhere in the world. Services are provided free of charge to all vessels irrespective of ownership or flag

Specific tasks of the Pira y Reporting Center are to:
- Report piracy incidents and armed robbery at sea to law enforcement agencies.
- Supply investigating teams that respond to acts of piracy and collect evidence for law enforcement agencies.
- Locate vessels that have been seized by pirates and recover stolen cargoes.
- Help bring pirates to justice.
- Assist owners and crews of ships that have been attacked.
- Collate information on piracy in all parts of the world.

The center broadcasts daily status bulletins by Inmarsat-C (SafetyNET), reporting acts of piracy against shipping in East Africa, the Indian subcontinent, Southeast Asia and the Far East regions.

The IMB also publishes a weekly piracy report, which is a summary of the Piracy Reporting Center's daily status bulletins. Each week's report is posted on Tuesday and may be accessed through the IMB Website at:

http://www.iccwbo.org/ccs/menu_imb_bureau.asp

The center may be contacted by:
- Telephone: 60-3-2078-5763.
- Fax: 60-3-2078-5769.
- Telex: MA 31880 IMBPCI.
- E-mail: imbkl@icc-ccs.org.uk.
24 hour Anti Piracy Helpline:
- Telephone: 60-3-2031-0014.

ANTI-SHIPPING ACTIVITY MESSAGES (ASAM) REPORTING: Piracy and other attacks against merchant shipping continue to be a worldwide problem. Information regarding these incidents often takes over a month to reach U.S. Government authorities. Delays in reporting these incidents can result in an ineffective response by the appropriate Government agency and, more importantly, will undermine the benefi to other mariners who may be transiting the affected geographic area.

At the request of a U.S. Government interagency working group on piracy and maritime terrorism, the Defense Mapping Agency (DMA) [now the National Geospatial-Intelligence Agency (NGA)] developed, in 1985, a system to offer the maritime community the most effective means of filin reports about attacks on shipping, storing the data on a computer and disseminating data to mariners and Government entities via telecommunications links.

The NGA system is the Anti-Shipping Activity Messages (ASAM) database accessed through the Maritime Safety Information Website. This system allows any user to send and record an ASAM or query the database for reported incidents by date, geographic subregion, victim's name or reference number.

All piracy, terrorism, attacks, hostile actions, harassments and threats while at sea, anchor or in port, should be reported. The primary means of reporting is through NGA's ASAM system, with acceptable secondary methods by telex/fax, telephone, and mail. An ASAM does not need to be file if a Ship Hostile Action Report (SHAR) has been issued-one will be generated following a SHAR.

This centralized database capability has been designed to be a major step toward monitoring the escalating problem of maritime crimes against life and property. The central location for filin reports of attacks against shipping is the firs step in supporting governmental responses, as well as warning the maritime community that they should avoid (or approach with caution) certain geographic areas.

Many ASAM reports are file each year; however, the number of reports as compared to worldwide incidents is quite low. The long range goal of the ASAM system is to assist Government official in the deterrence of such activities. Active participation by mariners is vital to the success of future deterrence. The U.S. Maritime Administration (MARAD) and NGA strongly encourage all mariners to participate and promptly report all incidents, whether against their vessel or observed against other vessels.

For further information pertaining to the ASAM system contact:

MARITIME DIVISION
NSS STAFF
ST D 44
4600 SANGAMORE ROAD
BETHESDA MD 20816-5003

Telephone: (1) 301-227-3147.
Fax: (1) 301-227-4211.
E-mail: webmaster_nss@nga.mil.

DISTRESS, EMERGENCY, AND SAFETY TRAFFIC

ANTI-PIRACY MEASURES: Merchant ships continue to be attacked by pirates in port and underway on the west coast of Africa, in and near the Strait of Malacca, in the South and East China Seas, in the Caribbean and in Brazilian and Ecuadorian waters. Pirates usually take money, radios, cameras and other property that is portable, valuable and easily sold. In some cases cargo has been raided. In this section "piracy" means all kinds of violent crimes against ships and small craft, including incidents in ports and in territorial and international waters, except incidents that are clearly political terrorism.

The following is a short checklist of prudent measures that ship's officer should consider when operating in regions where piracy has been reported:
– BE VIGILANT. ANTICIPATE TROUBLE
– Provide a security general alarm signal and security Station Bill to alert all crew members. Assign a ship's physical security office .
– Anti-piracy measures should be included in the ship's security plan. These measures should be designed to keep boarders off the ship. Repelling armed pirates already on deck can be dangerous.
– Piracy countermeasures should be exercised during regular emergency drills when in or approaching dangerous waters.
– Have water hoses under pressure with nozzles ready at likely boarding places when at sea and in port.
– Illuminate sides, bows and quarters while navigating in threat areas and in dangerous ports.
– Restrict access to vessel, close all ports, strong back doors, and secure spaces.
  In port:
– Ensure gangway watch can contact shipboard support if needed, preferably by hand-held radios.
– Ensure gangway watch can contact local security forces for assistance, if available.
– Maintain roving patrol on deck in port and at anchor, and ensure that patrol and gangway watch are in contact.
– Use rat guards on all mooring lines and illuminate the lines.
– Use covers on chain hawse and keep wash-down water running.
– Keep bumboats away and vendors off the ship.
  Underway:
– Keep good radar and visual lookout, including lookout aft.
– Have searchlights available to illuminate suspected boarding parties.
– Have signaling equipment, including emergency rockets, rocket pistols, and EPIRBs, available for immediate use.
  When suspected boarders are detected:
– Sound the general alarm.
– Establish VHF contact with shore stations and other ships in the vicinity.
– Increase speed and head into seas if practicable. Take evasive action by working rudder hard right and left if navigation permits.
– Fire warning rockets.
– Switch on outside lighting.
– Use searchlights to illuminate and dazzle suspects.
– CONTINUE TO MAINTAIN GOOD ALL-AROUND WATCH.
  After pirates have boarded:
– Barricade engine room and bridge, if practicable.
– Barricade the crew in secure areas, if practicable.
– Report the situation by radio and call for help, if available. Use Emergency Call-up Procedures in Chapter 4.
– DON'T BE HEROIC if the boarders are armed.

MARAD ADVISORIES: The U.S. Maritime Administration utilizes MARAD Advisories to rapidly disseminate information on maritime danger, safety, government policy, and other timely matters pertaining to U.S. fla and U.S. owned vessel operations. MARAD Advisories are issued by the Offic of Ship Operations to vessel Masters, operators, and other U.S. maritime interests via message. MARAD Advisories are also published in NGA's Notice to Mariners and maintained on NGA's Maritime Safety Information Center Website.

MARAD has established an internet Website at:
http://www.marad.dot.gov
to disseminate the latest information pertaining to the U.S. maritime industry. The following information is available:

– Ready Reserve Force news.
– Treasury Department's Office of oreign Assets Control.
– Maritime Security Act/Program.
– MARAD Advisories.
– Maritime Security Reports.
– Current maritime related legislation.
– Current press releases.
– Cargo preference.
– International and domestic marketing.
– Calendars of trade events.
– General public sales information.

For further information regarding MARAD Advisories contact:

MARITIME ADMINISTRATION
OFFICE OF SHIP OPERATIONS (MAR-613)
400 SEVENTH STREET SW
WASHINGTON DC 20590

Telephone: (1) 202-366-5735.
Fax: (1) 202-366-3954.
E-mail: opcenter1@marad.dot.gov.

400F. Emergency Position Indicating Radio Beacons (EPIRBs)

Emergency position indicating radio beacons (EPIRBs), devices which cost from $200 to $1500, are designed to save lives by alerting rescue authorities and indicating distress location. EPIRB types are described as follows:
– Class A (121.5/243 MHz): Float-free, automatically activating, detectable by aircraft and satellite. Coverage limited (see chart). An alert from this device to a RCC may be delayed 4-6 or more hours. No longer recommended.

- Class B (121.5/243 MHz): Manually activated version of Class A. No longer recommended.
- Class S (121.5/243 MHz): Similar to Class B, except that it floats or is an integral part of a survival craft. No longer recommended.
- Category I (406/121.5 MHz): Float-free, automatically activated EPIRB. Detectable by satellite anywhere in the world. Recognized by GMDSS.
- Category II (406/121.5 MHz): Similar to Category I, except manually activated. Some models are also water activated.
- Inmarsat-E (1646 MHz): Float-free, automatically activated EPIRB. Detectable by Inmarsat geostationary satellite. Recognized by GMDSS.

121.5/243 MHz EPIRBs (Class A, B, S): These are the most common and least expensive type of EPIRB, designed to be detected by overflyin commercial or military aircraft. Satellites were designed to detect these EPIRBs but are limited for the following reasons:
- Satellite detection range is limited for these EPIRBs (satellites must be within line of sight of both the EPIRB and a ground terminal for detection to occur) (see chart).
- Frequency congestion in the band used by these devices cause a high satellite false alert rate (99.8%); consequently, confirmatio is required before SAR forces can be deployed.
- EPIRBs manufactured before October 1989 may have design or construction problems (i.e., some models will leak and cease operating when immersed in water) or may not be detectable by satellite. Such EPIRBs may no longer be sold.
- Location ambiguities and frequency congestion in this band require two or more satellite passes to determine if the signal is from an EPIRB and to determine the location of the EPIRB, delaying rescue by an average of 4 to 6 hours. In some cases, a rescue can be delayed as long as 12 hours.
- Cospas-Sarsat is expected to cease detecting alerts on 121.5 MHz.

Class A, B, and S (121.5 MHz) EPIRBs have not been manufactured, imported, or sold in the U.S. since 1 February 2003; use of these EPIRBs in the U. S. shall be prohibited after 31 December 2006.

NOTE: The International Cospas-Sarsat Program has announced plans to terminate satellite processing of distress signals from 121.5/243 MHz emergency beacons on 1 February 2009. Mariners, aviators and other users of emergency beacons will need to switch to those operating at 406 MHz in order to be detected by satellites. The termination of 121.5/243 MHz processing is planned far enough in advance to allow users adequate time for the transition to the 406 MHz beacon.

The decision to terminate 121.5/243MHz satellite alerting services was made in response to guidance from the International Maritime Organization (IMO) and the International Civil Aviation Organization (ICAO). These two agencies of the United Nations are responsible for regulating the safety of ships and aircraft on international transits and handle international standards and plans for maritime and aeronautical search and rescue. In addition, problems within this frequency band inundate search and rescue authorities with false alerts, adversely impacting the effectiveness of lifesaving services. Although 406 MHz beacons are more costly, they provide search and rescue agencies with more reliable and complete information to do their job more efficiently and e fectively.

Individuals who plan on buying a new distress beacon need to be aware and take the Cospas-Sarsat decision into account.

406 MHz EPIRBs (Category I, II): The 406 MHz EPIRB was designed to operate with satellites. The signal frequency, 406 MHz, has been designated internationally for use only for distress; other communications and interference are not allowed on this frequency. Its signal allows a satellite local user terminal (LUT) to accurately locate the EPIRB (much more accurately than 121.5/243 MHz devices) and identify the vessel (by matching the unique identificatio code transmitted by the beacon to a registration database) anywhere in the world (there is no range limitation). These devices are detectable not only by Cospas-Sarsat satellites which are polar orbiting, but also by geostationary GOES weather satellites. EPIRBs detected by the GEOSAR system, consisting of GOES or other geostationary satellites, provide rescue authorities an instant alert, but without location information unless the EPIRB is equipped with an integral GPS receiver. EPIRBs detected by Cospas-Sarsat (i.e., TIROS N) satellites provide rescue authorities location of distress, but location and sometimes alerting may be delayed as much as an hour or two. These EPIRBs also include a 121.5 MHz homing signal, allowing aircraft and rescue craft to quickly fin the vessel in distress. These are the only type of EPIRBs which must be certifie by Coast Guard approved independent laboratories before they can be sold in the United States.

An automatically activated, floa free version of this EPIRB is designated for use in the GMDSS and has been required on SOLAS vessels (cargo ships over 300 tons and passenger ships on international voyages) since 1 August 1993. Coast Guard regulations require U.S. commercial fishin vessels to carry this device. The U.S. Coast Guard Navigation and Vessel Inspection Circular (NVIC) No. 3-99 provides a complete summary of EPIRB equipment requirements for U.S. fla vessels, including those vessels operating on the Great Lakes. This circular is available from the U.S. Coast Guard Homepage at:

http://www.uscg.mil/hq/g-m/nvic/

A new type of 406 MHz EPIRB, having an integral GPS navigation receiver, became available in 1998. This EPIRB provides accurate location, as well as identificatio information, to rescue authorities immediately upon activation through both geostationary (GEOSAR) and polar orbiting satellites.

DISTRESS, EMERGENCY, AND SAFETY TRAFFIC

COMPARISON OF THE 406 MHz AND 121.5 MHz DISTRESS BEACONS

406 MHz Beacons	121.5 MHz Beacons
Coverage:	
–Global.	–Ground station dependent; ground stations have an effective radius of about 1800 nm (2300 km). Both ground station and beacon must be in satellite footprint. Current coverage is about two-thirds of the world.
False Alerts:	
–All alerts come from beacons. Satellite beacon transmissions are digital, coded signals. Satellites process only encoded data, other signals are rejected. –About 1 in 12 alerts are actual distress. –Beacon-unique coding/registration allows rapid incident corroboration. Registration mandatory since 1994. 90% beacons registered. About 70% of false alerts are resolved by a phone or radio call to registration POCs prior to launching SAR assets.	–Only about 1 in 5 alerts come from beacons. Satellites can't discern beacon signals from many non-beacon sources. Beacons transmit anonymously with no unique identifie . –Fewer than 2 in 1000 alerts and 2 in 100 composite alerts are actual distress. –Since 121.5 MHz beacons transmit anonymously, the only way to ascertain the situation is to dispatch resources to investigate--a costly disadvantage.
Alerting:	
–First alert warrants launch of SAR assets. Earlier launches puts assets on scene sooner--average 3 hrs saved in maritime, 6 hrs in inland. –Average initial detection/alerting by orbiting satellites is about 45 minutes. –Average subsequent satellite passes every 60 minutes. –Vessel/aircraft ID, point of contact information provided with alerts allows rapid verification or stand-d wn. –Allows false alert follow-up to continuously improve system integrity/reliability. –Near instantaneous detection by geostationary satellites. System provides world-wide coverage.	–High false alert rate makes first-alert launch unfeasible Absent independent distress information means RCCs must wait for additional alert information. –Same as 406 MHz. –Same as 406 MHz. –Alerts are anonymous. 121.5 MHz analog technology not capable of transmitting data. –No false alert follow-up capability. –No GEO detection capability means no instantaneous detection.
Position Information:	
–1-3 nm (2-5 km) accuracy on average. Position calculated by Doppler shift analysis. –Less than 100 yard accuracy with GPS-equipped beacons. GPS position processed with initial alert. Major beacon enhancement.	–12-15 nm (15-25 km) accuracy on average. Position calculated by Doppler shift analysis. –No GPS capability.
Locating the Target:	
–Superior alert (non-GPS) position accuracy limits initial search area to about 25 sq. nm (65 sq. km). –GPS-equipped beacons reduce search area to a significantly smaller area –121.5 MHz homing signal facilitates target location by radio detection finder equipped search units	–Initial position uncertainty results in 500 sq. nm (800 sq. km) search area on average. –No GPS capability. –Same as 406 MHz.
Power Output:	
–5.0 Watts (strong power output).	–0.1 Watt (weaker power output)--hard for satellites to detect.
Cost:	
–Average cost is $1000 (GPS-equipped EPIRB). –Average cost is $500 (Personal Locator Beacon. –Average cost is $1500 - $3000 (ELT).	–Average cost is $200 - $400 (EPIRB). –Average cost is $600 - $1200 (ELT). –121.5 MHz beacons are being phased out.

DISTRESS, EMERGENCY, AND SAFETY TRAFFIC

Mariners should be aware of the differences between capabilities of 121.5/243 MHz and 406/121.5 MHz EPIRBs, as they have implications for alerting and locating of distress sites, as well as response by SAR forces. The advantages of 406/121.5 MHz devices are substantial, and are further enhanced by EPIRB-transmitted registration data on the carrying vessel. Owners of 406/121.5 MHz EPIRBs furnish registration information on their vessel, onboard survival gear, and emergency points of contact ashore, all of which greatly enhance both timely and tailored SAR response. The database for U.S. vessels is maintained by the National Oceanic and Atmospheric Administration (NOAA), and is accessed worldwide by SAR authorities to facilitate SAR response.

BEACON REGISTRATION: FCC regulations require that all 406 MHz EPIRBs carried on U.S. vessels be registered with NOAA. The U.S. Coast Guard is enforcing the FCC registration rule. FCC fines of up to $10,000, may be incurred for false activation of an unregistered EPIRB (e.g., as a hoax, or through gross negligence, carelessness, or improper storage and handling). The EPIRB must be updated with NOAA upon the change of vessel or EPIRB ownership, transfer of EPIRB to another vessel, or any other change in registration information, such as the owner's address or primary telephone number.

NOAA's National Beacon Registration Database is now available online. EPIRB owners can register and update their beacons directly via the internet at:

http://www.beaconregistration.noaa.gov/

Owner's of previously registered EPIRBs can access registration information with the unique beacon ID (i.e., 15 character hexadecimal Beacon Identification Code)

Registration forms and inquiries may also be obtained from:

NOAA SARSAT
E/SP3, RM 3320, FB-4
5200 AUTH ROAD
SUITLAND MD 20746-4304

- Telephone: (1) 888-212-SAVE (toll free), (1) 301-457-5678, or (1) 301-457-5430.
- Fax: (1) 301-568-8649.
- E-mail: osdpd.dsd.reception@noaa.gov.

TESTING 121.5/243 MHz EPIRBs: The U.S. Coast Guard urges EPIRB owners to periodically check for water tightness, battery expiration date, and signal presence. FCC rules allow Class A, B, and S EPIRBs to be turned on briefl (for three audio sweeps, or 1 second only) during the firs 5 minutes of any hour. Signal presence can be detected by an FM radio tuned to 99.5 MHz, or an AM radio tuned to any vacant frequency and located close to an EPIRB.

MONTHLY EPIRB INSPECTION PROCEDURES: For all compulsory vessels that are required to carry 406 MHz EPIRBs in U.S. waters (that is, all vessels over 300 gross tons, all commercial fishin vessels regardless of tonnage operating in waters greater than 3 nautical miles offshore, and all inspected vessels engaged in transporting 6 or more persons for hire regardless of tonnage) mandatory testing of a vessel's 406 MHz EPIRB is required on a monthly basis.

The following information has been developed by NOAA and the U.S. Coast Guard to provide EPIRB owners and maintainers a generic list of recommended procedures for conducting monthly EPIRB inspections. These inspection procedures are intended to provide general guidance and do not supersede the recommended procedures provided by the International Maritime Organization (IMO) or by the EPIRB manufacturer. All owners and maintainers should follow the inspection and self-testing procedures of their EPIRB manufacturer accordingly. Throughout the inspection and testing process, great care must be taken to avoid the transmission of a false distress alert.

- Inspection of the EPIRB housing: The firs test of an EPIRB should be to inspect the unit housing the EPIRB. 406 MHz EPIRBs should be fitte in an unobstructed "floa free" mounting and positioned away from any overhead obstructions to reduce the risk of the EPIRB becoming trapped when released. In such a mounting the EPIRB should be held in place by a Hydrostatic Release Unit (HRU), an Automatic Release Mechanism (ARM), or a manual release bracket. In the case of the HRU, it is designed to sense the increasing water pressure if a vessel sinks and at a predetermined depth (usually 3-5 meters) the HRU releases the mount, allowing the EPIRB to floa to the surface. If the EPIRB is a Category I beacon, the mounting unit will allow the EPIRB to switch itself on as it is released, so it will operate automatically if the vessel sinks. Category II EPIRBs differ in that they are not released automatically via the HRU; they activate manually or through immersion in water.
- Expiration date: If the EPIRB is retained in its mount or casing by an HRU, then the expiration date or service date label on the HRU should be noted and clearly visible. These units must be replaced every 2 years including any associated plastic bolts, rods, springs, and/or spacing washers. The HRU should be free of any signs of corrosion, cracking, water ingress, etc. Any damage should be repaired in accordance with the manufacturer's procedures, or the unit replaced.
- EPIRB lanyard: Presence of a firml attached lanyard in good condition should also be verified The lanyard should be neatly stowed, and must not be tied to the vessel or the mounting bracket.
- Checking for physical damage: The EPIRB should be examined thoroughly for any physical damage. If there appears to be any damage, corrosion, cracking, water ingress, etc., the EPIRB should be replaced with a backup immediately. In turn, this replacement EPIRB should meet each of the inspection and testing criteria listed here as well.
- Proper registration: An inspection of the EPIRB registration decal from NOAA should also be completed for all U.S.A.-coded EPIRBs. The registration decal should be properly placed on the EPIRB and clearly visible for U.S. Coast Guard inspectors. If there appears

DISTRESS, EMERGENCY, AND SAFETY TRAFFIC

to be any damage to the decal, NOAA should be notifie immediately. U.S. law requires that all 406 MHz EPIRBs must be properly registered with NOAA. Every two years NOAA will seek an update of the registration information to ensure accuracy. However, if at anytime the registration information does change (such as a new phone number, new address, new emergency contact, etc.) NOAA must be informed immediately.
– EPIRB battery: The expiration date of the EPIRB's battery should also be inspected. This is usually given on the EPIRB manufacturer's label or on another plate affi ed to the EPIRB. Battery life for most EPIRBs is 5 years. The battery must be replaced on or before the expiration date or if the EPIRB has been used in an emergency regardless of the length of time. EPIRB batteries are designed to operate the beacon for a minimum of 48 hours and therefore must always be fully charged.
– Self-testing: After the EPIRB has been properly inspected, a self-test of the EPIRB can be conducted following the instructions provided by the EPIRB manufacturer. It is important that the manufacturer's instructions be followed to ensure that the EPIRB is working properly and to avoid an accidental activation. Most EPIRBs have a visible test switch that is usually spring loaded so it cannot be left on inadvertently and thus reduce the life of the battery. A light will indicate that the test circuits are operating correctly. Sometimes this light will also activate the strobe light. It is recommended that the self-test switch be held for no more than 2 flashe of the strobe light or no longer than 1 minute after the firs self-test mode burst transmission. When operating a 406 MHz EPIRB self-test, the EPIRB is allowed to radiate a single burst which is specially coded so that it is ignored by the Cospas-Sarsat system. The EPIRB must never be tested by actual operation. If it is accidentally activated in the transmit mode, then it should be turned off at once and the false alert cancelled by calling the nearest U.S. Coast Guard Station and have them contact the nearest Rescue Coordination Center.
– Log-keeping: For compulsory vessels all EPIRB tests must be logged. Usually this is recorded in the GMDSS Station Log which requires compulsory vessels to conduct and record tests of the vessel's GMDSS system on a routine basis. The GMDSS Station Log is required under 47 CFR 80.409.

When used in an emergency, some EPIRBs must be floatin in the water for their antenna to operate at peak efficien y. The EPIRB manufacturer's instructions will indicate if the EPIRB should be operating afloa or if it can be kept inside the liferaft. In either event, once the EPIRB is activated in a distress situation leave it switched on until you have been rescued or until the batteries are exhausted.

ANNUAL TESTING OF EPIRBs: The annual testing of 406 MHz satellite EPIRBs is required by SOLAS regulation IV/15.9. The IMO has issued MSC/Circ.1040 (dated 28 May 2002) which provides the following guidelines on annual testing of 406 MHz satellite EPIRBs:

The testing should be carried out using suitable test equipment capable of performing all the relevant measurements required in these guidelines. All checks of electrical parameters should be performed in the self-test mode, if possible.

The examination of the installed 406 MHz satellite EPIRB should include:
– checking position and mounting for float-free operation
– verifying the presence of a firml attached lanyard in good condition; the lanyard should be neatly stowed, and must not be tied to the vessel or the mounting bracket;
– carrying out visual inspection for defects;
– carrying out the self-test routine;
– checking that the EPIRB identificatio (15 Hex ID and other required information) is clearly marked on the outside of the equipment;
– decoding the EPIRB 15 Hexadecimal Identificatio Digits (15 Hex ID) and other information from the transmitted signal, checking that the decoded information (15 Hex ID or MMSI/callsign data, as required) is identical to the identificatio marked on the beacon;
– checking registration through documentation or through the point of contact associated with that country code;
– checking the battery expiration date;
– checking the hydrostatic release and its expiration date, as appropriate;
– checking the emission in the 406 MHz band using the self-test mode or an appropriate device to avoid transmission of a distress call to the satellites;
– if possible, checking emission on the 121.5 MHz frequency using the self-test mode or an appropriate device to avoid activating the satellite system;
– checking that the EPIRB has been maintained by an approved shore-based maintenance provider at intervals required (i.e., not exceeding 12 months, see 47 CFR 80.1105(k));
– after the test, remounting the EPIRB in its bracket, checking that no transmission has been started; and
– verifying the presence of beacon operating instructions.

INMARSAT-E EPIRBs: Inmarsat-E EPIRBs operate on 1.6 GHz (L-band) and transmit a distress signal to Inmarsat geostationary satellites, which includes a registered identity similar to that of the 406 MHz EPIRB, and a location derived from a GPS navigational satellite receiver inside the EPIRB. Inmarsat-E EPIRBs may be detected anywhere in the world between 70°N and 70°S. Since geostationary satellites are used, alerts are transmitted almost instantly to a RCC associated with the Inmarsat Land Earth Station (LES) receiving the alert. The distress alert transmitted by an Inmarsat-E EPIRB is received by two LESs in each ocean region, giving 100 percent duplication for each ocean region in case of failures or outages associated with any of the LESs. Alerts received over the Inmarsat Atlantic Ocean Regions are routed to the Coast Guard Atlantic Area command center in Portsmouth, and alerts received over the Inmarsat Pacifi Ocean Region are routed to the Coast Guard Pacifi Area command center in Alameda. This type of EPIRB is designated for use in the GMDSS, but it is not sold in the United States or approved for use by U.S. flag essels.

NOTE: Inmarsat will withdraw its L-band EPIRB service (Inmarsat-E) on 1 December 2006.

THE COSPAS-SARSAT SYSTEM: Cospas-Sarsat (Cospas is a Russian acronym for "Space System for Search of Distress Vessels;" Sarsat signifie "Search and Rescue Satellite-Aided Tracking") is an international satellite-based search and rescue system established by the U.S., Russia, Canada, and France to detect and locate emergency radiobeacons transmitting on the frequencies 121.5 and 406 MHz. Since its inception, the Cospas-Sarsat system has contributed to the saving of over 15,700 lives in approximately 4,500 SAR events.

The Cospas-Sarsat system provides distress and location data to RCCs for 121.5 MHz beacons, within the coverage area of Cospas-Sarsat ground stations (Local User Terminals - LUTs), and for 406 MHz beacons, activated anywhere in the world. The system is composed of:
– distress radiobeacons (EPIRBs for maritime use) which transmit signals during distress situations;
– instruments on board satellites in geostationary and low-altitude Earth orbits which detect the signals transmitted by distress radiobeacons;
– ground receiving stations, referred to as Local User Terminals (LUTs), which receive and process the satellite downlink signal to generate distress alerts; and
– Mission Control Centers (MCCs) which receive alerts produced by LUTs and forward them to RCCs, SAR Points of Contacts (SPOCs), or other MCCs.

The Cospas-Sarsat system includes two types of satellites:
– polar orbiting, or low-altitude Earth orbit (LEO), satellites which form the LEOSAR System;
– geostationary Earth orbit (GEO) satellites which form the GEOSAR System.

The 406 MHz LEOSAR System provides global non-continuous coverage using a limited number of polar orbiting satellites and 406 MHz beacons. The coverage is not continuous because polar orbiting satellites can only view a portion of the earth at any given time. However, the satellite is able to store distress beacon information and continuously broadcast it until the satellite comes within view of a LEOLUT, thereby providing global coverage. Doppler processing techniques are used to calculate the position of the beacon. In the case of second generation 406 MHz beacons, the location information is acquired from global satellite navigation systems, through an internal or external navigation receiver, and encoded in the beacon message.

The 121.5 MHz LEOSAR System coverage is neither global nor continuous because the detection of the distress signal can only occur when the satellite simultaneously views the transmitting beacon and the ground receiving station. Doppler processing techniques are used to calculate the position of the beacon; however, the location accuracy of 121.5 MHz beacons is not as good as the accuracy achieved with 406 MHz beacons because of the relatively poorer frequency stability performance of these older generation beacons. Furthermore, a second satellite pass is normally required to resolve postion ambiguity.

The 406 MHz GEOSAR System provides continuous coverage of all areas of the globe to about 75 °latitude. This system provides almost immediate alerting in the footprint of the GEOSAR satellite, however it has no independent location capability. To provide rescuers with position information, the beacon location must be either:
– acquired by the beacon through an internal or an external navigation receiver and encoded in the beacon message; or
– derived, with possible delays, from the LEOSAR system Doppler processing.

The USCG receives data from international sources via the USMCC. See the following table:

LIST OF COSPAS-SARSAT MCCs AND LEOLUTs
(Extracted from ANNEX 10 of the IMO GMDSS Master Plan)

| Country | MCC | | | LEOLUT | | Associated RCC |
	Location	Designator	Status	Location	Status	
Algeria	Algiers	ALMCC	Operational	Ouargla	Operational	RCC Algiers
Argentina	Ezeiza	ARMCC	Operational	Parana Rio Grande	Operational	MRCC Puerto Belgrano
Australia	Canberra	AUMCC	Operational	Albany Bundaberg	Operational	RCC Australia
Brazil	Brasilia	BRMCC	Operational	Brasilia Manaus Recife	Under development	Salvamar/Salvaero
Canada	Trenton	CMCC	Operational	Churchill Edmonton Goose Bay	Operational	

DISTRESS, EMERGENCY, AND SAFETY TRAFFIC

LIST OF COSPAS-SARSAT MCCs AND LEOLUTs
(Extracted from ANNEX 10 of the IMO GMDSS Master Plan)

Country	MCC			LEOLUT		Associated RCC
	Location	Designator	Status	Location	Status	
Chile	Santiago	CHMCC	Operational	Easter Island Punta Arenas Santiago	Operational	MRCC Chile
China	Beijing	CNMCC	Operational	Beijing	Operational	
France	Toulouse	FMCC	Operational	Toulouse	Operational	MRCC Gris Nez MRCC La Garde
Hong Kong	Hong Kong	HKMCC	Operational	Hong Kong	Operational	MRCC Hong Kong
India	Bangalore	INMCC	Operational	Bangalore Lucknow	Operational	
Indonesia	Jakarta	IDMCC	Operational	Jakarta	Operational	RCC I; Soekarta-Hatta Airport, Jakarta RCC II; Djuanda Airport, Suraybaya RCC III; Hasanudin Airport, Ujung Pandang RCC IV; Frans Karseifo Airport, Biak
Italy	Bari	ITMCC	Operational	Bari	Operational	MRCC Roma
ITDC[1]	Taipei	TAMCC	Operational	Chi-lung (Keelung)	Operational	
Japan	Tokyo	JAMCC	Operational	Yokohama	Operational	RCC Otaru RCC Shiogama RCC Yokohama RCC Nagoya RCC Kobe RCC Hiroshima RCC Kitakyushu RCC Maizuru RCC Niigata RCC Kagoshima RCC Naha
Republic of Korea	Taejon	KOMCC	Operational	Taejon	Operational	RCC Inchon RCC Kimpo
New Zealand	Canberra[2]	AUMCC	Operational	Wellington	Operational	RCC Lower Hutt
Nigeria	Abuja	NIMCC	Under development	Abuja	Under development	
Norway	Bodø	NMCC	Operational	Tromso Spitzbergen	Operational	MRCC Bodø MRCC Stavanger
Pakistan	Lahore	PAMCC	Under development	Lahore	Operational	CAA Lahore MSA Karachi

DISTRESS, EMERGENCY, AND SAFETY TRAFFIC

LIST OF COSPAS-SARSAT MCCs AND LEOLUTs
(Extracted from ANNEX 10 of the IMO GMDSS Master Plan)

Country	MCC			LEOLUT		Associated RCC
	Location	Designator	Status	Location	Status	
Peru	Callao	PEMCC	Operational	Callao	Operational	MRCC Callao
Russian Federation	Moscow	CMC	Operational	Arkhangelsk	Operational	
				Moscow[3]	Not operational	
				Nakhodka	Operational	
Saudi Arabia	Jiddah	SAMCC	Operational	Jiddah	Operational	RCC Jiddah
Singapore	Singapore	SIMCC	Operational	Singapore	Operational	Singapore Port Operations Control Center
South Africa	Cape Town	ASMCC	Operational	Cape Town	Operational	
Spain	Maspalomas	SPMCC	Operational	Maspalomas	Operational	RCC Madrid RCC Baleares RCC Canarias
Thailand	Bangkok	THMCC	Operational	Bangkok	Under development	RCC Bangkok
United Kingdom	Kinloss	UKMCC	Operational	Combe Martin	Operational	MRCC Falmouth ARCC Kinloss
United States	Suitland	USMCC	Operational	Alaska California Guam Hawaii Puerto Rico Texas	Operational	RCC Boston RCC Norfolk RCC Miami RCC New Orleans RSC San Juan RCC Cleveland RCC Seattle RCC Honolulu RSC Guam RCC Juneau RCC Alameda Langley AFB, VA Ft Richardson, AK
Vietnam	VNMCC	Haiphong	Under development	Haiphong	Under development	MRCC Vietnam

Notes:
[1] The International Telecommunication Development Corporation.
[2] The NZ LUT is directly connected to the Australian MCC (AUMCC).
[3] Out of operation from 15 October 2001 due to relocation.

LIST OF COSPAS-SARSAT GEOLUTs
(Extracted from ANNEX 10 of the IMO GMDSS Master Plan)

Country	GEOLUT	
	Location	Status
Argentina	Ezeiza	In operation, commissioned
Brazil	Brasilia Recife	In operation, commissioned In operation, commissioned
Canada	Trenton (1) Trenton (2)	In operation, commissioned In operation, commissioned
Chile	Santiago	In operation, commissioned
France	Toulouse	In operation[1]
India	Bangalore	In operation[1]
New Zealand	Wellington (1) Wellington (2)	In operation, commissioned Under development
Spain	Maspalomas (1) Maspalomas (2)	In operation, commissioned Under development
United Kingdom	Combe Martin	In operation, commissioned

Notes:
[1] GEOLUTs have not been commissioned, however, alert data are used operationally.

DISTRESS, EMERGENCY, AND SAFETY TRAFFIC

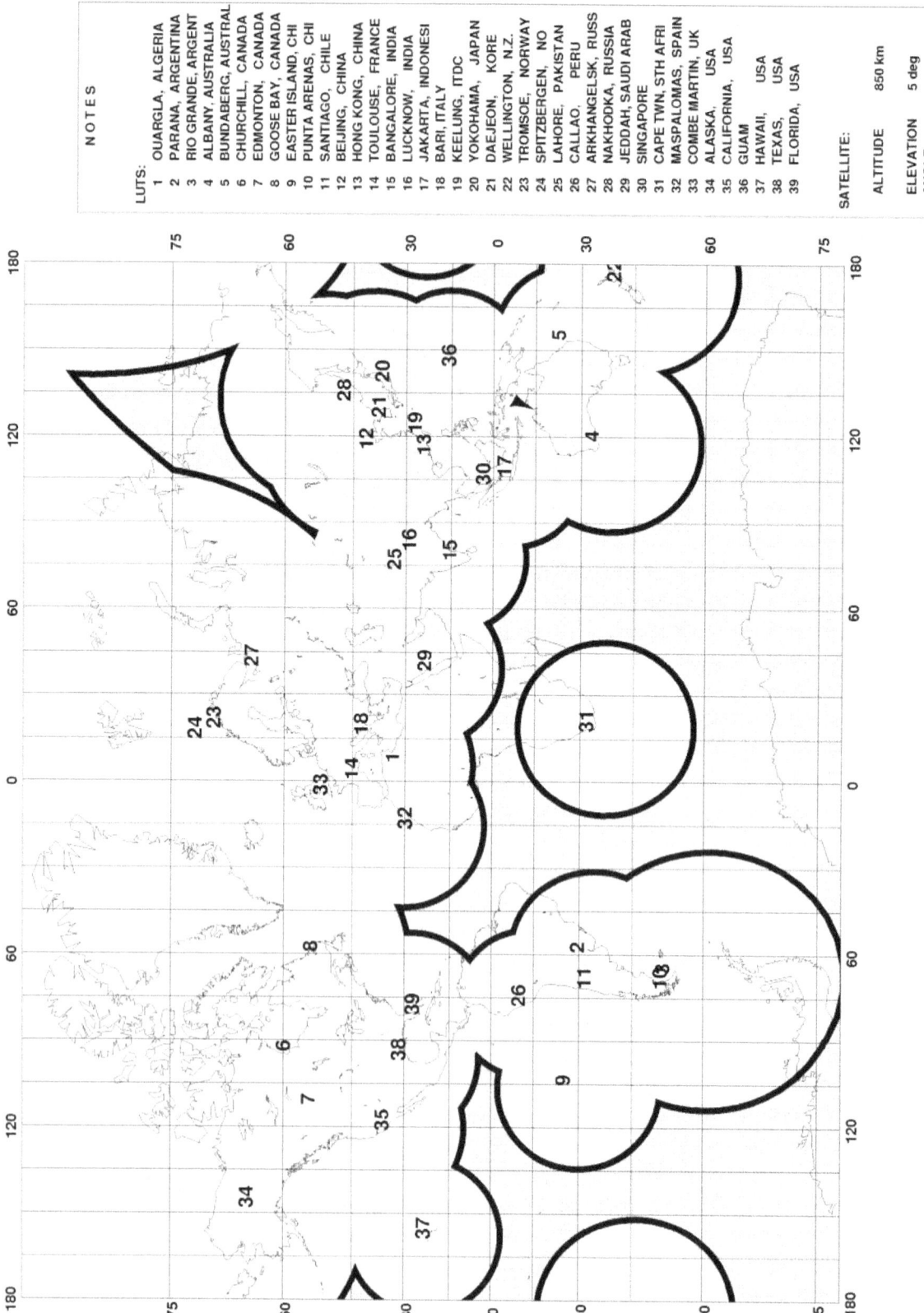

Cospas-Sarsat LEOLUTs - white area: 406 & 121.5 MHz coverage; gray: only 406 MHz coverage

4 - 27

DISTRESS, EMERGENCY, AND SAFETY TRAFFIC

400G. Global Maritime Distress and Safety System (GMDSS)

The Global Maritime Distress and Safety System (GMDSS) represents a significant improvement in marine safety over the previous system of short range and high seas radio transmissions. Its many parts include satellite as well as advanced terrestrial communications systems. Operational service of the GMDSS began on 1 February 1992, with full implementation achieved on 1 February 1999.

The GMDSS was adopted by amendments in 1988 by the Conference of Contracting Governments to the International Convention for the Safety of Life at Sea (SOLAS), 1974. The GMDSS offers the greatest advancement in maritime safety since the enactment of regulations following the Titanic disaster in 1912. It is an automated ship-to-ship, shore-to-ship and ship-to-shore system covering distress alerting and relay, the provision of Maritime Safety Information (MSI) and basic communication links. Satellite and advanced terrestrial systems are incorporated into a modern communications network to promote and improve safety of life and property at sea throughout the world. The equipment required on board ships will depend not on their tonnage, but rather on the sea area in which the vessel operates. This is fundamentally different from the previous system, which based requirements on vessel size alone. The greatest benefi of the GMDSS is that it vastly reduces the chances of ships sinking without a trace and enables search and rescue (SAR) operations to be launched without delay.

SHIP CARRIAGE REQUIREMENTS: By the terms of the SOLAS Convention, the GMDSS provisions apply to cargo ships of 300 gross tons and over and ships carrying more than 12 passengers on international voyages. Unlike previous shipboard carriage regulations that specifie equipment according to size of vessel, the GMDSS carriage requirements stipulate equipment according to the area the vessel operates in. These areas are designated as follows:

– Sea Area A1 - An area within the radiotelephone coverage of at least one VHF coast station in which continuous Digital Selective Calling (DSC - a radio receiver that performs distress alerting and safety calling on HF, MF and VHF frequencies) is available, as may be define by a Contracting Government to the 1974 SOLAS Convention. This area extends from the coast to about 20 miles offshore.
– Sea Area A2 - An area, excluding sea area A1, within the radiotelephone coverage of at least one MF coast station in which continuous DSC alerting is available, as may be define by a Contracting Government. The general area is from the A1 limit out to about 100 miles offshore.
– Sea Area A3 - An area, excluding sea areas A1 and A2, within the coverage of an Inmarsat geostationary satellite in which continuous alerting is available. This area is from about 70°N to 70°S.
– Sea Area A4 - All areas outside sea areas A1, A2 and A3. This area includes the polar regions, where geostationary satellite coverage is not available.

The GMDSS rules are found in subpart W of Part 80 (Code of Federal Regulations, Title 47, Part 80). Carriage requirements for GMDSS radio equipment can be summarized as follows:
– Sea Area A1 ships will carry VHF equipment and either a satellite or VHF EPIRB.
– Sea Area A2 ships will carry VHF and MF equipment and a satellite EPIRB.
– Sea Area A3 ships will carry VHF, MF, a satellite EPIRB and either HF or satellite communication equipment.
– Sea Area A4 ships will carry VHF, MF and HF equipment and a satellite EPIRB.
– All ships will carry equipment for receiving MSI broadcasts and equipment for survival craft.

Ships at sea must be capable of the following functional GMDSS requirements:
– Ship-to-shore distress alerting (by two independent means, each using a different communication service).
– Shore-to-ship distress alerting.
– Ship-to-ship distress alerting.
– SAR coordination.
– On-scene communications.
– Transmission and receipt of emergency locating signals.
– Transmission and receipt of MSI.
– General radio communications.
– Bridge-to-bridge communications.

To meet the requirements of the functional areas above the following is a list of the minimum communications equipment needed for all ships:
– VHF radio capable of transmitting and receiving DSC on channel 70 and radiotelephony on channels 6, 13, and 16.
– Radio receiver capable of maintaining a continuous DSC watch on VHF channel 70.
– Search and rescue transponders (SART) (two on every passenger vessel and cargo vessels of 500 gross tons and over and at least one on every cargo vessel 300 gross tons and over but less than 500 gross tons) operating in the 9 GHz band.
– Receiver capable of receiving NAVTEX broadcasts anywhere NAVTEX service is available.
– Receiver capable of receiving either SafetyNET or HF NBDP (if service is provided) anywhere NAVTEX is not available.
– Satellite EPIRB capable of being activated manually or float-free self-act vated.
– Two-way hand held VHF radios (two sets minimum on 300-500 gross tons cargo vessels and three sets minimum on cargo vessels of 500 gross tons and upward and on all passenger ships).

Additionally, each sea area has its own requirements under GMDSS which are as follows:
– Sea Area A1:
Vessels that operate only in Sea Area A1 must meet the above requirements for all ships and the following:
– 1. General VHF radiotelephone capability.
– 2. Capability of initiating a distress alert from a navigational position by using either:
– (a) VHF DSC; or
– (b) Category I 406 MHz EPIRB (this requirement may be met by either installing the 406 MHz

DISTRESS, EMERGENCY, AND SAFETY TRAFFIC

EPIRB required for all ships near the navigational position or by having remote activation capability); or
– (c) MF DSC; or
– (d) HF DSC; or
– (e) an Inmarsat Ship Earth Station (SES).

– Sea Areas A1 and A2:
Vessels that operate in Sea Areas A1 and A2 must meet the above requirements for all ships and the following:
– 1. An MF radio installation capable of distress and safety communications from a navigational position on:
  – (a) 2187.5 kHz using DSC; and
  – (b) 2187.5 kHz using radiotelephony.
– 2. Equipment capable of maintaining a continuous DSC watch on 2187.5 kHz (may be combined with MF installation in paragraph (1)(a) of this section, but must have separate receiver).
– 3. Capability of initiating a distress alert from a navigational position by using either:
  – (a) Category I 406 MHz EPIRB (this requirement may be met by installing the 406 MHz EPIRB near the navigational position or by having remote activation capability); or
  – (b) HF DSC; or
  – (c) an Inmarsat SES.
– 4. Capability of transmitting and receiving general radio communications using radiotelephony or direct-printing telegraphy by either:
  – (a) an MF or HF radio installation operating on working frequencies in the bands 1605-4000 kHz, or 4000-27500 kHz (this capability may be added to the MF installation in paragraph (1) of this section); or
  – (b) an Inmarsat SES.

– Sea Areas A1, A2 and A3:
Vessels that operate in Sea Areas A1, A2 and A3 must meet the above requirements for all ships and either, paragraphs (1) - (4) or (5) - (8) of the following:
– 1. An Inmarsat SES capable of:
  – (a) transmitting and receiving distress and safety communications by means of direct-printing telegraphy;
  – (b) transmitting and receiving distress priority calls;
  – (c) maintaining watch for shore-to-ship distress alerts including those directed to specificall defined geographical areas
  – (d) transmitting and receiving general radio communications using either radiotelephony or direct-printing telegraphy.
– 2. An MF radio installation capable of distress and safety communications on:
  – (a) 2187.5 kHz using DSC;
  – (b) 2187.5 kHz using radiotelephony.
– 3. Equipment capable of maintaining a continuous DSC watch on 2187.5 kHz (may be combined with MF installation in paragraph (2)(a) of this section, but must have separate receiver).
– 4. Capability of initiating a distress alert by either of the following:
  – (a) Category I 406 MHz EPIRB (this requirement may be met by installing the 406 MHz EPIRB near the navigational position or by having remote activation capability); or
  – (b) HF DSC; or
  – (c) an Inmarsat SES.
– 5. An MF/HF radio installation capable of transmitting and receiving on all distress and safety frequencies in the bands between 1605-27500 kHz using DSC, radiotelephony, and narrow-band direct-printing telegraphy.
– 6. Equipment capable of maintaining DSC watch on 2187.5 kHz, 8414.5 kHz and on at least one of the distress and safety DSC frequencies 4207.5 kHz, 6312 kHz, 12577 kHz, or 16804.5 kHz, although it must be possible to select any of these DSC distress and safety frequencies at any time (the watch-maintaining receiver may be separate from or combined with the MF/HF installation in paragraph (5) of this section).
– 7. Capability of initiating a distress alert by either of the following:
  – (a) Category I 406 MHz EPIRB (this requirement may be met by installing the 406 MHz EPIRB near the navigational position or by having remote activation capability); or
  – (b) a separate Inmarsat SES.
– 8. Capability of transmitting and receiving general radio communications using radiotelephony or direct-printing telegraphy by an MF/HF radio installation operating on working frequencies in the bands 1605-4000 kHz and 4000-27500 kHz (this capability may be added to the MF/HF installation in paragraph (5) of this section).

NOTE: It must be possible to initiate transmission of distress alerts by the radio installations specifie in paragraphs (1), (2), (4), (5), and (7) of this section from the position from which the ship is normally navigated.

– Sea Areas A1, A2, A3 and A4:
Vessels that operate in Sea Areas A1, A2, A3 and A4 must meet the above requirements for all ships and the following:
– 1. An MF/HF radio installation capable of transmitting and receiving on all distress and safety frequencies in the bands between 1605-27500 kHz using DSC, radiotelephony, and narrow-band direct-printing telegraphy.
– 2. Equipment capable of maintaining DSC watch on 2187.5 kHz, 8414.5 kHz and on at least one of the distress and safety DSC frequencies 4207.5 kHz, 6312 kHz, 12577 kHz, or 16804.5 kHz, although it must be possible to select any of these DSC distress and safety frequencies at any time (the watch-maintaining receiver may be separate from or combined with the MF/HF installation in paragraph (1) of this section).
– 3. Capability of initiating a distress alert by both of the following:
  – (a) Category I 406 MHz EPIRB (this requirement may be met by installing the 406 MHz EPIRB

DISTRESS, EMERGENCY, AND SAFETY TRAFFIC

near the navigational position or by having remote activation capability); and
- (b) the MF/HF installation using DSC on any of the above DSC distress alerting frequencies. It must be possible to initiate the distress alert by this means from the position from which the ship is normally navigated.
- 4. Capability of transmitting and receiving general radio communications using radiotelephony and direct-printing telegraphy by an MF/HF radio installation operating on working frequencies in the bands 1605-4000 kHz and 4000-27500 kHz (this capability may be added to the MF/HF installation in paragraph (1) of this section).

GMDSS information, provided by the U.S. Coast Guard Navigation Center, is internet accessible through the World Wide Web at:

http://www.navcen.uscg.gov/marcomms/default.htm

The information available includes worldwide NAVTEX and Inmarsat SafetyNET schedules, U.S. NAVTEX service areas, U.S. SAR areas, status of shore-side implementation, regulatory information, NAVAREA chart, HF narrow band direct printing and radiotelephone channels used for distress and safety calling, information on GMDSS coast stations, AMVER and International Ice Patrol information, information concerning radiofacsimile and other maritime safety broadcasts, and digital selective calling information.

400H. The Inmarsat System

Inmarsat, a limited private company of more than 600 partners worldwide, is an important element within GMDSS providing maritime safety communications for ships at sea. In accordance with its convention, Inmarsat provides the space segment necessary for improving distress communications, efficien y and management of ships, and maritime correspondence services.

The basic components of the Inmarsat system include the Inmarsat space segment, Land Earth Stations (LESs), and mobile Ship Earth Stations (SESs).

The Inmarsat space segment is comprised of four communications satellites in geostationary orbit that provide primary coverage. Five additional satellites in orbit serve as spares.

The higher polar regions are not visible to the operational satellites and coverage is available between 70°N and 70°S. Satellite coverage is divided into four ocean regions, which are:
- Atlantic Ocean Region - East (AOR-E).
- Atlantic Ocean Region - West (AOR -W).
- Pacific Ocean R gion (POR).
- Indian Ocean Region (IOR).

The LESs provide the interface between the satellite network and the public switched telephone network (PSTN), public data network (PDN), and various private line services. These networks link registered information providers to the LES. The data then travels from the LES to the Inmarsat Network Coordination Station (NCS) and then down to the SESs on ships at sea. Communications between the LES and the Inmarsat satellite are in the 6 GHz band (C-band). The satellite routes ship to shore traffi to the LES in the 4 GHz band (C-band). The SESs provide two-way communications between ship and shore. Communications between the SES and the satellite are in the 1.6 GHz band (L-band), while the satellite routes shore to ship traffic to the SES in the 1.5 GHz band (L-band)

Inmarsat provides four satellite communications systems:
- Inmarsat-A, the original Inmarsat system, operates at a transfer rate of up to 9600 bits per second and provides two-way direct-dial phone, telex, facsimile (fax), electronic mail and data communications. Although Inmarsat-A is approved for fittin in ships as part of their GMDSS equipment, it is not mandatory and does not contribute any unique functionality that is not also provided by other equipment in the full GMDSS suite. NOTE: The scheduled withdrawal of Inmarsat-A services will take effect on 31 December 2007.
- The Inmarsat-B system also provides two-way direct-dial phone, telex, fax and data communications at a transfer rate of up to 9600 bits per second, but uses digital technology to provide high quality, reliable and cost effective communication services.
- Inmarsat-C provides a store and forward data messaging capability (but no voice) at 600 bits per second, and is qualifie by the IMO to comply with the GMDSS requirements for receiving MSI data on board ship. Various equipment manufacturers produce this type of SES, which is small, lightweight, and utilizes an omnidirectional antenna.
- Inmarsat Fleet F77 is a fully integrated satellite communication service incorporating voice and data applications. It meets the latest distress and safety requirements, as specifie in IMO Resolution A.888 (21), for voice pre-emption and prioritization within the GMDSS. Inmarsat Fleet F77 recognizes four levels of priority:
  - distress,
  - urgency,
  - safety, and
  - other routine communications

and provides access to emergency communications in both ship-to-shore and shore-to-ship directions for distress, urgency and safety traffi originated by RCCs or other SAR authorities.

NOTE: Inmarsat-A and -B terminals are used for voice and high speed data capability. These terminals must be used in conjunction with a SafetyNET receiver or an Inmarsat-C transceiver. The Inmarsat-C/A and -C/B is the preferred combination for the following reasons:
- A satellite-option vessel must have a transmit capability on either Inmarsat-C/A or -C/B. If the vessel is Inmarsat-A or -B equipped, then the Inmarsat-C provides redundancy.
- The USCG and the National Weather Service strongly encourage vessels which participate in the voluntary AMVER position reporting and weather observing programs to equip with Inmarsat-C since its data

DISTRESS, EMERGENCY, AND SAFETY TRAFFIC

reporting capability enables a much less costly report than does the Inmarsat-A or -B, or HF radioteletype formats. These voluntary ship reports will be accepted by the government at no cost to the ship. The data reporting service is also available at very low cost for other brief reports which can be compressed to 32 bytes of data or less.

– Redundancy in selective equipment is not only very desirable but, under GMDSS rules, gives the vessel greater options in how GMDSS equipment is maintained. Ship owners/operators must generally provide shore-based maintenance, onboard maintenance, and limited equipment duplication.

– Vessels are tracked automatically when a navigation receiver is connected to an Inmarsat terminal by programming an automatic transmission of ship position at specifie times or by random polling from shore. This is done with the owner/operator's permission. When a navigation receiver is available, it should be connected to the Inmarsat-C, since the Coast Guard distress alerts are broadcast to all ships within a specifie distance from a distress scene. The Inmarsat-C processor will print the alert if the ship's position is within the specifie area. Alternatively, the ship's position must be entered manually every four hours to facilitate this safety service.

If a ship will accommodate an Inmarsat-C or SafetyNET receiver in addition to an Inmarsat-A or -B receiver, the separate omnidirectional antenna should be used rather than the stabilized, tracking antenna of the Inmarsat-A or -B. The reason for this is to have a completely separate system in case of an Inmarsat-A or -B antenna failure. There is also a primary designated satellite for SafetyNET broadcasts in each of 16 NAVAREAs worldwide, and the Inmarsat-C should guard that designated satellite when in areas of overlapping coverage (i.e., the Inmarsat-C can track the satellite designated for MSI broadcasts and the Inmarsat-A or -B can track the other satellite, if preferred). Ships with both Inmarsat -A/B and -C terminals should designate one as the primary GMDSS terminal. In most cases the Inmarsat-C will be selected to minimize the emergency power requirements.

INMARSAT SERVICES: Enhanced Group Call (EGC) is a message broadcast service within the Inmarsat-C Communications System. It allows terrestrial registered information providers to pass messages or data to mobile Enhanced Group Call (EGC) receivers, class 2 or class 3 SESs, or Inmarsat-A and Inmarsat-B SESs equipped with EGC receivers. EGC messages are sent to the LES by registered shore-based information providers using terrestrial facilities, such as Telex. The messages are processed at the LES and forwarded to a Network Coordination Station (NCS) which transmits them on an NCS common channel. There are two basic services offered by EGC: SafetyNET and FleetNET. SafetyNET is a service provided primarily for the dissemination of MSI, such as ship to shore distress alerts, weather forecasts, and coastal warnings. FleetNET is a commercial communication service which allows registered terrestrial information providers to send messages to predefine groups of subscribers (see EGC Receiver Addressing).

INMARSAT SES CAPABILITY: An EGC receiver is define as a single channel receiver with a dedicated message processor. SES classes 2 and 3 provide an EGC capability in addition to shore to ship and ship to shore messaging capabilities. The mandatory capabilities of an EGC receiver are defined as

– Continuous reception of an NCS common channel and processing the information according to EGC protocol.
– Automatic recognition of messages directed to a fxed geographic area, and service codes as selected by the receiver operator.

Additional optional capabilities are required for the reception of FleetNET:

– Automatic recognition of uniquely addressed messages directed to a particular receiver.
– Automatic recognition of messages directed to a group to which the receiver operator subscribes.
– Automatic response to group ID updates directed to that EGC receiver, adding or deleting group IDs as commanded.

The EGC receiver shall be capable of being tuned to any channel in the band 1530.0 MHz to 1545.0 MHz in increments of 5 kHz. The EGC receiver shall be equipped with facilities for storing up to 20 NCS channel numbers. Four of these will be permanently assigned global beam frequencies, which are:

NCS	NCS Common Channel Channel No.	Frequency
AOR-W	11080	1537.7 MHz
AOR-E	12580	1541.45 MHz
POR	12580	1541.45 MHz
IOR	10840	1537.1 MHz

These four numbers shall be stored in ROM and shall not be alterable. The remaining list of NCS Common Channel Frequencies (approximately 16 valid) will be published by Inmarsat and assigned as expansion common channels. These shall be held in non-volatile but alterable storage, and be capable of operator alteration in the event that Inmarsat decides to update the frequency plan by adding, deleting, or changing allocations.

MESSAGE PROCESSING: Message processing will be based on the header field For messages with a double header, the two packets must be regarded as a single message and will not be printed until completely received, even in the case of multipacket messages. Acceptance or rejection of service code-types shall be under operator control with the following exceptions:

– Receivers shall always receive navigational warnings, meteorological warnings, SAR information, and shore-to-ship distress alerts (which are directed by the geographical area within which the receiver is positioned).
– Unique and group identities shall not be programmable.

EGC RECEIVER ADDRESSING: The fve basic methods of addressing EGC receivers are:

– All ships call - urgent marine information.
– Inmarsat System message addressing - receives messages according to type and priority.

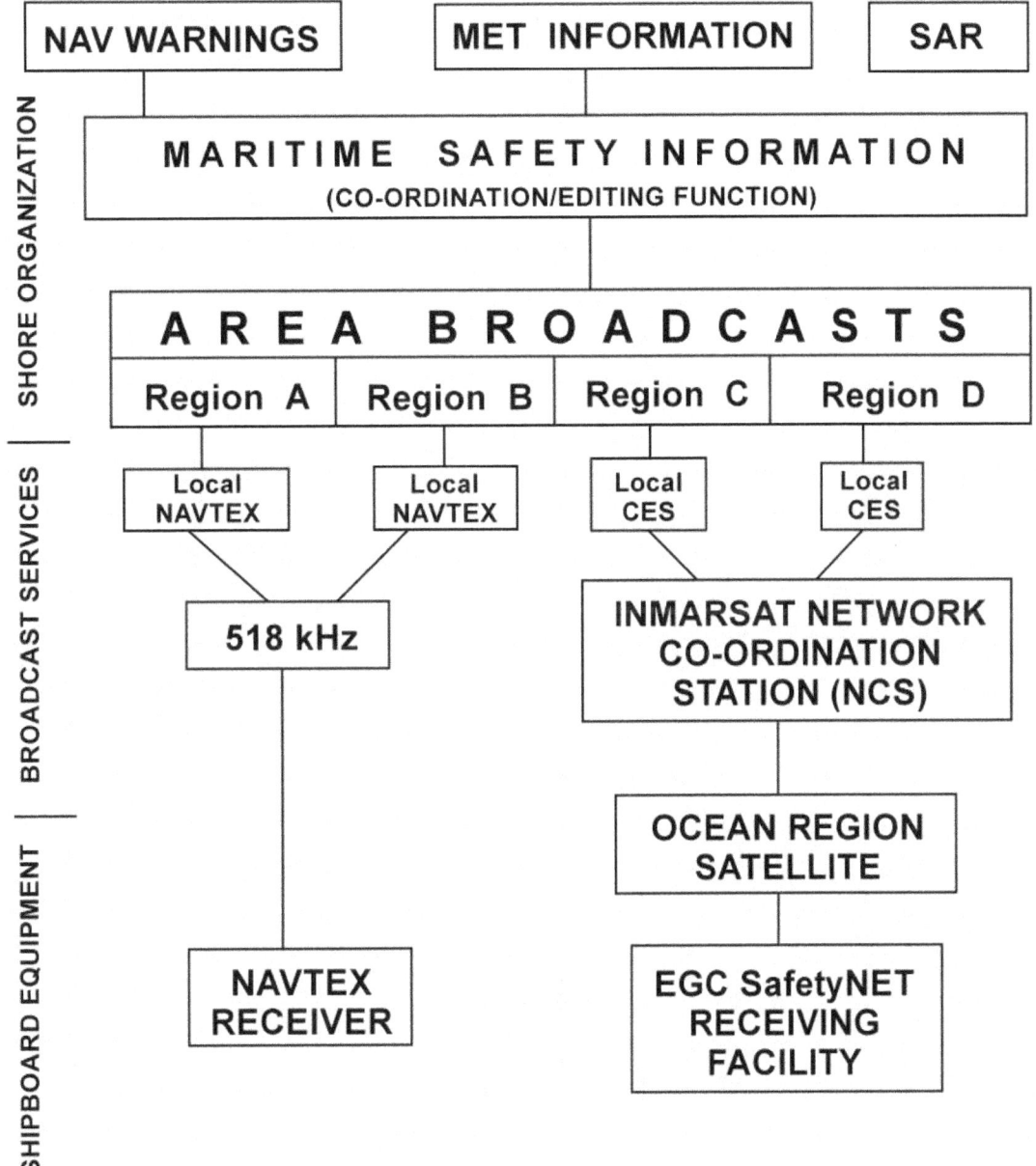

DISTRESS, EMERGENCY, AND SAFETY TRAFFIC

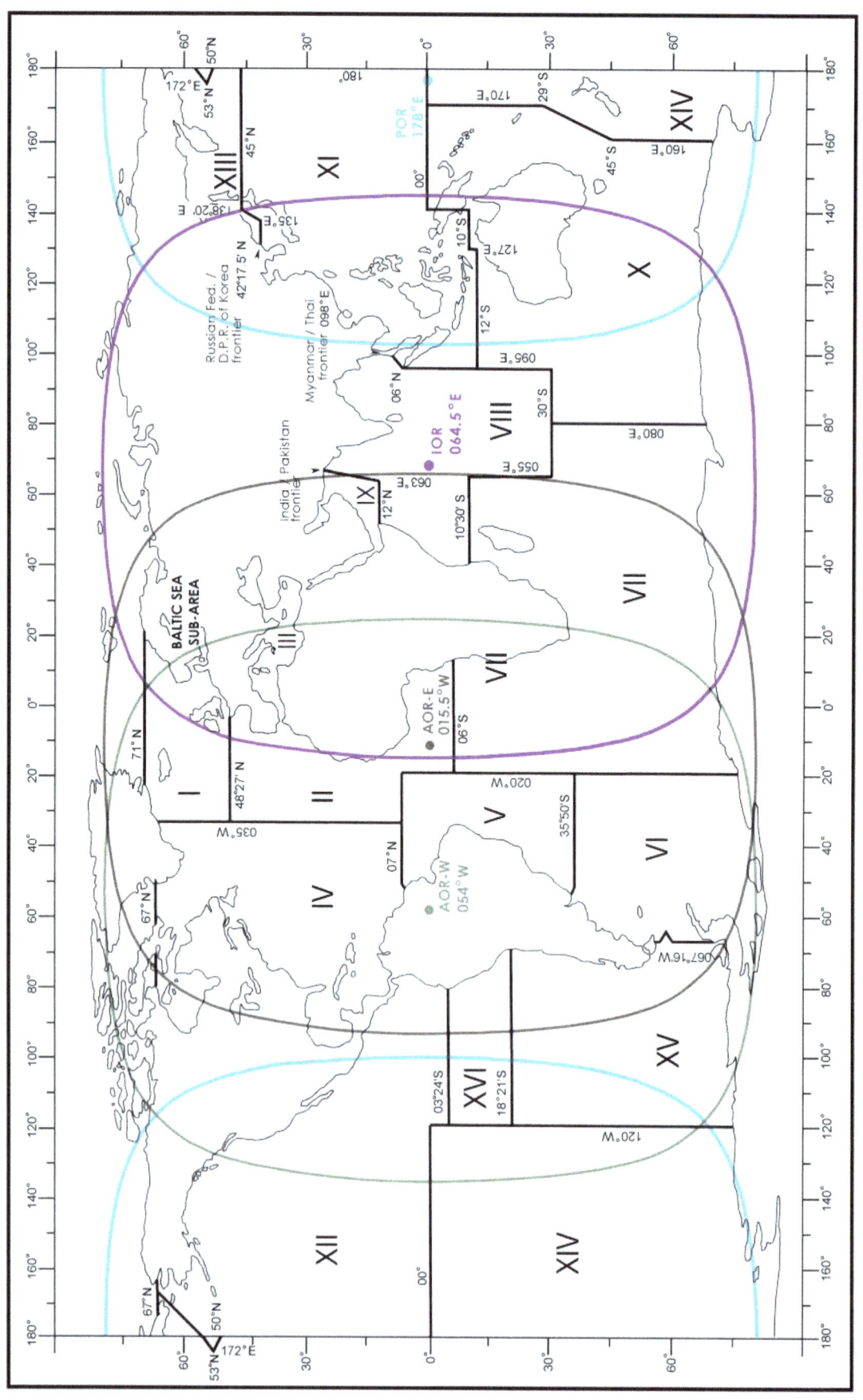

COVERAGE OF INMARSAT SATELLITES IN RELATION TO THE EXISTING NAV/MET AREAS

DISTRESS, EMERGENCY, AND SAFETY TRAFFIC

– Group addressing - FleetNET, group ID stored within receiver, which is accessible only by RF path.
– Unique addressing - FleetNET, allocated by Inmarsat.
– Geographic addressing - messages sent by ship's position.

NOTE: The type of address used in the header of an EGC packet is uniquely determined by the service code field

Both FleetNET and SafetyNET services make use of a fl xible addressing technique to allow the reception of messages from a variety of service providers depending on the particular requirements of the user. The SafetyNET service utilizes geographic area addressing technique to direct messages to ships within a defined boundar .

The FleetNET service employs closer user group and unique receiver addressing to provide secure transmission of a message from the registered terrestrial information provider to the desired recipient(s) (See sec. 400I.).

MESSAGE SEQUENCING: All messages will be transmitted with a unique sequence number and originating LES ID. Each subsequent transmission of the message will contain the original sequence number. When a message has been received error-free and a permanent record made, the unique 16 bit sequence number, the LES ID, and the service code fiel associated with that message are stored in memory and the information used to inhibit the printing of repeated transmissions of the same message. The EGC receiver should be capable of internally storing at least 255 such message identifications These message identification should be stored with an indication of the number of hours that have elapsed since the message was received. Subsequent reception of the same message identificatio shall reset the timer. After between 60 and 72 hours, message identification may automatically erase. If the number of received message identification exceeds the capacity of memory allocated for the store, the oldest message identification may be erased

TEXT PARAMETERS: For the EGC service, the International Reference Version of the International Alphabet, as define in the Consultative Committee on International Telephony and Telegraphy (CCITT) Red Book Rec. T.50, is used. Characters are coded as eight bits using odd parity. Other character sets according to International Standards Organization (ISO) 2022 or CCITT Red Book Rec. T.61 are used optionally for certain services. Inmarsat recommends that EGC equipment capable of receiving messages composed using International Telegraph Alphabet No. 2 do not make use of national options for Numbers 6, 7, and 8 in figur case to avoid varying interpretations in the Inmarsat-C System.

ERROR DETECTION: The EGC message will employ three levels of error detection:
– An arithmetic checksum is used to detect packet errors.
– An arithmetic checksum is used to detect header errors.
– Parity checking is used to indicate character errors in the information field

Only packets with header field received without error shall be processed for local message recording (even if the packet itself contains an error). In the case of double header messages the message may be processed (even if one header has been received correctly). A parity check on all incoming characters shall be performed, and in the event of a parity error in a received character, the "low line" character shall be displayed and/or printed. Outputs for multi-packet messages which have been received incomplete should provide a positive indication of the position of the missed packet(s). Subsequent receptions of messages printed with mutilated characters shall be output again until received error-free.

DISTRESS PRIORITY MESSAGES: Receipt of a valid distress or urgency priority message will cause the receiver to give an audible alarm. Provision shall be made to extend this alarm to the station from which the ship is normally navigated or other remote stations. This alarm should be reset in manual mode only.

MESSAGE OUTPUT: Inmarsat recommends that the EGC receiver have a printer. The display or printer, if fitted must be capable of presenting at least 40 characters per line of text. The EGC receiver should ensure that if a word cannot be accommodated in full on its line, it shall be transferred to the next line. Where a printer is fitted a local low paper audible alarm should be installed to give advance warning of a low paper condition. This alarm should be of a different pitch/tone so as not to confuse this alarm with that of the distress alarm. All SafetyNET messages shall be annotated with the time (UTC) and date received. This information shall be displayed or printed with the message.

NOTE: The time can be deduced from the frame count.

OPERATOR CONTROLS: The following control functions and displays shall be provided as a minimum indication of EGC carrier frame synchronization (or loss of synchronization):
– Selection of an EGC carrier frequency.
– Means of inputting ship's position, current NAVAREA, or current NAVTEX service coverage area.

Receivers shall be fitte with the operator controls to allow the operator to select the desired geographic area and message categories as previously described (see THE INMARSAT SYSTEM, INMARSAT SES CAPABILITY, and EGC RECEIVER ADDRESSING).

NAVIGATIONAL INTERFACE: In order that a receiver's position be automatically updated for geographically addressed messages, SOLAS requires that Inmarsat-C equipment have an integral navigation receiver or be externally connected to a satellite navigation receiver. A suggested standard interface is National Marine Electronics Association (NMEA) 0183 Standard for Interfacing Electronic Marine Navigational Devices.

400I.   The SafetyNET System

SafetyNET is a service of Inmarsat-C's Enhanced Group Call (EGC) system. The EGC system is a method used to specificall address particular regions or ships. Its unique addressing capabilities allow messages to be sent to all vessels in both fi ed geographical areas or to predetermined groups of ships. SafetyNET is the service designated by the IMO through which ships receive Maritime Safety Information.

DISTRESS, EMERGENCY, AND SAFETY TRAFFIC

SafetyNET is an international direct-printing satellite-based service for the promulgation of navigational and meteorological warnings, distress alerts, forecasts, and other safety messages. It fulfill an integral role in GMDSS as developed by the IMO. The ability to receive SafetyNET service information will be generally necessary for all ships that sail beyond coverage of NAVTEX (approximately 200 miles offshore) and is recommended to all administrations having the responsibility for marine affairs and mariners who require effective MSI service in waters not served by NAVTEX.

SafetyNET can direct a message to a given geographic area based on EGC addressing. The area may be fi ed, as in the case of a NAVAREA or weather forecast area, or it may be uniquely define by the originator. This is particularly useful for messages such as local storm warnings or a shore-to-ship distress alerts for which it would be inappropriate to alert ships in an entire ocean region.

SafetyNET messages can be originated by a Registered Information Provider anywhere in the world and broadcast to the appropriate ocean area through an Inmarsat-C LES. Messages are broadcast according to their priority (Distress, Urgency, Safety, or Routine).

Virtually all navigable waters of the world are covered by the operational satellites in the Inmarsat System. Each satellite broadcasts EGC traffi on a designated channel. Any ship sailing within the coverage area of an Inmarsat satellite will be able to receive all the SafetyNET messages broadcast over this channel. The EGC channel is optimized to enable the signal to be monitored by SESs that are dedicated to the reception of EGC messages. This capability can be built into other standard SESs. It is a feature of satellite communications that reception is not generally affected by the position of the ship within the ocean region, atmospheric conditions, or time of the day.

Messages can be transmitted either to geographic areas (area calls) or to groups of ships (group calls):
– Area calls can be to a f xed geographic area, such as one of the 16 NAVAREAs, or to a temporary geographic area selected by the originator. Area calls will be received automatically by any ship whose receiver has been set to one or more fi ed areas or recognizes a temporary area by geographic position.
– Group calls will be received automatically by any ship whose receiver acknowledges the unique group identity associated with a particular message.

Reliable delivery of messages is ensured by forward error correction techniques. Experience has demonstrated that the transmission link is generally error-free and low error reception is achieved under normal circumstances.

Given the vast ocean coverage by satellite, some form of discrimination and selectivity in printing the various messages is required. Area calls will be received by all ships within the ocean region coverage of the satellite; however, they will be printed only by those receivers that recognize the fi ed area or the geographic position in the message. The message format includes a preamble that enables the microprocessor in a ship's receiver to decide to print those MSI messages that relate to the present position, intended route, or a f xed area programmed by the operator (See sec. 400H: THE INMARSAT SYSTEM; OPERATOR CONTROLS.). This preamble also allows suppression of certain types of MSI that are not relevant to a particular ship. As each message will also have a unique identity, the reprinting of messages already received correctly is automatically suppressed.

MSI is promulgated by various information providers around the world. Messages for transmission through the SafetyNET service will, in many cases, be the result of coordination between authorities. Information providers will be authorized to broadcast through SafetyNET by IMO. Authorized information providers are:
– National hydrographic offices for n vigational warnings.
– National weather services for meteorological warnings and forecasts.
– RCCs for shore-to-ship distress alerts and other urgent information.
– International Ice Patrol for North Atlantic ice hazards.

Each information provider prepares their SafetyNET messages with certain characteristics recognized by the EGC service. These characteristics, known as "C" codes, are combined into a generalized message header format as follows: C1:C2:C3:C4:C5. Each "C" code controls a different broadcast criterion and is assigned a numerical value according to available options. A sixth "C" code, "C0," may be used to indicate the ocean region (e.g., AOR-E, AOR-W, POR, IOR) when sending a message to an LES that operates in more than one ocean region. Because errors in the header format of a message may prevent its being released, MSI providers must install an Inmarsat SafetyNET receiver to monitor the broadcasts it originates. This also ensures quality control.

The "C" codes are transparent to the mariner but are used by information providers to identify various transmitting parameters. C1 designates the message priority from distress to urgency, safety, and routine. MSI messages will always be at least at the safety level. C2 is the service code or type of message (for example, long range NAVAREA warning or coastal NAVTEX warning). It also tells the receiver the length of the address (the C3 code) it will need to decode. C3 is the is the address code. It can be the two digit code for the NAVAREA number for instance, or a 10 digit number to indicate a circular area for a meteorological warning. C4 is the repetition code that instructs the LES in how long and when to send the message to the NCS for actual broadcast. A six minute echo (repeat) may also be used to ensure that an urgency (unscheduled) message has been received by all ships affected. C5 is a constant and represents a presentation code, International Alphabet number 5, "00."

Broadcasts of MSI in the international SafetyNET service are in English. The different types of MSI broadcast over the SafetyNET service include:
– Coastal warnings (broadcast to areas where NAVTEX MSI is not provided):
  – Navigational and meteorological warnings;
  – Ice reports;
  – Search and rescue information;

DISTRESS, EMERGENCY, AND SAFETY TRAFFIC

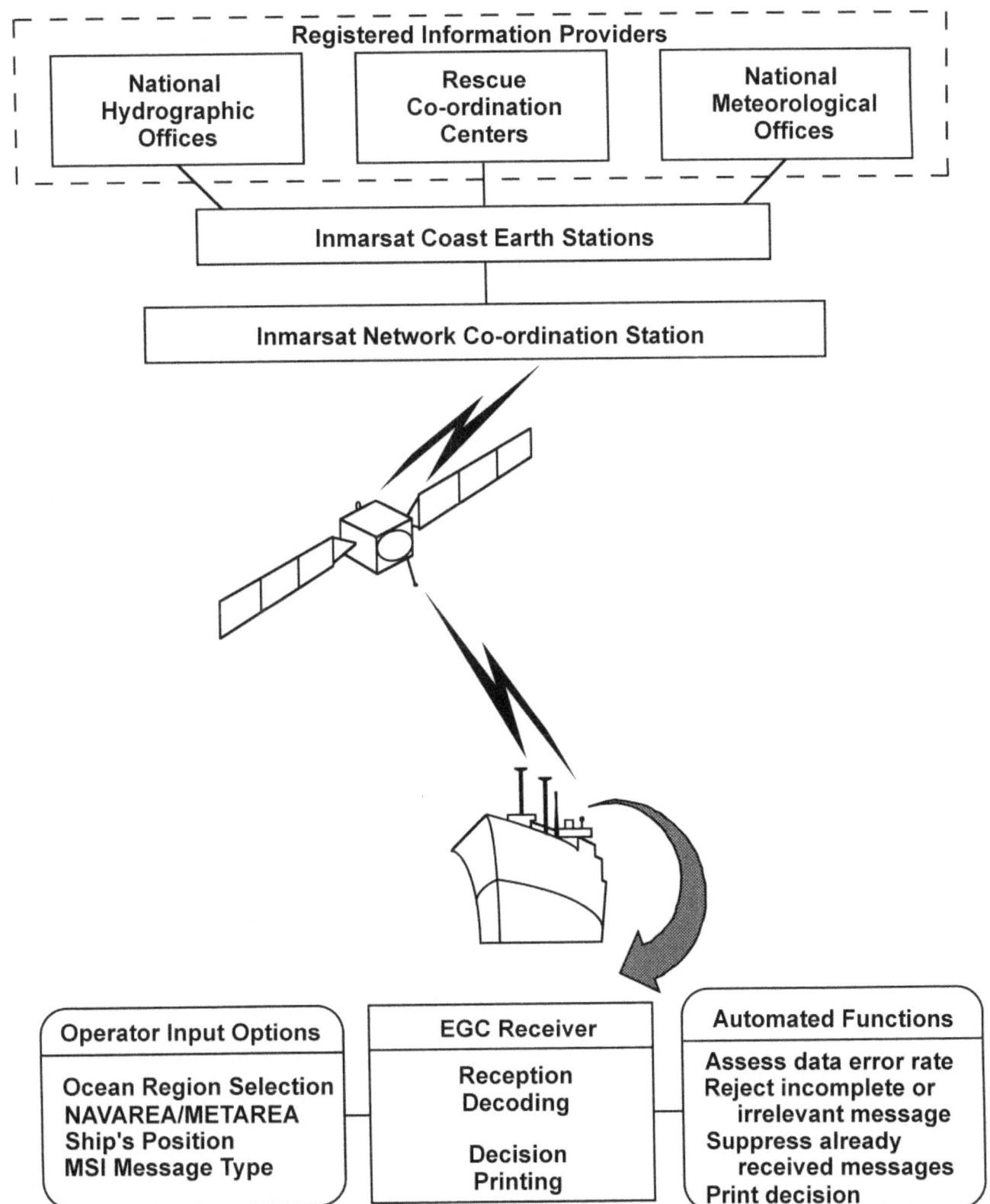

The International SafetyNET Service system

DISTRESS, EMERGENCY, AND SAFETY TRAFFIC

STATUS OF MARITME SAFETY INFORMATION BROADCASTS
INTERNATIONAL SafetyNET SERVICE

NAVAREA/ METAREA	NAV WARNINGS	MET FORECASTS & WARNINGS	SAR ALERTS	OCEAN REGION FOR SCHEDULED BROADCASTS
I (UK)	X	X	X	AOR-E
II (France)	X	X	X	AOR-E + AOR-W
III (Spain/Greece)	X	X	X	AOR-E
IV (USA)	X	X	X	AOR-W
V (Brazil)	X	X	X	AOR-E
VI (Argentina)	X	X	X	AOR-W
VII (South Africa)	X	X	X	AOR-E + IOR
VIII (India/Mauritius/La Reunion)	X	X (Note 3)	X	IOR
IX (Pakistan)	X	X	X	IOR
X (Australia)	X	X	X	IOR + POR
XI (Japan/China)	X	X	X	IOR + POR
XII (USA)	X	X	X	POR + AOR-W
XIII (Russian Federation)	X	X	X	POR
XIV (New Zealand)	X	X	X	POR
XV (Chile)	X	X	X	AOR-W
XVI (Peru/USA)	X	X	X	AOR-W

Notes:

1. X = Full Service now available

2. IMO has decided that routine broadcasts of navigational warnings and meteorological forecasts will be made at scheduled times over a single nominated satellite for each NAVAREA/METAREA. Unscheduled broadcasts of SAR Alert Relays and severe weather warnings will be made over all satellites which serve the area concerned. See the Inmarsat Maritime Communications Handbook for further guidance.

3. India provides meteorological forecasts and warnings for METAREA VIII north of the equator through LES Arvi (IOR). Mauritius/La Reunion provide meteorological forecasts and warnings for METAREA VIII south of the equator through LES Burum, Station 12 (IOR).

DISTRESS, EMERGENCY, AND SAFETY TRAFFIC

- Meteorological forecasts;
- Pilot service messages;
- DECCA, LORAN and SATNAV system messages;
- Other electronic navaid messages;
- Additional navigational messages.
- Meteorological and NAVAREA warnings and meteorological forecasts to ships within specifie NAVAREAs/METAREAs.
- Search and rescue coordination to fi ed areas.
- Search and rescue coordination to ships within specifie circular areas.
- Urgency messages, meteorological and navigational warnings to ships within specified circular areas
- Shore-to-ship distress alerts to ships within specifie circular areas.
- Urgency messages and navigational warnings to ships within specified rectangula .

MSI messages are generally broadcast with a key word in their header indicating the priority of the message, i.e., Distress or MAYDAY for Priority 3, URGENCY or PAN PAN for Priority 2, and SAFETY or SECURITE for Priority 1.

In order to avoid excessive duplication of MSI broadcasts, the IMO has authorized the following arrangements:
- For a given NAVAREA/METAREA which is covered by more than one ocean region satellite, scheduled broadcasts of MSI, such as navigational warnings and meteorological information, are made only through a single nominated satellite/ocean region.
- For a NAVAREA/METAREA which is covered by more than one ocean region satellite, unscheduled broadcasts of MSI, such as gale warnings and distress alert relays, are made through all satellites/ocean regions which cover the area concerned.

SOLAS-compliant vessels must meet the following requirements for receiving MSI broadcasts:
- Watch-keeping - every ship, while at sea, shall maintain a radio watch for broadcasts of Maritime Safety Information on the appropriate frequency or frequencies on which such information is broadcast for the area in which the ship is navigating.
- Logging messages - a written record shall be kept in the radio log of the time and identity of all safety messages received. A printed copy shall be kept of the text of all distress traffic

In addition to these mandatory requirements, the IMO recommends that all current navigational and meteorological messages be retained on the bridge, for as long as they are applicable, for the use of the person in charge of the navigational watch.

It is recommended that the EGC receiver be updated at least every four hours with the ship's position for the following reasons:
- To decide if the receiver should print a message which it has received addressed to a specific geographic area
- To print only messages for the required areas (if the ship's position has not been updated for 12 or 24 hours, the receiver will automatically print or store all geographically addressed messages within the entire ocean region);
- To ensure that the correct position is given if a distress alert has to be sent.

SOLAS regulations now require that Inmarsat-C equipment have an integral satellite navigation receiver, or be externally connected to a satellite navigation receiver, i.e., a GPS receiver.

Although an EGC receiver will receive and can print all SafetyNET broadcasts made throughout an entire ocean region, many messages may not be useful to a ship, i.e., those applicable to NAVAREAs beyond the ship's planned voyage, or those on subjects not relevant to the ship's circumstances. Every receiver is supplied with software that stores the geographical boundaries of the NAVAREAs: it can be programmed to print only essential messages applicable to the current area, in addition to any other areas programmed by the operator, and to reject all other messages. The receiver is unable to reject "all ship" messages, such as shore-to-ship distress alerts and MET/NAV warnings.

Under SOLAS requirements, it is mandatory for vessels to receive the following types of SafetyNET MSI messages:
- Shore-to-ship distress alert relays for the current NAVAREA;
- Navigational warnings for the current NAVAREA;
- Meteorological warnings for the current METAREA.

If the ship's EGC receiver does not automatically select these mandatory message types, the operator must program the receiver manually.

In addition, the IMO recommends a ship's EGC receiver be programmed to receive the following messages:
- Meteorological forecasts;
- MSI for any other NAVAREAs in which the ship is expected to sail.

The transmission schedule for the full GMDSS service broadcasts of routine weather bulletins (including warnings) and navigational warnings for the high seas is given in Tables I and II for the different ocean areas (extracted from ANNEX 8 of the IMO GMDSS Master Plan). The actual ocean region satellites through which these bulletins and warnings are transmitted are also indicated.

DISTRESS, EMERGENCY, AND SAFETY TRAFFIC

TABLE I - GMDSS TRANSMISSION SCHEDULE FOR INTERNATIONAL SAFETYNET SERVICE BROADCASTS OF ROUTINE WEATHER BULLETINS

NAV/MET AREA	Issuing Country	LES	Broadcast Schedule (UTC)	Ocean Region Satellite
I	United Kingdom	Goonhilly	0930, 2130	AOR-E
II	France	Aussaguel	0900, 2100	AOR-E/AOR-W
III	Greece[1]	Thermopylae	1000, 2200	AOR-E
IV	United States	Southbury	0430, 1030, 1630, 2230	AOR-W
V	Brazil	Tangua	0730, 1930	AOR-E
VI	Argentina	Southbury	0230, 1730	AOR-W
VII	South Africa	Burum	0940, 1940	AOR-E/IOR[2]
VIII	India	Arvi	0900, 1800 (N of 0°)	IOR
	Mauritius/La Reunion	Aussaguel	0130, 1330 (S of 0°) 0000[3], 0600[3], 1200[3], 1800[3] (S of 0°)	IOR
IX	Pakistan	Perth	0700	IOR
X	Australia	Perth	1030, 2330	IOR
			1100, 2300 0210[4], 0645[4], 1300[4], 1950[4] (Bass Strait)[5] 0815, 2015 (Northern Territory)[6]	POR
			0800, 2000 (Western Australia)[7]	IOR
XI	China	Beijing	0330, 1015, 1530, 2215	IOR
	Japan[8]	Yamaguchi	0230, 0830, 1430, 2030 (N of 0°) 0815, 2015 (S of 0°)	POR
XII	United States	Southbury/Santa Paula	0545, 1145, 1745, 2345	AOR-W/POR
XIII	Russian Federation	Eik	0930, 2130	POR
XIV	New Zealand	Albany (Auckland)	0930, 2130 0130, 1330 (NZ coast only) 0330, 1530 (warnings only)	POR
XV	Chile	Southbury	1845	AOR-W
XVI	United States	Southbury	0515, 1115, 1715, 2315	AOR-W

[1] Scheduled bulletins and warnings for the western Mediterranean Sea are prepared by France.
[2] Forecast for area 30°S-50°S / 50°E-80°E and tropical cyclone warnings are prepared by La Reunion.
[3] Tropical Cyclone warnings, if any, issued by La Reunion as unscheduled broadcasts.
[4] 1 hour earlier during Australian Eastern Daylight Saving Time.
[5] Coastal warnings and forecasts transmitted only to SafetyNET Coastal Area D in NAVAREA X.
[6] Coastal warnings and forecasts transmitted only to SafetyNET Coastal Areas G and H in NAVAREA X.
[7] Coastal warnings and forecasts transmitted only to SafetyNET Coastal Areas F and G in NAVAREA X.
[8] Scheduled bulletins and warnings for south of the equator prepared by Australia.

DISTRESS, EMERGENCY, AND SAFETY TRAFFIC

TABLE II - GMDSS TRANSMISSION SCHEDULE FOR INTERNATIONAL SAFETYNET SERVICE BROADCASTS OF NAVAREA WARNINGS

NAV/MET AREA	Coordinator	LES	Broadcast Schedule (UTC)	Ocean Region Satellite
I	United Kingdom	Goonhilly	1730 & as appropriate	AOR-E
II	France	Aussaguel	1630	AOR-E
III	Spain	Thermopylae	1200, 2400 & on receipt	AOR-E
IV	United States	Southbury	1000, 2200	AOR-W
	French Antilles (C[1])		0900, 2100	
	French Guiana (A[1])			
V	Brazil	Tangua	0400, 1230	AOR-E
	French Guiana (A[1])	Southbury	0900, 2100	
VI	Argentina	Southbury	0200, 1400	AOR-W
VII	South Africa	Burum	1940	AOR-E/IOR
	La Reunion (D[1])	Aussaguel	0040, 1240	IOR
	Mayotte (V[1])		0330, 1530	
	Kerguelen (K[1])		0140, 1340	
VIII	India	Arvi	1000	IOR
	La Reunion (D[1])	Aussaguel	0040, 1240	IOR
	Mayotte (V[1])		0330, 1530	
IX	Pakistan	Perth	0800	IOR
X	Australia	Perth	0700, 1900 & on receipt	IOR/POR[2]
	New Caledonia (N[1])	Southbury	0140, 1340	POR
XI	Japan	Beijing/Yamaguchi	0005, 0805, 1205	IOR/POR
XII	United States	Southbury/Santa Paula	1030, 2230	AOR-W/POR
XIII	Russian Federation	Eik	0930, 2130	POR
XIV	New Zealand	Albany (Auckland)	On receipt & every 12 hrs.	POR
	New Caledonia (N[1])	Southbury	0140, 1340	POR
	Wallis and Futuna (D[1])		0030, 1230	
	French Polynesia (R[1])		0250, 1450	
XV	Chile	Southbury	0210, 1410, 2210	AOR-W
XVI	Peru	Southbury	0519, 1119, 1719, 2319	AOR-W

[1] Coastal area code for Coastal Warnings.
[2] NAVAREA X Warnings and Australian Coastal Warnings (coastal area codes A to H).

DISTRESS, EMERGENCY, AND SAFETY TRAFFIC

400J.   Inmarsat-C SES Maintenance

The USCG has issued the following Safety Alert concerning the loss of Inmarsat-C safety messages. This advisory notifie users of Inmarsat-C Ship Earth Stations (SESs) that urgent marine information, weather warning and navigational warning broadcast messages, distress-related messages, as well as routine messages may be lost if a printer is not connected to and maintained with the Inmarsat-C terminal, or if flop y drive maintenance is not regularly performed on the terminal. Additionally, certain non-GMDSS-approved software (i.e., windows-based software) may freeze up if this maintenance is not performed.

All GMDSS versions of Inmarsat-C have approved data terminal equipment (DTE) that interfaces with the user. DTE generally refers to the computer and screen, keyboard, and printer (or user interface). These terminals are required to use only Inmarsat approved hardware and software. However, users need to understand that proper usage and housekeeping maintenance of the equipment is essential to ensure optimum user availability.

To avoid problems, and to ensure that unnecessary and irrelevant messages are not received, the recommended operating procedures in the manufacturer's equipment operating handbook and the below procedures should be followed:

MESSAGE/ARCHIVE LOG: All ingoing and outgoing messages are recorded on a disk in special log files Each log fil may hold a limited number of messages (limited by disk size or PC storage capacity). When the free disk space falls below a certain size, the terminal will display an error message asking to insert an empty disk. A new message/archive log fil will then be generated on the new disk.

DISK DIRECTORY: If so configured ingoing and outgoing messages (OUT.xxx, IN.xxx, EGC.xxx) can be stored on a disk (this is different than the message/archive log), where they can be viewed, erased, printed, and copied to different directories. On some models the directory shows the number of file (messages) stored on the disk/directory and this number is limited to 112 file (messages) regardless of the free space left. If the disk already holds 112 messages, you will not be able to store any more messages. When the disk is full, use the "erase/delete" command to delete unwanted file and create free space for new messages.

MESSAGE ROUTING: Check the message routing option on the terminal. Incoming mail should be routed to at least one of the output media—disk or printer. Enhanced Group Call (EGC) SafetyNET messages with Urgency and Distress priority will be printed out automatically, if a printer is fitted EGC SafetyNET messages with Safety priority can be printed out (user option), otherwise they will be stored on the disk. EGC FleetNET messages can be printed out (user option), otherwise they will be stored on the disk. If the Inmarsat-C is connected to a separate PC, a path for saving incoming and outgoing mail and EGC messages should be inserted/specifie per the manufacturer's handbook.

EGC SAFETYNET SET UP: Ensure that you are logged into the appropriate satellite for the scheduled maritime safety information (MSI) that you wish to receive. Otherwise log in to the satellite that broadcasts the MSI for your required area of operation. Timetables of broadcast and nominated satellites can be found in various national/international publications, such as Pub. 117, Radio Navigational Aids (See Tables I and II in sec. 400I.), the IMO GMDSS Master Plan (GMDSS/Circ.8), or the Admiralty List of Radio Signals, Volume 5. Ensure that your position (Lat/Long) on the SES position screen is valid. Otherwise you will receive and print ALL EGC SafetyNET messages broadcast via the satellite. If automatic position updating is not available, it is essential to manually update the position on a regular basis, i.e., every 4 hours. Instructions for doing this are in the manufacturer's handbook.

If properly set up, your SES will automatically receive all relevant NAVAREA/METAREA and other maritime safety information addressed to the area where you are in. If you require additional information for adjacent area(s), you must program your terminal to receive this information. Be careful if using the "EGC only" option. If this option is selected, the terminal will, effectively, be logged out and you will not be able to receive normal messages (mail) on your terminal. Also, if you choose "EGC only," previous EGC settings may be ignored and the terminal may receive all EGC messages within the ocean region.

If Inmarsat-C is used for communication (not as a supervisory control and data acquisition (SCADA) or "black box" terminal), it MUST have a DTE terminal which includes a keyboard, Video Display Unit, and printer. Every Inmarsat-C terminal, if properly configured set up and maintained, will receive all relevant messages addressed to it. These messages will be displayed or printed out, stored, or both. Improper settings, including printer settings, not in accordance with the manufacturer's instructions, will degrade the performance.

400K.   Digital Selective Calling (DSC)

Digital Selective Calling (DSC) is an integral part of the GMDSS used primarily for transmitting distress alerts from ships and for transmitting the associated acknowledgments from coast stations. DSC is a digital calling system which uses frequencies in the MF, HF or VHF bands. The advantages of DSC include faster alerting capabilities and automatic transmission of information such as ship's identity, time, nature of distress, and position. IMO and ITU regulations both require that the DSC-equipped VHF and MF/HF radios be externally connected to a satellite navigation receiver (i.e., GPS). This connection will ensure that accurate location information is sent to a RCC if a distress alert is transmitted. FCC regulations require that the ship's navigation position is entered, either manually or automatically through a navigation receiver, into all installed DSC equipment at least every four hours while the ship is underway (47 CFR 80.1073).

DISTRESS, EMERGENCY, AND SAFETY TRAFFIC

Since 1 February 1999, the GMDSS provisions to the SOLAS Convention require all passenger ships and most other ships 300 gross tons and over on international voyages, including all cargo ships, to carry DSC-equipped radios. A listening watch aboard GMDSS-equipped ships on 2182 kHz ended on that date. In May 2002, the IMO decided to postpone cessation of a listening watch aboard GMDSS-equipped ships on VHF Channel 16 (156.8 MHz). That listening watch had been scheduled to end on 1 February 2005. Once SOLAS vessels are allowed to disband watchkeeping on VHF radiotelephone, it will not be possible to initiate radio communications with these vessels outside the U.S. territorial limit without DSC-capable radios. The U.S Coast Guard recommends that VHF, MF and HF radiotelephone equipment carried on ships should include a DSC capability as a matter of safety. To achieve this, the FCC requires that all new VHF and MF/HF maritime radiotelephones type accepted after June 1999 to have at least a basic DSC capability.

The content of a DSC call includes the numerical address of the station (or stations) to which the call is transmitted, the self-identificatio of the transmitting station, and a message which contains several field of information indicating the purpose of the call. Various types of DSC calls are available in one of four priorities: Distress, Urgency, Safety or Routine. Routine calls could indicate that a routine communication, i.e., telephony or telegraphy, is required; or they could include calls related to the operation of the ship, e.g., calls to port authorities, pilots.

A receiving station accepting a DSC call receives a display or printout of the address, the self-identificatio of the transmitting station, and the content of the DSC message, together with an audible or visual alarm (or both) for distress and safety related calls. To increase the probability of a DSC distress call or relay being received, it is repeated several times. The transmission speed of a DSC call is 100 baud at MF and HF and 1200 baud at VHF. Error correction coding is included, involving the transmission of each character twice, together with an overall message check character which is to ensure the technical integrity of the DSC system.

In an effort to reduce the number of DSC relays of distress alerts on all shipboard DSC equipment, the IMO has issued COMSAR/Circ.25 (dated 15 March 2001) which provides new procedures for responding to VHF/MF and HF distress alerts.

Circ.25 is summarized as follows:
- Distress relays and acknowledgments of all types should only be sent on the Master's authority.
- Ships should not acknowledge DSC alerts by sending a return DSC call; they should acknowledge only by radiotelephony.
- Ships receiving a DSC distress alert on VHF Ch. 70 or MF 2187.5 kHz are not permitted to relay the call by DSC under any circumstances (they may relay by other means).
- Ships receiving a DSC distress alert on HF should wait for a period of 5 minutes of manual watchkeeping to ascertain whether it has been acknowledged by DSC,
radiotelephony or NBDP. If a DSC relay is then judged to be necessary, it should be initiated manually only to the appropriate coast station.
- Ships may only send a distress relay call (distress alert on behalf of another vessel), if the following two conditions both apply:
  - the ship in distress is not itself able to transmit its own distress alert, and
  - the Master of the ship considers that further help is necessary.

The distress relay call should be addressed to "all ships" or to the appropriate coast station.

Flow diagrams, which describe the actions to be taken aboard ships upon receipt of DSC distress alerts from other ships, can be found on pgs. 4-51 and 4-53. The IMO recommends that these fl w diagrams be displayed on the ship's bridge.

In an effort to manage and reduce the number of test calls on the MF/HF DSC distress and safety frequencies, the IMO has issued COMSAR/Circ.35 (dated 21 May 2004), with the following recommendation: to ensure that excessive test calls on DSC do not overload the system, live testing on DSC distress and safety frequencies with coast stations should be limited to once a week.

The following DSC Operational Procedures for Ships were adapted from Annex 3 of ITU Recommendation M.541-9, Operational Procedures for the use of Digital Selective-Calling (DSC) Equipment in the Maritime Mobile Service. Operating procedures may vary somewhat among different radios, depending upon radio design, software configuration and the DSC processor/radio transceiver connection.

1 DISTRESS:

1.1 Transmission of DSC distress alert: A distress alert should be transmitted if, in the opinion of the Master, the ship or a person is in distress and requires immediate assistance. A DSC distress alert should as far as possible include the ship's last known position and the time (in UTC) when it was valid. The position and the time may be included automatically by the ship's navigational equipment or may be inserted manually.

The DSC distress alert is transmitted as follows:
- tune the transmitter to the DSC distress channel (2187.5 kHz on MF, channel 70 on VHF (see Note 1 below));
- if time permits, key in or select on the DSC equipment keyboard (in accordance with the DSC equipment manufacturer's instructions):
  - the nature of the distress;
  - the ship's last known position (latitude and longitude);
  - the time (in UTC) the position was valid;
  - type of subsequent distress communication (telephony).
- transmit the DSC distress alert;
- prepare for the subsequent distress traffi by tuning the transmitter and the radiotelephony receiver to the distress traffi channel in the same band, i.e., 2182 kHz on MF, channel 16 on VHF, while waiting for the DSC distress acknowledgment.

NOTE 1: Some maritime MF radiotelephony transmitters shall be tuned to a frequency 1700 Hz lower

DISTRESS, EMERGENCY, AND SAFETY TRAFFIC

than 2187.5 kHz, i.e., 2185.8 kHz, in order to transmit the DSC distress alert on 2187.5 kHz.

1.2 Actions on receipt of a distress alert: Ships receiving a DSC distress alert from another ship should normally not acknowledge the alert by DSC since acknowledgment of a DSC distress alert by use of DSC is normally made by coast stations only. (Ships receiving a DSC distress alert from another ship should set watch on an associated radiotelephone distress and safety traffi frequency and acknowledge the call by radiotelephony. See also section 6.1.4.).

If a ship station continues to receive a DSC distress alert on an MF or VHF channel, a DSC acknowledgment should be transmitted to terminate the call only after consulting with a Rescue Coordination Center (RCC) or a Coast Station and being directed to do so.

Ships receiving a DSC distress alert from another ship should also defer the acknowledgment of the distress alert by radiotelephony for a short interval, if the ship is within an area covered by one or more coast stations, in order to give the coast station time to acknowledge the DSC distress alert first

Ships receiving a DSC distress alert from another ship shall:
- watch for the reception of a distress acknowledgment on the distress channel (2187.5 kHz on MF and channel 70 on VHF);
- prepare for receiving the subsequent distress communication by tuning the radiotelephony receiver to the distress traffi frequency in the same band in which the DSC distress alert was received, i.e., 2182 kHz on MF, channel 16 on VHF;
- acknowledge the receipt of the distress alert by transmitting the following by radiotelephony on the distress traffi frequency in the same band in which the DSC distress alert was received, i.e., 2182 kHz on MF, channel 16 on VHF:
  - "MAYDAY;"
  - the 9-digit identity of the ship in distress, repeated 3 times;
  - "this is;"
  - the 9-digit identity or the call sign or other identification of wn ship, repeated 3 times;
  - "RECEIVED MAYDAY."

1.3 Distress traffic On receipt of a DSC distress acknowledgment the ship in distress should commence the distress traffi by radiotelephony on the distress traffi frequency (2182 kHz on MF, channel 16 on VHF) as follows:
- "MAYDAY;"
- "this is;"
- the 9-digit identity and the call sign or other identification of the ship
- the ship's position in latitude and longitude or other reference to a known geographical location;
- the nature of the distress and assistance wanted;
- any other information which might facilitate the rescue.

1.4 Transmission of a DSC distress relay call: In no case is a ship permitted to transmit an all ships DSC distress relay call on receipt of a DSC distress alert on either VHF or MF channels. If no aural watch is present on the relative channel (2182 kHz on MF, channel 16 on VHF), the coast station should be contacted by sending an individual DSC distress relay call.

1.4.1 Transmission of a DSC distress relay call on behalf of someone else: A ship knowing that another ship is in distress shall transmit a DSC distress relay call if:
- the ship in distress is not itself able to transmit the distress alert;
- the Master of the ship considers that further help is necessary.

The DSC distress relay call is transmitted as follows:
- tune the transmitter to the DSC distress channel (2187.5 kHz on MF, channel 70 on VHF);
- select the distress relay call format on the DSC equipment;
- key in or select on the DSC equipment keyboard:
  - All Ships Call (VHF), Geographic Area Call (MF/HF) or the 9-digit identity of the appropriate coast station;
  - the 9-digit identity of the ship in distress, if known;
  - the nature of the distress;
  - the latest position of the ship in distress, if known;
  - the time (in UTC) the position was valid (if known);
  - type of subsequent distress communication (telephony).
- transmit the DSC distress relay call;
- prepare for the subsequent distress traffi by tuning the transmitter and the radiotelephony receiver to the distress traffi channel in the same band, i.e., 2182 kHz on MF and channel 16 on VHF, while waiting for the DSC distress acknowledgment.

1.5 Acknowledgment of a DSC distress relay call received from a coast station: Coast stations, after having received and acknowledged a DSC distress alert, may if necessary, retransmit the information received as a DSC distress relay call, addressed to all ships (VHF only), all ships in a specifi geographical area (MF/HF only), or a specific ship

Ships receiving a distress relay call transmitted by a coast station shall not use DSC to acknowledge the call, but should acknowledge the receipt of the call by radiotelephony on the distress traffi channel in the same band in which the relay call was received, i.e., 2182 kHz on MF, channel 16 on VHF.

Acknowledge the receipt of the distress relay call by transmitting the following by radiotelephony on the distress traffi frequency in the same band in which the DSC distress relay call was received:
- "MAYDAY RELAY;"
- the 9-digit identity or the call sign or other identificatio of the calling coast station;
- "this is;"
- the 9-digit identity or call sign or other identificatio of own ship;
- "RECEIVED MAYDAY RELAY."

1.6 Acknowledgment of a DSC distress relay call received from another ship: Ships receiving a distress relay call from another ship shall follow the same procedure as for acknowledgment of a distress alert, i.e., the procedure given in section 1.2 above.

DISTRESS, EMERGENCY, AND SAFETY TRAFFIC

1.7 Cancellation of an inadvertent distress alert: A station transmitting an inadvertent distress alert shall cancel the distress alert using the following procedure:
- **1.7.1** Immediately cancel the distress alert aurally over the telephony distress traffi channel associated with each DSC channel on which the "distress alert" was transmitted.
- **1.7.2** Monitor the telephony distress traffi channel associated with the DSC channel on which the distress was transmitted, and respond to any communications concerning that distress alert as appropriate.

2 URGENCY:
2.1 Transmission of urgency messages: Transmission of urgency messages shall be carried out in two steps:
- announcement of the urgency message;
- transmission of the urgency message.

The announcement is carried out by transmission of a DSC urgency call on the DSC distress calling channel (2187.5 kHz on MF, channel 70 on VHF). The urgency message is transmitted on the distress traffi channel (2182 kHz on MF, channel 16 on VHF). The DSC urgency call may be addressed to all stations at VHF, or a geographic area at MF/HF, or to a specifi station. The frequency on which the urgency message will be transmitted shall be included in the DSC urgency call.

The transmission of an urgency message is thus carried out as follows:

Announcement:
- tune the transmitter to the DSC distress calling channel (2187.5 kHz on MF, channel 70 on VHF);
- select the appropriate calling format on the DSC equipment (all ships (VHF only), geographical area (MF/HF only) or individual);
- key in or select on the DSC equipment keyboard (in accordance with the DSC equipment manufacturer's instructions):
  - specifi area or 9-digit identity of the specific station, if appropriate;
  - the category of the call (urgency);
  - the frequency or channel on which the urgency message will be transmitted;
  - the type of communication in which the urgency message will be given (radiotelephony).
- transmit the DSC urgency call.

Transmission of the urgency message:
- tune the transmitter to the frequency or channel indicated in the DSC urgency call;
- transmit the urgency message as follows:
  - "PAN PAN," repeated 3 times;
  - "ALL STATIONS" or called station, repeated 3 times;
  - "this is;"
  - the 9-digit identity and the call sign or other identification of wn ship;
  - the text of the urgency message.

2.2 Reception of an urgency message: Ships receiving a DSC urgency call announcing an urgency message addressed to more than one station shall NOT acknowledge the receipt of the DSC call, but should tune the radiotelephony receiver to the frequency indicated in the call and listen to the urgency message.

3 SAFETY:
3.1 Transmission of safety messages: Transmission of safety messages shall be carried out in two steps:
- announcement of the safety message;
- transmission of the safety message.

The announcement is carried out by transmission of a DSC safety call on the DSC distress calling channel (2187.5 kHz on MF, channel 70 on VHF). The safety message is normally transmitted on the distress and safety traffi channel in the same band in which the DSC call was sent, i.e., 2182 kHz on MF, channel 16 on VHF. The DSC safety call may be addressed to all ships (VHF only), ships in a specifi geographical area (MF/HF only), or to a specifi station. The frequency on which the safety message will be transmitted shall be included in the DSC call.

The transmission of a safety message is thus carried out as follows:

Announcement:
- tune the transmitter to the DSC distress calling channel (2187.5 kHz on MF, channel 70 on VHF);
- select the appropriate calling format on the DSC equipment (all ships (VHF only), geographical area (MF/HF only), or individual);
- key in or select on the DSC equipment keyboard (in accordance with the DSC equipment manufacturer's instructions):
  - specifi area or 9-digit identity of specifi station, if appropriate;
  - the category of the call (safety);
  - the frequency or channel on which the safety message will be transmitted;
  - the type of communication in which the safety message will be given (radiotelephony).
- transmit the DSC safety call.

Transmission of the safety message:
- tune the transmitter to the frequency or channel indicated in the DSC safety call;
- transmit the safety message as follows:
  - "SECURITE," repeated 3 times;
  - "ALL STATIONS" or called station, repeated 3 times;
  - "this is;"
  - the 9-digit identity and the call sign or other identification of wn ship;
  - the text of the safety message.

3.2 Reception of a safety message: Ships receiving a DSC safety call announcing a safety message addressed to more than one station shall NOT acknowledge the receipt of the DSC safety call, but should tune the radiotelephony receiver to the frequency indicated in the call and listen to the safety message.

4 PUBLIC CORRESPONDENCE:
4.1 DSC channels for public correspondence:
- **4.1.1 VHF:** The VHF DSC channel 70 is used for DSC for distress and safety purposes as well as for DSC for public correspondence.
- **4.1.2 MF:** International and national DSC channels separate from the DSC distress and safety calling channel 2187.5 kHz are used for digital selective-calling on MF for public correspondence. Ships calling a coast

DISTRESS, EMERGENCY, AND SAFETY TRAFFIC

station by DSC on MF for public correspondence should preferably use the coast station's national DSC channel. The international DSC channel for public correspondence may as a general rule be used between ships and coast stations of different nationality. The ships transmitting frequency is 2189.5 kHz, and the receiving frequency is 2177 kHz. The frequency 2177 kHz is also used for DSC between ships for general communication.

4.2 Transmission of a DSC call for public correspondence to a coast station or another ship: A DSC call for public correspondence to a coast station or another ship is transmitted as follows:
– tune the transmitter to the relevant DSC channel;
– select the format for calling a specifi station on the DSC equipment;
– key in or select on the DSC equipment keyboard (in accordance with the DSC equipment manufacturer's instructions):
  – the 9-digit identity of the station to be called;
  – the category of the call (routine);
  – the type of subsequent communication (normally radiotelephony);
  – a proposed working channel if calling another ship. A proposal for a working channel should NOT be included in calls to a coast station; the coast station will in its DSC acknowledgment indicate a vacant working channel;
– transmit the DSC call.

4.3 Repeating a call: A DSC call for public correspondence may be repeated on the same or another DSC channel, if no acknowledgment is received within 5 minutes. Further call attempts should be delayed at least 15 minutes, if acknowledgment is still not received.

4.4 Acknowledgment of a received call and preparation for reception of the traffic On receipt of a DSC call from a coast station or another ship, a DSC acknowledgment is transmitted as follows:
– tune the transmitter to the transmit frequency of the DSC channel on which the call was received;
– select the acknowledgment format on the DSC equipment;
– transmit an acknowledgment indicating whether the ship is able to communicate as proposed in the call (type of communication and working frequency);
– if able to communicate as indicated, tune the transmitter and the radiotelephony receiver to the indicated working channel and prepare to receive the traffic

4.5 Reception of acknowledgment and further actions: When receiving an acknowledgment indicating that the called station is able to receive the traffic prepare to transmit the traffic as foll ws:
– tune the transmitter and receiver to the indicated working channel;
– commence the communication on the working channel by:
  – the 9-digit identity or call sign or other identificatio of the called station;
  – "this is;"
  – the 9-digit identity or call sign or other identificatio of own ship.

It will normally rest with the ship to call again a little later in case the acknowledgment from the coast station indicates that the coast station is not able to receive the traffi immediately. In case the ship, in response to a call to another ship, receives an acknowledgment indicating that the other ship is not able to receive the traffi immediately, it will normally rest with the called ship to transmit a call to the calling ship when ready to receive the traffic

5 TESTING THE EQUIPMENT USED FOR DISTRESS AND SAFETY:
Testing on the exclusive DSC distress and safety calling frequency 2187.5 kHz should be avoided as far as possible by using other methods. Test calls should be transmitted by the ship station and acknowledged by the called station. Normally there would be no further communication between the two stations involved.

A VHF and MF test call to a station is transmitted as follows:
– tune the transmitter to the DSC distress and safety calling frequency (i.e., channel 70 and 2187.5 kHz);
– key in or select the format for the test call on the DSC equipment in accordance with the DSC equipment manufacturer's instructions;
– key in the 9-digit identity of the station to be called;
– transmit the DSC call after checking as far as possible that no calls are in progress on the frequency;
– wait for acknowledgment.

6 SPECIAL CONDITIONS AND PROCEDURES FOR DSC COMMUNICATION ON HF:
General: The procedures for DSC communication on HF are—with some additions described in 6.1 to 6.3 below—equal to the corresponding procedures for DSC communications on MF/VHF. Due regard to the special conditions described in 6.1 to 6.3 should be given when making DSC communications on HF.

6.1 DISTRESS:
6.1.1 Transmission of DSC distress alert: DSC distress alert should be sent to coast stations - i.e., in A3 and A4 sea areas on HF - and on MF and/or VHF to other ships in the vicinity. The DSC distress alert should as far as possible include the ship's last known position and the time (in UTC) it was valid. If the position and time is not inserted automatically from the ship's navigational equipment, it should be inserted manually.

Ship-to-shore distress alert (Choice of HF band): Propagation characteristics of HF radio waves for the actual season and time of the day should be taken into account when choosing HF bands for transmission of DSC distress alert. As a general rule the DSC distress channel in the 8 MHz maritime band (8414.5 kHz) may in many cases be an appropriate firs choice. Transmission of the DSC distress alert in more than one HF band will normally increase the probability of successful reception of the alert by coast stations.

DSC distress alert may be sent on a number of HF bands in two different ways:
– (1) either by transmitting the DSC distress alert on one HF band, and waiting a few minutes for receiving acknowledgment by a coast station;

DISTRESS, EMERGENCY, AND SAFETY TRAFFIC

if no acknowledgment is received within 3 minutes, the process is repeated by transmitting the DSC distress alert on another appropriate HF band etc.;
– (2) or by transmitting the DSC distress alert at a number of HF bands with no, or only very short, pauses between the calls, without waiting for acknowledgment between the calls.

It is recommended to follow procedure (1) in all cases, where time permits to do so; this will make it easier to choose the appropriate HF band for commencement of the subsequent communication with the coast station on the corresponding distress traffic channel

Transmitting the DSC distress alert (see Note 1 below):
– tune the transmitter to the chosen HF DSC distress channel (4207.5, 6312, 8414.5, 12577, 16804.5 kHz) (see Note 2);
– follow the instructions for keying in or selection of relevant information on the DSC equipment keyboard as described in section 1.1;
– transmit the DSC distress alert.

In special cases, for example in tropical zones, transmission of DSC distress alert on HF may, in addition to ship-to-shore alerting, also be useful for ship-to-ship alerting.

NOTE 1: Ship-to-ship distress alert should normally be made on MF and/or VHF, using the procedures for transmission of DSC distress alert on MF/VHF described in section 1.1.

NOTE 2: Some maritime HF transmitters shall be tuned to a frequency 1700 Hz lower than the DSC frequencies given above in order to transmit the DSC distress alert on the correct frequency.

6.1.2 Preparation for the subsequent distress traffic
After having transmitted the DSC distress alert on appropriate DSC distress channels (HF, MF and/or VHF), prepare for the subsequent distress traffi by tuning the radiocommunication set(s) (HF, MF and/or VHF as appropriate) to the corresponding distress traffi channel(s).

Where multiple frequency call attempts are transmitted the corresponding distress traffi frequency should be 8291 kHz.

If method (2) described in section 6.1.1 has been used for transmission of DSC distress alert on a number of HF bands:
– take into account in which HF band(s) acknowledgment has been successfully received from a coast station;
– if acknowledgments have been received on more than one HF band, commence the transmission of distress traffi on one of these bands, but if no response is received from a coast station then the other bands should be used in turn.

The distress traffic frequencies are

HF (kHz):

Telephony	Telex
4125	4177.5
6215	6268
8291	8376.5

HF (kHz):

Telephony	Telex
12290	12520
16420	16695

MF (kHz):

Telephony	Telex
2182	2174.5

VHF:

Channel 16 (156.800 MHz)

6.1.3 Distress traffic The procedures described in section 1.3 are used when the distress traffi on MF/HF is carried out by radiotelephony.

The following procedures shall be used in cases where the distress traffic on MF/HF is carried out by radiotel x:
– the forward error correcting (FEC) mode shall be used;
– all messages shall be preceded by:
  – at least one carriage return;
  – line feed;
  – one letter shift;
  – the distress signal "MAYDAY."
– the ship in distress should commence the distress telex traffi on the appropriate distress telex traffi channel as follows:
  – carriage return, line feed, letter shift;
  – the distress signal "MAYDAY;"
  – "this is;"
  – the 9-digit identity and call sign or other identificatio of the ship;
  – the ship's position if not included in the DSC distress alert;
  – the nature of distress;
  – any other information which might facilitate the rescue.

6.1.4 Actions on reception of a DSC distress alert on HF from another ship: Ships receiving a DSC distress alert on HF from another ship shall not acknowledge the alert, but should:
– watch for reception of a DSC distress acknowledgment from a coast station;
– while waiting for reception of a DSC distress acknowledgment from a coast station:
  prepare for reception of the subsequent distress communication by tuning the HF radiocommunication set (transmitter and receiver) to the relevant distress traffi channel in the same HF band in which the DSC distress alert was received, observing the following conditions:
  – if radiotelephony mode was indicated in the DSC distress alert, the HF radiocommunication set should be tuned to the radiotelephony distress traffi channel in the HF band concerned;
  – if telex mode was indicated in the DSC distress alert, the HF radiocommunication set should be tuned to the radiotelex distress traffi channel in the HF band concerned. Ships able to do so should additionally

watch the corresponding radiotelephony distress channel;
- if the DSC distress alert was received on more than one HF band, the radiocommunication set should be tuned to the relevant distress traffi channel in the HF band considered to be the best one in the actual case. If the DSC distress alert was received successfully on the 8 MHz band, this band may in many cases be an appropriate first choice
- if no distress traffi is received on the HF channel within 1 to 2 minutes, tune the HF radiocommunication set to the relevant distress traffi channel in another HF band deemed appropriate in the actual case;
- if no DSC distress acknowledgment is received from a coast station within 5 minutes, and no distress communication is observed going on between a coast station and the ship in distress:
  - inform a Rescue Coordination Center (RCC) via appropriate radiocommunications means;
  - transmit a DSC distress relay call.

6.1.5 Transmission of DSC distress relay call: In case it is considered appropriate to transmit a DSC distress relay call:
- distress relay calls on HF should be initiated manually;
- tune the transmitter(s) to the relevant DSC distress channel, following the procedures described in section 6.1.1 above (except the call is sent manually as a single call on a single frequency);
- follow the instructions for keying in or selection of call format and relevant information on the DSC equipment keyboard as described in section 1.4;
- transmit the DSC distress relay call.

6.1.6 Acknowledgment of a HF DSC distress relay call received from a coast station: Ships receiving a DSC distress relay call from a coast station on HF, addressed to all ships within a specifie area, should NOT acknowledge the receipt of the relay alert by DSC, but by radiotelephony on the telephony distress traffi channel in the same band(s) in which the DSC distress relay call was received.

6.2 URGENCY:
Transmission of urgency messages on HF should normally be addressed:
- either to all ships within a specified geographical area
- or to a specific coast station

Announcement of the urgency message is carried out by transmission of a DSC call with category urgency on the appropriate DSC distress channel. The transmission of the urgency message itself on HF is carried out by radiotelephony or radiotelex on the appropriate distress traffi channel in the same band in which the DSC announcement was transmitted.

6.2.1 Transmission of DSC announcement of an urgency message on HF:
- choose the HF band considered to be the most appropriate, taking into account propagation characteristics for HF radio waves at the actual season and time of the day; the 8 MHz band may in many cases be an appropriate first choice

- tune the HF transmitter to the DSC distress channel in the chosen HF band;
- key in or select call format for either geographical area call or individual call on the DSC equipment, as appropriate;
- in case of area call, key in specificatio of the relevant geographical area;
- follow the instructions for keying in or selection of relevant information on the DSC equipment keyboard as described in section 2.1, including type of communication in which the urgency message will be transmitted (radiotelephony or radiotelex);
- transmit the DSC call; and
- if the DSC call is addressed to a specifi coast station, wait for DSC acknowledgment from the coast station. If acknowledgment is not received within a few minutes, repeat the DSC call on another HF frequency deemed appropriate.

6.2.2 Transmission of the urgency message and subsequent action:
- tune the HF transmitter to the distress traffi channel (telephony or telex) indicated in the DSC announcement;
- if the urgency message is to be transmitted using radiotelephony, follow the procedure described in section 2.1;
- if the urgency message is to be transmitted by radiotelex, the following procedure shall be used:
  - use the forward error correcting (FEC) mode unless the message is addressed to a single station whose radiotelex identity number is known;
  - commence the telex message by:
    - at least one carriage return, line feed, one letter shift;
    - the urgency signal "PAN PAN;"
    - "this is;"
    - the 9-digit identity of the ship and the call sign or other identification of the ship
    - the text of the urgency message.

Announcement and transmission of urgency messages addressed to all HF equipped ships within a specifie area may be repeated on a number of HF bands as deemed appropriate in the actual situation.

6.3 SAFETY:
The procedures for transmission of DSC safety announcement and for transmission of the safety message are the same as for urgency messages, described in section 6.2, except that:
- in the DSC announcement, the category SAFETY shall be used;
- in the safety message, the safety signal "SECURITE" shall be used instead of the urgency signal "PAN PAN."

400L. Use of GMDSS Equipment for Routine Telecommunications

GMDSS telecommunications equipment should not be reserved for emergency use only. The IMO has issued COMSAR/Circ.17 (dated 9 March 1998) which recommends and encourages mariners to use that equipment for routine as well as safety

DISTRESS, EMERGENCY, AND SAFETY TRAFFIC

telecommunications. The following recommendation is extracted from Circ.17:

Use of GMDSS equipment for transmission of general radiocommunications is one of the functional requirements specifie in SOLAS chapter IV, regulation 4. Regular use of GMDSS equipment helps to develop operator competency and ensure equipment availability. If ships use other radiocommunication systems for the bulk of their business communications, they should adopt a regular program of sending selected traffi or test messages via GMDSS equipment to ensure operator competency and equipment availability and to help reduce the incidence of false alerts. This policy extends to all GMDSS equipment suites including Digital Selective Calling (DSC) on VHF, MF and HF, to the Inmarsat-A, -B and -C systems, and to any duplicated VHF and long-range communications facilities.

400M. Instructions for Canceling Inadvertent Distress Alerts

A false alert is any distress transmitted for any reason when a real distress situation does not actually exist. Most such alerts are inadvertent and can be traced to equipment problems and human error (caused by improper use of GMDSS equipment). A few, however, are deliberately transmitted as a hoax, made easier by GMDSS equipment that is not properly registered. Many are from non-GMDSS sources, especially in the 121.5 MHz frequency band.

False alerts obstruct efficien and effective SAR services and are detrimental because they:
– Cause delays which may cost lives and prolong or worsen human suffering.
– Adversely affect mariner safety.
– Waste limited resources.
– Erode the confidenc of both mariners and SAR personnel.
– Divert SAR facilities, making them less available should a real distress situation arise.
– Congest and drive up the costs of communications.

The following instructions, extracted from IMO Resolution A.814(19), are for canceling an inadvertent distress alert:

– DIGITAL SELECTIVE CALLING:
  – VHF:
    – Switch off the transmitter immediately (this applies when the false alert is detected during transmission);
    – Switch equipment on and set to Channel 16;
    – Make broadcast to "All Stations" giving name of vessel, call sign and DSC number, and cancel the false distress alert.
Example:
All Stations, All Stations, All Stations
This is NAME, CALL SIGN, DSC NUMBER, POSITION.
Cancel my distress alert of DATE, TIME UTC.

=Master, NAME, CALL SIGN, DSC NUMBER, DATE, TIME UTC

  –MF
    –Switch off the transmitter immediately (this applies when the false alert is detected during transmission);
    –Switch equipment on and tune for radiotelephony transmission on 2182 kHz;
    –Make broadcast to "All Stations" giving name of vessel, call sign and DSC number, and cancel the false distress alert.
Example:
All Stations, All Stations, All Stations,
This is NAME, CALL SIGN, DSC NUMBER, POSITION.
Cancel my distress alert of DATE, TIME UTC.
=Master, NAME, CALL SIGN, DSC NUMBER, DATE, TIME UTC

  –HF:
    –As for MF but the alert must be canceled on all the frequency bands in which it was transmitted: the transmitter should be tuned consecutively to the radiotelephony distress frequencies in the 4, 6, 8, 12 and 16 MHz bands, as necessary.

– INMARSAT-C:
  – Notify the appropriate Rescue Coordination Center (RCC) to cancel the alert by sending a distress priority message via the same CES through which the false distress alert was sent.
Example:
This is NAME, CALL SIGN, IDENTITY NUMBER, POSITION.
Cancel my Inmarsat-C distress alert of DATE, TIME UTC.
=Master +

– EPIRBS:
  – If, for any reason, an EPIRB is activated accidentally, the ship should contact the nearest coast station or an appropriate coast earth station or RCC and cancel the distress alert.
NOTE: Keep the EPIRB activated until an appropriate RCC can be contacted to cancel the alert. (This reduces incomplete alerts and uncertainty associated with why an EPIRB signal ceased.)

Notwithstanding the above, a ship may use any means available to them to inform the appropriate authorities that a false alert has been transmitted and should be canceled. No action will normally be taken against any ship or mariner for reporting and canceling a false distress alert. However, in view of the serious consequences of false alerts, and the strict ban on their transmission, Governments may prosecute in cases of repeated violation.

The following guidelines, extracted from IMO Resolution A.814(19), are recommended for reducing the chance of a false distress alert aboard ship:

DISTRESS, EMERGENCY, AND SAFETY TRAFFIC

- Ensure that all GMDSS certificate personnel responsible for sending a distress alert have been instructed about, and are competent to operate, the particular radio equipment on the ship.
- Ensure that the person(s) responsible for communication during distress incidents give the necessary instructions and information to all crew members on how to use GMDSS equipment to send a distress alert.
- Ensure that as part of each abandon ship drill, instruction is given on how emergency equipment should be used to provide GMDSS functions.
- Ensure that GMDSS equipment testing is only undertaken under the supervision of the person responsible for communications during distress incidents.
- Ensure that GMDSS equipment testing or drills are never allowed to cause false distress alerts.
- Ensure that coded identities of satellite EPIRBs, which are used by SAR personnel responding to emergencies, are properly registered in a database accessible 24 hours a day or automatically provided to SAR authorities (Masters should confir that their EPIRBs have been registered with such a database, to help SAR services identify the ship in the event of distress and rapidly obtain other information which will enable them to respond appropriately (See sec. 400F.)).
- Ensure that EPIRB, Inmarsat and DSC registration data is immediately updated if there is any change in information relating to the ship such as owner, name or flag and that the necessary action is taken to reprogram the ship's new data in the GMDSS equipment concerned.
- Ensure that, for new ships, positions for installing EPIRBs are considered at the earliest stage of ship design and construction.
- Ensure that satellite EPIRBs are carefully installed in accordance with the manufacturers' instructions and using qualifie personnel (sometimes satellite EPIRBs are damaged or broken due to improper handling or installation. They must be installed in a location that will enable them to floa free and automatically activate if the ship sinks. Care must be taken to ensure that they are not tampered with or accidently activated. If the coding has to be changed or the batteries serviced, manufacturers' requirements must be strictly followed. There have been cases where EPIRB lanyards were attached to the ship so that the EPIRB could not floa free; lanyards are only to be used by survivors for securing the EPIRB to a survival craft or person in the water).
- Ensure that EPIRBs are not activated if assistance is already immediately available (EPIRBs are intended to call for assistance if the ship is unable to obtain help by other means, and to provide position information and homing signals for SAR units).
- Ensure that, if a distress alert has been accidently transmitted, the ship makes every reasonable attempt to communicate with the RCC by any means to cancel the false distress alert using the instructions given above.
- Ensure that, if possible, after emergency use, the EPIRB is retrieved and deactivated.
- Ensure that when an EPIRB is damaged and needs to be disposed of, if a ship is sold for scrap, or if for any other reason a satellite EPIRB will no longer be used, the satellite EPIRB is made inoperable, either by removing its battery and, if possible, returning it to the manufacturer, or by demolishing it.

NOTE: If the EPIRB is returned to the manufacturer, it should be wrapped in tin foil to prevent transmission of signals during shipment.

DISTRESS, EMERGENCY, AND SAFETY TRAFFIC

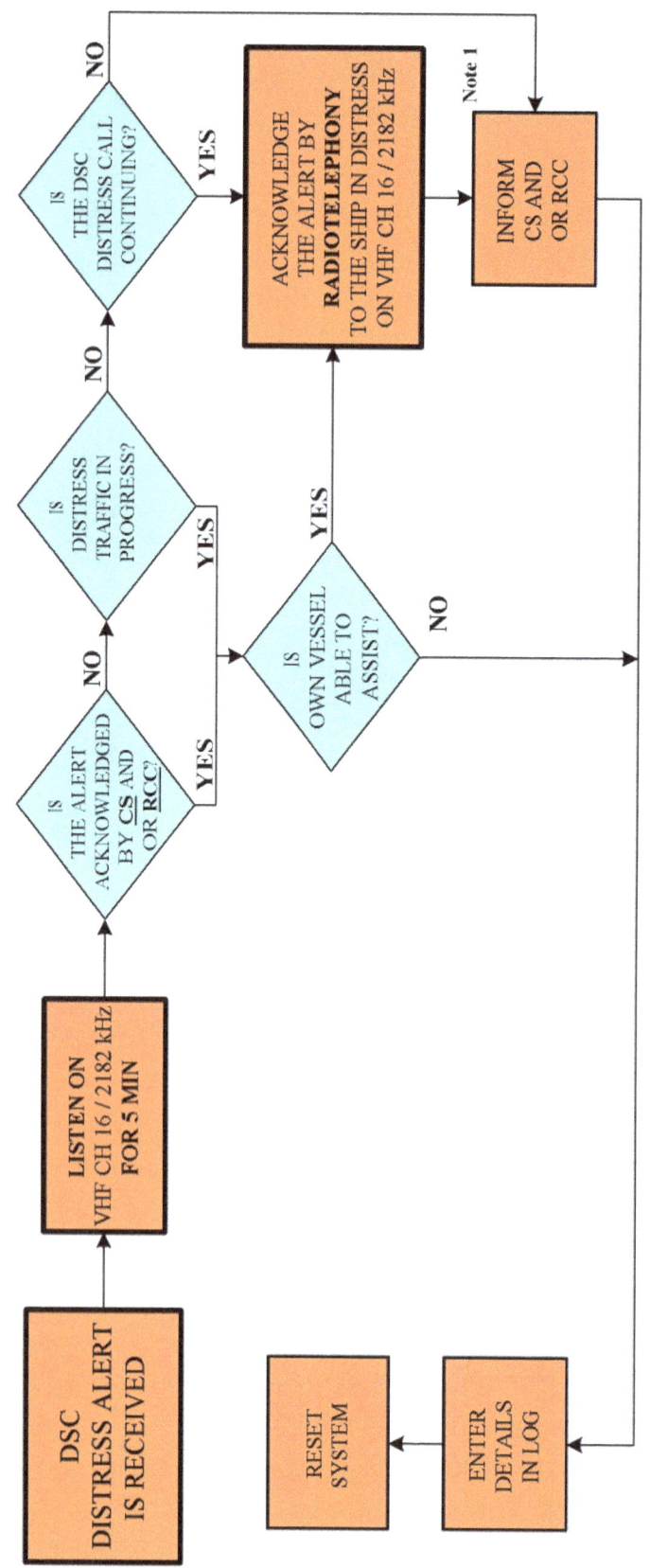

REMARKS:
Note 1: Appropriate or relevant RCC and/or Coast Station shall be informed accordingly. If further DSC alerts are received from the same source and the ship in distress is beyond doubt in the vicinity, a DSC acknowledgment may, after consultation with an RCC or Coast Station, be sent to terminate the call.

Note 2: In no case is a ship permitted to transmit a DSC distress relay call on receipt of a DSC distress alert on either VHF Channel 70 or MF Channel 2187.5 kHz.

CS = Coast Station   RCC = Rescue Coordination Center

4 - 51

DISTRESS, EMERGENCY, AND SAFETY TRAFFIC

ACTIONS BY SHIPS UPON RECEPTION OF **HF** DSC DISTRESS ALERT

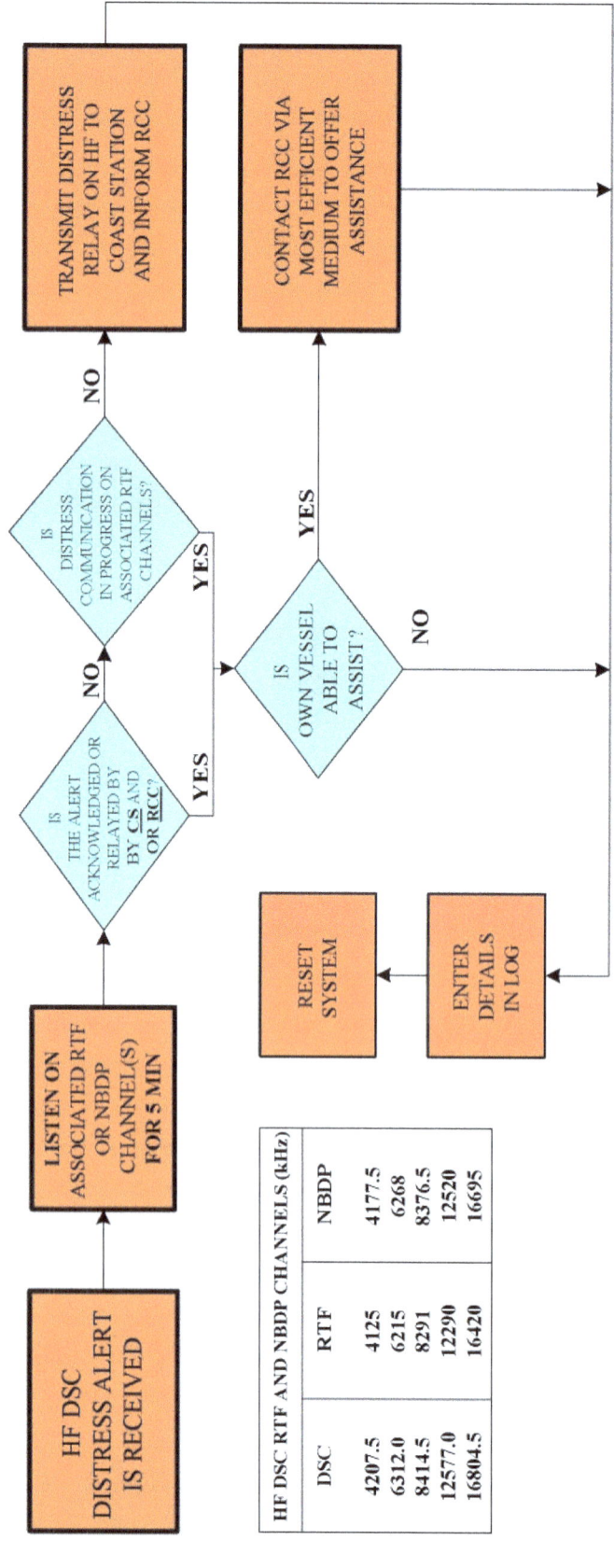

HF DSC RTF AND NBDP CHANNELS (kHz)

DSC	RTF	NBDP
4207.5	4125	4177.5
6312.0	6215	6268
8414.5	8291	8376.5
12577.0	12290	12520
16804.5	16420	16695

REMARKS:
Note 1: If it is clear the ship or persons in distress are not in the vicinity and/or other crafts are better placed to assist, superflou communications which could interfere with search and rescue activities are to be avoided. Details should be recorded in the appropriate logbook.

Note 2: The ship should establish communications with the station controlling the distress as directed and render such assistance as required and appropriate.

Note 3: Distress relay calls should be initiated manually.

CS = Coast Station   RCC = Rescue Coordination Center

4 - 53

DISTRESS, EMERGENCY, AND SAFETY TRAFFIC

LIST OF OPERATIONAL VHF DSC COAST STATIONS FOR SEA AREAS A1
(Extracted from ANNEX 2 of the IMO GMDSS Master Plan)

NAV/MET Area	Country	VHF DSC Coast Station				Associated RCC
		Name	MMSI	Position	Range (NM)	
I	Belgium	Antwerpen	002050485	51-13N 04-23E	25	Oostende
		Oostende	002050480	51-11N 02-48E	25	
	Denmark	Lyngby	002191000	-	-	SOK, Aarhus
		København		55-41N 12-36E	29	
		Vejby		56-04N 12-07E	30	
		Roesnaes		55-44N 10-56E	35	
		Ånholt		56-42N 11-35E	28	
		Fornaes		56-26N 10-56E	32	
		Vejle		55-40N 09-30E	42	
		Als		54-57N 09-33E	41	
		Svendborg		55-01N 10-37E	20	
		Karleby		54-52N 11-11E	36	
		Mern		55-03N 11-59E	45	
		Aarsballe		55-08N 14-52E	42	
		Laesoe		57-17N 11-03E	34	
		Frejlev		57-00N 09-49E	44	
		Blåvand		55-33N 08-06E	33	
		Skagen		57-44N 10-34E	29	
		Hirtshals		57-31N 09-57E	31	
		Hanstholm		57-06N 08-39E	34	
		Bovbjerg		56-31N 08-10E	34	
		Torshavn (Færoes)	002311000	-	-	MRCC Torshavn
		Torshavn		62-01N 06-49W	56	
		Fugloy		62-20N 06-19W	68	
		Mykines		62-06N 07-35W	64	
		Suderoy		61-25N 06-44W	57	
	Estonia	Tallinn	002761000	59-24N 24-40E	20	MRCC Tallinn
		Toila		59-25N 27-31E	30	
		Eisma		59-33N 26-17E	30	
		Aabla		59-35N 25-31E	30	
		Merevälja		59-30N 24-51E	30	
		Suurupi		59-28N 24-23E	30	
		Dirhami		59-12N 23-30E	30	
		Köpu		58-55N 22-12E	35	
		Orissaare		58-34N 23-04E	35	
		Undva		58-31N 21-56E	30	
		Torgu		57-59N 22-05E	28	
		Ruhnu		57-48N 23-15E	28	
		Töstamaa		58-18N 23-59E	30	
	Finland	Turku	002300230	-	-	MRCC Turku
		Kemi	002303000	65-49N 24-32E	30	MRSC Vaasa
		Hailuoto		65-02N 24-36E	27	

DISTRESS, EMERGENCY, AND SAFETY TRAFFIC

NAV/MET Area	Country	VHF DSC Coast Station				Associated RCC
		Name	MMSI	Position	Range (NM)	
I	Finland (cont.)	Kalajoki	002303000	64-18N 24-11E	47	MRSC Vaasa
		Kokkola		63-50N 23-09E	34	
		Raippaluoto		63-22N 21-19E	32	
		Kristiinankaupunki	002301000	62-16N 21-24E	36	MRCC Turku
		Pori		61-36N 21-27E	16	
		Rauma		61-08N 21-33E	28	
		Uusikaupunki		60-49N 21-26E	32	
		Geta		60-23N 19-51E	38	
		Brandö		60-25N 21-03E	25	
		Järsö		60-01N 20-00E	36	
		Korppoo		60-10N 21-33E	30	
		Naantali		60-27N 22-03E	32	
		Utö	002302000	59-47N 21-22E	23	MRSC Helsinki
		Hanko		59-50N 22-56E	26	
		Porkkala		59-59N 24-26E	30	
		Santahamina/Helsinki		60-09N 25-02E	30	
		Sondby		60-16N 25-51E	26	
		Kotka		60-29N 26-53E	29	
		Virolahti		60-36N 27-50E	32	
	France	Gris Nez (CROSS)	002275100	50-52N 01-35E	23	MRCC Gris Nez
		Dunkerque		51-03N 02-21E	22	
		Saint Frieux		50-36N 01-38E	38	
		L'Ailly		49-55N 00-57E	28	
		Jobourg (CROSS)	002275200	49-41N 01-54W	42	MRCC Jobourg
		Antifer		49-41N 00-10E	33	
		Ver-sur-Mer		49-20N 00-31W	27	
		Gatteville		49-42N 01-16W	26	
		Granville		48-50N 01-37W	26	
		Roches Douvres		49-06N 02-49W	24	
		Corsen (CROSS)	002275300	48-25N 04-47W	27	MRCC Corsen
		Cap Frehel		48-41N 02-19W	28	
		Ile de Batz		48-45N 04-01W	27	
		Stiff Ouessant		48-28N 05-03W	34	
		Bodic		48-48N 03-05W	25	
		Pointe du Raz		48-02N 04-44W	24	
	Germany	Bremen Rescue Radio	002111240	53-05N 08-48E	25	MRCC Bremen
		Rügen		54-21N 13-45E	27	
		Arkona		54-35N 13-37E	31	
		Darss		54-24N 12-27E	30	
		Rostock		54-10N 12-06E	33	
		Kiel		54-18N 10-07E	37	
		Lübeck		54-13N 10-43E	46	
		Flensburg		54-44N 09-30E	29	
		Norddeich		53-34N 07-06E	24	

DISTRESS, EMERGENCY, AND SAFETY TRAFFIC

NAV/MET Area	Country	VHF DSC Coast Station				Associated RCC
		Name	MMSI	Position	Range (NM)	
I	Germany (cont.)	Cuxhaven	002111240	53-50N 08-39E	24	MRCC Bremen
		Helgoland		54-11N 07-53E	33	
		Sylt		54-55N 08-18E	28	
		Eiderstedt		54-20N 08-47E	24	
		Hamburg		53-33N 09-58E	44	
	Ireland	MRCC Dublin	002500300	-	-	MRCC Dublin
		Dublin		53-23N 06-04W	40	
		Carlingford		54-04N 06-19W	40	
		Wicklow Head		52-58N 06-00W	30	
		Rosslare		52-19N 06-34W	44	
		Mine Head		52-00N 07-35W	30	
		MRSC Valentia	002500200	-	-	MRSC Valentia
		Cork		51-51N 08-29W	40	
		Bantry		51-38N 10-00W	60	
		Valentia		51-52N 10-21W	54	
		Shannon		52-31N 09-36W	50	
		MRSC Malin Head	002500100	-	-	MRSC Malin Head
		Clifden		53-30N 09-56W	50	
		Belmullet		54-16N 10-03W	25	
		Glen Head		54-44N 08-40W	47	
		Malin Head		55-22N 07-16W	49	
	Latvia	Riga Rescue Radio	002750100	57-02N 24-05E	20	MRCC Riga
		Vitrupe		57-36N 24-23E	25	
		Mersrags		57-22N 23-07E	25	
		Kolka		57-45N 22-35E	20	
		Jaunupe		57-32N 21-41E	20	
		Uzava		57-13N 21-26E	20	
		Akmenrags		56-50N 21-03E	20	
		Jurmalciems		56-18N 20-59E	20	
	Lithuania	Klaipeda Rescue	002770330	55-43N 21-06E	18	MRCC Klaipeda
		Nida		55-18N 20-59E	24	
		Shventoji		56-01N 21-05E	20	
	Netherlands	Netherlands Coast Guard	002442000	-	-	JRCC Den Helder
		Woensdrecht		51-26N 04-20E	25	
		Westkappelle		51-32N 03-27E	25	
		Renesse		51-44N 03-49E	25	
		Scheveningen		52-06N 04-15E	25	
		Schoorl		52-43N 04-39E	25	
		Den Helder		52-57N 04-47E	25	
		West Terschelling		53-21N 05-13E	25	
		Schiermonnikoog		53-29N 06-09E	25	
		Appingedam		53-20N 06-52E	25	
		Kornwerderzand		53-04N 05-20E	25	

DISTRESS, EMERGENCY, AND SAFETY TRAFFIC

NAV/MET Area	Country	VHF DSC Coast Station				Associated RCC
		Name	MMSI	Position	Range (NM)	
I	Netherlands (cont.)	Hoorn	002442000	52-39N 05-06E	25	JRCC Den Helder
		Wezep		52-27N 06-00E	25	
	Norway	Tjøme	002570100	-	-	MRCC Stavanger
		Halden		59-11N 11-26E	53	
		Oslo		59-59N 10-40E	62	
		Drammen		59-40N 10-26E	24	
		Tjøme		59-05N 10-25E	30	
		Porsgrunn		59-14N 09-42E	66	
		Risør		58-43N 09-12E	35	
		Arendal		58-27N 08-45E	36	
		Kristiansand		58-04N 07-59E	36	
		Rogaland	002570300	-	-	MRCC Stavanger
		Lindesnes		58-01N 07-04E	40	
		Farsund		58-04N 06-45E	29	
		Storefjell		58-09N 06-43E	52	
		Bjerkreim		58-38N 05-58E	66	
		Stavanger		58-56N 05-43E	40	
		Bokn		59-13N 05-26E	50	
		Haugesund		59-25N 05-20E	47	
		Valhall (Rig)		56-17N 03-24E	30	
		Ekofisk (Rig		56-32N 03-13E	30	
		Ula (Rig)		57-07N 02-51E	30	
		Draupner (Rig)		58-11N 02-28E	30	
		Sleipner A (Rig)		58-22N 01-54E	30	
		Stord		59-52N 05-30E	74	
		Sotra		60-19N 05-07E	53	
		Bergen		60-25N 05-22E	65	
		Lindas		60-35N 05-20E	59	
		Grimo		60-24N 06-40E	69	
		Oseberg (Rig)		60-30N 02-50E	30	
		Florø	002570500	-	-	MRCC Stavanger
		Gulen		61-02N 05-09E	73	
		Sogndal		61-10N 07-07E	93	
		Kinn		61-34N 04-46E	52	
		Bremanger		61-52N 05-00E	74	
		Raudeberg		62-00N 05-09E	38	
		Sagtennene		61-54N 06-07E	85	
		Snorre (Rig)		61-27N 02-09E	31	
		Gullfaks (Rig)		61-11N 02-11E	30	
		Nerlandshorn		62-21N 05-33E	59	
		Hjørunganes		62-21N 06-07E	19	
		Aksla		62-29N 06-12E	41	
		Gamlemsveten		62-35N 06-19E	80	
		Orskogfjellet		62-31N 06-52E	69	

DISTRESS, EMERGENCY, AND SAFETY TRAFFIC

NAV/MET Area	Country	VHF DSC Coast Station				Associated RCC
		Name	MMSI	Position	Range (NM)	
I	Norway (cont.)	Hellesylt	002570500	62-08N 06-56E	42	MRCC Stavanger
		Geiranger		62-07N 07-10E	57	
		Molde		62-45N 07-08E	59	
		Reinsfjell		62-57N 07-56E	84	
		Kristiansund		63-07N 07-42E	34	
		Litlefonni		63-23N 08-43E	56	
		Forbordsfjell		63-32N 10-54E	66	
		Mosvik		63-46N 10-58E	55	
		Kopparen		63-48N 09-45E	64	
		Yttervåg		64-18N 10-18E	34	
		Namsos		64-27N 11-32E	58	
		Rørvik		64-53N 11-14E	43	
		Draugen (Rig)		64-21N 07-47E	30	
		Åsgård B (Rig)		65-07N 06-47E	30	
		Heidrun (Rig)		65-20N 07-19E	30	
		Bodø	002570700	-	-	MRCC Bodø
		Vega		65-38N 11-54E	75	
		Horva		66-01N 12-49E	57	
		Mo i Rana		66-12N 13-45E	71	
		Traenfjord		66-32N 12-49E	53	
		Meløy		66-51N 13-38E	50	
		Rønvikfjell/Bodø		67-18N 14-27E	41	
		Fornesfjell		67-26N 15-27E	68	
		Værøy		67-40N 12-38E	59	
		Steigen		67-50N 15-00E	77	
		Fredvang		68-06N 13-11E	21	
		Hagskaret		68-10N 13-42E	36	
		Kvalnes		68-21N 13-58E	40	
		Raften/Svolvaer		68-24N 15-07E	18	
		Storheia/Hadsel		68-33N 14-53E	61	
		Myre/Vesteralen		68-57N 15-01E	30	
		Stamnes		68-49N 15-29E	13	
		Andenes		69-17N 16-01E	54	
		Lødingen		68-24N 15-58E	13	
		Harstad		68-48N 16-31E	36	
		Veggen/Narvik		68-28N 17-10E	48	
		Kistefjell		69-18N 18-08E	85	
		Tromsø		69-39N 18-57E	36	
		Tønsnes		69-43N 19-08E	47	
		Hillesoy		69-39N 18-00E	41	
		Bjørnøya		74-31N 19-01E	40	
		Vardø	002570800	-	-	MRCC Bodø
		Torsvag		70-15N 19-30E	23	
		Trolltind		70-04N 20-26E	78	

4 - 59

DISTRESS, EMERGENCY, AND SAFETY TRAFFIC

NAV/MET Area	Country	VHF DSC Coast Station				Associated RCC
		Name	MMSI	Position	Range (NM)	
I	Norway (cont.)	Skjervoy	002570800	70-01N 20-59E	37	MRCC Bodø
		Helligfjell		70-07N 22-56E	63	
		Fuglen		70-39N 21-58E	55	
		Tyven		70-38N 23-42E	57	
		Havoysund		71-00N 24-36E	49	
		Honningsvåg		70-59N 25-54E	56	
		Oksen		70-58N 27-21E	51	
		Mehamn		71-03N 28-07E	49	
		Berlevåg		70-52N 29-05E	40	
		Tana		70-28N 28-13E	65	
		Båtsfjord		70-40N 29-42E	49	
		Vardø		70-20N 31-02E	40	
		Varangefjord		70-05N 29-49E	41	
		Kirkenes		69-45N 30-08E	44	
		Svalbard	002570900	-	-	MRCC Bodø
		Isfjord		78-02N 13-40E	23	
		Longyearbyen		78-15N 15-24E	21	
		Kongsvegpasset		78-45N 13-30E	78	
	Poland	Witowo	002610210	-	-	MRCC Gdynia
		Swinoujscie		53-55N 14-15E	20	
		Grzywacz		53-57N 14-30E	35	
		Kolowo		53-20N 14-41E	40	
		Kolorzeg		54-11N 15-33E	25	
		Barzowice		54-28N 16-30E	30	
		Rowakol		54-39N 17-13E	35	
		Rozewie		54-50N 18-20E	25	
		Oksywie		54-33N 18-32E	30	
		Krynica Morska		54-24N 19-30E	20	
	Russian Federation	Saint Petersburg	002733700	59-53N 30-13E	27	MRCC Saint Petersburg
		Primorsk		60-20N 28-43E	30	
		Vyborg	002734415	60-42N 28-43E	17.5	
		Kaliningrad	002734417	54-58N 19-59E	26	MRSC Kaliningrad
		Murmansk	002734420	68-58N 33-01E	18	MRCC Murmansk
		Arkhangel'sk	002734414	64-32N 40-32E	25.6	MRSC Arkhangel'sk
		Mudyug		64-51N 40-17E	24.5	
	Sweden	Göteborg	002653000	-	-	MRCC Göteborg
		Umeå		63-50N 19-49E	59	
		Väddö		59-58N 18-50E	37	
		Svenska Högarna		59-27N 19-30E	21	
		Stockholm		59-18N 18-10E	50	
		Skellefteå		64-46N 20-57E	49	
		Seskarö		65-44N 23-44E	24	
		Luleå		65-32N 21-55E	36	
		Mjällom		62-59N 18-23E	48	

DISTRESS, EMERGENCY, AND SAFETY TRAFFIC

NAV/MET Area	Country	VHF DSC Coast Station				Associated RCC
		Name	MMSI	Position	Range (NM)	
I	Sweden (cont.)	Härnösand	002653000	62-36N 17-55E	40	MRCC Göteborg
		Sundsvall		62-24N 17-28E	40	
		Hudiksvall		61-42N 16-51E	60	
		Gävle		60-38N 17-08E	42	
		Öregrund		60-30N 18-24E	30	
		Västerås		59-38N 16-24E	45	
		Södertälje		59-13N 17-37E	35	
		Torö		58-49N 17-51E	31	
		Norrköping		58-40N 16-28E	49	
		Gotska Sandön		58-23N 19-14E	27	
		Fårö		57-52N 19-00E	30	
		Visby		57-35N 18-22E	48	
		Hoburgen		56-56N 18-13E	30	
		Västervik		57-43N 16-26E	50	
		Borgholm		56-51N 16-42E	30	
		Ölands Södra		56-14N 16-27E	28	
		Karlskrona		56-14N 15-39E	32	
		Kivik		55-40N 14-09E	44	
		Trelleborg		55-28N 13-16E	36	
		Helsingborg		56-02N 12-41E	32	
		Falkenberg		56-50N 12-41E	39	
		Göteborg		57-41N 12-03E	47	
		Hunnebostrand		58-25N 11-25E	34	
		Strömstad		58-55N 11-10E	30	
		Vänersborg		58-19N 12-16E	27	
		Kinnekulle		58-36N 13-24E	48	
		Karlsborg (Vättern)		58-40N 14-34E	38	
	United Kingdom	Falmouth	002320014	50-08N 05-07W	26	MRCC Falmouth
		Lizard		49-59N 05-12W	27	
		Scillies		49-56N 06-18W	26	
		Lands End		50-08N 05-39W	44	
		St. Ives		50-13N 05-28W	19	
		Trevose Head		50-33N 05-02W	30	
		Bude		50-49N 04-33W	20	
		Brixham	002320013	-	-	MRSC Brixham
		Rame Head		50-19W 04-13W	30	
		East Prawle		50-13N 03-42W	34	
		Dartmouth		50-21N 03-35W	31	
		Berry Head		50-24N 03-29W	27	
		Portland	002320012	-	-	MRSC Portland
		Grove		50-33N 02-25W	33	
		Bincleaves		50-36N 02-27W	16	
		Hengistbury Head		50-43N 01-46W	21	
		Beer Head		50-41N 03-06W	35	

4 - 61

DISTRESS, EMERGENCY, AND SAFETY TRAFFIC

NAV/MET Area	Country	VHF DSC Coast Station				Associated RCC
		Name	MMSI	Position	Range (NM)	
I	United Kingdom (cont.)	Solent	002320011	-	-	MRSC Solent
		Boniface (Tx)		50-36N 01-12W	44	
		Stenbury (Rx)		50-37N 01-14W	44	
		Selsey Bill		50-44N 00-48W	19	
		Newhaven		50-47N 00-03W	27	
		Guernsey (Channel Islands)	002320064	49-26N 02-36W	50	
		Jersey Radio (Channel Islands)	002320060	49-11N 02-14W	35	
		Dover (Rx)	002320010	51-08N 01-21E	33	MRCC Dover
		West Hougham (Tx)		51-07N 01-15E	45	
		Fairlight		50-52N 00-40E	34	
		North Foreland		51-22N 01-25E	25	
		Thames	002320009	51-52N 01-16E	18	MRSC Thames
		Shoeburyness		51-31N 00-46E	17	
		Bradwell		51-44N 00-53E	16	
		Bawdsey		52-00N 01-25E	24	
		Yarmouth	002320008	52-36N 01-42E	20	MRCC Yarmouth
		Lowestoft		52-29N 01-42E	19	
		Trimingham		52-55N 01-20E	30	
		Langham		52-57N 00-57E	24	
		Skegness		53-09N 00-21E	18	
		Trusthorpe		53-19N 00-16E	23	
		Humber	002320007	-	-	MRSC Humber
		Easington		53-39N 00-06E	25	
		Flamborough		54-08N 00-06W	26	
		Whitby		54-29N 00-36W	30	
		Hartlepool		54-42N 01-10W	19	
		Cullercoats		55-04N 01-28W	25	
		Newton		55-31N 01-37W	24	
		Forth	002320005	56-17N 02-35W	21	MRSC Forth
		St. Abbs		55-54N 02-12W	42	
		Craigkelly		56-04N 03-14W	49	
		Inverbervie		56-51N 02-16W	37	
		Aberdeen	002320004	-	-	MRCC Aberdeen
		Gregness		57-08N 02-03W	25	
		Peterhead		57-31N 01-46W	19	
		Windy Head		57-39N 02-14W	45	
		Banff		57-38N 02-31W	33	
		Thrumster		58-24N 03-07W	39	
		Rosemarkie		57-38N 04-05W	43	
		Foyers		57-14N 04-31W	44	
		Noss Head		58-29N 03-03W	22	
		Dunnet Head		58-40N 03-22W	30	

DISTRESS, EMERGENCY, AND SAFETY TRAFFIC

NAV/MET Area	Country	VHF DSC Coast Station				Associated RCC
		Name	MMSI	Position	Range (NM)	
I	United Kingdom (cont.)	Ben Tongue	002320004	58-30N 04-24W	50	MRCC Aberdeen
		Durness		58-34N 04-44W	26	
		Shetland	002320001	60-09N 01-08W	26	MRSC Shetland
		Wideford Hill		58-59N 03-01W	44	
		Compass Head		59-52N 01-16W	33	
		Fitful Head		59-54N 01-23W	47	
		Collafirth Hil		60-32N 01-23W	46	
		Saxa Vord		60-50N 00-50W	44	
		Stornoway	002320024	-	-	MRSC Stornoway
		Butt of Lewis		58-28N 06-14W	24	
		Forsnaval		58-13N 07-00W	44	
		Port Naguran		58-15N 06-10W	23	
		Rodel		57-45N 06-57W	29	
		Clettraval		57-37N 07-27W	37	
		Scoval		57-27N 06-42W	48	
		Skriaig		57-23N 06-14W	57	
		Barra		57-01N 07-30W	30	
		Melvaig		57-51N 05-47W	48	
		Arisaig		56-55N 05-50W	35	
		Clyde	002320022	55-58N 04-48W	20	MRCC Clyde
		Pulpitt Hill		56-19N 05-21W	35	
		Torosay		56-27N 05-44W	58	
		Glengorm		56-38N 06-08W	47	
		Tiree		56-30N 06-57W	35	
		Law Hill		55-42N 04-50W	41	
		Rhu Stafnish		55-22N 05-32W	44	
		Kilchiaran		55-46N 06-27W	37	
		South Knapdale		55-55N 05-28W	62	
		Belfast	002320021	-	-	MRSC Belfast
		Orlock Head		54-40N 05-35W	23	
		Slieve Martin		54-06N 06-10W	61	
		Black Mountain		54-35N 06-01W	62	
		West Torr		55-12N 06-05W	33	
		Limavady		55-06N 06-53W	53	
		Liverpool	002320019	53-30N 03-03W	17	MRSC Liverpool
		Moel-Y-Parc		53-13N 03-19W	57	
		Langthwaitet		54-02N 02-46W	37.5	
		Snaefell		54-16N 04-28W	70	
		Spanish Head		54-04N 04-46W	37	
		Caldbeck		54-44N 03-03W	65	
		Holyhead	002320018	53-19N 04-38W	17	MRSC Holyhead
		Rhiw		52-50N 04-38W	51	
		South Stack		53-18N 04-42W	38	
		Great Orme		53-20N 03-51W	43	

4 - 63

DISTRESS, EMERGENCY, AND SAFETY TRAFFIC

NAV/MET Area	Country	VHF DSC Coast Station				Associated RCC
		Name	MMSI	Position	Range (NM)	
I	United Kingdom (cont.)	Milford Haven	002320017	-	-	MRSC Milford Haven
		Tenby		51-42N 04-41W	29	
		St. Ann's Head		51-40N 05-11W	33	
		Dinas Head		52-00N 04-54W	43	
		Blaenplwyf		52-22N 04-06W	50	
		Swansea	002320016	-	-	MRCC Swansea
		Gower		51-34N 04-17W	27	
		Mumbles Hill		51-34N 03-59W	29	
		St. Hilary		51-27N 03-24W	50	
		Severn Bridge		51-37N 02-39W	33	
		Combe Martin		51-10N 04-03W	47	
		Ilfracombe		51-13N 04-05W	27	
		Hartland Point		51-01N 04-31W	35	
II	Benin	Cotonou	006100001	06-21N 02-26E	29	
	France	Etel (CROSS)	002275000	47-40N 03-12W	26	MRCC Etel
		Penmarc'h		47-48N 04-22W	28	
		Groix		47-39N 03-30W	24	
		Belle Ile		47-19N 03-14W	27	
		Kerrouault		47-27N 02-30W	33	
		Armandeche		46-42N 01-55W	21	
		Ile D'Yeu		46-43N 02-23W	24	
		Soulac		45-32N 01-06W	24	
		Chassiron		46-03N 01-25W	22	
		Cap Ferret		44-38N 01-15W	22	
		Contis		43-48N 01-18W	23	
		Hourtin		45-09N 01-10W	23	
		Biarritz		43-32N 01-32W	26	
	Ghana	Tema	006270000	-	-	Harbor Master's Office Accr
		Winneba		05-21N 00-37W	60	
		Afla		06-07N 01-11W	60	
		Tema		05-38N 00-00	60	
		Cape Coast		05-07N 01-15W	60	
		Half Assini		05-03N 02-53W	60	
		Takoradi		04-54N 01-45W	60	
		Axim		04-52N 02-14W	60	
		Ada		05-47N 00-38W	60	
	Spain	Bilbao (CCR)	002241021	-	-	MRCC Bilbao
		Pasajes		43-17N 01-55W	35	
		Bilbao		43-16N 03-02W	35	
		Santander		43-25N 03-36W	35	
		Cabo Penas		43-26N 05-35W	35	
		Navia		43-25N 06-50W	35	

DISTRESS, EMERGENCY, AND SAFETY TRAFFIC

NAV/MET Area	Country	VHF DSC Coast Station				Associated RCC
		Name	MMSI	Position	Range (NM)	
II	Spain (cont.)	MRCC Bilbao*	002240996	43-21N 03-02W	30	MRCC Bilbao
		MRSC Santander*	002241009	43-28N 03-43W	30	MRSC Santander
		MRCC Gijon*	002240997	43-34N 05-42W	30	MRCC Gijon
		MRSC Coruna*	002240992	-	-	MRSC Coruna
		Cabo Priorino		43-28N 08-20W	30	
		Coruna		43-22N 08-23W	30	
		Coruna (CCR)	002241022	-	-	
		Cabo Ortegal		43-35N 07-47W	35	MRCC Finisterre
		Coruna		43-10N 08-18W	35	MRSC Coruna
		Vigo		42-10N 08-41W	35	MRSC Vigo
		La Guardia		41-53N 08-52W	35	MRCC Finisterre
		Finisterre		42-55N 09-17W	35	
		MRCC Finisterre*	002240993	-	-	
		Monte Beo		43-20N 08-50W	40	
		Finisterre		42-42N 08-59W	40	
		Monte Xastas		43-02N 09-16W	40	
		Monte Taume		42-36N 09-03W	40	
		MRSC Vigo*	002240998	42-14N 08-43W	30	MRSC Vigo
		MRSC Huelva*	002241012	37-14N 06-57W	30	MRSC Huelva
		MRSC Cadiz*	002241011	36-32N 06-18W	30	MRSC Cadiz
		MRCC Tarifa*	002240994	-	-	MRCC Tarifa
		Cape Trafalgar		36-12N 06-01W	30	
		Tarifa		36-01N 05-35W	30	
		Punta Almina		35-54N 05-17W	30	
		MRSC Algeciras*	002241001	36-07N 05-26W	30	MRSC Algeciras
		Malaga (CCR)	002241023	-	-	MRCC Tarifa
		Huelva		37-13N 07-07W	35	MRSC Huelva
		Cadiz		36-32N 06-18W	35	MRSC Cadiz
		Tarifa		36-03N 05-33W	35	MRCC Tarifa
		Tenerife (CCR)	002241025	-	-	
		Arrecife		29-08N 13-31W	35	MRCC Las Palmas
		Fuerteventura		28-33N 13-55W	35	
		Las Palmas		27-58N 15-33W	35	
		Gomera		28-06N 17-06W	35	
		Hierro		27-48N 17-55W	35	MRCC Tenerife
		Tenerife		28-27N 16-23W	35	
		La Palma		28-39N 17-50W	35	
		MRCC Tenerife*	002241007	28-29N 16-14W	30	
		MRCC Las Palmas*	002240995	-	-	MRCC Las Palmas
		Las Palmas		28-09N 15-25W	30	
		La Isleta		28-10N 15-25W	30	

*NOTE: The primary responsibility for the receipt of VHF DSC distress alerts for Spain is carried out via the Coast Radio Stations. VHF DSC facilities maintained at various MRCCs and MRSCs are only complementary to the Coast Radio Stations network.

DISTRESS, EMERGENCY, AND SAFETY TRAFFIC

NAV/MET Area	Country	VHF DSC Coast Station				Associated RCC
		Name	MMSI	Position	Range (NM)	
III	Bulgaria	Varna	002070810	43-15N 27-57E	52	MRCC Varna
		Bourgas		42-29N 27-28E	45	
	Croatia	Split	002380100	-	-	MRCC Rijeka
		Savudrija		45-29N 13-29E	30	
		Ucka		45-17N 14-12E	90	
		Kamenjak		44-46N 14-47E	50	
		Susak		44-31N 14-18E	50	
		Celavac		44-16N 15-47E	80	
		Ugljan		44-04N 15-10E	40	
		Labistica		43-35N 16-13E	80	
		Vidova Gora		43-17N 16-37E	50	
		Hum (Otok Vis)		43-01N 16-07E	70	
		Uljenje		42-54N 17-29E	70	
		Srd		42-39N 18-07E	50	
		Hum (Otok Lastovo)		42-45N 16-52E	40	
		Rijecka	002380200	45-20N 14-25E	30	
		Dubrovnik	002380300	42-39N 18-05E	30	
		MRCC Rijecka	002387010 002387020	45-19E 14-27E	15	
		MRSC Zadar	002387400 002387401	44-07N 15-13E	7	MRSC Zadar
		MRSC Sibenik	002387500 002387501	43-44N 15-54E	7	MRSC Sibenik
		MRSC Split	002387040 002387030	43-30N 16-27E	10	MRSC Split
		MRSC Dubrovnik	002387800 002387801	42-39N 18-05E	15	MRSC Dubrovnik
	Cyprus	Cyprus	002091000	-	-	RCC Larnaca
		Pissouri		34-39N 32-42E	50	
		Olympus		34-56N 32-51E	120	
		Kionia		34-55N 33-12E	100	
	Egypt	Alexandria	006221111	31-11N 28-55E	23	RCC Cairo
		Marsa Matruh		31-21N 27-14E	23	
		Ras Alhkima		31-09N 27-49E	25	
		El Dab'a		31-02N 28-28E	27	
		El' Alamein		30-51N 28-55E	25	
		Sidi Kerier		31-02N 29-39E	25	
		Rashid		31-27N 30-22E	27	
		Baltim		31-33N 31-05E	27	
		Port Said	006221113	31-15N 32-19E	21	
		Ras el Barr		31-30N 31-50E	27	
		Beir Al Abd		31-02N 33-00E	27	
		Arish		31-07N 33-48E	27	
		Ismailia		30-36N 32-16E	24	

DISTRESS, EMERGENCY, AND SAFETY TRAFFIC

NAV/MET Area	Country	VHF DSC Coast Station				Associated RCC
		Name	MMSI	Position	Range (NM)	
III	Egypt (cont.)	Suez	006221113	29-58N 32-33E	22	RCC Cairo
		Zhafarana		29-07N 32-39E	27	
	France	La Garde (CROSS)	002275400	43-06N 05-59E	23	MRCC La Garde
		Bear		42-31N 03-08E	30	
		Pic Neoulos		42-29N 02-57E	94	
		Agde		43-17N 03-30E	31	
		Espiguette		43-29N 04-08E	19	
		Place du Planier		43-12N 05-14E	25	
		Mont Coudon		43-10N 06-10E	72	
		La Garoupe		43-34N 07-08E	30	
		Cap Camarat		43-12N 06-40E	30	
		Pic de l'Ours		43-28N 06-54E	62	
		Aspretto (Sous CROSS)	002275420	41-55N 08-46E	30	MRCC La Garde/ MRSC Corse
		Ersa		42-58N 09-23E	64	
		Serra Di Pigno		42-52N 09-24E	83	
		Piana		42-14N 08-38E	69	
		Punta		41-57N 08-42E	75	
		Serragia		41-31N 08-59E	58	
		Conca		41-44N 09-23E	54	
	Georgia	Batumi	002130100	41-39N 41-39E	50	MRCC Georgia
		Poti	002130300	42-09N 41-39E	50	RSC Poti
	Greece	Olympia	002371000	38-01N 23-50E	-	JRCC Piraeus
		Gerania		38-00N 23-20E	98	
		Poros/Darditsa		37-30N 23-27E	73	
		Thassos		40-47N 24-43E	90	
		Sfendami		40-25N 22-31E	41	
		Thira		36-25N 25-26E	66	
		Chios		38-23N 26-03E	78	
		Kefallinia		38-08N 20-40E	107	
		Kerkyra		39-45N 19-52E	82	
		Kythira		36-09N 22-59E	52	
		Limnos		39-52N 25-04E	59	
		Sitia (Mare)		35-12N 26-06E	75	
		Mytilini		39-04N 26-21E	84	
		Parnitha		38-10N 23-44E	98	
		Petalidi		36-56N 21-52E	83	
		Pilio		39-22N 22-57E	104	
		Rodhos		36-16N 27-56E	78	
		Syros		37-27N 24-56E	57	
		Knossos		35-17N 24-53E	87	
		Patmos		37-18N 26-32E	46	
		Moustakos		35-18N 23-37E	84	
		Tsoukalas		40-23N 23-28E	68	

DISTRESS, EMERGENCY, AND SAFETY TRAFFIC

NAV/MET Area	Country	VHF DSC Coast Station				Associated RCC
		Name	MMSI	Position	Range (NM)	
III	Greece (cont.)	Faistos	002371000	35-00N 25-12E	84	JRCC Piraeus
		Astypalea		36-36N 28-26E	59	
		Karpathos		35-28N 27-10E	66	
		Brochas Kritis		35-19N 25-44E	65	
		Lichada		38-52N 22-53E	60	
		Skiros		38-50N 24-30E	68	
		Andros		37-56N 24-46E	55	
		Milos		36-41N 24-23E	78	
		Aspropirgos	002391000	38-03N 23-35E	30	
	Israel	Haifa	004280001	32-49N 35-00E	50	Haifa Radio
	Italy	Roma	002470001	-	-	
		Conconello		45-40N 13-47E	38	MRSC Trieste
		Piancavallo		46-05N 12-32E	70	
		Monte Cero		45-15N 11-40E	45	MRSC Venezia
		Ravenna Bassette		44-24N 12-12E	20	MRSC Ravenna
		Forte Garibaldi		43-36N 13-31E	39	MRSC Ancona
		Monte Conero		43-33N 13-26E	60	
		Monte Secco		42-58N 13-52E	38	
		Silvi Paese		42-33N 14-05E	40	
		Porto Cervo Eliporto		41-08N 09-32E	25	MRSC Cagliari
		Monte Moro		41-06N 09-30E	40	
		Monte Limbara		40-51N 09-10E	55	
		Osilo		40-44N 08-40E	40	
		Campu Spina		39-22N 08-34E	55	
		Margine Rosso		39-13N 09-14E	19	
		Monte Serpeddi		39-22N 09-17E	55	
		Badde Urbara		40-09N 08-37E	55	
		Monte Tului		40-15N 09-35E	55	
		Monte Paradiso		42-05N 11-51E	50	MRSC Roma
		Monte Cavo		41-45N 12-42E	60	
		Formia Ascatiello		41-15N 13-36E	30	
		Monte Argentario		42-23N 11-10E	40	MRSC Livorno
		Gorgona		43-25N 09-53E	40	
		Monte Nero		43-29N 10-21E	40	
		Zoagli		44-19N 09-15E	37	MRSC Genova
		Castellaccio		44-25N 08-56E	45	
		Monte Bignone		43-52N 07-43E	50	
		Palermo	002470002	-	-	
		Monte Calvario		42-04N 14-39E	45	MRSC Ancona
		Abbate Argento		40-52N 17-17E	50	MRSC Bari
		Monte Parano		40-26N 17-25E	35	
		Monte Sardo		39-52N 18-20E	39	
		Casa D'orso		41-49N 15-59E	55	

DISTRESS, EMERGENCY, AND SAFETY TRAFFIC

NAV/MET Area	Country	VHF DSC Coast Station				Associated RCC
		Name	MMSI	Position	Range (NM)	
III	Italy (cont.)	Capo Colonna	002470002	39-01N 17-09E	37	MRSC Reggio Calabria
		Punta Stilo		38-26N 16-34E	26	
		Capo dell'Armi		37-57N 15-40E	31	
		Serra del Tuono		39-55N 15-50E	55	
		Ustica		38-42N 13-10E	40	MRSC Palermo
		Monte Erice		38-02N 12-35E	55	
		Pantelleria		36-46N 12-01E	70	
		Lampedusa		35-30N 12-37E	25	
		Caltabellotta		37-34N 13-13E	65	
		Gela		37-04N 14-14E	19	
		Siracusa Belvedere		37-05N 15-12E	40	MRSC Catania
		Augusta Campolato Alto		37-16N 15-12E	31	
		Forte Spuria		38-16N 15-37E	32	
		Cefalu		38-01N 13-57E	40	MRSC Palermo
		Capri		40-33N 14-15E	40	MRSC Napoli
		Napoli Posillipo		40-48N 14-11E	36	
		Varco del Salice		40-17N 15-02E	60	
	Romania	Constanta	002640570	-	-	Constanta Harbor Master
		Constanta		44-06N 28-38E	25	
		Enisala		44-51N 28-52E	44	
		Mahmudia		45-05N 29-04E	45	
		Sfintu Gheo ghe		45-18N 29-34E	24	
	Russian Federation	Novorossiysk	002734411	44-41N 37-47E	26	MRCC Novorossiysk
		Doob		44-36N 37-58E	51	
		Anapa		44-50N 37-21E	52	
		Sochi		43-32N 39-51E	71	
		Taganrog		47-14N 38-56E	19	
		Temrujk		45-19N 37-13E	28	
		Tuapse	002734413	44-06N 39-02E	46	
		Rostov-na-Donu	002734422	47-13N 39-44E	21	
		Eisk	002734422	46-43N 38-16E	23	
		Kosa Dolgaya		46-40N 37-45E	25	
		Astrakhan (Caspian Sea)	002734419	46-30N 48-00E	22.5	MRCC Astrakhan
		Iskusstvennyi		45-23N 47-47E	25	
		Makhachkala	002734423	42-59N 47-30E	23	
	Serbia and Montenegro	Bar	002790001	42-03N 19-09E	35	MRCC Bar
		Obosnik	002790002	42-25N 18-37E	35	
	Slovenia	Koper	002780200	45-32N 13-59E	86	MRCC Koper
	Spain	Malaga (CCR)	002241023	-	-	MRCC Tarifa
		Malaga		36-36N 04-36W	35	
		Melilla		35-19N 02-57W	35	MRCC Almeria
		Motril		36-53N 02-48W	35	
		Cabo Gata		36-43N 02-10W	35	

DISTRESS, EMERGENCY, AND SAFETY TRAFFIC

NAV/MET Area	Country	VHF DSC Coast Station				Associated RCC
		Name	MMSI	Position	Range (NM)	
III	Spain (cont.)	MRCC Almeria*	002241002	-	-	MRCC Almeria
		Almeria		36-50N 02-29W	30	
		Cabo Gata		36-43N 02-11W	30	
		MRSC Cartagena*	002241003	37-35N 00-58W	30	MRSC Cartagena
		MRCC Valencia*	002241004	39-27N 00-20W	30	MRCC Valencia
		Valencia (CCR)	002241024	-	-	
		Cartagena		37-35N 00-58W	35	MRSC Cartagena
		Alicante		38-20N 00-42W	35	MRCC Valencia
		Castellon		39-52N 00-19W	35	
		Cabo de la Nao		38-43N 00-10E	35	
		Tarragona		41-21N 01-32E	35	MRSC Tarragona
		Barcelona		41-25N 02-07E	35	MRCC Barcelona
		Bagur		41-57N 03-14E	35	
		Menorca		39-59N 04-07E	35	MRCC Palma
		Palma de Mallorca		39-44N 02-43E	35	
		Ibiza		38-55N 01-16E	35	
		MRSC Castellon*	002241016	39-58N 00-01E	30	MRSC Castellon
		MRSC Tarragona*	002241006	41-06N 01-14E	30	MRSC Tarragona
		MRCC Barcelona*	002240991	41-20N 02-09E	40	MRCC Barcelona
		MRCC Palma*	002241005	-	-	MRCC Palma
		Palma		39-34N 02-39E	30	
		Cabo Cala Figuera		39-27N 02-31E	30	
	Turkey	Samsun	002712000	-	-	MRCC Ankara
		Pazar		41-08N 40-49E	60	
		Hidirnebi		40-58N 39-26E	99	
		Uçpinar		41-19N 36-06E	94	
		Dütmen		41-26N 35-28E	107	
		Inebolu		41-53N 33-43E	85	
		Zonguldak		41-23N 31-49E	67	
		Istanbul	002711000	-	-	
		Akçakoca		40-58N 31-12E	66	
		Keltepe		40-38N 30-05E	105	
		Sarköy		40-41N 27-01E	70	
		Camlica		41-01N 29-04E	45	
		Mahyadagi		41-47N 27-37E	85	
		Kayalidag		39-58N 26-38E	79	
		Akdag		38-33N 26-30E	92	
		Antalya	002713000	-	-	
		Dilektepe		37-39N 27-09E	93	
		Palamut		36-45N 27-03E	79	
		Yumrutepe		36-15N 29-27E	88	

*NOTE: The primary responsibility for the receipt of VHF DSC distress alerts for Spain is carried out via the Coast Radio Stations. VHF DSC facilities maintained at various MRCCs and MRSCs are only complementary to the Coast Radio Stations network.

DISTRESS, EMERGENCY, AND SAFETY TRAFFIC

NAV/MET Area	Country	VHF DSC Coast Station				Associated RCC
		Name	MMSI	Position	Range (NM)	
III	Turkey (cont.)	Markiz	002713000	36-43N 30-29E	80	MRCC Ankara
		Anamur		36-02N 32-45E	61	
		Cobandede		36-31N 36-15E	108	
	Ukraine	Odessa	002723660	46-25N 30-46E	25	MRCC Odessa
		Theodosia	002723663	45-01N 35-23E	35	
		Kerch	002723659	45-21N 36-32E	25	
		Mariupol	002723650	47-03N 37-30E	23	
IV	Bermuda	Bermuda Harbor	003100001	32-23N 64-41W	30	RCC Bermuda
	Canada	Labrador	003160022	-	-	JRCC Halifax
		Nain		56-33N 61-43W	40	
		Hopedale		55-27N 60-13W	40	
		Cartright		53-44N 56-58W	40	
		Goose Bay		53-18N 60-33W	40	
		St. Anthony	003160021	51-30N 55-50W	40	
		Fox Harbor		52-22N 55-40W	40	
		L'Anse aux Meadows		51-34N 55-30W	40	
		Conche		50-54N 55-53W	40	
		Twillingate		49-41N 54-48W	40	
		Comfort Cove		49-15N 54-53W	40	
		St. John's	003160020	47-37N 52-40W	40	
		Lumsden		49-17N 53-35W	40	
		Cape Bonavista		48-42N 53-05W	40	
		Victoria		47-47N 53-17W	40	
		Placentia	003160019	-	-	
		Cape Pine		46-37N 53-32W	40	
		Cuslett		46-58N 54-09W	40	
		Freshwater Hill		47-16N 53-59W	40	
		Arnold's Cove		47-46N 54-00W	40	
		St. Lawrence		46-55N 55-23W	40	
		Fortune Head		47-04N 55-51W	40	
		Bay L'Argent		47-37N 54-52W	40	
		Hermitage		47-34N 55-57W	40	
		Port aux Basques	003160018	47-41N 59-16W	40	
		Ramea Island		47-31N 57-25W	40	
		Stephenville		48-33N 58-46W	40	
		Pinetree		48-35N 58-40W	40	
		Mount Moriah		48-58N 58-03W	40	
		Bonne Bay		49-36N 57-57W	40	
		Point Riche		50-42N 57-25W	40	
		Riviere au Renard	003160025	49-01N 64-24W	40	
		Harrington Harbor		50-30N 59-29W	40	
		La Romaine		50-13N 60-41W	40	
		Natashquan		50-09N 61-48W	40	

DISTRESS, EMERGENCY, AND SAFETY TRAFFIC

NAV/MET Area	Country	VHF DSC Coast Station				Associated RCC
		Name	MMSI	Position	Range (NM)	
IV	Canada (cont.)	Havre St. Pierre	003160025	50-16N 63-41W	40	JRCC Halifax
		Forillon		48-50N 64-16W	40	
		Heath Point		49-05N 61-42W	40	
		Newport		48-14N 64-48W	40	
		Carleton		48-08N 66-07W	40	
		Cap-aux-Meules		47-23N 61-52W	40	
		Sydney	003160017	46-11N 59-54W	40	
		Point Escuminac		47-04N 64-48W	40	
		North Cape		47-03N 64-00W	40	
		Cape Egmont		46-24N 64-08W	40	
		Montague		46-11N 62-40W	40	
		Cheticamp		46-35N 60-59W	40	
		Cape North		47-01N 60-26W	40	
		Kilkenny Lake		46-13N 60-10W	40	
		St. Columba		46-00N 60-51W	40	
		Halifax	003160016	-	-	
		Fox Island		45-20N 61-05W	40	
		Ecum Secum		44-58N 62-09W	40	
		Shannon Hill		44-41N 63-37W	40	
		Ketch Harbor		44-28N 63-37W	40	
		Kingsburg		44-17N 64-17W	40	
		Saint John	003160015	45-14N 65-59W	40	
		Scotch Mountain		45-46N 65-48W	40	
		Cape Blomidon		45-13N 64-24W	40	
		Grand Manan		44-36N 66-54W	40	
		Tiverton		44-23N 66-14W	40	
		Yarmouth		43-44N 66-07W	40	
		Lockeport		43-40N 65-08W	40	
	Mexico	Tampico	003450110	22-12N 97-51W	80	MRCC Ciudad Madero
		Veracruz	003450310	19-06N 96-08W	80	MRCC Veracruz
		Chetumal	003451120	18-30N 88-17W	80	MRCC Chetumal
		Cozumel	003451110	20-28N 86-58W	80	MRSC Isla Cozumel
		Ciudad del Carmen	003450710	18-39N 91-51W	80	MRSC Lerma-Campeche
		Progreso	003450910	21-16N 89-41W	80	MRSC Yukalpeten
		Coatzacoalcos	003450320	18-09N 94-26W	80	MRCC Veracruz
		NOTE: The following local VHF DSC stations assist with SAR communications within their individual coastal areas:				
		Isla Mujeres	003451171	21-14N 87-00W	20	MRSC Isla Mujeres
		Tuxpan	003450372	20-57N 97-22W	20	MRSC Tuxpan
		Lerma	003450772	19-49N 90-35W	20	MRSC Lerma
		Matamoros	003450172	25-44N 97-33W	20	MRSC Matamoros

DISTRESS, EMERGENCY, AND SAFETY TRAFFIC

NAV/MET Area	Country	VHF DSC Coast Station				Associated RCC
		Name	MMSI	Position	Range (NM)	
IV	Mexico (cont.)	NOTE: The following local VHF DSC stations assist with SAR communications within their individual coastal areas:				
		Mezquital	003450173	25-15N 97-27W	20	MRSC Mezquital
		Cayo Arcas	003450974	20-13N 91-58W	20	MRSC Cayo Arcas
		Isla Holbox	003451174	21-32N 87-17W	20	MRSC Isla Holbox
		Isla Contoy	003451175	21-30N 84-48W	20	MRSC Isla Contoy
		Playa Linda	003451176	21-08N 86-47W	20	MRSC Playa Linda
	Netherlands Antilles	Curaçao	003061000	-	-	JRCC Curaçao
		Seru Gracia (Curaçao)		12-20N 69-08W	40	
		Jamanota (Aruba)		12-29N 69-56W	35	
		Sibu Rincon (Bonaire)		12-14N 68-20W	30	
		Mt. Scenery (Saba)		17-38N 63-14W	70	
VI	Argentina	Argentina Radio	007010111	34-36S 58-28W	35	MRCC Buenos Aires
		Buenos Aires	007010001	34-27S 58-37W	35	
		Mar del Plata (Armada)	007010221	38-03S 57-32W	35	MRCC Puerto Belgrano
		Mar del Plata	007010003	38-03S 57-32W	35	
		Comodoro Rivadavia	007010008	45-51S 67-25W	35	
		Rio Gallegos	007010010	51-37S 69-03W	35	MRCC Ushuaia
		San Blas	007010006	40-33S 62-14W	35	MRSC Bahia Blanca
	Uruguay	Montevideo	007703870	-	-	MRCC Montevideo
		Armada Radio		34-56S 56-09W	30	
		Carmelo Radio		33-59S 58-17W	30	
		Colonia Radio		34-28S 57-50W	30	
		Piriapolis Radio		34-52S 55-16W	30	
		Chafalote Radio		34-28S 54-26W	30	
		Santa Teresa Radio		34-00S 53-33W	30	
VIII	India	Daman	004192201	20-25N 72-52E	20	MRCC Mumbai
		Porbander	004192202	31-38N 69-37E	25	
		Mumbai	004192203	18-55N 72-50E	25	
		New Mangalore	004192204	12-55N 74-48E	25	
		Kochi	004192205	09-58N 76-16E	20	
		Goa	004192206	15-25N 73-48E	25	
		Okha	004192207	22-28N 69-05E	20	
		Chennai	004194401	13-06N 80-18E	25	MRCC Chennai
		Vishakhapatnam	004194402	17-41N 83-17E	20	
		Paradip	004194403	20-16N 86-42E	25	
		Haldia	004194404	22-02N 88-06E	25	
		Tuticorn	004194405	08-45N 78-12E	20	
		Mandapam	004194406	09-17N 79-05E	20	
		Diglipor	004194407	13-18N 93-04E	25	MRCC Port Blair
		Campbell Bay	004194408	07-00N 93-55E	30	
		Port Blair	004194409	11-41N 92-46E	30	

DISTRESS, EMERGENCY, AND SAFETY TRAFFIC

NAV/MET Area	Country	VHF DSC Coast Station				Associated RCC
		Name	MMSI	Position	Range (NM)	
VIII	Mauritius	Mauritius Radio	006452700	-	-	MRCC Mauritius
		Albion		20-13S 57-24E	25	
		Belle Mare		20-11S 57-46E	25	
		Cap Malheureux		19-59S 57-36E	25	
		Souillac		20-31S 57-31E	25	
	Myanmar (Burma)	Yangon (Rangoon)	005060100	16-42N 96-17E	25	MRCC Yangon
		Myeik	005060200	12-26N 98-36E	25	
IX	Egypt	Quseir	006221112	26-06N 34-17E	28	RCC Cairo
		Ras Gharib		28-22N 33-04E	28	
		Zeitiya		27-49N 33-35E	29	
		Hurghada		27-15N 33-48E	28	
		Safaga		26-45N 33-56E	28	
		Sharm-El-Sheikh		27-51N 34-13E	24	
		Dahab		28-29N 34-29E	23	
	Iran	Kharg (Island)	004225306	29-16N 50-15E	25-30	HQ PSO Tehran
		Khorramshahr	004225309	30-20N 48-23E	25-30	
		Lengeh	004225307	26-33N 54-53E	25-30	
		Bandar Abbas	004225304	27-07N 56-04E	25-30	
		Bahonar	004225308	27-18N 57-17E	25-30	
		Bandar Khomeyni	004225300	30-30N 49-09E	25-30	
		Bushehr	004225302	28-58N 50-50E	25-30	
		Anzali (Caspian Sea)	004225305	37-25N 49-20E	25-30	
		Nowshahr (Caspian Sea)	004225303	36-40N 51-30E	25-30	
		Neka (Caspian Sea)	004225311	36-50N 53-15E	25-30	
	Israel	Haifa	004280001	-	-	Haifa Radio
		Elat		29-30N 34-58E	50	
	Jordan	Aqaba Radio	004381234	29-27N 34-58E	25	Harbor Master Aqaba
		Aqaba Port Control		29-30N 34-59E	25	
	Kuwait	Kuwait Radio	004472188	29-22N 47-59E	N.I.	
	Pakistan	Karachi	004634060	24-52N 67-01E	40	MRCC Karachi
		Ormara	004634056	25-13N 64-38E	40	
		Gwadar	004634052	25-08N 64-20E	40	
	Qatar	Mesaieed Port	004661001	25-56N 51-35E	50	Dept. of Customs & Ports
	Saudi Arabia	Jiddah	004030000	-	-	RCC Jiddah
		Duba		27-21N 35-42E	33	
		Al Wajh		26-14N 36-27E	33	
		Umm Lajj		25-01N 37-16E	33	
		Yanbu		24-05N 38-03E	33	
		Rabigh		22-48N 39-01E	33	
		Sharm Abhur		21-43N 39-06E	33	
		Jiddah		21-15N 39-10E	30	
		Al Shoaibah		20-40N 39-31E	35	
		Al Lith		20-08N 40-16E	35	

DISTRESS, EMERGENCY, AND SAFETY TRAFFIC

NAV/MET Area	Country	VHF DSC Coast Station				Associated RCC
		Name	MMSI	Position	Range (NM)	
IX	Saudi Arabia (cont.)	Al Qunfudhah	004030000	19-07N 41-05E	35	RCC Jiddah
		Al Birk		18-12N 41-32E	35	
		Al Shaqiq		17-43N 42-01E	35	
		Jizan		16-53N 42-32E	35	
		Khafji		28-26N 48-29E	33	
		Al Jubayl		27-00N 49-39E	33	
		Dammam		26-26N 50-06E	33	
		Aziziyah		26-15N 50-10E	33	
	United Arab Emirates	Emirates Radio	004700000	-	-	RCC Abu Dhabi
		Fujayrah		25-04N 56-21E	25	
		Khawr Fakkan		25-21N 56-22E	25	
		Ras al Khaymah		25-47N 55-59E	25	
		Umm al Qaywayn		25-32N 55-32E	25	
		Jabal Ali		25-02N 55-06E	25	
		Abu Zaby (Abu Dhabi)		24-28N 54-22E	25	
		Ruways (Jabal Dhanna)		24-06N 52-44E	25	
		Zirkuh		24-53N 53-04E	25	
X	New Caledonia	Noumea	005401000	-	-	MRCC Noumea
		Noumea		22-16S 166-28E	40	
		Mont Do		21-45S 166-00E	95	
		Kafeate		21-02S 164-43E	51	
		Mandgelia		20-24S 164-32E	84	
		Ouvea		20-39S 166-32E	27	
		Lifou		21-06S 167-24E	36	
		Mare		21-28S 168-02E	28	
		Oungone		22-19S 166-55E	68	
XI	China	Dalian	004121300	38-50N 121-31E	25	MRCC Liaoning
		Fuzhou	004122600	26-02N 119-18E	25	MRCC Fujian
		Guangzhou	004123100	23-08N 113-29E	25	MRCC Guangdong
		Haikou	004123500	20-01N 110-17E	25	MRSC Haikou
		Lianyungang	004122300	34-42N 119-18E	25	MRCC Lianyungang
		Ningbo	004122400	30-01N 121-30E	25	MRSC Ningbo
		Qingdao	004122200	36-10N 120-28E	25	MRSC Qingdao
		Qinhuangdao	004121200	39-33N 119-31E	25	MRCC Hebei
		Shanghai	004122100	31-06N 121-32E	25	MRCC Shanghai
		Tianjin	004121100	39-03N 117-25E	25	MRCC Tianjin
		Xiamen	004122700	24-35N 118-06E	25	MRSC Xiamen
		Yantai	004121400	37-32N 121-22E	25	MRSC Yantai
		Zhanjiang	004123300	21-09N 110-21E	23	RSC Zhanjiang
	Indonesia	Amboina (Ambon)	005250006	03-41S 128-11E	20	MRSC Amboina
		Balikpapan	005250009	01-16S 116-49E	20	MRSC Balikpapan

DISTRESS, EMERGENCY, AND SAFETY TRAFFIC

NAV/MET Area	Country	VHF DSC Coast Station				Associated RCC
		Name	MMSI	Position	Range (NM)	
XI	Indonesia (cont.)	Batu Ampar	005250012	01-09N 104-00E	20	MRSC Tanjung Pinang
		Belawan	005250003	03-46N 98-41E	20	MRSC Medan
		Benoa	005250014	08-44S 115-12E	20	MRSC Denpasar
		Biak	005250031	01-12S 136-05E	20	MRCC Biak
		Bitung	005250005	01-26N 125-10E	20	MRSC Menado
		Cilacap	005250030	07-47S 109-02E	20	MRCC Jakarta
		Dumai	005250004	01-39N 101-26E	20	MRSC Pekanbaru
		Fak-Fak	005250026	02-56S 132-17E	20	MRSC Sorong
		Jakarta	005250000	06-07S 106-51E	20	MRCC Jakarta
		Jayapura	005250007	02-31S 140-43E	20	MRSC Jayapura
		Kendari	005250019	03-58S 122-34E	20	MRCC Ujung Pandang
		Kupang	005250010	10-12S 123-37E	20	MRSC Kupang
		Lembar	005250022	08-43S 116-04E	20	MRSC Denpasar
		Makassar	005250002	05-06S 119-26E	20	MRCC Ujung Pandang
		Manokwari	005250023	00-51S 134-04E	20	MRCC Biak
		Merauke	005250021	08-28S 140-23E	20	MRSC Merauke
		Panjang	005250013	05-28S 105-19E	20	MRSC Palembang
		Pantoloan	005250018	00-39S 119-44E	20	MRSC Menado
		Pontianak	005250016	00-01S 109-19E	20	MRSC Pontianak
		Sanana	005250025	02-03S 125-38E	20	MRSC Amboina
		Sei Kolak Kiang	005250029	00-51N 104-36E	20	MRSC Tanjung Pinang
		Semarang	005250008	06-56S 110-19E	20	MRCC Surabaya
		Sibolga	005250028	01-44N 98-46E	20	MRSC Medan
		Sorong	005250011	00-53S 131-18E	20	MRSC Sorong
		Surabaya	005250001	07-11S 112-43E	20	MRCC Surabaya
		Tahuna	005250024	03-36N 125-30E	20	MRSC Menado
		Tanjung Pinang	005250029	00-56N 104-29E	20	MRSC Tanjung Pinang
		Tarakan	005250017	03-17N 117-35E	20	MRSC Balikpapan
		Ternate	005250020	00-47N 127-35E	20	MRSC Amboina
	Malaysia	Pinang	-	05-26N 100-24E	-	MRCC Port Klang
		Gunung Jerai	005330001	05-47N 100-26E	95	
		Gunung Berinchang	005330003	04-31N 101-23E	117	
		Ulu Kali	005330004	03-26N 101-47E	114	
		Gunung Ledang	005330005	02-03N 102-34E	95	
		Tioman	005330006	02-48N 104-12E	27	
		Kuala Rompin	005330007	02-48N 103-29E	38	
		Kemuning	005330008	04-19N 103-28E	57	
		Kuala Terengganu	005330009	05-18N 103-08E	55	
		Machang	005330010	05-43N 102-17E	70	

DISTRESS, EMERGENCY, AND SAFETY TRAFFIC

NAV/MET Area	Country	VHF DSC Coast Station				Associated RCC
		Name	MMSI	Position	Range (NM)	
XI	Malaysia (cont.)	Kuching	005330011	01-35N 110-11E	85	MRCC Port Klang
		Bintulu	005330012	03-13N 113-05E	48	
		Kota Kinabalu	005330013	06-02N 116-12E	75	
		Labuan	005330014	05-17N 115-15E	22	
	Republic of Korea	Inchon Maritime Police	004401001	37-30N 126-30E	25	RCC Inchon
		Donghae Maritime Police	004401002	37-31N 129-07E	25	RCC Donghae
		Mokpo Maritime Police	004401003	34-46N 126-23E	25	RCC Mokpo
		Busan Maritime Police	004401004	35-07N 129-02E	25	RCC Busan
		Cheju Maritime Police	004401005	33-21N 126-49E	25	RCC Cheju
		Inchon	004400001	37-34N 126-41E	25	RCC Inchon
		Kangnung	004400601	37-45N 128-53E	25	RCC Donghae
		Mokpo	004400301	34-48N 126-30E	25	RCC Mokpo
		Busan	004400101	35-06N 129-03E	25	RCC Busan
		Seoul	004400002	37-29N 128-43E	25	RCC Donghae
	Singapore	Singapore Port Operations Control	005630002	01-16N 103-51E	25	Singapore Port Operations Control Center
	Taiwan	Chi-lung (Keelung)	004162019	-	-	
		Anmashan (North)		24-16N 121-01E	86	
		Anmashan (West)		24-16N 121-01E	86	
		Chi-lung		25-08N 121-45E	21	
		Chinmen (Mainland)		24-28N 118-22E	32	
		Fukueichiao		25-14N 121-31E	40	
		Hotien Shan		23-53N 121-35E	45	
		Hsichuan Chuan		22-34N 121-01E	51	
		Lung Chuan		22-56N 120-26E	21	
		Matsu (Mainland)		26-13N 119-59E	32	
		San-I		24-24N 120-44E	43	
		Shou Shan		22-38N 120-15E	39	
		Suao		24-37N 121-52E	21	
		Taiho Shan		22-15N 120-52E	45	
		Taping		23-34N 120-36E	48	
		Taping Ting		22-01N 120-41E	30	
		Tsaoshan		25-06N 121-52E	51	
		Yingtzuling (North East)		24-54N 121-48E	64	
		Yingtzuling (South East)		24-54N 121-48E	64	
	Thailand	Bangkok Radio (Nonthaburi)	005671000	-	-	RCC Bangkok
		Sriracha		13-06N 100-55E	27	
		Petchaburi		12-59N 100-03E	27	
	Vietnam	Ben Thuy	005742009	18-39N 105-42E	30	Cua Lo Port Authority
		Cua Ong (Cam Pha)	005742008	20-01N 107-22E	30	Quang Ninh Port Authority

DISTRESS, EMERGENCY, AND SAFETY TRAFFIC

NAV/MET Area	Country	VHF DSC Coast Station				Associated RCC
		Name	MMSI	Position	Range (NM)	
XI	Vietnam (cont.)	Da Nang	005741999	16-04N 108-13E	30	Da Nang Port Authority
		Hai Phong	005741996	20-52N 106-41E	30	Hai Phong Port Authority
		Ho Chi Minh City	005741993	10-46N 106-43E	30	Saigon Port Authority
		Hon Gai (Quang Ninh)	005742006	20-57N 107-04E	30	Quang Ninh Port Authority
		Hue	005742010	16-33N 107-38E	30	Thien Hue Port Authority
		Mong Cai	005742007	21-32N 107-58E	30	Quang Ninh Port Authority
		Nha Trang	005742001	12-12N 109-13E	30	Nha Trang Port Authority
		Vung Tau	005742004	10-21N 107-06E	30	Vung Tau Port Authority
	Hong Kong (Associate Member of IMO)	Hong Kong Maritime Rescue	004773500	22-24N 114-07E	50	MRCC Hong Kong
		Victoria Peak (Alternative)		22-16N 114-08E		
XII	Canada	Prince Rupert	003160013	-	-	JRCC Victoria
		Dundas		54-31N 130-55W	40	
		Mount Hayes		54-17N 130-18W	40	
		Naden Harbor		53-57N 132-57W	40	
		Mount Gil		53-16N 129-12W	40	
		Cumshewa		53-10N 132-00W	40	
		Klemtu		52-35N 128-34W	40	
		Rose Inlet		52-13N 131-13W	40	
		Calvert		51-35N 128-00W	40	
		Comox	003160014	49-45N 124-57W	40	
		Port Hardy		50-42N 127-42W	40	
		Texada		49-42N 124-26W	40	
		Discovery		50-19N 125-22W	40	
		Tofin	003160012	-	-	
		Holberg		50-38N 128-08W	40	
		Eliza Dome		49-52N 127-07W	40	
		Esperanza		49-50N 126-48W	40	
		Nootka		49-36N 126-37W	40	
		Estevan Point		49-23N 126-32W	40	
		Port Alberni		49-13N 124-49W	40	
		Mount Ozzard		48-58N 125-30W	40	
		Amphitrite Point		48-55N 125-32W	40	
		Victoria	003160011	-	-	
		Bowen		49-21N 123-23W	40	
		Annacis Island		49-12N 122-55W	40	
		Mount Parke		48-50N 123-18W	40	

DISTRESS, EMERGENCY, AND SAFETY TRAFFIC

NAV/MET Area	Country	VHF DSC Coast Station				Associated RCC
		Name	MMSI	Position	Range (NM)	
XII	Canada (cont.)	Mount Newton	003160011	48-37N 123-27W	40	JRCC Victoria
		Helmcken		48-24N 123-34W	40	
		Vancouver	003160010	-	-	
		Watts Point		49-39N 123-13W	40	
	Ecuador	Guayaquil	007354750	02-11S 79-53W	30	Guayaquil Coast Guard
		Esmeraldas	007354752	00-57N 70-39W	30	
		Bahia	007354753	00-35S 80-25W	30	
		Manta	007354754	00-57S 80-43W	30	
		Salinas	007354755	02-12S 80-52W	30	
		Puerto Bolivar	007354756	03-16S 80-00W	30	
		Ayora	007354757	00-44S 90-20W	30	
		Baquerizo Moreno	007354758	00-54S 89-37W	30	
	Mexico	Mazatlan	003450810	23-10N 106-26W	80	MRCC Mazatlan
		Ensenada	003450210	31-51N 116-37W	80	MRCC Ensenada
		Manzanillo	003451410	19-01N 104-19W	80	MRSC Puerto Vallarta
		Acapulco	003451810	16-50N 99-56W	80	MRSC Acapulco
		Lazaro Cardenas	003451610	17-57N 102-12W	80	MRSC Lazaro Cardenas
		Puerto Vallarta	003451210	20-46N 105-32W	80	MRSC Puerto Vallarta
		NOTE: The following local VHF DSC stations assist with SAR communications within their individual coastal areas:				
		Guaymas	003450671	27-55N 110-52W	20	MRSC Guaymas
		Salina Cruz	003452071	16-11N 96-12W	20	MRSC Salina Cruz
		La Paz	003450471	24-08N 110-21W	20	MRSC La Paz
		Puerto Penasco	003450672	31-18N 113-35W	20	MRSC Puerto Penasco
		Topolobampo	003450872	25-35N 109-09W	20	MRSC Topolobampo
		Puerto Madero	003452271	14-42N 92-24W	20	MRSC Puerto Madero
		Puerto Cortez	003450472	24-33N 111-45W	20	MRSC Puerto Cortez
		Isla de Cedros	003450272	28-12N 115-15W	20	MRSC Isla de Cedros
		Isla Guadalupe	003450273	29-02N 118-17W	20	MRSC Isla Guadalupe
		San Felipe	003450274	31-01N 114-50W	20	MRSC San Felipe
		Los Cabos	003450473	22-52N 109-53W	20	MRSC Los Cabos
		Santa Rosalia	003450474	27-20N 112-15W	20	MRSC Santa Rosalia
		Isla Socorro	003450475	18-36N 110-58W	20	MRSC Isla Socorro
		Isla Clarion	003451472	18-22N 115-44W	20	MRSC Isla Clarion
		Huatulco	003452072	15-45N 96-08W	20	MRSC Huatulco

DISTRESS, EMERGENCY, AND SAFETY TRAFFIC

NAV/MET Area	Country	VHF DSC Coast Station				Associated RCC
		Name	MMSI	Position	Range (NM)	
XII	Mexico (cont.)	NOTE: The following local VHF DSC stations assist with SAR communications within their individual coastal areas:				
		Paredon	003452272	16-03N 93-52W	20	MRSC Paredon
		San Blas	003450174	21-32N 105-17W	20	MRSC San Blas
XIII	Russian Federation	Vladivostok	002734412	43-07N 131-55E	55	MRCC Vladivostok
		Nakhodka		42-51N 132-50E	45	
		Tumannaya (Posiet)		42-34N 131-11E	70	
		Yuzhno-Sakhalinsk	002733733	-	-	MRSC Yuzhno-Sakhalinsk
		Korsakov		46-45N 142-27E	42	
		Kholmsk		47-02N 142-03E	31	
		Nevelsk		46-38N 141-51E	40	
		Magadan	002734416	59-33N 150-43E	19	MRSC Petropavlovsk-Kamchatskiy
XV	Chile	Arica	007250010	18-29S 70-19W	39	MRSC Iquique
		Iquique	007250020	20-21S 70-06W	64	
		Tocopilla	007250030	22-05S 70-12W	14	
		Mejillones	007250040	23-05S 70-27W	14	
		Antofagasta	007250050	23-40S 70-24W	30	
		Taltal	007250060	25-24S 70-29W	14	MRSC Valparaiso
		Chanaral	007250070	26-21S 70-38W	14	
		Caldera	007250080	27-04S 70-49W	14	
		Huasco	007250090	28-27S 71-13W	14	
		Isla de Pascua	007250100	27-11S 109-25W	44	
		Coquimbo	007250110	29-56S 71-20W	62	
		Los Vilos	007250120	31-54S 71-31W	14	
		Quintero	007250125	32-46S 71-31W	14	
		Valparaiso	007251860	33-04S 71-36W	63	
		San Antonio	007250140	33-34S 71-37W	31	
		Juan Fernandez	007250130	33-37S 78-49W	14	
		Constitucion	007250150	35-19S 72-24W	14	MRSC Talcahuano
		Talcahuano	007250170	36-37S 73-04W	32	
		Valdivia	007250220	39-48S 73-15W	14	
		Corral	007250210	39-53S 73-25W	14	
		Puerto Montt	007250230	41-39S 73-10W	34	MRCC Puerto Montt
		Corona	007250235	41-47S 73-52W	26	
		Ancud	007250240	41-52S 73-50W	14	
		Castro	007250250	42-29S 73-46W	14	
		Chaiten	007250260	42-55S 72-43W	14	
		Quellon	007250270	43-07S 73-37W	14	
		Isla Guafo	007250290	43-34S 74-49W	33	
		Melinka	007250280	43-54S 73-44W	14	
		Puerto Aguirre	007250294	45-09S 73-31W	14	
		Aysen	007250300	45-24S 72-43W	16	
		Puerto Chacabuco	007250298	45-26S 73-49W	14	

DISTRESS, EMERGENCY, AND SAFETY TRAFFIC

NAV/MET Area	Country	VHF DSC Coast Station				Associated RCC
		Name	MMSI	Position	Range (NM)	
XV	Chile (cont.)	Cabo Raper	007250310	46-49S 75-37W	21	MRCC Punta Arenas
		San Pedro	007250320	47-42S 74-53W	18	
		Puerto Eden	007250330	49-08S 74-27W	14	
		Puerto Natales	007250340	51-45S 72-32W	14	
		Faro Evangelistas	007250350	52-23S 75-06W	21	
		Bahia Felix	007250370	52-44S 73-46W	19	
		Faro Fairway	007250360	52-57S 74-05W	19	
		Punta Arenas	007250380	53-09S 71-02W	64	
		Punta Delgada	007250390	52-27S 69-33W	17	
		Punta Dungeness	007250400	52-24S 68-26W	20	
		Espiritu Santo	007250410	52-39S 68-36W	24	
		Puerto Williams	007250420	54-56S 67-36W	22	
		Wollaston	007250430	55-36S 67-25W	28	
		Diego Ramirez	007250440	56-31S 68-42W	28	
		Bahia Fildes	007250450	62-11S 58-55W	14	
		Bahia Paraiso	007250470	64-49S 62-51W	14	
XVI	Peru	Zorritos	007600120	03-40S 80-40W	40	MRSC Zorritos
		Talara	007600122	04-34S 81-16W	40	MRSC Talara
		Paita	007600121	05-05S 81-07W	40	MRCC Paita
		Pimentel	007600123	06-57S 79-52W	40	MRSC Pimentel
		Salaverry	007600124	08-13S 78-59W	40	MRSC Salaverry
		Chimbote	007600126	09-05S 78-38W	40	MRCC Chimbote
		Supe	007600127	10-49S 77-43W	40	MRSC Supe
		Huacho	007600128	11-07S 77-37W	40	MRSC Huacho
		Callao	007600125	12-03S 77-09W	40	MRCC Callao
		Pisco	007600130	13-43S 76-14W	40	MRSC Pisco
		San Juan	007600131	15-21S 75-09W	40	MRSC San Juan
		Mollendo	007600129	17-01S 72-01W	40	MRCC Mollendo
		Ilo	007600132	17-38S 71-21W	40	MRSC Ilo

DISTRESS, EMERGENCY, AND SAFETY TRAFFIC

LIST OF OPERATIONAL MF DSC COAST STATIONS FOR SEA AREAS A2
(Extracted from ANNEX 3 of the IMO GMDSS Master Plan)

NAV/MET Area	Country	MF DSC Coast Station				Associated RCC
		Name	MMSI	Position	Range (NM)	
I	Belgium	Oostende	002050480	51-11N 02-48E	115	Oostende
	Denmark	Lyngby	002191000	-	-	SOK, Aarhus
		Blåvand		55-33N 08-07E	153	
		Skagen		57-44N 10-34E	148	
		Torshavn (Færoes)	002311000	62-00N 06-47W	225	MRCC Torshavn
	Estonia	Tallinn	002761000	59-24N 24-40E	150	MRCC Tallinn
		Undva		58-29N 21-59E	150	
		Kuressaare	002760120	58-15N 22-29E	150	
	Finland	Turku	002300230	-	-	MRCC Turku
		Sondby	002302000	60-16N 25-51E	185	MRSC Helsinki
		Mariehamn	002301000	60-07N 19-57E	185	MRCC Turku
		Hailuoto	002303000	65-02N 24-32E	185	MRSC Vaasa
		Raippaluoto		63-18N 21-10E	185	
	France	Corsen (CROSS)	002275300	-	-	MRCC Corsen
		Ouessant (Tx)		48-28N 05-03W	300	
		Corsen (Rx)		48-24N 04-24W	300	
	Iceland	Reykjavik	002510100	64-05N 21-51W	-	MRCC Kefl vik
		Arnarnes (Tx)		66-05N 23-02W	200	
		Garoskagi (Rx)		64-04N 22-41W	200	
		Grimsey (Rx)		66-31N 17-59W	200	
		Holl (Rx)		65-35N 14-15W	200	
		Hornafjorour (Tx)		64-15N 15-13W	200	
		Nes (Tx)		65-09N 13-42W	200	
		Raufarhofn (Tx)		66-27N 15-56W	200	
		Rjupnahaeo (Tx)		64-05N 21-50W	200	
		Saefjall (Tx)		63-25N 20-16W	200	
		Streite (Rx)		64-43N 13-59W	200	
		Storhofdi (Tx)		63-24N 20-17W	200	
		Thverfjalli (Rx)		66-02N 23-18W	200	
	Ireland	Malin Head	002500100	55-21N 07-20W	150	MRSC Malin Head
		Valentia	002500200	51-55N 10-20W	150	MRSC Valentia
	Latvia	Riga Rescue Radio	002750100	57-02N 24-05E	150	MRCC Riga
		Uzava		57-13N 21-26E	120	
		Akmenrags		56-50N 21-03E	120	
	Lithuania	Klaipeda Rescue	002770330	55-43N 21-06E	100	MRCC Klaipeda
	Netherlands	Netherlands Coast Guard	002442000	-	-	JRCC Den Helder
		Scheveningen (Tx)		52-06N 04-15E	240	
		Appingedam (Tx)		53-20N 06-52E	150	
		West Terschelling (Rx)		53-21N 05-13E	150	
		Noordwijk (Rx)		52-18N 04-28E	150	
	Norway	Tjøme	002570100	-	-	MRCC Stavanger
		Jeloy		59-26N 10-37E	200	

DISTRESS, EMERGENCY, AND SAFETY TRAFFIC

NAV/MET Area	Country	MF DSC Coast Station				Associated RCC
		Name	MMSI	Position	Range (NM)	
I	Norway (cont.)	Rogaland	002570300	-	-	MRCC Stavanger
		Bergen		60-43N 04-53E	200	
		Farsund		58-04N 06-45E	200	
		Vigre		58-39N 05-36E	200	
		Florø	002570500		-	
		Florø		61-36N 05-00E	200	
		Ørlandet		63-40N 09-33E	200	
		Bodø	002570700	-	200	MRCC Bodø
		Sandnessjøen		66-01N 12-37E	200	
		Andenes		69-17N 16-01E	200	
		Jan Mayen		70-57N 08-40W	200	
		Bjørnøya		74-31N 19-01E	200	
		Vardø	002570800	-	200	
		Tromsø		69-39N 18-57E	200	
		Hammerfest		70-40N 23-40E	200	
		Berlevåg		70-52N 29-04E	200	
		Svalbard	002570900	78-02N 13-40E	200	
	Poland	Witowo	002610210	54-32N 16-32E	150	MRCC Gdynia
		Barzowice (Tx)		54-28N 16-30E	N.I.	
		Gdynia/Oksywie (Tx)		54-33N 18-32E	N.I.	
		Grzywacz (Rx)		53-57N 14-30E	N.I.	
	Russian Federation	Kaliningrad	002734417	54-45N 20-35E	125	MRSC Kaliningrad
		St. Petersburg	002733700	-	-	MRCC St. Petersburg
		Primorsk (Rx)		60-20N 28-43E	150	
		Karavaldayskiy (Tx)		59-59N 29-07E	150	
		Murmansk	002734420	68-52N 33-05E	170	MRCC Murmansk
		Arkhangel'sk	002734414	64-21N 40-37E	1	MRSC Arkhangel'sk
	Sweden	Göteborg	002653000	57-28N 11-56E	210	MRCC Göteborg
		Bjuröklubb		64-28N 21-36E	210	
		Hoburg		56-56N 18-13E	250	
		Stockholm (Rx)		59-16N 18-42E	210	
	United Kingdom	Aberdeen	002320004	57-25N 01-51W	150	MRCC Aberdeen
		Humber	002320007	54-05N 01-10W	150	MRSC Humber
		Cullercoats		55-04N 01-28W	150	
		Stornoway	002320024	58-13N 06-20W	150	MRSC Stornoway
		Holyhead	002320018	53-19N 04-38W	150	MRSC Holyhead
		Falmouth	002320014	50-08N 05-07W	150	MRCC Falmouth
		Clyde	002320022	55-58N 04-48W	150	MRCC Clyde
		Milford Haven	002320017	51-41N 05-03W	150	MRSC Milford Haven
		Shetland	002320001	60-09N 01-08W	150	MRSC Shetland
II	Benin	Cotonou	006100001	06-21N 02-26E	150	

DISTRESS, EMERGENCY, AND SAFETY TRAFFIC

NAV/MET Area	Country	MF DSC Coast Station				Associated RCC
		Name	MMSI	Position	Range (NM)	
II	France	Corsen (CROSS)	002275300	-	-	MRCC Corsen
		Ouessant (Tx)		48-28N 05-03W	300	
		Corsen (Rx)		48-24N 04-24W	300	
	Ghana	Tema	006270000	05-39N 00-03W	200	Harbor Master's Office Accr
	Spain	Bilbao (CCR)	002241021	-	-	
		Machichaco		43-27N 02-45W	150	MRCC Bilbao
		Cabo Penas		43-39N 05-51W	150	MRCC Gijon
		MRCC Bilbao*	002240996	43-21N 03-02W	150	MRCC Bilbao
		MRCC Gijon*	002240997	43-34N 05-42W	150	MRCC Gijon
		Coruna (CCR)	002241022	-	-	
		Finisterre		42-54N 09-16W	150	MRCC Finisterre
		Coruna		43-22N 08-27W	150	MRCC Coruna
		MRCC Finisterre*	002240993	42-42N 08-59W	150	MRCC Finisterre
		MRCC Tarifa*	002240994	36-01N 05-35W	150	MRCC Tarifa
		Malaga (CCR)	002241023	-	-	
		Chipiona		36-41N 06-24W	150	
		Conil		36-17N 06-05W	N.I.	
		Tarifa		36-03N 05-33W	150	
		MRCC Tenerife*	002241007	28-29N 16-14W	150	MRCC Tenerife
		MRCC Las Palmas*	002240995	28-09N 15-25W	150	MRCC Las Palmas
		Las Palmas (CCR)	002241026	-	-	
		Arrecife		29-08N 13-31W	150	
		Las Palmas		27-45N 15-36W	150	
		Tenerife		28-25N 16-20W	150	
III	Bulgaria	Varna	002070810	43-04N 27-46E	200	MRCC Varna
	Croatia	MRCC Rijecka	002387010	45-19N 14-27E	160	MRCC Rijecka
	Cyprus	Cyprus	002091000	35-02N 33-17E	200	RCC Larnaca
	Egypt	Alexandria	006221111	31-11N 29-51E	200	RCC Cairo
		Port Said	006221113	31-19N 32-18E	200	
	France	La Garde (CROSS)	002275400	-	-	MRCC La Garde
		Porquerolles (Tx)		42-59N 06-12E	200	
		La Garde (Rx)		43-06N 05-59E	200	
	Georgia	Batumi	002130100	41-39N 41-39E	150	MRCC Georgia
	Greece	Olympia	002371000	38-01N 23-50E	-	JRCC Piraeus
		Iraklion		35-20N 25-07E	200	
		Kerkyra		39-37N 15-55E	200	
		Limnos		39-52N 25-04E	200	
		Rodos		36-26N 28-15E	200	
		Piraeus JRCC[2,3]	237673000	37-58N 23-40E	130	
		Kerkira[3]	237673190	39-38N 19-55E	130	
		Patrai[3]	237673140	38-14N 21-44E	130	

*NOTE: The primary responsibility for the receipt of MF DSC distress alerts for Spain is carried out via the Coast Radio Stations. MF DSC facilities maintained at various MRCCs are only complementary to the Coast Radio Stations network.

DISTRESS, EMERGENCY, AND SAFETY TRAFFIC

NAV/MET Area	Country	MF DSC Coast Station				Associated RCC
		Name	MMSI	Position	Range (NM)	
III	Greece (cont.)	Pylos[3]	237673230	36-54N 21-41E	130	JRCC Piraeus
		Iraklion[3]	237673180	35-20N 25-08E	130	
		Rodhos[3]	237673150	36-27N 28-14E	130	
		Thessaloniki[3]	237673210	40-38N 22-56E	130	
		Mytilini[3]	237673220	39-06N 26-35E	130	
		Aspropirgos[2]	002391000	38-03N 23-35E	200	
	Israel	Haifa	004280001	32-49N 35-00E	150	MRCC Israel
	Italy	Roma	002470001	-	-	
		Trieste		45-40N 13-46E	200	MRSC Trieste
		Ancona		43-36N 13-28E	200	MRSC Ancona
		Cagliari		39-13N 09-14E	200	MRSC Cagliari
		Roma		41-37N 12-29E	200	MRSC Roma
		Genova		44-25N 08-56E	200	MRSC Genova
		Palermo	002470002	-	-	
		Palermo (Punta Raisi)		38-11N 13-06E	200	MRSC Palermo
		Mazara del Vallo		37-39N 12-36E	200	
		Augusta		37-14N 15-14E	200	MRSC Catania
		Bari		40-26N 17-25E	200	MRSC Bari
	Romania	Constanta	002640570	44-06N 28-37E	100	Constanta Harbor Master
	Russian Federation	Novorossiysk	002734411	44-36N 37-58E	173	MRCC Novorossiysk
		Taganrog		47-14N 38-56E	70	
		Temrujk		45-19N 37-13E	70	
	Serbia and Montenegro	Bar	002790001	42-01N 19-08E	150	MRCC Bar
	Spain	Valencia (CCR)	002241024	-	-	
		Bagur		42-17N 03-15E	N.I.	MRCC Barcelona
		Cabo la Nao		38-43N 00-10W	150	MRCC Valencia
		Cabo de Gata		36-43N 02-12W	150	MRCC Almeria
		Palma		39-21N 02-59E	150	MRCC Palma
		MRCC Almeria*	002241002	36-50N 02-29W	150	MRCC Tarifa
		MRCC Valencia*	002241004	39-27N 00-20W	150	MRCC Valencia
		MRCC Barcelona*	002240991	41-20N 02-09E	150	MRCC Barcelona
	Turkey	Izmir	002715000	38-21N 26-35E	146	MSRCC Ankara
		Antalya	002713000	36-53N 30-42E	146	
		Samsun	002712000	41-17N 36-20E	146	
		Istanbul	002711000	40-59N 28-49E	146	
IV	Bermuda	Bermuda Harbor	003100001	32-23N 64-41W	200	RCC Bermuda
	Greenland (Denmark)	Aasiaat	003313000	-	-	MRCC Grønnedal
		Upernavik		72-47N 56-10W	280	
		Sisimiut		66-55N 53-40W	270	
		Nuuk		64-04N 52-01W	250	

*NOTE: The primary responsibility for the receipt of MF DSC distress alerts for Spain is carried out via the Coast Radio Stations. MF DSC facilities maintained at various MRCCs are only complementary to the Coast Radio Stations network.

DISTRESS, EMERGENCY, AND SAFETY TRAFFIC

NAV/MET Area	Country	MF DSC Coast Station				Associated RCC
		Name	MMSI	Position	Range (NM)	
IV	Greenland (Denmark) (cont.)	Qeqertarsuaq	003313000	69-14N 53-31W	250	MRCC Grønnedal
		Qaqortoq	003311000	-	-	
		Paamiut		62-00N 49-43W	250	
		Ikerasassuaq		60-04N 43-10W	220	
		Simiutaq		60-41N 46-36W	250	
		Ammassilik	003314000	65-36N 37-38W	280	
	Mexico	Tampico	003450110	22-13N 97-52W	150	MRCC Ciudad Madero
	Netherlands Antilles	Curaçao (Seru Gracia)	003061000	12-20N 69-08W	400	JRCC Curaçao
	United States	Boston	003669991	41-39N 70-30W	200	RCC Boston
		Chesapeake	003669995	36-44N 76-01W	200	RCC Norfolk
		Miami	003669997	25-37N 80-23W	200	RCC Miami
		New Orleans	003669998	29-53N 89-57W	200	RCC New Orleans
VI	Argentina	Argentina Radio	007010111	34-36S 58-28W	200	MRCC Buenos Aires
		Mar del Plata	007010221	38-03S 57-32W	150	MRCC Puerto Belgrano
		Comodoro Rivadavia	007010008	45-51S 67-25W	150	
		Rio Gallegos	007010010	51-37S 69-03W	150	MRCC Ushuaia
		San Blas	007010006	40-33S 62-14W	150	MRSC Bahia Blanca
	Uruguay	Montevideo	007703870	-	-	MRCC Montevideo
		Armada Radio		34-56S 56-09W	100	
VIII	India	Port Blair	004194409	11-41N 92-46E	200	MRCC Port Blair
		Porbandar	004192202	21-38N 69-37E	200	MRCC Mumbai
		Haldia	004194404	22-02N 88-06E	200	MRCC Chennai
		Mandapam	004194406	09-17N 79-05E	200	
		Daman	004192201	20-25N 72-52E	200	MRCC Mumbai
	Mauritius	Mauritius Radio	006452700	-	-	MRCC Mauritius
		Cassis		20-12S 57-28E	150	
	Myanmar (Burma)	Yangon (Rangoon)	005060100	16-42N 96-17E	100	MRCC Yangon
IX	Egypt	Quseir	006221112	26-07N 34-17E	200	RCC Cairo
	Jordan	Aqaba	004381234	29-33N 34-59E	350	Harbor Master Aqaba
	Kuwait	Kuwait Radio	004472188	29-22N 47-59E	N.I.	
	Pakistan	Karachi	004634060	24-52N 67-01E	250	MRCC Karachi
	Saudi Arabia	Jiddah	004030000	21-23N 39-11E	500	RCC Jiddah
XI	China	Basuo	004123600	19-06N 108-37E	100	MRSC Basuo
		Beihai	004123400	21-29N 109-04E	100	MRSC Beihai
		Dalian	004121300	38-50N 121-31E	100	MRCC Liaoning
		Fuzhou	004122600	26-01N 119-18E	100	MRCC Fujian
		Guangzhou	004123100	23-08N 113-29E	100	MRCC Guangdong
		Lianyungang	004122300	34-42N 119-18E	100	MRCC Lianyungang
		Ningbo	004122400	30-01N 121-30E	100	MRSC Ningbo

4 - 86

DISTRESS, EMERGENCY, AND SAFETY TRAFFIC

NAV/MET Area	Country	MF DSC Coast Station				Associated RCC
		Name	MMSI	Position	Range (NM)	
XI	China (cont.)	Qingdao	004122200	36-02N 120-28E	100	MRSC Qingdao
		Sanya	004123700	18-14N 109-30E	100	MRSC Sanya
		Shanghai	004122100	31-07N 121-33E	100	MRCC Shanghai
		Shantou	004123200	23-21N 116-40E	100	MRSC Shantou
		Tianjin	004121100	39-03N 117-25E	100	MRCC Tianjin
		Wenzhou	004122500	28-02N 120-39E	100	MRSC Wenzhou
		Xiamen	004122700	24-35N 118-06E	100	MRSC Xiamen
		Yantai	004121400	37-32N 121-22E	100	MRSC Yantai
		Zhanjiang	004123300	21-10N 110-22E	100	RSC Zhanjiang
	East Timor	Dili	005250015	08-33S 125-34E	100	MRSC Kupang
	Indonesia	Amboina (Ambon)	005250006	03-41S 128-11E	100	MRSC Amboina
		Balikpapan	005250009	01-16S 116-49E	100	MRSC Balikpapan
		Batu Ampar	005250012	01-09N 104-00E	100	MRSC Tanjung Pinang
		Belawan	005250003	03-46N 98-41E	100	MRSC Medan
		Benoa	005250014	08-44S 115-12E	100	MRSC Denpasar
		Biak	005250031	01-12S 136-05E	100	MRCC Biak
		Bitung	005250005	01-26N 125-10E	100	MRSC Menado
		Cilacap	005250030	07-45S 109-02E	100	MRCC Jakarta
		Dumai	005250004	01-39N 101-26E	100	MRSC Pekanbaru
		Fak-Fak	005250026	02-56S 132-17E	100	MRSC Sorong
		Jakarta	005250000	06-07S 106-51E	100	MRCC Jakarta
		Jayapura	005250007	02-31S 140-43E	100	MRSC Jayapura
		Kendari	005250019	03-58S 122-34E	100	MRCC Ujung Pandang
		Kupang	005250010	10-12S 123-37E	100	MRSC Kupang
		Lembar	005250022	08-43S 116-04E	100	MRSC Denpasar
		Makassar	005250002	05-06S 119-26E	100	MRCC Ujung Pandang
		Manokwari	005250023	00-51S 134-04E	100	MRCC Biak
		Merauke	005250021	08-28S 140-23E	100	MRSC Merauke
		Panjang	005250013	05-28S 105-19E	100	MRSC Palembang
		Pantoloan	005250018	00-39S 119-44E	100	MRSC Menado
		Pontianak	005250016	00-01S 109-19E	100	MRSC Pontianak
		Sanana	005250025	02-03S 125-38E	100	MRSC Amboina
		Sei Kolak Kiang	005250029	00-51N 104-36E	100	MRSC Tanjung Pinang
		Semarang	005250008	06-59S 110-19E	100	MRCC Surabaya
		Sibolga	005250028	01-44N 98-46E	100	MRSC Medan
		Sorong	005250011	00-53S 131-18E	100	MRSC Sorong
		Surabaya	005250001	07-11S 112-43E	100	MRCC Surabaya
		Tahuna	005250024	03-36N 125-30E	100	MRSC Menado
		Tarakan	005250017	03-17N 117-35E	100	MRSC Balikpapan
		Ternate	005250020	00-47N 127-35E	100	MRSC Amboina

DISTRESS, EMERGENCY, AND SAFETY TRAFFIC

NAV/MET Area	Country	MF DSC Coast Station				Associated RCC
		Name	MMSI	Position	Range (NM)	
XI	Japan	Otaru	004310101	-	-	RCC Otaru
		Shakotan		43-20N 140-32E	150	
		Hakodateyama		41-45N 140-43E	150	
		Kushiro	004310102	-	-	RCC Kushiro
		Tokotan		43-00N 144-53E	150	
		Souyamisaki		45-31N 141-56E	150	
		Nemuro		43-21N 145-35E	100	
		Monbetsu		44-21N 143-22E	150	
		Shiogama	004310201	-	-	RCC Shiogama
		Komagamine		38-18N 141-32E	150	
		Same		40-29N 141-37E	150	
		Kamaishi		39-16N 141-54E	150	
		Akita		39-44N 140-04E	150	
		Yokohama	004310301	-	-	RCC Yokohama
		Chikura		34-56N 139-56E	150	
		Chosi		35-44N 140-52E	150	
		Shimoda		34-40N 138-57E	150	
		Nagoya	004310401	-	-	RCC Nagoya
		Asamagatake		34-27N 136-49E	150	
		Tanabe	004310502	33-43N 135-24E	150	RCC Kobe
		Kochi	004310503	-	-	
		Tosayama		33-36N 133-32E	150	
		Kobe	004310501	-	-	
		Senzan		34-22N 134-50E	60	
		Hiroshima	004310601	-	-	RCC Hiroshima
		Noro		34-15N 132-40E	60	
		Moji	004310701	-	-	RCC Kitakyushu
		Yukawayama		33-52N 130-33E	150	
		Wakayama		33-11N 131-44E	60	
		Mokkoku		34-08N 129-12E	150	
		Sasebo	004310702	-	-	
		Ishimoriyama		33-14N 129-44E	150	
		Maizuru	004310801	-	-	RCC Maizuru
		Sorayama		35-33N 135-25E	150	
		Nawa		35-31N 133-32E	150	
		Niigata	004310901	37-54N 139-03E	150	RCC Niigata
		Kagoshima	004311001	-	-	RCC Kagoshima
		Yoko-o		31-19N 130-49E	150	
		Aburatsu		31-35N 131-25E	150	
		Naze		28-23N 129-30E	100	
		Naha	004311101		-	RCC Naha
		Tamagutsuku		26-09N 127-46E	150	
		Ishigaki	004311102	-	-	
		Miyara		24-21N 124-12E	150	

DISTRESS, EMERGENCY, AND SAFETY TRAFFIC

NAV/MET Area	Country	MF DSC Coast Station				Associated RCC
		Name	MMSI	Position	Range (NM)	
XI	Malaysia	Pinang	-	-	-	MRCC Port Klang
		Kuantan	005330008	04-06N 103-23E	200	
		Kuching	005330011	01-49N 109-46E	200	
		Kota Kinabalu	005330013	05-57N 116-02E	200	
		Permatang Pauh	005330002	05-22N 100-18E	200	
	Republic of Korea	Inchon Maritime Police	004401001	37-30N 126-30E	120	RCC Inchon
		Donghae Maritime Police	004401002	37-31N 129-07E	120	RCC Donghae
		Mokpo Maritime Police	004401003	34-46N 126-23E	120	RCC Mokpo
		Busan Maritime Police	004401004	35-07N 129-02E	120	RCC Busan
		Cheju Maritime Police	004401005	33-21N 126-49E	120	RCC Cheju
		Inchon	004400001	37-34N 126-41E	120	RCC Inchon
		Kangnung	004400601	37-45N 128-53E	120	RCC Donghae
		Mokpo	004400301	34-48N 126-30E	120	RCC Mokpo
		Busan	004400101	35-06N 129-03E	120	RCC Busan
		Seoul	004400002	37-29N 128-43E	120	RCC Donghae
	Taiwan	Chi-lung (Keelung)	004162019	-	-	
		Chi-lung		25-08N 121-45E	97	
		Hua-lien (Rx)		23-53N 121-35E	100	
		Linyuan		22-29N 120-24E	97	
		Sanchih (Rx)		25-16N 121-28E	90	
		Taping Ting (Rx)		22-01N 120-42E	100	
		Yenliaoken		23-54N 121-36E	97	
		Yüanli (Rx)		24-26N 120-38E	90	
	Thailand	Bangkok Radio (Nonthaburi)	005671000	-	-	RCC Bangkok
		Sriracha		13-06N 100-55E	162	
	Vietnam	Ben Thuy	005742009	18-39N 105-42E	200	Cua Lo Port Authority
		Cua Ong (Cam Pha)	005742008	21-01N 107-22E	200	Quang Ninh Port Authority
		Da Nang	005741999	16-04N 108-13E	200	Da Nang Port Authority
		Hai Phong	005741996	20-52N 106-41E	200	Hai Phong Port Authority
		Ho Chi Minh City	005741993	10-45N 106-43E	200	Saigon Port Authority
		Hon Gai (Quang Ninh)	005742006	20-57N 107-04E	200	Quang Ninh Port Authority
		Hue	005742010	16-33N 107-38E	200	Thien Hue Port Authority
		Mong Cai	005742007	21-32N 107-58E	200	Quang Ninh Port Authority
	Hong Kong (Associate Member of IMO)	Hong Kong Maritime Rescue	004773500	22-12N 114-15E	200	MRCC Hong Kong
		Mt. Butler		22-16N 114-12E	200	

DISTRESS, EMERGENCY, AND SAFETY TRAFFIC

NAV/MET Area	Country	MF DSC Coast Station				Associated RCC
		Name	MMSI	Position	Range (NM)	
XII	Mexico	Mazatlan	003450810	23-10N 106-27W	150	MRCC Mazatlan
	United States	Point Reyes	003669990	37-56N 122-44W	200	RCC Alameda
		Kodiak	003669899	57-46N 152-34W	150	RCC Juneau
		Honolulu	003669993	21-26N 158-09W	200	RCC Honolulu
XIII	Russian Federation	Yuzhno-Sakhalinsk	002733733	-	-	MRSC Yuzhno-Sakhalinsk
		Nevelsk (Rx)		46-39N 141-52E	165	
		Seleznevo (Tx)		46-37N 141-50E	165	
		Vladivostok	002734412	42-45N 133-02E	150[4]	MRCC Vladivostok
XIV	Fiji	RCC Suva	005201100	18-07S 178-25E	200	RCC Wellington RCC Funafuti RCC Nadi Nat. Surv. Center Samoa Mar. Div. Tarawa RCC Canberra
XV	Chile	Arica	007250010	18-29S 70-19W	180	MRSC Iquique
		Iquique	007250020	20-12S 70-06W	180	
		Antofagasta	007250050	23-40S 70-24W	180	
		Caldera	007250080	27-04S 70-49W	180	MRSC Valparaiso
		Isla de Pascua	007250100	27-11S 109-25W	180	
		Coquimbo	007250110	29-56S 71-20W	180	
		Valparaiso	007251860	33-04S 71-36W	180	
		San Antonio	007250140	33-34S 71-37W	180	
		Juan Fernandez	007250130	33-37S 78-49W	180	
		Talcahuano	007250170	36-37S 73-04W	180	MRSC Talcahuano
		Puerto Montt	007250230	41-39S 73-10W	180	MRSC Puerto Montt
		Aysen	007250300	45-24S 72-43W	180	
		San Pedro	007250320	47-42S 74-53W	180	MRSC Punta Arenas
		Bahia Felix	007250370	52-44S 73-46W	180	
		Punta Arenas	007250380	53-09S 71-02W	180	
		Punta Delgada	007250390	52-27S 69-33W	180	
		Puerto Williams	007250420	54-56S 67-36W	180	
XVI	Peru	Paita	007600121	05-05S 81-07W	200	MRCC Paita
		Callao	007600125	12-03S 77-09W	200	MRCC Callao
		Mollendo	007600129	17-01S 72-01W	200	MRCC Mollendo

[1] White Sea (Beloye More) to 66-00N.
[2] MF DSC stations operated by Hellenic Coast Guard.
[3] MF DSC stations owned by Hellenic Coast Guard, using ship station MMSI numbers.
[4] 150nm radius from 42-45N 133-02E starting at Korean coast to 42-33N 136-25E to Cape of Olarovskiy.

DISTRESS, EMERGENCY, AND SAFETY TRAFFIC

LIST OF OPERATIONAL HF DSC COAST STATIONS FOR SEA AREAS A3 AND A4
(Extracted from ANNEX 4 of the IMO GMDSS Master Plan)

NAV/MET Area	Country	HF DSC Coast Station				Associated RCC
		Name	MMSI	Position	Frequency Band[1]	
I	Denmark	Lyngby	002191000	55-50N 11-25E	4,6,8,12,16 MHz	SOK, Aarhus
	Iceland	Reykjavik	002516200	64-05N 21-51W	4,6,8,12,16 MHz	MRCC Oceanic
II	Ghana	Tema	006270000	05-37N 00-00	4,6,8,12,16 MHz	Harbor Master's Office Accr
	Spain	Madrid (CCR)	002241078	40-22N 03-17W	8,12 MHz	MRCC Madrid
		MRCC Madrid*	002241008	-	8,12 MHz	
III	Bulgaria	Varna	002070810	43-04N 27-46E	4 MHz	MRCC Varna
	Cyprus	Cyprus	002091000	35-03N 33-17E	4,8,16 MHz	RCC Larnaca
	Egypt	Alexandria	006221111	31-12N 29-52E	4,6,8,12,16 MHz	RCC Cairo
	Greece	Olympia	002371000	37-36N 21-29E	4,6,8,12,16 MHz	JRCC Piraeus
		Piraeus JRCC[2]	237673000	37-58N 23-40E		
		Aspropirgos[2]	002391000	38-02N 23-35E		
	Romania	Constanta	002640570	44-07N 28-35E	4,6,8,12,16 MHz	Constanta Harbor Master
	Spain	Madrid (CCR)	002241078	40-22N 03-17W	8,12 MHz	MRCC Madrid
		MRCC Madrid*	002241008	-	8,12 MHz	
	Turkey	Istanbul	002711000	40-59N 28-49E	4,6,8,12,16 MHz	MRCC Ankara
IV	Canada	Iqaluit	003160023	63-44N 68-33W	4,6,8,12,16 MHz	RCC Trenton[3]
		Resolute (Rx)		74-45N 94-58W		
	United States	Boston	003669991	41-39N 70-30W	4,6,8,12,16 MHz	Atlantic SAR Coordinator (RCC Norfolk)
		Chesapeake	003669995	36-44N 76-01W		
		Miami	003669997	25-37N 80-23W		
		New Orleans	003669998	29-53N 89-57W		
V	Brazil	Manaus	007100003	03-07S 59-55W	4,6,8,12,16 MHz	MRCC Brazil (Rio de Janeiro)
		Recife	007100002	08-04S 34-55W		
		Rio	007100001	22-58S 43-41W		
VI	Argentina	Argentina Radio	007010111	34-36S 58-28W	4,6,8,12,16 MHz	MRCC Buenos Aires
		Comodoro Rivadavia	007010008	45-51S 67-25W		
		Mar del Plata	007010003	38-03S 57-32W		MRCC Puerto Belgrano
		Rio Gallegos	007010010	51-37S 65-03W		MRCC Ushuaia
	Uruguay	Montevideo	007703870	34-56S 56-09W	4,6,8,12,16 MHz	MRCC Montevideo
VII	South Africa	Cape Town	006010001	33-40S 18-43E	4,6,8,12,16 MHz	MRCC Cape Town
VIII	India	Port Blair	004194409	11-41N 92-46E	4,6,8,12,16 MHz	MRCC Port Blair
		Porbandar	004192202	21-38N 69-37E		MRCC Mumbai
		Haldia	004194404	22-02N 88-06E		MRCC Chennai
		Mandapam	004194406	09-17N 79-05E		

*NOTE: The primary responsibility for the receipt of HF DSC distress alerts for Spain is carried out via Madrid (CCR) Radio. The HF DSC facility maintained at MRCC Madrid is only complementary to the Coast Radio Stations network.

NAV/MET Area	Country	HF DSC Coast Station				Associated RCC
		Name	MMSI	Position	Frequency Band[1]	
VIII (cont.)	India	Daman	004192201	20-25N 72-52E	4,6,8,12,16 MHz	MRCC Mumbai
	Myanmar (Burma)	Yangon (Rangoon)	005060100	16-42N 96-17E	4,6,8,12,16 MHz	MRCC Yangon
IX	Kuwait	Kuwait Radio	004472188	29-22N 47-59E	4,6,8,12,16 MHz	
	Pakistan	Karachi	004634060	24-52N 67-01E	4,6,8,12,16 MHz	MRCC Karachi
X	Australia	RCC Australia	005030331	-	-	RCC Australia
		Charleville		26-20S 146-16E	4,6,8,12,16 MHz	
		Wiluna		26-21S 120-34E		
XI	China	Shanghai	004122100	31-06N 121-32E	4,6,8,12,16 MHz	MRCC Shanghai
	Indonesia	Amboina (Ambon)	005250006	03-41S 128-10E	4,6,8 MHz	MRCC Ujung Pandang
		Balikpapan	005250009	01-16S 116-49E	8 MHz	MRCC Surabaya
		Belawan	005250003	03-46N 98-41E	4,6,8,12,16 MHz	MRCC Jakarta
		Bitung	005250005	01-26N 125-10E	4,6,8,12,16 MHz	MRCC Ujung Pandang
		Dumai	005250004	01-41N 101-27E	4,6,8,12,16 MHz	MRCC Jakarta
		Jakarta	005250000	06-07S 106-51E	4,6,8,12,16 MHz	
		Jayapura	005250007	02-30S 140-43E	4,6,8,12,16 MHz	MRCC Biak
		Kupang	005250010	10-09S 123-34E	8 MHz	MRCC Ujung Pandang
		Makassar	005250002	05-06S 119-25E	4,6,8,12,16 MHz	
		Semarang	005250008	06-56S 110-25E	8 MHz	MRCC Surabaya
		Sorong	005250011	00-53S 131-00E	8 MHz	MRCC Biak
		Surabaya	005250001	07-12S 112-44E	4,6,8,12,16 MHz	MRCC Surabaya
		Cilacap	005250030	07-45S 109-02E	8 MHz	MRCC Jakarta
		Merauke	005250021	08-28S 110-23E	8 MHz	MRSC Merauke
	Japan	Tokyo Sea Patrol Radio	004310001	35-40N 139-45E	4,6,8,12,16 MHz	RCC Otaru RCC Shiogama RCC Yokohama RCC Nagoya RCC Kobe RCC Hiroshima RCC Kitakyushu RCC Maizuru RCC Niigata RCC Kagoshima RCC Naha
	Republic of Korea	Inchon Maritime Police	004401001	37-30N 126-30E	4,6,8,12,16 MHz	RCC Inchon
		Donghae Maritime Police	004401002	37-31N 129-07E		RCC Donghae
		Mokpo Maritime Police	004401003	34-46N 126-23E		RCC Mokpo
		Busan Maritime Police	004401004	35-07N 129-02E		RCC Busan
		Cheju Maritime Police	004401005	33-21N 126-49E		RCC Cheju
		Inchon	004400001	37-34N 126-41E		RCC Inchon

DISTRESS, EMERGENCY, AND SAFETY TRAFFIC

NAV/MET Area	Country	HF DSC Coast Station				Associated RCC
		Name	MMSI	Position	Frequency Band[1]	
XI	Republic of Korea (cont.)	Kangnung	004400601	37-45N 128-53E	4,6,8,12,16 MHz	RCC Donghae
		Mokpo	004400301	34-48N 126-30E		RCC Mokpo
		Busan	004400101	35-06N 129-03E		RCC Busan
		Seoul	004400002	37-29N 128-43E		RCC Donghae
	Taiwan	Chi-lung (Keelung)	004162019	25-08N 121-45E	4,6,8,12,16 MHz	
	Thailand	Bangkok Radio (Nonthaburi)	005671000	13-34N 100-39E	4,6,8,12 MHz	RCC Bangkok
	Vietnam	Ho Chi Minh City	005741993	10-46N 106-40E	8 MHz	Saigon Port Authority
		Hai Phong	005741996	20-52N 106-42E	4,6,8,12,16 MHz	Hai Phong Port Authority
		Da Nang	005741999	16-04N 108-13E	6,8 MHz	Da Nang Port Authority
	Hong Kong (Associate Member of IMO)	Hong Kong Maritime Rescue	004773500	22-12N 114-15E	4,6,8,12,16 MHz	MRCC Hong Kong
XII	United States	Point Reyes	003669990	37-56N 122-44W	4,6,8,12,16 MHz	Pacific SA Coordinator (RCC Alameda)
		Kodiak	003669899	57-46N 152-34W		
		Honolulu	003669993	21-26N 158-09W		
XIV	Fiji	RCC Suva	005201100	18-08S 178-26E	4,6,8,12,16 MHz	RCC Funafuti RCC Tonga RCC Nadi Nat. Surv. Center Samoa Mar. Div. Tarawa RCC Canberra
	New Zealand	Taupo Maritime Radio	005120010	38-52S 176-26E	4,6,8,12,16 MHz	RCC New Zealand
XV	Chile	Antofagasta	007250050	23-40S 70-25W	4 MHz	MRSC Iquique
		Isla de Pascua	007250100	27-11S 109-25W		MRSC Valparaiso
		Valparaiso	007251860	33-01S 71-39W	4,6,8,12,16 MHz	
		Talcahuano	007250170	36-42S 73-06W	4 MHz	MRSC Talcahuano
		Puerto Montt	007250230	41-47S 73-53W		MRSC Puerto Montt
		Punta Arenas (Magallanes)	007250380	53-10S 70-54W	4,8 MHz	MRSC Punta Arenas
XVI	Peru	Paita	007600121	05-05S 81-07W	8 MHz	MRCC Paita
		Callao	007600125	12-03S 77-09W		MRCC Callao
		Mollendo	007600129	17-01S 72-01W		MRCC Mollendo

[1] The following frequencies are allocated for HF DSC distress and safety communication by Radio Regulation (Article N38):
  4 MHz = 4207.5 kHz   6 MHz=6312 kHz   8 MHz = 8414.5 kHz   12 MHz = 12577 kHz   16 MHz = 16804.5 kHz
[2] Hellenic Coast Guard, for reasons of additional safety only, keeps 24 hour watch on HF DSC frequencies, using its own stations.
[3] Operational during navigation season only, approximately June 25 to November 30.

PART II

410A. Requests for U.S. Navy Assistance in Emergency Situations

In view of the current and continuing threat of possible terrorist activity, seizure by hostile military forces, or piracy against U.S. fla and effective U.S. controlled (EUSC) merchant ships on the high seas, the requirement exists for the establishment and promulgation of emergency call-up procedures between U.S. merchant ships and units of the U.S. Navy for protection and assistance.

The following situations warrant immediate use of emergency communications to request assistance from the U.S. Navy:
- Attacks, threats of attack, or other hostile actions by military forces. Warning shots and/or observation of mining operations in international waters are included.
- Harassment by military forces. Threats or attempts of boarding and seizure or hostage taking are included.
- Terrorist attack (or threat) or seizure.
- Piracy.
- Request for rescue in the event of natural disaster if no acknowledgment is received through use of established distress and safety communications procedures.

COMMUNICATIONS PROCEDURES: Emergency communications from merchant ships in crisis situations essentially involve the reporting of incidents and requests for U.S. Navy protection or assistance on a real time basis. Requests for assistance will be submitted to Navy Fleet Command Centers by either commercial satellite (Inmarsat) or HF media. Commercial telephone numbers for Fleet Command Centers, Navy Communications Stations, and USCG Communications Stations are listed in Appendix A.
- Inmarsat Equipped Ships: Direct dial the appropriate Navy Fleet Commander Operations Control Center (OPCONCEN) to report the situation and request U. S. Navy assistance. If the direct dial attempt is unsuccessful, place a call via Inmarsat operator to the appropriate Navy Command Center.

If the call cannot be completed to the Fleet Commander, dial the appropriate Naval Computer and Telecommunications Area Master Station (NCTAMS) Joint Fleet Telecommunications Operations Center (JFTOC) or Naval Computer and Telecommunications Station (NAVCOMTELSTA) for patching relay to the Fleet Commander OPCONCEN. If direct dial effort is unsuccessful, place call to the communications station via the Inmarsat operator.

If contact cannot be made with the area NCTAMS JFTOC or NAVCOMTELSTA, a merchant ship should request the Inmarsat operator to place the call to USCG Area Operations Center (OPCEN) for notificatio to Fleet Commander. U.S. flag/EUS ships operating in the North Arabian Sea and Persian Gulf area requiring assistance from U. S. Navy ships of COMUSNAVCENT should call NAVCOMTELSTA Guam for direct patching via FM non-secure voice satellite communications.
- HF Equipped Ships: Upon establishing HF voice communications with the HF public coast radio station serving the merchant ship, request that the marine operator place a call to the appropriate Fleet Commander OPCONCEN for assistance, giving information in the prescribed format.

If a voice call via the coast station marine operator cannot be completed to the Fleet Commander OPCONCEN, the call should be placed to the closest NCTAMS JFTOC or NAVCOMTELSTA, USAF Communications Station, or USCG Communications Station for relay to the appropriate Navy Command Center.

If a merchant ship uses U.S. military HF facilities (Navy, Air Force, or Coast Guard Communications Stations) for a direct emergency voice communication request for assistance, the message will be relayed by the receiving facility to the appropriate Navy OPCONCEN for action. A listing of available HF frequencies by military facility and area is in Appendix B.

Ship to ship communications may be initiated by use of 2182 kHz or one of the Navy HICOM or tactical HF frequencies listed in Appendix B. However, Fleet Commander OPCONCEN approval is necessary prior to establishment of extended ship to ship communications between merchant ships and U. S. Navy afloat units
- VHF Communications: 156.8 MHz (Ch. 16) is recommended for use by ships at line-of-sight or extended line-of-sight (15-30 miles) communications ranges.
- Direct Ship to Ship Communications Connectivity: If a Fleet Commander OPCONCEN considers it essential for a merchant ship to establish direct non-secure voice communications with U.S. Navy surface units, the merchant ship will be directed to call the appropriate NCTAMS or NAVCOMTELSTA Guam for a patch to be made between the commercial media (Inmarsat, HF) and the Navy's Fleet Satellite Communications (FLTSATCOM) system to a Navy ship by use of a conference bridge. If direct HF voice connectivity is required, the merchant ship and Navy unit will be assigned an appropriate frequency for coordination purposes.
- COMSC Charter Ships: Except in crisis situations, U.S. merchant ships under charter to COMSC would continue to use the procedures stated in the effective edition of MSC Communications Policies and Procedures Manual (CPPM).
- Billing: Billing will be in accordance with tariff regulations applicable to Inmarsat and HF public coast radio stations.

NAVY ACTION: Upon receipt of emergency transmission by the Fleet Commander OPCONCEN, the Navy will determine what action will be taken in response,

DISTRESS, EMERGENCY, AND SAFETY TRAFFIC

e.g., dispatch of forces, establishing direct communications between the merchant ship and a Navy afloa unit, or providing guidance. Decision factors affecting Navy response are contingent upon U. S. Navy units available, proximity of U. S. Navy units to the merchant ship, and/or rules of engagement applicable to the theater of operations.

CALL-UP PROCEDURES: The following voice call-up procedure should be used by merchant ships if an indefinit call-up address is to be employed:

ANY NAVY/AIR FORCE/COAST GUARD STATION GUARDING THIS NET, THIS IS SS EXAMPLE, EMERGENCY MESSAGE FOLLOWS.

If the merchant ship is calling a specifi Navy, Air Force, or Coast Guard station ashore, the voice calls listed in Appendix B apply. Merchant ships are cautioned that Navy shore stations and/or afloa units guarding HICOM or other tactical HF nets may respond with an alphanumeric daily changing call sign and advise the merchant ship to send traffic and will not reveal the Navy unit's name to prevent compromise of the call sign.

Procedures for emergency incident reporting and/or requests for U. S. Navy assistance emphasize the use of voice communications between the merchant ship and the commands/facilities ashore and afloa as define in Appendix A. Frequencies for HF voice and radiotelex (NBDP) communications are listed in Appendix B. Inmarsat equipped ships should fil voice or telex traffi via appropriate earth stations. Emergency or distress messages received by non-U.S. Navy facilities will be immediately forwarded to the appropriate Navy Command Center.

MESSAGE FORMAT: The following format is recommended to provide for brevity and uniformity in reporting procedure:
– To Fleet Commander, Operations Control Center (as appropriate).
– Name of ship.
– International radio call sign and Inmarsat ID.
– Position (latitude/longitude).
– Date and time (GMT).
– Brief description (military attack, seizure, terrorist attack, mining, piracy, natural disaster).

Example:

TO COMPACFLT OPCONCEN
A. SS NOGALES
B. KCSD/1509999
C. LAT. 05N, LONG. 105E
D. 231800Z JAN 89
E. SHIP UNDER ATTACK BY MACHINE GUN AND RIFLE FIRE BY SMALL PATROL CRAFT AND BEING BOARDED BY PIRATES OR TERRORISTS. PERSONNEL CASUALTIES ON DECK.
F. REQUEST IMMEDIATE ASSISTANCE.

SHAR: The guidance provided above does not eliminate the need for submission of SHARs by merchant ships to NGA. Emergency procedures provide for transmission of a request for assistance to precede the SHAR.

TESTING OF PROCEDURES/FACILITIES: U.S. Navy and Air Force HF voice communications nets are dedicated to command and control of military units and air traffi control. These nets are not to be used for training purposes unless specificall designated by the Services and/or operational commanders for use by merchant ships as part of a scheduled exercise. Commercial communications systems (Inmarsat, HF) aboard ship may be used for personnel training and equipment check-out procedures by merchant ships by placing calls to the Fleet Commander OPCONCEN. Tests should be initiated from the merchant ship by dialing the appropriate Fleet Commander OPCONCEN for the ocean area involved. Shipping line owners are required to fund costs incurred for tests initiated by their ships. The Fleet Commander will determine if the calls should be extended to U. S. Navy afloa units via the FLTSATCOM interface at the NCTAMS or NAVCOMTELSTA Guam. The Fleet Commander may desire to use HF HICOM for exercise and training with COMSC chartered merchant ships as well as U.S. fla merchant ships not under Navy control during Naval Cooperation and Guidance for Shipping (NCAGS) exercises or for test prior to in-chop.

In addition to requesting direct assistance from the U.S. Navy, mariners should report acts of terrorism to the following:
– In the waters and ports of the United States, the FBI and the USCG.
– In areas outside U.S. territorial limits, the nearest U.S. Consulate Offic (Regional Security Officer) the U. S. State Department (Operations Center), at (1) 202-647-1512, and NGA.

DISTRESS, EMERGENCY, AND SAFETY TRAFFIC

APPENDIX A

OCEAN AREAS AND COMMAND CENTERS/COMMUNICATIONS FACILITIES

The following provides a listing of U.S. Navy and Coast Guard Command Centers and Communications Stations, showing area of command and/or communications coverage:

Ocean Area - Navy Operations Control Centers and Communications Facilities, USCG Command Centers and Communications Facilities	Telephone Number
Mediterranean, Baltic, Gulf of Guinea	
UKMTO (United Kingdom Maritime Trade Operations)	971505523215/6007
MARLO (Maritime Liaison Office) Bahrain (24x7)	973-3940-1395
JFTOC NAPLES IT (24x7)	39-081-568-6057
COMLANTAREA COGARD PORTSMOUTH VA	(1) 757-398-6700, Telex 127775
CNE-CNA-CGF Maritime Operations Center (Battle Watch Floor)	39-081-568-4551/4552
Atlantic, Caribbean, Atlantic Approaches to Panama Canal, North Sea	
COMUSFLTFORCOM OPCONCEN NORFOLK VA	(1) 757-836-5397
NCTAMS LANT JFTOC NORFOLK VA	(1) 757-444-2124/4182
COMLANTAREA COGARD PORTSMOUTH VA	(1) 757-398-6231, Telex 127775
COGARD CAMSLANT CHESAPEAKE VA	(1) 757-421-6240/6247
Eastern Pacific, Mexico, Central America	
COMPACFLT OPCONCEN PEARL HARBOR HI	(1) 808-471-3201/5200
NCTAMS PAC JFTOC HONOLULU HI	(1) 808-653-5377/1760/0090
NAVCOMTELSTA SAN DIEGO CA	(1) 619-545-8928
COMPACAREA COGARD ALAMEDA CA	(1) 510-437-3701, Telex 172343
COGARD COMMSTA KODIAK AK	(1) 907-487-5778
COGARD CAMSPAC PT REYES CA	(1) 415-669-2047
Mid Pacific, Northern Pacific, Pacific Approaches to Panama Canal, South America	
COMPACFLT OPCONCEN PEARL HARBOR HI	(1) 808-471-3201/5200
NCTAMS PAC JFTOC HONOLULU HI	(1) 808-653-5377/1760/0090
NAVCOMTELSTA SAN DIEGO CA	(1) 619-545-8928
COMPACAREA COGARD ALAMEDA CA	(1) 510-437-3701, Telex 172343
COGARD COMMSTA KODIAK AK	(1) 907-487-5778
COGARD CAMSPAC PT REYES CA	(1) 415-669-2047
Western Pacific, South Pacific, Southeast Asia, Straits of Malacca, Sea of Japan, Indian Ocean	
COMPACFLT OPCONCEN PEARL HARBOR HI	(1) 808-471-3201/5200
NAVCOMTELSTA GUAM	671-355-5513/5326/5327/5328
NAVCOMTELSTA FAR EAST	81-311-743-7510
COGARD COMMSTA KODIAK AK	(1) 907-487-5778

DISTRESS, EMERGENCY, AND SAFETY TRAFFIC

Ocean Area - Navy Operations Control Centers and Communications Facilities, USCG Command Centers and Communications Facilities	Telephone Number
Persian Gulf, Red Sea	
COMUSNAVCENT/BATTLEWATCH CAPTAIN BAHRAIN	973-17-85-3879/4577
NAVCOMTELSTA BAHRAIN	973-17-85-4185
(For Ships in the Persian Gulf)	
NAVCOMTELSTA GUAM	671-355-5513/5326/5327/5328
NAVCOMTELSTA BAHRAIN	973-17-85-4185
(For Ships in the Red Sea)	
JFTOC NAPLES IT	39-081-568-6057
COMLANTAREA COGARD PORTSMOUTH VA	(1) 757-398-6700, Telex 127775

Navy Communications Facilities With FLTSATCOM Interface Capability:

Upon direction from Fleet Commander OPCONCEN, calls will be placed to the following Navy Communications Stations with conference bridge capability to establish unclassified ship to ship voice connectivity with Navy afloat units via Navy FLTSATCOM:

NCTAMS LANT NORFOLK VA	(1) 757-445-9988/9989
JFTOC NAPLES IT	39-081-568-6141
NCTAMS PAC HONOLULU HI	(1) 808-653-0321
NAVCOMTELSTA GUAM	671-355-5513/5326/5327/5328

DISTRESS, EMERGENCY, AND SAFETY TRAFFIC

APPENDIX B

HIGH FREQUENCIES GUARDED BY AIR FORCE, NAVY, COAST GUARD, AND COMMERCIAL STATIONS

AIR FORCE

Area	Control Station	Voice Call	SSB (carrier) Frequencies (in kHz)	Hours of Watch (GMT)
Southwest Pacific Micronesia	ANDERSEN AFB GUAM	ANDERSEN	6738 8967 11176 13201 18002	0200-1200 24 hr. 24 hr. 24 hr. 2200-0700
Northwest Pacific, Se of Japan,	YOKOTA AB JA	YOKOTA	4747 6738 8967 11236 13201 18002	1000-2100 0900-2400 24 hr. 24 hr. 2100-1000 0001-0900
Mid Pacifi	HICKAM AFB HI	HICKAM	3144 6738 8964 11179 13201 18002	0600-1700 0400-0900 24 hr. 24 hr. 1700-0600 0001-0900
Northern Pacifi	ELMENDORF AFB AK	ELMENDORF	6738 8989 11176 13201	24 hr. 24 hr. 24 hr. 24 hr.
Eastern Pacific, est Coast Continental U.S., Mexico	MCCLELLAN AFB CA	MCCLELLAN	4746 6738 8989 11239 15031 18002	0400-1600 0400-1600 24 hr. 24 hr. 1600-0400 1600-0400
Central and South America, (Atlantic and Pacific), Cuba Hispaniola	ALBROOK AB PM	ALBROOK	5710 6683 8993 11176 15015 18019	0200-1200 0001-1400 24 hr. 24 hr. 1200-0200 0900-2400

4 - 98

DISTRESS, EMERGENCY, AND SAFETY TRAFFIC

Area	Control Station	Voice Call	SSB (carrier) Frequencies (in kHz)	Hours of Watch (GMT)
Northern Atlantic, East Coast Continental U.S., Canada, Caribbean, Gulf of Mexico	MACDILL AFB FL	MACDILL		Northern North Atlantic
			5688	0001-1400
			8989	24 hr.
			11179	0900-2400
			13244	0900-2400
			18019	0900-2400
				Central North Atlantic
			4746	0001-0900
			6750	0001-0900
			11179	0900-2400
			11246	24 hr.
			13244	0900-2400
				Southern North Atlantic
			4746	0001-0900
			6750	0001-0900
			8993	24 hr.
			11246	24 hr.
			13244	0900-2200
				Gulf of Mexico
			4746	0001-0900
			6750	0002-0900
			8993	24 hr.
			11246	24 hr.
Northern North Atlantic, Canada, Greenland	THULE AB GREENLAND	THULE	6738	
			8967	
			13201	(slight delay in answering)
Eastern North Atlantic, Iceland, North Sea, Baltic Sea	CROUGHTON AB, UK	CROUGHTON	3076	2300-0500
			5703	2100-0800
			6750	24 hr.
			9011	0500-2300
			11176	24 hr.
			13214	0800-2100
Eastern North Atlantic, Spain, Western Mediterranean, North Africa	LAJES AB PO (Acores)	LAJES	3081	2100-1000
			4746	2100-1000
			6750	24 hr.
			8967	24 hr.
			11226	1000-2100
			13244	1000-2100

DISTRESS, EMERGENCY, AND SAFETY TRAFFIC

Area	Control Station	Voice Call	SSB (carrier) Frequencies (in kHz)	Hours of Watch (GMT)
South Atlantic, Cape of Good Hope, Western Indian Ocean, Red Sea	ASCENSION ISLAND AUXILIARY AB	ASCENSION	6753 8993 11176 13244 15015	2000-0800 24 hr. 1800-1000 1000-1800 0800-2000
Central and Eastern Mediterranean, Strait of Hormuz, Persian Gulf, Northern Red Sea	INCIRLIK AB TU	INCIRLIK	6738 11176 13244 15015	24 hr. 24 hr. 24 hr. 24 hr.

DISTRESS, EMERGENCY, AND SAFETY TRAFFIC

NAVY

Area	Control Station	Voice Call	SSB (carrier) Frequencies (in kHz)
Mediterranean, Eastern and Northern North Atlantic (COMUSNAVEUR HICOM NET)	NCTAMS EURCENT DET ROTA SP NAVCOMTELSTA SICILY IT Designated afloat unit	AOK NSY "ANY NAVY STATION THIS NET"	2200-0600 Carrier Frequency: 6720 Upper Sideband: 6721.5 0600-2200 Carrier Frequency: 11255 Upper Sideband: 11256.5
Atlantic, Caribbean (COMUSFLTFOR COM)	NCTAMS LANT NORFOLK VA NCTAMS LANT DET KEY WEST FL NAVCOMTELSTA PUERTO RICO PR NAVCOMTELSTA KEFLAVIK IC	NAM NAR NAU NRK	24 hr. Carrier Frequency: 6687 Upper Sideband: 6698.5
HICOM Net	Navy Command Centers Ashore Designated afloat unit	"ANY NAVY STATION THIS NET"	24 hr. Carrier Frequency: 23287 Upper Sideband: 23288.5
Indian Ocean Voice Net	NAVCOMTELSTA DIEGO GARCIA Designated afloat unit	NKW "ANY NAVY STATION THIS NET"	0200-1300 Carrier Frequency: 23315 Upper Sideband: 23316.5 1300-0200 Carrier Frequency: 11205 Upper Sideband: 11206.5
Western Pacifi HICOM Net	NAVCOMTELSTA GUAM NAVCOMTELSTA FAR EAST Designated afloat unit	NPN NDT "ANY NAVY STATION THIS NET"	24 hr. Carrier Frequency: 6720 Upper Sideband: 6721.5 Carrier Frequency: 11205 Upper Sideband: 11206.5 Carrier Frequency: 11255 Upper Sideband: 11256.5 Carrier Frequency: 18009 Upper Sideband: 18010.5
Eastern and Central Pacific HICO	NCTAMS PAC HONOLULU HI COMTHIRDFLEET NAVCOMTELSTA SAN DIEGO CA	NPM "ANY NAVY STATION THIS NET"	0600-1700 Carrier Frequency: 4415.4 Upper Sideband: 4417.7 24 hr. Carrier Frequency: 8777.4 Upper Sideband: 8779.2 1700-0600 Carrier Frequency: 13156.4 Upper Sideband: 13182.8

DISTRESS, EMERGENCY, AND SAFETY TRAFFIC

COAST GUARD (HF RADIOTELEPHONE)

Area	Station (Call Sign)	ITU Channel	SSB (carrier) Frequencies (in kHz)		Hours of Watch (GMT)
			Shore	Ship	
Atlantic	Boston MA (NMF)	424	4426	4134	2300-1100
		601	6501	6200	24 hr.
		816	8764	8240	24 hr.
		1205	13089	12242	1100-2300
		1625	17314	16432	on request
	CAMSLANT Chesapeake VA (NMN)	424	4426	4134	2300-1100
		601	6501	6200	24 hr.
		816	8764	8240	24 hr.
		1205	13089	12242	1100-2300
		1625	17314	16432	on request
	Miami FL (NMA)	424	4426	4134	2300-1100
		601	6501	6200	24 hr.
		816	8764	8240	24 hr.
		1205	13089	12242	1100-2300
		1625	17314	16432	on request
	New Orleans LA (NMG)	424	4426	4134	2300-1100
		601	6501	6200	24 hr.
		816	8764	8240	24 hr.
		1205	13089	12242	1100-2300
		1625	17314	16432	on request
Pacifi	Kodiak AK (NOJ)		4125	4125	24 hr.
		424	4426	4134	on request
		601	6501	6200	24 hr.
		816	8764	8240	on request
		1205	13089	12242	on request
		1625	17314	16432	on request
	CAMSPAC Point Reyes CA (NMC)	424	4426	4134	24 hr.
		601	6501	6200	24 hr.
		816	8764	8240	24 hr.
		1205	13089	12242	24 hr.
		1625	17314	16432	on request
	Honolulu HI (NMO)	424	4426	4134	0600-1800
		601	6501	6200	24 hr.
		816	8764	8240	24 hr.
		1205	13089	12242	1800-0600
		1625	17314	16432	on request
	Guam (NRV)	601	6501	6200	0900-2100
		1205	13089	12242	2100-0900

Note: Miami, Boston and New Orleans receive remoted to CAMSLANT Chesapeake (NMN). Honolulu and Guam receive remoted to CAMSPAC Point Reyes (NMC).

DISTRESS, EMERGENCY, AND SAFETY TRAFFIC

COAST GUARD (HF RADIOTELEX)

This net provides for common medium and long range radioteletype communications between all ship stations and COMMSTAs for safety and liaison traffic Calling and working frequencies between shore and ships are in the paired duplex frequency modes indicated below. Stations follow the indicated schedule for frequency guards. Any changes wanted by area commanders to meet operational needs will be included in this schedule.

Area	Station (Call Sign)	ITU Channel	SITOR or NBDP (assigned) Frequencies (in kHz)		
			Shore	Ship	Hours of Watch (GMT)
Atlantic	CAMSLANT Chesapeake VA (NMN) Selcall: 1097 MMSI: 003669995	404 604 824 1227 1627 2227	4212 6316 8428 12592.5 16819.5 22389.5	4174 6264.5 8388 12490 16696.5 22297.5	on request 2300-1100 24 hr. 24 hr. 24 hr. 1100-2300
Pacifi	Kodiak AK (NOJ) Selcall: 1106 MMSI: 003669899	407 607 807	4213.5 6317.5 8419.5	4175.5 6266 8379.5	HN 24 hr. HJ
	CAMSPAC Point Reyes CA (NMC) Selcall: 1096 MMSI: 003669990	412 620 820 1242 1620 2220	4215.5 6323.5 8426 12600 16816.5 22386	4178 6272.5 8386 12497.5 16693 22294	on request HN 24 hr. on request HJ on request
	Honolulu HI (NMO) Selcall: 1099 MMSI: 003669993	404 604 827 1220 1627 2227	4212 6316 8429.5 12589 16819.5 22389.5	4174 6264.5 8389.5 12486.5 16696.5 22297.5	on request on request 24 hr. 24 hr. on request HJ
	Guam (NRV) Selcall: 1096 MMSI: 003669994	412 612 812 1212 1612 2212	4215.5 6319.5 8422 12585 16812.5 22382	4178 6268.5 8382 12482.5 16689 22290	on request on request HN 24 hr. 24 hr. HJ

Notes:
(1) Selcall number is used for radiotelex (sitor). The Maritime Mobile Service Identity (MMSI) is used for Digital Selective Calling (DSC) and may also be used for radiotelex.

(2) For radiotelex the frequencies listed are assigned. The carrier or dial frequency is located 1.7 kHz below the assigned frequency.

(3) Honolulu and Guam are operated remotely by CAMSPAC Point Reyes (NMC).

(4) Time definitions

HJ — Daytime (2 hours after sunrise until 2 hours before sunset, local time).

HN — Nighttime (2 hours before sunset until 2 hours after sunrise, local time).

DISTRESS, EMERGENCY, AND SAFETY TRAFFIC

RADIOTELEX SERVICES AVAILABLE

COMMAND	EXPLANATION	RESPONSE
OBS+	WEATHER OBSERVATION (message must be in standard format)	MOM11+ MSG+
AMV+	AMVER MESSAGE (message must be in standard format)	MOM01+ MSG+
MED+	MEDICAL EMERGENCIES (signals an alarm at the coast station)	MOM07+ MSG+
URG+	SHIPBOARD DISTRESS/EMERGENCIES (signals an alarm at the coast station)	MOM20+ MSG+
TFC+	MISCELLANEOUS ROUTINE MESSAGES	MOM16+ MSG+
VES+	U.S. FISHERIES, POLLUTION OR OTHER REQUIRED VESSEL REPORT	MOM13+ MSG+
OPR+	OPERATOR ASSISTANCE	
FREQ+	FREQUENCY GUARD SCHEDULE LIST	
MSG+	DOWNLOADS SHORE-TO-SHIP MESSAGES (limited to government vessels)	
BRK+	BREAK OFF COMMUNICATIONS	
HELP+	LIST OF AVAILABLE COMMANDS	

COMMERCIAL STATIONS (HF RADIOTELEX/NBDP)

Location	Station (Call Sign)	ITU Channel	Frequencies (kHz)	
			Shore	Ship
Mobile, Alabama, U.S.A.	Mobile (WLO) Selcall: 1090 MMSI: 003660003 Hours of watch: 24 hr.	406 606 806 810 815 1205 1211 1605 1615 1810 2215 2510	4213 6317 8419 8421 8423.5 12581.5 12584.5 16809 16814 19685.5 22383.5 26105.5	4175 6265.5 8379 8381 8383.5 12479 12482 16685.5 16690.5 18875 22291.5 25177.5
Republic, Washington, U.S.A.	Republic (KKL) Selcall: 1150 Hours of watch: 1700-0100 GMT	824	2523.4 4016.4 8183.4 8429.4 12104.4 16345.4 19685.4 26105.4	2523.4 4016.4 8183.4 8389.4 12104.4 16345.4 18874.9 25177.4

Notes: (1) Station WLO is part of the ShipCom Radio Network. Frequencies listed are assigned.

(2) Radiotelex frequencies listed for Station KKL are ARQ carrier center frequency. When calling KKL ARQ, call for at least 60 seconds. KKL uses scanning transceivers on all frequencies except 2522.0 kHz. Each channel is scanned for approximately 10 seconds.

(3) AMVER messages may be sent free of charge through any of the above coast radio stations.

DISTRESS, EMERGENCY, AND SAFETY TRAFFIC

COMMERCIAL STATIONS (HF RADIOTELEPHONE)

Location	Station (Call Sign)	ITU Channel	SSB (carrier) Frequencies (in kHz)	
			Shore	Ship
Marina del Ray, California, U.S.A.	Marina del Ray (KNN) Hours of watch: 24 hr.	416 814 1203 1616 2214	4402 8758 13083 17287 22735	4110 8234 12236 16405 22039
Mobile, Alabama, U.S.A.	Mobile (WLO) Hours of watch: 24 hr.	405 414 607 824 830 1212 1226 1607 1641 1807 2237 2503	4369 4396 6519 8788 8806 13110 13152 17260 17362 19773 22804 26151	4077 4104 6218 8264 8282 12263 12305 16378 16480 18798 22108 25076
Mobile, Alabama, U.S.A.	Mobile (WCL) Hours of watch: 24 hr.	403 802 1206 1601 2243	4363 8722 13092 17242 22822	4071 8198 12245 16360 22126
Republic, Washington, U.S.A.	Republic (KKL) Hours of watch: 1700-0100 GMT	421 606 821 1221 1621 1806	4417 6516 8779 13137 17302 19770	4125 6215 8255 12290 16420 18795
Seattle, Washington, U.S.A.	Seattle (KLB) Hours of watch: 24 hr.	417 805 1209 1624	4405 8731 13101 17311	4113 8207 12254 16429

Notes: (1) Stations KLB, KNN and WCL are part of the ShipCom Radio Network, operated remotely from Mobile (WLO).

(2) AMVER messages may be sent free of charge through any ShipCom Radio Network station.

DISTRESS, EMERGENCY, AND SAFETY TRAFFIC

COMMERCIAL STATIONS (HF DSC)

Location	Station (Call Sign)	ITU Channel	Frequencies (in kHz)	
			Shore	Ship
Mobile, Alabama, U.S.A.	Mobile (WLO) MMSI: 003660003		4219	4208
			6331	6312.5
			8436.5	8415
			12657	12577.5
			16903	16805

FREQUENCY SELECTION GUIDE

Time at Coast (Local)	Distance (NM)		
	200-750	750-1500	>1500
0000	3-5 MHz	6-9 MHz	6-11 MHz
0400	3-5 MHz	4-7 MHz	6-9 MHz
0800	3-7 MHz	6-11 MHz	11-22 MHz
1200	4-7 MHz	8-13 MHz	13-22 MHz
1600	4-7 MHz	8-13 MHz	13-22 MHz
2000	3-7 MHz	6-11 MHz	11-22 MHz

DISTRESS, EMERGENCY, AND SAFETY TRAFFIC

LIST OF INMARSAT COAST EARTH STATIONS

(Extracted from ANNEX 5 of the IMO GMDSS Master Plan)

NAV/MET Area	Country	Location	Ocean Area	Inmarsat Satellite Service	Associated RCC
I	Netherlands	Burum (Xantic) (LES ID x12 and x22)	AOR-E (12)	-A,-B,-C,-E	MRCC Den Helder
			AOR-E (22)	-C	
			AOR-W (12)	-A,-B,-C,-E	
			AOR-W (22)	-C	
			IOR (12)	-A,-B,-E	
	Norway	Eik	AOR-E	-A,-B,-C	MRCC Stavanger
			AOR-W	-A,-B,-C	
			IOR	-A,-B,-C	
	Poland	Psary	AOR-E	-A,-B,-C	RCC Gdynia
			IOR	-A,-B,-C	
	United Kingdom	Goonhilly	AOR-E	-A,-B,-C,-E	MRCC Falmouth
			AOR-W	-A,-B,-C,-E	
			IOR	-A,-B,-C	
			POR	-A,-B,-C	
II	France	Pleumeur-Bodou	AOR-E	-A	MRCC Gris-Nez (MRCC Bremen for Inmarsat-E)
			AOR-W	-A	
			IOR	-A	
			POR	-A	
		Aussaguel	AOR-E	-B,-C,-E	
			IOR	-B,-C,-E	
	Portugal	Sintra	AOR-E	-C	MRCC Lisbon
III	Greece	Thermopylae	AOR-E	-A,-B,-C	Piraeus JRCC
			IOR	-A,-B,-C	
	Italy	Fucino	AOR-E	-A,-B,-C	MRCC Roma
			IOR	-A,-B,-C	
	Turkey	Ata	AOR-E	-A,-C	MRCC Ankara
			IOR	-A,-C	
	Ukraine	Odessa	AOR-E	-A	
			IOR	-A	
IV	Canada	Laurentides	AOR-E	-B	RCC Halifax
			AOR-W	-B	
	United States	Southbury	AOR-E	-A,-B,-C	RCC Norfolk
			AOR-W	-A,-B,-C	
V	Brazil	Tangua	AOR-E	-A,-B,-C	Salvamar-Su Este; Rio de Janeiro
VIII	India	Arvi	IOR	-A,-B,-C	
IX	Egypt	Maadi	AOR-E	-A	RCC Cairo
	Iran	Boumehen	IOR	-A,-C	
	Saudi Arabia	Jiddah	IOR	-A	RCC Jiddah

DISTRESS, EMERGENCY, AND SAFETY TRAFFIC

NAV/MET Area	Country	Location	Ocean Area	Inmarsat Satellite Service	Associated RCC
IX	United Arab Emirates	Towi Al Sawan	IOR	-B	
X	Australia	Perth (Xantic) (LES ID x12 and x22)	IOR (12)	-C,	MRCC Australia (Canberra)
			IOR (22)	-A,-B,-C,-E	
			POR (12)	-A,-B,-C,-E	
			POR (22)	-A,-B,-C,-E	
XI	China	Beijing	IOR	-A,-B,-C	MRCC China
			POR	-A,-B,-C	
	Indonesia	Jatiluhur	IOR	-B	
	Japan	Yamaguchi	IOR	-A,-B,-C	RCC Yokohama RCC Nagoya RCC Kobe RCC Hiroshima RCC Kitakyushu RCC Maizuru RCC Niigata RCC Kagoshima RCC Naha
			POR	-A,-B,-C	RCC Otaru RCC Shiogama
	Malaysia	Kuantan	IOR	-A,-B	MRCC Port Klang
	Republic of Korea	Kumsan	IOR	-A,-C	RCC Inchon
			POR	-A,-C	
	Singapore	Sentosa	IOR	-A,-B,-C	Singapore Port Operations Control Center
			POR	-A,-B,-C	
	Thailand	Nonthaburi	IOR	-B,-C	RCC Bangkok
	Vietnam	Haiphong	IOR	-B,-C	MRCC Viet Nam
	Hong Kong (Associate Member of IMO)	Cape D'Aguilar	IOR	-A,-B	MRCC Hong Kong
			POR	-A,-B	
XII	United States	Santa Paula	POR	-A,-B,-C,-E	RCC Alameda
		Southbury	AOR-W	-A,-B,-C	RCC Norfolk
XIII	Russian Federation	Nakhodka	POR	-A	MRCC Vladivostok
		Nudol	AOR-E	-C	SMRCC Moscow
			IOR	-C	

4 - 108

DISTRESS, EMERGENCY, AND SAFETY TRAFFIC

LIST OF RESCUE COORDINATION CENTERS USING SHIP EARTH STATIONS

(Extracted from ANNEX 6 of the IMO GMDSS Master Plan)

NAV/MET Area	Country	RCC Name	RCC Position	SES DETAIL ID	SES DETAIL Type	SES DETAIL Ocean Region Accessed
I	Estonia	MRCC Tallinn	59-24N 24-40E	492480040	Inmarsat-C	AOR-E
	Finland	RCC Turku	60-26N 22-15E	423002211	Inmarsat-C	AOR-E
	France	MRCC Gris Nez	50-52N 01-35E	422799256	Inmarsat-C	AOR-E
	Germany	MRCC Bremen	53-04N 08-48E	492621021	Inmarsat-C	AOR-E
	Latvia	MRCC Riga	57-02N 24-05E	427518510	Inmarsat-C	AOR-E
	Lithuania	MRCC Klaipeda	55-43N 21-06E	Tel: 327703310 Fax: 327703312 Tlx: 327703314	Inmarsat-B	AOR-E or IOR
	Russian Federation	MRCC Saint Petersburg	59-54N 30-14E	492509012	Inmarsat-C	AOR-E, IOR
	Sweden	MRCC Göteborg	57-28N 11-56E	Tel: 326590010 Fax: 326590011 Tlx: 326590013	Inmarsat-B	AOR-E, AOR-W, IOR
				426590010	Inmarsat-C	AOR-E, AOR-W, IOR
	United Kingdom	MRCC Falmouth	Falmouth	1441532	Inmarsat-A	AOR-E
				423200159	Inmarsat-C	AOR-W
				423200158	Inmarsat-C	AOR-E
II	France	MRCC Etel	47-40N 03-12W	422799025	Inmarsat-C	AOR-E
III	Croatia	MRCC Rijeka	45-20N 14-27E	423816510	Inmarsat-C	AOR-E
	Cyprus	RCC Larnaca	34-52N 33-37E	Tel: 321099990 Fax: 321099991 Tlx: 321099992	Inmarsat-B	AOR-E, IOR
				421099999	Inmarsat-C	AOR-E, IOR
	Greece	Piraeus JRCC	37-58N 23-40E	1133207	Inmarsat-A	AOR-E, IOR
				423767310	Inmarsat-C	AOR-E, IOR
	Russian Federation	MRCC Novorossiysk	44-41N 37-47E	Tel: 327325510 Fax: 327325515 Tlx: 327325518	Inmarsat-B	IOR
	(Caspian Sea)	MRCC Astrakhan	46-20N 48-00E	427310985	Inmarsat-C	IOR
	Ukraine	MRCC Odessa	46-29N 30-44E	492550019	Inmarsat-C	AOR-E
IV	Bermuda	RCC Bermuda	32-23N 64-41W	431010110	Inmarsat-C	AOR-E
	Canada	MRSC St. John's	-	431699930	Inmarsat-C	AOR-W
			-	431699931	Inmarsat-C	AOR-E
		JRCC Halifax	-	Tlx: 331699943	Inmarsat-B	AOR-W
			-	493020114	Inmarsat-C	AOR-E
			-	493020115	Inmarsat-C	AOR-W
		JRCC Trenton	-	431699928	Inmarsat-C	AOR-W
			-	431699929	Inmarsat-C	AOR-E
		JRCC Victoria	-	431699932	Inmarsat-C	AOR-W
			-	431699933	Inmarsat-C	POR
	France (Martinique)	MRCC Fort-de-France	14-36N 61-04W	422799244	Inmarsat-C	AOR-E
				422799024	Inmarsat-C	AOR-W

DISTRESS, EMERGENCY, AND SAFETY TRAFFIC

NAV/MET Area	Country	RCC Name	RCC Position	SES DETAIL ID	Type	Ocean Region Accessed
IV	United States	RCC Norfolk	36-43N 76-12W	430370680	Inmarsat-C	AOR-W
				430370670	Inmarsat-C	AOR-E
V	Brazil	MRCC Brazil	22-53N 43-10W	471009910	Inmarsat-C	AOR-E, AOR-W
VI	Argentina	MRCC Puerto Belgrano	38-53S 62-06W	470128910	Inmarsat-C	AOR-E, AOR-W
VII	France (La Reunion)	MRCC La Reunion	20-56S 55-17E	422799193	Inmarsat-C	IOR
VIII	France (La Reunion)	MRCC La Reunion	20-56S 55-17E	422799193	Inmarsat-C	IOR
IX	Egypt	Suez Canal Authority	Ismailia Radio	1622570	Inmarsat-A	AOR-E
X	Australia	RCC Australia	35-15S 149-05E	450300458	Inmarsat-C	POR
	France (New Caledonia)	MRCC Noumea	22-17S 166-26E	422799194	Inmarsat-C	POR
XI	China	Beijing	N.I.	N.I.	N.I.	N.I.
	Hong Kong (Associate Member of IMO)	MRCC Hong Kong	Hong Kong	447735010	Inmarsat-C	POR
XIII	Russian Federation	MRCC Vladivostok	43-07N 131-53E	492500379	Inmarsat-C	POR
		MRSC Yuzhno-Sakhalinsk	46-59N 142-43E	427311122	Inmarsat-C	POR
	(White Sea)	MRSC Arkhangelsk	64-32N 40-32E	492509110	Inmarsat-C	AOR-E, IOR
XIV	French Polynesia	MRCC Papeete	17-32S 149-35W	422799192	Inmarsat-C	POR

CHAPTER 5

STATIONS TRANSMITTING MEDICAL ADVICE

500A. General. 5-3
500B. Station List. 5-3

CHAPTER 5

STATIONS TRANSMITTING MEDICAL ADVICE

500A. General

This chapter is to assist ships at sea, with no medical personnel embarked, experiencing a medical emergency onboard. The text of any message should be formatted in plain language and should describe the medical emergency as follows:
– General description of medical resources.
– Name of next port of call.
– List of ports visited where exotic or infectious diseases could have been contracted.
– Patient data:
  – Sex.
  – Age.
  – Clinical antecedents.
  – Vital signs (temperature in degrees centigrade).
  – Symptoms.
  – Presumed cause of illness or accident.
  – Observations.

If language is a limiting factor, the International Code of Signals (CDPUBNV102) can be used by itself, or in conjunction with English or another language specified by the coast station called.

Messages are generally addressed RADIOMEDICAL followed by the name of the coast station to which the message is sent. The priority of the message should depend on the severity of the ailment. In extreme emergency the urgency signal (PAN PAN) should precede the address on the address line (example: PAN PAN RADIOMEDICAL HALIFAX RADIO).

Messages are sent using distress and safety frequencies (See chapter 4.) by radiotelex, radiotelephony, or Inmarsat.

500B. Station List

Detailed information concerning stations transmitting medical advice is contained in the List of Radiodetermination and Special Service Stations of the International Telecommunication Union. A brief listing of medical advice stations, alphabetical by country, follows.

STATIONS TRANSMITTING MEDICAL ADVICE

(1) No.	(2) Name	(3) Address	(4) Name of Coast Station	(5) Remarks
		For all addresses in this table, the letters "XXX" are for use in radiotelegraphy; they are replaced by the words "Pan Pan Pan" in radiotelephony.		
5010	Algeria	XXX RADIOMEDICAL; station call sign.	Algiers (7TA). Annaba (7TB). Oran (7TO).	Message must be in English or French.
5020	Argentina	CONSULTA RADIO-MEDICA; name of coast station. In urgent cases the prefi "XXX" or "PAN" may be used.	Any coast radio station.	Message must be in Spanish. It should include the following information: (a) patient's sex; (b) age; (c) medical history; (d) symptoms; (e) probable cause of the illness or circumstances leading to the accident; (f) any additional information that may aid diagnosis and treatment such as pulse rate, temperature (°C), and cause and severity of the wound. Message must be signed by the Master. This service, provided by Servicio de Asistencia Medica de Emergencia (SAME) (Emergency Medical Assistance Service), assumes no liability for information given in medical consultations.
5030	Australia	RCC Australia; MMSI 005030001.	RCC Australia (VIC).	Vessels at sea can request medical advice via HF DSC radio or Inmarsat satellite services. The service has been put into place for SOLAS vessels but other craft may use the service in emergencies. This service is free and is available via Inmarsat-C fitte vessels using access code 32, HF DSC fitted essels through RCC Australia (VIC) using Urgency priority DSC Call or, for non-SOLAS vessels, by contacting RCC Australia on (61) 2 6230 6868 who will put the vessel in contact with the Duty Medical Officer at the R yal Flying Doctor Service (RFDS) Telemedical Advice Center (TMAC) at Cairns, Queensland.
5050	Bahrain	Health Office , Bahrain.	Bahrain (A9M).	
5060	Bangladesh	Medical Services, Port Health Office , Chittagong. In urgent cases the prefi "XXX" may be used.	Chittagong (S3D).	Message should include description of patient's symptoms and description of ship's medical chest. It must be signed by the Master.
5070	Barbados	Health Office , Barbados.	Barbados (8PO).	
5080	Belgium	RADIOMEDICAL Oostende. In urgent cases the prefi "XXX" may be used.	Oostende (OST).	Message must be in Dutch, English, French or German. It should include description of ship's medical chest and patient's symptoms, age, sex, vital signs and medical history. Message must be signed by the Master.
5090	Benin	XXX RADIOMEDICAL Cotonou.	Cotonou (TYA).	Message must be in French. It should include description of ship's medical chest and patient's symptoms, age, sex, vital signs and medical history. Message must be signed by the Master.
5100	Bermuda	Health Office , Bermuda.	Bermuda Radio (VRT)(ZBM).	
5101	Burma	Medical Service, Rangoon.	Rangoon (XYR).	
5110	Cameroon	XXX RADIOMEDICAL Douala.	Douala (TJC).	Message must be in French. This service assumes no liability.
5120	Canada	RADIOMEDICAL; station call sign.	Any coast radio station.	Message must be signed by the Master.
5130	Chile	MEDICO; station call sign. In urgent cases the prefi "XXX" may be used.	Antofagasta (CBA). Magallanes (CBM). Talcahuano (CBT). Valparaiso (CBV).	

STATIONS TRANSMITTING MEDICAL ADVICE

(1) No.	(2) Name	(3) Address	(4) Name of Coast Station	(5) Remarks
5140	China	MEDICO; station call sign. In urgent cases the prefi "XXX" may be used.	Dalian (XSZ). Guangzhou (XSQ). Qingdao (XST). Shanghai XSG). Tianjin (XSV).	
5141	Comoros	RADIOMEDICAL Dzaoudzi.	Dzaoudzi (FJN).	Message must be in English or French.
5150	Congo	XXX RADIOMEDICAL Pointe Noire.	Pointe Noire (TNA).	Message must be in French. This service assumes no liability.
5160	Costa Rica	DH MEDICO Limon.	Limon (TIM).	
5165	Croatia	RADIOMEDICAL; name of coast station.	Any coast radio station.	Message must be in English or Croatian. It should include: (a) symptoms noted and those experienced by patient; (b) patient's age and sex; (c) date of the accident or onset of illness; (d) temperature, pulse, general condition, and position of the patient; (e) medical equipment carried by the ship. Message must be signed by the Master. Stations provide medical advice to ships of all nationalities. The radiomedical service is free of charge.
5170	Cuba	DH MEDICO; station call sign.	Habana (CLA)(CLT). Santiago De Cuba (CLM).	
5180	Cyprus	MEDICO DMO Nicosia.	Cyprus (5BA).	
5190	Denmark	RADIOMEDICAL; station call sign.	Blaavand (OXB). Lyngby (OXZ). Ronne (OYE). Skagen (OXP). Torshavn (OXJ).	Message must be in Danish, English, French, German, Norwegian or Swedish. It should include ship's name and position and patient's symptoms and vital signs. Message must be signed by the Master.
5200	Djibouti	Service Quarantenaire Djibouti (J2A). In urgent cases the prefi "XXX" may be used.	Djibouti (J2A).	Message must be in English or French. This service assumes no liability.
5210	Dominican Republic	RADIOMEDICO Santo Domingo Piloto.	Santo Domingo Piloto (HIA).	
5220	Egypt	XXX RADIOMEDICAL; station call sign.	Alexandria (SUH). Kosseir (SUK).	Message must be signed by the Master. This service assumes no liability.
5245	Fiji Islands	RADIOMEDICAL Suva.	Suva (3DP).	
5250	Finland	RADIOMEDICAL; station call sign. In urgent cases the prefi "XXX" may be used.	Any coast radio station except Kemi, Turku or Port.	Message must be in English, Finnish or Swedish. It should include patient's symptoms and cause of illness. Message must be signed by the Master. Consultations with doctors of central hospitals of Helsinki and Turku University are free of charge. Other doctors consulted set their own fees.

STATIONS TRANSMITTING MEDICAL ADVICE

(1) No.	(2) Name	(3) Address	(4) Name of Coast Station	(5) Remarks
5260	France	XXX RADIOMEDICAL; name of CROSS/Sous-CROSS station.	Any coast radio station or CROSS/Sous-CROSS station. CCMM telex: 530333F telephone: 33 5 61 49 33 33	Message must be in French, English, or International Code (CDPUBNV102). The French Center for Maritime Medicine (CCMM) is part of the Urgent Medical Aid Service (SAMU) in Toulouse and is available continuously to give advice to ships at sea. After analyzing the patient's situation, CCMM advises the ship's Master of the recommended treatment: Type 1 - treatment onboard without altering voyage. Type 2 - treatment onboard with change of voyage plan. Type 3 - urgent evacuation without doctor (EVA-SAN). Type 4 - urgent evacuation with doctor (EVA-MED). Type 5 - onboard transfer of medical team followed by evacuation. For treatment types 3, 4, and 5 (interventions by CCMM), the Master is advised to send his request by telex or radiotelephone to the nearest CROSS station; Étel and La Garde CROSS stations specialize in providing medical advice. CCMM can be contacted by: (1) Radiotelephone via any CROSS or Sous-CROSS station or coast radio station. (2) Radiotelex (MED+) via any coast radio station. (3) Inmarsat telephone call using code 38.
5290	Gambia	Health Office, Banjul.	Banjul (C5G).	
5300	Germany	Funkarzt; station call sign. In urgent cases the prefi "XXX" may be used.	Any coast radio station.	Message must be in English or German.
5320	Ghana	Port Health Office, Takoradi.	Takoradi (9GA).	
5330	Greece	RADIOMEDICAL; station call sign. In urgent cases the prefi "XXX" may be used.	Any coast radio station.	Message must be in English, French or Greek. This service assumes no liability.
5340	Greenland	RADIOMEDICAL Julianehab.	Qaqortoq (OXF).	Message must be in Danish, English, French, German, Norwegian or Swedish.
5350	Guadeloupe	XXX RADIOMEDICAL Pointe-a-Pitre.	Pointe-a-Pitre (FFQ).	Message must be in French.
5360	Guinea	XXX RADIOMEDICAL Conakry.	Conakry (3XC).	Message must be in French. It should include patient's symptoms, age, sex, vital signs and medical history. This service assumes no liability. Conakry guards 2182 kHz 0700-1900 and 3 minutes at the beginning of every hour 2000-2200.
5370	Guyana	Health Office, Georgetown.	Demerara (8RB).	
5380	Hong Kong (China)	Porthealth Hong Kong.	Hong Kong (VRX).	
5390	India	Medical service; station call sign. In urgent cases the prefi "XXX" may be used.	Any coast radio station.	Message should include patient's symptoms and description of ship's medical chest. It must be signed by the Master.
5400	Indonesia	RADIOMEDICAL Jayapura. In urgent cases the prefi "XXX" may be used.	Jayapura (PNK).	Message must be in Dutch or English. It should include description of ship's medical chest and patient's sex, age, medical history, symptoms and vital signs. Message must be signed by the Master.
5410	Iraq	Port Medical Office, Ma'aqal. In urgent cases the prefi "XXX" may be used.	Basrah Control (YIR).	
5420	Ireland	(No specifi format).	Any coast radio station.	If a doctor from shore is wanted, the request should be addressed as a radiotelegram to the medical office of the nearest convenient port.
5430	Israel	MEDICO Haifa. In urgent cases the prefi "XXX" may be used.	Haifa (4XO).	Message must be signed by the Master. This service assumes no liability.

STATIONS TRANSMITTING MEDICAL ADVICE

(1) No.	(2) Name	(3) Address	(4) Name of Coast Station	(5) Remarks
5440	Italy	MEDRAD CIRM Roma.	Any coast radio station. The following coast radio stations will relay messages to CIRM: Italian coast radio stations (asking for CIRM) (address: MEDRAD CIRM Roma). USCG stations (Atlantic and Gulf coasts) (address: DH MEDICO CIRM Roma). USCG stations (Pacifi coast) (address: DH MEDICO CIRM Roma via PREWI). CIRM can be contacted 24 hours by: telephone: (39) 06 592 3331/3332 facsimile: (39) 06 592 3333 telex*: (43) 612068 CIRM I (both satellite or radio telex) E-mail: telesoccorso@cirm.it Website: http://www.cirm.it Maritec system	The International Radio Medical Center (CIRM) provides 24-hour free radio medical assistance to patients onboard vessels of any nationality anywhere in the world. CIRM can also decide and coordinate, wherever possible, the Medevac of a patient from a vessel by naval craft or helicopter, cooperating mainly with National MRCCs and if necessary with other rescue organizations, such as the USCG. Message must be in English, French or Italian. When requesting radio medical assistance, the vessel should communicate the following information regarding: the vessel: (a) Vessel's name/call sign. (b) Position, port of departure and destination, ETA, route and speed. (c) Medicine chest available. the patient: (d) Name, age and nationality. (e) Temperature, blood pressure, pulse and respiratory rates. (f) Patient's symptoms, location and type of pains, and any relevant information concerning the illness. (g) Other medical problems, with special reference to drug or other allergies, chronic illness and their treatment. (h) In case of accident, in addition to the symptoms, where and how the accident occurred. (i) Treatment already administered to the patient.

*NOTE: Requests via telex should be addressed MEDRAD or DH MEDICO to obtain priority of transmission.

(1) No.	(2) Name	(3) Address	(4) Name of Coast Station	(5) Remarks
5450	Ivory Coast	XXX RADIOMEDICAL Abidjan.	Abidjan (TUA).	Message must be in French. It should include patient's age, sex, symptoms, medical history and vital signs. Message must be signed by the Master. This service assumes no liability. Abidjan guards 2182 kHz, but only distress and safety traffic ar handled 2000-0800.
5460	Jamaica	Health Offic , Kingston.	Kingston (6YI).	
5470	Japan	MDC; station call sign and hospital name if applicable. In urgent cases the prefi "XXX" may be used.	Any coast radio station. The following hospitals also respond under the call signs listed: NKEB - Kobe Moji Nagasaki Nagoya Osaka Otaru Shiogama Tokyo Yokohama SHKB - Osaka Tokyo Yokohama Japanese vessels with doctors aboard will also respond to requests for medical advice (address: ship's Master).	Message must be in English, French, German or Japanese. It must be signed by the Master.
5480	Kenya	Medical Port Health Office , Mombasa.	Mombasa (5ZF).	Message must be signed by the Master.
5485	Latvia	(No specifi format).	Riga (UKB).	
5500	Madagascar	XXX RADIOMEDICAL; station call sign.	Antseranana (5RL). Mahajango (5RO). Taomasina (5RS). Toliara (5RT).	Message must be in English, French or Malagasy. This service assumes no liability.
5510	Malaysia	RADIOMEDICAL; station call sign. In urgent cases the prefi "XXX" may be used.	Kelang (9MP). Kota Kinbalu (9WH). Kuantan (9MK). Kuching (9WW20). Miri (9WW21). Pinang (9MG). Sandakan (9WH21).	Message should include patient's symptoms and description of ship's medical chest.
5520	Malta	Medical Office , Malta.	Malta (9HD).	

STATIONS TRANSMITTING MEDICAL ADVICE

(1) No.	(2) Name	(3) Address	(4) Name of Coast Station	(5) Remarks
5540	Martinique	XXX RADIOMEDICAL Fort de France Radio.	Fort de France (FFP).	Message must be in French. This service assumes no liability.
5541	Mauritius	Superintendent, Victoria Hospital, Quatre-Bornes, Mauritius.	Mauritius (3BA).	Message must be in English or French.
5542	Monaco	(No specifi format).	Monaco (3AC).	Message must be in English, French or Italian.
5550	Morocco	XXX RADIOMEDICAL; station call sign.	Agadir (CND). Casablanca (CNP). Saf (CND3). Tangier (CNW).	Message must be in French. This service assumes no liability.
5560	Namibia	Porthealth, Walvis Bay.	Walvis Bay (ZSV).	Message must be in International Code (CDPUBNV102) supplemented, if necessary, with Afrikaans or English. It should include patient's symptoms and brief description of ship's medical chest. This service assumes no liability.
5565	Nauru	RADIOMEDICAL Nauru.	Nauru (C2N).	
5570	Netherlands	Radio Medical Advice (RMA).	Netherlands Coastguard Radio (PBK).	Message must be in Dutch or English. Radiotelephone (VHF)-Sea Area A1: (a) Call Netherlands Coastguard Radio (PBK) on VHF DSC Ch. 70 MMSI 002442000 or Ch. 16. (b) State vessel's name, callsign and position, and ask for Medical Advice. (c) The vessel will be assigned a VHF working channel (Ch. 23 or 83) and connected to the duty RMA doctor. (d) Use the Radio Medical Advice questionnaire to give the doctor clear information. Radiotelephone (MF)-Sea Area A2: (a) Call Netherlands Coastguard Radio (PBK) on MF DSC 2187.5 kHz MMSI 002442000 requesting a transfer to 2182 kHz. (b) After establishing contact on 2182 kHz state vessel's name, callsign and position, and ask for Medical Advice. (c) The vessel will be assigned a working frequency and connected to the duty RMA doctor. (d) Use the Radio Medical Advice questionnaire to give the doctor clear information. Inmarsat-A/-B/-M Telephone (via Burum-Station 12): (a) Contact Station 12 by entering code 12. (b) For priority use code 32-Medical Advice or code 38-Medical Evacuation. (c) State vessel's name, Inmarsat number and position. (d) Vessel will be connected to the duty RMA doctor. (e) Use the Radio Medical Advice questionnaire to give the doctor clear information. Inmarsat-A/-B/-C Telex* (via Burum-Station 12): (a) Contact Station 12 by entering code 12. (b) For priority use code 32-Medical Advice or code 38-Medical Evaluation.

*NOTE: For Inmarsat -A/-B Telex, the vessel will be automatically relayed to the RMA computer and will receive the host (MEDIC SERVICE NL). Vessel's host will be called in. Send the message and end with: NNNN. Disconnect but do not switch off the Inmarsat terminal as the RMA computer will automatically send a reply from the doctor.
For Inmarsat-C Telex, the vessel will be automatically relayed to the store and forward system of Station 12. Send the message and end with: NNNN. Disconnect but do not switch off the Inmarsat terminal as the RMA computer will automatically send a reply from the doctor.

(1) No.	(2) Name	(3) Address	(4) Name of Coast Station	(5) Remarks
5580	Netherland Antilles	RADIOMEDICUS Curacao.	Curacao (PJC).	Message should include description of ship's medical chest, last/next ports of call and patient's age, sex, symptoms, vital signs and medical history. It must be signed by the Master.
5590	New Caledonia	RADIOMEDICAL Noumea.	Noumea (FJP).	Message must be in French. It should include patient's symptoms and description of ship's medical chest. Message must be signed by the Master.
5600	New Zealand	RADIOMEDICAL; station call sign. In urgent cases the prefi "XXX" may be used.	Taupo Maritime Radio (ZLM).	Message should include patient's symptoms and description of ship's medical chest. It must be signed by the Master.

STATIONS TRANSMITTING MEDICAL ADVICE

(1) No.	(2) Name	(3) Address	(4) Name of Coast Station	(5) Remarks
5610	Nigeria	Health Office, Lagos.	Lagos (5OW).	
5620	Norway	(No specifi format).	Any coast radio station.	Message must be in Danish, English, German, Norwegian or Swedish.
5630	Oman	Health Office, Muscat.	Muscat (A4M).	
5640	Pakistan	Medical Services, Port Health Office, Karachi. In urgent cases the prefi "XXX" may be used.	Karachi (ASK).	Message should include patient's symptoms and description of ship's medical chest. It must be signed by the Master.
5650	Panama	DH MEDICO.	Canal (HPN60).	Canal guards 500 kHz.
5660	Papua New Guinea	RADIOMEDICAL; station call sign.	Port Moresby (P2M). Rabaul (P2R).	
5665	Peru	Centro Medico Naval Callao.	Callao (OBC3).	Message must be in Spanish. It should include patient's sex, age, symptoms, medical history and vital signs, description of ship's medical chest, position and next port of call.
5670	Philippines	MEDICO Manila.	Manila (DZR).	
5680	Poland	RADIOMEDICAL; station call sign. In urgent cases the prefi "XXX" may be used.	Gdynia (SPC)(SPH). Szczecin (SPE)(SPO). Witowo (SPN)(SPS).	Message must be in English or Polish.
5690	Portugal	XXX RADIOMEDICAL; station call sign.	Lisboa (CUL). Madeira (CUB). Sao Miguel (CUG).	Message must be in English, French or Portuguese. It should inlude cause and symptoms of illness. Message must be signed by the Master. This service assumes no liability.
5705	Russia	(No specifi format).	Arkhangel'sk (UGE). Murmansk (UMN). St. Petersburg (UDB). Vladivostok (UIK).	Message must be in English or Russian.
5710	Reunion Island	XXX RADIOMEDICAL St. Denis.	St. Denis (FFD).	Message must be in French. This service assumes no liability.
5720	St. Helena	Medical Office, St. Helena.	St. Helena (ZHH).	
5725	St. Pierre and Miquelon	RADIOMEDICAL St. Pierre.	St. Pierre (TXU).	Message must be in French.
5730	Saudi Arabia	(No specifi format).	Dammam (HZG). Jiddah (HZH). Ra's Tannurah (HZY).	Stations guard 500 kHz.
5740	Senegal	XXX RADIOMEDICAL Dakar.	Dakar (6VA).	Message must be in French. It should include patient's age, sex, medical history, vital signs and symptoms. Dakar guards 2182 kHz, but only distress and safety traffi are handled 2000-0800.
5740.5	Serbia and Montenegro	RADIOMEDICAL Bar.	Bar (YUW).	Message must be in English or Serbo-Croat. It should include patient's age, sex, medical history, symptoms and vital signs, date of the accident or of the onset of the illness, and description of ship's medical chest.
5741	Seychelles	Health Office, Seychelles.	Seychelles (S7Q).	
5750	Sierra Leone	Health Office, Freetown.	Freetown (9LL).	
5755	Singapore	RADIOMEDICAL Singapore.	Singapore (9VG).	
5760	Slovenia	RADIOMEDICAL; station call sign.	Any coast radio station.	Message should include patient's age, sex, medical history, symptoms and vital signs and description of ships medical chest.

STATIONS TRANSMITTING MEDICAL ADVICE

(1) No.	(2) Name	(3) Address	(4) Name of Coast Station	(5) Remarks
5770	South Africa	Porthealth; station call sign.	Capetown (ZSC). Durban (ZSD). East London (ZSA). Port Elizabeth (ZSQ). Richards Bay (ZSU).	Message must be in International Code (CDPUBNV102) supplemented, if necessary, with Afrikaans or English. It should include patient's symptoms and description of ship's medical chest. This service assumes no liability.
5780	Yemen Aden	Health Office, Aden.	Aden (7OA).	
5790	Spain	MEDRAD; station call sign. In urgent cases the prefi "XXX" may be used.	Any coast radio station.	Message must be in Spanish or International Code (CDPUBNV102).
5800	Sri Lanka	Medical Service, Colombo. In urgent cases the prefi "XXX" may be used.	Colombo (4PB).	Message should include patient's symptoms and description of ship's medical chest. It must be signed by the Master.
5810	Suriname	Medical Advice, Director of Health, Paramaribo.	Paramaribo (PZN).	Message should include description of ship's medical chest and patient's sex, age, symptoms and medical history. It must be signed by the Master.
5820	Sweden	(No specifi format).	MRCC Goteborg.	MRCC Goteborg can be contacted by: telephone: (46) 31 699050 fax: (46) 31 648010 telex: (54) 20180 (MRCCGBG S) email: radiomedical@amrcc.sjofartsverket.se If possible, try to contact MRCC Goteborg by phone first when sending e-mail
5820.5	Svalbard	(No specifi format).	Svalbard (LGS). Ny-Alesund (LJN).	Message must be in Danish, English, German, Norwegian or Swedish (French over radiotelegraph only).
5821	Switzerland	RADIOMEDICAL Bern.	Bern (HEB)(HEC).	Message may be in English, but preferably in French or German.
5822	Tahiti	RADIOMEDICAL Mahina.	Mahina (FJA).	Message must be in English or French.
5823	Tonga	RADIOMEDICAL Nukualofa.	Nukualofa (A3A). In urgent cases the prefi "PAN PAN" may be used.	Message should be in English. It should include patient's symptoms and description of ship's medical chest.
5824	Togo	RADIOMEDICAL Lome.	Lome (5VA).	Message must be in French.
5840	Tunisia	XXX RADIOMEDICAL; station call sign.	Bizerte (3VB). Mahdia (3VM). Sfax (3VS). Tunis (3VX)(3VT).	Message must be in French.
5845	Ukraine	(No specifi format).	Odessa (UDE).	
5850	United Kingdom	(No specifi format).	Any coast radio station.	Radiotelephone (VHF): Vessels should call on DSC Ch. 70 or on VHF Ch. 16 and will be directed to a working channel. After contact is established on the working channel, the vessel will be connected to a casualty doctor by simplex radiotelephone. Radiotelephone (MF): After an initial call on DSC 2187.5 kHz using the Urgency priority and contact is established on 2182 kHz, the vessel will be assigned a working frequency. After contact is established on the working frequency, the vessel will be connected to a casualty doctor by simplex radiotelephone. Alternatively, vessels may call direct on 2182 kHz. Inmarsat-A/-B/-M/Mini-M Telephone (via Goonhilly): Vessels should use code 32 for medical advice and will be automatically connected to a doctor. Vessels requiring urgent medical assistance should use code 38 and will be automatically connected to the HM Coast Guard.

STATIONS TRANSMITTING MEDICAL ADVICE

(1) No.	(2) Name	(3) Address	(4) Name of Coast Station	(5) Remarks
5860	United States (Atlantic and Gulf)	DH MEDICO; station call sign; group count (number of words in message).	Massachusetts: Boston (NMF), USCG. Virginia: CAMSLANT Chesapeake (Portsmouth) (NMN), USCG. Florida: Miami (NMA), USCG. Louisiana: New Orleans (NMG), USCG.	Telephone calls from ships to doctors or hospitals are handled as regular phone calls in accordance with legally applicable tariffs. Ships requesting medical advice with no specifi telephone number will be connected by the USCG. No charge is made for the call when the ship states it is an emergency involving the safety of life or property at sea. Message must be signed by the Master. Messages transmitted to a USCG station are routed to the nearest medical facility. This service (inquiry and reply) is free of charge. Numerous USCG stations continuously guard 2182 kHz (USB) and 156.8 MHz (VHF-FM) and will facilitate the provision of medical advice through their associated Rescue Coordination Center (RCC). The use of the signal "CQ" from the International Code (CDPUBNV102) for medical messages is discouraged.
5861	United States (Great Lakes)	DH MEDICO; station call sign; group count (number of words in message).		Telephone calls from ships to doctors or hospitals are handled as regular phone calls in accordance with legally applicable tariffs. ships requesting medical advice with no specifi telephone number will be connected by the USCG. No charge is made for the call when the ship states it is an emergency involving the safety of life or property at sea. Messages must be signed by the Master. Messages transmitted to a USCG station are routed to the nearest medical facility. This service (inquiry and reply) is free of charge. Numerous USCG stations continuously guard 2182 kHz (USB) and 156.8 MHz (VHF-FM) and will facilitate the provision of medical advice through their associated Rescue Coordination Center (RCC). The use of the signal "CQ" from the International Code (CDPUBNV102) for medical messages is discouraged.
5862	United States (Pacific)	DH MEDICO; station call sign; group count (number of words in message).	Alaska: Kodiak (NOJ), USCG. California: CAMSPAC Point Reyes (San Francisco) (NMC), USCG. Hawaii: Honolulu (NMO), USCG. Mariana Islands: Guam (NRV), USCG.	Telephone calls from ships to doctors or hospitals are handled as regular phone calls in accordance with legally applicable tariffs. Ships requesting medical advice with no specifi telephone number will be connected by the USCG. No charge is made for the call when the ship states it is an emergency involving the safety of life or property at sea. Message must be signed by the Master. Messages transmitted to a USCG station are routed to the nearest medical facility. This service (inquiry and reply) is free of charge. Numerous USCG stations continuously guard 2182 kHz (USB) and 156.8 MHz (VHF-FM) and will facilitate the provision of medical advice through their associated Rescue Coordination Center (RCC). The use of the signal "CQ" from the International Code (CDPUBNV102) for medical messages is discouraged.
5866	Uruguay	Montevideo Trouville (CWC39).	Any coast radio station.	Message must be in International Code (CDPUBNV102).
5868	Vietnam	RADIOMEDICAL; station call sign.	Ho Chi Minh Ville (XVS). Haiphong (XVG).	

CHAPTER 6

LONG RANGE NAVIGATIONAL AIDS

PART I LORAN-C

600A.	General.	6-3
600B.	Operation.	6-3
600C.	Receivers.	6-4
600D.	Station List.	6-4

PART II SATELLITE NAVIGATION

610A.	General.	6-10
610B.	GPS.	6-10
610C.	DGPS.	6-11
610D.	GLONASS.	6-12

Notes: Greater detail on the theory, principles, and operation of long range navigational aids may be found in The American Practical Navigator (Bowditch)(NVPUB9).

The U.S. Naval Observatory Website provides LORAN-C and GPS user information and data at:
http://tycho.usno.navy.mil/gps.html

The U.S. Coast Guard Navigation Center Website provides Loran-C, GPS, DGPS and general radionavigation user information and status at:
http://www.navcen.uscg.gov/
http://www.navcenter.org (Mirror site)

GPS status is also broadcast from WWV and WWVH (See sec. 200H.).

CHAPTER 6

LONG RANGE NAVIGATIONAL AIDS

PART I LORAN-C

600A. General

LORAN is a long range system which operates on the principle that the difference in time of arrival of signals from two precisely synchronized transmitting stations describes a hyperbolic line of position (LOP). This time difference is measured with a LORAN receiver, and is either converted into geographic LOPs for use with nautical charts overprinted with LORAN lines or directly into latitude and longitude readouts. Since at least two LOPs must be determined to establish a position, the user must be within the range of two pairs of transmitting stations or, as is normally the case, a LORAN chain where a centrally located station serves as a timing reference for the other stations in the chain. This station is called the master station (designated M) and the secondaries are usually designated by the letters V, W, X, Y, or Z. In the United States, LORAN-C is operated by the U.S. Coast Guard. Developed in the late 1950's, LORAN-C operates on a frequency of 100 kHz. Each LORAN-C chain operates on a different pulse group repetition interval (GRI). This allows the operator to make at least two time difference (TD) measurements without changing channels on the receiver. The low frequency of LORAN-C permits usable groundwave signals over several hundred miles.

600B. Operation

The LORAN-C GRI rate structure is such that a GRI between 40,000 and 99,990 microseconds is chosen for each chain. The chain designations are four digit numbers which indicate the GRI in tens of microseconds. For example, the northeast U.S. LORAN-C chain is designated 9960 and has a GRI of 99,600 microseconds.

The accuracy of a LORAN-C fi is determined by the accuracy of the individual lines of position used to establish the fix as well as by their crossing angle of intersection. The accuracy of the individual lines of position depends on the following factors:
– Synchronization of the transmitting stations.
– Operator skill.
– Type of receiver and its condition.
– Skill in plotting the line of position.
– Position of user relative to the transmitting stations.
– Accuracy of charts.
– Accuracy of corrections to compensate for the overland path.

Some LORAN-C receivers employ a coordinate converter function, which is designed to internally compute the latitude and longitude and directly display these values. This eliminates the need for charts overprinted with LORAN-C time difference lines. (CAUTIONARY NOTE: The conversion computation on some models is based upon an all sea water propagation path. This leads to errors if the LORAN-C signals from the various stations involve appreciable overland paths. It is recommended that operators using coordinate converters check the manufacturer's operating manual to determine if and how corrections are to be applied to compensate for overland paths.)

Each LORAN-C rate is continuously monitored to determine that proper synchronization is being maintained. When the synchronization error exceeds the advertised tolerance, the user is advised by the blinking of pulses of the affected secondary and is warned not to use the signal for navigational purposes. The blink signal will cause most receivers to indicate by an alarm that the navigational data displayed is in error. Mariners should check equipment manuals to determine if their receivers are equipped with a Blink Alarm and, if not, should exercise caution when near known hazards or when in restricted waters.

LORAN-C position determinations on or near the baseline extensions are subject to significan errors and should be avoided wherever possible. A great circle line between two LORAN stations is a baseline; the baseline extension is the extension of that line beyond either station.

LORAN-C coverage presently exists along the western coast of North America from the Bering Sea southward along the Gulf of Alaska, western Canada, and the U.S. west coast to the Mexican border. Along the eastern coast of North America, LORAN-C coverage exists from Newfoundland to the southern tip of Florida. Gulf Coast coverage exists from the southern tip of Florida to the Texas-Mexico border. Coverage of Lakes Superior, Michigan, and Huron is provided by the Great Lakes chain, rate 8970. Coverage of Lakes Huron, Erie, and Ontario is provided by the Northeast U.S. chain, rate 9960. Coverage over the central region of the U.S. is provided by the North and South Central chains, rates 8290 and 9610, respectively. For foreign LORAN-C coverage (including that described above) refer to the LORAN-C Plotting Charts diagram in the latest edition of NGA Catalog of Maps, Charts, and Related Products Part 2-Volume I Hydrographic Products (CATP2V01U).

Detailed LORAN-C information is contained in the U.S. Coast Guard's LORAN-C User Handbook (COMDTPUB P16562.6).

NOTE: While the United States continues to evaluate the long-term need for continuation of the Loran-C radionavigation system, the Government will operate the Loran-C system in the short term. The U.S. Government will give users reasonable notice if it concludes that

Loran-C is not needed or is not cost effective, so that users will have the opportunity to transition to alternative navigation aids. With this continued sustainment of the Loran-C service, users will be able to realize additional benefits Improvement of GPS time synchronization of the Loran-C chains and the use of digital receivers may support improved accuracy and coverage of the service. Loran-C will continue to provide a supplemental means of navigation.

For further information and/or operational questions regarding LORAN-C in the United States, contact:

COMMANDING OFFICER
U.S. COAST GUARD NAVIGATION CENTER
7323 TELEGRAPH ROAD
ALEXANDRIA VA 22315-3998

Telephone: (1) 703-313-5900.
Fax: (1) 703-313-5920.

The Navigation Information Service (NIS) is internet accessible through the U.S. Coast Guard Navigation Center Website at:
http://www.navcen.uscg.gov/
http://www.navcenter.org (Mirror site)

FOREIGN LORAN-C COVERAGE: In 1992, the U.S. Coast Guard, which operated LORAN-C overseas for the Department of Defense, initiated plans to accomplish transfer or closure of U.S. Coast Guard LORAN-C stations located on foreign soil. As a result of these efforts, new LORAN-C systems have developed in areas of the world previously covered by the U.S. chains.

The countries of Norway, Denmark, Germany, Ireland, the Netherlands and France have established a common LORAN-C system known as the Northwest European Loran-C System (NELS). The developing system will be comprised of nine stations forming four chains. Since 1995, two chains, Bo and Ejde, have been in experimental (continuous) operation. The Sylt chain became operational in late 1995, but users are warned of its unstable condition. The Lessay chain became operational in September 1997.

For further information regarding NELS, contact:

NELS COORDINATING AGENCY OFFICE
LANGKAIA 1
N-0150 OSLO NORWAY

Telephone: 47 2309 2476.
Fax: 47 2309 2391.
Internet: http://www.nels.org

The countries of Japan, the People's Republic of China, the Republic of Korea and the Russian Federation have established an organization known as the Far East Radionavigation Service (FERNS). Japan took over operation of the former U.S. Coast Guard stations in its territory and they are currently operated by the Japanese Maritime Safety Agency (JMSA). In 1996, f ve chains (Korea, North China Sea, East China Sea, South China Sea, and Russian) became operational.

600C.   Receivers

There are many types of LORAN-C receivers available. Each type employs various techniques for acquiring and tracking LORAN-C signals, and for indicating the time difference or position information to the user. A LORAN-C receiver which will be useful within the limits of the Coast Guard's coverage for the U.S., and which is capable of measuring positions with the accuracy which is advertised for LORAN-C, has the following characteristics:
– It acquires the LORAN-C signals automatically, without the use of an oscilloscope.
– It identifie master and secondary groundwave pulses automatically.
– It tracks the signals automatically once they have been acquired.
– It displays two time difference readings, to a precision of at least one tenth of a microsecond, and/or latitude and longitude.
– It has notch filter to minimize the effects of radio frequency interference in the area of its operation.
– It automatically detects blink and alerts the operator.

Proper LORAN-C receiver installation is necessary to ensure optimum results. Some of the essential elements of good LORAN-C receiver installations are:
– Use of the correct antenna and antenna coupler. Mount the antenna as high as possible and away from all metal objects, stays, and other antennas. Do not connect any other equipment to a LORAN-C antenna.
– Connect both the antenna coupler and the receiver to a good ground. LORAN-C, operating at low frequency, requires proper grounding.
– Electrical and electronic interference, or noise, can come from many sources, both aboard the vessel as well as from the surrounding environment. Onboard noise comes from anything that generates or uses electricity; it is a more severe problem at 100 kHz than at higher frequencies, and it must be suppressed in order to have good results from LORAN-C. Alternators, generators, ignition systems, electrical motors, fluorescen lights, radars, and television sets are examples of interfering sources. Interference suppression may include installation of filters shields, grounds, and capacitors. Interference suppression should be accomplished with the vessel engine running.
– Protection of the LORAN-C receiver from excessive heat, dampness, salt spray, and vibration must be ensured. Do not mount the receiver in direct sunlight or within one meter of your magnetic compass. Provide adequate ventilation.

600D.   Station List

LORAN-C stations, grouped geographically by chains, are contained in the following list.

LONG RANGE NAVIGATIONAL AIDS

(1) No.	(2) Name	(3) Type	(4) Component	(5) Position	(6) Freq.	(7) Remarks
			NORTH PACIFIC CHAIN			
6100	St. Paul, AK 9990 (SS1).	LORAN-C	Master	57 09 12N 170 15 06W		
	Attu Is., AK 9990-X.		Secondary	52 49 44N 173 10 50E		
	Port Clarence, AK 9990-Y.		Secondary	65 14 40N 166 53 12W		
	Kodiak, AK 9990-Z.		Secondary	57 26 20N 152 22 11W		
			RUSSIAN (CHAYKA)-AMERICAN CHAIN			
6105	Petropavlovsk, Russia 5980.	LORAN-C	Master	53 07 48N 157 41 43E		
	Attu Is., AK 5980-X.		Secondary	52 49 44N 173 10 50E		
	Alexandrovsk, Russia 5980-Y.		Secondary	51 04 43N 142 42 05E		
			RUSSIAN CHAIN			
6110	Alexandrovsk, Russia 7950.	LORAN-C	Master	51 04 43N 142 42 05E		
	Petropavlovsk, Russia 7950-W.		Secondary	53 07 48N 157 41 43E		
	Ussuriysk, Russia 7950-X.		Secondary	44 32 00N 131 38 23E		
	Tokachibuto, Hokkaido, Japan 7950-Y.		Secondary	42 44 37N 143 43 10E		
	Okhotsk, Russia 7950-Z.		Secondary	59 25 02N 143 05 23E		
			NORTHWEST PACIFIC CHAIN			
6120	Nii Jima, Japan 8930 (SS3).	LORAN-C	Master	34 24 12N 139 16 19E		
	Gesashi, Okinawa, Japan 8930-W.		Secondary	26 36 25N 128 08 57E		
	Minami-tori Shima (Marcus Island), Japan 8930-X.		Secondary	24 17 08N 153 58 54E		
	Tokachibuto, Hokkaido, Japan 8930-Y.		Secondary	42 44 37N 143 43 10E		
	Pohang, South Korea 8930-Z.		Secondary	36 11 05N 129 20 27E		

LONG RANGE NAVIGATIONAL AIDS

(1) No.	(2) Name	(3) Type	(4) Component	(5) Position	(6) Freq.	(7) Remarks
			KOREA CHAIN			
6122	Pohang, South Korea 9930.	LORAN-C	Master	36 11 05N 129 20 27E		
	Kwangju, South Korea 9930-W.		Secondary	35 02 24N 126 32 27E		
	Gesashi, Okinawa, Japan 9930-X.		Secondary	26 36 25N 128 08 57E		
	Nii Jima, Japan 9930-Y.		Secondary	34 24 12N 139 16 19E		
	Ussuriysk, Russia 9930-Z.		Secondary	44 32 00N 131 38 23E		
			NORTH CHINA SEA CHAIN			
6124	Rongcheng, China 7430.	LORAN-C	Master	37 03 52N 122 19 26E		
	Xuancheng, China 7430-X.		Secondary	31 04 08N 118 53 10E		
	Helong, China 7430-Y.		Secondary	42 43 12N 129 06 27E		
			EAST CHINA SEA CHAIN			
6126	Xuancheng, China 8390.	LORAN-C	Master	31 04 08N 118 53 10E		
	Raoping, China 8390-X.		Secondary	23 43 26N 116 53 45E		
	Rongcheng, China 8390-Y.		Secondary	37 03 52N 122 19 26E		
			SOUTH CHINA SEA CHAIN			
6128	Hexian, China 6780.	LORAN-C	Master	23 58 04N 111 43 10E		
	Raoping, China 6780-X.		Secondary	23 43 26N 116 53 45E		
	Chongzuo, China 6780-Y.		Secondary	22 32 35N 107 13 22E		
			GULF OF ALASKA CHAIN			
6130	Tok, AK 7960 (SL4).	LORAN-C	Master	63 19 43N 142 48 31W		
	Kodiak, AK 7960-X.		Secondary	57 26 20N 152 22 11W		
	Shoal Cove, AK 7960-Y.		Secondary	55 26 21N 131 15 19W		
	Port Clarence, AK 7960-Z.		Secondary	65 14 40N 166 53 12W		

LONG RANGE NAVIGATIONAL AIDS

(1) No.	(2) Name	(3) Type	(4) Component	(5) Position	(6) Freq.	(7) Remarks
			WEST COAST CANADA CHAIN			
6140	Williams Lake, B.C., Canada 5990 (SH1).	LORAN-C	Master	51 57 59N 122 22 02W		
	Shoal Cove, AK 5990-X.		Secondary	55 26 21N 131 15 19W		
	George, WA 5990-Y.		Secondary	47 03 48N 119 44 39W		
	Port Hardy, B.C., Canada 5990-Z.		Secondary	50 36 30N 127 21 28W		
			WEST COAST U.S. CHAIN			
6150	Fallon, NV 9940 (SS6).	LORAN-C	Master	39 33 07N 118 49 56W		
	George, WA 9940-W.		Secondary	47 03 48N 119 44 39W		
	Middletown, CA 9940-X.		Secondary	38 46 57N 122 29 44W		
	Searchlight, NV 9940-Y.		Secondary	35 19 18N 114 48 17W		
			EAST COAST CANADA CHAIN			
6160	Caribou, ME 5930 (SH7).	LORAN-C	Master	46 48 27N 67 55 37W		
	Nantucket, MA 5930-X.		Secondary	41 15 12N 69 58 39W		
	Cape Race, Nfld., Canada 5930-Y.		Secondary	46 46 32N 53 10 28W		
	Fox Harbor, Nfld., Canada 5930-Z.		Secondary	52 22 35N 55 42 28W		
			NEWFOUNDLAND EAST COAST CHAIN			
6165	Comfort Cove, Nfld., Canada 7270.	LORAN-C	Master	49 19 54N 54 51 43W		
	Cape Race, Nfld., Canada 7270-W.		Secondary	46 46 32N 53 10 28W		
	Fox Harbor, Nfld., Canada 7270-X.		Secondary	52 22 35N 55 42 28W		
			GREAT LAKES CHAIN			
6170	Dana, IN 8970.	LORAN-C	Master	39 51 08N 87 29 12W		
	Malone, FL 8970-W.		Secondary	30 59 39N 85 10 09W		
	Seneca, NY 8970-X.		Secondary	42 42 51N 76 49 33W		
	Baudette, MN 8970-Y.		Secondary	48 36 50N 94 33 18W		
	Boise City, OK 8970-Z.		Secondary	36 30 21N 102 53 59W		

LONG RANGE NAVIGATIONAL AIDS

(1) No.	(2) Name	(3) Type	(4) Component	(5) Position	(6) Freq.	(7) Remarks
			NORTHEAST U.S. CHAIN			
6180	Seneca, NY 9960 (SS4).	LORAN-C	Master	42 42 51N 76 49 33W		
	Caribou, ME 9960-W.		Secondary	46 48 27N 67 55 37W		
	Nantucket, MA 9960-X.		Secondary	41 15 12N 69 58 39W		
	Carolina Beach, NC 9960-Y.		Secondary	34 03 46N 77 54 46W		
	Dana, IN 9960-Z.		Secondary	39 51 08N 87 29 12W		
			SOUTHEAST U.S. CHAIN			
6190	Malone, FL 7980 (SL2).	LORAN-C	Master	30 59 39N 85 10 09W		
	Grangeville, LA 7980-W.		Secondary	30 43 33N 90 49 43W		
	Raymondville, TX 7980-X.		Secondary	26 31 55N 97 50 00W		
	Jupiter, FL 7980-Y.		Secondary	27 01 59N 80 06 53W		
	Carolina Beach, NC 7980-Z.		Secondary	34 03 46N 77 54 46W		
			EJDE CHAIN			
6205	Ejde, Faroe Is., Denmark 9007.	LORAN-C	Master	62 17 59N 7 04 26W		
	Jan Mayen Is., Norway 9007-W.		Secondary	70 54 51N 8 43 56W		
	Bo, Norway 9007-X.		Secondary	68 38 06N 14 27 47E		
	Vaerlandet, Norway 9007-Y.		Secondary	61 17 49N 4 41 46E		
			BO CHAIN			
6215	Bo, Norway 7001.	LORAN-C	Master	68 38 06N 14 27 47E		
	Jan Mayen Is., Norway 7001-X.		Secondary	70 54 51N 8 43 56W		
	Berlevag, Norway 7001-Y.		Secondary	70 50 43N 29 12 15E		
			SYLT CHAIN			
6220	Sylt, Germany 7499.	LORAN-C	Master	54 48 29N 8 17 36E		
	Lessay, France 7499-X.		Secondary	49 08 55N 1 30 17W		
	Vaerlandet, Norway 7499-Y.		Secondary	61 17 49N 4 41 46E		

LONG RANGE NAVIGATIONAL AIDS

(1) No.	(2) Name	(3) Type	(4) Component	(5) Position	(6) Freq.	(7) Remarks
			LESSAY CHAIN			
6225	Lessay, France 6731.	LORAN-C	Master	49 08 55N 1 30 17W		
	Soustons, France 6731-X.		Secondary	43 44 23N 1 22 49W		
	Sylt, Germany 6731-Z.		Secondary	54 48 29N 8 17 36E		
			NORTH SAUDI ARABIAN CHAIN			
6240	Afif, Saudi Arabia 8830.	LORAN-C	Master	23 48 37N 42 51 18E		
	Salwa, Saudi Arabia 8830-W.		Secondary	24 50 02N 50 34 13E		
	Al Khamasin, Saudi Arabia 8830-X.		Secondary	20 28 02N 44 34 53E		
	Ash Shaykh Humayd, Saudi Arabia 8830-Y.		Secondary	28 09 16N 34 45 41E		
	Al Muwassam, Saudi Arabia 8830-Z.		Secondary	16 25 56N 42 48 05E		
			INDIA (BOMBAY) CHAIN			
6260	Dhrangadhara 6042.	LORAN-C	Master	23 00 14N 71 31 39E		
	Veraval 6042-W.		Secondary	20 57 07N 70 20 13E		
	Billimora 6042-X.		Secondary	20 45 40N 73 02 17E		
			INDIA (CALCUTTA) CHAIN			
6270	Balasore 5543.	LORAN-C	Master	21 29 08N 86 55 18E		
	Patpur 5543-W.		Secondary	20 26 48N 85 49 47E		
	Diamond Harbor 5543-X.		Secondary	22 10 18N 88 12 25E		

LONG RANGE NAVIGATIONAL AIDS

PART II SATELLITE NAVIGATION

610A. General

Satellite navigation presently consists of two global systems. Each may be considered a refinemen of celestial navigation, using artificia earth-orbiting satellites to form an electronic "constellation", serviced by land-based control and tracking stations, and passively "sighted" by mobile receivers. Both systems provide precise, global, and continuous position-fixin capabilities, in all weather, to a properly equipped user.

The U.S. Air Force system is the NAVSTAR Global Positioning System (GPS). GPS development began in 1973 and reached full operational capability in 1995. (The U.S. Navy system, the Navy Navigation Satellite System (NAVSAT, also known as Transit) became operational in 1964 and ceased operation as a positioning and timing system on December 31, 1996. Users should recognize that navigational equipment using the NAVSAT system should no longer be used since any signals received will no longer provide valid position or timing references.)

The Russian system is the Global Navigation Satellite System (GLONASS). GLONASS became fully operational in January 1996.

610B. GPS

GPS is a highly precise satellite-based radionavigation system providing three-dimensional positioning, velocity, and time information. GPS is an all-weather system with continuous and worldwide coverage. GPS consists of three segments: space, control, and user.

The Space Segment is composed of 24 operational satellites in six orbital planes. The satellites operate in circular 20,200 km (10,900 nm) orbits at an inclination angle, relative to the equator, of 55° and with a 12-hour period. The satellites are spaced in orbit so that at any time, a minimum of six satellites are observable from any position on earth, providing instantaneous position and time information.

Each satellite transmits on two L band frequencies: 1575.42 MHz (L1) and 1227.6 MHz (L2). Three pseudo-random noise (PRN) ranging codes are in use:
- The coarse/acquisition (C/A) code has a 1.023 MHz chip rate, a period of one millisecond, and is used primarily to acquire the P-code.
- The precise (P) code has a 10.23 MHz rate, a period of seven days, and is the principal navigation ranging code.
- The Y-code is used in place of the P-code whenever the anti-spoofing (A-S) mode of operation is act vated.

L1 carries a P-code and a C/A-code. L2 carries the P-code. A navigation data message is superimposed on the codes. The same navigation data message is carried on both frequencies. This message contains satellite ephemeris data, atmospheric propagation correction data, and satellite clock bias.

Selective Availability (SA), the denial of full accuracy, is accomplished by manipulating the navigation message orbit data (epsilon) and/or the satellite clock frequency (dither). Anti-spoofin (A-S) guards against fake transmissions of satellite data by encrypting the P-code to form the Y-code.

The Control Segment consists of f ve monitor stations, three of which have uplink capabilities, located in Colorado, Hawaii, Kwajalein, Diego Garcia, and Ascension Island. The monitor stations use a GPS receiver to passively track all satellites in view, accumulating ranging data from the satellites' signals. The information from the monitor stations is processed at the Master Control Station (MCS), located in Colorado Springs, Colorado, to determine satellite orbits and to update the navigation message of each satellite. The updated information is transmitted to the satellites via ground antennas. The ground antennas, located at Kwajalein, Diego Garcia, and Ascension Island, are also used for transmitting and receiving satellite control information.

The User Segment consists of antennas and receiver-processors that provide positioning, velocity, and precise timing to the user. The GPS receiver makes time-of-arrival measurements of the satellite signals to obtain the distance between the user and the satellites. The distance calculations, known as pseudoranges, together with range rate information, are converted to yield system time and the user's three-dimensional position and velocity with respect to the satellite system. A time coordination factor then relates the satellite system to earth coordinates. A minimum of four pseudoranges are needed to produce a three-dimensional fi (latitude, longitude, and altitude). GPS receivers compute fi information in terms of the World Geodetic System (1984), which may need datum shift correction before it can be accurately plotted on a chart.

There are three different types of receivers. Sequential receivers track only one satellite at a time, computing a f x after a series of pseudoranges have been sequentially measured; these receivers are inexpensive but slow. Continuous receivers have at least four channels to process information from several satellites simultaneously; these process fi information the fastest. Multiplex receivers switch at a fast rate from satellite to satellite, receiving and processing data from several satellites simultaneously, producing a fix by a sort of "round-robin" process

GPS provides two levels of service for position determination:
- The Standard Positioning Service (SPS) for general public use. (Until 1 May 2000, the SPS signal accuracy was intentionally degraded to protect U.S. national security interests through the process of Selective Availability.)
- The encoded Precise Positioning Service (PPS) primarily intended for use by the Department of Defense.

Accuracy of a GPS fi varies with the capability of the user equipment. SPS is the standard level of positioning and timing accuracy that is available, without restrictions, to any user on a continuous worldwide basis. SPS provides positions with a horizontal accuracy of approximately 100 meters. (This accuracy specificatio includes the effects of SA.) PPS provides full system accuracy to designated users. Selective Availability was set to zero (ceased) as of midnight (EDT) 1 May 2000. Users should experience a GPS horizontal accuracy of 10-20 meters or better.

NOTE: The following information is provided for informational purposes only and does not relieve any existing domestic or international safety, operational, or material requirement:

It has come to the attention of the U.S. Coast Guard and Federal Communications Commission that certain consumer electronics-grade active VHF/UHF marine television antennas are causing operational degradation in the performance of GPS receivers. This interference may be realized as a display of inaccurate position information or a complete loss of GPS receiver acquisition and tracking ability.

The interference is not limited to the GPS equipment onboard the vessel with the installed active marine television antennae. There have been reports of interference occurring on other vessels and installations operating up to 2000 feet away from vessels using such antennas.

In one particular case, the interference caused the position of the vessel as displayed on the electronic chart to move erratically and dramatically, often across large expanses of land. Various data displays indicated erroneous information such as excessive speeds. In these instances the problem would occasionally correct itself while at other times required resetting the system.

If you are experiencing recurring outages or degradation of your GPS receiver you should perform an on-off test of your TV antenna. If turning off the power to the antenna results in improvement in the GPS receiver performance, the antenna may be the source of interference in the GPS band. In that case, you should contact the manufacturer of the antenna and identify the symptoms. If the test is not positive and the GPS interference persists, contact the watchstander at the Coast Guard Navigation Information Service at:

Telephone: (1) 703-313-5900.
E-mail: nisws@navcen.uscg.mil.

The following antennae models were indentifie during investigations of GPS interference:
– TDP (Tandy Distribution Products) Electronics - MINI STATE Electronic Amplifie UHF/VHF TV Antenna - Models 5MS740, 5MS750, 5MS921
– Radio Shack Corporation - Long Range Amplifie Omni Directional TV Antenna - Model 15-1624
(For further information see:
http://support.radioshack.com/SUPPORT_VIDEO/DOC68/68779.HTM)

– Shakespeare Corporation - SeaWatch - Models 2040/Code Date 02A00, 2050/Code Date 03A00 (Code Dates are found on the antenna power supply.)
(For further information see:
http://www.shakespeare-marine.com/ANTENNAS/TV/SAFETYALERT-TVANTENNAS.HTM

610C. DGPS

The U.S. Coast Guard Navigation Center operates the Maritime Differential GPS (DGPS) Service and the developing Nationwide DGPS (NDGPS) Service, consisting of two control centers and over 60 remote broadcast sites. The service broadcasts correction signals on marine radiobeacon frequencies to improve the accuracy of and integrity to GPS-derived positions. The system is operated to International Telecommunications Union (ITU) and Radio Technical Commission for Maritime Services (RTCM) standards. More than forty foreign maritime nations have implemented standard DGPS services modeled after the U.S. Coast Guard's system to significantl enhance maritime safety in their critical waterways.

The U.S. Coast Guard's Maritime DGPS Service provides 10-meter (2 dRMS) navigation accuracy in all established coverage areas, integrity alarms for GPS and DGPS out-of-tolerance conditions within 10 seconds of detection, and an availability of 99.7% per month. Typically the positional error of a DGPS position is 1 to 3 meters, greatly enhancing harbor entrance and approach navigation. The system provides service for coastal coverage (to a minimum range of 20 nm from shore) of the continental U.S., the Great Lakes, Puerto Rico/U.S. Virgin Islands, portions of Alaska and Hawaii, and a greater part of the Mississippi River Basin.

DGPS reference stations determine range errors and generate corrections for all GPS satellites in view. The DGPS signals are broadcast, using existing Coast Guard radiobeacons, on frequencies in the 285-325 kHz band. Monitor stations independently verify the quality of the DGPS broadcast.

The Maritime DGPS service achieved Full Operational Capability (FOC) on 15 March 1999. The Coast Guard advises that Coast Guard DGPS broadcasts should not be used under any circumstances where a sudden system failure or inaccuracy could constitute a safety hazard. Users are further cautioned to use all available navigational tools to ensure proper evaluation of positioning solutions.

The U.S. Department of Transportation is coordinating the implementation of the Nationwide DGPS (NDGPS) Service. NDGPS is an expansion of the Maritime DGPS network and, when complete, this service will provide uniform differential GPS coverage of the continental U.S. and selected portions of Hawaii and Alaska regardless of terrain, man made, and other surface obstructions. The predictable accuracy of the NDGPS service within all established coverage areas is specifie 10 meters (2dRMS) or better. Typical system performance is better than 1 meter in the vicinity of the broadcast site. Achievable accuracy degrades at an approximate rate of 1 meter for each 150 km distance from the broadcast site. The service also provides a GPS integrity monitoring capability; it gives an alarm to users within 6 seconds of detecting a fault with the signal from any GPS satellite in view. Availability, on a per site per month basis, will be 99.9% for dual coverage areas and 99.7% for single coverage areas. The NDGPS Service will achieve FOC when it provides dual coverage of the continental U.S. and selected portions of Hawaii and Alaska with single coverage elsewhere.

A complete list of all U.S. Coast Guard DGPS broadcast sites is available from the Navigation Center. For further information and/or operational questions regarding GPS or DGPS, or to report GPS/DGPS service degradations, outages, and other incidents or anomalies, contact:

COMMANDING OFFICER
U.S. COAST GUARD NAVIGATION CENTER
7323 TELEGRAPH ROAD
ALEXANDRIA VA 22315-3998

Telephone: (1) 703-313-5900.
Fax: (1) 703-313-5920.

The Navigation Information Service (NIS) is internet accessible through the U.S. Coast Guard Navigation Center Website at:

http://www.navcen.uscg.gov/
http://www.navcenter.org (Mirror site)

610D. GLONASS

The Russian Global Navigation Satellite System (GLONASS), similar to GPS, is a space-based navigation system that provides continuous, global, all-weather, precise position, velocity and time information. The space segment consists of 24 satellites in three orbital planes at an altitude of 19,100 km. The satellites operate in circular orbits with an inclination of 64.8° and a period of 11h 15m. All satellites transmit simultaneously, using two carrier frequencies in the L band, to allow users to correct for ionospheric delays of the transmitted signals. However, each satellite is allocated a particular frequency within the band, determined by the frequency channel number of the satellite. These different frequencies allow the user's receiver to identify the satellite. The L1 band ranges from 1602.5625 MHz to 1615.5 MHz in increments of 0.5625 MHz, while the L2 band ranges from 1246.4375 MHz to 1256.5 MHz in increments of 0.4375 MHz. Superimposed to the carrier frequency, the GLONASS satellites modulate their navigation message by using either or both a 5.11 MHz precision (P) code and/or and a 0.511 MHz coarse/acquisition (C/A) code. The satellites also transmit ephemeris data, an almanac of the entire constellation, and correction parameters to the time scale. The coordinate system of the GLONASS satellite orbits is define by the PZ-90 system, formerly the soviet Geodetic System 1985/1990.

The Coordinational Scientifi Informational Center (CSIC) of the Russian Space Forces provides officia information on GLONASS status and plans, information and scientifi method services to increase the efficien y of GLONASS applications. For further information contact:

CSIC OF RUSSIAN SPACE FORCES
PO BOX 14
MOSCOW 117279
RUSSIA

Telephone: 7 095 333 72 00.
Fax: 7 095 333 81 33.
E-mail: sfcsic@space.ru.

Internet: http://www.glonass-center.ru/frame_e.html/

CHAPTER 7

AMVER

700A.	Amver Participation Instructions.	7-3
700B.	Communication Methods for Filing Amver Reports.	7-3
700C.	Special Warnings to Mariners.	7-4
700D.	Amver Voyage Report Types.	7-4

CHAPTER 7

AMVER

700A. Amver Participation Instructions

Amver is a worldwide voluntary vessel reporting system operated by the U.S. Coast Guard to promote safety of life and property at sea. Amver's mission is to quickly provide search and rescue (SAR) authorities, on demand, accurate information on the position and characteristics of vessels near a reported distress. Any merchant vessel on a voyage of greater than 24 hours to anywhere on the globe is welcome to participate in Amver. In general, international participation is voluntary regardless of owner's nationality or vessel's flag voyage origin, or destination. However, there are requirements for certain U.S. fla or U.S. interest vessels.

According to U.S. Maritime Administration (MARAD) regulations, the following vessels must report and regularly update their voyages and positions to the Amver Center:
– United States fla merchant vessels of 1,000 gross tons or more, operating in foreign commerce.
– Foreign fla vessels of 1,000 gross tons or more, for which an Interim War Risk Insurance Binder has been issued under the provisions of Title XII, Merchant Marine Act, 1936.

In accordance with Title 47, Code of Federal Regulations (CFR), Ch. 1, Sec 80.905, the following vessels must participate in the Amver system while engaged on any voyage where the vessel is navigated in the open sea for more than 24 hours:
– United States vessels which transport more than six passengers for hire, operated more than 200 nautical miles from the nearest land.

Information voluntarily provided by vessels to Amver is kept strictly confidential and is protected by the Coast Guard. It will be released only for safety purposes.

Amver's greatest use is in providing SURface PICtures, or SURPICs, to Rescue Coordination Centers (RCCs). A SURPIC either lists latitude/longitude or provides a graphical display of vessels near the position of a distress. It is used by RCCs to coordinate the efforts of merchant vessels and other resources to provide the best and most timely assistance possible to distressed vessels or persons at sea.

There are four types of Amver reports: Sailing Plan, Position Report, Deviation Report, and Arrival Report. NOTE: Departure Reports have been eliminated in favor of the more common practice of filin a combined Sailing Plan/Departure Report upon departure. This combined report is now called simply a Sailing Plan and it should be sent within a few hours before or after departure. The information required for Position and Deviation Reports has been increased to ensure enough information is provided to keep Amver accurate. Also, an end-of-report (Z line) line has been added to facilitate automatic processing of Amver reports.

What and when to report to Amver:

– Sailing Plan, containing complete routing information, should be sent within a few hours before, upon, or within a few hours after departure.
– Position Report should be sent within 24 hours of departure, and subsequently at least every 48 hours until arrival. The destination should also be included in Position Reports.
– Deviation Report should be sent as soon as any voyage information changes which could affect Amver's ability to accurately predict the vessel's position. Changes in course or speed due to weather, ice, change in destination, or any other deviations more than 25NM from the original Sailing Plan should be reported as soon as possible.
– Arrival Report should be sent upon arrival at the port of destination.
– At the discretion of the Master, reports may be sent more frequently than the above schedule; for example, in heavy weather or under other adverse conditions.

Amver also needs information that describes communications equipment, Inmarsat numbers, radio watch schedule, medical personnel on board, and so forth. This information is collected separately, retained in the automatic data processing system, periodically validated, and used only for search and rescue purposes.

700B. Communication Methods for Filing Amver Reports

The following methods are recommended for ships to transmit Amver reports:

ELECTRONIC MAIL VIA THE INTERNET: If a ship already has an inexpensive means of sending electronic mail to an internet address, this is a preferred method. Electronic mail may be sent via satellite or via HF radio, depending on the ship's equipment and arrangements with communications providers ashore. Ships must be equipped with a personal computer, an interface between the computer and the ship's communications equipment, and the appropriate software. NOTE: The e-mail path on shore to the Amver Center is essentially free, but the communications service provider may still charge from ship-to-shore. Amver Address: amvermsg@amver.org or amvermsg@amver.com.

AMVER/SEAS "COMPRESSED MESSAGE" (INMARSAT-C VIA TELENOR): Ships equipped with an Inmarsat Standard C transceiver with flop y drive and capability to transmit a binary fil (ship's GMDSS Inmarsat-C transceiver can be used); an IBM-compatible computer (not part of the ship's GMDSS System) with hard drive, 286 or better PC, VGA graphics; an interface between them; and the Amver/SEAS software (available free of charge from the U.S. National Oceanic and Atmospheric Administration, NOAA), may send combined

AMVER

Amver/Weather observation messages free of charge via Telenor Land Earth Stations at:

- 001 Atlantic Ocean Region-West (AORW)-Southbury.
- 101 Atlantic Ocean Region-East (AORE)-Southbury.
- 201 Pacific Ocean R gion (POR)-Santa Paula.
- 321 Indian Ocean Region (IOR)-Aussaguel.

Amver Address: NOAA phone number entered in the "addressbook" (for further information on how to fin the NOAA phone number and to correctly setup the addressbook, see the instruction sheet for your specifi brand of Inmarsat-C transceiver).

Amver/SEAS software can be downloaded from the NOAA SEAS Website at:
   http://seas.amverseas.noaa.gov/seas/
or requested from:

TELENOR SATELLITE SERVICES, INC.
1101 WOOTTON PARKWAY
ROCKVILLE MD   20852

Telephone: (01) 301-838-7800 or 1-800-685-7898.
E-mail: customer.care@telenor.com.

HF RADIOTELEX: Amver reports may be file via the HF radiotelex service of U.S. Coast Guard Communications Stations. Further information on how to send Amver messages by this method is provided in Chapter 4, Appendix B (see COAST GUARD (HF RADIOTELEX)), or at the U.S. Coast Guard Navigation Center Website:
   http://www.navcen.uscg.gov/marcomms/high_frequency/call.htm

HF RADIO: Amver reports may also be file by HF radio at no cost via U.S. Coast Guard contractual agreement with the following ShipCom Radio Network public coast stations (see Chapter 4, Appendix B, for complete frequency listing):
 – Mobile Marine Radio (WLO)
 – Mobile (WCL)
 – Marina del Ray (KNN)
 – Seattle (KLB)
  Internet: http://www.wloradio.com or
       http://www.shipcom.com

TELEX: Amver reports may be file via telex using either satellite (code 43) or HF radio. Ships must pay the tariffs for satellite communications. Telex is a preferred method when less costly methods are not available. Amver Address: (0) (230) 127594 AMVER NYK.

TELEFAX: In the event other communications media are unavailable or inaccessible, Amver reports may be faxed directly to the Amver Computer Center. However, this is the least desirable method of communications, since it involves manual input of information to the computer vice electronic processing. NOTE: Do not fax reports to the Amver Maritime Relations Offic in New York, since it is not staffed 24 X 7, and relay and processing of reports is delayed pending normal (Mon.-Fri.) business hours. The telefacsimile phone number to the U.S. Coast Guard Operations Systems Center in Martinsburg, West Virginia is (01) 304-264-2505.

The following method is discouraged:

CW (MORSE CODE): Due to the decline in its usage, the number of coast stations supporting it, its high cost, potential for error, and the mandatory carriage of upgraded GMDSS communications capabilities, ships are discouraged from using this medium.

For more information regarding Amver reporting, visit the Amver Website at http://www.amver.com or contact:

Mr. Rick Kenney
AMVER MARITIME RELATIONS OFFICE
USCG BATTERY PARK BUILDING
1 SOUTH STREET
NEW YORK NY   10004-1499

Telephone: (1) 212-668-7762.
Fax: (1) 212-668-7684.
E-mail: RKenney@BatteryNY.uscg.mil.

700C.   Special Warnings to Mariners

Special Warnings reflec U.S. Government policy on international incidents with political ramifications The content of such Special Warnings is the responsibility of the Department of State and National Geospatial-Intelligence Agency (NGA). NGA is the disseminating agency for such messages since its Radio Navigational Warning Broadcast System can be received by all U.S. flag merchant ships

United States fla vessels in an affected area are required to acknowledge receipt of a Special Warning through the use of the Remarks line (X line) in their next regular Amver report. For the purpose of this requirement, all vessels are deemed to be in an affected area if within 500 miles or 1 day's steaming of a reported incident.

700D.   Amver Voyage Report Types

There are four types of Amver Reports: Sailing Plan, Position, Deviation, and Arrival Reports.

REPORTING FORMAT: Each Amver message consists of report lines. There are 15 types of lines. The firs line in every report begins with the word "AMVER" followed by a slash (/), a two letter code identifying the report type, and ends with a double slash (//). Each remaining line begins with a specifi letter followed by a slash (/) to identify the line type. The remainder of each line contains one or more data field separated by single slashes (/). Each line ends with a double slash (//). All reports should end with an end-of-report line (Z line).

REPORTING DATA: Amver participants need to be familiar with the four types of reports. Report identifier are as follows:

AMVER/SP// denotes Sailing Plan.
AMVER/PR// denotes Position Report.
AMVER/DR// denotes Deviation Report.
AMVER/FR// denotes Arrival Report.

AMVER

An example and explanation of each of the four types of the Amver reports follows. Numbers in parentheses refer to footnotes at the end of the section.

SAILING PLAN: A Sailing Plan should be sent within a few hours before, upon, or within a few hours after departure. It must include enough information to predict the vessel's actual position within 25 nautical miles at any time during the voyage, assuming the Sailing Plan is followed exactly. The L lines are used to report route information. These lines are the most complex lines in an Amver report but they are critical to Amver's success. Complete route information should be provided in all Sailing Plans and also in Deviation Reports when the vessel's route or destination changes.

Example:

AMVER/SP//
A/SANDY JOAN/ABCD//
B/110935Z//
E/145//
F/126//
G/NOVOROSSIYSK/4470N/03780E//
I/GIBRALTAR/3600N/00600W/140730Z//
L/RL/140/4130N/02910E/112000Z//
L/RL/140/4010N/02620E/112300Z//
L/RL/140/3630N/02330E/120300Z//
L/RL/140/3650N/01520E/121500Z//
L/RL/140/3760N/01000E/130100Z//
L/RL/060//
M/GKA/GKM//
V/MD/NURSE//
X/NEXT REPORT 120900Z//
X/SITOR INSTALLED. SELCALL NUMBER IS 99999//
Y/MAREP//
Z/EOR//

Explanation:
  Required items:
    AMVER line/SP//
    line A/vessel name/International Radio Call Sign//
    line B/time//(1)
    line E/current course//(5)
    line F/estimated average speed//(6)
    line G/port of departure/latitude/longitude//(2) (3)
    line I/destination/latitude/longitude/ estimated time of arrival//(1)(2)(3)
    line L/route information //(1)(3)(4)
    line Y/relay instructions//(9)
    line Z/end of report//(10)

  Optional items:
    line M/current coastal radio station or satellite number/next coastal radio station, if any//
    line V/onboard medical resources//(7)
    line X/up to 65 characters of amplifying comments//(8)

POSITION REPORT: A Position Report should be sent within 24 hours of departing port and at least once every 48 hours thereafter. The destination should be included, at least in the firs few reports, in case Amver has not received the Sailing Plan information.

Example:
AMVER/PR//
A/SANDY JOAN/ABCD//
B/120300Z//
C/3630N/02330E//
E/145//
F/126//
I/GIBRALTAR/3600N/00600W/140730Z//
M/GKM//
X/NEXT REPORT 131800Z//
Y/MAREP//
Z/EOR//

Explanation:
  Required items:
    AMVER line/PR//
    line A/vessel name/International Radio Call Sign//
    line B/time of position//(1)
    line C/latitude/longitude//(2)(3)
    line E/current course//(5)
    line F/estimated average speed//(6)
    line Y/relay instructions//(9)
    line Z/end of report//(10)
  Recommended items:
    line I/destination/latitude/longitude/ estimated time of arrival//(1)(2)(3)
  Optional items:
    line M/current coastal radio station or satellite number/next coastal radio station, if any//
    line X/up to 65 characters of amplifying comments// (8)(9)

DEVIATION REPORT: Deviation Reports should be sent whenever the vessel deviates significantl (more than 25NM) from its Sailing Plan. Other situations in which Deviation Reports should be sent include, but are not limited to: Change in destination, diverting to evacuate a sick or injured crewmember, diverting to avoid heavy weather, any change of route (as, for example, change based on recommendations from a vessel routing service), stopping to make repairs or await orders, change in anticipated average speed of one knot or more, etc.

Example:

AMVER/DR//
A/SANDY JOAN/ABCD//
B/120600Z//
C/3600N/02245E//
E/095//
F/220//
I/NEW YORK US/4040N/07380W/180800Z//
L/GC/220//
M/GKA/WSL/NMN//
X/DIVERTING BEST SPEED TO NEW YORK//
Y/MAREP//
Z/EOR//

AMVER

Explanation
  Required items:
    AMVER line/DR//
    line A/vessel name/International Radio Call Sign//
    line B/time of position//(1)
    line C/latitude/longitude//(2)(3)
    line E/current course//(5)
    line F/estimated average speed//(6)
    line Y/relay instructions//(9)
    line Z/end of report//(10)
  Required items if destination or route changes:
    line I/destination/latitude/longitude/ estimated time of arrival//(1)(2)(3)
    line L/route information//(4)
  Recommended items (in cases when not required):
    line I/destination/latitude/longitude/ estimated time of arrival//(1)(2)(3)
  Optional items:
    line M/current coastal radio station or satellite number/next coastal radio station, if any//
    line X/up to 65 characters of amplifying comments//(8)

ARRIVAL REPORT: Arrival Reports should be sent upon arrival in the immediate vicinity of the destination port, such as at the sea buoy or pilot station. This report properly terminates the voyage in Amver's computer and ensures the vessel will not appear on an Amver SURPIC until its next voyage.

Example:

AMVER/FR//
A/SANDY JOAN/ABCD//
K/NEW YORK/4040N/07380W/180830Z//
X/PROBLEMS WITH MF XMTR. AGENT ADVISED//
Y/MAREP//
Z/EOR//

Explanation:
  Required items:
    AMVER line/FR//
    line A/vessel name/International Radio Call Sign//
    line K/port name/latitude/longitude/time of arrival//(1)(2)(3)
    line Y/relay instructions//(9)
    line Z/end of report//(10)
  Optional items:
    line X/up to 65 characters of amplifying comments//(8)

Footnotes:
(1) Indicates the time associated with the position given in the C and G lines of the report. All times must be expressed as a six-digit group giving date of month (first two digits), hours and minutes (last four digits). Only Universal Coordinated Time (i.e., Greenwich mean time) is to be used. The six-digit date-time-group is to be followed by either Z, GMT or UTC. The month is optional. If addition of the month is deemed appropriate, the first three letters of the English language month are used. The following examples are acceptable:
  B/290900Z//
  B/290900Z DEC//
  B/290900GMT//
  B/290900UTC//
(2) Both port name and geographic position are required from U.S. flag essels.
(3) Latitude is a four-digit group expressed in degrees and minutes, suffi ed with N for north or S for south. Longitude is a f ve-digit group expressed in degrees and minutes, and suffi ed with E for east or W for west. For example:
  G/4000N/03500W//.
(4) The L lines contain most of the sailing plan information. As many L lines as needed may be used to describe the vessel's intended route. Detailed route information caused by maneuvering over short distances near coasts should not be included. An approximate route using fewer turn points and the "coastal" navigation method should be provided. However, enough turn points should be provided to keep Amver's plot of the vessel's position within 25 nautical miles of the vessel's true position. All L lines except the last one in the report require the following information: /navigation method/leg speed/latitude/longitude/port or landmark name/ETA/estimated time of departure. For example:
  L/RL/125/0258N/07710W/ABACO/111200Z//.
  L/RL/125/0251N/07910W/NWPROVCHAN/112145Z//.
  L/RL/125/0248N/08020W/120255Z//.
  L/RL/125//.
The navigation method is required. There are three types of navigation methods recognized by Amver: Rhumb Line (RL), Great Circle (GC) and Coastal (COASTAL).
Leg speed is useful, but is not required. See footnote (6).
Latitude/longitude are required. See footnote (3).
Port or landmark name is useful, but is not required.
ETA is required. See footnote (1).
ETD is required if the ship will layover at an intermediate point. See footnote (1).
A fina navigation method is required to route the ship to its destination.
Final leg speed is useful, but not required.
(5) True course is a three-digit group.
(6) Speed is a three-digit group in knots and tenths of knots. For example, 20.5 knots would be expressed as 205, without a decimal point.
(7) If the optional V line is used, one or more of the following is required:
  /MD/ for medical doctor or physician.
  /PA/ for physician's assistant or paramedic.
  /NURSE/ for trained nurse.
  /NONE/.
For example:
  V/MD/NURSE//

7 - 6

AMVER

It is important to accurately report a vessel's medical resources EVERY VOYAGE. Medically trained personnel are very scarce on the high seas and this makes them extremely valuable in cases where a member of a vessel's crew becomes ill or injured.

(8) Any information provided in the remarks line will be stored in Amver's automatic data processing system for later review. However, no particular action will be taken, nor will the information be routinely passed to other organizations. The remarks line cannot be used as a substitute for sending information to other search-and-rescue authorities or organizations. However, Amver will, at the request of other SAR authorities, forward remarks line information to the requesting agencies.

Changes in vessel data: When a vessel changes name, flag owners, etc., it is important to include the number assigned the ship in Lloyds Register of Shipping to ensure the Amver database is kept current.

(9) The Y line is used to request relay of the Amver report to certain other reporting systems. In accordance with Title 46 CFR, all U.S. fla merchant vessels and certain other vessels are REQUIRED to report their positions to MARAD via participation in the Amver system. Such vessels must include the keyword "MAREP" in the Y line of every Amver report.

Presently, Amver and the Japanese Regional Reporting System (JASREP) cooperate with each other by accepting and complying with relay requests. For example:

Y/MAREP//
Y/JASREP//
Y/JASREP/MAREP//
Y/AMVER//
Y/AMVER/MAREP//

(10) EOR (End of Report) must be the last line in every Amver report as it is used by the Amver computer to signal the end of the report.

For example:

Z/EOR//

CHAPTER 8

COMMUNICATION INSTRUCTIONS FOR U.S. MERCHANT SHIPS

Chapter 8 sets forth instructions and procedures for U.S. merchant vessels to establish communucations in order to receive and send information to/from the Homeland Defense (HLD) organization, Naval Cooperation and Guidance for Shipping (NCAGS), during normal operations or times of crisis.

PART I U.S. NAVAL COOPERATION AND GUIDANCE FOR SHIPPING (NCAGS)

800A.	General.	8-3
800B.	History of NCAGS	8-3
800C.	NCAGS Organization	8-3
800D.	Questions and Comments	8-4

PART II COORDINATION WITH NCAGS

810A.	General.	8-6
810B.	Elements of the NCAGS	8-6

PART III COMMUNICATIONS WITH NCAGS

820A.	General.	8-7
820B.	Methods of Communication	8-7
820C.	Forms and Message Formats	8-7

PART IV CONTAMINATION PREDICTION SYSTEM FOR MERCHANT SHIPS AT SEA AND THE MERWARN SYSTEM

830A.	Significance of NBC Warnings	8-9
830B.	The MERWARN System, Warnings to Merchant Ships at Sea	8-9
830C.	MERWARN Originating and Diversion Authorities	8-9
830D.	Precedence of NBC Messages	8-9
830E.	Method of Promulgation	8-9
830F.	Relay Responsibilities	8-9
830G.	Danger Zones	8-9
830H.	MERWARN NBC EDM	8-9
830I.	MERWARN NBC 3 NUC, Standard Format	8-10
830J.	MERWARN NBC 3 NUC, Plain Language Format	8-10
830K.	MERWARN NBC CDM	8-10
830L.	MERWARN NBC 3 CHEM	8-11
830M.	MERWARN DIVERSION ORDER	8-11
830N.	Other Warnings	8-11
830O.	Ground Zero	8-11
830P.	Effective Downwind Direction and Downwind Speed	8-12
830Q.	Fallout Pattern Criteria	8-12
830R.	Fallout Plotting in Merchant Ships	8-12
830S.	Plotting from MERWARN NBC 3 NUC	8-12
830T.	Contamination Plotting in Merchant Ships	8-13
APPENDIX A	Instruction to Masters in an Emergency on Defense Against Nuclear Fallout	8-15

CHAPTER 8

COMMUNICATION INSTRUCTIONS FOR U.S. MERCHANT SHIPS

PART I U.S. NAVAL COOPERATION AND GUIDANCE FOR SHIPPING (NCAGS)

800A. General

The purpose of this section is to provide guidance to ship owners, operators, Masters, and officer on the arrangements for Naval Cooperation and Guidance for Shipping (NCAGS) in order to enhance the safety of merchant ships and to support military operations. It provides information on the provision of NCAGS support.

In periods of crisis, conflict national emergency or war, naval authorities may direct the movement of merchant ships (including routing and diversion) so that they may be better protected from hostilities and not interfere with possible active Naval and/or Joint Military Operations. The NCAGS organization is the principal U.S. resource to carry out this function. The purpose of NCAGS is to ensure the efficient management and safe passage of merchant ships

This mission primarily involves:
– the establishment of an organization and framework for communicating directions, advisories, concerns, and/or information among operational forces, merchant shipping, and maritime organizations;
– the deconflictio of merchant vessel sailings/operations, for safety to preclude interference with naval activities;
– and making recommendations to the theater/ operational commander on the extent and type of protection that may be provided to merchant shipping.

800B. History of NCAGS

NCAGS was formerly known as NCAPS (Naval Coordination and Protection of Shipping). NCAPS was originally established to meet a Cold War-era national need to protect merchant shipping against a global open ocean threat. NCAPS policy included escorting and routing of large convoys of merchant shipping.

The threat to merchant shipping has changed and so has the Naval Control of Shipping (NCS) mission. The primary threat to U.S. merchant vessels is no longer considered to be traditional naval vessels under the fla of a known enemy; instead, the threat is terrorism. The NCAGS mission is to provide U.S. military commanders the information necessary to provide Maritime Domain Awareness (MDA). The goal of MDA is to assist in Homeland Defense (HLD) by maintaining as much real-time information as possible regarding merchant shipping, such as positions, destinations, cargo, etc. As a result, the NCAGS organization can provide U.S. and allied merchant vessels the information needed to help prevent terrorist attacks at sea or inport.

800C. NCAGS Organization

NCAGS doctrine has evolved with the changing threat posed both on merchant shipping and by merchant shipping in the context of regional operations and maritime HLD. The NCAGS organization addresses both the traditional protection and control of shipping in a region and the emerging requirement of maritime HLD, where merchant shipping may be either the protagonist, or target, requiring the establishment of communications to increase maritime situational awareness of merchant shipping. NCAGS doctrine applies to maritime HLD, contingency support, and general economic shipping.

Types of contingency support shipping include naval vessels of the Military Sealift Command (MSC), shipping operated or chartered by the U.S. Government to support naval operations or to meet U.S. policy objectives, crisis response shipping, and relief shipping chartered by government agencies.

Types of economic shipping include vessels engaged in normal commercial trade worldwide, regardless of fla or ownership, or such other shipping that is not under the control or direction of the U.S. Government.

Specifi to maritime HLD operations in the United States Northern Command (USNORTHCOM) Area of Responsibility (AOR), a new organization was developed in an effort to execute the required mission to improve maritime HLD and to support the USCG as the lead federal agency for maritime Homeland Security (HLS). As an element of the Joint Force Maritime Component Commander (JFMCC), the NCAGS organization provides direct support to USNORTHCOM's mission of conducting operations to deter, prevent, and defeat maritime threats and aggression. NCAGS works jointly with the United States Coast Guard (USCG). The NCAGS organization consists of Shipping Coordination Centers (SCCs) geographically positioned to assist in improving merchant shipping coordination and providing positional information of merchant vessels operating in the USNORTHCOM AOR. The SCCs are the firs step in creating a global merchant vessel tracking capability for the maritime domain.

800D. Questions and Comments

Ship's Officers ship owners, and operators are encouraged to submit questions and comments on procedures outlined in this chapter to:

U.S. FLEET FORCES COMMAND
MR. ERIC SHAFFER N35
1562 MITSCHER AVENUE SUITE 250
NORFOLK VA   23551-2487

COMMUNICATION INSTRUCTIONS FOR U.S. MERCHANT SHIPS

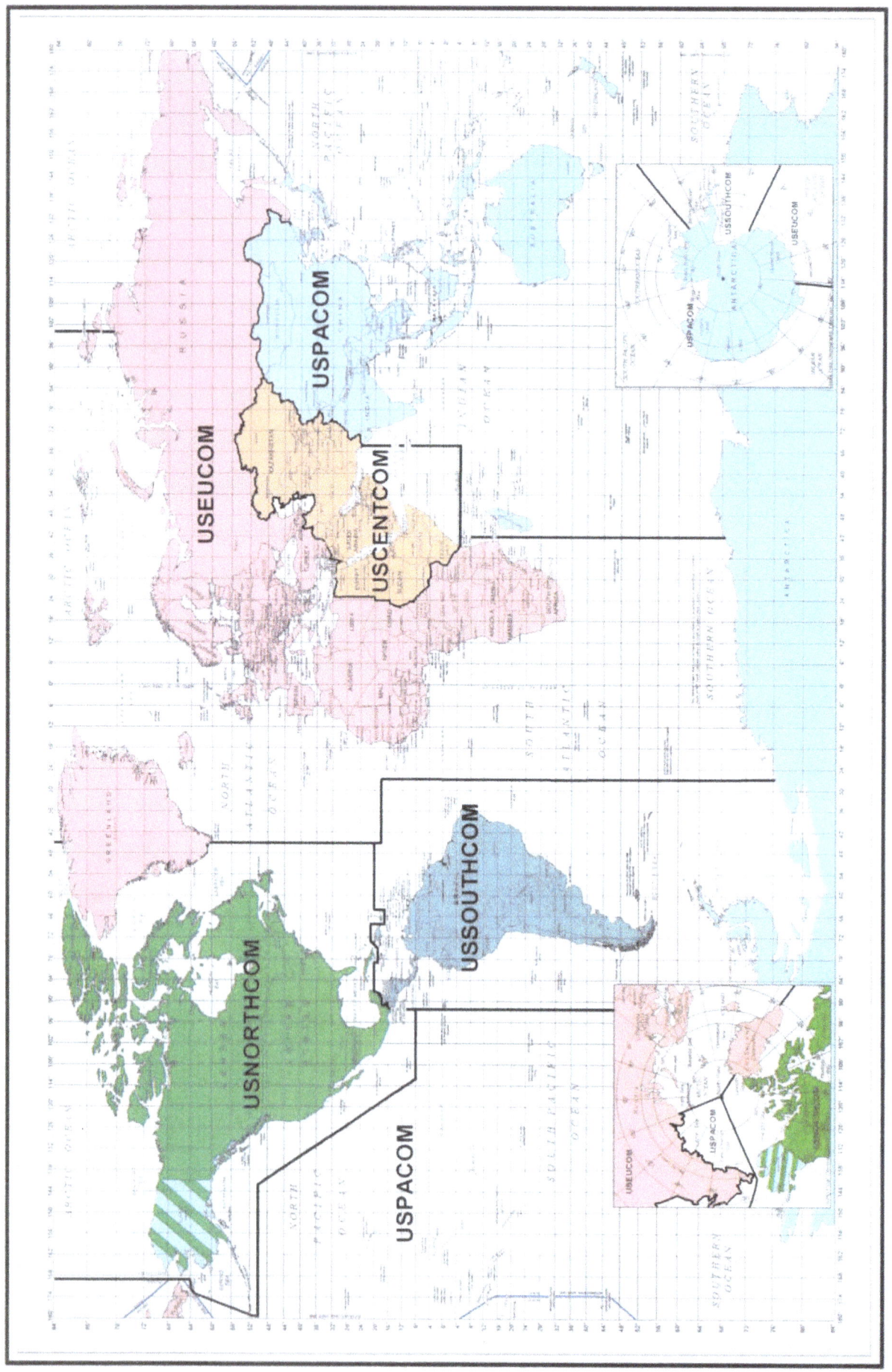

THE WORLD WITH U.S. COMMANDERS' AREAS OF RESPONSIBILITY

PART II COORDINATION WITH NCAGS

810A. General

The primary organization responsible for executing the NCAGS mission is the Shipping Coordination Center (SCC). A SCC bridges the gap between military leaders responsible for HLD and U.S. merchant shipping. NCAGS support provided by the SCC includes military cooperation, guidance, advice, assistance, and supervision to merchant shipping to enhance the safety of U.S. and allied merchant ships and to support military operations by maintaining awareness of merchant shipping positions around the U.S. The purpose of NCAGS is to make use of cooperation between military and civil maritime authorities and agencies and the commercial shipping industry in order to facilitate an uninterrupted fl w of maritime commerce in periods of peace and conflic and simultaneously minimize disruption to military operations.

The cooperation and frequent exchange of information achieve this goal. An accurate assessment of the merchant shipping picture is critical to the accomplishment of this goal. Masters will be asked to provide basic information concerning their ship, cargo, and voyage details. In times of increased tension or conflict additional information may be requested. The response of Masters to information requests is one of the most important aspects of NCAGS. The commercial sensitivity of the information supplied by the merchant shipping community will be respected and protected.

The NCAGS organization will in turn ensure that appropriate military authorities are advised of these details for monitoring during the voyage. If deemed necessary, they will provide the merchant Master with up-to-date information concerning the situation and specifi information on the voyage. This information can range from basic situation briefs to the provision of routes, lead through, or escort. Safe passage responsibility remains with the Master.

The principal benefit of NCAGS to merchant shipping include:
– Improved safety and security.
– Minimized disruptions to passages through areas where military operations are being conducted.
– Quicker reaction to terrorism.
– A better understanding of military constraints.
– Minimized disruption to commercial schedules.

The principal benefit of NCAGS to the military commander include:
– A more comprehensive picture of merchant activity and positions of merchant ships.
– Deconfliction of merchant ships in military operations
– Enhanced safety and security of merchant ships.
– Improved effectiveness of military operations.
– A better understanding of commercial constraints.

810B. Elements of the NCAGS

The NCAGS is fl xible in order to meet the needs of the military commander and merchant shipping. It may comprise some or all of the following elements tailored to suit the situation depending on the level of NCAGS support required.
– Shipping Coordination Center (SCC): The SCC is a permanent organization, tasked with establishing and maintaining links with the military, merchant shipping, HLD and HLS agencies, such as the USCG. The SCC will:
  – Provide MDA by maintaining a merchant shipping plot of the assigned AOR.
  – Generate Notice to Mariners (NOTMARs) as necessary regarding acts of terrorism or military operations.
  – Advise civil maritime authorities, via Maritime Administration (MARAD), of general shipping risks in the area.
  – Establish Shipping Risk Areas (SRAs) and recommend routing of shipping.
– Shipping Coordination Team (SCT): The SCT is an expeditionary team that can be deployed to a specifi region to gather information on local merchant shipping and naval operations and will provide the means to brief merchant shipping on risks, routing, and organization for protection. The SCT will, depending on the level of an operation, encompass coordination and guidance to local military commanders and merchant Masters. The location of SCTs can be ashore or afloat The SCT liaises with local and regional authorities including port authorities, shipping agents, and local shipping companies and reports ship movements to local military commanders to help deconflic military operations with merchant shipping.
– NCAGS Liaison Office (LNO): An office deployed aboard a merchant ship to provide liaison between the merchant ship Master and military authorities. The LNO is the naval advisor to the merchant Master. His position on board does not affect the Master's responsibilities for the safe navigation and safe handling of the ship. The LNO makes military knowledge available to the Master to allow the Master to understand the naval and military requirements that are applicable.
– Shipping Risk Area (SRA): When necessary, a SRA may be recommended by a SCC or SCT. A SRA is a geographically define portion of the NCAGS area where an elevated risk to merchant shipping exists. Risks can include potentially hostile acts, navigational restrictions that require an elevated closer management of shipping traffic or naval forces operations that may conflic with routine safe passage. More than one SRA can be established within an NCAGS area. SRAs are established by the local military commander.

COMMUNICATION INSTRUCTIONS FOR U.S. MERCHANT SHIPS

PART III COMMUNICATIONS WITH NCAGS

820A. General

The role of NCAGS in keeping the seas safe and providing the essential framework needed to allow commercial and military shipping to operate together in a crisis is dependent on effective communications with merchant shipping at sea or inport. The SCC or SCT will exchange data at the unclassifie level with merchant shipping authorities and with elements of the NCAGS organization. This part provides guidance to Masters who may need to communicate with military forces. Communications with merchant ships by the military are accomplished via the Global Maritime Distress and Safety System (GMDSS) and other commercial means. Under normal circumstances, ships working with NCAGS will maintain their normal peacetime communications. However, if the situation so dictates, they may be required to maintain additional communications methods.

820B. Methods of Communication

GMDSS: Every effort is made by the NCAGS organization to provide communications for merchant vessels to either the SCC or SCT so that ships can communicate easily and regularly with them using Inmarsat-C. Generally telex, fax, email, and voice, when available, are used as the primary means for the NCAGS organization to contact ships either through owners, directly to the ships if this has been made available, or via commercial organizations who specialize in passing messages.

Navigational Warnings (NAVWARNs)/Notice to Mariners (NOTMARs): The military authorities will pass safety information for the NCAGS AOR, promulgated by broadcast methods, via NAVWARNs, NOTMARs, and MARAD Advisories. These warnings will describe possible military operations in an AOR. Notices will include toll free telephone numbers a merchant Master or agent can call to obtain real-time information regarding an ongoing crisis or military operation.

Military Points of Contact: A SCC, SCT, or NCAGS LNO can provide merchant shipping with their main means of communications in an elevated risk situation via GMDSS, NAVWARNs/NOTMARs, or embarked LNO.

Communication Reporting Gate (CRG): In an AOR, there is a good possibility that your ship will be called, or challenged, by naval vessels or military aircraft on the VHF calling frequency. To allow merchant ships to contact naval vessels in the AOR, information will be distributed directly to the Master via LNO, naval vessels in the local area, or local advisory notices by various means including, but not limited to, NOTMARs, e-mail, or websites. However, naval units can normally be contacted through standard calling VHF frequencies.

CRG is established to provide a position/line for merchant ships to call NCAGS in order to establish initial contact or to update previous information. A CRG should be positioned in such a way that a minimum notice period of 36 hours is available to merchant ships to contact their owners/operators for onward passage instructions before reaching the AOR. The CRG will normally be represented as lines of latitude or longitude that encompasses the area concerned.

Ships will be notifie of the CRG details for the AOR and the reporting requirements will be promulgated to merchant ships through a variety of means, such as by the SCC, SCT advisory notices, or NAVWARNs. Instructions will normally contain details of the information required, the occasions of reporting, and to whom the report is to be sent. Ships will be asked to forward a Format Alfa before arriving at the CRG.

820C. Forms and Message Formats

(Ref: ATP-2, Vol. II)

Format Alfa: Format Alfa is the principal means by which merchant ship data is collected for use by the NCAGS. The Format Alfa will be requested to be forwarded at least 24 hours prior to entering the area of operations and then, if possible, every 6 hours until exiting the area of operations. The form is divided into four sections:
– Section A covers basic details of the vessel.
– Section B covers details of the current voyage.
– Section C covers details of the ship's operator.
– Section D covers cargo data.
NOTE: Date and Time should be entered either by the date followed by a four digit time (18.Oct 97 21.00 UTC) or a Date-time Group (DTG). The military method of expressing date and time is contained within the DTG and is written in the following manner:
DDHHMMZ MON YY
therefore, the DTG 182100Z JUL 98 describes a time of 21:00 (GMT/UTC) on the 18 July 1998. Military units routinely describe GMT/UTC as time zone "Zulu" abbreviated to "Z."

– Section A - Ship Data:
 (1) Ship's name.
 (2) International callsign.
 (3) Type of vessel.
 (4) Flag of registry.
 (5) IMO number.
 (6) Port of registry.
 (7) Overall length.
 (8) Vessel's width.
 (9) Maximum draft for present voyage.
 (10) Vessel's gross tonnage.
 (11) Speed:
  (a) Service speed.
  (b) Maximum speed.

COMMUNICATION INSTRUCTIONS FOR U.S. MERCHANT SHIPS

(c) Minimum speed.
(12) Significan appearance of vessel for optical recognition.
(13) Inmarsat/DSC number.
(14) Name of communication station being copied.
(15) State whether pocket-sized automatic crypto equipment (PACE) and keying material is held.
(16) Fax number.
(17) Email address or telex number.
(18) Other communication means.

– Section B - Voyage Data:
(19) Intended movement - description of passage.
(20) Last port/country of call including actual date and time of departure from last port.
(21) Next port of call, including ETA at next port of call.
(22) Current position.
(23) Date/time and position entering the region.
   (a - x) Waypoints of intended track through AOR (date/time - latitudes/longitudes).
(24) Position and date/time of departing the region.

– Section C - Operator Data:
(25) Name of ship owner/operator including address of ship owner, name of charterer (if any), and address of operator/charterer.
(26) Flag of ship operator.
(27) Email address of the above.
(28) Telephone number of above.
(29) Fax number of above.

– Section D - Cargo Data:
(30) Quantity and nature of main/relevant cargo.
(31) Shippers of main/relevant cargo (name and address).
(32) Origin of main/relevant cargo.
(33) Consignee of main/relevant cargo.
(34) Final destination of main/relevant cargo.
(35) Special queries appropriate to current operation such as "State if any cargo/person is carried being subject to UN sanctions, by YES or NO (if the answer to the query is YES, then describe on a separate sheet)."

Ship Data Cards: Ship Data Cards are amplification of the information provided by the merchant ship on the Format Alfa that is used to facilitate cooperation between merchant ships and military assets. Masters will be asked to supply only information that is not available from other open sources, such as agents and the Internet.

Sailing Instructions (SI): SI are issued to all ships transiting a SRA and any other ships requiring specifi guidance. The issue of a SI indicates that the Master has accepted the routing guidance contained within the SI. NCAGS will monitor the ship's passage and divert the ship if the threat or risk changes and a diversion message will be sent to the Master.

Diversion Order: A message from NCAGS ordering a diversion from the existing route for any reason. The firs words of the text will be the identifie "DIVERSION ORDER" followed by:
(1) The reason for diversion.
(2) The position or time at which the diversion is to take place.
(3) New positions through which ships are to pass. Each position is to be preceded by its two letter designator.
(4) The immediate destination and amended ETA.

Example:
DIVERSION ORDER
(1) Acts of terrorism in your vicinity.
(2) Divert at position AB.
(3) Pass through new positions BL 4245N04800W, BM 4230N05500W, then to original position AE and original track.
(4) Amended ETA Baltimore 160800Z Jan.

Passage Amendment: This message is to be sent by a ship to report passage amendments involving changes in destination or differences of greater than 6 hours variance from the original passage plan intentions reported by Format Alfa. The message will be addressed to the original addressee of the Format Alfa. The firs words of the text will be the identifie "FORMAT ALFA PASSAGE AMENDMENT" followed by:
(1) The international call sign, IMO number, and name of the ship.
(2) Position at . . . . . .
(3) Great circle or rhumb line track and speed.
(4) Name of next port of call.
(5) ETA at next port of call.

Example:
FORMAT ALFA PASSAGE AMENDMENT
(1) WGLW, 9076236, SS YOUNG AMERICA.
(2) 4315N 03515W at 181500Z Aug.
(3) Rhumb line/l9.
(4) Baltimore.
(5) 221200Z Aug.

PART IV CONTAMINATION PREDICTION SYSTEM FOR MERCHANT SHIPS AT SEA AND THE MERWARN SYSTEM

830A. Significance of NBC Warnings

Radioactive fallout from nuclear explosions and chemical and biological contamination (hereafter collectively referred to as contamination) on sea and land targets, particularly the latter, may affect large areas of adjacent waters. The areas affected will depend upon the prevailing wind conditions, and any ship close to or approaching these areas will be in grave danger. It is therefore essential that shipping should be warned of the fallout hazards and contamination in order that:
– Passive defense measures, such as activating washdown systems, may be taken.
– Course may be altered, if necessary, to avoid the dangerous zones.

830B. The MERWARN System, Warnings to Merchant Ships at Sea

A simplifie contamination warning system has been established throughout NATO for broadcasting, via MERCOMMS and coastal radio stations, warnings of contamination dangerous to merchant shipping. This system calls for the origination, by NATO naval authorities, of f ve types of messages:
– MERWARN NBC Effective Downwind Message (MERWARN NBC EDM).
– MERWARN NBC 3 NUC.
– MERWARN NBC Chemical Downwind Message (MERWARN NBC CDM).
– MERWARN NBC 3 CHEM.
– MERWARN DIVERSION ORDER.

In some cases it may be better to provide warning of contamination by means of general plain language messages rather than by these formats.

830C. MERWARN Originating and Diversion Authorities

MERWARN Originating and Diversion authorities will be designated by national or NATO commanders before commencement of operations.

830D. Precedence of NBC Messages

All MERWARN NBC messages should be given FLASH (Z) precedence to ensure rapid handling on any military circuit between the originating authority and the MERCOMMS and/or coastal radio stations. This precedence should not be used where the rules for the use of the international safety signal (SECURITAY for voice circuits) apply.

830E. Method of Promulgation

All MERWARN NBC EDM, MERWARN NBC CDM, MERWARN NBC 3 CHEM and NBC 3 NUC messages will be transmitted in plain language, using GMT, preceded by the international safety signal, from the appropriate MERCOMMS station and from all the coastal radio stations of the area concerned. Masters need not concern themselves with the identity of the MERWARN originators, but only with the sea areas covered by each message.

830F. Relay Responsibilities

Originating authorities are responsible for relaying to:
– The appropriate Coast Earth Station (Inmarsat CES), Coast Radio Station (CRS) under their control, and/or other CRS in their geographic area.
– Their own national authorities (for transmission to merchant ships not yet copying MERCOMMS).
– Adjacent MERWARN originators and shipping diverting authorities within the geographical area affected by each MERWARN NBC 3 NUC message.
NOTE: Adjacent MERWARN originators are responsible for relaying to CES/CRS under their control as necessary.

830G. Danger Zones

All shipping in waters out to 200 nautical miles from any coast at the outset of war must be regarded as being in an area of possible fallout danger from nuclear attacks on shore.

830H. MERWARN NBC EDM

MERWARN NBC EDM is a prediction, for a specifie sea area and time interval, of the fallout which will result from a 1 megaton (MT) nuclear surface explosion. It will give the Master of a ship, observing a nuclear explosion, an immediate indication of the area likely to be affected by fallout.

MERWARN NBC EDM will be issued at 12 hour intervals from the time of activation of the MERCOMMS system, and will be valid 12 hours ahead from the date and time given in the firs line of the message (line A). In the event of changing meteorological conditions it may be necessary for the originating authorities to issue MERWARN NBC EDM more frequently. The original MERWARN NBC EDM will automatically be overruled by the latest MERWARN EDM issued.

The following standard format will be used:

COMMUNICATION INSTRUCTIONS FOR U.S. MERCHANT SHIPS

A. Message identifie (MERWARN NBC EDM) and date-time group (GMT) from which valid for 12 hours ahead.
B. Specified sea area for which alid.
C. Effective downwind direction (in degrees, three digits) and effective downwind speed (in knots, three digits).
D. Downwind distance of Zone 1 (in nautical miles, three digits).
E. Additional information.

Example:

A. MERWARN NBC EDM 180600ZSEP1999
B. BALTIC SEA WEST OF 15°00'E
C. 045-020
D. 078
E. NIL

NOTE: Sets B, C, and D may be repeated for different sea areas should this be considered necessary.

830I. MERWARN NBC 3 NUC, Standard Format

MERWARN NBC 3 NUC will be issued after a nuclear attack producing fallout, and gives fallout data for a specifi explosion or series of explosions, which will be identified in the message

MERWARN NBC 3 NUC messages are issued as soon as possible after the attack, and at 6 hour intervals (to the nearest hour) thereafter, for as long as fallout danger exists. They contain information which enables the Master of a ship to plot the danger area.

The standard format of MERWARN NBC 3 NUC contains the sets ALFA, DELTA, FOXTROT, and PAPAB of the military NBC 3 NUC message.

The MERWARN NBC 3 NUC has the following structure:

MERWARN NBC 3 NUC (Message identifier

ALFA: Strike Serial Number (as define by the naval authority).
DELTA: Date-time Group of detonation (GMT).
FOXTROT: Location of attack (latitude and longitude, or geographical place name) and qualifie (two digits as follows: AA=Actual Location, EE=Estimated Location).
PAPAB: Effective wind speed (three digits and unit of measurement), downwind distance of Zone 1 (three digits and unit of measurement), cloud radius (two digits and unit of measurement), left and right radial line of the predicted fallout hazard area (three digits and unit of measurement each).

Example:

MERWARN NBC 3 NUC

ALFA/UK/NBCC/02-001/N//
DELTA/021405ZSEP1999//
FOXTROT/451230N014312E/AA//
PAPAB/012KTS/028NM/02NM/272DGT/312DGT//

830J. MERWARN NBC 3 NUC, Plain Language Format

The MERWARN NBC 3 NUC standard format may not be suitable after a multiple nuclear attack which produces fallout from several bursts in a large or complex target area. In such cases warnings will be plain language statements of a more general nature, indicating area affected and expected movement of the fallout.

Example 1:

MERWARN NBC 3 NUC

ALFA/UK/02-001/N//
DELTA/021405ZSEP1999//
Fallout extends from Glasgow area to eastern Ireland at 021405Z and is spreading westwards with 12 Knots. Irish Sea is likely to be affected within an area of 60 nautical miles of the British coast.

Example 2:

MERWARN NBC 3 NUC

ALFA/IT/15-001/N//
DELTA/150630ZFEB1999//
Fallout is estimated to be occurring at 150830Z over Adriatic Sea east of the coast line Bari/Brindisi up to a distance of 30 nautical miles. Fallout is moving south-eastwards with 016 Knots, getting weaker. It is not expected to be dangerous after 151000Z.

830K. MERWARN NBC CDM

The MERWARN NBC CDM message contains information needed for CHEM/BIO hazard prediction by the master of a merchant ship. The MERWARN NBC CDM will be issued as required via the MERCOMMS and will be valid as specified In the event of changes in the meteorological conditions, the MERWARN NBC CDM will be updated as required.

The following standard format will be used:

ALFA: Message identifie (MERWARN NBC CDM), date-time group (GMT) from which valid 6 hours ahead.
BRAVO: Specified sea area for which alid.
CHARLIE: Representative downwind direction (degrees, 3 digits) and representative downwind speed (knots, 3 digits).
DELTA: Maximum downwind hazard distance (nautical miles, 3 digits).

COMMUNICATION INSTRUCTIONS FOR U.S. MERCHANT SHIPS

ECHO: Additional information.

Example:

ALFA   MERWARN NBC CDM 180600ZSEP1999//
BRAVO   BALTIC SEA WEST OF 15°00'E//
CHARLIE 045/020//
DELTA   010//
ECHO   NIL//

830L. MERWARN NBC 3 CHEM

This message is issued to pass immediate warning of a predicted chemical contamination and hazard area. MERWARN NBC 3 CHEM reports are issued as soon as possible after each attack. They contain sufficien information to enable the master of a ship to plot the downwind hazard area.

The following standard format will be used for MERWARN NBC 3 CHEM:

MERWARN NBC 3 CHEM (Message identifier

ALFA: Strike Serial Number (as define by the naval authority).
DELTA: Date-time group (Z) of start and end of attack.
FOXTROT: Location of event.
GOLF: Delivery Means.
INDIA: Release Information.
PAPAA: Predicted attack and hazard area.

NOTE: If representative downwind speed is 5 knots or less, or variable, this letter item will consist of three (3) digits instead of coordinates, representing the radius of a circle in nautical miles centred on the location of the attack contained in set FOXTROT.

YANKEE: The representative downwind direction and speed.
ZULU: Information on actual weather conditions.
GENTEXT: Remarks.

NOTE: Some of the letter items above may not be completed in the report that is received, but there will be sufficien information for a Downwind Hazard plot to be carried out.

The MERWARN NBC 3 CHEM standard format may not be suitable after a multiple chemical attack, which produces a hazard from several attacks or depositions in a large or complex target area. In such cases warnings will be plain language statements of a more general nature, indicating areas affected and expected movement of the hazard.

Example 1:

MERWARN NBC 3 CHEM

ALFA/DA/NBCC-4/003/C//
DELTA/020300ZSEP1999//
GENTEXT/PERSISTENT NERVE AGENT VAPOR HAZARD EXISTS FROM NORFOLK TO HATTERAS AT 020300Z SEP 1999 AND IS SPREADING SOUTH-EASTWARDS AT 017 KNOTS. SEA AREA OUT TO 100 NAUTICAL MILES FROM COAST LIKELY TO BE AFFECTED BY 020600ZSEP1999//

Example 2:

MERWARN NBC 3 CHEM

ALFA/DA/NBCC-3/003/C//
DELTA/020300ZSEP1999//
GENTEXT/PERSISTENT NERVE AGENT VAPOR HAZARD AT 020600Z SEP 99 IS ESTIMATED TO BE OCCURRING OVER MOST OF THE SEA AREAS OUT TO 40 MILES EAST OF THE COAST LINE FROM NORFOLK TO HATTERAS. HAZARD IS EXPECTED TO HAVE DISPERSED BY 021000Z SEP1999//

830M. MERWARN DIVERSION ORDER

In addition to the origination of MERWARN NBC EDM and MERWARN NBC 3 NUC messages, naval authorities may, if circumstances dictate, broadcast general diversion orders, based upon the fallout threat, whereby merchant ships proceeding independently will be passed evasive routing instructions of a more general nature, using the standard NCS identifie MERWARN DIVERSION ORDER.

Example:
A. MERWARN DIVERSION ORDER
B. English Channel closed. All shipping in North Sea remain north of 052 degrees N until 031500ZSEP1999.

830N. Other Warnings

ATP-2, Vol II, gives instructions for the display of signals by ships which have received a MERWARN NBC 3 NUC message which affects their area. Ships arriving from sea but remaining beyond visual/aural range of shore stations should continue to keep radio watch in order to receive MERWARN messages.

830O. Ground Zero

The point at the surface on sea or land immediately below or above a nuclear explosion is called Ground Zero (GZ).

COMMUNICATION INSTRUCTIONS FOR U.S. MERCHANT SHIPS

830P. Effective Downwind Direction and Downwind Speed

Winds in the atmosphere vary considerably with height, both in direction and speed, and have a major influenc on the distribution of radioactive fallout from a nuclear cloud.

The worst contamination will fall to the surface along a path represented by the average wind between the surface and the middle of the nuclear cloud.

Based upon meteorological information on the wind conditions in the airspace between the surface and the height of the nuclear cloud, NBC Collection Centers will compute the average direction and speed of the radioactive particles' path from the nuclear cloud to the surface.

The results of this computation make up the fallout prediction, expressed in the terms of effective downwind direction and speed. It should be noted that the direction of the effective downwind is the direction towards which the wind blows. This direction is also known as the fallout axis.

The surface wind will usually be considerably different from the effective downwind, both in direction and speed, and the surface wind should never be used to estimate the drift of fallout.

830Q. Fallout Pattern Criteria

The predicted fallout area consists of two zones, Zone 1 and Zone 2, with the following characteristics:
- Zone 1 is the zone of immediate concern. Within this zone there will be areas where exposed, unprotected personnel may receive doses of 150 cGy (rads) or greater, within 4 hours. Casualties among personnel may occur within portions of this zone.
- Zone 2 is the zone of secondary hazard. Within this zone the total dose received by exposed, unprotected personnel is not expected to reach 150 cGy (rads) within a period of 4 hours after the actual arrival of fallout, not even when the radioactive fallout remains on the deck of the ship.

Outside these two zones the risk will be negligible.

830R. Fallout Plotting in Merchant Ships

When a nuclear explosion is reported in a MERWARN NBC 3 NUC message, the Master of a merchant ship should immediately plot the fallout area on a chart, using the information contained in the message. A plot example accompanies the next section.

When a MERWARN NBC 3 NUC is not available (for example, when a nuclear detonation is observed from the ship) the data contained in the current MERWARN NBC EDM should be used. The plotting procedures are almost identical in the two cases.

For purposes of simplification merchant ships are to use cloud radii and safety distance as follows:
- Plotting from MERWARN NBC EDM: Use cloud radius 10 nautical miles and safety distance 15 nautical miles in all cases.
- Plotting from MERWARN NBC 3 NUC: Use the cloud radius given in the MERWARN NBC 3 NUC and, in all cases, a safety distance of 15 nautical miles.

Plotting should be performed in the following manner:
- Plot the location of the detonation (ground zero) on the chart. Look up the fourth and fift fiel of set PAPAB (left and right radial line of the fallout area) and calculate the bisector. This line is the equivalent to the downwind direction. Draw a downwind axis from GZ in the downwind direction, as calculated above. Draw two additional downwind radial lines from GZ, 20° to either side of the downwind axis.
- Using GZ as center and the downwind distance of Zone 1 (second fiel of set PAPAB) as radius, draw an arc between the two radial lines on each side of the downwind axis. Draw a second arc between the radial lines to represent Zone 2, doubling the downwind distance for radius.
- Using GZ as center, draw a semicircle upwind (opposite the downwind axis and radials) using the cloud radius (third field of set APAB).
- From the intersections of the Zone 1 arc with the two radial lines, draw straight lines to the ends of the cloud radius semicircle.
- To determine the area in which fallout deposition is predicted to occur at any given time after the detonation:
- Multiply the effective downwind speed (firs fiel of set PAPAB) by the time after the burst (in hours), the result being a distance in nautical miles.
- To and from this distance add and subtract a safety distance of 15 nautical miles to allow for finit cloud size, diffusion, and wind fluctuations The result will be two distances.
- With GZ as center and the two safety distances obtained above as radii, draw arcs across the plotted fallout area.
- The area enclosed between the two arcs will contain, in most cases, the area of deposition of fallout at this particular time after the burst.

830S. Plotting from MERWARN NBC 3 NUC

Example:

Given:
MERWARN NBC 3 NUC

ALFA/UK/NBCC/09-001/N//
DELTA/091715ZSEP1999//
FOXTROT/PLYMOUTH/AA//
PAPAB/018KTS/040NM/05NM/275DGT/315DGT//

Problem: Determine the predicted fallout area and the area within which fallout is predicted to deposit at the surface at 091845ZSEP1999.

Solution (See figure.)
- On the chart plot GZ. Calculate the downwind direction 295 degrees as bisector from left and right radial line (from set PAPAB, fourth and fifth field). Draw a downwind axis from GZ on a bearing of 295° for a

distance of 80 nautical miles. Draw two radial lines from GZ, bearing 275° and 315°, both 80 nautical miles long. (80 is twice the downwind distance of Zone 1.)
- Using GZ as center, draw arcs between the radial lines at 40 nautical miles downwind to mark Zone 1, and at 80 nautical miles downwind to mark Zone 2.
- From the third fiel of set PAPAB, the cloud radius is 5 nautical miles. With GZ as center and 5 nautical miles as radius, draw the cloud radius semicircle upwind of GZ.
- From the intersections of the Zone 1 arc with the radial lines, draw straight lines to the ends of the cloud radius semicircle.
- 091845Z is 1.5 hours after the burst. From the firs fiel of set PAPAB, obtain the effective downwind speed; 18 knots:

18 kts x 1.5 hr = 27 nautical miles.

The safety distance is always 15 nautical miles.

27 + 15 = 42 nautical miles, and 27 - 15 = 12 nautical miles.
- With GZ as center and 42 and 12 nautical miles as radii, draw arcs across the fallout pattern. The area enclosed by the two arcs and the boundary of the pattern is the area within which fallout is predicted to deposit at the surface at 091845ZSEP1999.

830T. Contamination Plotting in Merchant Ships

When a chemical attack is reported in a MERWARN NBC 3 CHEM message, the following procedure should be followed:
- Plot the location of the attack from the details in set FOXTROT.
- Plot the coordinates or radius of the circle contained in set PAPAA.

COMMUNICATION INSTRUCTIONS FOR U.S. MERCHANT SHIPS

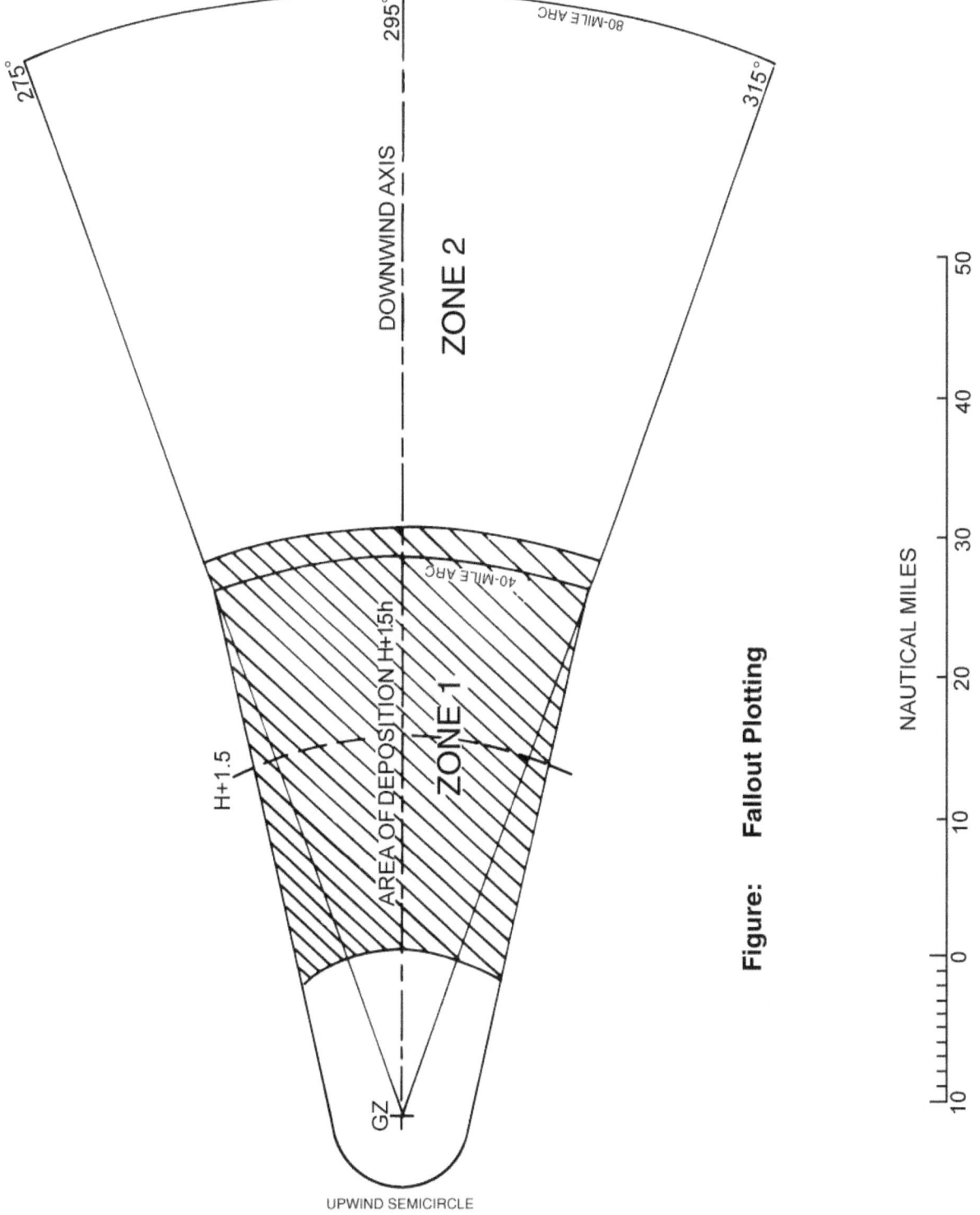

Figure: Fallout Plotting

COMMUNICATION INSTRUCTIONS FOR U.S. MERCHANT SHIPS

APPENDIX A

INSTRUCTION TO MASTERS IN AN EMERGENCY ON DEFENSE AGAINST NUCLEAR FALLOUT

Attacks with nuclear weapons may be expected on land targets adjacent to your route. Such attacks are likely to result in radioactive fallout being deposited over large areas of sea, through which you may have to pass. It may be possible to issue a general warning to indicate which areas are likely to be dangerous at any particular time.

As fallout will probably be in the form of fin dust which may be invisible, you should observe the following precautions during nuclear fallout.

If your ship is equipped with the necessary instruments to detect fallout, these precautions may be relaxed accordingly.

PRECAUTIONS TO BE TAKEN: If your ship has a prearranged radioactive countermeasure plan prepared, ensure that all measures laid down in that plan are carried out. If no such plan is in existence, improvise measures as indicated below:

– Select a group, or groups, of compartments as low in the ship and as far removed from the ship's side as possible within which the crew can take shelter. These spaces should be equipped with washing and lavatory facilities, and sufficien food should be stowed there to last for the passage through the dangerous area. Spaces selected should be capable of being completely shut down with all ventilation and other openings secured.

– Strike below or cover as much gear on the weather decks as possible, particularly absorbent materials such as line, awnings, etc. Ensure that food stores and galleys are secured with all openings closed. Stop all ventilation fans and close or cover all ventilation and other openings which are not essential for running machinery and continued steaming. In the absence of suitable closures, the use of canvas covers, adhesive tape, etc., is recommended.

– Rig all available fire-fighti and deck washing hoses and nozzles to spray water continuously over as much of the weather decks and superstructure as possible, to prevent contamination settling. If complete coverage is impossible, concentrate effort on the navigating position, over the top of the shelter position(s), and above the machinery spaces.

– If a continual spraying of the upper works is impracticable, organize working parties at frequent intervals to wash down the weather decks and superstructure to reduce the buildup of contamination.

– Reduce the number of your crew who must remain on the weather decks or in positions near the weather decks, or in machinery spaces, to the bare minimum required for safe steaming, and keep the remainder in the selected shelter position(s).

– Ensure that all who must remain in exposed positions (including machinery spaces, unless ventilation can be stopped) are fully clothed, preferably in foul weather clothing, with all the skin covered so far as practicable.

– During the passage, so far as the numbers of appropriately skilled personnel allow, change around those manning exposed or relatively unsheltered positions (including the machinery spaces) as often as possible in order to spread the radiation dosage. Remember that this advice also applies to the Master, who should take as much shelter as the safe navigation of the ship will permit.

– Ensure that all who have been exposed remove at least their outer clothing on returning to shelter, wash thoroughly their exposed skin (especially hands, face, and neck) as soon as possible, and in any case before drinking or eating.

– Restrict unnecessary movement throughout the ship to minimize the possible spread of contamination.

– Unless absolutely necessary, do not distill water for drinking while in a dangerous area.

– As soon as possible after clearing a dangerous area, carry out a thorough hosing down of the all weather decks and superstructure.

INDEX I

RADIO AIDS TO NAVIGATION BY COUNTRY

A

Acores	3456.2
Albania	3498.1
Algeria	3550, 5010
American Samoa	3948
Angola	3629
Antarctica	3209
Argentina	2080, 3182, 5020
Australia	1665, 2600, 3876, 5030

B

Bahrain	3716, 5050
Bangladesh	3731, 5060
Barbados	5070
Belarus	2150
Belgium	3378, 5080
Benin	3610, 5090
Bermuda	3135, 5100
Bjornoya	3216
Brazil	2050.5, 3150
Bulgaria	1187.61, 3510
Burma	5101
Burma (Myanmar)	3733

C

Cameroon	3620, 5110
Canada	1001, 2020, 5120
Canada - Arctic and Atlantic	3017
Canada - Pacific	3671
Channel Islands	3410
Chile	1895, 2445, 3645.4, 5130
China	2485.1, 3740, 5140
Colombia	1850
Comoros	5141
Congo	5150
Congo (Brazzaville)	3630
Costa Rica	5160
Cote D'Ivoire (Ivory Coast)	3600
Croatia	3499, 5165
Cuba	3119, 5170
Cyprus	3509, 5180
Czech Republic	2091

D

Denmark	3359, 5190
Djibouti	5200
Dominican Republic	5210

E

Ecuador	2051, 3646
Egypt	5220
Egypt - Mediterranean	3537
Egypt - Red Sea	3713.2
Estonia	3334

F

Faroe Islands	3215
Fiji	3945
Fiji Islands	5245
Finland	3314, 5250
France	1182, 1273, 2380, 5260
France - Channel and Atlantic	3421
France - Mediterranean	3471
French Polynesia	3943

G

Gambia	5290
Georgia	3519
Germany	1205, 2320, 5300
Germany - North Sea	3370
Ghana	3605, 5320
Greece	3500, 5330
Greenland	3001.5, 5340
Guadeloupe	5350
Guam	3913
Guinea	3590, 5360
Guyana	5370

H

Hong Kong	5380
Hong Kong (China)	3739

I

Iceland	3212
India	2476, 3722, 5390
Indonesia	2633, 5400
Indonesia - Irian Jaya	3840
Indonesia - Java	3820
Indonesia - Moluccas	3836
Indonesia - Sulawesi	3830
Indonesia - Sumatera	3816
Iran	3715
Iraq	5410
Ireland	3405, 5420
Islas Baleares	3464
Islas Canarias	3579

INDEX I

RADIO AIDS TO NAVIGATION BY COUNTRY

Israel 3534, 5430
Italy 2410, 3475, 5440
Ivory Coast 5450

J

Jamaica 3135.5, 5460
Jan Mayen 3214
Japan 1530, 2500, 3753, 5470

K

Kenya 5480
Kyrgyzstan 2211

L

Latvia 1198, 3333, 5485
Libya 3538
Lithuania 1199, 3332

M

Madagascar 5500
Malaysia 5510
Malaysia - Peninsular 3734
Malaysia - Sabah 3803
Malaysia - Sarawak 3805
Malta 3498.05, 5520
Martinique 3140, 5540
Mauritania 3583
Mauritius 3710, 5541
Mexico 2040, 3118
Monaco 3474, 5542
Morocco 1320, 3560, 5550

N

Namibia 3627, 5560
Nauru 5565
Netherland Antilles 5580
Netherlands 1218, 3375, 5570
Netherlands Antilles 3145
New Caledonia 3940, 5590
New Zealand 1625, 3904, 5600
Nigeria 3615, 5610
Norway 1204, 3242, 5620

O

Oman 3713.8, 5630

P

Pakistan 1188, 3720, 5640
Panama 5650
Papua New Guinea 3866, 5660
Peru 2461, 3646.1, 5665
Philippines 2530, 3792, 5670
Poland 1200, 3336, 5680
Portugal 1295, 3441, 5690
Puerto Rico 3138

Q

Qatar 3713.9

R

Republic of Korea 1520, 2505, 3742
Reunion 3711
Reunion Island 5710
Romania 3512
Russia 1190, 2202, 5705
Russia - Baltic Coast 3325
Russia - Black Sea 3520
Russia - Caspian Sea 3522
Russia - Northern Coasts 3224
Russia - Pacific 3748

S

Saudi Arabia 5730
Saudi Arabia - Persian Gulf 3714.2
Saudi Arabia - Red Sea 3713.6
Senegal 3584, 5740
Serbia and Montenegro 3499.5, 5740.5
Seychelles 5741
Sierra Leone 5750
Singapore 3735, 5755
Slovenia 5760
South Africa 3641, 5770
Spain 1300, 5790
Spain - North Coast 3430
Spain - South and Mediterranean 3458
Sri Lanka 2480, 3730, 5800
St. Helena 5720
St. Pierre and Miquelon 3050, 5725
Suriname 5810
Svalbard 3218, 5820.5
Sweden 1203, 3288, 5820
Switzerland 2400, 5821

T

Tahiti 5822

INDEX I

RADIO AIDS TO NAVIGATION BY COUNTRY

Taiwan. 2635, 3785
Thailand 1480, 3736
Togo 5824
Tonga 3949, 5823
Trinidad and Tobago. 3143
Tunisia. 3540, 5840
Turkey. 3528.1

U

Ukraine 1305, 3514, 5845
United Kingdom 1055, 1237, 2351, 3390, 5850
United States. 1720, 2000, 5860, 5861, 5862
United States - Alaska. 3692.5
United States - Atlantic and Gulf 3083

United States - Hawaii 3703
United States - Pacific. 3646.5
United States and Canada - Lakes. 3068
Uruguay. 3168, 5866
Uzbekistan. 2212

V

Venezuela 2043
Vietnam. 3737, 5868

Y

Yemen Aden 5780

INDEX II

RADIO AIDS TO NAVIGATION BY STATION

A

Aasiaat	3015
Aberdeen	3390
Abidjan	3600
Adelaide	3885
Agadir	3570
Alexandria	3537
Alger	3552
Alicante	3459
Alistro	1187.4
Almeria	3459.65
Amboina	3836
Ammassalik	3002
Ancona	3477.5
Annaba	3550
Antalya	3528.1
Antofagasta	3645.75
Antwerpen	3378
Arkhangel'sk	2209, 3226
Arrecife	3579
Astoria, OR	3665
Astrakhan	3522
Athens	3504
Atlantic City, NJ	3090.7
Auckland	1625
Augusta	3477.2
Ault	1182.5
Aveiro	1295

B

Bagur	3462.5
Bahia Blanca	3192
Bahrain	3716
Baltimore, MD	3092
Bandar Abbas	3715.2
Bandar Khomeyni	3715
Bangkok	3736
Banks	1002.36
Bar	3499.5
Barcelona	3459.55
Barfleur	1183.1
Bari	3495
Barra	1055
Barry Inlet	1002.6
Base Prat, Greenwich Island (South Shetland Islands)	3645.8
Batumi	3519
Batz	1183.7
Bawdsey	1060
BBC-Radio 1	2360
BBC-Radio 2	2361
BBC-Radio 3	2362
BBC-Radio 4	2363
BBC-World Service	2370
Bec de L'Aigle	1186.2
Beg Melen	1184.2
Beg-Meil	1184.1
Belawan	3817
Belem	3150
Belem Radio Liberal	3151
Belem Radio Marajoara	3152
Belfast	3404.5
Bergen	3252
Bermuda Harbor	3135
Berry Head	1065
Berwick Bay, LA	1730
Bilbao	3430.2
Bisan Seto	1550
Bitung	3832
Bjornoya	3216
Bodo	3244
Bombay	3722.05
Bombay Naval	3722
Boniface	1066
Boston, MA	3086
Botlek	1231
Boulogne	1182.4
Brehat	1183.6
Bremen	3370
Brignogan	1183.75
Brixham	3400.2
Brougham	1002.37
Buenos Aires	2080, 2081, 3182
Buffalo, NY	3076
Busan	1520, 3746
Bushehr	3715.1

C

Cabo de Gata	3459.7
Cabo de la Nao	3459.35
Cabo Ortegal	3430.6
Cabo Penas	3430.8
Cadiz	3458
Cagliari	3476
Cairns	3876
Calcutta	3728.3
Callao	3646.1
Caloocan	3792.5
Calvert Island	1002.65
Cambria, CA	3646.6
Cap Bear	1185.6
Cap Camarat	1186.5
Cap Cepet	1186.3
Cap Corse	1186.9

I-5

INDEX II

RADIO AIDS TO NAVIGATION BY STATION

Cap Couronne	1186
Cap de la Chevre	1183.95
Cap du Dramont	1186.6
Cap Ferrat	1186.8
Cap Ferret	1184.8
Cap Leucate	1185.7
Cap-aux-Meules	1001
Cape Croker	1002.38
Cape Hatteras, NC	3099
Cape Naval (NAVCOMCEN Cape)	3645.1
Cape Town	3644
Cartagena	3462
Carteret	1183.3
Casablanca	1320, 3572
Casey	3209
Castellon	3459.4
Centro Meteorologico Antartico Vcom. Marambio	3210
Centro Meteorologico Presidente Eduardo Frei, King George Island (South Shetland Islands)	3645.77
Cerrito	3170
Chah Bahar	3715.3
Chapultepec	2040
Charleston, SC	3100
Charleville	3901
Chassiron	1184.65
Cheju	3742.5
Chemoulin	1184.5
Chesapeake, VA	3096
Chi-lung	3785
Chincoteague, VA	3093
Chipiona	3459.3
Chittagong	3731
Chukpyon	3746.5
Chung-Li	2635
Cienfuegos	3121
Civitavecchia	3482
Clyde	3402
Cobourg	1002.4
Cochin	3728
Colombo	2480, 3730
Colonia	3177
Comodoro Rivadavia	3196
Comox, B.C.	3672
Compass Head	1070
Conakry	3590
Constanta	3512
Corpus Christi, TX	3116
Corse	3473
Corsen	1287, 3423
Coruna	3434
Cotonou	3610
Crosslaw	1072
Crotone	3493
Cullercoats	1073, 3392
Cumshewa	1002.7
Curacao	3145
Cyprus	3509

D

Da Nang	3737.5
Daet	3802
Dakar	3584
Dalian	3740.3
Dammam	3714.2
Danish Radio (Kalundborg)	3362
Darlowo	1201
Darwin	3900
Davao	3799
Delfzijl	1218.5
Den Helder	1219
Detroit, MI	3077
Deutschlandfunk	3373
Dickson	3232
Die Elbe	1205
Die Ems	1217
Die Jade	1216
Die Weser	1215
Dieppe	1182.6
Doha	3713.9
Dordrecht	1226
Douala	3620
Dover	3397.1
Dublin	3405
Dubrovnik	3499.05
Dumai	3816
Dundas Island	1002.75
Dunkerque	1182.3, 1273
Dunnet Head	1075
Durban	3643
Durres	3498.1

E

Easington	1080
East London	3645
East Prawle	1082
Eemshaven	1218
Etel	1184.15, 3423.5

F

Fairlight	1086
Falmouth	3400.3
Faro	3445
Farsund	3256
Fecamp	1182.7
Fedje	1204

INDEX II

RADIO AIDS TO NAVIGATION BY STATION

Fife Ness	1087
Finisterre	3433
Flamborough	1088
Floro	3251
Fort Collins, CO	2000
Fort de France	3140
Fort Macon, NC	3099.5
Forth	3391
Fortune Head	1001.3
France Inter (Allouis)	2380
Frunze	2211
Fuerteventura	3579.5
Fuzhou	3740.4

G

Galveston, TX	3112
Genova	3478
Gijon	3430.9
Gladstone	3876.5
Goa	3726
Gomera	3581.3
Gorky	2203
Goteborg	1203
Grand Haven, MI	3078
Gravesend Radio	1254
Great Ormes Head	1089
Greenland Radio	3003
Gris-Nez	1182, 1274, 3421
Grosses-Roches	1001.35
Grove Point	1090
Guam	3913
Guangzhou	3740
Guayaquil	2051
Guayaquil Naval	3646
Guernsey	1090.5

H

Habana	3131
Hai Phong	3737
Haifa	3534
Halifax, N.S.	3045
Hamburg	1210
Hartel	1232
Hartland	1091
Hartlepool	1091.2
Harwich	1262
Havre St.-Pierre	1001.45
Hellas	3507
Hellenic Radio-Television	3506
Hengistbury Head	1092
Hierro	3581.6
Hiroshima	3766

Ho Chi Minh Ville	3738
Hobart	3884
Hoek van Holland	1230
Holyhead	3400.6
Homet	1183.2
Hong Kong	3739
Honolulu, HI	3703, 3703.5
Horta	3456.3
Houston-Galveston, TX	1740
Hua-lien	3787
Humber	3394
Humboldt Bay, CA	3661

I

Ibiza	3465
Icelandic State Broadcasting Service	3212.5
Ijmuiden	1220
Ile Rousse	1187
Iloilo	3801
Inchon	3742
Inuvik, N.W.T.	3018
Inverbervie	1093
Iqaluit, N.T.	3017
Iraklion	3502
Irkutsk	2205, 2205.5
Ishigaki	3769
Isla de Pascua (Easter Island)	3645.76
Ismailia (Serapeum)	3713.4
Istanbul	3533
Izmir	3529

J

Jakarta	2633, 3820
Jamaica Coast Guard	3135.5
Jan Mayen	3214
Jayapura	3840
Jersey	1093.5, 3410
Jiddah	3713.6
Jobourg	1182.1, 3421.5
Juncao	3166
Juneau, AK	3692.5

K

Kagoshima	3767
Kaliningrad	3325
Kandla	3723
Kangnung	3745
Kanmon Kaikyo	1540
Kao-Hsiung	3790
Karachi	1188, 3720
Karachi Naval	3721

I-7

INDEX II

RADIO AIDS TO NAVIGATION BY STATION

Kekaha, Kauai, HI	2001
Kerch	3517.5
Kerkira	3500
Key West, FL	3106
Khabarovsk	2206
Kholmsk	3750
Kiev	3518
Kilchiaran	1094
Klaipeda	1199, 3332
Klemtu	1002.8
Kobe	3764
Kochi	3772.2
Kodiak, AK	3695
Kolobrzeg	1202
Kunsan	3744
Kushiro	1570, 3753

L

L'Espiguette	1185.9
La Chiappa	1187.3
La Garde	1185.5, 3471
La Garoupe	1186.7
La Gironde	1290
La Goulette Port	3540
La Guardia	3430
La Hague	1183.25
La Heve	1182.8
La Loire	1288
La Palma	3581.9
La Paloma	3168
La Parata	1187.1
La Seine	1280
Labrador, Labr.	3019.5
Lac D'aigle (Sept Iles)	1001.6
Laem Chabang	1480
Lagos	3615
Lampedusa	3490
Lands End	1094.1
Langdon Battery	1094.2
Laoag	3797
Las Palmas	3580
Law Hill	1094.5
Le Grouin (Cancale)	1183.45
Le Havre	1275
Le Roc	1183.35
Le Stiff (Ile d'Ouessant)	1183.8
Le Talut	1184.4
Leba	1200
Leixoes	3441
Lerwick	1237
Les Baleines	1184.6
Les Escoumins, Que.	3038
Liblice	2091
Limnos	3508
Liverpool	1270, 3400.7
Livorno	3480
Lizard	1095
Llandilo, Penrith	2601
Long Beach, CA	3646.5
Long Island Sound, CT	3088.5
LOOP Deepwater Port (Louisiana Offshore Oil Port)	1735
Lowestoft	1095.5
Luanda	3629
Lucena	3796
Luderitz	3627
Lyngby	3359

M

Maasboulevard	1234
Machichaco	3436
Madras	3728.2
Magadan	3751
Magallanes	3645.7
Mahina	3943
Mainflingen	2320
Maizuru	3773
Makasar	3830
Malaga	3459.6
Malin Head	3406
Malolos	3793
Malta	3498.05
Mandaluyong	3795.5
Mangalore	3727
Manila	2530, 3795
Mar del Plata	3184
Mariupol	3517
Mariupol (Zhdanov)	1315
Mauritius	3710
Mayport, FL	3102
Mazara del Vallo	3489
Medway	1250
Melbourne	3883
Menorca	3464.5
Messanges	1184.82
Messina	3486
Miami, FL	3104
Milford Haven	3400.5
Milwaukee, WI	3079
Miri	3805
Mobile, AL	3111
Moji	3772.4
Mokpo	3743
Mollendo	3646.3
Molodechno	2150
Monaco	3474
Monsanto	3444

INDEX II

RADIO AIDS TO NAVIGATION BY STATION

Montevideo Trouville	3176.1
Mont-Louis	1001.85
Montmagny	1001.9
Montreal, Que.	3036
Moriches, NY	3088.6
Moskva	2202, 2202.5
Mount Gil	1002.85
Mount Hays	1002.9
Murmansk	1196, 3224
Muscat	3713.8

N

Naden Harbor	1002.95
Nagoya	1555, 3760
Naha	3777
Nakhodka	1194
Napoli	3484
Natashquan	1001.95
Navia	3430.5
Netherlands Coast Guard	3375
New Delhi	2476
New Orleans, LA	3108
New York, NY	1720, 3088.7
Newhaven	1096
Newport	1002
Newton	1097
Niigata	3772.8
Niton	3398
North Bend, OR	3664
North Foreland	1098
North Post	3143
Northwood	3395
Nos Galata Lt	1187.61
Noss Head	1098.2
Nouadhibou	3583
Noumea	3940
Novorossiysk	1192, 3520
Novosibirsk	2204
Nueva Palmira	3178
Nukualofa	3949
Nuuk (Kook Island)	3005

O

Observatorio Naval Caracas	2043
Odessa	1305, 3514
Offenbach/Pinneberg	3371
Okhotsk	3751.5
Olinda	3157
Oostende	3380
Oran	3554
Orlandet	3248
Orlock Head	1098.5
Osaka	1530
Otago Harbour	1630
Otaru	3775
Ottawa, Ont	2020

P

Pago Pago	3948
Paita	3646.2
Palembang	3819
Palermo	3487
Palma	3464
Palmer Station	3211
Pasajes	3430.3
Penmarc'h	1184.05
Penta Comstat, Firefly	3877
Perth	3886
Pertusato	1187.2
Peru National Radio	2461
Petropavlovsk-Kamchatskiy	3749.5
Pevek	3235
Pinang	3734
Piriac	1184.45
Placentia, Nfld.	3027.5
Ploumanach	1183.65
Point Reyes, CA	3657
Pointe au Baril	1002.45
Pointe de Grave	1184.75
Pointe du Raz	1184
Pointe Heath	1002.1
Pointe Noire	3630
Polo	3792
Ponta Delgada	3456.2
Ponta do Ceu	3153
Porquerolles	1186.4
Port Angeles, WA	3667
Port aux Basques, Nfld.	3021
Port Blair	3729
Port Dampier	1675
Port Elizabeth	3641
Port Harcourt	3617
Port Hedland	1665, 3892
Port Louis	3710.5
Port Moresby	3866
Port-en-Bessin	1183
Portland	3400
Portland, ME	3084
Portland, OR	3666
Portnaguran	1098.3
Porto Cervo	3477.3
Porto Santo, Madeira	3456
Porto Torres	3477.4
Portpatrick	3401
Prangins	2400

INDEX II

RADIO AIDS TO NAVIGATION BY STATION

Station	Page
Prescott, Ont.	3069
Primera Angostura	1900
Prince Rupert, B.C.	3677
Prince William Sound, AK	1770
Puerto Covenas, Floating Storage Unit	1850
Puerto Madryn	3193
Puerto Montt	3645.4
Puerto Princesa	3798
Puget Sound, WA	1760
Punta Carretas	3169.5
Punta del Este	3169
Pyonsan	3744.5

Q

Station	Page
Qaqortoq	3001.5
Quebec, Que.	3032
Quequen	3191
Quseir	3713.2

R

Station	Page
Radio Australia	2600
Radio Finland (Yleisradio)	3315
Radio Nacional de Macapa	3154
Radio Victoria	2462
Rame Head	1105
Rangoon	3733
Ratnagiri	3725
Ravenna	3477.6
Recalada Rio de la Plata	3186
Reunion	3711
Reykjavik	3212
Rhiw	1105.2
Riga	3333
Rijeka	3499.1
Rio de Janeiro	2050.5
Rio de Janeiro Naval	3161
Rio Gallegos	3204
Riviere du Loup	1002.2
Riviere-au-Renard	1002.15
Riviere-au-Renard, Que.	3040
Roches-Douvres	1182.2
Rodel	1106
Rodhos	3503
Rogaland	3254
Roma	2410, 3475
Rouen	1285
Rugby	2351

S

Station	Page
S. Quay Portrieux	1183.55
Safi	3574
Sagro	1187.5
Saint John, N.B.	3047
Saint-Cast	1183.5
Saint-Julien	1184.3
Saint-Mathieu	1183.85
Saint-Sauveur	1184.55
Saint-Vaast	1183.05
Samsun	3531
San Benedetto del Tronto	3496
San Francisco, CA	1750
San Juan, PR	3138
Sandakan	3803
Sankt-Peterburg	1190
Santander	3430.4
Santiago de Cuba	3119
Sanwa	2500, 2501
Sanya	3740.1
Sarnia, Ont.	3070
Sasebo	3772.5
Sault St. Marie, MI	3074
Savannah, GA	3101
Scheveningen	1225
Seattle, WA	3668
Selsey	1115
Sete	1185.8
Sevastopol	3516
Shanghai	2485.1, 3741
Shetland	3404.1
Shiogama	3754
Shoeburyness	1116
Singapore	3735
Skegness	1117
Slupsk	3337
Snaefell	1120
Socoa	1184.85
Solent	3397.2
Southampton Vessel Traffic Services Centre	1265
Southwest Harbor, ME	3083
Split	3499
St. Ann's Head	1108
St. Anthony, Nfld.	3020
St. John's, Nfld.	3023
St. Mary's, Isles of Scilly	1109
St. Petersburg, FL	3107.8
St. Pierre Radio	3050
Stad	1233
Stockholm	3288
Stornoway	3404
Strait of Gibraltar	1300
Sullom Voe Harbour	1240
Surabaya	3824
Suva	3945
Svalbard	3218
Swansea	3400.4

INDEX II

RADIO AIDS TO NAVIGATION BY STATION

Sydney 3882
Sydney, N.S. 3042

T

Tacubaya 2041
Taedok 2505
Tai-Chung 3790.5
Talcahuano 3645.6
Tallinn 3334
Tanabe 3772
Tanger 3560
Tarifa 3460
Tarragona 3459.5
Tashkent 2212
Taupo Maritime Radio 3904
Tees 1245
Tema 3605
Tenerife 3581
Thames 3397
Thunder Bay, Ont. 3080
Tianjin 3740.2
Tiree 1150
Tjome 3258
Tobermory 1002.5
Tofino, B.C. 3675
Tokyo 3756
Tokyo Wan 1560
Torino 2411
Torshavn 3215
Toulinguet (Camaret) 1183.9
Trafalgar 1002.55
Trevose Head 1155
Trieste 3498
Trimingham 1160
Tripoli 3538
Tunis 3542
Turku 3314
Tuticorin 3728.1
Twillingate 1002.35
Tynemouth 1165

U

Ullung 3747
Ushuaia 3208

V

Valdez, AK 3696.5

Valencia 3459.37
Valentia 3408
Valenzuela 3794
Valparaiso 1895
Valparaiso Playa Ancha 3645.5
Valparaiso Playa Ancha Radiomaritima 2445
Van Inlet 1003
Vardo 3242
Varna 3510
Ventspils 1198
Veracruz 3118
Victoria, B.C. 3671
Vigo 3430.1
Villerville 1182.9
Vishakhapatnam 3722.1
Vishakhapatnam Naval 3722.2
Vladivostok 3748

W

Walney Island 1170
Walvis Bay 3628
Wanganui 1635
West Torr 1171
Westport 1640
Whitby 1172
Wiarton, Ont 3068
Wideford Hill 1175
Wiluna 3902
Windyhead 1180
Witowo 3336
Woods Hole, MA 3087
Woolwich Radio 1255

X

Xian 2490

Y

Yarmouth 3396
Yeosu 3747.5
Yokohama 3757
Yuzhnyy 1310

Z

Zatoka Gdansk VTS 3338

CROSS REFERENCE – INTERNATIONAL vs. U.S. RADIO AIDS

Inter.	– U.S. –			
2-0001	1055,	1060,	1065,	1066,
	1070,	1072,	1073,	1075,	1080,
	1082,	1086,	1087,	1088,	1089,
	1090,	1091,	1091.2,	1092,	1093,
	1094,	1094.1,	1094.2,	1094.5,	1095,
	1095.5,	1096,	1097,	1098,	1098.2,
	1098.3,	1105,	1105.2,	1106,	1108,
	1109,	1115,	1116,	1117,	1120,
	1150,	1155,	1160,	1165,	1170,
	1172,	1175,	1180		
2-0155	1090.5,	1093.5		
2-0175	1098.5,	1171		
2-0815	1182,	1182.1,	1182.2,	1182.3,
	1182.4,	1182.5,	1182.6,	1182.7,	1182.8,
	1182.9,	1183,	1183.05,	1183.1,	1183.2,
	1183.25,	1183.3,	1183.35,	1183.45,	1183.5,
	1183.55,	1183.6,	1183.65,	1183.7,	1183.75,
	1183.8,	1183.85,	1183.9,	1183.95,	1184,
	1184.05,	1184.1,	1184.15,	1184.2,	1184.3,
	1184.4,	1184.45,	1184.5,	1184.55,	1184.6,
	1184.65,	1184.75,	1184.8,	1184.82,	1184.85
2-1040	1185.5,	1185.6,	1185.7,	1185.8,
	1185.9,	1186,	1186.2,	1186.3,	1186.4,
	1186.5,	1186.6,	1186.7,	1186.8,	1186.9,
	1187,	1187.1,	1187.2,	1187.3,	1187.4,
	1187.5				
2-1282	1187.61			
2-2147	1188			
2-3510	1002.6,	1002.65,	1002.7,	1002.75,
	1002.8,	1002.85,	1002.9,	1002.95,	1003
2-4326	1001.3,	1001.35,	1001.45,	1001.6,
	1001.85,	1001.9,	1001.95,	1002,	1002.1,
	1002.15,	1002.2,	1002.35		

www.ingramcontent.com/pod-product-compliance
Lightning Source LLC
Chambersburg PA
CBHW080836230426
43665CB00021B/2854